WITHDRAWN

Frank Buchman: a life

By the same author

BRAVE MEN CHOOSE
JOHN WESLEY, ANGLICAN
GOOD GOD, IT WORKS!
REBIRTH OF A NATION?
STRANGELY WARMED
GOD'S POLITICIAN: WILLIAM WILBERFORCE'S STRUGGLE

With Sir Arnold Lunn
THE NEW MORALITY
THE CULT OF SOFTNESS
CHRISTIAN COUNTER-ATTACK

With Sydney Cook
THE BLACK AND WHITE BOOK

Garth Lean

FRANK BUCHMAN:
—— A LIFE ——

Constable · London

First published in Great Britain 1985
by Constable and Company Limited
10 Orange Street, London WC2H 7EG
Copyright © 1985 Garth Lean
Set in Linotron Ehrhardt 11pt by
Rowland Phototypesetting Limited
Bury St Edmunds, Suffolk
Printed in Great Britain by
St Edmundsbury Press
Bury St Edmunds, Suffolk

British Library Cataloguing in Publication Data
Lean, Garth
Frank Buchman : a life.
1. Buchman, Frank N.D.   2. Evangelists –
Great Britain – Biography
I. Title
269'.2'0924   BV3785.B8

ISBN 0 09 466650 4

CONTENTS

ILLUSTRATIONS

PREFACE

Working on this book for the past five years has been for me the renewal of an old comradeship and the making of a new acquaintance. I knew Frank Buchman well for thirty years, but I would not claim that I wholly understood him. Talking to hundreds of people of the most varied opinions, in the course of my researches, has brought me many new insights, as well as additional information.

I worked with Buchman in the Oxford Group and Moral Re-Armament from 1932, but was not, except during a few years in the thirties, one of his closer colleagues. After those years, I saw him regularly, but often found myself working in a different country from him. I liked and greatly respected him, though we often disagreed and sometimes clashed which, as he once said, was apt to 'hold things up'.

On one occasion, quite early in our association, he hinted to me that I might some day write his biography. I do not know how seriously he meant it, and did not expect to take up the suggestion. But it seemed wrong, twenty years after his death, that no full biography had been written, and important to produce an objective assessment while the last generation who knew him well was still alive. So, after hoping for some time that others would undertake it, I decided to make the attempt.

I have inevitably approached the task with a continued and strong belief in the ideas which Buchman put forward, but I have tried to maintain an open mind about the man himself and his achievement. I have repeated nothing which I cannot vouch for, and I have sought to investigate, as fully as I can, the various claims made for and against him. My researchers and I have had access to his private papers, as well as to the archives kept by Moral Re-Armament in various countries, and many unpublished diaries and autobiographies. We have read the relevant material in the Public Records Office and the libraries of Lambeth Palace and Church House in London, the Bodleian in Oxford, the Library of Congress in Washington, the Document Centre in Berlin, and the Bundesarchiv in Koblenz.

I have been particularly fortunate in the generosity of two friends. The first did very extensive research during the years immediately after

Buchman's death, and the other interviewed many dozens of people about Buchman in more recent years. Both have made their material available to me; neither wishes to be publicly thanked. Since then many more interviews and investigations have taken place, and any quotation in this book for which no numbered reference is given is the fruit of an interview with the person named in the text.

My thanks are due not only to those who gave these interviews but also to those who assisted in my own researches, including Kenneth Belden, Alan Faunce, Michael Hutchinson, Svend Major, Mary Meekings, Michel Sentis, Pierre Spoerri, Erika Utzinger and a host of others. I am also grateful to John Bright-Holmes, Peter Harland, Graham and Jean Turner and my son, Geoffrey, and daughter, Mary, for reading the book and giving professional advice, and to Peter and Margaret Sisam for co-ordinating the photographs. My day-to-day editor has been Ailsa Hamilton, whose help has been invaluable and has often amounted to co-authorship. Needless to say, I alone am responsible for the conclusions in the final text and for whatever judgements, misjudgements and opinions it expresses.

Among many who have typed or committed to the word-processor the various drafts, I am particularly indebted to Hazel Clark, and to John Charlton, Jane Harrison, Catherine Hutchinson, Janet Mace, Margaret O'Kane and Janet Paine. Without their generous service, and the stead-fast encouragement and support of my wife, Margot, the book could not have been completed.

GDL

THE BUCHMAN CONTROVERSY

This is the story of a man who set out to remake the world. That must be said at the outset because it is only possible to understand Frank Buchman in the context of that aim. Everything he did in his adult life was a part of it, and scarcely anything he did could, in his eyes, be separated from it. That aim conditioned where and how he lived, how he approached people and situations, and what he did from hour to hour.

No sane person looking round the world of 1961, when Buchman died at the age of 83, would have described that bid as successful. On the other hand, it would be equally hard to judge his life a failure. Some remarkable streams of events sprang from his initiatives; others are still breaking surface today. It is at least arguable that few of them would have emerged if his aim had been smaller.

Buchman was always – and still is – a controversial figure. In the thirties Archbishop Lang of Canterbury stated that he was being 'used to bring multitudes of human lives in all parts of the world under the transforming power of Christ', while Bishop Henson of Durham accused him of 'megalomaniacal self-confidence'. In 1940 the British Minister of Information, Brendan Bracken, said that he would be arrested immediately America entered the war, while the United States Department of Justice described his work as 'essential to the defence effort'. The author and Member of Parliament for Oxford University, A. P. Herbert, called him a 'canting cheat' in the House of Commons, and Tom Driberg, later to be Chairman of the Labour Party, attacked the Home Secretary for allowing a man who had never denounced Hitler to re-enter Britain in 1946. The Gestapo condemned him in reports from 1936 onwards and he was periodically attacked on Moscow Radio. His work was investigated at different times by Princeton University, by the Secretariat of the International Confederation of Free Trades Unions, and by a working party of the Church of England's Social and Industrial Council. In 1953 the Holy Office in Rome issued a warning to Catholics, a 'misunderstanding' which was only cleared up years later. Meanwhile he was decorated by seven countries, including France, Germany, Greece, Japan and the

Philippines, for his effect on their relations with other countries. When I had nearly finished this book, I was introduced at an Oxford reception to Cardinal Franz König, Archbishop of Vienna. He asked me what I was writing, and I mentioned Frank Buchman. 'He was a turning-point in the history of the modern world through his ideas,' he said immediately. In the next week he sent me his reasons for saying so.

Such a variety of opinions calls for a more thorough investigation than has yet appeared. A more detailed description of the man himself, his character, beliefs and lifestyle, is overdue. For even some who frequently met him found him puzzling. Sir Arnold Lunn, the author and inventor of the slalom and down-hill races in skiing, used often to question me about him. After criticising Buchman in several books, Lunn decided to visit the Moral Re-Armament centre at Caux in Switzerland, to study him and his work at first-hand. Thereafter, he went there most years over a ten-year period, partly because he enjoyed the company. Yet still Buchman puzzled him.

'He has no charisma that I can see,' he said. 'He isn't good-looking, he is no orator, he has never written a book and he seldom even leads a meeting. Yet statesmen and great intellects come from all over the world to consult him, and a lot of intelligent people have stuck with him, full-time without salary, for forty years, when they could have been making careers for themselves. Why?'

Why indeed? G. K. Chesterton once remarked that it is well for there to be something enigmatic about the subject of a biography because 'it preserves two very important things – modesty in the biographer and mystery in the biography'. This book aims to give a living picture of a well-known, yet largely unknown, man.

SMALL-TOWN BOY

Frank Buchman was born in Pennsburg, Pennsylvania, on 4 June 1878. The town had one main street of plain brick houses, a Lutheran Reformed church, a general store, a millinery shop, a small cigar factory, a hotel, and a newly-built railway station patronised by four passenger trains and two freights a day. Its 1,200 inhabitants were virtually all Pennsylvania Germans – the name by then corrupted to Pennsylvania Dutch – most of them descended from settlers who had trekked up the valleys from Philadelphia during the previous century and a half. To the east lay the Perkiomen River, named after an Indian chief, and all around stretched the rolling, fertile farmland which had made Pennsburg a comfortable and prosperous township.

Like the rest of Pennsylvania Dutch society, Pennsburg was a conservative and intensely close-knit place. 'I could lie awake at night', said Buchman later, 'and think who lived in every house from one end of Pennsburg to the other.' German, in a dialect which sounded like a mixture of Swabian and Swiss German, was still the language of everyday speech, and to the end of his days Buchman's father was more at home with German than with English. Most of the area's local newspapers were printed in German, sermons were delivered in German and many of the customs of the homeland survived intact. At Christmas the trees were heavy with red apples and cookies decorated with red sugar; on Shrove Tuesday there were special doughnuts, known as Fawsanochdkucha (*Fastnachtkuchen*). It was all part of a culture quite different from anything outside the area.

The people, too, strongly resembled their prototypes in Europe. They were serious, dutiful and apt to take a sombre view of life, and their morality embodied a keen appreciation of the value of material things. They believed in hard work, frugality and a scrupulous honesty in their dealings. Buchman once described them as 'people who are conservative, stubborn, suspicious. Not to excel in something is just too bad.'

Abstinence from alcohol was regarded as preferable, and the only permissible vice was overeating. To the Pennsylvania Dutch, indeed, the

[3]

delights of the table were among the principal joys of life. This was the land which originated the waffle and shoo-fly pie, the land of chicken corn soup and dandelion salad. Everyone was expected to provide a good meal at short notice and anyone who was not a good trencherman was apt to be suspect.

The first 'German' settlers arrived in the late seventeenth century. For them, Pennsylvania was a land of refuge from religious persecution. They had come at the invitation of the English Quaker in 1680, William Penn, to whom Charles II had granted a tract of 45,000 square miles in his newest colonial domain. Penn's mother was German and he was thus particularly sensitive to the plight of those who were being harried for their beliefs by either Catholic Hapsburgs or Lutheran princes, or both. So they poured across the Atlantic – Mennonites, Schwenkfelders, Seventh-Day Adventists, Amish and Moravians as well as Lutherans. Most came from Swabia and southern Germany, from eastern Switzerland and from the Tyrol.

Buchman's ancestors travelled from eastern Switzerland half a century or so later, not so much to avoid persecution as to take up free land in a thriving and congenial community. The family's Swiss citizenship was in the town of Bischofszell. The most noted bearer of the name had been Thomas Bibliander*, who succeeded Zwingli as Professor of Theology in the Academy at Zurich in 1531. At the time when the Turks were besieging Vienna and every pulpit was thundering against the 'Mohammedan enemies of Christ', he issued a medieval translation of the Koran into Latin, the universal language of scholarly Europe. His printer was imprisoned, and he himself was only with the greatest difficulty restrained by his friends from setting off for the Middle East. Frank Buchman, in later years, took much delight in the assumption – suggested to him by a Buchman he met in Paris – that he was descended from Bibliander; but the extent of the kinship is uncertain.[1]

The Buchmans who emigrated to Pennsylvania were Martin and his brother Jacob. They left Switzerland in 1750, sailed for Philadelphia from Rotterdam on the *Phoenix* on 28 August, and then trundled by wagon the sixty miles to Cetronia, where both soon became modestly successful farmers. Martin's son and son-in-law fought in the Revolutionary War, as major and captain respectively, in the Northampton County Militia. Meanwhile in 1738 Buchman's mother's forebear, Jacob Greenwalt,[2] had left the canton of Bern with his wife and three sons, become indentured to a farmer for two years to pay for their passage and then settled in the same Northampton county.

---

* Following the custom of the time, he had adopted the classical rendering of the family name.

[4]

Young men from both families went West to seek their fortunes. One of Frank Buchman's maternal uncles, Aaron Greenwalt, settled in Anoka, Minnesota. He was one of the first in the state to enlist for the North in the Civil War, and died at the battle of Gettysburg. Buchman's own father, Franklin, got as far as Indiana, where he worked as a road builder – on the 'corduroy' roads of those days, made from tree trunks – but then caught malaria and had to be brought home to the family farm. He met Sarah Anna Greenwalt at a picnic and, on 5 January 1875, they were married and went to live at the Greenwalt farm in the lovely hill country around Weisnersville.

Franklin Buchman senior was both restless and enterprising. Within a year he had left the farm and set up as a merchant, and eighteen months later he and Sarah moved again, this time to Pennsburg, where he bought a general store at 772 Main Street, selling everything from meat and molasses to paraffin. Business prospects must have looked promising. The Philadelphia and Reading Railroad had already opened its Perkiomen branch from Philadelphia to Pennsburg, and planned to extend the line to Emmaus and Allentown.

Franklin and Sarah Buchman's first child, a son, called John William, was born in Pennsburg in 1876, but died from diphtheria before he was two. Five months later their second boy was born in the first-floor bedroom above the store.* He was named Franklin after his father, and Nathaniel Daniel after his Buchman and Greenwalt grandfathers. As he said, 'When I was born, they tried to keep everybody happy.' The Buchmans had no more children of their own, but twenty-one years later they adopted their nephew Dan, eighteen years younger than Frank, who became a much-loved if troublesome member of the family.

The store flourished and, after a time, Franklin Buchman senior was able to emulate his own father, who had been an inn-keeper as well as a farmer, and buy the small hotel down by the railroad station. It had thirteen rooms, a saloon bar, and a wooden balcony which ran the full length of the frontage. It now became the Buchman House Hotel, offering 'Best accommodation for travellers, salesmen and drovers. House furnished with steam heat. Teams to hire at reasonable rates.' 'There was one rule,' Frank Buchman recalled: 'if you weren't in by one o'clock, no lunch. It was a family affair. I used to have to dry the dishes.'

So the young Frank spent a formative period in his childhood in a small railway hotel. The experience played a vital part in shaping his character. The railway tracks were like a river which, every week, brought in a new tide of demanding, hurrying humanity. Through them, the boy caught the

* The building, now Markley's Pharmacy, is marked by a plaque put up by the community as part of the centenary celebrations of Buchman's birth.

[5]

echoes and flavours of the great world outside to which otherwise he might have had little access; and he saw his parents acting as hosts to a wide assortment of travellers, taking the meticulous care in preparing rooms and serving meals which was to be a practice with him all his life.

It was, by his own account, a delightful childhood. 'I could walk the tracks from Greensboro to Pennsburg and never get off. I squashed pennies on the track.' Six days a week in the holidays, he went fishing for catfish, sunfish and bass on the upper Perkiomen River and, next morning, fried his catch for breakfast. At Easter, he hunted for eggs which his mother had hidden in the garden, in summer there was swimming, in the winter tobogganing and sleigh-rides. Later, his father took him each Saturday to the races in their carriage, drawn by 'two spanking black horses' – though he was not allowed to bet. He had a new red velocipede and a dog called Nickie, and there seemed all the time in the world for everything. The memory of that childhood remained with him through a long life of travel. 'There is nothing I like so much as Pennsylvania in June,' he once said. 'I love the red soil and the flowers, the loveliness of the Blue Mountains . . . I'm glad I was surrounded by so much beauty.'

When Buchman was eight, his parents sent him to a private school a few blocks along the tracks. Perkiomen Seminary* was run by the Schwenk-felders, the most liberal of the German sects which had colonised the area. They believed that the Lutheran Reformation was too rigid and state-dominated and that a more personal and spiritual religion was needed, with less liturgy and ritual. To the study of the Bible, they added 'the inner light' which, they considered, came through the direct inspiration and rule of the Holy Spirit. Closer to the Quakers than to the fundamentalist sects like the Amish and Mennonites, they were in many ways ecumenists before their time. Whether their influence on Buchman was permanent is not known – in later years he could not list their beliefs – but in any event it was not a narrow one. Although his family were orthodox Lutherans, he sometimes walked six miles to the nearest Catholic church with a friend who was going to early Mass.

At the seminary he had a formal education in languages (including Latin and Greek), rhetoric, mathematics, science and music. In the classroom, he seems to have been eager and hard-working, though no more than an average pupil. Outside it, he was a sociable extrovert, 'a rapidly growing boy of clear skin and eye and ruddy colour, often monopolised by the "fairer sex" ', according to a family friend.[3] When thirteen, he founded a club for boys and girls which he called the PGB Society: the initials, he explained, were merely designed to provoke curiosity.[4]

---

* Now the centre of a large campus, drawing students from several countries.

If this kind of levity was rare in Pennsylvania German society, another side of the young Buchman had already begun to show itself. His mother, whose cousin had been a distinguished divine, cherished the desire that her son, too, should become a minister, and the boy appears to have accepted the commission readily enough. He recalled, at the age of 83, one incident which may have helped to form his early mind. A well-known Pennsburg drunk appeared one Sunday on the penitent's stool in church, thus signalling a decision to reform. 'I was about five at the time,' related Buchman. 'It was the first time I grasped that religion could change someone's way of living.' His Sunday School teacher noted that he seemed 'to crave the power to lead others aright' and soon he was practising sermons at home.

All the same, he seems to have been subject to most of the peccadilloes of youth. 'When I was eleven I kissed a girl,' he said. 'The girl wouldn't have anything to do with me for a week.' He stole money from his mother to buy sweets, had his mouth washed out with soap for swearing, and years later, when a young man shamefacedly told him that he gave way to a common temptation, asked cheerfully, 'How old are you?' 'Twenty-two.' 'You've got one year to go,' replied the middle-aged Buchman. 'I didn't finally get free of that till I was twenty-three.'

There was no high school in Pennsburg, and so, when Buchman was sixteen, his father sold the hotel and the family moved to Allentown, only eighteen miles to the north but, at that time, a three-hour journey by horse and buggy. It was a major shift in environment and status. They took a comfortable, newly-built terraced house with a porch, at 117 N 11th Street,* looking out across a dirt road to farmland – said to be among the most fertile in the United States. Frank Buchman senior opened a restaurant and saloon at 533 Hamilton Street, at a stone's throw from the court-house, which soon became a centre of political and social discussion. At that time, even the main street was still unpaved and the only form of public transport was a trolley, drawn by two scrawny mules. But – like the rest of America – Allentown was expanding at an explosive rate. Its population, only 18,000 in 1880, was to double by 1900, and new smoke-stacks were constantly going up along the banks of the Lehigh River. There were good telephone, telegraph and rail links with New York and Philadelphia: by the time the Buchmans arrived, twenty trains a day in each direction.

The move did not impair young Buchman's high spirits. At Allentown High School – three and a half blocks from his new home – he and a friend

---

* In what is now the Old Allentown Historic District. The house is open to the public, and has been preserved by the Lehigh County Historical Society almost exactly as it was when the Buchman family lived there.

decided to explore the loft, which meant crawling around on the exposed rafters. Buchman slipped and one leg went through the ceiling of the classroom below, to the delight of the pupils and the annoyance of the master. As at Perkiomen, he contributed items of gossip to the school magazine. 'Why does a certain lass carry a picture of Athletics Team '95 to school?' he asked. 'She surely has a reason!' At the same time, he was telling a friend that, although he loved dancing, he would give it up when he was twenty-one because he was going to be a minister.

He duly entered Muhlenberg College, a liberal arts institution owned and run by the Lutheran Ministerium, whose prime purpose was to provide the church with a steady stream of ministers. Buchman himself 'was pining to go to Princeton', but his father was adamant that Muhlenberg, just a mile from home on 11th Street, was more suitable. The students wore black suits and ties; theology, together with German and Greek, loomed large in the curriculum; and those who aspired to the cloth were expected to teach Sunday School and visit the sick. Buchman took a Sunday School class at a local mission and spent a good deal of time visiting hospitals and orphanages. But, in other ways, he scarcely comported himself in the accepted earnest fashion.

To begin with, he took painting lessons. He also attended Mrs Chapman's dancing academy on Hamilton Street and was not slow to put into practice what he had learnt. Sometime in 1897 a party was given by Mrs Chapman's pupils, to which each invited a young lady. Afterwards, said the local newspaper, they 'repaired to Peters and Jacoby's where they enjoyed oysters on the half-shell, fried oysters, chicken . . . ice-cream and cake'. On this occasion, it added, 'There was only one toast, 'Pitch in.' Its repetition was not deemed necessary.'[5]

In the winter, there were sleighing parties to villages as far away as Nazareth. 'We'd go and dance all night', recalled Buchman, 'and then drive home fourteen miles by sled in the early morning.' On a visit to Allentown later in life, he pointed out the Alpha Tau Omega Fraternity house where he had taken twelve girls to a dance: 'I couldn't bear to disappoint them.'

At college, he was business manager of the paper, drew cartoons for the year book, the *Ciarla* – Prohibition appears as a severe and crusty old man – was an enthusiastic member of the tennis and bicycle clubs, won a physical culture prize, was class vice-president for the second half of his senior year, and amused himself writing dramatic sketches and poetry of a romantic character and acting in the freshman play.

Buchman's home background was even more unusual for the average ordinand of those days. In 1897 his father opened a wholesale wine and liquor business in Emmaus, five miles south of Allentown, and this, combined with his passion for the turf, hardly made him the Lutheran establishment's idea of a model parent for one of their future pastors. In fact, a local minister preached against him and said he would go to hell. However, Frank's father, meeting the minister on the railway station, pulled his leg about the sermon and offered him a drink. This was accepted, and they became friends. Meanwhile his business prospered, and his teams supplied wines, liquor, and soft drinks like sarsaparilla to establishments in four counties.

Buchman's mother was always ready, in the tradition of the area, to provide hospitality for his friends at the shortest notice. 'Frank always loved a party,' said a neighbour, 'and his mother did too.' He often referred to her as a 'great provider'. In the frozen studio portraits of the period, she appears distinctly stern-faced and forbidding. A Scotsman, meeting her in her old age, said she was built like 'a great square-rigger'. 'She was tall, her face full of wrinkles, but when she smiled it was like a sunflower,' he added. Contemporaries stress her sense of humour. At all events, the stern exterior in the photo cloaked an exceptionally tolerant nature, at least so far as her only son was concerned.

By comparison, Buchman's father looks indecisive. But 'he was', said a friend, 'a successful business man who was out to back his son to the limit.'[6] He was also generous with friends who got into difficulties; and the years spent in restaurants and behind the bar had given him a shrewd and charitable insight into human nature. That, perhaps, is why his son used later to tell younger men that what they needed, in trying to help people, were the qualities of a good barman – sympathy, willingness to listen and intuition. Buchman said he learnt from his father how to understand people, while he inherited from his mother his personal reserve and a sense of order and of the line that divides right from wrong.

Theirs was a comfortable home in the German style, with a good deal of dark and rather heavy furniture, relieved by pleasant oils and water-colours – several of them, showing considerable sensitivity, painted by the young Frank – and a number of elegant ornaments, including a beautiful Limoges tea service. They had two servants, and wine was regularly served at table.

Sarah Buchman, always to be seen with a crisp white frill at her neck, her hair drawn back in a bun, was both proud that she came from a family of some means* and determined that her son should have the kind of upbringing which she felt their standing as a family merited. Like any good Pennsylvania German, she had an acute sense of the proper order of things; like any good *bourgeoise*, she longed to see her offspring rise in that order. She hoped he would make his mark in the world, but as a local man

---

* 'My grandmother came (from Switzerland) with corsets and lace. Few people had corsets in those days,' related Buchman. (Martin diaries, 12 May 1941.)

of God. In her ambition for him at this time, the temporal and the spiritual were closely intertwined.

Buchman spent his summer holidays either on cycle trips (one year he and a school friend, Arthur Keller, went by train and boat as far as Montreal, making side trips by bicycle or on foot) or at Chautauqua, the religious and cultural centre in New York State, where an annual series of lectures and recitals provided what seems to have been a cross between a holiday and a summer finishing school. Its programme included lectures on subjects ranging from Milton to cookery and temperance, prayer meetings and sports, and was enlivened by a variety of entertainments, among them orchestral concerts, Swiss yodellers and college girl octettes. The lecturers included evangelists like Henry Drummond, though Buchman never met him, and writers like Mark Twain.

While at Muhlenberg, Buchman visited Woonsocket, Rhode Island, at the invitation of a Miss Florence Thayer, whom he had evidently met either in Chautauqua or at a social gathering in Allentown, and whose father ran five satinette mills. The splendour of the Thayers' home quite dazzled him. The house, he told his mother, was in a very aristocratic quarter, in the finest street in Woonsocket, and right next to the home of a former governor of Rhode Island. It had a large hall, a large reception room in gold and white, and there were Wilton carpets on the floor, fine draperies at the windows and handsome pictures on the walls. One room alone, he calculated with the eye of a hotelier's son, must have cost $1,500 to furnish, if not more. The Thayers, he concluded, had no less than three carriages.[7]

The social life was equally captivating. He went to dances with Miss Thayer and was 'entertained at cards' by her friends. One was a multi-millionaire's son who had recently graduated from Harvard. He was, Buchman reported, 'a splendid young fellow, interested quite a bit in racehorses but seems to be a Christian'. His own delight was all the greater because he felt in such demand. 'I am perfectly lionised here,' he told his mother. 'They want me at the house all the time.'[8] As for Miss Thayer herself, 'She did not disappoint me in the least.'[9] It is clear that the young Frank regarded Florence as a possible fiancée. She is on his list of those who gave him Christmas presents in 1897 and 1898; although several other ladies also appear on the latter list. Another young lady was the recipient of Buchman's fraternity pin, such an exchange in those days often being a precursor of engagement and marriage; while the daughter of a third is convinced that had Buchman married, it would have been to her mother, Bertha Werner.

The young Buchman, then, was full of natural contradictions. He relished the gaiety of bourgeois social life, he was dazzled by the elegance and wealth of a world he had only just begun to explore and, whatever might happen after he had reached the age of twenty-one, he had no intention of conforming before then with the standard image of the future Lutheran divine.

At the same time, he was clearly looking for some path of religious or social self-giving. His essays on religious subjects* displayed a warmth and breadth of vision beyond obligatory piety. 'God's greatest gift to man,' he wrote on 'Friendly Service', 'is love. Man rises or falls in the scales of greatness as he possesses this gift . . . The danger is . . . that our adhesion to one political party means wholesale denunciation of the other – that in upholding our own city, we abuse others, or in loving our own nation, we hate others. Most of us need to lead broader lives, not only in our thoughts but in our hearts. The cultivation of that spirit must begin with the individual if it is ever to influence a nation. He who will do his share to help it must broaden his life, extend his sympathies and make no bounds for his generosity and helpfulness.'

His hopes for the future were displayed in an orotund commencement speech delivered in 1899, entitled 'The Dawn': 'When, in the twilight of the coming century, the roll will be called of those who figure prominently in the moulding and guiding of our nation, may we hope that the names of some of us may appear thereon. Though our names may not appear on earth's scroll of fame, may they appear on Heaven's roll of honour.'

This was more than a young man's rhetoric. Buchman already sensed that sacrifice would be required if such an ambition was to be fulfilled. When a cousin, Fred Fetherolf, told him that Bacon had remarked somewhere in his *Essays* that a single man could do better work than a married man, Buchman continually pestered him to find the exact quotation. It reads: 'He that hath wife and children hath given hostages to fortune; for they are impediments to great enterprises, either of virtue or mischief.'[10]

Even then, recalled Fetherolf later, Buchman's idea was that a man should have a single aim in life: his own was to win people to God. 'If ever a man had a fixed purpose,' Fetherolf added, 'it was Frank Buchman, though he made himself unpopular with some of the fellows because of it.'

His natural ebullience and gregariousness accompanied a deeper instinct to stand, and walk, alone. His character was a compound of ambition, an abundant self-confidence and that growing sense of calling.

In the summer of 1899, aged 21, Buchman graduated from Muhlenberg with honourable mention and the Butler Analogy Prize of twenty-five dollars in gold for an examination paper on Bishop Butler's classic

---

* Found in Buchman's home, among other essays in support of 'The Dance', 'Women Bicyclists' and one entitled 'Cuba Will Be Free', as well as some love poetry, a play and notes for gossip columns in the school magazine.

[11]

defence of Christianity, *Analogy of Religion*.[11] That same autumn, he went to Philadelphia to attend the Lutheran theological seminary at Mount Airy in Germantown. For the time being at least, his sense of calling was leading him towards the church of his forefathers.

LIFE-WORK ENDED?

The move from Muhlenberg to Mount Airy took Buchman from one part of the Pennsylvania German culture to another. The seminary, owned by the Ministerium, mirrored its dutiful earnestness. The buildings them-selves conveyed an impression of austerity, even grimness, and suggested that a career in the Lutheran Church was not something to be undertaken lightly. At the same time, Mount Airy was situated in the exciting city of Philadelphia, the birthplace of the American Constitution and a major port, which still looked to Europe as the centre of gravity of the world. That great world, of which Buchman read and dreamed, seemed a good deal nearer now than it had in Allentown.

At first Buchman was intensely lonely, and compensated by taking a somewhat lordly attitude towards his classmates at the seminary. They were, he thought, rather colourless and narrow. Very few, he wrote his mother, had much general knowledge. They knew nothing apart from what they had studied in books. That was well and good, but a man needed a knowledge of the 'doings of men'.

At the same time, in the manner of many young men who have newly left home, he was giving his parents a glimpse of his ambitions. They were grandiose in the style of an America saturated with the log-cabin-to-the-White-House philosophy of Horatio Alger, 200 million copies of whose books had been sold in the previous twenty-five years. 'A man in order to be great must do extraordinary things, not ordinary,' Buchman wrote to his parents. 'By the grace of God, I intend to make the name of Buchman shine forth. By earnest toil and labour I can accomplish it.' Dr Luther, he remarked, had not written hymns until he was forty; and his own ambition was to be a famous author and hymn-writer. 'Never before', he con-cluded, 'have I revealed my mind to you like this but often I have laid awake and thought of all these things.'[1]

Not only did he take himself seriously, he also expected others to follow suit. For example, he not infrequently chided his mother for the stationery she used when writing to him. 'I hate to receive letters on such poor paper,' he told her briskly. 'It looks so careless and I want to keep them. So please do me the favour to use better paper in the future. Every woman ought to have good paper.'[2] 'Don't feel hurt about the stationery question,' he added in another letter, 'I meant it in all kindness.'[3]

By March he had adjusted to the more reserved company he found himself in, and 'recovered from the blues'.[4] There were, also, a good range of things to be enjoyed in Philadelphia in the intervals between taking examinations in Hebrew, and as well as playing tennis, riding and boating, Buchman was soon making his number with young ladies of good position, fortified by a new pair of patent leather shoes. He had been invited, he wrote to his parents, to visit a Miss Taylor who was staying with family friends in Philadelphia – 'very aristocratic people' – and later he reported on the success of the visit. The shoes, he declared, had looked stunning; he only wished they could have seen him.[5]

Almost immediately he was invited to attend the wedding of Florence Thayer's sister in Woonsocket, and he started to lay careful siege to his father's pocket-book. It would, he told his parents, be a great education 'to see the beautiful decorations, the people and the like', the chance of a lifetime, in fact. He didn't expect ever again to get an invitation to such a fine wedding because he had but one millionaire family on his acquaintance list. The only other wedding he could expect to attend was his own – 'that is if I ever marry a girl like Miss Thayer, who can afford such a wedding'.

Then, no doubt recalling his previous letter about the visit to Miss Taylor, he seeks to reassure them that his affections are not promiscuous and that, this time, their money would be spent on the true object of his heart. 'I think I must stick to Miss Thayer', he declares, with perhaps a touch of remorse, 'as she seems more devoted than ever.'[6]

Fearing his first effort may have no fruit, Buchman tries again. 'You may think', he writes, 'that I want too much, but it will only be a few years more and then I shall enter on my life's work. Then I cannot taste these pleasures.' 'A man who enters the ministry', he adds, 'must of a necessity be social . . . It's the getting out into the world that opens one's eyes.' The letter also contains a poetic description of an afternoon sky, which he had sat and watched for two hours, bolstered by comments on the moral purpose of beauty.[7] 'My ambition is some day to become an author,' he added next day. 'I am going to aim high. An author cannot describe a scene unless he has seen and experienced it. If he wishes to describe a fashionable wedding, he cannot imagine it, he must see one. I could never have described to you yesterday's sky had I not seen it. Do you catch the force of my argument?'[8]

His mother evidently did catch the force, anyway of his determination. So, having asked her to send him his 'nose-pinchers'* – 'because they are

* Pince-nez.

[14]

more becoming' – and having suggested that she might care to let the Allentown *Chronicle* know of his visit to Woonsocket,[9] which she did, he set off for Rhode Island.

The occasion turned out to be all he could have hoped for. There was, he wrote his parents, such a crowd watching that 'it took four policemen to keep the mob in subjection'. The luncheon was excellent, with salads and oysters 'in every style'; words were inadequate to describe the pretty dresses; there were jewels and laces galore; and a butler in full livery gave each of the departing guests a piece of wedding-cake.[10]

As the months went by, Buchman took advantage of the joys of the great city, and peppered his parents with enthusiastic reports. 'We saw the pew in St Peter's which George Washington occupied and not only saw it, but sat in the very place he was wont to sit ... I bicycled all up Wissahickon Drive yesterday; the scenery is grand ... Yesterday Bernard and I went to a cricket match at Manheim. I saw a real live Prince. He is called Prince Ranji and is a champion cricketer. You can read about him in the Sunday Press ... Dewey* will be in Philadelphia on Thursday. I advise you to come. I wouldn't miss the chance to see Dewey as he is one of the biggest men of the century.'[11] He heard Mlle Nerada, who 'frequently' sang before Queen Victoria, saw Henry Irving and Ellen Terry in *Robespierre* and Bernhardt playing Ophelia.[12] He loved the splendour of grand opera – one year, he complained, he hadn't seen a single one 'and the season almost over'[13] – and relished being invited to a private showing of new paintings at the local Academy to which 'a great many Parisians have sent work over'.[14] He also wrote a paper on 'Art in Worship' for the Melanchthon Society.[15]

Beneath Buchman's relish for a fashionable social life lay the insecurity and touchiness of a young man who could easily be wounded. One of his fellow-students had evidently been spreading minor items of gossip about him in Allentown: to wit, that a professor had said he did not have sufficient will-power to do his work (a grave charge in the German community), that he blushed a great deal – and that this blushing was not unconnected with his interest in a young lady called Marie.

Buchman retorted with heat. No professor, he told his mother, had ever hinted that he was not doing good work. As for the suggestion of a romantic attachment, 'where Marie comes in and the blushing I do not know. I know no one by name Marie in Mount Airy, except Mary Fry and she is every bit of thirty-five and perhaps older ... About my blushing that is the worst rot.'[16]

So far as work was concerned, Buchman provoked no complaint from his tutors. To enter Mount Airy, he had had to pass a qualifying

* Commodore George Dewey, hero of the Spanish–American War.

examination which involved translating St Augustine from the Latin and passages of the New Testament from the Greek. Soon he was reading the Old Testament in the original Hebrew. Morning prayers were conducted alternately in German and English, and the students read Luther in the original German at the *Luther Abend* society to which Buchman belonged.[17] His own speech, too, was seasoned with words which were literal translations from the German ('homelike' from *heimlich*); but he wrote to his mother apologising for finding it too time-consuming to write letters in Pennsylvania German and asking her to translate for his father anything he did not understand.[18] He was also evidently taking elocution lessons, possibly to iron out the typical Allentown brogue, at the same time as relishing a visit from a friend who 'enjoys a good joke in the Pennsylvania German'.[19]

Sometime in 1900 he went to stay at the Hotel Walton, advertised as 'the only absolutely fire-proof hotel in Philadelphia', and from there took a momentous step. 'If you won't say anything, I'll tell you a secret,' he wrote home. 'I received three dollars for my first sermon. . . . It was a splendid experience for me. . . . My life work has begun.'[20]

At this time the Church was increasingly emphasising its mission to the poor, the destitute and the aged. Given the state of American society, it was an obvious and crying need. In the years after the Civil War, the United States had expanded rapidly but painfully. Between 1860 and 1890 the national wealth had almost quintupled, from 16 billion to 78 billion dollars; the coast-to-coast rail link had been completed in 1869 and 100,000 miles of new railroad track were laid in the 1880s alone; and enormous fortunes were made by the new business potentates, men like Rockefeller, Carnegie, Harriman and John Pierpont Morgan. Some of the new plutocrats might have their teeth set with diamonds and provide cigarettes wrapped in hundred-dollar bills, but on New York's East side people lived in squalor, 290,000 to the square mile. In 1895 the Salvation Army served 150,000 Christmas dinners in Boston alone. In New York there were 10,000 destitute children on the streets; while in the Bowery, in one small area six blocks long and seven wide, there were no fewer than 200 saloons. Alcoholism was rife, prostitution flourished; and the thousands of strikes which took place between 1881 and 1894 were merely an outward expression of the desperation of the poor.

In 1901, Buchman attended a meeting of the Lutheran Church's Inner Mission Society and was considerably moved by what he heard. 'The idea of the movement', he told his parents, 'is to bridge over the widening gulf which separates and alienates the masses from the Church by personal hand-to-hand work in densely populated districts, to visit the sick, lift up the fallen, counsel the tempted, cheer the aged, instruct the ignorant and reclaim the children.'[21] This, he wrote the following year, was the thing which lay nearest his own heart. 'Perhaps', he noted in his diary, 'the Lord will open this way of serving Him for me.'

By this time, he had already become involved in a wide variety of social work and flung himself into it with the same ardour as he showed in his social life. He joined the Sunshine Society, founded to help orphans, and visited hospitals and the aged.[22] In 1901 he and a group of colleagues opened a new Sunday School in Kensington, one of the poorest districts of the city. On the first Sunday fifty-one children were present, unprecedented in Philadelphia, wrote Buchman to his mother; on the second, seventy-four, though the collection amounted to only $1.06. 'I have charge of the infant department. . . . They are all interesting and all have beaming faces.' He had a distinctly lively sense of the wider significance of what he was doing. 'We are', he said, 'making history for the Lutheran Church in Kensington.'[23]

In the summer of 1901 he had been to the Northfield Student Conference in Massachusetts, founded by the evangelist Dwight L. Moody and now run by John R. Mott, the Assistant General Secretary of the YMCA and perhaps the dominant figure in the student evangelical movement. The visit, Buchman reported, 'completely changed' his life.[24] 'Never have I had such a splendid week.'[25] It seems to have been there that he decided that winning people to Christ must be his main objective in life, and that therefore he ought to win at least one person before he got back to Allentown. A visit to New York diverted him from this resolution, recalled as he was buying his train ticket home. The first person he laid eyes on at this juncture was a black porter. Buchman launched in.

'George, are you a Christian?'

'No.'

'Then you ought to be.'

The conversation continued in this vein, ending with, 'Now, George, you've got to be a Christian.'

'Thus ended', recalled Buchman, 'my first crude attempt to bring the unsearchable riches of Christ to another man. Whether he became a Christian or not . . . I can't tell. But that day the ice was broken on a new life-work.'[26]

Another influence on Buchman at this time was said to have been his Aunt Mary, who had a habit of asking him over Sunday lunch, 'Well, Frankie, how many people got converted today?' 'Meeting Mary is as good as going to church ten times over,' said Buchman's father.

His letters at this time display a marked increase in piety, frequently ending with a text or motto for his parents' edification. He also developed a deeper interest in his fellow-students. 'The other week', Buchman wrote to his parents in 1901, 'I did a work for one of my fellow-students which has changed his entire life. He was on the verge of leaving the

[17]

Seminary, feeling that he was not leading the true kind of a life. Today that man is the happiest fellow here. He is such a fine fellow and today he owes all he has in way of position in this institution to me.'[27] The tone is self-important, the theology no doubt unsound, but Buchman's desire to help individuals seems to have been starting to bear fruit.

He graduated from Mount Airy in the summer of 1902, having meantime succeeded in reviving a chapter of the Pennsylvania Alpha Iota fraternity there, and was one of the three members of his class chosen to speak at the commencement ceremony. Florence Thayer came down from Woonsocket to attend it. By now, Buchman was a little sad to be leaving – 'I shall miss these beautiful surroundings and the fellowship of the boys,'[28] he wrote to his parents – but conscious, too, that he was about to take up his vocation.

His parents had already vetoed a number of notions about what he might do next – at one time he had wanted to go to India, at another to spend a year at university in Leipzig – but he still cherished the ambition that he might be called to an important city church. Therefore when, in August, he was asked to take over the Oliver Mission in the city, he promptly refused. Then he talked with an old college friend from Allentown, Bridges Stopp, the son of wealthy parents but crippled and often in ill health. Buchman spoke of his hope of being offered a place in a big city church. 'You're going out to get a fat job,' retorted Stopp, 'but what am I going to get?' The remark stung Buchman's pride and redirected his ambition – or, perhaps, determined him to prove his lack of it. When, on the day of his ordination,* he was asked to start a new church in one of Philadelphia's growing suburbs, he agreed.

Overbrook, the charge which Buchman accepted, was an area embracing extremes of social class. There were mansions belonging to the city's prosperous business men and, on the other side of the railway tracks, the shacks and tenements of the poor. When he started work there was no church building, the room where he slept had no carpet on the floor, he was given a bed but no mattress. The letter appointing him said that he should begin work as soon as possible but added that the question of a salary 'must for the present be left unstated'. It did not take long to discover what that implied. 'They have just enough to pay their debts,' wrote Buchman to his parents, 'and nothing left for me.'[29]

The whole of his first month was spent tramping the streets trying to whip up a congregation and acquire suitable premises. All Buchman could find was a triangular three-storey building, on the corner of Lancaster Avenue and 62nd Street, the ground floor of which had been a store. This had to serve both as church and living quarters. One friend

---

* 10 September 1902, at St John's Lutheran Church, Allentown.

offered to pay the first month's rent, another to lend some chairs, providing that Buchman could arrange to have them picked up in Philadelphia. A month after he had arrived in Overbrook, the Church of the Good Shepherd opened its doors. There were eighty at the first evening service and the collection was $10.35.

It was hard and often dispiriting work. 'I do so miss the home life,' he wrote. 'Everything is so quiet, but I shall again be accustomed to it ere long. Pray for me and that I may have strength to continue.'[30] Buchman ate his meals off an old trunk covered with a cloth and, when his mother eventually sent a rug for the floor, he wrote that it made him feel as if he were living again. Nor was there any longer the consoling prospect of marriage. During the years at Overbrook, the relationship with Florence Thayer seems quietly to have faded away, even though at a reunion of his Muhlenberg class of '99 he was proposing the toast of 'Our Sweethearts'.

Buchman took an active interest in the School for the Blind in Overbrook. He enlisted the pupils to help him, and invited their chorus to sing in public. Genevieve Caulfield, blind since the age of three months, was one of these pupils, and forty years later was decorated by President Kennedy for her life-work for the blind in Asia. She had never forgotten Buchman. 'He was very interested to know that even then I was thinking of going to Japan,' she recalled. 'He asked me all about it when he took us out to the park or the zoo. He knew how children liked to eat, and he knew just what we liked to eat. . . . I never forgot him. He was kind without being patronising, and didn't take us out because he thought we were blind, but treated us as if we were real people whom he expected to do something in the world.'[31]

Following a pattern which persisted throughout his life, Buchman spent himself entirely on his work at Overbrook, and by the following summer was so exhausted that his doctor prescribed a long holiday. In June 1903 he sailed for Europe on the *Vancouver*, with a college friend, Howard Woerth. Buchman had hoped that his wealthier parishioners would provide the fare. It seems, however, to have come from his father, who at first was outraged at the thought of added expense after three years of college fees but then relented and won over his wife, for once disinclined to generosity towards her son. It was, in fact, most unusual for any but the wealthiest of Pennsylvania Dutch families to send their sons abroad.

The two young men made friends with a party of young ladies from Quincy, Massachusetts, organised by Miss Edith Randall. Soon they were all calling each other 'cousin', and for a time travelled together. Landing in Genoa, they visited Florence and Venice, and then went over the Simplon Pass by 'diligence' into Switzerland. Edith Randall later wrote to

Buchman, 'How many years have gone by since I first saw you drenched with sea-water on the deck . . . ! Shall we ever forget the perils of the Gorner glacier which we braved together, or the sunrise at 4 am (ouch) on the Rochers-de-Naye.'[32] At the Grand Hotel on the Rochers-de-Naye, two thousand metres above Montreux on Lake Geneva, Buchman found awaiting him a card from a Polish-German acquaintance staying half-way down the mountain at the Caux Palace, where he visited him next day.*

For Buchman, however, the holiday soon became more than a pleasant sightseeing trip in amiable company. As an ardent and ambitious young pastor, he was constantly looking for new ideas. Both in Switzerland and in Germany, he stayed in Christian Hospices (*Christliches Hospiz*) set up by the Lutheran Inner Mission to provide lodgings for young men who were away from home. Might he not, he wondered, be able to open a similar home in Philadelphia?

In the same enquiring spirit, Buchman visited Friedrich von Bodelschwingh, the son of a Prime Minister of Prussia, who had founded a colony of farms, hospitals and workshops for epileptics and the mentally sick at Bethel, near Bielefeld. Buchman was deeply impressed with von Bodelschwingh's attempt not merely to create the atmosphere of a Christian family but also to give everyone a worthwhile job to do.

Back in Overbrook again, the Church of the Good Shepherd flourished modestly. During the first year Buchman had depended heavily on an allowance from his parents. The first anniversary celebration, however, raised $310 and the executive committee were so overjoyed that they agreed to give their pastor $130 in back pay. That, at least, enabled him to pay off his debts. From now on he received his salary of $50 a month regularly.

It was little enough to meet the sort of expenses which Buchman began to incur. Immediately he arrived back from Europe, he had discussed with a group of young business men the idea of opening a *Hospiz* on the European pattern. Soon, necessity overtook planning. One snowy night there was a knock at Buchman's door. It turned out to be a house-boy from one of the nearby mansions who had been driven out into the night for some trivial misdemeanour. Buchman took him in and, eventually, found him a new job.

Then he heard of a college student who was literally starving. Buchman wanted to invite him, too, to share what he had, but realised that he did not even have a spare bed. One of his young friends in the congregation soon resolved that problem. He told Buchman to buy a bed at Wanamaker's and let him have the bill.

---

* Forty-three years later, it was this hotel which became the centre of Buchman's European work.

It was the same young man, Gus Bechtold, who told Buchman of a boy he had seen in the tuberculosis ward of a local Home for the Indigent and Insane. The boy's father had just died of *delirium tremens* and his mother, who had once been cook to the Governor of Pennsylvania, was addicted to laudanum, the alcoholic tincture of opium. Mary Hemphill and her two boys were living in a tenement, of the type known as 'three rooms straight up', in one of the most squalid parts of Philadelphia – searching the garbage-bins for food. Buchman called on her and found her washing herself thin over the laundry-tub trying to make a living, a woman totally without hope. He needed a housekeeper, and invited her to join him along with her two boys.

Meeting this family made him decide to give up drinking alcohol. If Mary took a drop, she would return to her addiction; so he too must not touch it. The decision, a genuine sacrifice for one of his upbringing, lasted his lifetime.

Nor were the Hemphills the only poor family whom Buchman helped. 'No one will ever know how much he did,' said Bechtold later. 'He was very close-mouthed about it. In all the years I knew Frank his first love was to serve the poor.'[33]

'That work', said Buchman afterwards, 'was a fellowship in a store, where it was easier for workers and domestic help to gather together. It was literally the church in the house. Some walked miles because they felt the poor would find an understanding heart and ear, but also a home. With them I gladly shared my all and learnt the great truth that where God guides, He provides.' Increasingly, he depended on gifts of food and money. Money was pushed through the letterbox, baskets of food left on the doorstep.

In May 1904 Buchman formally founded a *Hospiz*.[34] By November his own warmth of heart, Mary's cooking and the insatiable need in the district, had filled the house.

Indeed, the *Hospiz* was almost too successful. It soon had more applicants than beds. The Church's Home Missions Board, however, were not slow on the uptake. Within weeks they were beginning to talk about opening a full-scale hospice, with room for fifty young men. Buchman was delighted. The local Ministerium consulted him fully and seemed only too happy to go along with the kind of institution he had in mind. He had no intention of setting up an austere hostel which merely offered basic amenities: he wanted something much closer in spirit to the Buchman House Hotel.

'It is his (Buchman's) and the Board's purpose', record the Ministerium's minutes for June 1905, 'to actualise as nearly as possible the Christian family life, with all its comforts, refinements and wholesome influences.' Nor, at this stage, did either Buchman or the Ministerium consider economic self-sufficiency critical. Although it was hoped to make the hospice self-sustaining, the minutes went on, 'its very purpose might be defeated were an effort made to make it altogether so . . . The deficit . . . will have to be covered from the Treasury of the society.' The Ministerium had rented premises for this first Luther Hospice for Young Men at 157 N 20th Street for $2,000 a year, a sum which, in fact, made breaking even virtually impossible.

That was the understanding on which Buchman took the job of 'housefather', at $600 a year, with 'general charge of the house in material and spiritual things under the direction of the Board'.[35] Unfortunately, the chairman of the Board, Dr J. F. Ohl, was determined that the hospice should make the balancing of its books a priority and, indeed, regarded fund-raising as one of the housefather's principal jobs. Although he had, as Superintendent, been the sole signatory of the original terms of reference as set out in the minutes, it soon became clear that, so far as he was concerned, they might never have existed. Ohl was a musician, a liturgical scholar and a student of social movements, and known as a prickly character.

The two men found themselves in disagreement even before the hospice opened. Buchman had rented a cottage at Northfield, where he was taking daily Bible studies, as he did each year, and had invited Mary Hemphill, her sons and some of the young men from the Overbrook *Hospiz* to attend the Student Conference there with him. He was appointed as from 1 September and, having told the Board that he planned to return to Philadelphia on 26 August in ample time for the opening on 15 September, he was astonished to get a letter from Ohl pressing him to return sooner. It was essential, Ohl wrote, that the hospice should be completely full on the day it opened. Did Buchman not realise the cost if it were not? 'Furthermore,' he added, 'I must point out that the Board does not like the word "Hospice" spelt "Hospiz".'[36] Buchman replied that he could not leave Northfield before the 26th, to which Ohl sent a charitable acquiescence.

The new hospice flourished as the old one had done. Buchman chose as housemother an elderly New Englander called Sarah Ward, who was a close family friend of Dwight Moody and whom Buchman had first met at Northfield. Between them, Buchman and Miss Ward managed to create an atmosphere which was both homely and friendly.

'I believe I was expected, but certainly not that night,' wrote one college student who stayed there for a summer. 'Practically everyone had gone to bed; Mr Buchman had, I know. He was up immediately, however, and welcomed me in his dressing-gown as warmly as an old friend. I had scarcely been an hour in the town before I felt as much at home as in any place outside my native city.'

[22]

'Eating', he went on, 'was a most enjoyable affair . . . I remember one long table and two or three smaller ones. Mr Buchman sat at the head of the long table, some ten of us in a row down either side, and delightful Miss Ward sat at the foot. The meals were very simple, of course, but well-cooked, and there was always plenty of everything. Much was made of every occasion of note. Fourth of July, a distinguished guest, a birthday: all were made an excuse for some slight celebration at table. After breakfast, there were family prayers in the parlour.'[37]

'One sensed at once the spirit of the hospice,' wrote John Woodcock, a minister who lived there for a time. 'It was not an institution. It was a family. There were few rules beyond those in any well-ordered household.

'If one of the young men went out for the evening he knew that, after a certain hour, he would be admitted only in response to his ringing the doorbell. But, however late the hour, Frank was invariably there to open the door with never a sign that he had been put to any trouble, nor by any look that might embarrass the young man; but rather to invite him to share . . . something to eat. It is not strange that such an attitude frequently opened the way to further confidences and opportunities to help spiritually.'[38]

By the beginning of the following year, Buchman felt it was time for the hospice to extend its activities. He was much taken with the work being done in London at Toynbee Hall, a settlement in the East End founded by Canon Barnett in 1884. Barnett's idea had been to strengthen the mission work being done in the slums by setting up 'a resident club with a purpose', which would be run by a group of people who came to live in the slums and rehabilitate them from within. Instead of holding religious services in the settlements, he expected every member of the resident team to be a shining example of the Christian life. Faith, in other words, was to be caught, not taught. Buchman's ideas were modelled precisely on Barnett's. Having founded a hospice for poor boys, he wanted 'to keep them from becoming selfish through only receiving' by persuading them to care for people even poorer than themselves.

In the spring of 1906, therefore, he founded a settlement in one of the grimmest areas of downtown Philadelphia, on the corner of Callowhill and 4th Streets. According to a contemporary account it was a neighbourhood where immigrant families lived 'amid filth and squalor . . . under moral surroundings and influences that almost compel the angels to weep'. Here, Buchman persuaded a brewer to lend him a room above his stables where youngsters could meet on Saturday nights. Soon, immigrant children had begun to pour in from the streets – Polish, Italian and Turkish as well as German and Scandinavian, from Jewish and Catholic as well as Protestant families. On hot summer nights the ammonia stench from the stable straw came up through the floor. Buchman's home-town newspaper wrote, 'The Settlement House is thronged with children from the streets who find a warm, happy home. Boys learn carpentering, girls learn sewing, cooking and other domestic arts.'[39] When asked by some business friends what he was doing for these youngsters, Buchman replied, 'Well, I'm just teaching them how to live.'*

Both at the hospice and in the settlement Buchman found himself dealing with the social problems afflicting all rapidly expanding American cities. He wrote, for example, to the Water Street Mission in New York, where they had had a great deal of experience in helping to cure alcoholics, asking for advice. He was also learning to win the confidence of individuals. The story of 14-year-old George, which Buchman often told in later years, was typical.

'George', he would recall, 'was an orphan who came to live with me. We spent the first week happily together. I told him my best yarns. We had our meals together, and I gave him a great deal of attention but, with all this, I never gained his confidence. One Friday night he said he was going down town. I didn't think anything amiss about it. Round about 9.30 – it was one of those long summer evenings – I saw a form come up the street, sometimes zig and sometimes zag.

'My heart sank and the question came, what to do? I could see from my window he was trying to fit the key into the key-hole, but did not seem to make the connection. He began violently shaking the grating of the door, naturally blaming the door and thinking it to be at fault. Someone finally let him in, he made his way up to the room next to mine, and I saw that he was safely in bed without speaking to him or letting him know of my presence.

'Now, how to handle George? It came to me next morning not to go down to breakfast, because I thought if I saw the red in George's eye, I might say too much – so I waited until the middle of the morning and then went down to the place where George worked. I asked the manager whether I might see him. He said, 'Yes, any time.' The minute George saw me, his head fell. He thought, of course, that I had told the manager.

'I turned to George and said, "George, what about having some lunch together?" George gladly assented, so we went to a restaurant and began with oysters. George was as silent as a clam. We had fish and, while he was picking the bones, he said to me, "I was drunk last night", an awfully difficult thing for him to say, because he was fearful of what I might say. I didn't say anything. He then volunteered the information that it hadn't cost him very much, only twenty cents. He wanted to appeal to my sense of economy!

* Gus Bechtold became director of this settlement from 1914 to 1923.

'He then changed the subject and wanted to know about my Sunday School class, as he called the settlement. He wanted to talk religion. I knew that the time for that was not ripe yet, so I said my Sunday School class was going on all right. Then he knew he had to come to the point. He said, "You know, I thought to myself as I came up 20th Street last night, 'If he scolds me, I will go out and do it again.'"" We then smiled, and he left. He said, "I think I will come to your Sunday School next Sunday."'

Not surprisingly, the hospice was failing to balance its books, and Buchman's relations with Ohl and his Board became increasingly strained. Ohl kept up a constant barrage of criticism. The cooking at the hospice might be good, but was it not extravagant? Again, what about the rooms being occupied by Mary Hemphill and her sons, for which they paid nothing? Surely they could be let to paying guests?

On 3 May 1906 a special committee of the Board was set up 'to devise methods of decreasing expenditure and ensure the permanency of the Hospice'. It decided that a housekeeper should be taken on 'so that the housefather can give his time to spiritual care and, more important, the gathering of contributions, the collection of dues and securing of new members'. A housekeeper was duly hired. In addition, said the committee, there must be immediate economies: supplies should be bought at less expensive stores. Buchman, they implied, had been both careless and extravagant.

The new housekeeper naturally seems to have regarded herself as the committee's agent. The quality of the food fell sharply – Buchman said later that the butter was sometimes rancid, the fish stale – and she began a campaign to get rid of Mary Hemphill and her sons. Even under normal circumstances, Mary found it hard enough to stay away from her old addiction. Now, with a growing sense that the new housekeeper was determined to force her out, she began taking paregoric, a camphorated tincture of opium.

As the months went by, the situation became worse and Buchman found himself fighting a rearguard action. He put out at least one report, called *Hospice Incidents*, to try to illustrate for the Board the effectiveness of his work. There was the young man who had been 'in the rudderless class' but had decided to become a minister; a second who had been tempted to look for a prostitute ('the social sin') but who had then thought of the hospice and decided not to yield.

It was perfectly true, Buchman went on, that they had not succeeded with every young man, and that a handful had had to be asked to leave because they behaved 'in an antagonistic spirit', but every single one of them had asked if they could come back.

Why was it that they were not self-supporting? Well, replied Buchman, one of the young men earned only $4 a week in wages and paid all of it for his bed and board at the hospice. Another was paid $5 and he, too, handed over $4. In a third case, where both parents had died and two sisters were already in charitable institutions, a young man who earned only $3.50 a week had asked for a room. Should he have been turned away? He had since become confirmed.[40]

It was all to no avail. The conflict eventually came to a head in the summer of 1907. Buchman decided to make the matter an issue of confidence even at the risk of losing his job, though he seems to have felt there was very little danger of that.

First, he found a home for Mary Hemphill and her sons, with the future Mrs John Woodcock. Then, in October 1907, he submitted to the Board a seventeen-page handwritten document, signed by himself and Miss Ward. The hospice, he declared, was not a boarding house. 'The boarding house woman cannot afford to give them a dinner at Christmas and Thanksgiving that they can remember to the end of their days. It would be extravagant on the part of the boarding house. It does not pay.

'Out of my experience (I) consider these things necessary to . . . make the home attractive. These things cost. The saloonkeeper in the corner does not hesitate for one moment to spend money to make his place inviting and attractive. Surely the church will not hesitate to do the same to win the man for the church.'

Buchman then compared the hospice with similar institutions in other cities and countries. Their experience, he argued, suggested that a hospice needed to own its own building to stand a chance of breaking even, and many of those which did so still made a loss. To insist that the hospice be self-supporting was short-sighted and would mean its downfall. In any case, there was a much more important fact to be borne in mind. 'The results of this work', he declared, 'are not to be weighed in the scales of mammon.'

The work had been called a failure, yet young men flocked to it – no less than 300 had come under its influence. The hospice was universally well spoken of. Was it a failure because $1,000 a year was needed to make the place attractive enough to hold the men? The issue resolved itself into a simple question: 'What are you after?'

Then, there had been a number of occasions when his personal liberty had been interfered with and his actions questioned. If a man was old enough to be entrusted with such a work, he was also old enough to decide the minor details of his own conduct. 'If you are to have a *man* at the head of this work to bear a *man's* responsibilities, he must be treated as a *man* and not as a child.'

Next, Buchman laid down the conditions under which he felt prepared to continue. First of all, the Board must show its confidence in him: he had repeatedly had occasion, he said, to doubt men on the Board who were supposed to be behind him. All the hospice staff must be directly responsible to him. He must have the power to remove anyone who had proved unsuitable. In future, moreover, nobody should be appointed without his full knowledge and approval. He should be granted a month's vacation and his salary should be raised to $1,000 a year.

Finally, Buchman asked for a larger view of the work. The original commission, he said, could best be put in Jesus's own words describing the Last Judgement: 'Then shall the King say unto them on his right hand, Come, ye blessed of my Father, inherit the Kingdom prepared for you from the foundation of the world: For I was anhungered and ye gave me meat: I was thirsty and ye gave me drink: I was a stranger and ye took me in.'

'I insist', he ended, 'that whatever conclusion is reached be not from any mere motives of sympathy but that the question be squarely, dispassionately faced and such measures taken as shall ensure the healthy and normal growth of this work.'[41]

It was a passionate and uncompromising statement of Buchman's case. His tone suggests that he was entirely confident that he would win, perhaps because he regarded himself as indispensable.

That night the discussion with the Board went on until midnight. Led by the implacable Ohl, its six members insisted that the hospice must be financially self-supporting. That, Buchman knew, could mean only one thing: he would have to resign. Next morning, he did not appear for breakfast, and when John Woodcock knocked at his door he 'heard muffled sobs, and then "Come in."' 'I knew then what had happened and understood his feelings,' wrote Woodcock later. 'He responded, however, to the suggestion that he get up, have breakfast, and then go out into the country for the day. There, walking and talking seemed to help him to think more clearly and to arrive at some reasoned conclusions. That night he went before the Board and offered his resignation.'[42] The resignation was accepted on 24 October.

'I feel like a whipped cur, all tired out,' he wrote to his parents. Then, after saying that he had held a Settlement House service the evening before with some sixty children present, he added, 'Mary was brave, but you could see it was hard for her. Don't be anxious about me. All will go well. Greetings and love to all, loyally your son, Frank.'[43]

But all was far from well. Buchman's whole heart had been in the hospice. Now, his hopes had come crashing down. He had virtually been dismissed, he had been belittled by men who, he felt, simply did not grasp what he was trying to do. Ohl's attitude is apparent in his subsequent annual report in which, without even a formal mention of the founder of

the enterprise, he simply stated that it was 'now well-organised'.* Buchman's world was in ruins. He was an outcast in his own creation. As day
followed day and he relived again and again the fateful hours with the
Board, Buchman began to conceive a bitter hatred for those men.

The exhaustion due to months of unremitting work, added to the
turmoil in his spirit, made him ill. He saw a leading Philadelphia
physician, Weir Mitchell, who told him that he was worn out and
prescribed a long holiday abroad. His father gave him $1,000 and, on 29
January 1908, Frank Buchman sailed for Europe on the *SS Moltke*.

---

* The new director, the Revd Joseph Schantz, was, however, to write Buchman on the
25th anniversary of the hospice, in October 1930, urging him to attend: 'We would so like
to have you present. Will you do this, Frank? The Hospice has been a wonderful work in
spite of its poor plant. At least 25,000 men have lived in its atmosphere in its 25 years of
existence.'

AFTERNOON IN KESWICK

It began as another conventional journey of the kind which, four years earlier, had led to an 'illustrated lecture on "Travels through Europe" in Overbrook Church, tickets 25 cents, by the Revd F. N. D. Buchman'. Seville, Granada, Monaco, Cairo, Jerusalem, Athens, Constantinople, Vienna – it was a Grand Tour on a grand scale. The only trouble, as he said afterwards, was that 'I took myself with me'. Wherever he went, to the Alhambra, to the Greek islands in their shimmering, pellucid sea, to the Holy Places themselves, he felt harried and burdened by the unassuaged bitterness of his rejection by the Board. Off the island of Patmos, he said to a fellow-traveller, 'I'll never forgive those men.'

It seemed to him as if the Care personified in Horace's Ode – 'Black Care takes her seat behind the horseman' – was riding with him. 'I could feel its breath on the back of my neck,' he recalled. Often he felt more like a fugitive than a tourist. But, on the surface, he appeared cheerful most of the time. He took genuine interest in those around him, and people enjoyed his company. Travelling through the Mediterranean, he met an elderly American couple, the Dulls from Harrisburg in Pennsylvania; and, when Mrs Dull fell so seriously ill with pneumonia that she had to leave the ship at Athens, Buchman abandoned his own plans in order to look after them. He called on the American Embassy to report on Mrs Dull's progress and was invited to an Embassy party. There, a woman who had met him on the ship introduced him to Miss Angélique Contostavlos, Lady-in-Waiting to Crown Princess Sophie of Greece. Miss Contostavlos was interested by his kindness to the Dulls, and told her mistress about him. 'Today', she said, 'I met an American saint.'

'Impossible,' replied the Crown Princess. 'I'd like to meet him.'

Princess Sophie herself was, evidently, also much taken with Buchman: enough, anyway, to express a hope that he might help Greece and Turkey live at peace together and to arrange for him to meet the Turkish Sultan, Abdul Hamid, in Istanbul. Buchman seems to have taken this remarkable suggestion in his stride, and later described how he had been 'sent down in an armoured car – two men on the step, two men on the box' to the Sultan's reception. He also had breakfast with the Sultan.[1]

The extra expense of his stay in Athens left Buchman flat broke and he had to borrow from a friendly American doctor. His parents hurriedly cabled $150 but were clearly far from pleased. By June, his mother was writing reproachfully, 'I believe the only thing you like to do is travel. You know father's business is not what it was, he is getting older and is not as active as he used to be.'[2] Nevertheless, she would send enough money to enable him to stay in Europe until August.

In Germany, still sick at heart despite the outward liveliness, Buchman went to see von Bodelschwingh again. By July he was in Britain and decided to attend the Keswick Convention, an annual gathering of evangelical Christians. His hope was to see the reputed Congregational minister, F. B. Meyer, whom he had met at Northfield and who he believed might be able to help him. Meyer, however, was not there, and Buchman kept himself busy attending meetings and walking the Lakeland countryside.

Then, one Sunday, on a whim, he dropped in on a service in a little stone-built chapel. It was sparsely attended – a congregation of only seventeen – and a woman was leading the service. She was the evangelist Jessie Penn-Lewis, whose husband was a descendant of the family of William Penn. She spoke about the Cross of Christ. It was hardly a new subject to Buchman. He had heard the doctrine of the Atonement expounded on a score of occasions at Mount Airy, taken notes on it, answered examination questions on it, preached about it. This woman, however, spoke so movingly about the Cross that, for the first time, it became a living and life-giving experience for him. 'She pictured the dying Christ as I had never seen him pictured before,' he recalled later. 'I saw the nails in the palms of His hands, I saw the bigger nail which held His feet. I saw the spear thrust in His side, and I saw the look of sorrow and infinite suffering in His face. I knew that I had wounded Him, that there was a great distance between myself and Him, and I knew that it was my sin of nursing ill-will.

'I thought of those six men back in Philadelphia who I felt had wronged me. They probably had, but I'd got so mixed up in the wrong that I was the seventh wrong man. Right in my conviction, I was wrong in harbouring ill-will. I wanted my own way and my feelings were hurt.

'I began to see myself as God saw me, which was a very different picture than the one I had of myself. I don't know how you explain it, I can only tell you I sat there and realised how my sin, my pride, my selfishness and my ill-will, had eclipsed me from God in Christ. I was in Christian work, I had given my life to those poor boys and many people might have said 'how wonderful', but I did not have victory because I was not in touch with God. My work had become my idol.

'I did not need any other voice than the voice of the Man on the Cross. I thought of the lines, "This hast Thou done for me, What have I done for Thee, Thou Crucified?" I was the centre of my own life. That big "I" had to be crossed out. I saw my resentments against those men standing out like tombstones in my heart. I asked God to change me and He told me to put things right with them.

'It produced in me a vibrant feeling, as though a strong current of life had suddenly been poured into me and afterwards a dazed sense of a great spiritual shaking-up. There was no longer this feeling of a divided will, no sense of calculation and argument, of oppression and helplessness; a wave of strong emotion, following the will to surrender, rose up within me . . . and seemed to lift my soul from its anchorage of selfishness, bearing it across that great sundering abyss to the foot of the Cross.'³

The experience was as sudden as that which came to John Wesley in the upper room in Aldersgate, or to Francis at St Damiano when he 'fell before the crucifix and, having been smitten with unwonted visitations, found himself another man than he who had gone in'.

As he left the chapel Buchman's one thought was not so much to forgive those he had hated, but to ask their forgiveness for the way he had behaved. Back at the house where he was staying, he sat down and wrote letters to each member of the Board. One of the letters – the one to Dr Ohl, dated 27 July 1908 – has survived in the archives at Mount Airy.

'Am writing,' declared Buchman, 'to tell you that I have harboured an unkind feeling toward you – at times I conquered it but it always came back. Our views may differ but as brothers we *must* love. I write to ask your forgiveness and to assure that I love you and trust by God's grace I shall never more speak unkindly or disparagingly of you.

'The lines of that hymn have been ringing in my ears –

> When I survey the wondrous Cross
> On which the Prince of Glory died,
> My richest gain I count but loss
> And pour contempt on all my pride.'⁴

Buchman appended the same lines to each of the letters and, each time, felt the weight of the words in a completely new way. 'It's easy to repeat those lines,' he said later. 'I know because I'd done it over and over again myself. But that day those lines had become great realities. And the last line cost me most of all. I almost wrote it in my own blood.'*

* Buchman used to say that he had received no replies to these letters. Ohl noted on the back of his letter from Buchman, '. . . you will notice that he gives no address. Had he done so I surely would have written.' Among Buchman's papers is a brief note from Miss F. G. Crafts, the housekeeper, to whom a letter must also have gone. She wrote, 'I thank you very much for your kindness in forgiving me. For my part I have nothing to forgive. P.S. The dear little children missed you very much at the Settlement House.'

At tea that afternoon Buchman related what had happened to him, and among those who heard the story was a Cambridge undergraduate. 'I want to talk to you,' he said to Buchman. They walked around Derwentwater. Before they returned the young man, too, had found a release similar to Buchman's. 'That was the first man that I ever brought face to face with the central experience of Christianity,' Buchman commented.* From that day Buchman began to help people, not from a position of rectitude but from the reality of knowing that he too was a sinner and that he had been forgiven.

From Keswick, too, Buchman wrote to his mother. He told her how he now knew that he was the seventh wrong man.

'I was awfully put out about your letter that you did not know sooner to forgive and forget,' she replied. 'Put that out of your mind. We are counting the days till you come home.'⁵ It was some years before she measured the magnitude of what had taken place in her son's heart.

Back in America, the new Frank Buchman faced his first direct test. 'In church on Christmas morning, I saw sitting in front of me one of the very men against whom I had harboured ill-will. He had a bald spot on his head, and sitting opposite him in Committee meetings I used to think the letter "I" was written all over that spot. After the service, I reached out my hand and said "Merry Christmas". He could not meet my eye. But I had been kept from ill-will.'

Fifty years later, John Woodcock, the man who had helped Buchman to decide to resign on the morning after the hospice Board meeting, put the whole matter into longer perspective. 'I think we both felt that we were straight and they were wrong,' he wrote to Buchman. 'We do know now that what seemed to be the breakdown of your life's work was only the opening of the gate which God alone could open, through which we go to our *real* life's work.'⁶

---

* Fourteen years later, passing through Liverpool, Buchman telephoned this man, who told him that the talk had 'regenerated the whole principle of his life'. His name is not known.

PICKLE AT PENN STATE

It was indeed a very different Frank Buchman who arrived back in America – altogether calmer and happier, thought his friend John Woodcock.[1] He was, still, however, without a job and had very little idea what to do next. The Woodcocks knew that the post of YMCA Secretary at Pennsylvania State College was vacant, and Mrs Woodcock suggested he apply for it. Whether he did is not clear, but one way or another word got to John R. Mott's office at YMCA headquarters that Buchman might be available, and Mott's assistant, H. P. Anderson, wrote to the Chairman of the College 'Y' Committee, Professor J. M. Willard, recommending Buchman as a 'man of breadth and great personal attractiveness'.[2] The Dulls' nephew, Vance McCormick, then Chairman of the State Democratic Committee, was a College trustee and may also have intervened. The faculty members who had interviewed Buchman were soon urging him to come. 'We accepted your terms with the hope and expectation of prompt acceptance,' wrote the Professor of Romance Languages, Irving L. Foster.[3] But Buchman, now thirty, hesitated for over two months before accepting and, even then, only agreed to a six-month engagement, starting in January 1909, on a trial basis. The salary was $100 a month.

Buchman's hesitation was not altogether surprising. The YMCAs dominated the religious life of most American college campuses in the years before the 1914–18 war but, even so, 'Penn State' was scarcely an alluring prospect. Founded as an agricultural college where farmers' sons could acquire a liberal arts education as well as the rudiments of farming, Penn State had 1,400 students and was known neither for its intellectual excellence nor its sporting prowess. It was, moreover, remote and provincial, situated in the centre of the state, where a small town without social outlets, actually called State College, had grown up around it – 'out in the boondocks with a vengeance', as one local historian put it.[4]

In recent months, too, State College had earned itself an unenviable reputation. The YMCA Secretary would be in charge of the religious work in the college, and Mott had, according to Buchman, told him that he thought it 'the most godless university in the country'. Moreover, a

[33]

student strike – a rare phenomenon in those days – had only just been
settled. Class scraps often resulted in serious injuries, and one recent 'flag
scrap' had lasted for ninety hours. 'Hazing' – the custom of subjecting
new students to harassment – was often brutal, and, although saloons
were forbidden by state law, the supply of alcohol on the campus was
plentiful, much of it peddled by a local hostler and college janitor called
Gilliland. On the night Buchman arrived, there were a score of liquor
parties in progress. Gilliland did a particularly brisk trade before and after
college football matches. 'There were times when we sent six hundred to a
game, and they would all be drunk,' said Buchman of his first year. Few
games were won. Buchman soon found that you did not have to be a
student to get an unpleasant reception. He had not been in his room for
two hours before two hefty young men arrived with the idea of roughing
him up. Fortunately a friend had sent him a large box of chocolates, so
he hastily suggested they continue their talk over these. That saved the
day.

Perhaps Buchman was still nervous when he was introduced to the
student assembly. In any event, he could hardly have begun more ineptly.
'Greetings, students of State College,' he declared in a high-pitched
voice, and was duly greeted with howls of merriment and derision. At that
moment, the YMCA committee may have felt relieved that they had only
hired him for six months.

They need not have worried. Buchman attacked his new job with the
pent-up energy of a man just back from an eight-month holiday who was
determined not to fail and who, furthermore, had a deep experience to
share. Soon, his mother was complaining that he only sent her postcards
instead of the usual letters.[5] He was working eighteen to twenty hours a
day, had stepped up the YMCA's level of activity with a new programme
of classes and meetings, and seemed to be everywhere at once. 'He was
robust, always neatly dressed, rosy-cheeked and sparkling and distinguished-looking in his beaver hat,' recalled the college chaplain, Robert
Reed. 'He seemed to be going among people constantly. Every day you
would see him walking on the campus with one of the fellows, chatting and
laughing. He had a keen sense of humour and his chuckle and spontaneous laughter were very contagious.'[6]

The ridicule, however, continued. During his first year, Buchman
reckoned, he was probably the most unpopular man on campus. Some of
the students reacted sharply both to his earnestness and to what they felt
were his puritanical attitudes, and he was nicknamed 'Pure John', a jibe
derived from a contemporary cartoon figure. He became accustomed to
seeing 'Pure John – 99 per cent pure' scrawled on vacant sign-boards; he
was guyed in the college revue, caricatured in the college magazine.

He also seems to have irritated some of the faculty. 'Buchman', one professor is reported to have said later, 'oozed the oil of unctuous piety from every pore. I would not be interested in seeing him again if it were at the cost of having to shake hands with him.'[7]

The results of his vigour and friendliness, nevertheless, were impressive. Within two months of his arrival, Buchman was writing to his cousin and adopted brother Dan, 'We had 1,100 men at the meeting last night ... Entire fraternities are signing up to study the Bible.'[8] Within two years, membership of the 'Y' had more than doubled from 491 to 1,040. Within three years, it had more than seventy-five per cent of the student body on its books, compared with thirty-five per cent when Buchman arrived.[9]

Furthermore, he seemed to have a particular gift for attracting outstanding students. 'Before the end of that first year', wrote Lloyd Douglas, author of *The Robe*, who was then Director of Religious Education at Illinois State College and who visited Penn State several times, 'it was discovered that the men about the campus who were doing the real things, leaders in scholastic standing, athletics, oratory ... were spending whole evenings in Buchman's quarters ... It seemed easy for Buchman to collect about him the picked men of the campus. Of course, it was not easy, but Buchman had a Napoleonic gift of making people want to do hard things.'[10]

Buchman himself, however, was far from satisfied with the results of his work. The numbers were impressive, but were men just being influenced a little or were they experiencing the kind of change he himself had undergone in Keswick? Many were making initial decisions to let Christ into their lives. But how deep did these decisions go? The alcohol consumption, it had to be faced, had hardly decreased, and the general tone of the college had not greatly altered. Would the quality of the decisions being made reshape men's careers, and affect their communities in later life? Or would it just be the sorry tale of some reawakenings, where greater religious observance went along with a decline in morality in the community at large? He later described his dilemma: 'I was working eighteen hours a day and I was so busy that I had two telephones in my bedroom. People kept coming to me, but the changes in their lives were not revolutionary enough to be permanent.'

At this point he consulted a visitor to the college – almost certainly the F. B. Meyer he had sought in Keswick – about his inner questionings. 'You need to make personal, man-to-man interviews central, rather than the organising of meetings,' said Meyer.

'Since that time', remarked Buchman later, 'I no longer thought in terms of numbers but in terms of people.'

Meyer also asked, 'Do you let the Holy Spirit guide you in all you are doing?' Buchman replied that he did indeed pray and read the Bible in the

morning, and sometimes received inspirations then and at other times in
the day.

'But', persisted Meyer, 'do you give God enough uninterrupted time
really to tell you what to do?'

Buchman thought this over and decided to give at least an hour each
day in the early morning to listening to God, a period which he came to
refer to as a 'quiet time'. He chose from five to six o'clock before the
phones were likely to ring. The very first morning, he received an unusual
thought, the nickname of a student, 'Tutz, Tutz, Tutz' – and the first
person he met when he went out on to the campus was that same Tutz.

'Tutz', Buchman later recalled, 'regularly got tight on trips with the
Dramatic Club, but would always kneel down at night to say his prayers. I
first felt like funking him, but the insistent urge came that this was the time
to speak to him. I asked whether he would like to speak to a friend of mine
who knew how to put before people the great truths of life. He readily
assented, feeling it lots more important than a lecture. This friend was an
athlete, who had recently graduated from one of the large state universities of the West. Tutz came back to me after the interview and told me that
he had decided to give his life unreservedly to Christ. I said to him,
"Well, what are you going to do about it?"

'He said, "*Do* about it?"

'I said, "Are you not going to tell your friends about this new experience
of yours?"

"Why, they would all laugh at me!" he said.

'I said, "That's your game in the Dramatic Club, the more curtain calls
you get, the better you like it."

'Tutz had imagination, so when all his club-mates were sitting about
waiting for lunch, he walked in and said to the group, "I suppose you'll
laugh when I tell you what I did this morning." They were all agog, as they
thought Tutz had pulled the leg of a professor or heard some new funny
story. He announced simply and unemotionally, "I have decided to
change my life." Not a fellow cracked a smile . . . I met him seven years
afterwards, when he said that vital meeting was the means of changing his
whole life's direction.'

Buchman now began to brood on how to 'bring the whole college, as a
community, Godwards', which it seemed to him should be the logical
development from real changes in individuals. Three names came forcibly into his mind – Gilliland, the bootlegging hostler, who was commonly
known as Bill Pickle, Blair Buck, 'a Virginian graduate student with every
grace and charm', and the college Dean, Alva Agee, 'popular, easy of
access, hospitable, a man's man and an agnostic'.

Buchman knew that Blair Buck was not a man to be rushed, 'a type of
person', as he observed later, 'with whom you used intelligent restraint

and a nonchalant reserve'. 'I didn't ever talk to him about the things that meant most to me . . . We talked about everything else under the sun.' They also went riding – a passion with Buchman since boyhood – in the green hills around the town.* Buchman's intentions were to make friends with Buck, and to involve him in the conversion of Bill Pickle.

Bill Pickle was the illegitimate son of a colonel, and had served in the Civil War as a drummer boy. He sported a 'furious walrus moustache', 'looked like a roaring pirate' and had often been heard to declare that he would like to stick a knife in Buchman's ribs. Buchman was rather nervous about him, and was alarmed when one day Buck pointed him out as they walked through town together, because he knew he must make a move towards him or lose Buck's respect. 'I've got a big nose,' Buchman related later, 'so when I walked up to Bill, I put my hand on his biceps so that if he did haul off, he wouldn't haul so hard. The thought flashed into my mind, "Give him your deepest message." "Bill," I said, "we've been praying for you." To my surprise all the fight went out of him. He pointed to a church tower.

' "See that church over there?" he said. "I was there when the cornerstone was laid. There's a penny of mine under it." '

The conversation ended in an invitation for Buchman and Buck to visit Bill, his wife and their twelve children in their unpainted house on what everyone called 'Pickle Hill'. Buchman found that they shared a love of horses, and they became friends. After some months he talked Bill into going to a student conference in Toronto. Bill said he would go if Buchman gave him his cherished beaver hat – a price Buchman promptly, if sadly, paid.

In Toronto, Bill decided to become a Christian, and, as he found writing difficult, asked Buchman to write out his letter of apology to his wife for the way he had treated her in the past. Thereafter, despite efforts by some of the students to lure him back, Bill stopped both bootlegging and drinking, which brought a marked decline in the overall campus consumption.

Dean Agee, who had paid Bill's fare to Toronto as a kind of 'dare', was much impressed by the difference in him, and Buck henceforth began to drop the words 'If there is a God . . .' and to speak of One who 'had answered their prayer'. But there was a long way to go. One day, however, he told Buchman, 'There are lots of things I don't understand about the Bible and prayer and helping others.' 'Let's spend the summer vacation

---

* Buchman owned a horse called Mary during the early years at Penn State. When upkeep became too expensive, he sold her and gave the proceeds to a poor student. 'I have just had the good news that it has helped him and his brother through college. They have built quite an extensive laundry service round Mary,' he wrote Woodcock on 7 November 1916.

together,' replied Buchman, and during a couple of months, first on Mackinac Island in Michigan and then in Montana, where Buck's grandfather used to be Governor, and through the West, the younger man found the change he was seeking.[11]

Over the seven years at Penn State the hallmark of Buchman's work was his ability to bring such change into the lives of the most unlikely people. These included, besides those mentioned, Dick Harlow, who became football coach at Harvard; Henry Armstrong, one of the originators of the nickname 'Pure John'; Pete Weigal, who had stuffed his ears with cotton wool when forced to attend a meeting as horn-player in the college band, but became interested after the cotton wool fell out during an especially lively serenade; the football captain, Larry Vorhis; an athlete, Pete Johnson; and 'Pop' Golden, the tough football coach, whose dissipated life had affected generations of students. With most the alteration was lasting: Harlow introduced Buchman when he spoke at Colgate University some years later; Weigal succeeded Buchman as YMCA Secretary when he left Penn State; Blair Buck became a pioneer of black education in the South at Hampton Institute in Virginia and was closely in touch with Buchman all his life; Dean and Mrs Agee corresponded with him for many years; Armstrong invited Buchman to his home in 1931; and Mrs Pete Johnson came to Buchman's eightieth birthday party in 1958, her husband's factory having sent a gift of tiles to the American centre of Buchman's work. 'Pop' Golden's influence became, in Buchman's opinion, more important than that of a dozen preachers and, for whatever reason, the football team won 26 games and lost only two in the four years after his change.

All this time a wider impact was being felt in the college. 'In five years the permanent secretary at Penn State has entirely changed the tone of that one-time tough college,' wrote Maxwell Chaplin, the YMCA Secretary at Princeton, to a friend in 1914 after attending one of Buchman's annual 'Y Week' campaigns.

Lloyd Douglas took part in the same campaign. 'It was', he wrote afterwards, 'the most remarkable event of its kind I ever witnessed.

'There wasn't an idle moment for any man who had been summoned to the campaign as an associate. One night, Buchman decided we would pair off and visit the fraternity houses and put to each group the proposition of definite Christian decision. It was an impossible job and everybody realised the futility of it but Buchman. Well, there were great doings that night. One after another, prominent fraternity men . . . stood up before their fellows and confessed that they had been living poor, low-grade lives and from henceforth meant to make good. The faculty was back of it all heart and soul.'[12]

The campaign was not restricted to the campus. Buchman divided the town into ten sections, and made each the responsibility of a team of helpers whose job it was to invite everyone to the meetings. It was to be, he said, an 'everyman-out campaign'.

On the first day, all the stores and the town's solitary cinema closed to encourage people to attend. The college band played in the town before the meeting began and then marched to the hall. There were mass meetings addressed by well-known speakers on topics like 'The Secrets of a Victorious Life'. The town was 'running over with notables' according to one professor and, for that week, 'the college lived and talked and argued nothing but religion'.[13]

The following year, Buchman brought in 150 outside helpers from most of the major East Coast colleges. Each was given a student 'secretary', whose job was to see that their time was used to the full: frequently they conducted interviews until midnight and beyond. Some, like Professor Henry Wright of Yale, relished the intensity of the campaign. 'I spoke pretty nearly steadily for three days,' he wrote to a friend; 'it was a glorious work.'[14] Others found the pace decidedly testing. 'It took me a week to get over that strenuous day at State College,' one visitor wrote to Buchman. 'I wouldn't have missed it for a hundred dollars, nor repeat it for five hundred. You ought to confine your invitations strictly to Pennsylvania Dutchmen who are as steel-framed as you.'[15]

'Sooner or later', noted Fred Lewis Pattee, the Professor of English, 'there appeared on the campus every college religious leader in the nation to study Buchman's methods.'[16] His methods were not only studied, but applied. Thus the Yale University publication, *The Week*, on 3 March 1915, traced the genesis of a religious awakening in Yale to this same campaign. 'It really began at the Pennsylvania State College last year under Frank N. D. Buchman', the article stated, and concluded, 'This new evangelism of the second decade of the twentieth century is transforming our colleges.'

Thereafter, there were campaigns on the Penn State pattern at Yale, Illinois State, Williams, Cornell and other colleges, as well as student conventions in Rochester and Kansas City; Estes Park, Colorado; Eaglesmere, Pennsylvania; Silver Bay, New York; and Northfield, Massachusetts. To most of them Buchman was able to take teams of men whom he had trained. It was an old dream coming true. 'When I came to State College, I had the whole general line for our Eastern colleges in mind,' he wrote to an associate in China three years later. 'If you had asked me how that would have worked out, I could not have told you. Bill Pickle, the grandson of the Governor, the coach of the football team, and all the other fruit that came could not be planned in advance. When, however, other colleges saw that there was sustained change in Penn State, they asked that these same principles be carried back to their

[39]

institutions, but we must remember this was a programme of seven years. It had to grow naturally. Any plans "stuck" in to Penn State would have died a natural death.'[17]

For Buchman, in fact, the 'Y Week' was merely the high point in a year of intense activity. His summer holiday seems to have been conducted with the same vigour. Mrs Buchman had been complaining constantly of the lack of letters from her son; but now they were to spend the vacation as a family, and in June, Buchman, his parents and Dan sailed on the *President Lincoln*. They returned three months later, having been in England, Holland, Belgium, Germany and Italy. His father, by now two years retired, was 72 and already a semi-invalid.

Dan kept a diary. Four days out to sea, on 25 June, he notes: 'Cousin Frank held a service in the dining saloon. Good attendance.' On 6 July, in London, Buchman's attention seems to have wandered from the care of his family: 'Spent whole day in British Museum, got no dinner. Cousin Frank went to Eastbourne to see some lady-in-waiting to Queen of Greece.' 15 July, Antwerp: 'Met Edith Randall from Quincy, Mass. F. went to movies with E.R.' This was a year after her letter to Buchman reminiscing about their Swiss mountain climb in 1903. The next day, 'F. to Cathedral with E.R.' Again, his family seem to have been left to fend for themselves. Edith Randall also appears for dinner a week later, in Cologne, then vanishes for good. On 1 August, in Bad Homburg, Buchman is learning to play golf, and on the 12th all the family are at the English Church, at the invitation of the British chaplain, to see the Kaiser unveil a memorial to Edward VII of England.

At Bad Homburg, Buchman consulted a Dr Schäfer who diagnosed a 'floating kidney' linked with colitis. Schäfer prescribed a rich diet. 'A quiet mind at night and a rest of several hours during daytime will contribute to your well-being, and take Falstaff as an ideal – every pound you will put on will increase your health,' he wrote. 'Baths will be the hours when you may think of poetry and romances, and every drop of water will stimulate the heart and nervous systems. Begin with a hot bath of fifteen minutes duration and pour cold water down your back – where the floating kidney is a solid rock. . . .'[18] How much of the good doctor's advice Buchman took is doubtful – although he was never averse to a rich diet – but in later life he spoke of Schäfer as the man who had 'anchored my floating kidney'.

Back home again, Buchman paid a four-day visit to his old college, Muhlenberg, and asked the YMCA President there, Paul Krauss, to make arrangements for another 'everyman campaign'. The preparations apparently did not fully match his expectations because, when he got back to Penn State, he wrote Krauss a letter 'so you can gain some idea how largely we plan here'.

He had, he said, arrived back at State College late on Saturday. There followed a thumb-nail sketch of his programme. 'Got in touch at once with Flagg, one of our athletics managers, who was seriously hurt in the Gymnasium during the week. Went to our entertainment course. Had interviews with four men. Got to bed a little after twelve. Had more than two hundred at my Freshman Bible Class on Sunday morning. Had interviews both before and after the meeting. Took dinner with the Gilliland family . . . Came back to meet the Hugh McAllister Beaver Club.*

'Had appointment with our Athletics Director, who was leading our meeting in the evening. Students' communion at two o'clock. Meeting with student representative. Called on football coach and several athletes. Didn't have a chance to eat supper. Taught a Fraternity Bible Class, came back in time for a meeting of a thousand students . . . It lasted for an hour and thirty-five minutes. Coach Reed and "Pop" Golden, our athletic director, Professors Agee and Torrey spoke. It was a splendid meeting and the aim of it was to prepare the men for the Pittsburgh game. Had a meeting for conference and prayer afterwards. Arranged to help financially the man who was hurt in the Gymnasium. Went out to talk over some plans with our Chaplain. Got to bed at twelve. Am leaving for Pittsburgh to be gone until Saturday. I neglected to tell you that we had a special meeting for the Freshmen of the entire class and had a talk on the evils of drink and the problems of social purity.

'I know', concluded Buchman, 'that you men will push the work at Muhlenberg.'[19] This letter is a good illustration of how, all his life, Buchman unconsciously expected his colleagues to work at the same pace as he did, and often to use the same approach.

Buchman frequently invited to the campus what he called 'contagious' outside speakers like the evangelist Billy Sunday, the pioneer social worker Jane Addams and – despite opposition from some of his colleagues – Melinda Scott, a pioneer of the Catholic workers' movement who had taken up the cause of women workers in sweat-shops.

In 1912 he decided to set up a home on the campus where he could offer good food and a warm welcome. 'My plan', he wrote, 'would be to gather the men who do not have the advantage of friends, the lonely, the homesick, the discouraged, the tempted.'[20]

* This was a boys' club which he had started in the town. In a letter to Mrs Andrew Carnegie, who had sent 100 dollars to the Club and to whom he sent, on their behalf, a trailing arbutus in a tin, he wrote: 'They are the sons of the working people, and up until two years ago they were rather shiftless. I organised them into the Hugh McAllister Beaver Club, and started a baseball team, and in the fall a football team. They are holding together nicely, and instead of the Saturday night carousing, they have just lately organised themselves into a town YMCA.' (Buchman to Mrs Carnegie, 29 April 1912. Buchman first met Andrew Carnegie on 8 May 1907 at Princeton.)

[41]

He invited Mary Hemphill, whom he had placed with various friends since the days of the hospice and whose son, David, he was putting through college, to come back to him as housekeeper and cook. 'The master of a great art,' Buchman described her later, 'a noble soul, a ready wit, a self-effacing team-mate . . . The cooking of a good meal was her greatest delight.' Buchman also asked the college for extra facilities. 'I want to arrange for the extra room you wish,' replied the college President, Edwin Sparks. 'An organisation which can bring about an opening of college such as we have seen thus far is worthy of an entire dormitory if it wishes it.'[21] Buchman duly took an apartment on College Avenue and, with the help of Mary's omelettes and oyster stews, used it to entertain a steady stream of visitors.

Particularly in view of the generosity of his table, it was a mystery to other members of the faculty how he managed to pay his bills, despite the fact that his salary finally rose to $3,000 a year with another $250 for expenses. The President's wife, Mrs Sparks, recalled the time when, travelling back to Penn State, Buchman got to within thirty miles of the campus but, with only twenty-six cents in his pocket, had not enough to pay for the bus fare. Then 'he just happened to meet Mr Sparks and, of course, Mr Sparks invited him to ride home in his car and gave him dinner on the way.'

Buchman was also, added Mrs Sparks, 'very generous with what he had, giving away his overcoat or anything if he thought someone else needed it worse than he did'. He frequently made loans to students with little expectation of ever seeing the money again. Yet, by some mysterious and rather irritating alchemy, he always seemed to have enough. Somewhat to Mrs Sparks' chagrin, he was also able to borrow large sums of money from the bank without security of any kind; whereas she, the President's wife, could not. 'There were times I would get so provoked with Buchman that I'd vow not to do another thing for him, although I always did,' she wrote later, and added that he impressed her 'as having the most faith in God of anyone I ever knew'.[22]

President Sparks always backed Buchman in his work. But even he was given on occasion the same kind of treatment as his students. The draft of a letter to Sparks which Buchman wrote while he was on a tour of the Far East suggests that he was no respecter of persons. It begins: 'Dear President Sparks, I am talking to you as I talk to the men. I have repeatedly tried to bring you to a realisation of your spiritual needs but I have evidently not made myself clear.

'My chief concern is for your own soul. You show every symptom of not being a happy man. Your smile seems forced. You do not seem to find the real joy in your religious life. Your interest is commendable and far exceeds that of others I know, but it does not ring true. . . .'[23]

Not surprisingly, perhaps, if the tone of this letter was typical, Buchman had plenty of critics at Penn State. Some members of the faculty accused him of self-advertisement: his annual reports, which were quoted in evidence, seldom erred on the side of understatement. In 1914, for example, he wrote, 'Prominent people are keen to know about God's wonder-working in our midst . . . Penn State as a result of this year has become a world factor, and is making her influence felt in many centres.' The *North American Student* magazine, he went on, with evident satisfaction, had given extensive notice of Penn State's campaigns in two issues, while a campaign led by Mott at Columbia had only merited a few lines.[24] Buchman may well have believed that what had happened at Penn State was entirely the work of God – indeed he often said, 'I hadn't any part in all this except that I let God use me' – but he certainly sounded at times as if he was blowing his own trumpet, if only on behalf of the Almighty.

Some of the faculty also charged him with name-dropping. He was, declared one, 'always talking about important men and women he knew', an instance being a telegram explaining a postponed return 'which ended in a long list of the famous he was meeting'.[25] This could well have been after an occasion where the Andrew Carnegies invited him to meet various of their friends, including the heads of Yale, Cornell and other major educational institutions, when his work at Penn State was a matter of frequent remark.

Yet a contrasting characteristic was evident. A visitor to one of the 'Y Week' campaigns, Professor Norman Richardson, remarked to the college chaplain, Robert Reed, 'I have been interested in watching this man Buchman all day. He is always in the background, pushing others into places of leadership and responsibility.'[26]

He was also, it seems, ready to accept criticism which he felt justly applied to him. He wrote to a friend at Union Theological Seminary in New York, 'Thanks so much for your most helpful criticism. It is just this that I need most of all . . . I am just like a beginner . . . I have just spoken at Wesleyan, and . . . felt that it had not "come across".'[27]

Buchman was full of apparent contradictions. An ardent advertiser of his own activities, he was also surprisingly self-effacing; the product of a conservative and cautious religious tradition, he was strikingly radical in his methods; extrovert in manner, he was at heart profoundly reserved.

His work, too, was full of paradoxes. He concerned himself with the intimate details of people's lives yet encouraged them to have a global perspective: 'Think in continents,' he told students, although his own experience was so far limited to two.* In the same way, although he was at

* cf. Major Gordon Heron (Penn State 1915) to Buchman, 20 May 1932: 'I well remember how you used to tell us to "think in continents" and be a "world power" . . . It seems to me you have achieved what you used to advise for us.'

grips with the deepest human emotions, his work bore none of the marks of extravagant revivalism. 'As I have witnessed it,' wrote Blair Buck later, '(it) is not at all of the emotional variety characteristic of Billy Sunday or Aimee Semple Macpherson.'[28]

Those seven years in Penn State provided Buchman with a multitude of stories which he used for the rest of his life. He was no preacher. Where others used emotion or the fear of hell-fire, Buchman used stories. These encouraged the hearer to feel that if people like Bill Pickle, Blair Buck and Dean Agee could become different, then it was possible for anyone. He was a master raconteur, and people frequently said that a story which took him an hour to tell flashed by like ten minutes. Critics attributed this method to egotism, since – particularly in the early years – they were generally stories in which he had himself featured: it was only as others began to work with him that the stories as frequently centred around the adventures of others. Buchman used them in an age before films or television, to leave vivid pictures in people's minds.

ASIAN RECONNAISSANCE

In April 1915 Buchman left Pennsylvania State College, permanently as it turned out.* America still being neutral, Mott had asked if he would join a small 'flying squadron' of experienced workers for service among the prisoners-of-war in Europe;[1] then, a few days later, the evangelist, Sherwood Eddy, with Mott's agreement, pressed him to go instead to India to help to prepare a large-scale religious campaign. Buchman, as he well knew, had built up a reputation for lasting personal work at Penn State – Mott thought it 'the most thorough he had ever seen'[2] – and was therefore the man to help lay the groundwork for the new campaign. Buchman had longed since 1902 to visit India and, in spite of his mother's protests at his leaving America, fanned by her fears of German torpedoes, he went. He sailed on 28 June for Marseilles in the Italian ship *Patria*, and thence to Colombo on 16 July.

He found an India where the British Raj reigned supreme, if not secure. Gandhi, whom Buchman met briefly at the home of Bishop Whitehead in Madras, had only just come back from South Africa and was still a little-known figure on the fringe of political life. At that stage he seems to have made no particular impact on Buchman, nor Buchman on Gandhi. Buchman also stayed at the Viceregal Lodge while Lord Hardinge was Viceroy, and toured three of the princely states, in company with Sam Higginbotham, founder of the agricultural mission in Allahabad. Others from this period who became friends were Rabindranath Tagore and Amy Carmichael, creator of the Dohnavur Fellowship near Tinnevelly, which he described as 'the place nearer heaven than any spot on earth'.

During the next six months Buchman travelled throughout India, from Travancore in the south to Rawalpindi in the north, from Bombay to Calcutta, criss-crossing the continent many times, paying three visits to Madras. In Travancore, where his campaign began, Eddy claimed a total

* Sparks renewed his invitation to Buchman to return to Penn State in a letter of 9 October 1916.

in audiences of 400,000, and there were 60,000 at a single meeting which Buchman addressed. Buchman's main function, however, was to help to train the Christian workers whose job it was to follow up these vast meetings; in Travancore, he had a workers' group of 1,300, 'with the Metropolitan and clergy of the Mar Thoma Church in attendance'.*

The huge set-piece meetings, with platform speeches tediously relayed to the back of the throng by a chain of interpreters, struck Buchman as largely ineffective. It was 'like hunting rabbits with a brass band', he said. What was needed, he insisted, was 'personalised work', detailed dealing with the moral and spiritual needs of individual people, and definite decisions. 'We must simply rivet, rivet, rivet from the very first moment,' he wrote to E. C. Carter, the Joint General Secretary of the YMCA's National Council for India and Ceylon. 'Every leader must be permeated with this idea, and be incisive in his addresses and personal dealings. We need to study each man.'[3]

His ardour was fuelled by what he considered the ineffectiveness of the YMCA Secretaries he came across in city after city. As it seemed to him, many were religious bureaucrats whose energies were absorbed by administration. 'The Christian workers in India need to be taught the "how" of Christian service,' he wrote to Mott in November. 'There are agencies abundant and many Christian workers, but they do not seem to get into close, vital touch with the people . . . There is an utter lack of consciousness everywhere of the need of individually dealing with men.'[4]

'The danger', he wrote to Eddy in a later letter, 'is, we do not know our Secretaries. The International Committee think they know, but to be absolutely frank, they do not . . . We depend on hostels, organisation. We must go deeper. Otherwise, we will develop a constituency of parasites.

'Some do not even know *how* to deal with a man who has the simplest needs. Three Indian Secretaries worked side by side with one American. The problem of one of these men was dishonesty. The Indians knew about it. The community knew about it, and, most of all, the man himself knew about it. But no one seemed to know how to cure the dishonesty and make it the stepping-stone to a life of power. A simple twenty minutes changed the whole tenor of his life.' Buchman enclosed a letter from the man to illustrate the story.[5] His own eighteen-page letter gave many other instances of how he had found himself dealing with the same elementary moral problems as in Penn State and other American colleges. He also found in many the same need which Meyer had revealed to him in himself at Penn State – fruitless activism operating an unproductive organisation.

Some of Buchman's colleagues no doubt found this sort of criticism irritating, implying as it did that they had been missing the point.

* The South Indian church traditionally founded by St Thomas.

Nonetheless, his direct dealing with the moral weaknesses of individuals seems to have been both effective and welcomed at headquarters. 'This Buchman', wrote K. T. Paul to the other YMCA joint General Secretary for India, his colleague E. C. Carter, 'is a very great soul. On S., his effect has been marvellous. He has confessed how utterly wrong he was in regard to the Serampore money affair and how he has decided to return every pie of it. How I crave we could have Buchman in India for all time.'[6]

Among those affected by their contact with Buchman were the young American YMCA Secretary in Lahore, Howard Walter, and his wife Marguerite. Walter was, according to a friend, 'a rare combination of scholarly brain and child-like spirit, a born poet . . . with a marvellous sense of humour'. People had spoken of him to Buchman as the most Christlike person they knew. When they met in Lahore, he and Buchman immediately took to each other. Observing Buchman's persistence, Walter asked, 'What does the N.D. in your name stand for, is it "Never Despair"?'[7]

Buchman also, evidently, won the confidence of more senior members of the religious hierarchy. 'My overwhelming difficulty in dealing with English people is to know how to begin,' wrote Hubert Pakenham-Walsh, the Bishop of Assam, to Buchman with engaging humility. 'I am more and more learning to pray, I can preach, and of course if I get ice broken in preaching I can go ahead with individuals . . . but where I fail . . . is that I can't grasp the splendid opportunities which mixing with the Planters gives me, to open out on soul questions. I suppose it is really cowardice . . . if you think you can help me and have the time to do so, be as frank and brutal as ever you like.'[8]

The Bishop had first been interested in Buchman by meeting a once notoriously difficult schoolboy called Victor. 'You are Victor's friend,' he had said on meeting him. Buchman had met Victor at a boys' camp at Roorkee in the foothills of the Himalayas. The masters complained that he was in rebellion. He kept pulling out the tent pegs while people were inside the tents. He would have to be sent home.

'Have you talked to the boy?' asked Buchman.

'No, we've talked about him.'

Buchman agreed to talk to him, but Victor cut three appointments, preferring to row on the canal. 'Who could blame him?' said Buchman.

Next day Victor was discovered on a knoll playing with bamboo canes, which he twirled like a band-major's baton on parade. Buchman went up to him and said, 'You do that so well. I wish I could do it.'

'Well, try it,' said Victor, forgetting to run away.

Buchman tried and failed, much to Victor's delight. 'I once went to camp,' Buchman said casually. 'I hated it.'

'Were you like that? I am too,' said Victor, and began to tell Buchman

[47]

about the nuisance he was making of himself. 'There's something wrong inside me,' he concluded. 'I'm sorry.'

'How much sorry?' asked Buchman. 'Do you know what remorse is?'

'That's being sorry and then doing it again,' said Victor.

'Then what do you think you need?' asked Buchman.

'Repentance.'

'What's that?'

'Oh, that's when a fellow's sorry enough to quit!'

Buchman began to tell the boy about a companion who always understood, so interesting that people never wanted to run away from him. 'I know who that is,' said Victor, 'that's Christ. I'd like to be his friend, but I don't know how.'

Buchman talked about how to get rid of sin which always had a big 'I' in the middle. 'Where should we go to do that?'

'On our knees,' said Victor, and when, later, they knelt together, he prayed, 'Lord, manage me, for I can't manage myself.'

Walking back to the camp, he said to Buchman, 'It's as if a lot of old luggage has rolled away. I must go and tell my friends.'[9]

From St Stephen's College, Delhi, a year later, Victor wrote to Buchman, 'With the help of God I will do the duty assigned to me since that memorable day at Roorkee.' As for Buchman, he used Victor's definitions of remorse and repentance for the rest of his life.

Buchman revelled in the novelty of India's sights and sounds. He wrote to his mother of the women 'washing their pots of bright brass in the stream, dressed in scarlet, picturesque in the mellow saffron twilight' and reassured her that the food was 'excellent; I never once suffered on account of it', and train travel 'more comfortable than at home'.[10] To Dan he described the Taj Mahal, the festival of Diwali and a visit to a monkey temple. By now he was eager to return home, but he was planning first to visit the main focus of American missionary effort, China.

Eddy, who was himself to be in China the following year, was at first opposed to Buchman's visiting there,[11] feeling perhaps that his direct methods might make enemies for himself. He left him with only a loan of $100 and a return ticket to Seattle. But Buchman was determined to go, and an invitation arrived from the committee in China which was sponsoring Eddy's visit. Eddy, on his way back to the United States, seems to have changed his mind. 'The more I think of it, the more I think what a unique work you have done,' he wrote from Aden. 'Talk over the whole question of permeating our China campaign with personal work. It is the forgotten secret of the Church.'[12]

In February 1916 Buchman sailed for Canton. His effect there proved to be such that Eddy cancelled the $100 loan and declared himself ready to meet another $400 of Buchman's expenses.

The YMCA Secretary for South China, George Lerrigo, spoke of Buchman's 'wonderful directness' and how 'he came to us just as an old friend . . . Every man he touched was a key man, and you can realise what this will mean for our work;[13] while his visit to Shanghai 'promised large and permanent results'.[14] At Canton the US Asiatic Fleet was in. He met many of the men and the result was the creation in several ships and ports of what the seamen called 'Buchman Clubs'.*

All was not well at home, however. Buchman's father, now 76, was growing increasingly deaf and cantankerous, and there were signs of a mental deterioration which was to increase with age. Buchman's mother evidently needed trained help as early as the summer of 1915: he wrote from India asking her to tell him 'about the nurse and everything that goes on'.[15] Dan also was a cause of anxiety. He had been unable to keep up academically at the excellent Taft School in Connecticut to which Buchman had sent him, and had since been expelled from the technical school where he had gone to learn to be an electrician. Dan seems to have been, from his childhood, weak and unreliable. But Buchman wrote to him regularly, and always with encouragement. 'Yesterday I sat on the beach to listen to the waves as they go dashing in and my thoughts turned to you with love and affection,' he had written from Hohangabad,[16] and later, 'There is not a mean bone in your body and we are all proud of you.'[17]

In August 1916 he sailed for home on the *Empress of Russia*. Back in America, Buchman needed time to absorb all that he had experienced. 'For two months I didn't want to see anybody,' he said later. 'I wanted to think this thing through for myself, just take the letters that had come to me, and study the needs of the human heart as in a laboratory. I came to this conclusion, that the fundamental need is ourselves.'[18]

He was offered a part-time job at the Hartford Theological Seminary, a small non-sectarian college in New England with an evangelical tradition. The President, Douglas Mackenzie, was looking for someone who could give his students a thorough training in personal work and several people recommended Buchman, among them Howard Walter, temporarily back at Hartford, his old college, from India. From Buchman's own point of view the job was ideal. It gave him liberty, and an expense account, with which to travel, and the freedom to arrange his lectures when it suited him. He became Extension Lecturer in Personal Evangelism, initially for a year.

His arrival at Hartford was far from popular. His highly evangelistic approach upset students and staff alike. One student recalled later, with a continuing sense of shock, that Buchman had wanted to convert the *entire*

* Buchman found such a club still functioning in the Philippines two years later.

class.[19] Buchman also made it clear that he regarded a good many of the existing courses as more theoretical than 'vital'. So far as he was concerned, an ability to deal with the moral and spiritual needs of individuals was a great deal more important than a mastery of theological minutiae. Many of the middle-year students, he remarked, lost their faith, and the faculty did not seem to know what to do about it.

He was apparently surprised and hurt by the reactions to him. At Christmas Howard Walter wrote to reassure him. 'Frank,' he said, 'just don't worry about all the things people say . . . your real friends who've seen your work – its fundamental, sacrificial reality – will never get these unpleasant reactions. You ought to go serenely forward.'[20]

Meanwhile a small group of men was gathering around him in what he called 'a companionship of fellowship and silence'. Among them were Mott's son John, Howard Walter, and Sherwood Day, whom Walter had known in India. They supported Buchman's conviction that intensive work with individuals was the key to 'sustained evangelism', and that the first target should be China.

Their first objective, Buchman wrote to President Mackenzie in February 1917, was to transmit this passion for work with individuals to 'the leaders of China'. In Peking, for example, they hoped to bring together fifteen of the most influential Chinese Christians in the city and train them in the 'how' of Christian work. The fifteen were to include a general whom Mott had converted, an admiral, the Minister of the Interior, the Vice-Minister of Justice who had become a Christian the previous year, and the President of the Chinese Assembly, as well as a number of leading missionaries. The Hartford men, said Buchman, would then try to repeat these tactics in other Chinese cities. It was, he added, a superhuman task and they were attempting it only because they felt God had called them to it.[21]

It was, indeed, a bold programme. Buchman and his colleagues were planning to reform a vast country. Their principal target was its political leadership; and their principal co-workers were to be not other missionaries but influential Chinese. It was the first of Buchman's efforts to implement his conviction that a country, no less than a person, could become God-directed.

The plan seemed all the more ambitious in view of the anarchic state into which China had fallen. After a century in which the country had increasingly become the prey of European powers, the reigning Manchu dynasty had been overthrown by a revolution in 1912 and replaced by a republic under Sun Yat-sen. Within weeks, however, Sun's flimsy regime had also been swept away; and Yuan Shih-k'ai, the most powerful military figure of the old order, had seized power. Yuan himself died in 1916, leaving behind a pathetically weak and unstable central government in

Peking, while Sun and his allies tried to keep alive the ideals of the Young Revolutionaries from a southern base in Canton.

The country was massively in debt (its entire customs revenue was in foreign hands), demoralised, disunited and leaderless. Russia, Britain, Japan, France and Germany all claimed large areas as their particular 'spheres of influence', and the central government was a ready-made puppet for whichever group of generals happened to be in the ascendant.

China already contained the seeds of a revolution more fundamental than that of Sun Yat-sen. In the same year as Buchman set out on his second visit there, a student called Mao Tse-tung decided to adopt the ideal of 'the serene and dedicated philosopher-athlete', to talk 'only of large matters' and to rouse his fellow-students to dedicate their lives to the selfless service of the people.[22] Mao was not yet a Marxist – his philosophy was still based on a belief in absolute moral principles and the power of the mind – but his disillusionment with the way in which China was being governed was already complete.

To believe, as Buchman did, that the changing of individual lives could transform this highly volatile situation clearly leaves him open to charges of over-simplifying. This, after all, was not Penn State but a nation of countless millions. Buchman, however, saw no essential difference. He had become convinced that, if a few key people gave their lives wholly to Christ, whether at Penn State or in China, anything was possible. 'Who can tell the power of a man won for Jesus Christ?' he asked. 'If the selfish Yuan Shih-k'ai had been won, it might have changed the history of China.' It was the kind of personalisation of a vast problem for which he was often to be criticised: but in view of the influence later exerted by individuals like Mao Tse-tung and Chou En-lai, was he entirely wrong?

A number of prominent Chinese took the same view. Several of the Peking fifteen named in Buchman's plan – the Vice-Minister of Justice and later acting Prime Minister, Hsu Ch'ien, was one of them – passionately believed that Christianity alone could bring the unification of the country and 'national salvation'. So, too, did Mott and Eddy; at least they hoped it might be a fruit of their work. A good many of the missionaries who lived in China, however, felt that it was scarcely their business. To become involved in China's political turmoil, they thought, was both risky and not particularly Christian; and in any event, as in India, a fair proportion were more absorbed by administration than by the conversion of souls. In 1916 Buchman noted unhappily that the net gain in the communicant membership of the Christian churches (26,173) was actually less than the number of salaried missionaries (27,562).

Buchman's emphasis on the importance of a close partnership with educated and sometimes high-ranking Chinese was also untypical of the missionary community. After his own visit to China in 1890, Henry

Drummond had complained that the Chinese educated classes were not being reached at all. That was perhaps less true by 1917, but many missionaries were still apt to think of the Chinese as a people to be worked on from a superior level rather than as partners in a common task. Buchman's belief was exactly the opposite. These differing attitudes were to become an increasing cause of disagreement between him and an influential part of the missionary community.

In June 1917 Buchman sailed for China on the *Empress of Russia* with three Hartford friends and two Yale men. He had his father's blessing for the trip. 'Father was very eager to have me go,' he wrote later to Dan, 'and when I for a moment spoke of not being able to go, he said very decidedly, "Go, it is your duty, I do not want you to stay for me." '[23]

In these early months, Buchman himself learnt a basic lesson. During their ten-day voyage across the Pacific members of the party became critical of each other and of Buchman in particular. The reason is not entirely clear, but the undercurrents persisted when, the others having proceeded to their mission stations, only three of the party – Howard Walter, Sherwood Day* and Buchman – were left to work and travel together. They realised that they could hardly tackle division in China until the divisions within their own ranks had been healed. The three of them therefore sat at a round table in a sparsely furnished hotel room in Tientsin – 'a setting rather like a poker game, the light a little too high for comfort', according to Walter – and said honestly what they felt about each other.

Out of these talks, Sherwood Day wrote later, evolved the principle that no member of a team should say anything about someone to anyone else which he had not already told the person concerned.[24]

Howard Walter amplified the principle in a letter to Sherwood Eddy: 'I have come to a new realisation this summer of the importance of the utmost frankness within the circle of any group of people working together, combined with entire absence of criticism of others outside the group, or indeed anywhere in the absence of the person immediately concerned. In China I have seen how criticism of Frank, or of you, started perhaps in some careless joke and growing as it spread, has played havoc with our work and met us at every turn taking much time and trouble and prayer to overcome. Even within our little group of three we found the same danger . . . We finally got together for several long talks in which every critical thought ever cherished was brought to light, and we went forth with a new unity and mutual confidence, determined henceforth to keep on that firm basis with each other and with our fellow workers, just in

---

* Sherwood Day, a graduate of Yale and at one time YMCA Secretary there, worked and travelled with Buchman for twenty-two years, between 1916 and 1938.

so far as they would unite with us in this mutual understanding.'[25] Buchman, after the Tientsin meeting, always regarded complete open-ness as a prerequisite for effective teamwork.

Soon after the party arrived in China, they had lunch with the Foreign Minister and the Vice-Speaker of the Parliament (a former interpreter of Eddy's), but political titles meant little in a situation where the central government was so impotent. At about this time, too, Buchman met Chang Ling-nan, a leading corporation lawyer and diplomat.* Chang had a house in the beautiful mountainous country near Kuling, where Buch-man and his friends had gone to attend one of the missionary community's yearly summer conferences. One day, in breach of the normal social divide between Chinese and non-Chinese, Chang asked Buchman over for a game of tennis and a sumptuous Chinese dinner of thirty-six courses. 'We paused for an hour and a half between the eighteenth and nineteenth,' related Buchman. The lawyer drank a different wine with each course, and his nicotine-stained hands shook even when drinking cocktails before dinner. At a late hour Buchman departed in a chair ordered by the lawyer and carried by six coolies. 'I didn't need the chair to carry me home, though he certainly needed someone to carry him to bed,' commented Buchman later. 'But I gratefully agreed as I didn't want to upset him that night.'

Next evening the lawyer came to dinner with Buchman in Kuling, where he was staying with Mrs Adams, the widow of a Baptist missionary. Buchman told a story of how God had once guided him.

'Do you think God can speak to people like me?' Chang asked.

'Of course I do,' answered Buchman.

A great storm arose and Chang had to stay the night. He admitted that he did not want to stay because he had to take pills to go to sleep and other pills to wake up properly in the morning. But, after a long talk with Buchman and reading the Bible together, he slept soundly. The next morning he decided to make a new start in life. Shortly afterwards, at his own lunch table with Buchman present, and in front of the children and their nurse, he said to his wife, 'You married me thinking I was a real Christian. But I have not been.' His change, which was permanent and growing, led to a series of house-parties in his home, at which some eighty of his friends and relatives took part, many travelling long distances to do so. One by-product was the creation of a Chinese missionary society manned by Chinese and backed by Chinese money.[26]

The missionary community's two annual summer conferences, one amid the mountain grandeurs around Kuling and the other in the dry, bracing climate of Peitaiho on the Gulf of Chihli, to which Buchman went

* Chang's daughter married T. V. Soong, Madame Chiang Kai-shek's brother.

during August, must have seemed like another and almost wholly unrelated world. The delegates were virtually all missionaries, and the overwhelming majority non-Chinese. No committed Christians from the country's political leadership had been invited, nor had any of the 'interesting sinners' whom Buchman thought necessary to enliven any conference. They were simply private gatherings of Christian workers. Nor, as Buchman complained later, were they 'personalised'; in other words, too little effort was made to meet the moral and spiritual needs of those who did attend. 'There were walls that could not be penetrated,' he remarked.[27]

The conferences instead followed what was known as the 'old meeting plan': a series of gatherings culminated in a major 'inspirational' address which was intended to send the missionaries away with a sense of uplift. They were occasions which provided a welcome and no doubt necessary breathing-space in the busy missionary calendar, but seemed to Buchman to have little or no relevance to the state of China.

So far as he personally was concerned, the best thing which came out of them was a friendship with Cheng Ching-yi, the Secretary of the curiously-named China Continuation Committee,* an organisation whose aim was to foster co-operation among the missionaries. Cheng was keen to win over some of the politicians who had gone with Sun Yat-sen to Canton, and wanted to find a way of introducing Buchman to Sun.

By early autumn Buchman was hard at work preparing for Eddy's arrival. He was by now travelling round China with a team of fourteen including Dr E. G. Tewksbury, National Secretary of the China Sunday School Union, Miss Ruth Paxson of the National YMCA, and Dr H. W. Luce,** former Vice-President of Shantung University. The *Chinese Recorder* gave enthusiastic reports of this tour throughout the autumn of 1917 and winter of 1918.[28] That by Cheng Ching-yi was simply headlined 'Miracles'.[29] Buchman had found fresh financial backing, in the shape of the Stewart Evangelistic Fund, which had resources of $3 million. Characteristically, he wrote to Eddy, who had been tardy in supplying promised funds, that Bishop Lewis – the senior Methodist Bishop in China – had described the work he and his team were doing as 'the greatest movement that has yet come out of China',[30] and had 'allocated' the Trustee of the Stewart Fund, the Rev Harry Blackstone, to travel with him.

Such letters were apt to have the reverse effect of that which Buchman intended. Eddy had already received Walter's letter telling of the unity he, Day and Buchman had found in Tietsin, to which his reply had been

---

* The leading personalities of almost all the Protestant Christian groups in China, both Chinese and foreign, were on this Committee. Its chairman was Bishop Logan Roots.
** The father of the creator of *Time* magazine.

equivocal. The fact is that he wavered between pride and perturbation at Buchman's impact, rather like a mother hen who sees one of her brood take to the water. Others in headquarters, both in Shanghai and New York, found the success of new ways hard to bear because they implied criticism of the past. When enthusiastic reports came in from city after city, as much opposition as applause was provoked, even if the opposition was for the moment muted.

The meetings which Buchman held were usually small affairs, so that the problems of individuals could be thoroughly dealt with. 'Our meetings are all carefully planned for in groups of 25,' he wrote to his family from Nanking in October. 'I am conducting four of these a day in addition to many interviews. I have been lately spending 16 to 18 hours a day with men.'[31] At Whampoa in November Christian workers of every age and denomination had found freedom from the sins that were keeping them from spiritual power. In Canton in the same month 150 personal workers brought 150 nominal Christians to a Sunday afternoon meeting. 'The result is beyond telling,' wrote Buchman enthusiastically. 'One of the miracles was a Member of Parliament.'[32]*

It was during this tour that Buchman first met Samuel Moor Shoemaker, a recent Princeton graduate, who was working on the faculty of a business school which Princeton maintained to teach Chinese boys the rudiments of English and business methods. It was lodged in the Peking Christian Association. 'Few men got along with other people more easily than young Shoemaker,' writes his biographer, Irving Harris. 'He not only had what is tritely called "a winning personality" but he influenced most of those with whom he associated so that they in turn enjoyed a measurable increase in self-esteem. The younger Chinese lads in his classes delighted him, especially those in his Bible class.' He was, however, disturbed that attendance at this class had declined from twenty to seven in his first three meetings. His methods, he thought, must be faulty.

Hearing Buchman speak, he cornered him to explain his predicament. After many preliminaries, he said that if only Buchman could touch one or two of the leaders of his Bible class, they might affect the whole student body.

Buchman, who had been following Shoemaker's life story up to this point 'with flattering attention', suddenly leaned back and laughed. 'Tell me,' he said abruptly, 'why don't you get through to at least *one* of these fellows yourself?'

'The younger man was ready for almost anything but this,' continues

---

* Buchman also remarks, in a letter dated 18 April 1918: 'Just had tiffin with a descendant of Confucius.' This was apparently a 76th-generation descendant of the sage, and he and Buchman spent time in quiet together asking divine guidance on some local political matter.

Harris. 'Heretofore, religious leaders had invariably patted him on the back and told him how fine it was that he was going into the ministry. Now Shoemaker didn't like to be thus unexpectedly put on the spot; his pride was hurt and, since the best defence is often an offence, he countered with a question of his own: "If you know the trouble, why not tell me what it is?"'

'Might be sin,' Buchman replied, and then went on to describe how resentment in his own life had for over a year kept him from spiritual freedom and power.

'To say that Shoemaker was nettled would be greatly to understate his reaction. He quickly made his excuses, broke off the conversation and walked home alone across the city, determined to take no part in such "morbid introspection".

'But he couldn't get the conversation out of his mind, especially Buchman's reference to sin. He recalled that someone had once explained this three-letter word as any barrier, great or small, between oneself and God or between oneself and other people. He could see plenty of barriers in his own life. Several were what might be called "reserved areas". One had to do with his service in China. He had come out to the Far East on a short-term basis. Was he willing to stay on indefinitely should God indicate the necessity? . . .

'More troubled in mind than ever, as he ate supper he continued to consider the future – his personal life, marriage, the kind of a ministry that God might be calling him to – and then again (perhaps with animosity) he thought of Frank Buchman. How long this all took one would hesitate to guess, but there came a moment . . . when, unable to sleep . . ., he finally slipped to his knees and entered into a wholly fresh spiritual transaction. He now realised how greatly he needed forgiveness. It seemed to him that he heard someone saying, "You want to do My work but in your own way." As the sense of God's love enfolded him, he . . . agreed that he would serve him anywhere indefinitely.'

The next day, according to Harris, Shoemaker sought out Buchman. 'Frank,' he blurted out, 'you were right. I have been a pious fraud, pretending to serve God but actually keeping all the trump cards in my own hands. Now I've told Him how sorry I am, and I trust you'll forgive me for harbouring ill-will against you. This sprang up the moment you used that word sin!'

Buchman said that he freely forgave him. 'Now what's the next step?' he added.

Shoemaker told him he had a long-standing arrangement to have tea with one of the Bible-class boys. 'What shall I tell him?' he asked.

'Tell him just what you've told me. Be honest about yourself,' replied Buchman.

Shoemaker did exactly that – and the boy said, 'I wish it could happen to me.' 'They talked . . . of the honesty and purity and faith required of any individual who gives his total allegiance to God, and when the student expressed his readiness they prayed together,' concludes Harris. 'Each man felt deeply moved and very grateful.'[33] For Shoemaker this was the beginning of a twenty-year association with Buchman.

Buchman still wanted to meet with Sun Yat-sen. By the beginning of 1918 Hsu Ch'ien had joined the Southern Military Government at Canton as Chief Secretary to Sun. With the help of an introduction from Hsu, Buchman had at least two meetings with Sun in February 1918. Sun's own position at the time was insecure, as rivals within his own party were working towards demoting him from Generalissimo to being merely one in a committee of seven. Nonetheless, Buchman was convinced that Sun could become 'the great liberator of China', and their talks were unusually candid. At their first meeting, on 23 February, when various of Sun's associates were present, Buchman spoke of the moral weaknesses which Hsu had told him lay at the root of China's anarchic condition. Five days later they met again in a cement factory converted into working quarters for the President and situated on an island only reachable by water. There they had privacy.* Sun said, 'Politically we have succeeded. We have established a republic. But we have many problems that we can't answer. Can you help us? What do you think is wrong in China?' Buchman said, 'Three things. One is corruption – squeeze. Another is concubines. And the third is the poppy – smoking opium.'

Buchman then told Sun that even some of his own supporters said that he had too many wives. Sun had, in fact, divorced his first wife under Chinese law and married the woman who had previously been his concubine – Ching-ling Soong, sister of Madame Chiang Kai-shek and later Vice-President of Communist China.

After the interview Buchman received an indignant note from Sun, declaring that there must have been some misunderstanding. He had never, he said, had more than one wife and had divorced his previous wife quite correctly before marrying his present one.[34] Hsu, however, encouraged by Buchman, continued to press the point. He told Sun bluntly that his divorce might be justifiable under Chinese law but that it certainly did not conform to Christian teaching, which Sun admitted to be true. He gave Sun the Bible and asked him to read the story of David, Uriah and

---

* A young soldier on guard in the cement factory that day came forty years later to the Moral Re-Armament headquarters in Switzerland as a general, and told how astonished he and his colleagues had been that Sun should ask advice of an American.

Bathsheba. His first wife had, Hsu reminded him, married him when he was in great trouble, and it was against Chinese custom to desert a wife who marries you in such circumstances. Also, she had borne him a son.[35] If he did not obey the laws of God, asked Hsu, how could Sun have any power from God to save his country? Sun finally thanked Hsu for his 'faithful counsel'.[36]

At first sight, it seems odd that both Buchman and a practical politician like Hsu Ch'ien should be so persistent in this matter. However, Sun's action was not just a moral weakness but was leading to political weakness. The son of the President of the Parliament which elected Sun Yat-sen President and Generalissimo showed me, in 1983, a photograph of Sun among the parliamentary leaders with his secretary, Ching-ling Soong, sitting beside him in the place of honour, and his wife several seats away. Sun's insistence on this arrangement, he told me, shocked his father and Sun's other colleagues. The Soong family were also 'horrified', according to Emily Hahn, when their middle daughter announced her intention of marrying Sun Yat-sen, because 'she was going against the conventions of both Christianized and non-Christianized society in China'.[37] The whole affair weakened Sun's position. It contributed to the intrigues which led to the legislature stripping him of his military powers and transferring the government to an Administrative Committee of which he was only one in seven. In May 1918, when this Government Reorganising Bill was passed, Sun resigned and left Canton for Shanghai.

In June Buchman and Sun were travelling on the same train in Japan. Sun heard that Buchman was on the train and sent for him. Buchman wrote Hsu that 'he seemed mellow and very responsive to every suggestion . . . You did a courageous thing in speaking so frankly to him. You possess the fearlessness of a Lincoln . . . I believe God is going to use you in bringing about His great plan for China.'[38]

Buchman's message, meanwhile, was as straightforward as ever. 'If sin is the disease,' he told an audience of missionaries in Shanghai, 'we must deal with sin. Sin first of all in ourselves, the 'little sins' that rob us of power and keep us from being able to go out in deep sympathy to men in sin. Ill-will towards others, jealousy, ambition, self-will, criticism. And then sin in others. We fail to get at the sin which is keeping a man from Christ. Fear often holds us. We say we are too reserved, that no one should infringe upon another's personality . . . and all the time there are men about us who long to share the deepest things in their hearts . . . The woman at the well had no feeling that Jesus had infringed upon her personality when He put His finger upon the cause of her heartache.'

Eddy, who had by now arrived in China and was campaigning with Buchman, was evidently delighted by the effectiveness of Buchman's preparatory work. If the enthusiastic endorsements of this work which

Buchman was apt to quote sound overstated, Eddy echoed them. 'I may say at the outset,' he wrote to K. T. Paul in India in April, 'that Buchman's work in China has developed by a growth of evolution into a movement of immense proportions, far more powerful and fruitful than any similar preparatory movement we have ever had in the past in any country.'[39]

Yet, within three months, Buchman was to be asked to leave China.

CONFLICT IN CHINA

An opposition to Buchman had, in fact, been steadily growing. Many missionaries objected to his concept of personal work, and his style and personality also came in for criticism. There was, as well, the awkward fact that wherever he went people queued up for talks with him, which was not the case with all the others.

The opposition finally came to a head over Buchman's part in the 1918 summer conferences at Kuling and Peitaiho. He had been an invited observer at the 1916 conference, and had been asked to conduct the sector on 'Personal Work' in 1917. Now, along with Miss Paxson and Tewksbury, he was to lead the conferences. He was determined that they should not be a repetition of the previous years, and for two reasons. The first was that concentrated work with small groups of missionaries had convinced him that their moral and spiritual needs were a good deal more basic than he had previously suspected.

The second was that he wanted conferences which could both bring greater effectiveness to the missionary community and give hope to men like Hsu Ch'ien. Hsu saw Christianity as a potentially revolutionary force. The best way of feeding that faith, Buchman felt, was to demonstrate that it was true. 'It will be no ordinary conference,' he wrote of his plans for Kuling. 'There will be men like Cheng Ching-yi and Hsu Ch'ien who believe that Jesus Christ is the only hope of China; another group who feel that the returned students must become a force in the present political crisis . . . They will come from all over China and one of the results will, we hope, be an endeavour to laicise the Chinese Church.' There were to be no 'bench-warmers', no 'grand-stand quarter-backs'. Kuling was no longer to be a private event for the missionary community. It was to be a 'fully personalised' training centre for the national leadership of China.[1] All this, of course, totally upset the traditional pattern of the summer conferences.

At first, Buchman appeared to be getting his way. At a conference in Hangchow before Eddy left China, there was 'unanimous approval' from the missionary leaders both for the idea of inviting carefully selected foreigners and Chinese to Kuling and Peitaiho, and for the notion that both conferences should be intensive and selective.[2] Buchman concentrated on Kuling. He sent personal invitations to leading Chinese and other 'marginal men'* whose presence would ensure that the conference there would be in touch with the actual needs of the country.

One May morning in Changsha Buchman wrote in the flyleaf of his Bible, 'I have prepared you to help these men. You will release many. I will be with thee.' On Whit Sunday he wrote, 'I am calling you to a mighty and far-reaching work.' And on the Monday, 'Begin the conference by dealing with sin. Clear up everything in our lives. Activity versus reality.'

Some missionaries, however, disliked the idea of delegates who were not 'Christian workers'; others objected to the absence of major addresses in the old style; others again may reasonably have resented the fact that *their* summer conferences had been taken over by this brisk man of 40 who, after a fraction of their time in the country, claimed to know exactly what China needed.

By the time he arrived in Kuling early in July to make preparations for the conference, it was abundantly clear that all was not well. Harry Blackstone, who, as Trustee of the Stewart Fund, had undertaken to finance the conference, had been away in the United States and had still not provided the necessary guarantees; and neither of Buchman's co-organisers felt the need to arrive in Kuling until a week before the conference began, despite Buchman's persistent requests. Tewksbury delayed in Japan to meet Blackstone on his way to China, ostensibly about money, but Buchman suspected other reasons.

Buchman, by contrast, arrived a full month in advance, convinced that meticulous preparation was essential, not least to avoid a repetition of the conditions in which the previous year's conferences had been held. The conference buildings, he wrote to Tewksbury who was in charge of practical arrangements, were scantily furnished. Ought they not to invest in some long chairs for the foreign ladies? Then there were the beds. There had been bed-bugs the previous year, and his own bed had been 'impossible, just a succession of ridges'. He was equally unhappy about the food, and listed people who had fallen ill after previous conferences because of it. The flies and chipped crockery had certainly not invited delegates to a comfortable meal. The Chinese, too, he added, must have ample food of their own – 'we want a fine sense of fellowship and equality'. Unless they were careful about such details, they would alienate the very people they wanted to win. A sense of rest must pervade everything,

* 'Marginal men', in the jargon of the day, meant people who were not already committed Christians or full-time Christian workers.

because many of the delegates would come tired after a winter's work. It was the hotelier's son speaking.

Nor did he sympathise with Tewksbury's concern that so many of the delegates did not come into the 'Christian worker' category. 'You cannot standardise the Kuling conference,' he replied. 'The provision for marginal men will keep it from being academic . . . you can have Peitaiho, but I must keep Kuling.'[3]

Blackstone – who also by this time had serious, if undisclosed, reservations about Buchman – had still not pledged financial support by the time the conference began and, in his absence, Buchman wrote to his wife declaring that he was quite prepared to do without help from the Stewart Fund. 'I know what it means to live by faith and prayer,' he told her, 'and to be chargeable to no man's silver and gold.' Aware that he was being criticised for extravagance, he also sent Mrs Blackstone a personal cheque to cover anything, including medicine, which could be regarded as personal expenses.[4]

On the day before the conference opened, Buchman had a full-scale row with Tewksbury about who was running it, and was further burdened by a recent letter from his mother telling him that his father's illness was becoming increasingly serious. He nonetheless sailed full-tilt into a venture where, Sherwood Day being ill and Walter having returned to India, he was taking on a large section of the missionary community almost single-handed.

There were 200 at the first meetings on 5 August. Among them were Hsu Ch'ien, now acting Prime Minister in Sun Yat-sen's absence in Japan; General Wu, another of Sun's senior advisers; and S. T. Wen, former Commissioner for Foreign Affairs, as well as other Chinese and many of the leading missionaries. Their first job, said Buchman briskly, was to find out what real life there was in the conference.[5] Such life, he added, was spurious unless it was expressing itself in converting power in the lives of other people. What problem of life, he asked the delegates, who included bishops like Logan Roots of Hankow, did each of them want met during the conference? It might, he said, be a personal problem.

Later the same day, Hsu Ch'ien spoke, and made it clear that he was not interested in pious discussions which did not seek ways of tackling China's moral evils, which he described as 'despotism, militarism, autocracy, opium-smoking, liquor traffic, concubinage, foot-binding and slavery'. 'We have to discover our national sin,' he said, 'otherwise we cannot save our country. If we cannot save the country, we cannot save the world, but the Christians today are powerless in China because of their private sins.'

'I have the salvation of a nation in mind,' Hsu went on, 'therefore I consider this conference a very serious matter. I want to know the method for saving China. The foreign leaders of the church do not quite understand how to save China . . . we have been too slow. I believe we will save the nation by the direct method, that of personal work.'

During the next eight days Buchman spoke no fewer than thirteen times. It was a full exposition of what he had learnt during the Penn State years, illustrated by stories of his own experience both of failure and success. He also said that he had recently told a man a lie which he had just owned up to; that he had failed to meet a certain man's spiritual need because he had not had the courage to be drastic enough with him and was going shortly to see him; and that, during that very conference, he had realised that for some years he had availed himself of a reduced fare privilege on the Pennsylvania Railroad to which he was not strictly entitled. He had that morning sent a cheque for $150 to the railroad. He had been tempted not to sign his name because the vice-president of the railroad was a personal friend, and not to tell the conference because he, as its leader, would lose face.*

He remarked one day that it had only been in China that he had become convinced that the confession of one's own shortcomings privately or publicly was an important way to help others. 'My message is not mine; it is God's. It grows as various people contribute to it,' he said. 'When I came to China this last time, for example, I wasn't fully convinced that "a confessing Christian is a propagating Christian". It became a reality in my life when Bishop Moloney opened our retreat in Hangchow and said that if a Christian is to have power he must confess. A servant in his family had come and told him that he had taken "squeeze". The bishop then remembered that he had failed to pay a physician's bill which the physician was prepared to forget because of his position. He told his servant that he too had taken "squeeze", and then paid his bill. This had been the beginning of a revival in his diocese.'

All this was woven in with his theme that 'only one thing in the world can keep us from being miracle-workers – sin'. 'There is nothing else, absolutely nothing else,' he continued. 'You can't see sin in the life of the other person unless you see sin in your own.' 'It is not because you are better than anyone else that you can help another,' he added. 'It is because you are tempted like the other person, but through honesty you have power from Jesus Christ, who has the only power to save from sin.'

'There are certain things we will do,' he said on another day. 'We will come to China; teach in colleges, hold secretarial posts; but when it comes to intimate personal dealings with men we say, "No, I can't do that, I'm not

---

* Buchman at that moment was in financial straits, but a cheque had just come from a Mrs Woolverton in New York, and turned out to be the exact amount needed for this restitution. (Buchman to Mrs William H. Woolverton, 21 November 1918.)

built that way." You will never know the real need, the real China, unless you are willing to untie the bandages of the people around you. And you can never untie bandages for dead men about you unless you have untied bandages first in your own life.

'The first year I was here I merely touched the surface, last year I scratched it, and I hope that this year I will get down deeper... I thought I knew something about individual work when I first came to China. I am beginning to find out how little I actually know.'

When he first went to Penn State, he told them, he had found 'twenty-five uninteresting Christians in that university. They were regular rounders of the American YMCA. They had the form of goodness, but no power...' The thing to do, he continued, was go after the interesting sinner. He had gained the confidence of twelve fellows who went out stealing chickens together. Now *they* were interesting sinners. 'Some of you will say, "Oh, he's talking about himself,"' Buchman added tartly. 'If you feel that way, please go out of the room. One person can ruin a group.'

The twelve young men, he went on, had organised a Bible group, which they called the Royal Rooster Bible Class and which sometimes went on until 2.30 on Sunday morning; and one of them had eventually become student president of the YMCA. Some people, said Buchman, objected to using marginal men of that kind in Christian work. He wondered what they thought St Augustine was when he was in Milan in his early days. The Christian community in China as it was could not assimilate the marginal man.

The other thing he had done at Penn State, he went on, was to bring in contagious personalities from outside to help win the students. 'There are,' he declared, 'few people in this room who would have qualified.'

The effect of these comments was certainly not marginal. Some missionaries accepted what Buchman said, others were infuriated: Buchman, they told each other, was not merely arrogant and presumptuous, he was also an egoist who constantly paraded his own successes.

Buchman felt the force of the opposition to him keenly. In one of his later talks, on the subject of entering into the sufferings of Christ, which would come to all who took the path of total service, he referred to the temptation to drink the cup of peace and joy and happiness but shirk the cup of suffering. 'We decide for ourselves just how far we are willing to go. Our service ends when we begin to suffer,' he said. 'When a person says all sorts of things about you and is quietly scheming against you ... have you victory in Christ? No man can do it, only Christ can. At times I haven't the victory for things that are difficult. I just have to go away.' Indeed, one evening at this time he took a walk in the neighbouring hills and came upon a lake. For a moment he thought how peaceful it would be to lie at the bottom of it, away from the conflict. Nonetheless, he did not soften what he had to say, some of which seemed to discount the professional expertise of the missionaries. Effective Christian living, Buchman declared, was not a question of how much one knew or how much training one had had: it depended entirely on how much one was willing to co-operate with God. There were, he said on another occasion, too many who sat at their desks and were not in touch with people's real needs.

The Chinese present took much the same line. Christians, declared General Wu, had to revolutionise the church. Some pastors stood up, repeated prayers and then thought their work was finished – so the layman had to be his own pastor. 'I have decided to do personal work among the officials,' added General Wu. 'Many are rotten. We need to help them all to forge a new regime, a new force and a new army.'

Buchman also raised what proved to be an even touchier issue. 'When I came to China last year', he said, 'a man* who is a real physician of souls told me of one of the bandages which bind. He said, "Do give a strong message wherever you go on 'absorbing friendships'." He used a word that was new to me, "crushes". On these hilltops I have seen "absorbing friendships". I can't judge. I can only say this, they may be unhealthful. He knew far more than I do. I cannot do other than give you that word of caution from an old tried physician of souls.'

This time the reaction was explosive, and Bishop Roots was inundated with protests. The day before Buchman left Kuling, Roots complained to him about the offence he had caused. Two days later, apparently unabashed, Buchman wrote to Roots saying how surprised he had been that some of the 'Y' Secretaries should have taken personally what he had said.** He also told Roots that, insofar as his criticism of 'the God-given message' had been inconsistent and destructive, it was indicative of Roots' own need.[6]

Meanwhile, some of those present at Kuling were writing him grateful letters. 'I was very near to breakdown when God sent you to help me gain victory,' wrote one, while a Chinese added, 'I shall never forget our refreshing time on the Pines Rock . . . I can never thank you enough for what you brought into my life.' A third thanked him for his 'clear message on sin', while a 'bishop's daughter' said that several who were resentful for some days stayed to hear him right through and were 'won'. She added that some must have a mighty lot hidden away in their lives to be so afraid of Mr Buchman and his message.[7]

---

* It was, in fact, the Methodist Bishop Lewis.

** Throughout his life, when Buchman objected that a friend had taken a remark of his 'personally', he meant that the person had missed the love behind the criticism, which was intended not to depress but to liberate. He expected people to take the matter to God and find out from Him whether there was any truth in what he had said. His remarks were sometimes so vigorous, however, that this reaction was understandable.

[65]

Buchman set out for the second conference, at Peitaiho, knowing that he had left turmoil behind him. He sensed that a storm was brewing, while not suspecting that Blackstone, whose letters were friendly, was stirring it up.

In fact Blackstone, newly arrived from Japan, wrote from Peitaiho a confidential letter to Bishop Roots, the Chairman of the China Continuation Committee, who was now back in Hankow. He had heard, he said, that the Kuling conference had been a great blessing. On the other hand, a few things he had been told about Buchman's relation to the conference had raised serious questions in his mind as to the advisability of Buchman doing any further work in China for the moment.

'It has long been apparent to me', Blackstone went on, 'that there were certain disqualifications in Mr Buchman in the line of egoism, selfishness and extravagance, and yet ... I have stood behind him with all my strength, sometimes even against my own judgement and the opinion of others.'

Blackstone asked Roots whether he felt Buchman's work in China was finished for the present, and whether he thought something had come into Buchman's personal experience which was a hindrance to his message. 'I may say', remarked Blackstone, 'that there is a serious gloom cast over this conference because of his present condition, and I hardly find him to be the same man whom I left in the spring.' Could Roots please send his reply by telegram?[8]

The following night there seems to have been a noisy confrontation between Buchman and the other conference organisers on the porch of Blackstone's bungalow. The immediate issue was probably a complaint that Buchman was behaving as if he were running the conference single-handed. In any event, he said something which 'grieved' Tewksbury, and told Ruth Paxson in the heat of the moment that he never took orders from a woman. Nor did he feel able to agree to three points which the others put to him, more or less as an ultimatum. One was apparently that the word 'sin' should no longer be mentioned.[9] Another was a demand to return to the 'old meeting plan'. Tewksbury accused him of 'egotism', to which he replied that most of his message was derived from Henry Wright.*

The next day, however, he fell ill with dysentery and for several days ran a high fever, so the issue of who was supposed to be running the conference was no longer relevant. A few days later, on 31 August, a

---

* Three weeks later Buchman wrote to Wright: 'I am experiencing what you forecast – persecution. Much of the best of my message is yours ... You come nearer than any other man in the sphere of my acquaintance (to the one) who actually incarnates the principles of Christ' (20 September 1918). Professor Wright's influence on Buchman is discussed in Chapter 8.

telegram came to Blackstone from Bishop Roots in Hankow, carrying the code phrase Blackstone had suggested, 'Discontinue work'. A following letter set out his views in more detail.

He wanted, he told Blackstone, to bear witness to the value of the work Buchman had done in China. The life of the Christian community in Hankow had been 'permanently elevated and inspired'. Buchman's work had also 'been of inestimable value to me, and I shall never cease to be grateful to Buchman for it'.

On the other hand, he went on, he shared Blackstone's misgivings. The Kuling conference had done a great deal of good, particularly among those who had not encountered Buchman before, but all the older missionaries were disappointed. He had also observed in Buchman 'a kind of censorious and dictatorial attitude of mind'. One of Buchman's chief limitations was the difficulty he had in working with others, although he did seem to have co-operated 'in the most perfect fashion' with Eddy.

Roots added that he was 'deeply grieved to observe the change in Buchman himself of which you speak. What its cause is I am not wise enough to judge,' but at Kuling they had suffered from the same gloomy atmosphere to which Blackstone referred at Peitaiho. 'I am afraid, to speak with great frankness,' he concluded, 'that Buchman is in danger of a serious breakdown if he continues longer in China at the present time.' Buchman's work in China thus far had been 'a glorious success', but it ought in his view to be discontinued.[10]

It must have been a shattering blow for Buchman to be asked to leave China after fifteen months' passionate campaigning. Yet, whatever it was which had made Bishop Roots believe he might be in danger of a breakdown seems to have evaporated very rapidly. He and two friends, his secretary, Hugh McKay,* and Sherwood Day, had planned to take a month's complete rest and recreation after Peitaiho at Port Arthur, across the Gulf of Chihli, and since they now had two days to spare, they took the chance to visit en route the Great Wall of China and the Ming tombs. Within days Buchman was sending cheerful letters home, and on 12 September he wrote Blackstone to say that he had just been for a ten-mile walk and 'topped it off with a good sauerkraut supper'. He asked Blackstone, in passing, to deny the false rumour that he had 'physically gone to pieces' and had been sent back to America.[11] Blackstone replied warmly, but did not mention his part in getting Bishop Roots to take the action he had.[12]

It is hard to reconcile Bishop Roots' estimate with the impression which Harlan Beach, once Professor of Mathematics at Penn State and later the first Professor of Missions at Yale, had of Buchman in China. Notes taken

* The grandson of Hudson Taylor, founder of the China Inland Mission.

[67]

of one of his lectures give a very different picture: 'No flourish of trumpets, no rhetoric, a great human, strong personality . . . A friendly man who cheers, is conversational, talks like a brother, no parson lording it over us. Tells funny stories, jolly, yet most earnest and serious . . . He has a new conception, talking to one instead of masses . . . People criticised that he emphasised sin, that he was too severe. He talked about real things which are fundamental . . . He had generalship and he could work with a team . . . Whole total summary – the best thing that ever happened in China.'[13]

Reviewing at Port Arthur his last weeks in China, Buchman realised that he had treated Tewksbury and Miss Paxson badly and sent letters of apology to both;[14] but on the central issues which he felt were at stake, and particularly his attempt to deal with sins which he believed made the work of many of the missionaries ineffective, he remained totally unrepentant.

'The people at headquarters have never been won,' he wrote to Howard Walter in India, 'and the opposition was evident in most subtle forms. They have been trying for some time to use every conceivable means to get us out of China, as the shoe pinched harder and harder and we got deeper into the personal lives of men.'[15] In a second letter to Walter, Buchman said he was convinced that there were far deeper reasons for what had happened than they had yet fathomed.[16]

His letters to Bishop Roots were also far from apologetic. He conceded that the burden he was carrying at Kuling might have caused a certain 'harshness' in him, but only the harshness of one who was concerned about the failure of the churches and had applied that same harsh judgement to his own life first.

As for Kuling, he went on, he was more than ever convinced that he was merely 'scratching the surface'. Terms like that and 'spiritual bankruptcy' had been objected to, but nothing less expressed the real need. What made his heart heavy, he declared pointedly, was that as God had given him an increasingly clear diagnosis of conditions and his message had more nearly met the actual needs, 'there were some Christian leaders who turned back'.

He would, he concluded, respond warmly to the friendly tone of the Bishop's letters if he did not feel there was a danger of clouding the fundamental issue, and he warned Roots against thinking that their disagreement in Kuling had been purely a personal one. 'It is far deeper,' declared Buchman, 'a matter of principle which vitally affects the progress of the Kingdom.'[17]

To Blackstone he wrote explaining that he had not felt able to join in the picnics and the lighter side of the Kuling conference partly because he had a sense that his father's illness was growing much worse.[18] Buchman had, in fact, known for many months that his father's condition was deteriorating. A letter from his mother the previous Christmas had made it clear that his father's behaviour was now totally irrational and that she herself went in fear of what the old man might do to her.

'I cannot see how I can hold out any longer,' she had written in December 1917, 'it is so serious I don't know which way to turn. This week he was ready to go off and they kept him back from the train. I am in constant fear, the only hope I have is the Lord.'[19]

By the summer of the following year, the tone of her letters had become even more desperate. In June she wrote that 'your father left this morning with his suitcase, he told me he did not know when he would return. I am writing this with tears. I never thought I could go through what I am now . . . your mission is at home.'[20] At the end of July one of their neighbours in Allentown wrote to confirm that his mother was no longer safe at home. Something, she said, would have to be done.[21]

Then, while he was in Port Arthur, his mother wrote to say that the old man had been taken into hospital on doctor's orders. 'We had to take him,' she explained, 'this is hard to tell you, Frank, to take him out of his good home. He chased me through the house Monday morning in my night-clothes from one end of the house to the other and threatened. I left home and hid at Hirner's that day. They took him away very quietly, without a scene but, oh think of it, out of his home.'[22]

The astonishing thing is that, even now, Buchman did not set out post-haste for Allentown. One factor was the length of time which mail and travel, both by surface, took in those days. Partly because of this, there was also a tradition among Americans and Europeans, serving either as missionaries or in a civil capacity, to stick to their work abroad whatever the difficulties at home. Certainly, Buchman felt convinced at the time that he was where God meant him to be. 'I know just how much you want me,' he wrote to his mother from Peitaiho in August 1918, 'and I just want to do God's will.'[23] He sent fond letters regularly, often accompanied by presents or gifts of money – $300 for his mother's birthday – but never gave even the slightest hint that he was in any uncertainty that he must stay in the East. Indeed, at one point he suggested that she join him in China, presumably putting his father under suitable care.

Now he wrote from Port Arthur telling his mother that he had cabled Dr Willard Kline, a well-known Allentown specialist, to ask what could be done for his father. He also sent $600 to help pay for a male nurse. 'It is clear', he said, 'that the strain is too great for you, and you ought not to bear it any longer.' In his quiet hours God had given him real assurance 'that He will be a husband to you and that you are safe in His keeping'. He was, he added, starting out with a small party of friends on an evangelistic programme of his own. There had been invitations from both Korea and Japan.[24] 'We are going forth on faith and prayer', he wrote to Howard

Walter in India, 'with nothing but the Almighty's bank to draw upon. All of us are richer for these days of trial through which we have passed.'[25]

It seems likely, in view of his letter to Blackstone, that a subsidiary motive in undertaking the tours in Korea and Japan was a desire, conscious or unconscious, to make it quite clear that he had not been 'sent home' from Asia and to re-establish that, unhampered, his message could achieve wide acceptance. He was indeed enthusiastically received in both countries, and through the friendships he then formed laid the foundation for work which came to fruition in later years. In Japan, in addition to his usual work, he became friends with two of the creators of modern Japan, Baron Moriumura Kawasaki and Viscount Shibusawa, who chaired a meeting of the Concordia Society where Buchman spoke on 'Human Engineering'.

To Buchman's great sadness, Walter died of influenza in India that November, and there was constant anxiety about his parents; but otherwise these months in Korea and Japan seem to have been both happy and fruitful. Dr Kline's reply to his letter, through one delay and another, did not reach him till 8 February 1919. Thereupon he cancelled various engagements, and in March 1919 sailed for the United States.

He had not, as it turned out, heard the last of some of the leading characters in the drama of his departure from China. Harry Blackstone, it became known, had a weakness for Eurasian secretaries and, when one of them spoke publicly about their relationship in 1924, he was disgraced and left the church to go into business. In his misery, he wrote to Buchman for help.[26] 'I am so very sorry that all this has happened,' Buchman replied in April 1924. 'You can have anything at my disposal and I shall do all in my power to do what you want me to do. I shall stay straight by you to help, even though you say the sky is black as midnight. . . Do feel free to make any demands upon me and I will do my utmost to fulfil them.'[27]

As for Bishop Roots, Buchman never (according to Roots' daughter) mentioned the matter again either to him or to any of his family, although the Bishop and all his family, both before and after his retirement, came later to work closely with Buchman. 'You have forgiven us much,' the Bishop wrote to him in 1942. 'In particular you have forgiven me so much. I am slowly beginning to realise how much.'[28]

Hsu Ch'ien gradually became disillusioned with what he saw of Christianity in China. At Kuling he and a colleague had had a talk with Buchman, during which the 'National Society for the Salvation of China' had been conceived. After Kuling, he had had a three-hour talk with Sun Yat-sen who thought it 'a sincere and very deep idea' and later confirmed that he 'believed this fundamental principle is the only way China will be saved'. But early the next year Hsu wrote sadly to Buchman, 'At present the missionaries are only preaching about the *individual* righteousness but nothing about society and nations as a whole. Why should people be only righteous individually but not in political affairs?"[29] In 1923 an agent from Moscow called Michael Borodin arrived in Canton and, in due course, became adviser to both Sun Yat-sen and Hsu. Hsu felt that Borodin really appreciated his ability and idealism whereas, according to his daughter, 'he got little co-operation from the formal Christians in his large national schemes of applied Christianity'.[30] By 1925 he was living in an apartment in the Russian legation.

Many have wondered why Communism was able to capture the leadership of China so easily in spite of the vast missionary investment, both American and British, put into the country during the previous half-century. Arthur Holcome, Professor of Government at Harvard University, gives full weight to the Chinese disillusionment at their treatment by the 'Christian' Allied powers at the Versailles Peace Conference where the German concessions were handed over to Japan and the Allies retained their own, in spite of promises to the contrary. To this, he adds three more deep-seated reasons: 'the failure of Western missionaries to treat the Chinese as equals', their 'lack of unity' and their 'ignorance of China and the Chinese'. The missionaries, he says, were intent on changing Chinese culture, while the Russians, and particularly Borodin, sought to understand and use it.[31] All these three attitudes were ones which Buchman was trying to tackle while in China.

One can speculate what would have happened if there had been significant alteration on any or all of these points among the missionary community. If a considerable body of the Chinese leadership, with such backing, had set themselves to remedy the ills which Hsu and General Wu articulated, it is at least possible that there might have been an alternative dynamic enough to withstand the atheistic revolution which Borodin imported.

As it was, Hsu Ch'ien, Sun Yat-sen, Chiang Kai-shek, Mao Tse-tung, Chou En-lai and others succumbed to the persuasive personality of Borodin.* In their search for the unifying and cleansing principle, which Hsu and others had seen in the revolutionary Christianity offered by

---

* A young American journalist, one of Bishop Roots' sons, then writing for the *New York Times* in China, knew Borodin well. It was Chiang Kai-shek who introduced them in 1926. 'Borodin spoke of revolution,' he recalled later. 'He had worked his way several times through the New Testament. He said, "That man Paul, there was a revolutionary!" Then he suddenly turned with a distorted face, pounded his fist on the table till the teacups flew off on to the floor, looked me in the eye and shouted, "But where do you find men like him today? Give me one example. No, you cannot."' (John M. Roots writing in *Morgenbladet* (Oslo), 2 January 1962.) Partly as a result of this conversation, John Roots decided to work full-time with Buchman, and was later joined by the Bishop and several others of his family.

Buchman, they turned to Communism. Some later broke with it. Some were confused. Some were captured by it heart and soul.

For Buchman himself, the consequences of his Chinese experience were considerable. He had found himself in conflict with a sizeable part of the Christian establishment and had lost, but had learnt a good deal in the process. It was a great surprise to him. 'Simply because I attacked sin in China,' he noted when he arrived home. Of the reaction to his mention of 'absorbing relationships', he added, 'Had no idea such sin existed except in isolated cases. Being misunderstood opened my eyes. There is a clique that is impure.' In passing on Bishop Lewis' warning, he had simply thought that he was offering the assurance of inner freedom and of spiritual effectiveness to Christian workers who would be glad to receive it. In relating the story to Hartford President Douglas Mackenzie, he added, 'I believe that some of the criticism is traceable to the fact that the men felt I knew more than I actually did.'[32]

As he came back to America, ignorant still of Blackstone's manoeuvring, he felt that wider opposition to him was crystallising and he expected that rumours would have found their way not only to Hartford but to YMCA headquarters in New York. Meantime he wrote to Sherwood Day, 'I am not returning to Hartford tied in any way. I must have liberty of speech and action.'[33]

FIRST PRINCIPLES

By now Buchman's message, as well as some of his ways of working, was beginning to crystallise. It was not a new message – it had existed for nearly two thousand years – but through his experience and personality it was acquiring certain distinctive emphases. Its expression developed as the age produced new challenges; but its roots remained the same.

His home background, reinforced by his studies at Muhlenberg and Mount Airy, had left him with beliefs which, in the theological language of the day, may be summarised as the sovereignty and power of God, the reality of sin, the need for complete surrender of the will to God, Christ's atoning sacrifice and transforming power, the sustenance of prayer and the duty to witness to others. But these were for him, as he left Mount Airy, largely intellectual beliefs – assumptions, rather than vibrant convictions. 'Everybody went to church,' he once said of Pennsburg, 'but it didn't affect their lives, other than they were *very* moral. I only once saw anyone become different.' And of himself after Mount Airy, he recalled, 'I was a flat failure. I was the product of a mould, a conservative theological seminary. I was supposed to know how to preach, but I knew nothing about men or how to help them. I knew nothing about the Holy Spirit except as a dove.'

Yet his desire for growth was eager, and as he met new situations and challenges, long-assumed doctrines sprang to life. Meaning was poured into them, and a lesson once learnt was learnt for life.

Thus, during the years at Overbrook and the hospice, he had begun to understand human nature more thoroughly – and, also, to discover that God was reliable, that in a life of 'faith and prayer' practical needs were met. At Penn State he had found that people could change radically and that, through such change in individuals, the tone of an institution could be altered; and in China he had come to believe that what was true for a university could prove true for a nation. In his struggle to alter these larger situations he reached a conclusion which Augustine had remarked upon centuries before: that, although every soul is of the same value and needs the same care, conditions in society could only be affected at all quickly if key people – those with influence – were affected.* Whereas he spoke of Penn State as 'the laboratory' in which he tested the principles on which to work, he had seen China, as he approached it in July 1917, as 'the proving ground of the power to turn nations Godwards'. His mind was grappling with one of the largest challenges which could face a man of faith, and one which not many in his day were contemplating.

Buchman, however, always regarded his spiritual discoveries as having universal application. After his experience in the little church in Keswick, when he realised his own sin and experienced Christ's forgiveness, he never again considered that any other human being, however corrupted, was beyond the reach of the grace which had healed his own hate and pride.

Another decisive experience had resulted from F. B. Meyer's question to him at Penn State – whether he gave enough time each day to asking God what he should do. This can be seen as the time when Buchman decided to give his will, as distinct from his life in general, to God. Now he must do God's work not in his way, but in God's. His immediate response had been to set aside the hour between five and six in the morning not just to talk to God, but to listen as well. It was his personal discovery of the age-old discipline of silence before God. In carrying out this experiment, he was much encouraged by contact with Professor Henry Wright of Yale and by studying his book, *The Will of God and a Man's Lifework*, which was published in that same year of 1909.**[1]

The central theme of Wright's book was that an individual could, through 'two-way prayer' – listening for guidance as well as talking – find God's will for his life and for the ordinary events of the day. Wright himself set aside half an hour for such listening prayer first thing every morning. At such times – and indeed at any time in the day – he declared that what he called 'luminous thoughts' came from God, provided only that the human receiver was clean enough to pick them up. These thoughts Wright wrote down in a notebook and always tried to carry out.

Buchman saw his thought to tackle 'Tutz', followed by his immediate

---

* 'Further in so far as they are known widely, they guide many to salvation and are bound to be followed by many . . . Victory over the enemy is greater when we win from him a man whom he holds more strongly and through whom he holds more people.' *The Confessions of St Augustine*, translated by F. J. Sheed (Sheed and Ward, London 1944), Book 8, Section IV, pp. 128–9.

** Wright immediately sent a copy to Buchman at Penn State, who replied, 'Your book has just come and I am delighted with it . . . am teaching it myself to about a hundred' (Mark Guldseth, *Streams*, privately printed 1982, p. 87). Wright was at this time Assistant Professor of Latin History and Literature at Yale. In 1914 a special chair in Christian Methods was created for him at Yale Divinity School. Guldseth makes clear Buchman's debt – often acknowledged by Buchman himself – at this period to Wright, Moody and Drummond.

meeting with him, as an intimation to him from God. Similarly, a decisive moment for Ray Purdy, who became one of his life-long colleagues, was at a student camp in September 1919, when Buchman received such an unexpected prompting, suddenly got up and hurried to a tent at the far end of the camp, where he found a man seriously ill with acute appendicitis. In later life, too, Buchman would talk of 'that arresting tick' which could intrude into a person's ordinary thinking with particular authority. But his concept of listening was not mainly composed of such occurrences. 'Listening means an unhurried time when God really can have a chance to imprint His thoughts in your mind,' he said at Kuling.[2] 'For me personally at five o'clock or an earlier hour, I am awake and conscious of the presence of God. Some days it is simply a series of luminous thoughts of things God wants me to do that day. Some days it is just a sense of peace and rest and one or two outstanding things. Other days it is a sense of need for intercession on behalf of certain people. It takes all the fret, strain and worry out of life.'*

Such communing with God has been the practice of saints down the ages. Buchman's belief was that this contact was also available to everyone and anyone. 'This listening to God is not the experience of a few men,' he told the Chinese. 'It's the most sane, normal, healthful thing a person can do ... You begin to realise your own nothingness.'

To Sam Shoemaker in 1920, Buchman wrote a seven-page foolscap letter, citing a formidable array of Biblical and theological authority for the practice. 'It is, of course, constant in all the books of the Scripture,' he wrote, 'and I am absolutely convinced from my clinical reactions both at Princeton and in other places, that it is possible for babes in Christ to have this experience. Someone once compared the Bible to a lake, in which lambs could walk and an elephant could swim. The same analogy holds ... I want to make it available to the masses who are hungry but unaware of this very simple truth ...

'It is not a matter of temperament; much more of a willingness to become as little children. It is given to all alike if they will accept it in a childlike spirit. We have lived such poverty-stricken lives spiritually that the simple offends and seems peculiar. One of the reasons the truth did not flash upon me earlier was a lack of abandon on my part. It was my own stupidity in blundering so long.'

Buchman wrote this letter from a student camp and added, 'This is not without its humorous side. We live a very simple life, and I would have an inspiration, write it out, and then turn out the gas and go to bed, then

* The thoughts which arose in such times of seeking God's guidance in later years became known, in the verbal shorthand of Buchman and his friends, as 'guidance', although neither he nor they considered that all such thoughts came from God.

[75]

another one came, then the light out again, then another match. It took a box of matches and a lot of perseverance . . .'[3]

Buchman was aware that people who tried to listen to God needed safeguards. Human beings had an infinite capacity for self-deception and some of the most dangerous men in history had proclaimed their will as synonymous with God's. To guard against such excesses, he subjected his thoughts to 'a six-fold test'.

The first test was a willingness to obey, without self-interested editing. A second was to watch to see if circumstances intervened – for example, if he felt he should see somebody and that person turned out to be in another country, or if some other more urgent need in another person supervened. A third test was to compare the thought to the highest moral standards known to him: the standards of absolute honesty, purity, unselfishness and love which he had adopted as a rough and ready summary of the moral teaching in the Sermon on the Mount. His fourth testing point was whether any particular thought tallied with the overall teaching of the Scriptures. His fifth was the advice of friends who were also trying to live by God's guidance. If one was uncertain of a course of action, he felt, one should wait and seek out friends and listen with them, picking for the purpose the person least, rather than most, likely to agree with one's own predilections. The sixth was the experience and teaching of the Church.

The moral standards which he used as a test of directing thoughts also became central to Buchman's life and teaching: he took them as measuring rods for daily living. Here again he was indebted to Henry Wright. 'The absolutes' had originally been set out, as a summary of Christ's moral teaching, by Robert E. Speer in his book, *The Principles of Jesus*.[4] Buchman had several times heard Speer preach at Mount Airy, but it was in Wright's book that he first found the summarised standards 'in regard of which', Wright maintained, 'Christ's teaching is absolute and unyielding'. Wright described them as 'the four-fold touchstone of Jesus and the apostles' and maintained that an individual could apply them 'to every problem, great or small, which presents itself . . . if (anything) fails to measure up to any one of these four it cannot be God's will'.[5]*

Buchman's adoption of this expression of Christ's standards was, as so often with him, a practical choice. He was interested, above all, in what he called 'the how' – the way in which the life of faith, at its most demanding, could be grasped by the beginner as well as by the long-time believer. The standards of honesty, purity, unselfishness and love were something anyone, however simple or scholarly, could use to measure his life, and the

* Buchman made one alteration – in the order of the standards. Wright put 'absolute purity' first; Buchman placed 'absolute honesty' in first place.

addition of the prefix 'absolute', while setting an aim which no one could attain, had two obvious advantages. It stopped the honest seeker from letting himself off with a second or third best, or with the relativism which adjusts to the standards of the society around him; and it set so high a goal that anyone attempting to live by these standards would constantly be turned back to God for forgiveness, grace and strength. Buchman gained through the years an overwhelming sense that 'Christianity has a moral backbone': that spirituality cannot be divorced from the highest moral imperatives and survive.

Here, as elsewhere, he was striking out against the current of the day and of the age ahead. As William Hocking later observed, 'It is a mark of the shallowness of Western life that it should be thought a conceit to recognise an absolute and a humility to consider all standards relative, when it is precisely the opposite. It is only the absolute which rebukes our pride.'[6]

By standards Buchman did not mean rules. He had a horror of people who tried to live Christianity by rote or regulation, and when asked whether such and such a piece of conduct was permissible was apt to answer, 'Do anything God lets you.' 'If you want to go on working round here,' he admonished a young man in the last years of his life, 'please stop living by rules and live by the Cross.' For Buchman, 'living by the Cross' meant the voluntary laying down of anything in one's personal life which did not match Christ's standards, the abandoning of one's own will to do the will of God, and the daily experience of Christ's cleansing and healing power. The essence was the free choice of such a way of life, thus avoiding the need for rules and the danger of creating a movement or sect. 'The Cross is an alternative to living by the book,' he said on another occasion. His own criterion was to do nothing which robbed him of the power to help other people spiritually. The standards, in fact, were to be interpreted to the individual by the Holy Spirit.

C. H. Dodd wrote at about the same time that as the Christian approaches any practical problem of ethics, he should 'bring the mind of Christ to bear': 'The moral demand of letting Christ's Spirit rule you in everything is far more searching than the demand of any code, and at the same time it carries with it the promise of indefinite growth and development. It means that every Christian is a centre of fermentation where the morally revolutionary Spirit of Christ attacks the dead mass of the world.'[7]

Shortly before Buchman's second visit to China, Henry Wright was responsible for another important step in his development. While based at Hartford, teaching and gathering his team, Buchman used to travel four hours each way, once a week, to attend Wright's lectures at Yale. On the wall of Wright's lecture room he was confronted with Moody's words: 'The world has yet to see what God can do in, for, by and through a man whose will is wholly given up to Him.' Wright never began a lecture until two minutes had been spent silently considering those words. Then he would say, 'Will *you* be that man? Will *you* be that man?', and would always link his challenge with the Bible verse, 'I, if I be lifted up, will draw all men unto Me.'

Buchman said of those sessions, 'It took me six weeks until I came to absolute conviction and yielded myself to that principle.' Exactly what he meant is not known, but it was evidently a profound commitment – a break-out from a narrow to a universal conception of Christianity – for in repeating the phrases used by Moody and Wright, he always laid stress on the words 'world' and 'all'. This may have been the source of his thought of 'turning nations Godwards', and could help to account for the steadiness which kept him working towards this vision despite the setbacks which were to occur at different times throughout his life.

Perhaps it was also the origin of the quality to which Henry van Dusen of Union Theological Seminary later referred: 'Frank Buchman belongs to the tiny company of the centuries who have known themselves summoned to the surrender of all to the exacting demand of the Divine Will, and who, making that surrender, have pressed on through darkness and light in immovable confidence in the Divine Guardianship of their destiny. A like surrender he requires of every person who would share intimately in the leadership of his work.'[8]

Buchman's most immediate interest in these years in Penn State, Hartford and China was in studying and practising how to win individuals to God. Here another influence upon him was Henry Drummond, the Scots geologist and evangelist who in his undergraduate treatise *Spiritual Diagnosis* pioneered the science, as he liked to call it, of helping individuals one by one. Drummond contrasted the detailed clinical work required of every medical student with the total absence in the theological curriculum of 'any direct dealing with men'. Yet, he maintained, a minister could do far more by learning how to help individuals than by preaching sermons. Drummond's phrases were liberally used by Buchman in his talks in China and he is much quoted in *Soul Surgery*, the little book published in 1919 in which Howard Walter summarised his and Buchman's experience of life-changing. *Soul Surgery* was intended as an outline of a fuller book which the two friends planned to work upon at Hartford after the second visit to China, a hope frustrated by Walter's death in 1918.

The central thesis of Walter's book was simple, if explosive: if men and women were to be fundamentally changed, if they were to have a *real* conversion experience, the change must touch and transform the deepest areas of their lives, their root motives and desires. Too often the basic problems were untouched, and it was thought enough if someone declared himself saved – or, in today's parlance, 'born again' – if he joined the appropriate religious institution and began to use the name of Christ liberally, or subscribed generously to the institution's funds. The book's purpose was to explore the art of bringing the basic experience of change to others.

While on the ship with his Hartford friends, en route for China, a Miss Constance Smith asked Buchman one evening how he helped individuals. Next day, he answered her with a rough formula which he called 'the five Cs' – Confidence, Confession, Conviction, Conversion, Continuance, a summary which he often used in following years. Nothing could be done until the other person had confidence in you, and knew that you would keep confidences. Confession – honesty about the real state of the person's life – would lead to a conviction of the seriousness of sin and the desire to be freed from its control. For conversion to take place there must be a free decision of the will – often cold-blooded, seldom emotional. But far the longest and most neglected part was continuance. You were responsible for helping the newly orientated person to become increasingly the person God meant him or her to be. 'Personal work,' Buchman said on another occasion, 'means the unfolding of the possibilities which are in men.' 'What is the craving of the human heart?' he asked in Kuling. 'Fun, enjoyment, satisfaction, peace, joy – and they come when Jesus and the sinner are reconciled.'

He always stressed that 'life-changing', as he often called such helping of individuals, was not a technique. Only God could change a person, and the work of a 'life-changer' had to be done under His direction, which alone could provide the sensitivity and flexibility required. True diagnosis, too, was not a matter of mere psychology. 'A sacred responsibility rests with the person who has the courage to listen to God,' he said one day at Kuling. 'When a man tells you he has no spiritual power in his life, God will reveal to you why. He will give you the diagnosis of the problems of the very person with whom you are working.'

Such work must naturally be done privately – 'under four eyes', as Buchman sometimes described it. Often it would require the 'life-changer' first being honest about problems which had been, or still were on occasion, those which he found most difficult in his own life, as this gave the other the courage to be open about fundamental problems in turn. Often Buchman found that the problems which most troubled people were sexual, and he did not hesitate to enter this area, into which few others but Freud and himself – from profoundly different angles – dared at that time to venture. As far back as Penn State, he had seen sexual indulgence as one of the most common barriers to a full experience of Christ. It was self-evidently one of the places where the human will was most deeply rooted, and where clarity of decision was most necessary if a person was to become free and able to bring similar freedom to others.

Buchman realised that if he were to help others, he must live a pure life himself. 'I find I cannot listen to the slightest suggestive. I need to be antiseptic. I cannot play on the edge. O Lord, I want to give myself to the maximum,' he once noted. The act of giving himself more fully to God seems to have led to a sharper battle in his own heart. 'The temptations in an intensified form,' he noted a day later, 'are the preparation for greater victory. They give greater sympathy for the sinner.'

Buchman had learnt that temptation, of whatever kind, was best resisted at its earliest stage. It was easier, he sometimes said, to divert a small stream than to dam a river. He defined the progression of tempta-tion as 'the look, the thought, the fascination, the fall', and said that the time to deal with it was at the thought – 'Tackle temptation well upstream.' This was not a new idea. Thomas à Kempis, whose writings he would not likely have encountered at Mount Airy but whose *Imitation of Christ* went with him everywhere during his adult life, describes the same progression. 'The enemy is more easily overcome,' writes à Kempis, 'if he be not suffered in any wise to enter the door of our hearts but be resisted without the gate at his first knock.'[9]

A futher necessary element in becoming a free personality, Buchman believed, was to be prepared to make restitution, to put right as far as possible any wrong done. Hence, for example, his own letters from Kuling to the Pennsylvania Railroad Company and to the man to whom he had told a lie – even though, in the latter case, it was the seemingly trivial matter of having pretended to have read a book of which he had only read reviews.[10] Sometimes such restitutions might involve public confession, but only when it affected the public. 'If your sin is a public one, like that of the leader in a public quarrel, you ought to confess it. If it is sincere, people will sympathise with you.'

It was Bishop Moloney who had opened his eyes to a further use of confession, both private and public. Buchman had long known that people were more interested and more lastingly helped if he told them of his faults and how he had been freed from them, than if he set before them his virtues, real or supposed. But the revival in the Bishop's diocese which had begun with the Bishop's and his servant's mutual honesty confirmed for him that the principle might have much wider application. So, in the next decades, when he was deploying large teams of people and when his usual practice was for them to do the bulk of the speaking in any meeting, he encouraged speakers to be honest about the specific liberations which handing over control to God had brought to them. This, he found, was the surest way of showing people, whether believers or unbelievers, that God could help them in personal or public matters, that God was in fact a God of power. However, he set firm limits to what should be publicly confessed. Nothing must be mentioned which involved a third party, and where questions of sex were involved, he always said, 'If your sins were forms of impurity, never say what they were. Just say "impurity".'

The taboos of those days being what they were, Buchman's frank dealing with sexual problems, even in private, provoked criticism and rumours. Those who wished to attack him were apt to pounce on any lapse in discretion at any of his meetings, whether he could be considered responsible for them or not. Buchman, however, was undeterred. The facts were there and he could not shrink from dealing with them. 'Men used to come to me, a different man each half-hour,' he once said, recalling visits to summer conferences at Northfield. 'There it was – you could not underestimate it when you got it by the bushel.'

Buchman had also learnt by this time that if one proposed that people should hand over complete control of their lives to God, or even try to live by absolute moral standards, one provoked active opposition. Sometimes it was of the casual kind which had appeared among students in Penn State when Bill Pickle stopped drinking and bootlegging; at others, the more sophisticated – and, he had begun to think, planned – type of action which had removed him from China. This, of course, was quite a different matter from honest disagreement with his approach, or from the fact that his personality did not appeal to everyone. 'Thank God we can disagree without being disagreeable,' he was wont to say. He wrote to Shoemaker, 'Yes, I am liable to make mistakes as other men are and I always want you to feel you can tell me anything.'[11] He remained friends with hundreds of people who held sincere intellectual doubts on the way he went about things.

Sometimes, of course, sincere differences of opinion and active opposition coincided; and sometimes he overlooked this fact and took opposition to him and his message as a sign of resistance to truth itself. But his basic understanding of opposition grew through experience, and he was coming to recognise the edge of malice or even hatred which intruded when the opposition arose from people or groups who felt that his message threatened their ways of life or even their institutions. That Buchman provoked such opposition did not of itself prove the validity of his stand, but if he had not provoked persecution from any quarter, that would have indicated that he was not putting into practice the revolutionary quality of the great Christian tradition. He did not enjoy it, but he welcomed the test. 'Persecution is the fire that forges prophets – and quitters,' he said in later life.

To move out beyond accepted boundaries, which was to be the pattern of Buchman's life, was a consequence partly of temperament, and partly of the atmosphere in which he began to work and develop in Penn State and China. John Mott's crusade 'to evangelise the world in this generation' was the central theme among the Christians with whom he worked

[81]

most closely. Mott had become Student Secretary of the International Committee of the YMCA in 1888 and General Secretary of the World Student Christian Federation, which he largely created, in 1895. 'While the missionary enterprise should not be diverted from the immediate and controlling aim of preaching the gospel where Christ has not been named,' he wrote, 'this must ever be looked upon as a means of the mighty and inspiring object of enthroning Christ in the individual life, in family life, in social life, in national life, in international relations and in the relationships of mankind.'[12] The strategy for this tremendous enterprise was to mobilise students from as many countries as possible in order to build up 'the new world leadership' for carrying out an epochal change during 'this decisive hour of world history'. His primary aim was not so much to enlist large numbers, but 'to get the ablest, strongest men, those who in any walk of life would be leaders', and he quoted Drummond's saying, 'If you fish for eels you catch eels; if you fish for salmon, you catch salmon.'

Mott's strategy depended on the peace and freedom of movement and communications which preceded the First World War, and during that war its thrust slackened. The American YMCA, of which he was by now General Secretary, became more and more involved, after 1917, in providing amenities for the troops. Its Secretaries in the mission fields of India and China were inadequate to their primary task, and no match for a Communist missionary like Borodin. Buchman, on his return home after the war, found that the old modes of working – through the YMCA, Northfield and so on – no longer possessed the power which they had previously. He felt that something less organisational, much more dependent upon the kind of transparent fellowship which he and his friends had established through total honesty in Tientsin, was necessary. At the same time it becomes clear, as the story proceeds, that he had absorbed and retained much of the optimism and many of the tactics of Mott's great design.

Such optimism was greatly needed as Buchman faced the post-war world. Every major war brings demoralisation, but one where, in Churchill's words, 'torture and cannibalism were the only two expedients that the civilised, scientific, Christian states had been able to deny themselves',[13] drastically undermined both spiritual belief and traditional morality. 'At the beginning of the 1920s,' as one historian relates, 'the belief began to circulate, for the first time at a popular level, that there were no longer any absolutes: of time and space, of good and evil, of knowledge, above all of value.'[14] This belief coincided with – or perhaps was in part caused by – two other contemporary phenomena: the widespread acceptance of Freudianism, and the fact that Leninism, with its espousal of atheism and a totally relative morality, now controlled one of the major countries of the world. In fact, the age of relativism had arrived, and – much to Einstein's displeasure, for he himself believed passionately in absolute standards of right and wrong – his theory of relativity was used to give scientific respectability to the whole process. As moral relativism spread, it became the dominant theme of art and literature over many decades and penetrated every area of life, lay and ecclesiastical. Buchman, with his uncompromising beliefs, was to find himself more and more often swimming against the tide. It was to batter him, but not to turn him from his purpose.

That purpose was entirely positive. He never organised a protest against anything, still less denounced anyone in public. His response to every difficulty was the faith that God could change people, and the more serious he perceived the state of the world to be, the more intensely he concentrated on individuals. As the century progressed and moral relativism manifested itself in ever more powerful forms, he felt that his calling was to raise a world-wide force of God-directed people.

For the moment, he was returning to his job at Hartford and to the succour of his mother and father. But it became increasingly clear to him that he was intended to find new ways of working and, after his Chinese experience, he was less and less willing to let any job or institution stand in the way of following them.

'RESIGN, RESIGN'

Buchman returned home from the Far East in April 1919. Instead of playing down what had happened there, he wrote to Mott that the Christian effort in Asia was doomed to failure unless there was 'a radical reversal of direction from diffusion over the many to a deep penetration of the few'.[1] Of his own role, he wrote, 'If the policy of the Foreign Department . . . is to be first and last the Propagation of Life then you may be sure I am ready to pay the price that we have all got to pay if such a policy is to be followed. On any other basis I cannot honestly give my time and strength to the Association.'[2] He also wrote to Sherwood Day from Allentown, where he had gone to give his mother some sorely-needed help, 'I am perfectly willing that there should be a break with Hartford. That wouldn't be any particular wrench.'[3]

Nevertheless, after a good deal of soul-searching, he accepted Hartford's renewed offer. The arrangement was a generous one: it gave Buchman freedom to travel for nine months in the year, and only required him to give a series of lectures on the 'how' of personal evangelism at times agreed with President Mackenzie and Dean Jacobus.

Buchman considered that the purpose of a seminary was thoroughly to convert its students and then to send them out as skilled 'fishers of men'. If it did not serve those ends, theological scholarship became irrelevant. One of Buchman's students, Edward Perry, later described what it was like to study under him: 'His lectures were totally unlike any others in that sedate institution. Mostly they consisted of stories of people whose lives had been changed by God's power working through him. It was fascinating, up-to-date, real . . . His picture of a real ministry was not a matter of eloquent sermons and well-organized parish activities, but of meeting people's deepest needs one by one . . .

'He did not feel that his job was just to teach us *about* his subject, in this case the changing of people, as in other classes. He also felt responsible to see that we ourselves changed, for he recognized that no amount of technique or knowledge could make us effective "fishers of men" unless we found for ourselves the victory in Christ that must be our message for others.'

After describing the period when he recognised his own spiritual need and rebelled against the thought of asking for help – during which Buchman made no approach on a personal level, although they did have one game of tennis 'which neither of us played very well' – Perry continues: 'I asked him for "an interview". There, in his office, for the first time in my life I told another person what I was like inside – at least as far as I understood myself. He was not in the least shocked . . . About all that he said was, "What you need is to surrender your life completely to Jesus Christ. . . ." It was almost an insult. Was I not studying for the Christian ministry? But I knew what he was talking about was something far more than I had yet done. My earlier decisions had been sincere, but they had not been complete. I had decided to do certain things for God. What Buchman asked was that I turn over the management of my life to God.'[4]

Buchman's relationship with senior Hartford was somewhat uneasy almost from the beginning. The reasons are not far to seek. For one thing, there as in China, Buchman made no secret of his conviction that the more traditional approach was inadequate. 'The seminary today', he wrote to a friend, 'is an expensive luxury for propagating theology which is often-times wholly divorced from life.'[5] Another cause of friction was that Buchman wanted freedom to move wherever he felt the Spirit was leading him. Since he often seemed to feel led away from Hartford even when he was expected to be there, this fitted ill with the seminary's assumption that his prime obligation was to them.

The trouble was caused by the demand for Buchman from other colleges and later from abroad. The fact that Douglas Mackenzie retained him on the staff for so long says a great deal for Mackenzie's large-mindedness.

Mackenzie's position was difficult. He was conscious that although 'there were divided opinions among the professors, some of whom preferred the ivory-tower conception of academic life', Buchman 'won his way magnificently with the students'. In fact, he 'only knew of one or two of the students who did not confess that they had received personal help from his work'.[6]

All through this time Buchman was burdened by a sense that if the Protestant churches as a whole were to fulfil his idea of their calling, they must change their approach. Organised religion, he told his students, too often meant 'efficiently doing what is not the way'; the Church, he warned, might well tremble 'lest it be abandoned as a deserted city where buildings are standing and all the machinery of human life is silent'.[7]

Back from missionary service six months after the end of the war, he saw the symptoms of its aftermath everywhere in the victorious America to which he had returned. While President Woodrow Wilson was in Paris attempting to 'dictate a new world order under a League of Nations pledged to universal peace' and his Secretary of State was privately noting in his diary that his master was 'making impossible demands on the Peace Conference . . . what misery it will cause'[8], emotions held in check by war were bursting out at home. The closing of the munitions factories, a cut-back in the working week, a slump in the price of crops which for four years had poured into the granaries of the Allies, aggravated the situation. Veterans who had been promised homes found only suburban boxes at extravagant rents. Labour, which had been willing to forfeit the right to strike, now felt free to press very real grievances, in the face of employers who had done well out of the war and were flaunting their riches outrageously. An ugly witch-hunt against supposed Bolshevists and the black population got under way.

Buchman observed with concern the triumph of an atheist regime in Russia after the recent revolution, but he was much more disturbed by the deterioration in his own country. A radical reawakening of faith was, he believed, the only long-term answer. Convinced by now that a vast and progressive moral disintegration was beginning to take place not only in his own country but in the world – 'a breakdown of civilisation' – he saw that it would have to be a reawakening on a world-wide scale. He seems immediately to have assumed that this demanding undertaking was his responsibility, and to have launched into it alone: 'I was convinced after my time in Asia that God meant to bring a moral and spiritual reawakening to every country in the world, and I personally felt called to give my whole time to that work.'[9]

Among the legacies he inherited from his work with Mott was the belief that the place to look for leadership for this awakening was in the universities. It would take the energy and idealism of which young people were capable. They must be won, individually, to the most radical obedience to God. Young Americans, back from the war, were anxious to study again in Europe, and especially in Britain. As a genuine rebirth of life appeared in one place, he believed it would spread to others. Yale would kindle Cambridge; Princeton and Harvard men would be used to revive religion in Oxford and Cape Town. From the great universities, the influence would spread to the newer and smaller colleges, and then to communities, churches and the professions. The final outcome, the regeneration of the whole Church, could in turn affect governments.

He saw this as happening through 'peripatetic evangelism' – a world-wide movement by small bands of completely committed, disciplined, carefully trained men and women from different countries. As in the Acts of the Apostles, they would move through the world, bringing new life to individuals and binding them into close-knit fellowships. Contagion would be borne from group to group.[10]

The drab red-brick buildings of Hartford Seminary might seem an unlikely place from which to start such a movement, and a lone man of 41 at least optimistic, if not naive and presumptuous, to think that he could bring it off. Nevertheless, as a first step he conceived the idea of a conference at Hartford, drawing in students from different colleges in the Eastern states. Mackenzie and Jacobus strongly backed the venture, although, as in China, there were a few misunderstandings about the agenda, misunderstandings which were this time settled ahead of the occasion.[11] Invitations went to Yale, Harvard, Williams, Amherst and Cornell, among other colleges. After the first conference, demands came for return visits, and each time Buchman took men from Hartford or other colleges with him.

So Buchman sallied forth from Hartford, returning each week to give his lectures. He received a salary ($3,000, plus $500 expenses), but his resources for this rapidly expanding work were slender and he must have hoped for more substantial backing. Indeed, Dean Jacobus frequently mentioned the need for him to gain outside support. In 1920 he was approached to create and lead a movement financed by John D. Rockefeller and others, which would, in its initiators' phrase, 'use all the genius of American industry to carry Christ's message to the laymen of the world'.[12] It was being planned on a big scale and would have large resources behind it.

Remembering what had happened in China, however, Buchman turned down this offer and, apparently, others which he felt would cramp his work into an organisational framework. He wrote Sherwood Day of his 'hunger to get away for a deeper message, more time alone. I feel my own need . . . It is more of Christ for me. I feel about all these offers for next year great dangers. My thought from above is – "*wait and see what God hath wrought*". We need to sweep the decks clear. And travel with light baggage.'[13] When he refused one of these offers, he was warned that he could expect no money for his own work from them, or, it was hinted, from similar sources. 'My answer', he explained later, 'was, "Well, I will starve, because that particular work is not 'of the Spirit'."' It was becoming clearer and clearer to him that he was meant to find and follow an independent road.

Buchman's initial campaign from Hartford received a notable stimulus at the Northfield Conference in the summer of 1919. By then, he had taken his mother for a much-needed holiday and arranged for his father, who had suffered a stroke the previous autumn, to be cared for at a nursing home close to his own lodgings at Hartford.

At Northfield Buchman had a profound effect on the lives of some of the Princeton delegation. The result was that they decided to launch a much more vigorous programme and they suggested to the Princeton

President, John Hibben, that he appoint Sam Shoemaker, now an active colleague of Buchman, as Secretary of the Philadelphian Society, the university's student Christian association. Hibben, who was also a Presbyterian minister, was entirely in favour of the idea. He had been greatly impressed by the results of a visit Buchman had paid to the campus in 1915. William T. Ellis, the author and journalist, reports him as saying that he had never known the student body so interested in personal religion.

That winter and the following spring, Buchman visited Princeton almost once a month. Each time, a steady stream of undergraduates came to talk to him. 'I spent last Sunday at Princeton in interviews from nine o'clock in the morning until one o'clock at night,' he reported to Hartford towards the end of the year. 'The men insisted I return this Sunday and I am taking two men from Hartford with me.'[14] On another visit, he had only five hours' sleep in three days. Nor was Princeton unusual. At Yale, he conducted interviews until three in the morning on three successive nights in November 1919.

For whatever reason, men were frank with him about matters they had never spoken of to anyone else. 'It is to be accounted a remarkable thing', wrote a student from Princeton Theological Seminary, 'when a man tells another in the first half hour of their personal acquaintance anything which he had withheld from every other being . . . Yet that is what I did to Mr Buchman, and it was all done with such a frankness and calmness that there could be no doubt of the vital reality of it all.'[15]

The young men who had begun to use Buchman's approach were also hard at work in Princeton even when he himself was not there. 'How grateful I have been that you taught me some things about reaching men!' wrote Sam Shoemaker early in 1920. 'Two magnificent opportunities yesterday and today, and two miracles in consequence.'[16]

Not all Buchman's young friends were quite so self-confident. Henry van Dusen, then studying at Princeton, wrote of two whom he felt he had failed, the first because of 'talking religious instead of moral difficulty' and the second because he seemed unable to help him to become free of past memories of various kinds. 'I don't feel I have given him a bit of help and, frankly, I don't know how to.' For himself, he added, he would not have missed the last six months for all his other twenty-one and a half years. Van Dusen also reported that, after attending a meeting where students trained by Buchman spoke, 'The Dean said it was the manliest thing he had ever seen a group of Princeton men do.'[17]

Buchman had clearly taken considerable risks in encouraging a group of inexperienced young men to confront problems which older heads had seldom had the courage or insight to tackle. But his work at Princeton soon had marked results. Considerable numbers of young men, who had not been thinking of the church as a profession, took the cloth because of contact with him. In May 1920 twenty Princeton men who entered the ministry in that year presented Buchman with a pair of gold cuff-links and their grateful thanks. In 1934 van Dusen, who had by that time distanced himself from Buchman, wrote that 'of the fifty ablest Ministers on the Atlantic seaboard to-day, somewhere near half were directed into their vocation through his influence at that time'.[18]

At the same time Buchman was accused by a few of an abnormal and morbid emphasis on sex and of conducting an unwarranted inquisition into men's private lives. Stories of alleged sexual confessions went round the campus and there was talk of emotionalism and even hysteria. Robert P. Wilder, a senior Director of the Philadelphian Society, came to the conclusion that those who opposed Buchman did so because 'Frank strikes too close to them.'[19] By the spring of 1920 van Dusen had begun to think that Princeton would not stand for what he called 'apostolic work'. Buchman disagreed. So did Shoemaker. 'They talk about emotion,' he wrote to Buchman. 'I don't believe in working it up for its own sake but no man can come to the profoundest decision of his life without its having an emotional reaction afterwards which stirs him to the depths.'[20]

Shoemaker was equally definite about the accusation that there was an undue emphasis on sexual indulgence. 'Of the sins which root in the flesh, any fool knows that sexual sins are likely to insinuate themselves into the first place in people's minds. They are common. Men want help there where the battle rages and there we must help them if we have anything to help with. We emphatically do *not* believe that it is the basic trouble. The basic trouble is always the pride of trying to get along without God.'

On 3 July 1920 Buchman sailed for Europe, taking with him two students from Yale. They joined up with some of his Princeton friends who were in Britain on an athletics tour. The peripatetic fellowship was on the move. They attended an evangelical conference in England and travelled round Europe, and were shown something of each country's art and architecture, as well as meeting Buchman's friends.

In Lucerne he took them to a hotel to meet Queen Sophie of Greece. She, with her husband and their son, Prince Paul, were visiting Switzerland with their German relations, the Hesse family: Sophie's cousin, Princess Margaret, and her two sons, Richard and Christopher. This was the first time Buchman had met the Hesses, but he seems to have rapidly won their confidence. 'For us young people coming from a Germany impoverished as a result of the First World War, these were very dazzling and tempting surroundings, and Mother, with her keen instinct for the inner worth of a man, viewed them with real mistrust,' wrote Prince Richard nearly forty years later. 'Only in the case of Frank was it a quite different matter. He moved around in that atmosphere without being

[89]

contaminated or influenced by it, which gave us great confidence in him.'
What he chiefly remembered was Buchman's 'infectious laughter' which
'revived everyone's spirits just to hear it'.[21] Thereafter, Buchman and his
friends became regular summer visitors at Kronberg, the Hesse home
near Frankfurt; so regular, indeed, that in the family it became known as
'the Buchman season'.

The two Yale students returned to college. In his luggage one of them
found a reproduction of Andrea del Sarto's 'John the Baptist' with the
note: 'John the Baptist was simple in life and dress, fearless in utterance
and uncompromising with the shame and superficialities of his day. He
was the forerunner of a new age. Yale needs a man like that, and I believe
you are one who will pay the price and have the power.'[22]

In Rome Buchman received news that Dan, not quite 24, had died two
days earlier in Paris. Although Dan had only come to live with the family
after he had left to take up parish work, Buchman always said that, next to
his mother and father, he loved Dan more than anyone in the world.
Although, or because, he was good-looking and charming, life was always
difficult for him, and Buchman had felt constantly responsible for him.
His correspondence with Dan was continuous, even at his busiest times,
and often included gifts of money, as well as advice to get his teeth fixed,
obey the doctor, wear his overcoat and buckle down to studies. After
Dan's failures at the Taft School and the technical school, he had enlisted
in the army in 1917, where he developed what, at his death, was
discovered to be a tubercular infection.

After demobilisation, an abortive job and a failed marriage, he wrote his
brother in April 1920, 'I am leaving the United States to try my luck in a
foreign country. I am sick and disheartened . . . I did not realise the money
you gave me last summer represented your only reserve supply. I mean to
pay it all back and more, so I must strike out.' He shipped as a merchant
seaman to France and made three crossings. On the last of them he fell ill,
and collapsed with double pneumonia in Paris.

In July Buchman wrote an affectionate letter to Dan in Paris, suggesting
he come to be his secretary at Hartford – perhaps with the idea of finally
spending enough time with him to be able to help him to find the faith they
had so often corresponded about. He made a rendezvous with him at
Thomas Cook's in Paris.[23] Hurrying to Paris from Rome on receipt of the
news, he found his letter uncollected at the *poste restante*.

Buchman grieved but was not surprised. In October 1919 he had
written, 'Dan is dying by inches. He will not live long.' He co-officiated at
the funeral in the American Church, and Dan was buried in the cemetery
at St Germain. Mrs Buchman wrote from Allentown, sending a poem
which she had found among Dan's papers. Buchman later put the first two
stanzas on his parents' gravestones, and chose the third stanza for his own:

He lives! In all the past,
He lives! Nor to the last
Of seeing him again will I despair.
In dreams I see him now
And on his angel brow
I see it written, 'Thou shalt meet me there.'

On the day of Dan's funeral, a telegram arrived from Prince Paul of Greece saying that, following their talks in Lucerne, he would like to come to America with Buchman and attend college there. Buchman postponed his own return to wait for him, only to hear, some time later, that the plan had been cancelled because the Greek people had voted for the return of the monarchy. In the interval, Buchman went to Cambridge to fulfil a promise made in China to Bishops Moloney and White to visit their sons. He also found several Princeton friends there.

President Mackenzie, hearing he was going to Cambridge, had recommended Buchman to his old fellow-pupil, Professor John Oman, a University lecturer based on the Presbyterian seminary, Westminster College. There Buchman was received as part of the Senior Common Room. He attended Oman's lectures, but his main interest was the university men he met. 'I often had three breakfasts,' he told friends later, 'one with the working crowd, then the next with the non-workers and then with the Indian princes.' Soon he was writing his Princeton friends that 'it would be ruinous to leave at this time'[24] and to Dean Jacobus explaining that he must stay, or 'if my stay embarrasses you, I should sever my connection with Hartford if that is a way out of the difficulty'.[25]

President Mackenzie, plainly annoyed at this extra absence and reasonably so, replied that he did not want the connection to break, but that if Buchman offered his resignation he would be compelled to recommend it.[26] The situation was, however, patched up once more.

Buchman, in fact, did not return till just before Christmas, for which his parents joined him at Hartford. It was their last Christmas together. His father died in the Hartford nursing home on 7 March 1921. The doctor's telegram reached Mrs Buchman too late for her to leave Allentown to see him. Buchman, who had been summoned from Boston, wired her: 'Father's home-going was peaceful. Wonderful crossing the bar. He felt you here . . . I arrived in time for him to know me and he died holding my hand. Your letter was God-timed. Love, affection. We must be brave. Frank.'[27]

He wrote to a friend, 'I never knew death could be so wonderful. It was a glorious end and I spent the last two hours and a half with him. He was so happy to have me near.'[28] And when, many years later, a student in

Australia asked Buchman why he believed in life after death, he said, 'Because I saw my father die.'

Meanwhile, in January 1921, Buchman had invited three evangelical Cambridge undergraduates – Godfrey Buxton and the brothers Godfrey and Murray Webb-Peploe – to join him in America. Godfrey Webb-Peploe was prevented from going by a war wound, but the others had what his brother, a medical student, describes as 'a fascinating three months . . . in the eastern universities – mainly Harvard, Yale and Princeton, sharing the good news of Jesus Christ and our experiences of God's presence with us in the war'. Those weeks, he adds, 'were to convince us of the three fundamental and practical facts concerning the leading of God: that God does guide; that where he guides, he also provides; and that he works at the other end, confirming and preparing the way.'[29]

From America he wrote to Buxton's fiancée, 'I have learnt more in the last ten days than in all my life about this game. . . . This work has convinced me more than ever of the amazing truth of the Bible, every part of it, and of one's belief in what it teaches, but I have been seeing, I think, that I have been allowing my Christian doctrines to be a barrier between me and the man who needs a Saviour and a surgeon. I have been getting down to where men live, and sharing with them the mess I have been in and the temptations that come every day. . . . By this sharing one gets "cross-sections" of men's lives . . . in a way one never did before. Men seem to open up right away and one can ask plain questions and they like it when they realise we are both just plain sinners. . . . If one may generalise, though it is always dangerous to do so, we in England who are evangelical are getting our air and food – prayer and the Bible – but are short on exercise; really getting down to where men live and diagnosing a man's trouble – "getting his history" as we say in medicine.'[30]

Buxton recalled later, 'Buchman had an amazing gift for personal work – for leading individuals to Christ. He certainly based what he said on the Bible, but he rarely spoke from it directly or spoke holding one – he said it might put off worldly people. I don't think, however, that he used the Bible as realistically as Murray and I had learnt to do. He tended to specialize in converting the influential and the rich – the "up-and-outs" as he called them. He reckoned they were harder to reach than the down-and-outs, through having less sense of need.'[31]

The pair evidently underwent something of a cold douche from some of their evangelical friends on their return to Cambridge, but Murray, in particular, held on to what he had learnt and helped Buchman in Oxford later in the year.

In May Buchman was in Cambridge. On the first evening fifty people turned up to see him. He began to have the sense that God was calling him to a wider task. One moonlight night, as he was bicycling down Petty Cury, a sudden thought struck him: 'You will be used to remake the world.' This thought so staggered him that, as he used to recall, he almost fell off his bicycle. It seemed so preposterous that he was reluctant to acknowledge it.* Contrary to his custom, he did not write it down and told no one about it for several days. But the idea kept recurring. 'I wondered then – and I still wonder – why God should take a little runt of a fellow like me and pitchfork me into the world and tell me to do the impossible,' he said, relating the experience some years later.

From now on this sense of specific mission was always with Buchman. Its very impossibility prevented his considering it a personal crusade with himself as heroic leader; its size gave him the nerve to proclaim his purpose in season and out of season, and to try to enlist every likely and unlikely person who would take it on with him. This made him at times bewildering and even unattractive to people who did not discern his underlying motive. It gave him, as well, an unflagging impetus which made of him what can only be described as a revolutionary personality, with all the effect of creative discomfort which this implies.

From Cambridge he went to Oxford, filling a gap in the Westminster College tennis team as a chance to visit some of the Princeton graduates who had gone there as Rhodes Scholars. One, a Southerner called Alex Barton, was at Christ Church and, through Barton, Buchman met Loudon Hamilton, a handsome, humorous Scot who had fought on the Somme and at Passchendaele and was now reading philosophy and playing rugby intermittently for the university.

At a loss as to how to entertain him, Hamilton invited Buchman to his rooms that evening for a meeting of a college society known familiarly as the 'Beef and Beer Club'. Ninety per cent of the gathering, according to Hamilton, were ex-officers, veterans of twenty-one or twenty-two with rows of medals which they would never have dreamed of talking about. A number, like Hamilton and his room-mate 'Sandy', had been wounded; some were deeply embittered by their experiences. A future Chancellor of the Exchequer was there, together with future High Court judges and the sons of landed gentlemen. It was a slice of the Establishment in the making.

Buchman seemed hopelessly out of place. 'He looked rather like a prosperous business man,' said Hamilton, 'a bit on the stout side, with a dark suit and rimless glasses, and he was wearing those fancy American shoes, made of white goat-skin and brown leather.'

The discussion – a typical Oxford one on how to put the world to rights

---

* It was not, however, an entirely unusual concept at that time. The campaign card which the evangelist Billy Sunday asked converts to sign in 1915 declared, 'God helping me, I dedicate myself to the task of rebuilding the world according to Christian ideas.' Buchman had on occasion worked with Sunday.

[93]

– went on until well past eleven o'clock and still the visitor had said nothing. The chairman asked whether he would care to say a word. Buchman, Hamilton recalled, 'ignored the violently contradictory opinions which had been expressed, and remarked that "any real change in the world had to start with a change in people". He didn't use words like "conversion" but he did talk about God and he told us about young men very like ourselves who'd become different. Everybody there knew exactly what he was talking about. A sort of hush fell. People took their pipes out of their mouths. Everybody was thoroughly uncomfortable. The whole thing really narked us because we liked things kept academic and impersonal, and he'd had the courage to make it very personal.' Buchman had offended against one of the most important canons of contemporary British good taste: he had raised the subject of religion on an unscheduled occasion.

'There was a terrible silence,' recalled Hamilton, 'but then the clock struck midnight and that saved the day. Most of the people made a very hasty exit, but to my horror and astonishment my room-mate, who was an atheist, suggested that we invite Buchman to breakfast the next morning.'

Hamilton ordered a gargantuan meal – cereals, fish, eggs and bacon, toast and marmalade, strawberries and cream – with the idea of keeping Buchman as quiet as possible. 'We covered the weather, Henley, the Varsity match,' said Hamilton, 'and I thought, "Surely he's going to start to fire off soon." Then he told the story of a Chinese headmistress of dowager status who had complained that one of her girls was stealing money. Buchman had asked the headmistress, "When did *you* last steal yourself?" and when she replied, "When I was thirteen," Buchman had asked why she didn't tell that to the girl.'

'Suddenly,' Hamilton went on, 'Sandy said, "I haven't always been honest about money", and there was a simplicity and an honesty in his voice that I'd never heard before. Buchman just nodded. He didn't ask any direct personal questions, but it suddenly occurred to me that I'd been to the New College Commem Ball without paying for the ticket. I didn't say anything, but I spent the rest of breakfast wondering who I could borrow the money from if I did decide to pay it back.'

By now, Buchman had evidently begun to feel thoroughly at home in England. 'Dearest Mater,' he wrote, on Christ Church Boat Club paper, 'God is very good, oh so good. It is marvellous, wonderful! Here I have many old and new friends and one meets at every turn grateful ones whose lives have been changed.'[32]

Hamilton, in any event, was interested enough to want to get to know Buchman better. In August he went to a 'house-party' at Trinity Hall, Cambridge, arranged by Robert Collis, a young Irish rugby international whom Buchman had helped with personal problems.

The house-party, which became a characteristic feature of Buchman's work, was a way of bringing together an assortment of people for several days in a friendly, relaxed atmosphere where they might be able to take fundamental decisions for their lives. It had much the flavour of the contemporary social house-party but the same essential purpose as a religious retreat: the main difference was in the sort of people whom Buchman invited. Many, as Hamilton discovered, were 'thorough-going pagans' like himself.

'There were,' according to Robert Collis, 'old Rugbeian Blues, Etonian rowing men, Presidents of the Oxford Union, Firsts in Greats*, Naval officers, Americans, a British colonel, Indians, Chinese, a famous American lawyer and a well-known English MP. The two latter arrived rather drunk but rapidly sobered down.'[33]

Buchman had in fact brought the lawyer and the Member of Parliament from London himself, in a Rolls hired by the MP. The lawyer, who was distinctly the worse for wear, kept complaining that there was a creak in the car, to which Buchman drily retorted that there *was* a creak, but *not* in the car.

This house-party, which lasted five days, began with Buchman asking everyone to say who they were and why they had come. Hamilton said candidly that he had slipped a stitch in life and that he knew he would get nowhere until it was picked up. Soon, he recalled, the atmosphere had become so relaxed that 'you were talking to people to whom you'd not even been introduced'.

'Buchman,' wrote Collis, 'not only succeeded in harmonising this gathering, but by the end genuine friendliness replaced the strain intensely felt through the first meetings . . . Each had come wearing his mask . . . By the end of the house-party the masks had disappeared from each face . . . To describe the house-party as a success would be to understate the facts of the case. It was a very *tour de force*.'[34]

The theme, according to Hamilton, was what changes would be involved in people's lives if they decided to give themselves to God. After breakfast each day, one or two of Buchman's friends – people like Charles Haines, a rowing man from Princeton – would talk about their experiences, and Buchman himself spoke from time to time. Hamilton remembered him telling the story of Bill Pickle – 'forty minutes which seemed like ten'.

'It was all so real,' he said, 'and it was related to the world I understood. I felt great confidence in Frank. In the accepted sense of personal magnetism, he didn't have it – and he was a cautious man in many ways, absolutely the opposite of the blustering evangelical type. What attracted

* The traditional Oxford Degree of Philosophy and Ancient History.

me was the reality and conviction with which he spoke and got others to speak, and the relationship between the people around him. They called each other by their first names, which aroused suspicion in our circles, but there was no affectation. Previously, religion had seemed a rather gloomy business, but this was different.' On the Sunday Hamilton decided to stop 'teetering around on the diving board' and to give his life to God 'come what may'.

By the time Buchman sailed for America in November 1921 it had become clear to him that he would have to part company with Hartford. He approached the decision with a trepidation natural in a man over forty who had no other means of support. It finally crystallised one night when he was travelling to Washington to meet delegates to the current Disarmament Conference.* 'Resign, resign, resign,' the rhythm of the train's wheels seemed to say, and he jotted down, 'Resign on principle. Don't worry about finances. You must make an untried experiment. Step out alone.'

On 25 January 1922 he asked Mackenzie if he could give more periods of practical instruction to balance the weight of academic theological teaching in the curriculum. Mackenzie refused, saying that there were other courses which were 'vital' to personal conduct and inner life and that other professors were quite as anxious about that side of the work as Buchman. When rumours were later spread that Buchman had been asked to resign, Mackenzie commented, 'On the contrary, I did everything in my power to persuade Frank to stay.'[35] On 1 February Buchman sent in his formal letter of resignation, thanking Mackenzie and Jacobus for their 'many known and unknown courtesies and kindnesses to me'. At the same time he wrote his mother, 'Don't worry about things. Worry killed the cat and I have a peace which passeth all understanding . . . The best is yet to be.'

Never again was he to hold any paid position.

---

* 20 December 1921. Colonel David Forster, who was on the British Delegation, had invited the conference delegates to meet Buchman; thirty came.

MONEY AND MANPOWER

It was not a rosy prospect. Buchman had no regular income except a monthly payment of $50 from a family insurance, nor did he have a base from which to work. There were hundreds of people scattered around America, Britain and the Far East to whom he had brought a basic experience of Christ. He had shown, in miniature, that his idea of contagion through travelling teams worked. But the only cohesive groups which had developed were at Princeton and, in a very small way, at Oxford. His greatest needs, if his vision was to come true, were for the emphasis of his work to move to the team or groups in many countries, and for some to step out as his full-time companions. At present Sherwood Day was the only one. A man of singular charm, only a few years younger than Buchman, he in many ways complemented him: for example, where Buchman had creative thoughts, Day could often clothe them in compelling language. But clearly many more companions were now needed.

Some of those he had helped in America, hearing that he had resigned from Hartford, said they would raise $3,000 a year to support him, but the results were meagre: $1,000 collected in the first fifteen months. In the autumn of 1922, perhaps in an attempt to secure a broader base as well as to define his aims, Buchman and a few friends formed what they called 'A First Century Christian Fellowship'. 'It is', declared Buchman in a note to a supporter, 'a voice of protest against the organised, committeeised and lifeless Christian work' and 'an attempt to get back to the beliefs and methods of the Apostles'.[1]

The First Century Christian fellowship was never much more than a name, since it was composed mainly of supporters rather than people with a commitment equal to Buchman's. Within a few years it had faded away. The result was that, at this period, Buchman had to depend largely on gifts from a few wealthy New York women, of whom Mrs C. Richard Tjader, the widow of a Swedish-American business man, was the most generous.

Margaret Tjader had been a missionary in India as a girl, and she had decided to use a considerable inheritance to support Christian work in various parts of the world. In 1901 she had founded the International

Union Mission, which by 1922 had its headquarters in a former Rockefeller home on West 53rd Street. Here she gave Buchman the use of a sizeable room which served both as office and, when he was in New York, as bedroom. Her interest in Buchman originated from help he had given to her son, and her gifts to Buchman began in January 1923. Others who assisted him financially at this time were Mrs Finlay Shepard, and Mrs William Woolverton, whose husband was one of the two men who installed the first telephone in New York City. Buchman had probably met her at Northfield, as she was in the habit of taking parties there. She and her husband knew of the events at Penn State, and had been struck in particular by the change in Bill Pickle.

Buchman was no less forthright with benefactors than with anyone else. 'We left our friend through a crack in the door,' he wrote to Shoemaker in 1923 about a visit to one of them. 'She asked me what I thought she needed most and I told her "conversion". She said, "You are right." It is a great sense to feel that you are not going after people's cheques, but that you can check them to live the maximum. People don't like this, but then if they don't receive you at one place, follow Paul's plan, and let the dust from your feet blind them.'[2]

The amounts of money given to Buchman by backers in those early days of independence cannot have been large. Whereas from their earliest trips Buchman and his family had travelled first-class on transatlantic crossings, in June 1923 he went second-class for the first time 'because of the venture of Faith which compelled me to enlarge the work' – he was taking seven students to Europe. This letter was to a banker friend who was paying the passage of two of the students, and of them he wrote, 'I would very decidedly, if I were you, let them come first-class . . . because these men are to be the future leaders in their own country, and you want them to meet and know the men and women who are leaders in American life.'[3]

Buchman's bank statements for 1923 show that he never had more than $550 (then about £110) in his account, which often sank to $50 and once to $7.23. His average balance was about $100, and the income shown on his tax return for the year was $2,010. All the same, Mrs Finlay Shepard's contributions provoked a protest from Shoemaker. He wrote Buchman, 'You have very little feeling for social justice. You *say* you think reform is wanted but you see it all in terms of personal sin. I do not believe the anomaly of your rich friends being rich ever strikes you much. Hungry Coxe thinks you are a fearful snob . . . I am going to write him he has never seen you with Mary and Hannah and George . . . But, Frank, there is danger in too much hob-nobbing with the well-favoured classes of society.'[4]

These criticisms were to recur throughout Buchman's life. Since his days with the 'unprivileged' in Overbrook, his view had become that any really effective social or economic change had to spring from a thorough-going transformation in people of every class: the old principle of personal evangelism, he told Shoemaker, 'takes care of the social aspect when thoroughly thought through and sincerely applied'.[5] Without that trans-formation, he felt, any social or economic change was likely to be superficial. An event like the Russian Revolution, for example, might only substitute one form of oppression for another. Throughout his life, whatever the contemporary norm, he was more stringent in his challenges to the privileged than to the disadvantaged.*

It is clear that, feeling commissioned to try and change the world, Buchman regarded it as his duty to aim to change those people whose transformation would most quickly affect society at large. That, he believed, would create a more radical and lasting impact than any revolution of a purely political kind. 'Frank', said Eustace Wade,** who met him in 1921 as a Cambridge undergraduate, 'felt that leadership must come from the top. He saw a moribund establishment being reactivated by an inner spiritual power.' Dr Mahlon Hellerich, for many years Archivist of the Lehigh Valley Historical Society, regards it as most remarkable that a Pennsylvania Dutchman should undertake such a mission. They were brought up to be deferential to prominent people, but here was one actually trying to change them.

This meant that Buchman took care to go where he would meet such people, and also that he used their change or support – if they themselves had publicly stated it – to interest others. So he mentioned names – but he did not break the confidences that people, of whatever eminence, en-trusted to him, and if asked whether this or that person was associated with his work, would answer, 'Why don't you ask them?'

He had no wish to reach only the upper strata of society. 'I want to make it [the message] available to the masses who are hungry but unaware ...,' he wrote Shoemaker in 1920. 'The hunger for God is in every human breast. This is for everyone.'[6] 'We are after the kings and the poor and needy as well,' he said to another friend later. 'I know some poor and needy kings.'

His friendships, from 1909 onwards, with so many branches of the intertwined royal families of Europe, had sprung from the meeting with Princess Sophie of Greece in 1908. Undoubtedly he was initially amazed, and not a little excited, by the way an uncalculated act of kindness to two elderly Americans had led him into such intimate relations with the Greek

---

* At one of his first house-parties in Switzerland, where a well-to-do audience sang Luther's hymn 'A safe stronghold our God is still', his immediate comment was, 'I wonder how many of you really feel your safe stronghold is your bank account?'

** Later Chaplain of Downing College, Cambridge, and father of the Wimbledon tennis champion, Virginia Wade.

royal family and by the fact that they had passed him on to their relatives all over Europe. He felt that only God could have arranged such a sequence of events for a 'small-town boy', and so he took the responsibility seriously. Perhaps because he came from an age when a royal 'request' was a command, he was ready to change his plans to respond to the urgent calls from these quarters. Also, he was aware that any change of heart in such people, still then in power in their countries, could have particular importance for the world, and he never concealed that such change was his aim. However, the loss of power which befell so many in no way altered his care for or treatment of them.

Perhaps Buchman's clearest statement of his position on these matters was expressed in 1928 in a letter to Alexander Smith, then Executive Secretary of Princeton University and later US Senator for New Jersey, who had passed on a letter containing a criticism of his association with the eminent. 'The point is this: are we seeking titled people for any social position it can give us, or is our direction the changing of their lives?' he wrote. 'If it were the former I should say the criticism was justified. . . . I think there is a danger of a certain type of American who has such a false sense of democracy that he feels it is a form of snobbery to mention them. They are a part of the machinery of European life; and they have souls just the same as the middle and lower classes, and there are very few people who run the risk of the abuse that one naturally encounters in changing them. . . . The same is true in America. There are certain people whose names go down on committees. We have studiously avoided all such patronage. . . . I am frankly out to change the leaders and to create the leadership that will change present conditions.'[7]

Buchman's correspondence also shows that throughout his life he kept in equally close touch with the 'unprivileged'. In the 1920s these were often confined to two groups – his many old Pennsylvanian friends, like Bill Pickle and Mary Hemphill, and the staff of hotels or houses in which he had stayed, entire lists of whom appear in his revised address books until the day of his death. Not until the remarkable expansion of his work in Britain and elsewhere in the 1930s did he make deep friendships with many industrial workers and unemployed people.

Back in Oxford in March 1922 he was given two rooms at Christ Church by the Senior Censor, R. H. Dundas. 'Here is a man who could stir Oxford. How, I am at a loss to explain,' went one contemporary account of his stay there. 'He sat for two weeks in a room and by the end of it the College was sharply divided into pro and anti-FBs. He addressed a meeting in College soon after arrival at which an influential section of the undergraduates came with a concerted scheme for a "rag". But somewhere they felt their witticisms out of place, and the attack fell flat.' The occasion was probably a debate of the 19 Club on 'This House considers that man is his own worst enemy'. In a scribbled note he wrote, 'I didn't question their beliefs. I told them of the power of the Holy Spirit.'

When Loudon Hamilton invited a few friends to his own rooms to hear why he spent so much less time at the Mitre Hotel bar, forty-four turned up and they had to adjourn to the Junior Common Room. A cheerful undergraduate came in late, sat at the piano and drummed heavily on the keys whenever he heard something he disliked. At five minutes to ten he and three friends announced they were going out to get drunk, and did so.

On a later visit Buchman was staying at University College. Going to bed there, late one night, Buchman had the thought that the piano-player and a friend were on their way to see him. He got up again just in time to greet them. They were intent on demonstrating to him, by readings from *The Republic*, that Plato was superior to the Bible. Next morning early, Buchman wrote down some notes for a letter to the piano-player: 'I have found my norm in the Bible not Plato. Whenever I depart from Christ or Paul, I go wrong. The furniture of a man's soul can change in an instant. Your problem is not reason. It is moral. Faith transcends reason yet it is not unreasonable. You will change conclusions once this has gripped you. We need discipline for leadership. The athlete gladly denies himself. Why not for life?'

Buchman recognised a quality of leadership in the piano-player, a brilliant but wayward man, and, although rejected as no Platonist, kept intermittent touch with him. He once saw him off to America with a note ending 'Yours for the winning of an heiress', and later dined with him in New York, again stressing his responsibility for leadership in Britain.

On another occasion in America the young man replied to a lunch invitation with an abusive letter. Buchman asked Hamilton what he thought of it. Hamilton said indignantly that the young man needed 'a good kick in the pants'.

'No, no,' replied Buchman, 'it's a cry for help.'

On the boat back to England the young man dressed up as a waiter to attract the attention of a particularly beautiful American girl. In London Buchman asked him to bring the young lady to lunch.

'I am sorry I couldn't bring the lady,' he replied. 'One, if she had been in London. Two, if a jealous old husband would have allowed me. Three, if she and I were on speaking terms, I would be delighted to do so.

'No, my dear Frank, no new forces are at work. I am never free from a very old force though not without regrets for lost hopes. I disapprove of you but hold you in deep regard.'

This seems to have been the last letter the man wrote to Buchman. The friendship had not been strong enough to survive the pressures which he mentioned. Buchman was sad to hear that, after a brief but brilliant career, he died while still a young man.

[101]

Buchman spent the summer of 1922 travelling in England and Europe. He went with Hamilton to Eton for the Fourth of June celebrations* – 'a very interesting function', he told his mother, 'where one wears top hat and morning coat and white spats, and the young Etonians take great pleasure in wearing very swagger clothes'.[8] In July he led a house-party at the home of a banker at Putney Heath. Later the same month he was at the Keswick Convention meeting friends like Colonel David Forster of the Officers' Christian Union. It was here that Buchman met Eustace Wade again. After a couple of days Wade had had quite enough of the solemnity of the convention, and was on his way to the railway station when he ran into Buchman. Buchman said he had had clear guidance from God that they would meet. They talked over tea in the garden of the Keswick Hotel and Wade was interested enough to stay another two days. 'He expressed to my young spirit something I failed to see in humdrum church life,' recalled Wade in 1977. 'What he was doing seemed like real adventure, that's what drew me.'

Others at Keswick, like Julian Thornton-Duesbery (later Master of St Peter's College, Oxford), would have nothing to do with Buchman at that stage. 'A friend of mine in Oxford had told me awful stories about him,' said Thornton-Duesbery, 'something about unhealthy confessions of sex problems, so I was very careful to avoid him.' Later he met Buchman, found these stories untrue, and worked with him for the rest of his life.

Meanwhile, opposition to Buchman at Princeton had been steadily gaining in strength and his visits to the campus were becoming a matter of controversy. In December 1921 Charles Haines, who was now an Assistant Secretary of the Philadelphian Society, wrote that the student 'Cabinet' of the Society** had been discussing whether they should invite him to Princeton. Some, said Haines, thought he should come and have personal talks with students, but that the visit should not be advertised too openly 'on account of the general feeling on the campus'.[9] Others argued that this was too much like working under cover. Their conclusion was to invite him to address a large open meeting if he was willing to come.

Far from being inclined to keep his head down and avoid controversy, Buchman consistently encouraged his supporters at Princeton neither to water down their message nor to take themselves too seriously. In reply to a gloomy letter from Haines in January 1922 he wrote, 'I have gotten your bit of constipated atheism this morning and I am just chuckling to myself. I am still laughing, Chas, and that's what you need to have someone do to you fairly often. Just chuckle, chuckle, chuckle.'

Buchman goes on to suggest the name of another speaker they might

---

* The annual celebration by the school of the birthday of King George III.
** The 'Cabinet' was a group of 18 elected by the undergraduate body of the Society.

invite to Princeton, a man with 'fine humour and everything', just what the undergraduates needed. 'You certainly need a bomb under that crowd,' he declared. 'There needs to be a lot of dynamite loose if you are going to send them home convicted, converted and continued Christians.'[10]

By May of that same year, however, Shoemaker was writing to Buchman in Britain to say that he had been to see President Hibben and that Hibben 'feared too much sin emphasis, especially of the sort for which we are criticised'. He had also asked – 'in such a way as to make it impossible to decline' – that Shoemaker suggest to Buchman that he should not come to Princeton for a time, 'until some of the misunderstanding has been cleared up'.[11] Hibben, who had become President in 1912 with a mandate to restore peace to a campus which had been deeply divided by Woodrow Wilson's plan to reorganise it, had an administrator's natural dislike of controversy.

Neither Shoemaker nor Buchman seems to have regarded Hibben's prohibition as other than temporary. In November 1922 Buchman again spoke on the campus and had interviews with no less than forty students afterwards, none of which seems to have called forth any protest from the Princeton President. In April 1923 Shoemaker wrote to Buchman that the Hibbens were 'coming along splendidly';[12] and, in October, Buchman paid another, highly successful, visit to the campus.

This visit stirred Buchman's opponents into vigorous action. What seems to have happened is that a number of undergraduates began going, often in pairs, to see Hibben at intervals of four or five days to complain about Buchman's methods. In particular, they charged him with asking students highly personal questions which nobody had any right to ask. This campaign was master-minded by a small group of undergraduates who had sworn to have Buchman and his work outlawed from the campus.[13] Their leader, Neilson Abeel, told one of Buchman's supporters that, if he did nothing else in life, he would smash what Buchman was doing. Buchman's supporters believed that a number of their most active opponents were practising homosexuals who felt that Buchman's message posed a threat to their life-style.

Hibben became increasingly troubled by the situation. In December 1923, in an attempt to clear the air, he called a conference at his own home. To it he invited a number of his most trusted advisers, the campus doctor Donald Sinclair, some of the undergraduates who had criticised Buchman, Shoemaker, and Buchman himself. According to Shoemaker, Buchman was invited on the basis that his work was not going to be investigated, but that the university authorities would like to know more of the facts. Abeel turned up with a bottle of smelling salts which he periodically held to his nostrils, and he and his friends stated their case against Buchman.

Buchman then answered questions from some of the senior members of the university. 'The meeting', wrote Shoemaker to one of Buchman's critics later, 'brought out the complete lack of knowledge of the spiritual needs of the men in the university on the part of many of the faculty present; and to hear some of those dry old men correct Buchman, who knew and was doing more than they ever could concerning the realisation of religion in human lives, was infinitely pathetic. He quietly answered questions and the meeting broke up.'[14]

At some point in the evening Buchman seems to have spoken privately to Hibben about the needs of undergraduates as he saw them. Hibben evidently got the impression that Buchman asserted that 80 per cent of Princeton students were given to homosexual practices. This, Buchman declared, when he came to hear of it later, was entirely erroneous. What he *had* said was that 'from eighty to ninety per cent of all youths in the adolescent stage have sexual problems, and many of them are troubled by secret sins affecting their sex life. The term secret sins, which I used, does not connote homosexuality, but refers to the common variety of the problems of youth. They are in great need of sympathetic understanding and help from mature persons.'

'I believe we cannot help those youths to a victorious life with Christ in the centre unless we recognise this fact and enable them to face honestly and courageously these and other barriers that separate them from God and their fellow men,' Buchman added.[15]

In 1926 Hibben claimed that, on this occasion, he had forbidden Buchman to return to the campus. Neither Buchman nor any of his friends present were aware of this, and Sinclair denied it on several occasions.[16] Certainly, the letters exchanged between Hibben and Buchman in the months immediately after the conference show no signs of such an injunction, or of any residual doubts or misunderstandings. Hibben wrote to Buchman in that same December that he hoped the visit had not been too much of a strain,[17] and again in January expressed 'great confidence in Sam and the young men working with him' whom he knew to be products of Buchman's work, and trusted 'that the conference the other night will result in better understanding' all round.[18]

Any hopes which Hibben may have had that the conference would defuse the situation, however, were soon disappointed. In February 1924 Buchman's opponents prepared a pamphlet called 'The Cannonball'. Buchman's supporters alleged that Hibben was shown proofs of this, accompanied by the threat that it would be published unless the President made some more categorical statement condemning Buchman and his methods; and that Hibben extracted from Shoemaker a personal undertaking that Buchman would never again be invited to the campus.

Some major change in the situation – and in Hibben's attitude – does seem to have occurred, because in the spring of 1924 Buchman came to the conclusion quite suddenly that he should stay away from Princeton. 'Clear out of Princeton completely,' he noted during a time of meditation.

The gathering storm at Princeton had been provoked by the growth in Buchman's work there; and elsewhere, too, it was growing steadily. There were two house-parties at Yale early in 1922, and in March 1924 Buchman reported that Harvard was having its third house-party, while Williams and Vassar were each planning for their second.

A great many attended these not because of Buchman himself but because of the quality of the people around him. Garrett Stearly, who first met Buchman in 1924, was typical of these. The son of the Bishop of Newark, New Jersey, he had been to Yale but had very little idea what he wanted to do with his life apart from an inclination towards business. His father, however, packed him off to an episcopal training college in North Virginia. The young Stearly set off unenthusiastically and 'with a couple of quarts of whisky in my trunk'.

'While I was there', he recalled, 'I came across a dozen outstanding people who were studying theology because they had met Frank Buchman. They talked about him so much that I became curious and so, when they invited me over to Princeton for a weekend to meet him, I accepted.

'Well, it was the merriest time I'd had in years, not at all like a religious weekend as I understood it. Buchman's young friends all told stories of how they'd changed – so natural, so open, it was a new world to me. They didn't talk too much about God or Christ, but I knew it was there – and I went away envying their way of life and feeling a completely new respect for religion.

'As for Frank, he didn't behave the way I thought spiritual leaders were supposed to. He didn't end up the afternoon with a long talk and neither then, nor later, was there any prying or questioning. I just felt he was more interested in me than he was in himself.'

A different type of young man was James Newton, the son of a Philadelphia doctor. He had rejected a place at Dartmouth to go hoboing through America. In the course of his travels, mainly illicitly on freight trains, he had washed dishes, picked cotton, wrangled horses and punched cattle. Then at nineteen he became a salesman covering New England for a luggage company. One weekend he looked in for dinner at the Toytown Tavern in Winchengton, Mass., and, having observed three pretty girls in the dining room, strolled up to what he thought was a dance in an adjoining cottage afterwards. The girls were there all right, but it turned out to be a house-party of students from various New England universities. He stayed on, and talked with Sherwood Day. On Monday morning he set out to try to put moral standards into practice. He went back to his customers and was honest about the lies he had told them, and was astonished to find that they then trusted him more, not less. 'At the end of six weeks I found my whole life had begun to change,' he says.

By the time of Newton's weekend at the Toytown Tavern there were already a number who had given up their careers to work with Buchman full-time without salary. Loudon Hamilton, for example, decided against teaching at Eton, despite the fact that the headmaster, C. A. Alington, had asked him to undertake theological training and then take a permanent job at the school. Instead, he had gone to America with Buchman in the autumn of 1922. After eight months he had returned to Oxford – working his way back across the Atlantic as a stoker – to continue Buchman's work there with only a monthly allowance of $50 from Mrs Tjader to support him.

Although the number involved was still small, Buchman's work was slowly becoming more widely known. Back in Britain, Rudyard Kipling, after several meetings with Buchman, invited him to bring some of his undergraduate friends to his home, Batemans, in the village of Burwash. He took with him Harry P. Davison, later head of J. P. Morgan's Bank; Jim Douglas, later US Secretary for Air; and Hugh Auchincloss.*

Harold Begbie, a British political journalist who wrote under the pseudonym 'Gentleman with a Duster', became interested through meeting a wounded Royal Flying Corps officer whom Buchman had helped. Begbie asked if he could write a book about Buchman and his friends, who at that time shunned publicity. Buchman agreed provided that the young men remained anonymous and he himself be referred to only by the initials F.B. 'The character of these men, some of them so brilliant in scholarship, others so splendid in athletics, and all of them, without one exception, so modest and so disturbingly honest, was responsible for my reawakened interest,' Begbie wrote. 'It was impossible in their company to doubt any longer that the man who had changed their lives, and had made them also changers of other men's lives, was a person of very considerable importance.'[19]

He described Buchman as 'a young-looking man of middle life, tall, upright, stoutish, clean-shaven, spectacled, with that mien of scrupulous, shampooed, and almost medical cleanness or freshness' so typical of

---

* C. E. Carrington in his *Rudyard Kipling, His Life and Works* (Macmillan, 1955, p. 525) provides an interesting example of distorted history. He mentions the visit of 'Dr Frank Buchman with a team of young men', and continues, 'who gate-crashed and sang hymns on the lawn'. Kipling's letter of invitation still exists: 'It will give Mrs Kipling and myself great pleasure if you and your friends can come to Burwash on the 15th or 16th. I shall be at home and free in the afternoon of either day. I suggest a motor.' Hymn-singing on such occasions was even less in Buchman's line than gate-crashing.

Americans. 'His carriage and his gestures are distinguished by an invariable alertness. He never droops, he never slouches. You find him in the small hours of the morning with the same quickness of eye and the same athletic erectness of body which seem to bring a breeze into the breakfast-room. Few men so quiet and restrained exhale a spirit of such contagious well-being ... He strikes one on a first meeting as a warm-hearted and very happy man, who can never know what it is to be either physically tired or mentally bored. I am tempted to think that if Mr Pickwick had given birth to a son, and that son had emigrated in boyhood to America, he would have been not unlike this amiable and friendly surgeon of souls.'[20]

Begbie's book, *Life Changers*, appeared in 1923 and helped to increase interest in the doings of the mysterious F.B. His identity soon became known and later editions carried his name in full.

In January 1924 he took part in a drawing-room meeting at the home of Thomas Edison, the inventor of the electric lamp, in New Jersey. A nephew of Edison had encountered Buchman's work at Princeton, where he was studying, and the subsequent difference in him had caught Edison's attention. Edison had invited Buchman and Hamilton to visit him. It was a brilliant February night when they arrived at the front door through an avenue of snow. Edison answered their ring himself, stood looking up at the sky, and said to Buchman, 'Is Heaven lit up?'

'Sure,' said Buchman, 'that's been looked after long ago. You don't need to worry about that.'

Once inside, Edison, an agnostic, asked about his nephew's change, and then brought up the subject of divine guidance. 'It is through divine guidance that this miracle has happened to your nephew,' said Buchman.

'I know that I'm not supposed to believe in these things,' replied Edison. 'But I know that between my fingernail and knuckle there are ten thousand atmospheric forces. We inventors know that. Our only job is to invent an instrument delicate enough to tune in so that we can use those forces. That's your problem with guidance, Mr Buchman, isn't it?' Buchman agreed that it was. Lifelong friendships with both Edison and his wife began that evening.

In August Buchman was back in London, and had a long talk with the poet Siegfried Sassoon. 'My instinct tells me', wrote Sassoon afterwards, 'that your success in the work you are doing is made possible by simplicity. And I am learning, slowly, that simplification of life is more important than anything else. . . . Miracles can still be worked by it.'[21]

Buchman still felt that his most urgent need was to build a team of younger people who would be willing to carry the work with him. For almost a year he had pondered taking what he called 'an apostolic group' on a world tour which would include Europe, the Middle East, India, China and Australia. Maybe the situation at Princeton convinced him that

1924 was the right year to go. At any rate, it was at this time that he asked several young men to come on a prolonged expedition with him. Sherwood Day, Sam Shoemaker, Loudon Hamilton, Eustace Wade, Godfrey Webb-Peploe from Cambridge and Van Dusen Rickert from Princeton decided to join him, for some or all of the journey.

COMPANIONSHIP OF THE ROAD

Buchman sailed for England on the *SS Paris* in June 1924. In the weeks before leaving, he had seen a good deal of his mother, and included her in his activities when he felt that they would be congenial to her. He also maintained his interest in her daily life. Inviting her to a tea in New York, he adds, 'I suggest you wear your low shoes as it is a tea. If you wear the dress which you wore to New York the last time, which would be a good one, don't wear the white sleeves or under-vest. You can wear your coat till you get there so you won't catch cold.'[1] She attended the last house-party before his departure, and then preferred to return to Allentown rather than staying with him in New York until he sailed.[2] 'The parting is not pleasant, you know, but it looks that it has to be,' she wrote from there. 'God will take care of us. Everybody tells me that you are helping them so much. Think of me and the Lord will bless you.' The letter ended, 'Goodbye, hope to meet again sometime, somewhere.'[3]

On the same ship was Mrs Tjader. She was going to Sweden for her daughter's wedding and had provided substantial funds towards Buchman's present project, partly because he was going to visit some of the missionaries in India for whom she was responsible. Expecting to be away from America for at least two years, Buchman took no fewer than fourteen suitcases and valises, containing clothes suitable for every sort of occasion and the accumulated correspondence and memorabilia of a quarter of a century. Even the young Eustace Wade, who joined him in London – and whom Buchman had christened 'Nick' because he thought he looked like the Devil – had eight pieces of luggage, containing among other things a top hat, morning coat, dinner jacket and full evening dress as well as a topee for use in India. In those formal days every garment would be needed.

There was no doubt about the purpose of the journey. 'I am taking a group of younger people with me to train them,' Buchman wrote to Mrs Shepard before he left New York;[4] and he was equally explicit with Wade and Loudon Hamilton on the platform of Liverpool Street Station in

London. 'Mind you,' he told them, 'there'll be discipline on this trip.'

'We didn't know what he meant at the time,' remarked Hamilton, 'but we soon found out. He expected us to have the single-mindedness of St Paul, "this one thing I do", with no hold-back – and he wasn't going to have any tomfoolery.' In the breakfast-car of the train carrying them across Holland, Hamilton remarked jocularly that it was interesting to be behind enemy lines again. At this, Buchman, thinking of the neutral Dutch he was taking them to see, exploded. If he was going to talk in that way, he told Hamilton, he could leave the party and go home. 'Loudon went red,' recalled Wade, 'and I went white. It was a first-class raspberry, the size of a grapefruit!'

Their first stop was Baron van Heeckeren's home at Rhederoord, where they were joined by Sam Shoemaker. Buchman had met the Baroness's mother, Countess Bentinck, in England the previous year. After a tea-party in her London home* she said that her son-in-law had left a pair of pyjamas on his last visit and asked if Buchman would take them to him on his forthcoming visit to Holland. News thereupon reached the van Heeckeren family that a German student was arriving with the Baron's laundry. Clarification must have followed, as on arrival at Rhederoord, Buchman and his companions were among the guests at a ball followed by a house-party. The Baron held a senior position at Court where one of his daughters, Albertina, was a lady-in-waiting and, according to Wade, 'half the Dutch aristocracy came in'.

The Baron and Baroness were devout Christians, holding family prayers every morning. Their daughters, however, were not at all attracted to their parents' religion. 'We went to church because we were supposed to,' says Albertina, 'it wasn't something real.' 'Our aim in life was enjoyment,' says another daughter, Lily. 'Going to balls, being presented at Court, those were the things we liked.'

The van Heeckerens' friends were of much the same ilk. They thoroughly enjoyed the dance but went with mixed feelings to the house-party – to which they were invited by a card which announced, somewhat forbiddingly, that 'Mr Buchman will give an address'.

Actually, Buchman gave no formal address. Sitting down in the drawing room, 'among many question marks, some exclamation marks, many curious, others prepared to be bored,' records Albertina, 'he said, "I think I'll tell you a story . . .",' which he proceeded to do. Other stories of changed lives followed, and as the evening wore on he remarked cheerfully, 'I can see the walls coming down.' Next morning there was a bigger

---

* The hostess on this occasion followed her usual practice of getting all her guests on their knees for prayers after the second cup of tea. 'Oh God,' she began, 'bless Mr Bunkum.' Her subsequent letters were addressed to 'Dr Bookman'.

crowd. Sitting on the stairs in full evening dress was an agnostic student, Eric van Lennep, who asked Buchman afterwards why he had been looking at *him* during the whole morning. As a result of the ensuing conversation, van Lennep started on the road to faith, and worked with Buchman for many years to come.

The lives of the entire van Heeckeren family and household were permanently affected. As a result, a series of house-parties was held at Rhederoord during the next few years. After one, the Baroness felt that she had not been treating her servants properly and publicly apologised to them. She also apologised to an aunt with whom she had had a bitter quarrel, and faced up to and lost the hatred she felt towards the Germans because one of her brothers had been killed on the Somme. That, in turn, led to a reconciliation with the German branch of the Bentinck family.

The van Heeckeren children, then in their late 'teens and early twenties, were just as deeply influenced. Buchman played tennis with them, and they liked his relaxed manner – 'he had a real sense of humour and there was such a twinkle in his eye'. But what captivated them was his vision of what they might do for their country and the world. It was quite clear to them that Buchman was challenging them to live a revolutionary life. 'He talked about risking all our relationships,' adds Lily. 'He told us we needed an experience of the Cross, and I used to wonder what he meant. When we asked him what we should do, he said, "All that God tells you." '

So far as the van Heeckerens were concerned Buchman seems to have followed his own advice: he often spoke to them with great freedom and candour. 'You haven't enough Christianity to change a flea,' he once told Lily.*

From that first house-party onwards Buchman also spent a good deal of time with the family servants, particularly the nanny and chauffeur. 'How he cared for our nanny!' recalls Lily. 'He had long talks with her – she'd had a disagreement with the nanny at the German Bentincks, and she put that right – and he always wanted to know how she and the chauffeur were.'

After Rhederoord, Buchman and his friends went on to Germany. They visited Kurt Hahn's school at Salem, and Buchman's old friends at the von Bodelschwingh colony of Bethel, near Bielefeld. Like the rest of Germany, it was still suffering from the horrors of the post-war hyper-inflation, some of the patients 'lying on sawdust without blankets or sheets', according to Hamilton. It left an indelible mark on his mind, as it did on Buchman's. 'Everything was *ersatz*,' recalled Hamilton. 'People

---

* Several of the van Heeckeren children travelled with Buchman at various times; more than fifty years later, four daughters are still committed to his work.

were dying as they walked, shuffling about without shoes. Families sold their daughters.' Buchman had arranged four years earlier for three cows to be sent to Bethel, and now renewed his attempts to get American friends to help needy Germans.

In Southern Germany they met Frau Hanfstaengl, an American from a New England family, the Sedgwicks, whose ancestors included the general who 'marched through Georgia' in the Civil War. The young Adolf Hitler had become a regular visitor to the Hanfstaengl home after her son Ernst ('Putzi') had got to know him. Frau Hanfstaengl showed Buchman and his friends the room where Hitler had hidden after the Munich *Putsch* in the previous year. She had, she said, told Hitler that unless he changed his attitude to the Jews she would never support him. 'That I will never do,' he had replied.

In Florence Buchman, Hamilton and Wade had dinner with King George of Greece and his family. Buchman had seen a good deal of him in London, before he returned to Greece to take up the throne in 1922. The King had said to Hamilton, 'When are you men coming to Greece? Buchman is the only person we can trust not to be out for himself.' Now they met again in Italy, with the Queen Mother, Sophie, and King George's grandmother, Queen Olga. In 1923, King George had been forced to leave Greece once more, and the misery of exile often made him and his family turn to Buchman.

From Italy Buchman's party travelled on the Simplon-Orient Express to Constantinople. At Queen Sophie's request, he himself flew from there to Bucharest to visit her daughter Helen, who was married to Crown Prince Carol. Queen Marie of Roumania, an able high-spirited English princess, granddaughter of both Queen Victoria and Tsar Alexander II, invited him to join King Ferdinand and herself at Peles Castle at Sinaia and asked that one of his party should also come.

Hamilton immediately set out to join Buchman. His cabled announcement did not arrive, but at the station he was – as he later discovered – mistaken for visiting royalty and picked up in a large car. This mistaken identity got him through three road blocks en route for Peles Castle. On arrival at the heavily guarded castle, confusion was worse confounded when he asked for Mr Buchman, which also happened to be the name of the butler who opened the front door. Luckily, at this point, Frank Buchman looked out of the sitting-room window and called down, 'Oh, that's one of mine!' Finally ushered into Queen Marie's presence, Hamilton found Buchman recounting the story of the Beef and Beer Club.

Both Queen Marie and Crown Princess Helen wanted Hamilton to become tutor to Helen's young son Michael (later King Michael), but neither Hamilton nor Buchman felt he should take the job. After a week in which they formed friendships which were to last a lifetime, they left to rejoin the others in Constantinople.

There Buchman was asked to address the student body of Robert College. One of the audience later described the occasion: 'Before him were seated, besides most of the faculty, about seven hundred hard-boiled, cynical students of many ages and nationalities. There were no oratorical tricks, no attempt to make an impression. On the contrary, one could feel his intense earnestness. He told us what happened to a real boy, with real problems, when God came into his life. At the end he asked us all to repeat that boy's prayer: 'Oh God, manage me because I cannot manage myself.' It went straight to the heart of the matter.'[5]

The vitality of the group left behind in Constantinople was typical of those left at other places on the journey. The same student, George Moissides – then a minister in Canterbury, Connecticut – described later how he and his friends, Gregory Vlastos, Homer Kalcas, Dashem Hussein Shams-Davari and Rashid Alajaji, were affected. 'What a total change that one weekend fifty years ago brought to my personal life and to that of so many of my friends!' commented Moissides.[6] Most kept in touch with Buchman for many years, some till his death. Vlastos became Professor of Philosophy at Princeton, Kalcas taught in Turkey, and Shams-Davari managed the Persian Oil Company at Ahwaz, where he translated films and books about Buchman's work into Farsi.

The party sailed for Alexandria soon after the anniversary of the end of the 1914–18 war. Wade recalls that, as they passed through the Dardanelles, Buchman walked towards the stern of the ship, took off his hat, threw his Armistice Day poppy over the side and quietly spoke some lines of Rupert Brooke, who had died near there.

In Cairo they were joined by Sherwood Day and Van Dusen Rickert, an Oriental languages graduate from Princeton. Buchman was delighted to have Day with him again. Buchman said to the younger men, 'Sherry is dependable twenty-four hours in the day. It will be great when the rest of you get to that point. Sherry never maladapts.' In Cairo too, Shoemaker received a long-expected invitation to become the Rector of Calvary Church in Gramercy Park, New York, to which he replied, 'Judgement unfavourable now . . . writing.'[7]

By the time the party reached Palestine, the atmosphere had become distinctly strained. Individually, they were devout enough. There were, Wade recalled, no regulated observances but all the group normally kept a time of private prayer and meditation and shared such thoughts as they then had with their room-mates. They were also able to help many of the people they met. Nevertheless, as the journey proceeded, strains and irritations developed to the point where Buchman noted, 'You can be in the Holy Land and Hell at the same time.'

[113]

To begin with, there were natural jealousies and rivalries. There was also the fact that each had joined the trip for different motives: one or two were more interested in the delights of travel than in creating the kind of disciplined team which Buchman had in mind. Buchman also conducted affairs in a style which the younger men sometimes found baffling. According to Hamilton, for example, they were always delighted when a hostess asked Buchman, 'And where are you going next?' as this enabled them to discover what their itinerary was to be. Then, too, there were the natural preoccupations of able, ambitious young men. Shoemaker was much attracted to the offer from Calvary Church. This was a constant pull. Once he came back from a shopping expedition in Constantinople laden with Bokhara rugs and other ornaments, and his cabin-mate, Hamilton, asked what he had bought them for. 'They'll look good in my rectory,' replied Shoemaker.

Such preoccupations aside, there was another irritant: a dislike of the discipline which Buchman, the initiator of the venture and older than all his companions but Day by twenty years, sought to impose. For example, one of the party arranged to speak at a school. At the last moment, Buchman suggested that two others should go with him. It meant the sacrifice of a carefully-prepared solo speech, and the willingness to become one of a group. Buchman felt that they needed training to work as a team: self-will, pride, the prima donna element would have to be cured if their future work was to have any lasting effect. But young men of high calibre and considerable self-esteem did not see it that way. 'We were far from being a united team,' Hamilton commented. 'Sherry Day was the most loyal. The rest of us were raw, self-willed, undisciplined and egotistical. Our selfishness grated on each other. . . .' At the time, however, they were more apt to blame Buchman than themselves.

'The climax came later on board the ship between Suez and Colombo,' writes Hamilton. 'Frank was resting in his cabin for two or three days, and one day he said to Sam, "Sam, just list my laundry, will you, and give it to the steward?" Sam came up on deck very angry. He met me and told me of this request of Frank's, and said that he had absolutely refused to do it. He said, "I would rather preach five sermons than do what he asked me. I have surrendered my life to Jesus Christ, not to Frank Buchman."'

Shoemaker's reactions to the disciplines of the journey were not unexpected. He was a handsome, confident and charismatic young man. Shortly before this trip he had been invited to take part in a major evangelical campaign alongside Sherwood Eddy. Buchman had replied to Shoemaker's request for advice on this proposition: 'The warning no's have come in my quiet time with alarming constancy and I would not be faithful if I kept silent . . . You have been riding roughshod over experi-

ences which have forged Sherry and I into an intelligent, workable team
. . . You need a year's discipline in a team, such as a year's trip around the
world would give you. You need the drab, not the dramatic. . . . I can only
say this, – that if you are led to go and your convictions differ with mine
after you have checked with everyone . . . go, and God abundantly bless
you. With assurances of the finest spirit of affection and mutual confidence, whatever may be your choice.'[8]

They reached India on 10 December and spent Christmas in Madras.
Buchman disappeared on Christmas Eve, and reappeared with a Christmas tree, decorations and presents, and a signed photograph of Gandhi
for each of them – 'a priceless present', Wade observed.

It was plain, however, that the air needed to be cleared, and after
Christmas they kept a day free for that purpose. In many ways it was like
the conversations in the Tientsin Hotel room all over again. This,
however, was an even more painful confrontation: Wade and Rickert, as
relatively new boys, kept well clear of it, but as Hamilton recalled,
Shoemaker, Day and he all spoke their minds forcibly:* 'We all tried to say
what we felt and, from our side, we said fairly bluntly the things we felt
Frank had been – secretive, authoritarian, inconsiderate.'

Wade saw Buchman coming out, tears rolling down his cheeks.
'They're all against me, Nick,' he said. 'What have I done?'

Wade replied that he thought Buchman had been a bit outspoken.

'Do you *really* think so?' asked Buchman, in great distress.

'Yes,' said Wade, 'I do.'

'It isn't easy to get a profound unity of six people,' wrote Shoemaker to
Mrs Tjader, a few days later. 'All of us have our characteristic sins and
weaknesses . . . (Frank) is so in the habit of holding others in line that he
isn't always ready to be held himself.'[9]

Despite these private upheavals, the months in India were rewarding.
On 23 December Buchman had met Gandhi again at the Congress Party
conference at Belgaum, and photographs show them laughing vigorously
with Chakravarti Rajagopalachari, later first Governor-General of independent India, and the Ali brothers, the Muslim leaders in whose home
Gandhi had recently completed a 21-day fast. There, too, he first met the
young Jawaharlal Nehru, who afterwards sent Buchman his photograph
and asked for the book, *Life Changers*, which Buchman had promised to
send him. Unitedly the party took on the Student Christian meetings
with friends like Gandhi's confidant, C. F. Andrews**, and Bishop
Pakenham-Walsh.

* Godfrey Webb-Peploe, the last to join the party in Port Said, had by now carried out
his previous plan to visit Amy Carmichael's mission centre in Dohnavur.
** The Revd Charles F. Andrews, who died in 1940, was a missionary and author who
devoted himself to the rights of the Indian people both in India and in Africa.

Then some visited Amy Carmichael at the Dohnavur Fellowship. From there Buchman wrote a letter to Mrs Tjader, in which he described a growing dream: 'She is easily the greatest missionary I have yet met, and her place has the atmosphere we desire for The School of Life . . . We need a demonstration centre with living miracles all about us with reality as the keynote. . . . It will be a quiet, slow but expanding and multiplying work, just as people here flock from all the corners of the world and people are praying for it in fifteen countries. I am so happy today. . . .'[10] The regard seems to have been mutual. After this visit Amy Carmichael wrote in the *Dohnavur Letter*, 'Let no one judge this man by anything written about him. Frank Buchman is out for one thing only, to win men for Jesus Christ.'[11]*

They stayed with the Anglican Metropolitan of India, Foss Westcott, in Calcutta, and in February, while in Darjeeling, met Jan Masaryk, the future Czech Foreign Minister. In March they were the guests of Lord Reading at Viceregal Lodge. When Buchman lunched with the Viceroy, the Ali brothers came up in conversation. 'Those rascals,' said Reading, 'I have to keep putting them in gaol. What would you do with them?'

'If I were in your place,' Buchman replied, 'I would do to them what you have done for me – put them in the seats of honour at your table and get to know them.'

The Viceroy's senior ADC, Ralph Burton, introduced Buchman to the Maharajah of Gwalior. This eccentric character enjoyed setting fire to his courtiers' turbans for the pleasure of seeing them duck their heads into the nearest fountain to extinguish the flames. He also had an electric train which carried choice liqueurs around his dining table, with a secret switch beside him, which enabled him to speed up the train so that it passed any guest he wished to tease.

He was evidently much taken by Buchman and his friends. After dinner on the evening of a Hindu festival, Buchman and Wade were strolling under the moon when they encountered him. 'He said to Frank, "Come and talk to me," ' recalled Wade, 'and we all sat down on a marble bench. First there was a long silence, which Buchman did not attempt to break.

* In 1929 Buchman's colleagues in American converted Amy Carmichael's brother, which she described in writing Buchman on 4 August 1930 as 'my greatest joy of the last year on the human side'. She wrote her brother, 'In England, and Scotland too, all sorts of lies are being circulated about Mr Buchman and his friends. I have known him for years and always found him a true man . . . Well, the devil hates and, if he can, discredits such a man. . . .' In 1932 pressure from supporters of Dohnavur induced her to write that the Dohnavur fellowship had no connection with the Oxford Group, a step she had long resisted. She sent the statement to Buchman, saying, 'I hope you won't disown your friend and comrade in prayer', (6 January 1932), and warm letters continued between them until at least October 1938. Buchman, of course, had never suggested there was a connection, and used her prayers at meetings until the end of his life.

left Frank Nathaniel Daniel Buchman aged 3.
[cen]tre The Buchman family – Franklin and Sarah,
son Frank and adopted son Dan.
[top] right 'I could walk the tracks from Greensboro
[to Pe]nnsburg.'
[bot]tom right The Buchman home in Allentown,
[Penn]sylvania, to which the family moved in 1894.

5. *right* 'A little stone-built chapel' in Keswick.

6. *below* Thirty years later, Buchman recalls his experience in the chapel in 1908.

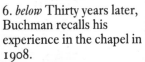

7. *below* Buchman with a group of Penn State students, and (on his left) Bill Pickle, the ex-bootlegger.

8. Blair Buck (left) vacationing Buchman in Minnesota, 1912

9. *above* Buchman (right) and Bishop Logan Roots of Hankow at the Kuling conference of 1918.

10. *left* Samuel Moor Shoemaker, a Princeton graduate working at a business training school for Chinese boys in Peking.

11. *right* Of his various meetings in India with Mahatma Gandhi, Buchman wrote: 'Walking with him was like walking with Aristotle.' Buchman is on the right and Howard Walter on the left.

12. *above* Buchman speaking at the 'Beef and Beer Club' in Loudon Hamilton's rooms in Oxford, 1921.
13. *right* Loudon Hamilton, Christ Church, Oxford.
14. *below* In South Africa, 1929. McGhee Baxter (2nd left), Sherwood Day, George Daneel, Lily van Heeckeren (7th left), and Buchman (right).

15. *above* Professor and Mrs.
B. H. Streeter with Buchman
(right) in Oxford. In the
background centre are Roland
Wilson and John Roots.

16. *above right* Rozi Evans (St. Hilda's College).
17. *left* H. Kenaston Twitchell (Princeton and Balliol College)
18. *bottom left* Harry S. Addison (Oriel College).
19. *below* Reginald A. E. Holme (New College), competitor
in the Isle of Man Amateur Tourist Trophy Races.

20–24. Buchman at a working session in the 1930s examining layouts for a forthcoming picture publication. With him are two Oxford colleagues, Basil Entwistle (St. John's College) and the author.

25. *bottom left* Buchman leading a meeting in Oxford, 1934.

26. *left* Buchman at Brown's Hotel. On the right is John Vinall.

28. *below* C. F. Andrews at an Oxford house-party.

27. *left* Lord Salisbury greets friends at the Oxford Group house-party in Oxford, 1935.

29. *below* The crowd of 6,000 people at the house-party.

30. *left* On a journey in the Middle East: Buchman (left) with Lady Minto (former Vicereine of India) and Cuthbert Bardsley (later Bishop of Coventry).

31. *bottom left* East London. Buchman's work began to be active in the 1930s.

32. *below* In the King's Head pub, West Ham, Buchman meets with his local 'team'. Top right: Bill Rowell, a leader of London's unemployed. Below him: Tod Sloan, watchmaker and friend of Ben Tillett. On Buchman's right: Bill Jaeger, the student who pioneered the work. Seated left: Mrs. Annie Jaeger, his mother, who sold her tiny shop in Stockport to go and help him in East London.

Then the Maharajah said, "Do I understand that you believe Jesus Christ can change human nature?" Frank replied, "That's exactly what we do believe, that's why we're here." '

Buchman wrote to the Maharajah a few days later, 'Further answering your question about God's guidance, I find that the appetites of the flesh are the most damaging factor in keeping us from knowing God. . . .'[12]

In a brief lull in the journeying, Van Dusen Rickert attempted 'to bring some order into Frank's chaotic correspondence. And it is an amazing correspondence, from people all over the world; religious workers and loafers, nobility, and celebrities and common people . . . and is a hopeless morass of letters, postcards, photos, cablegrams, bills, receipts, notes, wedding announcements, pamphlets, duplicates, guidance jottings, guide books, tracts, steamship booklets, reports, etc., all floundering stubbornly through 14 valises and trunks. A two-weeks' job to straighten it all up; and I have had a day and a half. And nothing must be thrown away, however useless – old barren envelopes, toothpicks, battered Roumanian hotel stationery – all are priceless . . . Well, I got two-thirds of it roughly classified, and stowed away the residue into the absurd black patent leather drum bag without a handle which completes his impedimenta.'[13]

A good many doors opened to Buchman and his friends because of their effect on the lives of those they met. In Madras, for example, they came across a prominent Scottish business man called George Kenneth, whose alcohol bill was reputed to be the largest in the city. Buchman called on him at his office, but was received with marked curtness. 'I am busy,' Kenneth told him flatly.

'So am I,' retorted Buchman with matching crispness; he left Kenneth with a copy of *Life Changers* and his name and address, and departed. Next day, Kenneth called, saying that he had read the book and had all the time in the world.

As a result of their talks, Kenneth became a practising Christian, gave up alcohol and dramatically altered the running of his business life. He began by calling together the dozen foremen of his printing company – most of whom were Hindus – and telling them about his change. 'This business', he said, 'has been a failure. From now on, Christ is to be the head of it, and we shall work together along entirely new lines. I have treated you like dogs and you have worked only because you feared me. Now, I would like you to help me put this business on a wholly new basis.' He then shook hands with each in turn. It was the change in Kenneth which first interested Lord Lytton, then Governor of Bengal, in Buchman and his work.

By March the whole travelling group had begun to disperse. In January Shoemaker had received another cable from Calvary Church, and this time accepted the job. Buchman was still convinced that he should not leave. 'I have an uneasy feeling that this decision of yours will lead to trouble,' he said. 'I'm leaving by train this very night,' Shoemaker replied.

Wade, who had always intended to be ordained, and Van Dusen Rickert went back to their respective countries, where they worked closely with Buchman in various ways. Hamilton left for home after a serious illness caused by drinking contaminated water, and when he had recovered, went back to Oxford, was given rooms free in Wycliffe Hall and continued the day-in, day-out work of training a group in the university. It was to be three years before he and Buchman met again, although they maintained intermittent contact.

It had been a journey which probably fell well below Buchman's hopes. Yet his vision of an explosive and revolutionary upheaval within the Christian world, led by the sort of young men with whom he had been travelling, remained undimmed. 'A new approach is needed to overcome the deadness,' he noted. 'Respectable Christianity will not do it . . . A band of young people who represent God in His attractiveness, in His excellence, and radiate His love by caring. . . . The Living Christ not every hour, but every minute of the day.'

Buchman and Sherwood Day remained in India. In the next few weeks, they again met an astonishing range of people, both British and Indian. They saw Gandhi twice more at the Sabarmati Ashram and in Foss Westcott's home in Calcutta. They met Nehru again at Allahabad. They were at Viceregal Lodge for the departure of Lord Reading and the inauguration of Lord Lytton as Acting Viceroy. Buchman particularly prized long talks with Lord Lytton, who, after one of them, visited two men awaiting sentence after a bomb attempt on his life. 'I would never have done that if I had not met you,' he told Buchman. 'You have taught me to talk to the ordinary man.'

By now, indeed, Buchman seemed to have won the confidence of many of the British Raj. Visiting Ralph Burton in hospital unexpectedly one day, he was approached by a senior nurse. 'Oh, Mr Buchman,' she said, 'the Commander-in-Chief is dying and Lady Rawlinson is in great distress. Can you come to her? We didn't know where to find you.'

More and more, however, he became convinced that the old regime was on the way out. 'The old gang – no good,' he noted. 'The East is going to correct the West. Gandhi is on the right track.' Of one of his meetings with Gandhi at this time he used to say in later life, 'Walking with him was like walking with Aristotle.'

In the midst of all this Buchman heard in April that his mother had fallen and broken her hip. He had kept up the flow of letters to her, some starting in Pennsylvania Dutch. His mother had been invited to spend Christmas of 1924 with Mrs Tjader and had greatly enjoyed it. Now Mrs

Tjader went to Allentown to be with her as she lay in hospital, and cabled Buchman, 'This week she will either go from us or recover.' Buchman cabled from Madras on 6 May, 'Many loving messages. God assures me all is well. In Jesus' keeping we are safe. No separation. Call in best consultant.' He travelled by night train to a house-party in Kodaikanal. There next day he received the news that his mother had died. Buchman sometimes related that he had been forewarned while travelling. 'At the moment of death, the carriage suddenly seemed lit up, as bright as day.'

In those days it would have been impossible to return for the funeral – which was attended by a thousand people and at which Buchman asked Shoemaker to speak; but on the same day, 12 May, at Kodaikanal, a memorial service was conducted by a clergyman from Calcutta Cathedral.

Buchman wrote, 'The memorial service was attended by Indians and Europeans. A triumphant note pervaded the service. The young Indian who shared my pew had spent two Christmases with our family in America.'[14] To Mrs Tjader he wrote, 'As you left home with mother, Sherry and I went down by the lakeside – and such a moon with the Southern Cross. It was wonderful beyond words. There was the lake and the fine lane of spruce and then the mist and the stars. It seemed as if God had planned it all . . . There has been a nearness and a peace that has been beyond description.'[15]

Mrs Buchman's influence on Frank Buchman had been profound. Her strong sense of right and wrong, her home-making qualities and down-to-earth common-sense remained with him. He wrote to her once, 'The liberty which I have always enjoyed is one of your strongest traits. It has taught me to think and act for myself.'[16] She had tried at first to form his future and, when he was in China, was often clamant that he should return home. He was loving in his letters, but clear that he must not waver from doing what he felt God asked of him, however painful he found it. Then, at a certain point, his mother yielded her attempts at control. This appears to have taken place during his time in China. At any rate, a change there was, and Buchman wrote later in his life, 'Her one wish for me was that I do God's will, and having decided that she backed me, even at difficult times when it meant I could not be near her.'[17] In later years, she always rejected the view of those who said her son should stay with her. During her last Christmas, she had said to a friend, 'Christ's work must go on. Yes, I miss Frank, but I would not interfere. He is under a higher authority.' Her last letter to her son, written on the day of her accident, ended, 'Some day we shall meet.'[18] It reached him in Australia, two months later.

Buchman's own account of his three months in Australia was characteristically enthusiastic. 'We arrived almost unknown. We began with a student at Melbourne University. Some twenty men came the first weekend with beliefs ranging from Hellenism to agnosticism, and one Rugger Blue told us he was an orthodox, nominal Anglican who did not believe in God. The Hellenist told us that the three weekends brought him back to a faith in Jesus Christ . . . The changed lives set Melbourne agog . . . We had interviews at all hours.'[19]

Thirty years later, one of those present, S. Randal Heymanson, by then the representative of the Australian Newspaper Service in Washington, described the scene: 'There must have been about a dozen of us. I remember Bob Fraser, now Director-General of the Independent Television Authority in Britain; "Mac" Ball, now Professor Macmahon Ball, who represented Australia on the Allied Council that governed Japan immediately after the war, and George Paton, now Vice-Chancellor of the University of Melbourne . . . Frank sat in a big arm-chair and the rest of us, preferring the floor, gathered in a semi-circle around him. We were a difficult group, and I blush for our youthful arrogance . . . All our criticisms and objections he must have heard and answered a thousand times, but he listened attentively to each of us as we paraded our store of learning and made our clever little points . . . For those who heard and those who would not hear, Frank Buchman had the same infinite kindness and understanding . . . From dawn till past midnight he was at the service of even the least promising, always cheerful, seemingly never discouraged.'[20] In introducing a radio talk by Buchman on 10 July, Frank Russell spoke of 'a number of our brightest young university men who have been captured, or at any rate captivated', and described him as 'a buccaneer of souls, making them walk a moral plank'.[21]

Among others he met was Prime Minister Stanley Bruce. 'I know you are changing lives,' Bruce remarked. 'What baffles me is how!' They also spent two hours with his immediate predecessor, the legendary Labour pioneer 'Billy' Hughes.

In September Day left for America – a business man had cabled, 'Need you for a hundred house-parties' – while Buchman decided to return via Asia and Europe. He went through Siam and Burma back to India, where he stayed for a weekend with Rabindranath Tagore and talked again with Lord Lytton. He wrote to a friend in January, with mixed accuracy of foresight, 'I was with Ghandi (sic) yesterday for two hours. He is no longer a political leader but the sphere of his usefulness will be sainthood, and a compelling one at that.'[22] He was unable to accept a subsequent cabled invitation from Gandhi to revisit the Sabarmati Ashram.

In Burma he had received an SOS from Queen Sophie in Rome. 'The atmosphere in the family here is rather troubled and all wrong and in my distress I thought I would turn to you first of all to ask for your prayers and then advice and help.'[23] In Rome he spent much time with her and the younger members of her family, as well as several days with Queen Olga, 'a marvellous Christian who has seen much sorrow'. He was extremely tired, but on receiving a rather desperate invitation from Queen Marie of Roumania,[24] he left for Bucharest where she asked him if he would stay a month. 'Don't leave me,' she begged. 'I can't speak to anyone else.' But Buchman could only manage two weeks. The Queen wrote of him 'spreading his kind, uniting atmosphere over us all'.[25] Back in London he found the head-waiter, housekeeper and manager of Brown's Hotel waiting up for him, and sat talking to them until almost one in the morning.

The rest of the summer was no less hectic. There were two house-parties at Rhederoord, several visits to Germany, a brief visit to Allentown for his mother's memorial service during which his old college, Muhlenberg, conferred on him an honorary Doctorate of Divinity, and lunch with Archbishop Söderblom of Sweden at Brown's Hotel in London. Queen Olga died in July and he went to her funeral.

Back in London he ran into concerted opposition. 'Damnable under-mining on the part of a well-known group of homosexuals has begun on one of our younger converts who has been going along splendidly,' he wrote to Day in September. 'They called for him in a luxurious motor at eleven o'clock at night. They took him to fly in an aeroplane. When they saw they could not seduce him, they asked him to sleep with one of the well-known political mistresses in London. When this was refused, he was accused of having slept with another fellow. Can you beat it?'[26]

In the years since he had left China, he had encountered many people whose lives were governed by their homosexual tendencies. Two men who had attended one of his house-parties in Surrey, for example, had been 'flagrantly troubled with it'. 'They are hard and difficult but unconvincing,' Buchman noted. 'I intend to follow a fearless programme, combined with charity, which considers one's self lest one also be tempted, and thus forge a message for myself and others that will transform lives.'

Through the years many lives were indeed transformed, and Buch-man's whole-time colleagues included people who had had homosexual tendencies but who had found a freedom which enabled them to use their lives for constructive ends. His approach to sex, in whatever form, was always the same. He believed it to be a natural gift of God to be used under His direction, not indulged in promiscuously. He understood the progression from indulgence to addiction, and regarded such addiction as a spiritual captivity, or, in plainer words, sin. 'Sin is the disease, Christ is the cure, the result is a miracle,' was his response to every level of such captivity. He was neither shocked nor prurient. He never condemned, still less exposed people. He felt that his task was to offer a cure which would set free people's creative qualities for the good of others and the world at large.

He did believe that active homosexuality was in danger of producing other problems of greater seriousness than itself: an exclusive attitude which kept out all other people and took precedence over every other loyalty, a vicious attitude to those outside the circle, and the squandering of often gifted lives. He also came to notice that some homosexuals had a crusading zeal for their way of life which, as in the case mentioned above, often brought them into collision with his work. But he never doubted that every person who wished could be liberated.

In the September of 1926 Buchman was in Geneva. He had lunch there one day with Nehru. By this time Nehru had read *Life Changers*, but had confessed in a letter that, despite Gandhi's influence, 'the way of faith does not fit with my present mentality'.[26]

While in Rome that February the talk was all of Mussolini, who had come to power four years before, and the social improvements which he was initiating in those early days. Buchman wrote to him asking for an interview. 'My mission is the development of constructive leadership in different countries,' he wrote.[27]

He also sent Mussolini a copy of *Life Changers*. 'Do not consign this book to a museum,' he said in a covering note to Mussolini's secretary. 'Suggest to His Excellency that he keep it for his son, Vittorio, for reading when he is a suitable age.'[28]

Later Buchman heard Mussolini speak in Perugia and apparently was impressed – 'He said some excellent things,' he wrote to Mrs Tjader[29] – but appends no comment on a subsequent interview which, from someone as ebullient as Buchman, appears to indicate that it was a failure or at least a disappointment. Years later, when Stanley Baldwin, as Prime Minister, asked him his impressions of Mussolini, he paused as if searching for the right word and then said, 'He seemed to me a poseur.'

Now it was time to return to America. At Geneva Buchman had received a cable from Queen Marie suggesting he travel on the same boat as she and her party did. He agreed, and they sailed on the *Leviathan* on 12 October. He spent a good deal of time with the royal family on the ship, and one night they gave a formal dinner for him. Afterwards they discussed the days in New York. The Queen said she wished to express publicly her debt to Buchman of which she had so often spoken privately. Prince Nicolas suggested that there should be a house-party for this purpose, in place of the one in Roumania which had been postponed because of the trip. In the end, however, it was agreed to make it a reception at the rooms which Mrs Tjader provided for Buchman at 11 West 53rd Street. Buchman cabled New York, 'Queen accepts tea twenty-fourth Ileana Nicolas accompany.'[30]

In New York, however, a major row about Buchman and his work was already brewing.

THE PRINCETON ENQUIRY

The trouble had begun that September of 1926, in a town in Connecticut called Waterbury. The occasion was a student mission, to which students from all the Eastern colleges were invited. Whether by design or simply because they were the ones enthusiastic enough to sacrifice the last ten days of their summer vacation, three-quarters of those who turned up were young men who had found a faith through Buchman's work; and Princeton provided easily the largest delegation, including several officers of the Philadelphian Society. Among them was Ray Purdy, Sam Shoemaker's successor as General Secretary, who had given up a job in Wall Street to go back to Princeton. Shoemaker himself had been invited to take the lead in the preparation days for the campaign.

During these preparations one of the young men from Princeton was able to help the rector of a local Episcopal church with some personal problems; and the rector subsequently told his congregation about his new experience of faith. This alarmed some of his brother clergy. One of them, in a preparatory meeting, declared at length that the clergy were *not* the target of the mission. When he had finished his speech, he asked Sherwood Day – who was sitting beside him – what he really thought of it. Somewhat taken aback, Day replied candidly, 'Oratory, empty oratory.'

The campaign seems to have been successful enough. Afterwards, however, a series of critical articles appeared in an Episcopal magazine called *The Churchman*, the editor of which, Guy Emery Shipler, was a long-term opponent of Buchman's work and said to be the inventor of the term 'Buchmanism'. They noted the fact that Princeton had supplied more missioners than any other college and inferred that it had been a plot of Buchman's devotees to take over the campaign. The articles, written by Ernest Mandeville, were described as 'distorted, untruthful and unworthy' in a letter signed by eight senior churchmen who had taken part in the campaign.[1] However, *Time* magazine, on 18 October 1926, reproduced some of the more offensive portions from these articles, without their qualifications, and described Buchman, under a picture, as 'Soul-surgeon and anti-auto-eroticist'. On the same day Buchman, whom *The*

New York Times had reported as having dined on board ship with Queen Marie and her family, arrived in New York.

Immediately the hunt was on. The apparent combination of royalty, religion and sex was irresistible to the newspapers, and both Buchman and his royal friends were eagerly pursued. The tea reception took place, but Queen Marie did not appear, although her son Prince Nicolas did. 'While Dr Frank N. D. Buchman, "surgeon of souls", sat patiently in his home, No 11 West 53rd Street, surrounded by 150 guests who had been asked to meet the Queen, Marie of Roumania forsook the engagement, if engagement it was,' reported the *New York Herald Tribune.*[2] Eventually, according to the reporter, Buchman phoned a message to the Queen, and his guests went off to a brief audience at her hotel, each with a blank admission card on which he had written in red pencil: 'Ambassador Hotel to meet Queen Marie'. *Time* added the false gloss that Buchman had only met the Queen when 'he was presented to her on the *Leviathan* a fortnight ago'.[3]

Buchman was from then on cast by the press at large as the leader of a strange and unhealthy sect, another Rasputin exploiting a brief encounter with royalty, who operated in 'darkened rooms', 'holding hands', 'hysterical', 'erotic', 'morbid'.*

Buchman was deeply hurt by these insinuations, especially hating being made to look like the leader of a new cult, the more so as his own name was used to describe what he regarded as God's work and not his. When he first heard the word 'Buchmanism', he said later, 'it was like a knife through my heart'. 'What is Buchmanism? There is no such thing,' he told the *New York-American*. 'We believe in making Christianity a vital force in modern life.'[4]

The whole affair was an ideal *casus belli* for Buchman's critics in Princeton. The student newspaper, *The Daily Princetonian*, summarised what *Time* had said about the Waterbury campaign and asked, in an editorial, what the graduate Secretaries of the Philadelphian Society were doing, dragging the good name of Princeton in the mud. To try to clear the air, the university authorities agreed to an open forum to debate the work of the Philadelphian Society. It was held in the largest lecture hall in the university, interest was intense and the hall was packed.

It turned out to be a debate more about Buchman's work than that of the Philadelphian Society. There was much angry talk about 'Buchmanism', though, as the campus doctor, Donald Sinclair, said later, 'no one ... seemed to have any definite idea what it was to which they were opposed'.[5]

---

* These allegations went into the newspaper files and for many years permeated most accounts of Buchman and his work in America.

The meeting enthusiastically carried a motion for an investigation into the work of the Philadelphian Society, the New York press took it up, and President Hibben agreed. A high level committee was set up,* and Hibben gave a number of press interviews, one of which quoted him as saying that 'there is no place for Buchmanism in Princeton'.[6]

When the committee started work they found very little evidence to justify the hullabaloo at the forum. They began, according to the Committee's minutes, by asking undergraduates to come forward and express their grievances. Not one appeared. They then approached Neilson Abeel and the group whose campaign had instigated the inquiry, and asked them to produce evidence. Abeel and his friends refused to appear, but they provided a list of twenty names, to whom the committee wrote letters. None came forward. Undergraduate members of the committee were then sent to interview the twenty young men individually. Eighteen said that they had no grievance, so why should they appear? Two did voice grievances but one later decided that he had misunderstood the situation and withdrew. The second made a complaint which the committee dismissed as being too vague to have any validity.

By contrast, the evidence given in support of the Philadelphian Society was impressive. The undergraduate 'Cabinet' of the Society gave its officers unanimous and unqualified endorsement, and their evidence was backed up by what the committee described in their report as 'a considerable number of undergraduates'. A young man called Dean Clark was typical. What he had learnt through contacts with people like Purdy, he said, had been 'the greatest help in life I have ever known'. 'There is nothing I can say which will fully express the debt of gratitude I feel I owe these men,' he went on. 'The talks I have had with them have done more for me than any other single thing in college. The claims of Christ upon a man's whole life and activity have been put by them in the most sincere and convincing way – no doctrines . . . or dogmas were expressed – nothing but the simple and heart-searching challenge of Christ himself.'[7]

Buchman also began to get a modest amount of support in the press. *Life* magazine (the predecessor of the *Time-Life* publication) commented editorially on what it called 'the inquisition at Princeton University into the qualifications of Frank Buchman as a religious influence'. 'What Mr Buchman seems to do', wrote the editor, E. S. Martin, 'is to give men new motives and driving power. The means which he seems to have at his disposal sometimes upset persons exposed to them, and none the less

---

* This committee was chaired by a senior member of the university's Board of Trustees, Edward D. Duffield, the President of Prudential Life Insurance, who was later to step in as acting President of Princeton when Hibben was killed in a motor accident. It consisted of two other trustees, four members of the faculty and several student representatives.

because they are spiritual means. That may be why he is scrutinised at Princeton. Or it may be that Princeton likes its students the way they are, and does not want new men made of them . . . what this world needs the most of anything is that a lot of people in it should be changed in many of their vital particulars. Our world needs to be born again, needs it badly, and is at least as reluctant to face that process as Princeton seems to be to have "F.B." transmogrify any of her children.'[8]

The result of all this was a marked change of atmosphere among the investigators, which was apparent when they called the officers of the Philadelphian Society before them for a second time. 'Whereas on our first appearances we had been treated as accused criminals,' recalled Howard Blake, then an Assistant Secretary, 'the whole atmosphere had changed by December.'[9]

The report appeared at the end of December.[10] The committee had, it said, looked into the charges: that members of the Society had practised an aggressive and offensive form of evangelism; that individual privacy had been invaded; that confessions of guilt had been required as a condition of Christian life; that meetings had been held where mutual confession of intimate sins had been encouraged; and that emphasis had been placed on confessions of sexual immorality. 'We have endeavoured in every way to secure any evidence which would tend to substantiate or justify these charges,' it stated. 'With the exception of a few cases which were denied by those implicated, no evidence has been produced before us which substantiates . . . or justifies them. . . . On the other hand, judged by results, the General Secretary's work . . . has been carried on with signal success . . . He has given to Princeton a reputation for efficient and fruitful Christian endeavour which is certainly not exceeded at this time by similar work carried on in any other institution.' The only criticisms were that the Secretary had made some mistakes largely through an 'excess of zeal' and that the officers of the Society had confined them-selves too closely to 'intensive work' and thus failed to appeal to the undergraduate body in general.

The committee, however, carefully skirted any direct judgement on Buchman and his work as being beyond its terms of reference, although its members knew that the activities of the General Secretary were based upon Buchman's principles. So the original press rumours were left unanswered. As a young Presbyterian minister in New York wrote to Ray Purdy, 'The investigating committee certainly leave Buchman high and dry, praising with faint damns.'[11] Buchman was acutely aware of this, and wrote to Purdy, 'Exoneration should have come from you and a few like-minded if the committee would not accord that finding'. The aim of their opponents had been 'to free you but discredit the work nationally'.[12]

The situation became once more acute when Hibben told Purdy that not only was he unwilling to have Buchman on the Princeton campus as a guest of any section of the university, but he also wanted to extend the ban to the town as well, although he conceded that he had no right to do so.

In any case, the editors of the campus newspaper had no intention of leaving the matter there. They told Purdy that they proposed to run a series of editorials condemning personal evangelism on the campus. Purdy felt 'in duty bound to answer',[13] and wrote a letter which *The Daily Princetonian* headed 'Practices of Buchmanism will stay while secretaries remain'.[14] It was accompanied by a similar letter from Blake and another Assistant Secretary, C. Scoville Wishard.[15]

These letters, of course, reopened the row which had led to the investigation. Hibben sent for Purdy and asked for an assurance that he and his colleagues would have no further contact with Buchman, and said he would give them until the end of the academic year in June to re-establish confidence in themselves.

Purdy and his friends had no intention of accepting Hibben's demand and, the following morning, were discussing how to word their reply when Hibben telephoned again. He told Purdy that he had been unable to sleep because he had not been entirely candid. Under *no* circumstances would Purdy and his colleagues be reappointed for the following year. They thereupon submitted their resignations, effective from the beginning of March.

The Princeton affair thus put Buchman on the map with a vengeance. It did so in the way he least wanted, as the supposed leader of a distinctly dubious sect or cult. However much he protested that what the newspapers labelled 'Buchmanism' was simply vital Christianity at work, in the public mind it was now a thing apart.

The events in Princeton, furthermore, continued for decades to cast a shadow over Buchman's work among influential sections in America. Hibben liked to insist that he never made any public statement about Buchman.[16] But he never required *The Daily Princetonian* or the New York newspapers involved to withdraw their assertion that he had. He was also very outspoken to other academics, like the President of Yale. His letters show how completely he had accepted the line of Abeel and Buchman's other critics, in direct contradiction to the findings of his own investigating committee. Meanwhile, a complete press silence on the committee's findings enabled *Time*, seven months later, to write that the Princeton authorities had 'forbidden Mr Buchman the practice of his system there' as 'unhealthy'.[17] The verdict of that committee was forgotten, even in Princeton.

Thus, when Buchman died in 1961, the old accusations were resurrected, and the only member of the investigating committee still living,

Alexander Smith, who had been United States Senator for New Jersey from 1944 to 1959, felt constrained to repeat its conclusions in the *Princeton Alumni Weekly*. 'In the present critical and confused state of the world we should all be deeply grateful for Frank Buchman and the great work he has done,' he added.[18] Again in 1978, in a semi-official book by Alexander Leitch, Secretary of Princeton University Emeritus, published by the Princeton University Press, the controversy is referred to in a way which perpetuates the criticisms, and, while mentioning the report, omits all the main findings of the investigating committee.[19]

The withdrawl of Queen Marie from his New York tea was a public embarrassment and a personal hurt for Buchman. His notes at the time reveal how disconcerted he was and how much in need of inner reassurance: 'Regain your poise . . . There is much to suffer. . . Cheer up, go strong, all is well. Forget it.' He suspected 'courtiers' of intervening, but a recent biography of the Queen lays the blame on her 'official hosts' and, by implication, on events. On arrival in the city, Queen Marie was given a tumultuous ticker-tape welcome and what the *New York Times* described as 'probably the most relentless camera bombardment . . . in the world's history'. 'Ebullient and enthusiastic, she never lost her composure or good humour, even with the often cynical representatives of the press.' After a visit to Washington to meet President Coolidge, she returned to New York with a heavy cold and only her 'royal training' enabled her to defy the doctor and remain on her feet. 'The object of uncontrolled social lust, the Queen was annoyed by the "fearful competition" among her sponsors for her attention . . . Pressed by their official hosts to push Buchman aside, Marie and her children balked. Public repudiation of an old friend, the Queen said, was against their royal "creed".'[20] On Sunday 24 October she attended Calvary Church in the morning, but only Prince Nicolas attended Buchman's reception.

Buchman drafted an immediate letter warning her against endangering 'the moral and spiritual development of her children'. Exactly what was sent is not known. 'Queen Marie unhappy since she received your letter. Will write fully,' he noted a little later. She had returned to Roumania where King Ferdinand's terminal illness had begun and where, with Prince Carol in Paris having renounced his right to succession, she was in the middle of a constitutional crisis. Her four-page handwritten letter addressed, as usual, to 'Uncle Frank' was dated 15 April 1927.

She thanked him for his welcome news and, as one martyr of unfair newspaper attacks to another, hoped he was coming clear and strong out of the difficulties accumulating on his 'brave way'. She asked him whether he thought she belonged to the foolish virgins who did not light their lamps, and said she tried to live as straight, think as straight, act as straight as she possibly could, though she knew she was not perfect.

Buchman replied thanking her for her 'frank letter': 'You are marvellous on a human basis, but the truth is that you lack the maximum power. . . Uncle Frank cannot and must not convict you of sin – it must be the Holy Spirit. I am thinking of future days . . . and if you had this power as a possession the future might be changed. . . I am sure you have enough Christianity to take you to heaven, but there's danger of your Christianity at times being sentiment. . . I feel that there is a great deal more that He wants to tell you if you maintain the discipline of an early morning quiet time and that surrender of self and of human plannings to His will and His way. . . .

'What hope is there for royalty or anyone else but rebirth? . . . can the "still, small voice" be the deciding factor in political situations, such as face you in these days of crises? . . . Let me say, with the utmost conviction, it is the only thing that will. . . .

'I am deeply touched when you ask me to keep a large spot in my heart for the children: I gladly do this always . . . Let mother and children go far enough for fun in the Christian life. It's an unbeatable romance! It's life's greatest adventure . . . With the rarest sense of fellowship with you . . . Your devoted friend.'[21]

Faced with the difficulties stemming from the Princeton fracas and the wide condemnatory publicity, Buchman reacted with a mixture of faith, obstinacy and hurt feelings. He wrote to George Stewart Jr, 'I have gone through these weeks with a peace that passeth human understanding, living in the great whirling vortex with utmost quiet, no resentment, no ill will . . .'[22] Certainly the *New York-American* article reported that 'he smiled quietly and denied without vehemence' the various charges brought against him. But his letter to Purdy complaining that he had not himself been exonerated also accused Purdy of disloyalty to him personally. This was unfair to Purdy, who had nailed his colours firmly to the mast both during the investigation and in a press release to Associated Press which the agency had not sent out. Purdy seems to have understood the hurt behind the personal accusation, and sent back a letter compassionately but firmly stating his view of events.

At the height of the crisis, Buchman said, 'We are internationally discredited,' and went away to be alone. He returned a few hours later saying that the whole situation would be 'a sounding-board to the nation'.

Seven years later, Henry van Dusen, who had spoken up for Buchman's colleagues before the committee but had distanced himself soon after, estimated that Buchman had been left with 'not over a half-dozen persons on both sides of the Atlantic' prepared to work with him.[23] This was a ridiculous underestimate, but one which showed how deeply the affair had affected the Princetonian mind.

OXFORD AND SOUTH AFRICA

When defeat threatened Buchman's instinct was to attack. So he arranged what turned out to be the largest American house-party so far, at Lake Minnewaska in New York State. J. Ross Stevenson, the Principal of Princeton Theological Seminary, who had backed Buchman throughout the controversy, and Professors Alexander Smith and W. B. Harris came from Princeton.

Five came from Oxford. One of them, J. F. Brock, a South African Rhodes Scholar at University College, had staggered his tutor by asking permission to postpone his final examinations for a year in order to attend. The college authorities debated it, thought it a mistake, but let him go because they felt that a genuine conviction underlay the request. Next year he was to take his finals with high honours, and he later became Professor of Medicine at Cape Town.

Within a month of resigning, the three leaders of the Philadelphian Society, together with Eleanor Forde,[1] a Canadian and the first woman to travel internationally with the Groups,* were in Oxford. Kenaston Twitchell from Princeton, who had married Alexander Smith's daughter Marion, was already studying at Balliol, and together they reinforced the work which had been building up since Loudon Hamilton's return.

Julian Thornton-Duesbery, then chaplain of Corpus Christi, held a weekly meeting in his study, but the numbers soon forced him to adjourn to the lecture room below, and fifty turned up for a house-party at nearby Wallingford in the summer of 1927. They were an average cross-section of the university, though some, like Dickie Richardson, soon to be captain of boxing, were enthusiastic sportsmen, and others, like Brock, outstanding scholars. There was also a handful of the senior members of the university, like the Revd G. F. Graham Brown, Principal of Wycliffe Hall, the Anglican theological college, whose interest stemmed from a small meeting in London, chaired by Buchman. He had entered the room to find an American, obviously drunk, abusing Buchman with the gossip of

* As Buchman's work was beginning informally to be known.

Princeton. Everyone seemed uncomfortable except Buchman, who let him finish, and then said, 'That's fine, now you will feel much better.' Next day the young American sought out Buchman's help with his own life. Graham Brown used to say that he learnt more from Buchman's handling of that incident than from many years of university teaching.

As at Princeton, the growth of interest did not depend on Buchman's presence, because he spent relatively little time in Oxford, and it sprang less from novelty of doctrine than from the evidence of changes in people's lives.

Some of the new converts set about recruiting their friends (and enemies) with extreme ardour; others displayed a nonchalance bordering on indifference. 'I used to play very second-rate golf with a theological student called Chutter,' says Alan Thornhill, then studying at Wycliffe Hall. 'He was a very undisciplined fellow, but suddenly he started getting up early in the morning, so I asked what had happened to him.

' "Oh," he said, in a very off-hand sort of way, "I met some interesting people."

' "Well, who are they?" I asked.

' "They're just a bunch of fellows round the university who're putting Christianity into practice."

' "Are others permitted to meet these mysterious people?" I said.

' "I'm not sure," said Chutter, "but I'll find out." Well, of course, that aroused my curiosity and, the next time I saw him, I asked if his friends had decided whether they'd deign to have me. "Yes," he said, "come tomorrow", so I went to a meeting after lunch in the library of the University Church, St Mary's.

'It was rather a plus-fours gathering,' recalls Thornhill, 'and one or two of them were already in rowing gear. I'd met Christians who button-holed you, but this wasn't like that at all. They struck me as being a very normal bunch and they talked about God and their own experience in a most natural way, with humour and honesty.

'At that point, of course, I hadn't even heard of Buchman's existence. Certainly nobody mentioned him at the meeting. Then I was invited to another meeting and there were thirty or so people there.

'Somebody suggested we all had a quiet time, but the idea of listening to God was a novelty to me and, when it came to my turn to speak, I hadn't the remotest idea what to say. So I told them that I'd been to the New Theatre the night before with a Chinese student. It was a rather seedy revue and he was a bit embarrassed by the chorus girls. I felt rotten afterwards, because he'd obviously not liked it. "Now, what is the right Christian thing to do in such circumstances?" I said – trying to start off an intellectual discussion in the approved Oxford style.

'A voice from somewhere behind me piped up and said, "And what *did* yer do?"

'I'd no idea who'd said it, but it pricked the bubble and went to the heart of the matter. "Well, nothing, as a matter of fact," I said, feeling rather uncomfortable.

'Then Buchman, because that's who it was, told a light theatrical story to put me at my ease. "But think," he added, "what a force for God the theatre could be in the world!" He was brisk and trim, with rimless glasses and a tweed suit, and he was very obviously American.

'When I got to know him a little, I thought he was nice but slightly maladroit, a good man who'd do useful work if only he understood Oxford better. He'd say things like, "The banana that leaves the bunch always gets skinned." "But, Frank," I said, "that's the whole purpose of a banana," but he just chuckled and repeated it four times. Then he used to say P-R-A-Y stood for Powerful Radiograms Always Yours. Such appalling taste, I used to think!'

Despite Buchman's lack of outward charisma, more and more people began to be intrigued by the changes which they could see taking place in the lives of their friends or pupils. As the interest grew, however, so did the opposition.

By the early months of 1928, the numbers of young men and women coming to meetings were so large that, in February, Buchman's friends decided to hire the ballroom of the Randolph, Oxford's biggest hotel. The *Daily Express* got wind of this and on 27 February ran a story under the headlines 'Revival Scenes at Oxford. Undergraduates' Strange New Sect. Prayer Meetings in a Lounge', which carried unmistakable echoes of Princeton.

The reporter said that 'a sensational religious revival is causing excitement, and some consternation, among Oxford undergraduates'. The main focus, he wrote, was a group which met every Sunday evening in the private lounge of Oxford's largest hotel, and the public confession of sin had been a feature of these meetings.

'Such an ordeal', he went on, 'naturally involves a violent emotional strain and, in the case of one or two young men of nervous temperament, the unfortunate results of their "conversion" have provoked severe comment, and are said to be attracting the attention of the university authorities.'

However, there was, apparently, little sign of these violent strains at the meeting he attended, nor could he report a single juicy confession made, or any specific unfortunate result. There were, he reported, fully 125 men present, almost all undergraduates. 'Their baggy grey trousers and the cigarettes which they smoked freely helped to create the atmosphere of informality which characterised the whole meeting. There was as much devotion as discussion during the two hours that they spent there, but an absence of even the elementary ceremonial of standing or kneeling. They just sat about in easy chairs, even when speaking.'[2]

The *Express* also carried, on the same day, a largely approving editorial saying that it was inspiring that there should be signs of a 'deep stirring of religious feeling' at Oxford, and that, while it was easy to deride such youthful quests into the reality of things spiritual, 'these are the adventures that, when undertaken with earnestness and sincerity, leaven life, keep materialism at bay and fortify the soul of the coming Generation'.[3]

Such inconsistency was doubtless the result of the editorial and the report being the work of different hands. The reporter was Tom Driberg, later chairman of the Labour Party, who had recently left Christ Church without a degree but with an exciting reputation for black magic parties and had joined the *Daily Express* on a trial basis.

Driberg followed up with a second piece the next day. 'Members of the new cult', he wrote, 'hold hands in a large circle and, one after another, apparently "inspired", make a full confession of his sins.'[4] Again no confessor was named or actual confession quoted.

An (unnamed) college head, he added, had told him that 'this indiscriminate divulging of one's feelings must certainly produce a kind of thrill among the listeners, which can scarcely be described by any other word than sensual'. It was, the college head was reported to have said, 'a morbid sensualism masquerading under the guise of religion'.

Given the nature of those supposed to be involved, the story sounds unlikely to say the least. The idea of the university boxing captain holding hands with a bunch of rowing men requires a considerable leap of imagination.* Driberg continued. 'American undergraduates here declared that the authorities of Princeton University, where the movement is reported to have originated, stopped it as soon as they learned of its existence.'

The third article, next day, was less sensational, possibly because four Oxford men had waited on the editor of the paper and demanded more accurate reporting.[5]

On the following Sunday, at the suggestion of the Revd Graham Brown, the meeting was moved from the Randolph Hotel to St Mary's, the University Church, and the *Daily Express* smugly reported that, due to

---

* Thornton-Duesbery comments: 'The articles do not state that the writer *heard* any such confessions, nor does he give a single name of anyone who so confessed or who claimed to have heard such confessions. No doubt, as a good journalist, he would have done so if he could. He could not because such things did not happen. I was present at virtually all these Oxford meetings, and no one held hands, nor were there any unsavoury or emotional confessions by undergraduates.' (*The Open Secret of MRA*, Blandford, 1964, pp. 10–11.)

their publicity, the Randolph ballroom was now too small.[6] Two contemporary letters to Buchman add some interesting background. 'The writer of the scurrilous articles in the *Express* last week,' reported the first, 'turned up last night with some 20 odd fellows from Christ Church headed by one who used to be at Princeton with the hope he could disturb the meeting. They did not realise it had been moved to St Mary's.' Finding the ballroom empty, they threw a few chairs about and departed. A later report added, 'Some of the men responsible for these articles have come into the group and told us of the half-cynical, prankish frame of mind which combined with fertile imaginations to produce them,' and stated that one of the undergraduates concerned had brought with him to the non-existent meeting a highly coloured account of its proceedings and of how they had broken it up in disgust.[7]

Doubtless the editor of the *Daily Express* was unaware of these antics, for it was this series – 'my first "scoop", the first story, I think, in a mass circulation paper' about the Oxford Group[8] – which confirmed Driberg in his job, which was later to develop into his long and brilliant term as the paper's columnist under the pen-name 'William Hickey'.

Buchman was not particularly down-hearted. On the day after the hostile article, he wrote down, 'Nothing to fear. Praise God. All is well. Sleep.'

The press attacks did, indeed, call forth a certain amount of support. The *Oxford Times* of 2 March declared that 'it is definitely not a new religious sect. It is an endeavour to realise more fully the value of Christianity as applied more especially to everyday life and problems', while the *Church Times*, which covered one of a series of At Homes given by Lady Beecham in her Grosvenor Square home, reported that 'One by one, young men stood up . . . and told in the simplest possible way how the influence of Frank Buchman . . . had completely altered their lives, making them real people instead of posers . . . Buchmanism is clearly not an "ism", in the sense that it has tenets of its own . . . Its effect on the individual is, so far as I could perceive, to convert conventional religion into a real and personal religion.'[9]

The attacks, nevertheless, continued. A. P. Herbert, one of the most amusing humorists of the day, produced a satire in *Punch* obviously based on the Driberg cuttings[10] and, at the beginning of the summer term, the Oxford undergraduate magazine *Isis* demanded the removal of the 'Buchmanites' from the university. 'Buchmanism,' it declared, 'is flourishing . . . In an atmosphere hovering between giggles and fanaticism, restraint is thrown aside.' The authorities, it continued, appeared to be alarmed but remained apathetic. It was time something was done.[11]

The *Isis* article had a negligible effect in Britain, but it was picked up by both *Time*[12] and by the *New York Times*, which added, as its own contribution, that the university authorities were urging the expulsion of Buchman and his followers.[13]*

Some senior members of the university had already risen to Buchman's defence. Then, on 23 June, a letter appeared in *The Times* over eleven academic signatures including the heads of two colleges, referring to reports which had been circulating about Buchman's work and declaring, 'From what we have observed of the results of this work, it is our belief that this criticism has arisen from misunderstanding and unfounded rumour, and misrepresents the spirit of the work.' On the same day, the *Manchester Guardian* described Buchman's work as 'extraordinarily impressive' and predicted that it would have 'a big and growing influence'.

The *Express* had meanwhile printed a statement by Canon L. W. Grensted, Chaplain and Fellow of University College and a university lecturer in psychology: 'I have seen a good deal of the leaders of the group, and I should like to bear testimony not only to the general sanity with which they have organised their efforts, but also to its real effectiveness. Men whom I have known – and they are only a few out of many – have not only found a stronger faith and a new happiness, but have also made definite progress in the quality of their study, and in their athletics, too.'[14]

That same summer of 1928 six Oxford men went to South Africa in the long vacation. Five, like Brock, were South Africans, and the party also included Loudon Hamilton and Eric van Lennep, the young Dutchman. The first problem was to raise their fares. 'We began to pray for money,' Hamilton recalled. 'I remember starting an account at the Chartered Bank with nothing in it, but by a variety of mysterious means the money began to come. We wrote not a line, no letters at all, but soon we had enough for those who, like me, needed money for their fare.' Others, like van Lennep, could well afford to pay for themselves.

Buchman was told of this enterprise after it was planned and made no attempt to control or direct their activities in South Africa. The one precaution he did take was to tell each of the party separately to be the person in charge – a stratagem which came to light on board ship when one of them called a meeting in his own cabin, only to meet resistance from all the others, who had been similarly instructed. 'It dawned on us,' said Hamilton, 'that he wanted us all to be equally in charge – to be a responsible team.' The only message Buchman sent during the entire trip was a cable saying that he would come himself the next year.

Despite their inexperience this team of young men made a considerable impression wherever they went. James Lang, the headmaster of Grey College, Brock's old school in Port Elizabeth, found 'something Francis-

* One of those who spread this rumour was the Revd F. D. V. Narborough who had been Chaplain of Worcester College, 1922–6.

can in the naturalness of approach and the simplicity of method',[15] and the most popular Presbyterian minister in Pretoria, Ebenezer Macmillan, spoke publicly of the new experience he had found through them. 'One had only to hear them,' he told his congregation, 'to realise that they have got hold of something we have not got, or once had and lost. L. P. Jacks speaks of the lost radiance of the Christian religion – that is just what they have found.'[16]

The visit had one unexpected side-effect. Almost from the outset, the newspapers – seeking for a simple catch-phrase to describe them – labelled them 'the Oxford Group'.* The story is told that a sleeping-car attendant, seeking for a name to put on their compartment, used the phrase for the group of young men who only had Oxford in common – and that the press meeting them picked it up. The name stuck because it so exactly described the party. Francis Goulding – a St John's graduate, by then working full-time with Buchman – remembers him receiving the news that this name was being generally used: 'He wasn't enthusiastic, but he said, "If it's got to be called something, that's as good as anything." '

In the early months after the Princeton difficulties, with *Time* snapping at his heels, Buchman seems to have felt some need to have the balance restored in his own country. In September 1927 he wrote to Mrs Tjader asking whether she could arrange to have his name put into the New York Social Register. 'I feel for the work's sake this ought to be done,'[17] he told her. He need not have worried. The demand for house-parties, both in Europe and America, grew steadily.

There was a series of sizeable gatherings in upstate New York and New England; three in a year at Rhederoord in Holland, a fourth at Wassenaar; two at Melrose in Scotland; two more in Cambridge; while a house-party at the Beauregard Hotel in Wallingford became a standard event before the beginning of each Oxford term.

These occasions had long ceased to be private affairs in private homes because of the growth in numbers. More and more they were held in hotels, and more and more they aroused the curiosity of every sort of investigator, amateur and professional.

Some, like Kenneth Irving Brown,[18] came away declaring that there had been 'no feeling of something uncanny, no conscious emotional exhilaration, no pious solemnity', that on the contrary 'religion was discussed with ease and humour and naturalness'. In a similar vein, the Revd Graham Baldwin[19] reported that, in meetings punctuated by regular outbursts of laughter, all barriers were broken down.

---

* The *Sunday News* of Durban (6 June 1939) attributed this to John Geary of the *Pretoria News*, who 'had a gift of coining phrases, the most famous of which is "The Oxford Group" '. First used, *Pretoria News*, 10 September 1928.

On the other hand, J. C. Furnas, reporting on a house-party at the end of 1927,[20] had clearly found the whole occasion repugnant. He spoke of Buchman's 'oily voice', 'decidedly stuffy' rooms, 'a puerile lust for morbid details'.

In view of the number of people who claim to have heard unwise public confessions, some must have taken place. However, I attended meetings from 1932 onwards myself and cannot recall hearing any. Cuthbert Bardsley, for some years a colleague of Buchman, said after his retirement from the Bishopric of Coventry, 'I never came across public confession in house-parties – or very, very rarely. Frank tried to prevent it – and was very annoyed if people ever trespassed beyond the bounds of decency.' Buchman is reported to have said once, when a clergyman did speak foolishly, 'I think it would have been wiser if he had been checked, but, of course, you can't expect every parson to speak sense. Some of them unfortunately don't.'

Different people, however, are apparently shocked by different things. When discussing this book with an old friend, a Socialist peer, in 1982, I was suddenly asked whether 'all those confessions' of the thirties still went on. Thinking he must mean the kind of thing recorded by Furnas, I asked, 'What confessions?' 'Well,' he replied, 'I once attended a meeting in Oxford, and Austin Reed (the Regent Street clothier) got up and said he had had to overhaul his whole price structure at his shops because he was charging too much.' It must have been painful for a man as reticent as Austin Reed to make such an admission, but it would seem to be the kind of remark which would incline other business men to search their consciences, something which one would expect a Socialist to welcome.

As usual, criticism does not seem to have deflected Buchman. When the *Atlantic Monthly* asked for an article about the movement, Buchman told its author, John Roots, that he must be quite categoric about the Oxford Group's attitude towards the subject of sex. 'We do', he wrote to Roots, 'unhesitatingly meet sex problems in the same proportion as they are met and spoken of in that authoritative record, the New Testament . . . No one can read the New Testament without facing it, but never at the expense of what they consider more flagrant sins, such as dishonesty and selfishness.'[21]

Dr J. W. C. Wand, then Dean of Oriel College and later Bishop of London, gave his impressions in the August 1930 issue of *Theology*. After stating that 'there were numerous recorded instances of Dr Buchman's marvellous success with individuals through bluntly revealing to them the actual sin in their own life', he added: 'This, be it noted, is sin interpreted as widely as in the gospels. One hears more of selfishness, pride, ill-will than anything else, and the charge that "Buchmanism" is unduly concerned with sexual matters had better be dismissed as the merest nonsense.'

In the spring of 1929 Buchman sailed for Europe en route for South Africa. His only travelling companion was a Yale graduate called McGhee Baxter. Baxter was an alcoholic who had already been divorced, but he had met Buchman the previous autumn and resolved to make a fresh start. While only too aware of his continuing problems, Buchman had the highest hopes for him.

'M.,' he noted one morning, 'could step forward into triumphant leadership. What is needed is God's clear light into every nook and cranny of our lives. The sub-cellars and the coal-bin need cleaning out. Never lose God's care for M. Have M. share with you any of his lonely, waking hours . . . M. a witness of the Spirit.'

He took Baxter with him wherever he went that summer, to house-parties at Wallingford and Scheveningen in Holland, to Baden-Baden and the Hesse home in Germany. For much of the time, Baxter stayed sober and, when Buchman sailed for South Africa a fortnight before the main body of his team, Baxter again went with him.

It was an extraordinary decision. This was the first time Buchman had taken a team abroad under its new Oxford Group label. A great deal of criticism had already been levelled at him, and he knew perfectly well that he would again be the focus of considerable press and public interest when he arrived. He seems to have been ready to take risks which anyone intent on building a prestigious work would have thought reckless.

On the *Arundel Castle* Baxter was faced with all the delightful temptations of life on board ship. 'M. difficult,' Buchman noted one morning. 'Be prepared for the worst.' At the same time he knew that he would never help Baxter by trying to cramp and confine him – and had no intention of doing so. 'In all actions with M. the sky is the limit,' he wrote in a time of quiet.

The evening before they landed at Cape Town, Baxter slipped into a last-night party and, by next morning, was helplessly drunk. Buchman struggled to get him dressed before the ship docked and, while Baxter was led quietly from the ship by Loudon Hamilton, who had remained in South Africa from the previous year, he answered questions from the press. Even then he did not lose faith in Baxter, who in fact proved to be an effective, if erratic, member of Buchman's team throughout the three and a half months in South Africa.

One of the party of twenty-nine who joined Buchman was Eleanor Forde, whom Baxter had for some time been pursuing with proposals of marriage. Just after the main party arrived in Cape Town, they went for a walk on a beach together. An alert newspaperman photographed them; the picture appeared in his paper. Eleanor feared that the picture would give a wrong impression, at the outset, of Buchman and his group, and retired to her room in tears. An hour later, there was a knock at the door.

Outside was Buchman, with a single red rose which he gave her without a word.

The tour consisted largely of five major house-parties, each in or near one of South Africa's bigger cities. Each of them lasted ten days, each took place in a sizeable hotel and all drew large numbers. Between 600 and 700 went to the house-party held twenty miles outside Cape Town.

'In Jo'burg I was just a traffic cop directing the crowds,' Loudon Hamilton said. 'We never seemed to be able to finish a meeting. If anyone in the audience got up to leave, there were always at least three others waiting to take their place.' The method at those meetings was very simple. 'Whoever happened to be leading would simply get other members of the travelling team to tell the story of their change.'

'The message in the meetings was direct and personal,' recalls Eleanor Forde. 'Queues of people would come up to us afterwards and ask for a talk. Before they left we made sure they had fully grasped the point of the absolute moral standards, and then made dates with them next day, one after the other, for twenty minutes. "Go through those standards before we get together and then we will talk about listening to God," we'd say.

'Of course, they would not come next day unless they meant business, but nearly everyone did. So they'd come and they'd mostly have it all written down, and boy! the things that came out were the deepest things in their lives. Then they'd get down on their knees and make a decision to give their lives to God, and then they'd go away and change other people. All ages – one was the head of a girls' school, and another was the matron of the big hospital in Johannesburg. That's why she asked us to come and stay in her nurses' home.'

'I was very impressed by them,' recalls Bremer Hofmeyr, then a university student who was shortly to become a Rhodes Scholar at Oxford. 'I was used to one-man shows but this wasn't like that. Buchman himself led some of the meetings – he was spick and span, and moved at a tremendous lick – but my overall impression was not of a person but a group.'

The Group's visit touched all kinds of people, some in spite of themselves. Bishop Karney of Johannesburg, preaching before the Governor-General, the Earl of Athlone, and his wife Princess Alice, admitted that he had gone to the house-party in Bloemfontein 'tired and jaded and not a little critical' but had come back 'feeling much humbler than I went. I was profoundly touched';[22] while Bishop Carey of Bloemfontein declared that he now felt 'the need of much more power to alter and recreate the lives of the people committed to me' and was 'seeking to discover where I may alter or change'.[23]

The Governor-General was a family friend of the van Heeckerens. Lily van Heeckeren stayed at Government House while they were in Pretoria, and Athlone waited up each evening to hear what the group had been doing that day. He invited Buchman to tea, and asked particularly how the group had reached an outstanding young Afrikaner like George Daneel, who had been a member of the 1928 Springbok Rugby team.

Daneel was at that time training to be a minister in the Dutch Reformed Church, and was still somewhat innocent. Buchman started to teach him how to deal with individual people. One evening he left him and a friend, Don Mackay, to keep an eye on Baxter, who was more than usually beset by his chronic problem and asleep on his bed. Daneel and Mackay had a long talk by the fire in the sitting-room next door. On his return, Buchman asked Daneel how it had gone.

'Fine, Frank – all quiet.'

'That sounds bad,' rejoined Buchman.

Investigation revealed Baxter's room not only quiet but empty, with the window wide open. Buchman sent Daneel and Mackay to find him. They were to divide the town in two, and visit every bar. Early in the morning they returned empty-handed. Baxter had staggered home on his own at 3 am.

The house-parties at that time were for whites but the group visited Lovedale and nearby Fort Hare, the only institutions of higher education for blacks in the Cape. Apart from this, their visit had little effect on what was then known as 'the Native Question', but which had not then posed itself as acutely as one would now imagine. The key question appeared to be the bitterness festering between English- and Afrikaans-speaking South Africans as a result of the treatment by the British Army of Afrikaner civilians during and after the Boer War.

At the final house-party at Bloemfontein in September Professor Edgar Brookes, Professor of Political Science at Pretoria University, addressed his English-speaking compatriots with considerable bluntness. 'We have the problem of racialism between English- and Dutch-speaking South Africans,' he said. 'Every one of us individually is going to do our best about this, but it is not going to be done easily or without sacrifice . . . You must ask God's guidance about learning Afrikaans. It is not everybody's duty, but is there anyone here who is too lazy or has been too proud to learn it? That is a first step.'

Brookes then challenged the audience on their attitude to 'the Native Question'. He did not, he said, have any simple solutions, but 'I do know that we must handle it as Christ would do if He were here . . . Not only have we failed to do it. We have actually been a stumbling-block.'[24] In later years Brookes went into African education and became a close friend of Chief Albert Luthuli, the President of the African National Congress, who described him as 'one of South Africa's greatest champions of public and private sanity and morality'.[25]

Brookes' words and the atmosphere of the house-party brought a deep response from many of the Afrikaners. The widow of an Afrikaner general who had died in a British prison camp had sworn that she would never again speak English. Now she stood up and, in broken English, asked forgiveness of the English-speakers for her hatred.

A test of the efficacy of this work was to come three years later in Brookes' own University of Pretoria. An English-speaking professor wrote a book which was offensive to the Afrikaner people. The author was tarred and feathered by the outraged Afrikaners, and in the ensuing rumpus the university became, in January 1933, wholly Afrikaans-speaking. English-speaking professors, including Brookes, lost their jobs. At the centre of this move was the Professor of Economics, Arthur Norval, whose father had been killed by the British in the Boer War.

Norval was induced by his wife to attend an Oxford Group meeting at the home of W. H. Hofmeyr, the headmaster of the Pretoria Boys' High School. One of the speakers was Dr Brookes. Norval wrote later: 'On my return from the meeting I spent one of the most dreadful nights in my life . . . I could not go on hating and fighting the English . . . but I could not face the costs as I realised it would mean . . . being looked upon as an outcast and betrayer amongst those whom I counted my dearest friends and with whom I had fought for years for a cause . . . I obeyed God and paid the price. On the very moment I accepted God's challenge, my hatred for the English passed completely out of my being, and in its place there came a love which I cannot describe, and which has grown in intensity ever since.'[26]

Soon afterwards Norval invited the national leadership of both communities to Pretoria City Hall. For twenty-five minutes he spoke to them in the English language he had sworn never to use again. Beside him stood Edgar Brookes. For many years, even up to World War II, such reconciliations remained a continuing influence. At one point C. F. Andrews travelled to South Africa to oppose some anti-Indian legislation. 'I was met by new friends and helpers in the Group,' he said on his return. 'Some were Afrikaners. Others were English. What had seemed impossible was accomplished. The hostile legislation was withdrawn.'[27]

Six of Buchman's party decided to stay on in South Africa. His team had not pleased everyone; and even some of those who had initially been helped broke away. Buchman, they declared, had not mentioned the Cross or the Blood of Jesus Christ often enough and they were going to correct the error. Calling themselves The New Experience, they were to be the first of several breakaways from Buchman's work during the 1930s. As later, Buchman's response was to do nothing. He had no intention of trying to enforce uniformity.

He arrived back in England in October 1929 with a sense that the future was bright. While he had been away, his work had flourished both at Oxford and elsewhere. In Oxford itself, the Group had grown steadily. The newest converts included founders of a University Motor Cycle Club who reckoned to live by the motto 'A temptation resisted is a temptation wasted'. One was Stephen Murray, son of Professor Gilbert Murray; another was Reginald Holme, a scholar of New College. 'We'd both ridden in the last amateur TT in the Isle of Man in 1929,' said Holme, 'we regularly went grass-track racing, which was strictly forbidden to undergraduates, and we'd burnt a Trojan van near the Martyrs' Memorial.

'When I came back in January 1930 I found that something had happened to Stephen. He wasn't womanising, he wasn't drinking, but he'd kept his sense of humour. We said, "The God men have got Stephen and he's drinking milk"; which was a very serious indictment, since I used to live on a diet of beer and Balkan Sobranies.' Murray, it turned out, had become interested in the Oxford Group.

A third member of the club, 'Chip' Lutman, still undecided as to whether he should throw in his lot with the Group, was invited by Buchman to join his team for a series of meetings in Edinburgh in the spring of 1930. Lutman wrote back and said that if Buchman represented God, he would represent the Devil. 'That was a step we all regarded as risky in the staid city of Edinburgh,' recalls Roland Wilson, who had joined Buchman when a Scholar at Oriel, 'and, sure enough, Chip arrived on a huge motor-bike which made a hell of a row *and* in his most truculent mood. He went with the rest of us to the meeting, which was absolutely laced with theological dignitaries who'd come to make up their minds whether Buchman was sound or not.'

Loudon Hamilton led the meeting: Buchman himself, as so often, was not even on the platform. 'Half-way through the meeting', Wilson goes on, 'Frank sent a message to Loudon telling him to ask Chip if he would speak. So up he got in his flannels and sports jacket – and nobody had any idea what he would say. He just said that he'd come up to Edinburgh in great need because he thought the Oxford Group might do something for him, that he'd lived a rotten life but intended to change and do something worthwhile with it. So those men in the front row who perhaps never reached that kind of fellow saw one in the process of change.' The next day Lutman got on his knees, gave his life to God and threw his tobacco pouch and pipe out of the window of the Roxburgh Hotel 'where', as Holme remarked, 'some thrifty Scot no doubt retrieved them'.

It was during this period in Scotland that Eric Liddell, the Scots Olympic gold medallist portrayed in the film *Chariots of Fire*, renewed his contact with the Oxford Group. Speaking at a house-party in Edinburgh in 1932, during his first furlough from missionary work in China, he described a walk with Loudon Hamilton in Galashiels eight years earlier when, he said, his heart had 'burned within him'. Now he had recently returned to Galashiels to stay with a tweed mill-owner and his wife, Stuart and Bina Sanderson, who were associated with the Oxford Group. Sanderson had 'put a finger on something hidden in his life' to which Liddell objected. Therefore, said Liddell, 'I really lied.' The following Sunday morning, feeling that he must put this right, he had telephoned Sanderson, 'who didn't seem pleased at having his Sunday disturbed'. However, Liddell motored over and they had 'a wonderful talk'.

He wanted to associate himself with the Oxford Group, he said, because it had challenged him to a keener life for Christianity, and he knew he was going back to China leading a fuller Christian life than when he first went out. The invitation to a house-party in St Andrews in September that year quotes Liddell: 'The Group has brought to me personally a greater power in my own life, discipline without the thoughts of discipline and a greater willingness to share the deepest things in my life. In my time in this country I have met no body of people who are so vitally active and through whom the Spirit of God works so closely as the Oxford Group.'*

* Liddell's biographers – D. P. Thomson (*Scotland's Greatest Athlete*, The Research Unit, Crieff, Perthshire, 1970) and Sally Magnusson (*The Flying Scotsman*, Quartet Books, 1981) – while apparently unaware of these statements, both pay generous tribute to the influence of the Oxford Group upon Liddell.

COMMUNISM AND ALCOHOLICS
ANONYMOUS

After spending Christmas 1930 at Oxford with his Princeton friends, Kenaston and Marion Twitchell, Buchman sailed for Lima, Peru, where he arrived on 10 February. He was taking up the invitation of the British ambassador, Sir Charles Bentinck, whom he had met through the van Heeckerens, relatives of his. The Prince of Wales and his brother, the Duke of Kent, were visiting South America to try and boost British commercial interests at a time of slump. Their first stop was Lima, and Bentinck had asked Buchman to come at the same time. They travelled on the same ship, and some, at least, of the Princes' entourage were prepared to repulse the assault which they imagined would take place. Buchman neither met nor tried to meet the Prince or his brother, though he was introduced to Major Humphrey Butler, the Duke's equerry, by a British Member of Parliament, Sir Burton Chadwick.

The Foreign Office had advised the Prince and the Duke to cancel their visit to Lima because of an impending left-wing revolution in Peru. Bentinck, however, relying on his faith in Spanish chivalry, encouraged their visit, and, sure enough, the garrison at Arequipa and the students of Lima refrained from acting until two days after the royal visitors had departed.[1] The disorder in Lima started with a taxi strike, and Buchman was surprised when, on its first morning, a taxi arrived for him as usual. He told the driver that, if he was really allowed to drive him, he would like to go and thank the strike organiser. 'Oh,' said the driver, 'we decided this morning that even if no other taxi moved, you could go where you liked. We had heard that when your previous driver fell ill, you went to visit him.'

Shortly afterwards, Buchman left for Mollendo, Arequipa and Cuzco, the ancient Inca capital. The revolution had spread to Cuzco, and on his first morning there the hotel manager routed him out and advised him to leave the hotel and get into the city. Buchman sought guidance, and received the thought, 'Whatever else you do, don't leave the hotel.' 'Everybody else moved out and I stayed all day and slept,' he related later. 'I didn't hear any shooting or anything. Around six, the others came back. They told me they had been potted at all day.' On 21 February Buchman wrote down, 'All is well. You will safely and unmolestedly pass the border [into Bolivia]. Very right you did not stay in Lima. Man fails. God is firm. Go Tuesday. Normal time to leave. Perfect peace and rest.'

The experience of this attempted revolution lived with him. 'It was a challenging time,' he wrote Baroness van Wassenaer. 'Think of girls of eighteen and nineteen in Cuzco University being propagandists for Communism. Have the Christians any answer for such a prepared programme?'[2]

His reaction to Communism was to admire the boldness and initiative of its advocates while disagreeing with their ideology. In the mid-1920s he had studied the theory of Communism and decided that it was not only built on moral relativism in an advanced form but was also militantly anti-God. Now the experience of one of his oldest friends was to reinforce that belief.

Chang Ling-nan, the lawyer he had helped in China fifteen years before, was now Chinese Minister in Chile, and Buchman went from Bolivia to Santiago to see him. Chang told him that when, in 1927 and 1928, he had been in charge of a district of Hankow, a Soviet agent of the post-Borodin era had threatened to cut off his head and carry it on a pole through the city unless he renounced Christianity. 'Jesus Christ is my personal friend. I will never betray him,' Chang had replied. Buchman, who usually absorbed his most lasting impressions from people rather than the printed word, was deeply affected by this.

Buchman's thinking was taken a step further when he reached Buenos Aires, where the Prince of Wales was opening the British Industrial Exhibition. All the talk among industrialists was of the Depression and Communism. Some said Communism was the cause of the Depression, others that the Depression caused Communism. This did not satisfy him, and he moved to the view that materialism, particularly in the upper classes, had 'prepared the soil for Communism'. 'Communism is the most organised and effective leadership abroad today,' he noted later in the tour. 'Vital Christianity is the only cure.'

In São Paulo, he addressed a group of Brazilian industrialists. His rough notes have survived: 'Commercial dumping and dishonesty are more dangerous than bombs. But this Depression could be our salvation if it killed the germs of materialism in us. These lands are spiritually bankrupt. The answer could be in this gathering. Christ of the Andes. What about a Christ of Rio or São Paulo. The new leadership which must challenge a bankrupt age. People want such leadership. Alone, no; a group. It is a company that will do it together.'

The more he thought of it, the more he felt that what he called 'moral Bolshevism' – the revolt against God and His absolute moral standards – was the greatest danger in the West. Reading of the Soviet persecution of

[147]

Christians and of the paralysis of the German Parliament in face of Hitler's rise, he noted, 'Collision is essential for the saving of Christianity. Christ must be liberated. Materialism prepared the soil for Communism. Humanism is not enough. Members of Parliament are fearful and diplomacy is impotent. I see no movement in all Christendom that gives an answer. Moral Bolshevism demands a mighty counter-move of God's Living Spirit. Can there be a powerhouse that generates the energy to change modern history? We need to change our temperament and our environment. Trade depression is God's way of reminding us.'

On the boat back to Britain, Buchman did have some contact with the Princes and their entourage. In planning a tea party for the Duke of Kent, he wrote down, 'Ask him, "How would you like to catch a live Communist and change him?" Kindle his imagination.' The Duke appreciated Buchman's freshness of approach, together with his restraint in not pushing himself forward, and kept in friendly touch until his untimely death.* Humphrey Butler talked to Buchman of the need for change which he saw in London and borrowed books about his work. Off Pernambuco Buchman was interested to see the Prince of Wales reading one of them while everyone else was dancing. But nothing is known of any contact between the two men.

The journey also gave him time to assess the future. One morning he wrote, 'This is the age of the ordinary man. Develop him. Plan for world-wide revival. The devil gets them if you don't. Much more initiative on your part. Much more dare. Trained Christian forces. They have been too apologetic. No conforming to the world's standards. You cannot avoid criticism. The ordinary man demands honesty, purity, unselfishness and love. Dedicate yourself to the people.'

Buchman's time in South America had a considerable effect on his thinking. The students he had been in contact with in America and Britain had not, up till now, been those who were turning to Communism. On this trip he came to believe that a half-hearted Christianity and the 'moral Bolshevism' of the privileged classes were taking the world into an age of conflict. He had been appalled, as well, to discover in Brazil that vast amounts of coffee had been thrown into the sea for commercial reasons, when people were going hungry. On his return to Britain he said to some of the young people working with him, 'In one country I was told two young Communists had made it their duty to attach themselves to each Cabinet Minister to win him to the Party line. Which of you will plan as thoroughly to bring a Christian revolution to your leaders?'

---

* The cuff-links Buchman wore in his portrait by Frank Salisbury, painted in 1938 and now hanging in the Westminster Theatre in London, are thought to be the pair given him by the Duke.

As a result of this visit to South America he was considering similar 'spiritual prospecting' in Spain and Portugal, when the clear thought came to him that he must stay in England because someone needed him immediately. Arriving at Brown's Hotel late one night he left word with White, the hall porter, to let him know at once if anyone called for him. Next morning early, White called to say a gentleman was downstairs asking for him. He found a man with every sign of having been drinking long and hard. Later this man told his own story:

'Men drink for various reasons – for company, for consolation, to celebrate or to forget. I drank simply because I was thirsty. I loved to drink. I drank mostly alone. I would go to my room with a bottle of whisky and a novel and not appear again until both were finished.

'It was after an all-night session in my flat spent in the usual way that I found myself facing an early London morning, with a hangover, a foul temper, and no more drink. I was extremely thirsty, and there being no supply available anywhere at such an hour, I strolled round to a friend of mine to knock him up and ask for a drink. This friend was an equerry to the Prince of Wales and lived in St James's Palace. He did not much like being disturbed at this unearthly hour and, in fact, was pretty fed up with me and my habits – as indeed were all my friends.

' "I'll give you a drink, Jim," he said, "on one condition."

' "What's that?" I said cheerfully. I would willingly have promised him the moon. I wanted a drink!

' "That you go round and see a friend of mine – I think he could do something for you."

' "Certainly, old man. I'll go round and see the King of England or the Pope of Rome. I want a drink."

' "Well, he's a fellow called Frank Buchman and he stays at Brown's Hotel. I met him on board ship and I'm sure you ought to see him."

'I had my drink and I kept my promise. We got on well from the start. We found we had many friends in common and Frank was full of stories. Pretty soon I found myself telling him my own story. Frank was a good listener. The only trouble was that talking made me thirsty, so I asked Frank for a drink. Frank said nothing but pressed the bell and the waiter came in. At that very moment an extraordinary thought struck me. It came with the force of a clap of thunder. "This is the last drink you will take." I quickly added a P.S. of my own, "Well, you'd better make it a double." I did. And it was! Before I left Frank that day we prayed together.'[3]

This man, Jim Driberg, a brother of Tom, had been an able surgeon who had already drunk himself out of Harley Street. He had had a good war record, and was a cheerful companion and a fearless gambler around the clubs. During the next months he was a source of help and inspiration to many who met him. The Bishop of London, Mahatma Gandhi and C. F. Andrews were among many who were struck by the obvious change in his behaviour. He returned to his old Oxford college, Brasenose, and was the guest of the Dean, an old drinking companion. His host was anxious to keep conversation in safe familiar channels. 'How is your golf, Jim? What's your handicap?' 'Mine's drink,' he replied cheerfully. 'What's yours?'

Different though he had become in many respects, Jim received little encouragement from his family. His brother, Tom, who was now firmly established at the *Daily Express*, responded to the news of his change with the remark, 'I knew you could sink very low, but I never thought you would sink so totally as to associate with those people.'[4] His mother was more realistically sceptical, saying he owed thousands of pounds. Buchman and his friends kept in constant touch with him, and his letters to Buchman – which were often daily – show that he was keeping free of drink, enjoying their fellowship, genuinely helping many people, and even returning to surgery.

Then suddenly, on 17 February 1932, in the same week in which he had sent Buchman letters of joy and comradeship – he was in Geneva, Buchman in Rome – he wrote saying he could no longer work with Buchman and the Oxford Group. His letter expressed his 'deep, deep gratitude for all you have done for me' and stated that he 'would never waver in his loyalty to the Group', but added that he had, ten days ago, seen an exaggeration concerning himself in a copy of a letter from Buchman to a third person which had 'shaken his confidence'. Buchman had written that Jim had been sent to him by 'the Princes through one of their ADCs'. Buchman immediately cabled him, 'Forgive and forget my mistakes,' and followed with a letter apologising for what he called his 'legally incorrect statement', while expressing himself 'puzzled that you should take such drastic action'. But Driberg firmly cut the links.

Whether this was the sole – or real – reason for his action was never clear. His elder brother John attributed the sudden move to the 'mental factor which has now and then sent Jim off on absurd tangents'.[5] Humphrey Butler, the equerry who had sent Jim to Buchman, wrote of his 'brain storms' being 'the fault of the war', and said he would try to 'persuade him to continue his work with the Group'.[6] He failed, and telephoned to say that he thought Buchman's 'little inaccuracy' was being used by Jim as 'a cloak to hide from other things'.[7] A year later Jim's former wife came into Brown's Hotel and confirmed that her ex-husband owed very large sums to medical colleagues and socialite friends, and it became clear that there were layers of difficulty to which Buchman and his friends had not penetrated.

Buchman and Major Butler, meanwhile, had consulted each other about the mental and emotional factors involved, and the Major found Driberg a post, at his own request, as a ship's surgeon. Before he left Driberg wrote Buchman, who was then in America, 'I would like to thank you and the Group once more for all you have done for me and to let you know my prayers are with you always.'[8]

Alas, Jim Driberg could not make it alone. As Tom, his brother, relates in *Ruling Passions,*[9] he soon turned back to the bottle and to massive borrowing. This defeated his attempt to establish himself as a surgeon in Brazil and, for many years, he lived as an awkward pensioner of his brother's, first at Bradwell Manor and then at a boarding house in Devon, where he died in November 1956.

Tom Driberg alleges in his book that 'according to MRA myth, it was I who, in sheer wickedness, lured him back to the demon drink'. Certainly if this statement was made – and, on occasion, it does seem to have been, in conversation – it was made without evidence. Equally, there is no evidence that Buchman himself took that line.

Buchman had given Jim Driberg the same attention he had given to McGhee Baxter the previous year. He had been prodigal of his time and care, and had taken many risks on his behalf. In 1938 he advised one of his friends to think again before taking responsibility for a certain person: 'At the request of Humphrey Butler, I spent a lot of time on a person like that. I am doubtful about ambulance cases like that, as they need very special handling.'[10]

Though he continued to help many in desperate straits, Buchman felt that his time should now be mainly spent in training people who could tolerate the pressures of his developing work.

Even as Buchman moved towards this decision, events were taking place independently in two American cities which were to lead to his principles being applied to such hospital cases by other people, first throughout America and then all over the world.

In Akron, Ohio, Jim Newton, the young salesman at the Toytown Tavern weekend who had since become personal assistant to Harvey Firestone, the tyre manufacturer, found that one of Firestone's sons was a serious alcoholic. He offered to try to help the young man, and took him first to a drying-out clinic on the Hudson River and then on to an Oxford Group conference in Denver. The young man gave his life to God, and thereafter enjoyed extended periods of sobriety. The family doctor called it a 'medical miracle'.

Firestone Senior was so grateful that, in January 1933, he invited Buchman and a team of sixty to conduct a ten-day campaign in Akron. They left behind them a strong functioning group which met each week in the house of T. Henry Williams, an inventor of machinery for making tyre moulds used by the chief American tyre-makers. Among them were an Akron surgeon, Bob Smith, and his wife Anne. Bob was a secret drinker and it was not until he had been attending Oxford Group meetings for some time that he told them the extent of his problem.

Meanwhile, in New York, a series of alcoholics – one of whom had been told by Carl Jung that his only hope was a vital spiritual experience – were cured through a group based with Sam Shoemaker at Calvary Church. Bill Wilson, a Wall Street man who had become an alcoholic following the stock-market crash of October 1929, had a dramatic cure in December 1934, and during the next months tried to sober up many other alcoholics but without success. He could not make out why, until someone said to him, 'You're preaching at these fellows, Bill. No one ever preached at you. Turn your strategy round.'

In May 1935 Wilson went to Akron on business. On a Friday night he found himself alone with only about ten dollars in his pocket. He was heavily tempted to get drunk, and in desperation telephoned a clergyman, picked at random out of the directory, to try and find some Oxford Group people in Akron. The clergyman gave him ten names, the first nine of whom were out. The tenth, Henrietta Seiberling, daughter-in-law of the founder of Goodyear Rubber, put him in touch with Bob Smith and T. Henry Williams' group. Wilson did not preach, but told Smith his experience and was, for the first time, able to help cure another alcoholic.

Bill and Lois Wilson lived with the Smiths for several months, and out of their experience blossomed Alcoholics Anonymous.

Late in life, T. Henry Williams was asked by a researcher where Alcoholics Anonymous had started. 'His eyes lit up. Pointing to a spot on his carpet, he said, "It started right there!"'[11] Newton quotes the agreement worked out in those years with the Oxford Group in Akron. 'You look after drunken men. We'll try to look after a drunken world,' Williams had said to Wilson and Smith, who became world-famous as 'Bill W. and Dr Bob of AA'.

As AA's official *Brief Biographies of the Co-Founders of Alcoholics Anonymous* more concisely states, 'In May 1935 a business trip to Akron led to his (Bill Wilson's) meeting with Dr Bob, who became the second successful recovery – and Alcoholics Anonymous was born.'[12] Bill Wilson himself wrote, 'The early AA got its ideas of self-examination, acknowledgement of character defects, restitution for harm done, and working with others, straight from the Oxford Groups and directly from Sam Shoemaker . . . and from nowhere else.'[13] Later AA developed the organisation and principles suitable for its precise mission, and, in turn, led to many other "spin-offs" dealing with specific social ills. There are currently estimated to be 500,000 self-help groups modelled on Alcoholics

Anonymous in the United States alone,[14] and AA itself is active in 116 countries.[15] Howard Clinebell, author of the classic textbook *Understanding and Counselling the Alcoholic*, describes Buchman as one of the foremost pioneers of the modern mutual-assistance philosophy.[16]

Paul Tournier, the Swiss psychiatrist, believes that Buchman's thought has also had considerable influence in certain developments in other fields – particularly in medicine and in the Protestant Church as he knows it. Of medicine, he says, 'The whole development of group therapy in medicine cannot all be traced back to Frank, but he historically personified that new beginning, ending a chapter of the purely rational and opening a new era when the emotional and irrational also were taken into account.' Of Buchman's effect on the Church, he adds, 'Before Buchman the Church felt its job was to teach and preach, but not to find out what was happening in people's souls. The clergy never listened in church, they always talked. There is still too much talking, but silence has returned. Frank helped to show again that the power of silence is the power of God.'

THE OXFORD GROUP

In the early thirties, Oxford was the place where the largest number of young people were prepared to take training for the task to which Buchman had set his hand. They and the Communists, who founded their October Club in 1932 and recruited three hundred members in the first year, were probably the most controversial bodies in the university. This was not because either group was sensationally numerous. Their significance resided in their radical commitment.

The first sign that many of the brighter spirits in Oxford were turning to Communism was the recruitment of poets like W. H. Auden, Stephen Spender and Cecil Day Lewis in the late twenties. Others followed them in the early thirties, mainly because of despair at the state of society. Three million Britons were unemployed, and living on a means-tested pittance not far from the starvation line. Successive governments, Conservative and Labour, seemed unwilling or unable to do anything about it. On the Continent Mussolini's dictatorial colours were now apparent, and in January 1933 Hitler came to power.

'No one who did not go through this political experience during the thirties', writes Day Lewis in his autobiography, 'can quite realise how much hope there was in the air then, how radiant for some of us was the illusion that man could, under Communism, put the world to rights.'[1]

There was generosity as well as naivety in this illusion, for Day Lewis and his friends seemed ready to dismantle their own pleasant way of life if they could thereby lessen the injustices of society and the world. Bearing in mind the pressures at home and abroad, the complacency of the establishment, and the almost total ignorance of how Communism was actually working in the Soviet Union, their attitude was understandable and worthy of respect. 'It would have been a disgrace not to have been a member of the Party in the mid-thirties,' claimed one adherent, who states that he left it in 1938.[2]

The extent of the migration among British intellectuals – particularly in Cambridge where it included such then unpublicized figures as Kim Philby, Guy Burgess, Anthony Blunt and Donald Maclean – was significant. George Orwell believed that 'for about three or four years the central stream of English literature was more or less under Communist control',[3] while Neal Wood writes of 'the dazzling array of intellectual virtuosi', many of whom achieved distinction in literature, the universities, the civil service and the sciences, who took the same road.[4]

Any examination of the lives of many of these intellectual Communists does much to indicate Buchman's belief that 'moral Bolshevism' among the intelligentsia, like the right-wing materialism of which he had warned the São Paulo business men, was an important factor in moving people towards Communism. The story is told in autobiography after autobiography. 'I was ripe for conversion because of my personal case-history,' wrote Arthur Koestler. 'Thousands of other members of the intelligentsia and the middle classes of my generation were ripe by virtue of their own case-histories: but, however much these differed from case to case, they had one common denominator: the rapid disintegration of moral values.'[5]

In Oxford at that time advocacy of such moral relativism was an active element in Communist propaganda. Hugh Elliott of Hertford College, a friend of the founder of the October Club, says, 'We met the Hunger Marchers on their way to London, sang the *Internationale* with them and bitterly criticised the Government's policy of "safety first". In the October Club we discussed a new social order. I began to question all my basic beliefs. A distinguished gynaecologist came to lecture to a mixed and packed audience. He told us we were all suffering from inhibitions about sex. Free love was both natural and normal. Many of my friends went the whole way with his teachings. Later, I saw real tragedy in their lives and understood the connection between discarding moral standards and the acceptance of the Communist ideology, which was the lecturer's frank intention. Myself, I hesitated . . .'

It was at that moment that Elliott met the Oxford Group. 'My friend who had introduced me to the October Club won my respect by his dedication,' Elliott continues, 'but I saw in those who worked with Buchman a greater dedication and self-discipline. They were so genuine. What they started in Oxford aroused a lot of controversy, but could not be talked down, and I joined them.'

Buchman and his colleagues did not decry Communism or support any other political tendency. They simply set before people uncompromising standards of absolute honesty, purity, unselfishness and love, and stated that God had a plan for the world – and for each person individually – which each could find and with which each could co-operate. Buchman asserted, though there was little contemporary evidence to back the assertion, that if they fully committed their lives to God they would, in the future, see transformations in social and national affairs around them.

For some the method seemed too slow, yet it had the virtue of facing both personal and social problems, of filling, in Day Lewis' words, 'the hollow in the breast where a God should be'.

The majority of those who composed the Oxford Group had not experienced Elliott's dilemma. The relative morality which had penetrated the Oxford poets was only beginning to affect the average undergraduate. Many had become agnostics – or nominal Christians – because they had never seen Christianity whole-heartedly lived out, but had been held back from 'the moral slum' of which Spender wrote concerning himself by the standards of their parents or a sneaking feeling that Christianity, if it were possible, was the right way to live. Most Oxford undergraduates had read the Bible – all at that time had to pass an examination on the Gospels and the Acts of the Apostles – and many of those who responded to Buchman's ideas saw in his Oxford friends the nearest thing to the Acts which they had encountered.

So, between 1931 and 1935, about a hundred and fifty undergraduates (myself among them), together with the Chaplains of Corpus, Hertford and Lincoln Colleges, and an occasional professor, met at 1.30 each day, between a hurried bread-and-cheese lunch and the afternoon's sport. The variety was wide though, from the nature of Oxford then, mainly middle-class. Harry Addison, the son of a clerk in a small coal agency in Sunderland, came from Newcastle University with the best classical degree of his year: painfully shy, a passionate scholar, wholly apolitical. Ray Nelson was the ebullient leader of a jazz band, with a penchant for railway timetables. Charis Waddy was the first woman to study oriental languages at the University. John Morrison had already studied theology at New College, Edinburgh, and in Germany under Barth and Bultmann. Kit Prescott, a rowing member of a famous rugby football family, narrowly collected a pass degree and left a string of transformed lives behind him.

The whole mobilisation, though very much in earnest, was conducted with a certain humorous abandon. In one college there was a sweepstake initiated by the 'unchanged' as to who would be 'changed' next. Prescott, spying an *Oxford Mail* poster 'Oxford Stroke Changed' in the weeks leading up to the Boat Race, acquired half a dozen and nailed them on the doors of his rowing friends in college. One young man who had heard that Roland Wilson was trying to be 'guided by God' followed him for a day to see where he went.

Paul Petrocokino, a faintly Wodehousian figure, who sported a leopard-skin waistcoat and composed in the manner of Handel, remembers the rumour in Exeter College that a certain high-spirited maiden, who always toured Oxford on a bicycle with a dog attached, had succumbed.

[156]

'Seen the "dog girl" lately?' he had asked one of her admirers in the Junior Common Room.

'Haven't you heard?'

'Heard what?'

'The Oxford Group have got her.'

They had, indeed, and to the amazement of the connoisseurs, she stuck to it. Buchman's idea was to 'out-live, out-love and out-laugh the pagan world', and she found that interesting.

The training, given and received, was serious. Of the lunch-time meetings, Alan Thornhill, then Chaplain of Hertford, says, 'They were not the usual discussion circles that Oxford loves. The aim was not discussion. It was to build a new world. These meetings were an intense spiritual training. There was complete informality and you could say what you liked, but the spiritual temperature was such that the dilettante and the armchair theorist soon found the pace too hot for him. People were blunt with themselves and each other. Absolute standards of honesty and unselfishness were applied not to some pleasant pipe-dream of the sweet by-and-by, but to details of the nasty now-and-now. What time do you get up these days? How about your times of prayer and listening? Are you winning your friends to this new way of life? Which comes first – ambition or God? These were the kind of questions flung out and fought out in those daily meetings. With them went the simple, practical training that every Christian university ought to give as a matter of course – the moral basis of Christianity, the steps involved in finding a personal experience of faith, the art of passing that experience on, how to listen to God, the building of an unbreakable fellowship.' It was a fellowship of travellers, a dedication without vows or rules, where no one had to do anything except what he or she felt God told them to do.

On one afternoon each week, all came together for a meeting where visiting speakers or distinguished Oxonians took matters wider and deeper. There were reports on the progress in other countries. L. W. Grensted, by now Nolloth Professor of the Philosophy of the Christian Religion, gave a series of talks on the psychology of life-changing and the Christian life. The afternoons finished with a half-hour service which the Professor conducted in the University Church. People went to their college chapel or other churches on Sunday.

Buchman was, as Thornton-Duesbery often said, 'soaked in the Bible', and made certain that it formed the basis of the training given in Oxford. His recipe for Bible-reading was, 'Read accurately, interpret honestly, apply drastically.' 'The Bible is a manual about fishing for fishermen,' he would sometimes say, in taking people through the stories of the man born blind whom Jesus cured and converted,[7] of the woman he met at Jacob's Well whose change affected her whole community,[8] or of Philip's daring encounter with the Treasurer of the Queen of Ethiopia.[9] He believed that, in order to grow, the infant Christian needed food (the Bible), air (two-way prayer) and exercise – and his young colleagues, here as in China or on his world tour, learnt much about their own natures and the further changes which were needed, as they went into action together.

Buchman insisted, at the beginning of one term, that each should aim to change the most difficult person in the college. With some it happened, and the skill and reticence he practised gradually began to develop in his young friends. Meanwhile, there was trial, and not a little error. 'Ambition came in a good deal with me, and did harm,' recalls Ian Sciortino of St Edmund Hall. 'I met our College Vice-Principal – he'd got a brilliant First in theology – and told him all about the spiritual life. He didn't like being assaulted by a brash young hearty and told me so. I also buttonholed the college chaplain. He was quite encouraging, but I learnt later that he had given me a very unpleasant nickname which went around the Senior Common Room.' Sciortino's Principal, A. B. Emden, however, frequently had him and his friends to his rooms, listened and prayed with them, and remained a life-long friend.

Families naturally reacted in different ways. When the *Isis* cartoonist, Reginald Hale, met the Oxford Group, his mother was anxious about the subject of 'guidance' and wrote to her uncle, Prebendary Carlile, the founder of the Church Army. Back came a reassuring postcard: 'Dear Marie, Guidance is love in action. Yours in the fight. Wilson Carlile.'[10] Margot Appleyard's[11] father, anxious that she might later regret her decision to give her whole time to Group work after leaving Oxford, allowed her four months to try it out and then took her on six months' world-wide travel. On their way back across the Mediterranean, she told him that she was more sure than ever that she should work with Buchman and his friends. Her father was content, and backed her in her decision for the rest of his life.

Others met with sterner opposition. One young man was cut out of his father's will, and other parents feared that 'faith and prayer' would mean that their offspring would get into financial difficulties which would put some obligation on them. But most parents, when they were sure their young people felt a deep call, agreed to their following it. Indeed, quite a few followed their children. When Rozi Evans, a cheerful agnostic from Herefordshire, joined Buchman, she was followed by her father and mother, three brothers, two sisters and numerous cousins. The surviving parents of Kit Prescott, Ray Nelson and Francis Goulding were among many who took an active part with them in the Oxford Group for the rest of their lives.

In the vacations the Oxford students – together with those from Cambridge and other universities – took part in campaigns in East

London and other industrial areas, as well as taking initiative in their own towns.

Thus, in Scotland, the North-East, Yorkshire, the Midlands and South Wales teams grew round them, and as in East London they moved particularly with the workers. In Newcastle, Harry Addison enlisted the Lord Mayor, Will Locke, who was a miner, and his friends. In Scotland, the Glasgow students raised a team of unemployed shipyard workers. In Yorkshire it was, amongst others, a group of mill-girls, in Birmingham engineering workers, and in Wales shipyard workers and miners. Oxford students, reinforced by some from other universities, were at the heart of Buchman's large-scale ventures in Canada and Scandinavia in the mid-thirties, and many – for some forty to fifty per cent of the Oxford recruits took on the work full-time – pioneered teams of their own in various countries.

At the same time those who had opted for active moral relativism or Communism, or both, went on to play a major part in the intellectual life of Britain, and of the great majority who had joined the Communist Party and later left it, many looked back to their past with nostalgia, feeling, in Koestler's words, that 'never before or since then had life been so brimful of meaning'.[12] Their ideas remained, in certain aspects, the antithesis of those the Oxford Group tried to practise, and in some among them the antipathy was so strong that they became active opponents in the coming decades.

Oxford had also become the centre of Buchman's activities in another way. Each year between 1930 and 1937 he hired one or more colleges for a house-party in the summer vacation. In 1930 it was a comparatively small affair at Lady Margaret Hall and St Hugh's. In the summer of 1933 5,000 guests turned up for some part of an event which filled six colleges and lasted seventeen days. Four main meetings ran simultaneously, with the principal speakers shuttling from one to the other; and a team of 400 met with Buchman at 7.30 each morning for training and to prepare the day. Almost 1,000 were clergy, including twelve bishops.

Even the relatively small numbers of 1930 caused some concern to Buchman's more cautious British associates. On 17 June he wrote to Eleanor Forde, recuperating from an illness in America, 'I go on to Oxford tomorrow. They are paralysed by the number of people coming, but I am not worried.'[13] Ten days later he wrote to her enthusiastically, 'We are now under a genuine avalanche. We have to run two concurrent house-parties to cope with all the numbers. We have wonderful weather, green lawns, sunny skies and everything needed to complete a perfect setting – only we do miss you and wish you were with us.'[14]

Paul Hodder-Williams, the son of the Dean of Manchester and later chairman of the family publishing firm, Hodder and Stoughton, attended the house-party in 1932 and recalled, in 1980, that it made 'the spiritual knowledge I was brought up with come real for the first time – practical rather than theoretical'. He persuaded his uncle to carry a weekly column about the Oxford Group in the *British Weekly*, and an eight-page supplement of the same paper on the subject ran to an edition of 119,000 copies.[15]

In 1932 Hodder and Stoughton also produced a racy account of Buchman and his work by A. J. Russell, a former literary editor of Beaverbrook's *Daily Express* and managing editor of the *Sunday Express*. The book, titled *For Sinners Only*, went through seventeen editions in England in two years and was translated widely, the French edition being even more provocatively titled *Ceci n'est pas pour vous*. The book brought in a flood of letters. George Bernard Shaw's niece read her uncle's copy. She wrote to a friend, 'G.B.S. met the Group in South Africa and felt they had got "the right thing", even if not altogether keen on some frills attached in the way of phraseology. He told me to get in touch and even offered to pay for me at a house-party.' He also urged his secretary to do the same, characteristically suggesting that, as she was the daughter of a clergyman, she needed to seize the chance.[16]

In 1934 the house-party ended with a meeting in Oxford Town Hall. Its principal interest, as far as Oxford was concerned, was the speech of the Provost of the Queen's College, Dr B. H. Streeter, an outstanding New Testament scholar with wide knowledge of world affairs and especially of the Far East. He said he had been watching the Oxford Group for two and a half years and compared his attitude to 'that taken towards the early Church by Gamaliel, that most amiable of the Pharisees'. 'The reason I have come here tonight', he continued, 'is to say publicly that I ought now to cease from an attitude of benevolent neutrality towards what I have come to believe is the most important religious movement of today. . . . The movement seems to be able not merely to change some bad people into good, but also to give new heart and a new courage and a new sense of direction to those who are already men of goodwill. That is why I have come to the conclusion that in an age of growing world despair it is my duty to associate myself with it.

'May I add,' he concluded, 'that I come to the Group, not as a person with some little reputation in his own sphere of study, or as the head of an Oxford College; I come as one who has already learned something from the Group, and hopes to learn more.'[17]

The numbers at Oxford house-parties kept on rising. Almost 1,000 people registered on one day in July 1935, twice the previous record for a day's arrivals, and there were 6,000 for a meeting on the lawns of Lady

Margaret Hall. Nor was it only Oxford which drew the crowds. In January 1935 1,400 went to a house-party in Malvern, called at the suggestion of the Bishop of Worcester; and this was followed by a series of meetings in Penge, in South London, to which 4,000 went and which the Bishop of Croydon welcomed in glowing terms.

For Buchman himself, however, life was not all moonlight and roses. That summer he was asked by General Lynden Bell to spend a day in the Buffs'* tent at Canterbury Cricket Week. J. L. Guise, the Oxford and Middlesex cricketer, drove him there from Oxford via London, as Buchman wanted to buy a suitable tie for the occasion. The tie of the Eton Ramblers took his fancy, and Guise only persuaded him to purchase something more neutral 'with considerable difficulty'. The whole occasion turned out something of a 'baptism of fire' for Guise, who relates: 'I shall never forget that day; until then I had not realised the degree of persecution and opprobrium Frank had to endure. Bishops, high-ranking soldiers and cricketers packed the marquee and most were holding Frank in suspicious sidelong glances. "There's Frank Buchman", one could hear them mutter to each other. For me it was the test of a lifetime, for I was well-known in the world of cricket and to be Frank's companion meant meeting the same hostility. Only one person was perfectly at ease in every conversation and introduction we had and that person was Frank; he remained his natural cheerful self throughout. . . . Driving home in the evening, Frank suddenly pointed to a small cottage . . . and asked me to stop as an old friend of his, a gardener, lived there whom he had not seen for many years. It was a full hour before he came out, very happy that he had found his old friend well and in good heart, though getting on in years.'[18]

The Group's younger and more ebullient supporters were, of course, the last to play down the significance of the sudden expansion of numbers. When four teams of students were commissioned to visit the South Coast, London, the Midlands and the North respectively, the Group's publicity declared that 'this marked in England and perhaps for the world a revival fully as significant as the Reformation'; while one young enthusiast regarded the arrival of 300 Canadians and Americans at the 1934 house-party as 'the most significant event since the sailing of the *Mayflower*'. Their history was faulty, to say the least. But a less biased witness, the unregenerate Malcolm Muggeridge, wrote in his book *The Thirties* that in half a decade the Oxford Group had generated the only genuine religious revival of the period.[19]

On the other side of the Atlantic, too, Henry van Dusen, a professor at Union Theological Seminary, was describing Buchman's work as

* Bell's exclusive regiment.

'perhaps the most powerful, and certainly the most striking spiritual phenomenon of our times'. Van Dusen expressed various criticisms, together with his assessment of Buchman's personality, in an article headed 'Apostle to the Twentieth Century' in *The Atlantic Monthly*.[20] His main criticisms were that Buchman was disdainful of the efforts of other Christians, while being 'hypersensitive to any criticism of his own vision'; that he saw the task of 'life-changing' as the *sine qua non* for every Christian, whatever his gifts, and allowed no division of responsibility for different talents; that he was a name-dropper and 'paid an uncritical, almost childlike, deference to people of birth or social position'; and that he was prone to exaggerations of various kinds which clashed with his avowed standard of 'absolute honesty'. At the same time, his final paragraph describes Buchman as 'one of the most extraordinary men in a period which may be distinguished in the annals of history as the Begetter of Great Leaders'.

'As with all men of genius,' he wrote, 'the secret of Mr Buchman's influence is not easily defined. One thinks at once of obvious qualities which distinguish him and make their contributions to his effectiveness – a quite extraordinary skill in administration; personal attention to the importance of the minutest detail; infinite solicitude for each person's needs and idiosyncrasies; tireless resilience of body and nerves; playful and unclouded gaiety of spirit; financial sagacity, not to say shrewdness; tenacious memory; a sense of strategy which might quicken the jealousy of a Napoleon; exuberant and contagious optimism.

'But one is driven to conclude that none of these is the gift of inborn equipment: all are products of some deeper secret. The ultimate sources of Mr Buchman's personal power are, I think, four: uncanny pre-vision of the future, expert understanding of the inmost problems of the human spirit, unclouded certainty in his own procedure and the absolute deliverance of self – his hopes, his necessities, his reputation, his success – into the direction of the Divine Intention, clearly and commandingly made known to him. How far the first three are themselves the result of the last, no human analysis can reveal.'

LIFE WITH BUCHMAN

Brown's Hotel in Dover Street, just off Piccadilly, had been Buchman's first stopping-place in London after World War I. This unpretentious-looking, Swiss-managed hotel, with its faithful clientele 'of country gentry, retired colonial administrators, distinguished service officers, not the aristocracy',[1] was, during the 1920s and most of the 1930s, Buchman's only permanent address for mail and co-ordination. On every visit to London he returned, and in the late twenties began to keep a permanent foothold there, a bedroom which others used when he was away.

Few people knew of Buchman's long-term link with Brown's. In 1932 Sir Henry Lunn, who ran the Lunn travel agency, questioned him about it and about his finances generally. 'I want you and your great work to be encased in triple brass against the darts of hostile criticism,' he wrote. He had heard it said that the Group people always travelled first-class, and why did Buchman make his headquarters at a West End hotel like Brown's?[2]

'Just in from two overnight journeys on the Continent,' replied Buchman, 'one happens to have been in a second-class carriage, the other the typical crossing in a boat on the North Sea, which was none too quiet.

'I enclose at once the statement of the American accounts. As far as my own personal finances are concerned, I have no investments; my mother had left me what she hoped to be a small annuity of several pounds a week when I was 65; this has all been wiped out in a single week by the closing of a bank.* I have no personal funds.

'As for Brown's Hotel, let us get at the facts. I pay ten shillings and sixpence a day when I am in residence, for which three rooms are placed at my disposal. In addition I receive stationery. I have the service, seven days

---

* The bank failed because of a dishonest cashier. Buchman was warned of the impending collapse and could have withdrawn his money, but said he would suffer with his fellow townsmen. On a later visit to Pennsylvania he called on the cashier in prison and on his wife. The $50 a month from his brother's insurance policy went after his mother's death in 1926 to his old cook, Mary Hemphill, until her death in 1937.

a week, of letters being forwarded, etc. This saves paying a secretary when I am out of town . . . The meals I take in the hotel are given at a reduction.

'If there is anyone who could give me a constructive answer to the problem of my being housed somewhere at less expense, and as efficiently, I should be very glad to have their suggestions.

'As to travelling, I do not know when any of the Group has travelled first-class. A telephone call to Cook's in Berkeley Street will tell you that they always travel tourist class.'[3]

Buchman's quarters in those days were described by a visitor as 'a tiny room almost completely filled by the bed, round which were large piles of a newspaper which he was sending out to friends around the world. The only light came from a small well going up past every floor to the outside air far above. On the other side of the bed was another door opening into a minute bathroom which had no right angle between any of its walls.'

The occasion was a typical one. The visitor was Francis Goulding, then an Oxford undergraduate, and the time about three in the afternoon. Buchman was lying on the bed. Goulding continues:

'Frank raised his head and said, "Well, what do you want?"

' "Oh, nothing really," I said. "I just wanted your advice on something. But I'm disturbing you."

' "No, no, no. Not at all. I was up till 4.30 this morning sending out these papers and I thought I'd have forty winks. I'll get up now. You go and ask Salvo to bring up tea for one and two cups. He knows."

'Salvo was happy to comply. Frank insisted I eat the cakes and we talked about my future.'*

In 1933 a new arrangement was made by which Buchman had the use of seven rooms, including a very large sitting room, for only forty-four shillings a day. His sleeping quarters do not seem to have improved much. Mrs Harold Taylor, wife of the headmaster of Cheam, remarks of this period, 'People used to say to us, "He must be a very rich man if he can live indefinitely at Brown's." Well, I saw his bedroom once. It was a coat-hanger, a bed and a bag.'[4]

The large sitting room included in the new bargain was hardly more adequate than Buchman's sleeping quarters. 'I remember being in that room when it was so crowded that if, by mischance, you lifted your foot off the ground, you had to be a stork for the rest of the time because your neighbour's foot had occupied your place,' recalled Nora Cochran-Patrick.[5]

'Brown's really was a hive of activity at that time,' wrote John Vinall,

---

* Salvo, an old Italian waiter, used to say, 'I should like to see the Ten Commandments plastered up in every street in London. They keep people cleaner than Pears soap!' Buchman was one of three, other than his family, present at his funeral.

who joined Brown's in his teens and became head porter. 'He was always surrounded by people. Dr Buchman would see about thirty or forty people in a day; he would never get flurried . . . I believe that more than half the visitors to Brown's were Dr Buchman's friends . . . Whenever there was a birthday party in Room 1, the staff would always go too. . . . At Christmas he went . . . through the kitchens and the steward's room – down mysterious passages he went, and . . . gave an envelope to each one of the staff. There were one hundred and fifty staff, and one hundred and fifty envelopes. . . . It was really a personal gift from a friend. . . . Dr Buchman was the making of me – you have got to model yourself on somebody, and for me that was Dr Buchman.'⁶ 'He was a very homely sort of man, seemed to fit in with everybody, rich or poor, talk to anybody, and talk with you and help you,' Vinall said in old age. 'I'm trying to do what Dr Buchman was doing. Not that what I'm doing it so good, but still, I'm trying in that way.'

From the first Brown's fitted Buchman perfectly. It was small enough to become a home, central enough that anyone could drop in and distinctive enough that anyone could be invited. It was here that he met people like Kipling and Siegfried Sassoon. King George II of Greece came to live at the hotel while in exile because Buchman was there, and often came to his room to talk. Workers from East London and miners from Wales and Scotland came too. 'He just treated everyone the same,' said Vinall.

Alan Thornhill remembers calling in one day, like Goulding, to talk about his future. He had lost his job at Hertford College and the Principal of the Oxford theological college, Wycliffe Hall, had asked him to join the staff. 'I was floundering a bit at the time and was not living as a Christian should. I had been hurt by the abrasive tongue of Principal Crutwell at Hertford College and I wanted Frank's approval for my plan. Frank asked me to tea. On the way, feeling unsettled and unhappy, I slipped into a show at the Windmill Theatre that wasn't too good for me.

'Frank was alone in the sitting room. He greeted me and I started to tell my plan, but he interrupted me in the first sentence, "Alan, could you straighten that picture on the wall. I don't like being in a room with something crooked." I started to do it. Frank bawled at me, "No, no. This way, not that way . . . no, no, no, that way, not this way!" I was swivelling it this way and that. Finally, he said, "That's fine." It was only afterwards that I realised what he was talking about, me and not the picture.

'I was very self-important. It was a great spiritual opportunity and so on. Frank listened. "How much will they pay you?" He registered it was less than what I had got at Hertford – "Uh-uh". Then he said, "My conviction is, nothing less than another St Francis." Such a shattering and, in a way, absurd remark. He repeated it two or three times.

'We had a quiet time. The sentence from him which I remember was,

"Alan needs persecution." Which annoyed me. I'd been thrown out of Hertford. I saw Wycliffe would be a softish job. He absolutely refused to discuss the job – that was for me to decide. He just gave me perspective. I accepted the job.'

Buchman's relationships took no account of age or gender. Where he found solid ground, he built on it. The young Canadian, Eleanor Forde, was a trusted colleague from their first meeting. 'You have a remarkable concept of the Gospel message,' he wrote her in 1925, 'and it is a privilege in these days of loose thinking to find one who has so thoroughly gripped the truths of Christ.'[7] From then on he confided in her his plans, his hopes, his thoughts and dilemmas about people, in much the same way as he did with his older male colleagues. 'I certainly want you to hold me to God's best,' he wrote to her, 'and I haven't forgotten that you want a full hour to tell me where I have fallen short.'[8] Buchman counted on her intuition and wisdom with individuals, as well as on her public leadership in his work. She describes how he sent her off one day in 1928 during her first visit to England. 'He got hold of me in Brown's one day and said, "I think you'd better go out into the country today and have lunch with Queen Sophie."

' "Frank, I can't go and see a Queen like that. What would I say? How would I behave?" I replied.

'He said, "Don't bother about behaving. Just tell her how you have changed, how you gave your life to God and what a difference it has made." I found he had made all the arrangements and off I went and did it. A year later, the Queen thanked me.'

Not all Buchman's team were so easily overawed. Cece Broadhurst, a cowboy singer straight from the Canadian prairies, used to call everyone 'George'. Bouncing into Brown's one morning, he greeted an unknown gentleman emerging from Buchman's quarters, 'Hiya, George!' The foreign gentleman bowed politely. 'I had no idea you knew His Majesty so well,' commented one of Cece's companions.[9]

Buchman himself treated royalty much like anyone else, even if he was more old-world in his greetings.

'Did you meet those princesses?' he asked Roger Hicks, an Oxford graduate who had joined him after teaching in India, when he came into Brown's at about this time.

'Yes.'

'How were they?'

'Very angry.'

'I thought they would be,' said Buchman. 'I told them the truth. If I can't have fellowship with them on that basis, I don't want it at all. Now let's go on.'[10]

Besides interviews of every kind, the rooms in Brown's were used to send off a mass of literature. 'We would make the midnight post in the box in the hall,' says Vinall. 'We were always catching that post! There was a tremendous lot of work to be done with the mail, and with the literature as well, sending it out all over the place.'[11]

All the secretarial work was done there, too. Stella Corderoy[12] describes some of the hazards involved. Once, when Buchman's usual secretary was away, she went to take dictation from him for the first time: 'He was marching about the room, talking to half a dozen people. He suddenly said, "My, you have started with a team." I waited. "My, you have started with a team," he repeated – and someone whispered, "That's the letter." It was to a Dutch couple who had just had twins. I started in, but I had to guess when he was talking to someone else and when he was dictating.

'On one occasion when he was off to America,' she continues, 'Grace Hay had taken dictation till the last moment in London and on the boat train, I was to take it on the boat, and Enid Mansfield was to type all the way to Cherbourg and send the letters back from there to be posted. We had thirty minutes on the boat, saying goodbye to innumerable people, walking up and down the deck, going up and down in the lift and in his cabin. I think I took seventeen letters in the time, nearly half of them to children – wonderful letters. Then everyone had to go ashore, so I stood at the top of the gangway with Frank waiting for the sailors to lift it. There we got some more down.'

'One of the endearing things about him', Stella Corderoy adds, 'was the way he saw that everyone possible was in on the big events. He took all of us who worked with him at Brown's to the Command Performance in honour of the French President at Covent Garden. Somehow, he got most of us in to the musical evening at the Austrian Embassy when the Trapp Family Singers first sang outside Austria. And this did not stop as the team grew larger. He found several hundred tickets for his friends and guests to see the Coronation procession in 1937, and we all went each year to the Albert Hall carols. Frank looked after you and saw you had a good time.'

At the same time he did not find so constantly public a life easy. When once for a short period he rented a small house, he said, 'I feel like a child with a new toy.' And during house-parties held in large hotels, he would at times choose to eat at a small table by himself.

Arthur Strong, a young and successful professional photographer, spent a weekend with him and his secretary, Michael Barrett, in the English Lake District in the late 1930s, partly with the aim of finding and photographing the chapel in Keswick where Buchman had had his decisive experience in 1909. Buchman was now aged 60. 'Frank's gaiety is immense and he chips Mike like a schoolboy,' Strong recorded in his diary. 'We had constant laughter. . . . In the car going there FB sang and whistled, he was so happy not to have any plans and engagements for two whole days. He sang old hymns and it was then that I realised his age. To Keswick. . . . Then the chapel. There were several possibilities . . . Frank warned us it was an ordinary place with nothing particular to distinguish it. Found the Tithebarn Methodist (Primitive) Church; opposite it is a bus depot.

'He sat where he had done thirty years before; then read the *News Chronicle* – he'd already read six other papers that day . . . Back at the hotel we changed for tennis and I played Frank. His energy is amazing; he serves well and has a good eye. He ran too.'

Strong was impressed by the vigour with which Buchman played, but as he had taken part in Junior Wimbledon that year, 'gave Frank pat-ball' at the beginning to try to make the game more even. Buchman strode to the net: 'You're not going full-out, Arthur! That's not fellowship!'

Strong had first worked with Buchman the previous year, taking time off from his flourishing business to help with a picture magazine Buchman was planning. At the Oxford house-party that year he had felt the need to make some spiritual sacrifice, and said in a meeting that he thought he should sell his cameras. After the meeting Buchman sent for him.

'I hear you feel you should sell your cameras,' he said. 'How much are they worth?'

'About £150,' replied Strong.

'Hand me my coat,' said Buchman, who then took out his wallet and handed over £150, almost all the money he had. Then he said, 'Now, Arthur, you can look after my cameras until I need them.' So Strong took the cameras and money, and used both for a photographing trip he had long wanted to make. A year later, he gave up his business and came to work full-time with Buchman.

At Whitsun 1935 Buchman's secretary, Joyce Machin, died suddenly of a tumour of the brain. Michael Barrett and another young Scot, Lawson Wood, volunteered to take on her duties. Barrett was the son of an Edinburgh printer and had been in the Oxford ju-jitsu team. Wood had read law at Aberdeen. Both were around 25, and each had an ample supply of Scots determination and pride. They learnt typing and speed-writing and set to work.

Barrett, who married one of Lloyd George's grand-daughters, re-marked recently that he much preferred A. J. Sylvester's to the other lives of Lloyd George 'because it showed how impossible it was to be his secretary'. 'Like Buchman,' he added with a smile.

For one thing, he explained, Buchman often seemed astonished if letters he dictated were not perfectly typed and ready for the post the moment they had left his mouth, besides expecting you to know to whom he was writing without being told. Once they were in Egypt together and, while they showed their travelling companions the citadel above Cairo, Buchman remarked, 'We must write So-and-so.' Directly they got into the taxi to return to Cairo, Buchman began dictating, and continued, without let-up, through a series of tunnels in complete darkness. 'I got most of it, and remembered or made up the rest,' said Barrett.

'Moving from one country to another, which was frequent, was always an all-night job,' Barrett recalls. 'Sometimes I would stop at two or three, while Lawson, who was tougher, went on another hour. Then we'd be up at five-thirty, to greet Buchman as he woke. He would survey matters, note a scarf we had missed, and remark, "It's wonderful how everything gets done." Then he'd wink. Of course, he was furious if either of us fell ill through over-work or pride.'

Lawson Wood loved driving long distances. In August 1937 he drove well over 600 miles – from London via Oxford and Glasgow to Acharacle on the West Coast of Scotland – to deliver a guest to Buchman, who was staying there. He arrived in time for breakfast and insisted he would drive on another 175 miles, without a break, to join his family in Aberdeen. Everyone tried to stop him; for he was obviously too tired to drive, though too stubborn to stop. Finally Buchman led him to the room which had been set aside for him and pointed to a card on the door with his name on it. 'You can't waste all that ink,' he said. Wood began to laugh, and stayed.

A year later, however, Wood relates, 'I was desperately ill at Partenkirchen in 1938, because I had driven on wilfully across Europe through ice and snow, leaning out through an open window because the windscreen was frozen over. So I deprived Frank of help he urgently needed. It was Christmas time and as I lay, unable to lift my head from the pillow, an exquisite Christmas tree was brought to my room, decked with white candles, each studded with little red hearts. Then the door opened a few inches and Frank's long nose and twinkling eye-glasses came round the edge. "Do you see all those candles? That is just to show how much we love you," he said.

'Later, when I was recovering but still in bed, Frank came to see me with Frankie Bygott. I received a royal wigging for my sins and particularly this one. Then Frank turned to Bygott and said, "Do you ever talk to him like that? If not, you ought to."'

On another occasion Wood experienced Buchman's tenacious attention when, leaving Germany during the Nazi years, he forgot to pack Buchman's precious address book, and left it in the hotel at Garmisch-Partenkirchen. 'I asked a friend to post it on to New York,' Wood remembers. 'Then I told Frank. He was furious. He knew that there was at least one Nazi agent on the staff. "Don't you realise, they'll photograph all our addresses and know who we are in touch with?" he roared. For three months he rubbed my mistake in to make sure I had learnt from it.'

Barrett has never forgotten a journey around the Middle East with Buchman and a party of fifteen, who included an East London leader of the unemployed and two sisters of over eighty, Lady Antrim and Lady Minto, the latter a former Vicereine of India. Barrett was detailed to get the ladies to cut down the quantity of their bags as some of the journey was to be by air – something neither had previously experienced. He managed to reduce the number from twenty-seven to eighteen. Then he impressed on Lady Minto the need to be ready to be picked up in time to catch the boat train. 'Catch?' was the reply. 'I am accustomed to trains waiting for me!'

The journey continued through Europe and the Balkans to Cairo, while it became ever clearer to Barrett that, apart from Buchman who was otherwise engaged, he seemed the one practical person in the party. The handling of luggage, tickets and hotels, as well as Buchman's typing, all fell on him. Finally, in Cairo, Buchman found him in tears, an unprecedented event for a Scot like Barrett. Buchman did not apologise, though he was sympathetic and tried to mobilise help for him. 'But he had expected me to enlist it myself,' says Barrett.

When asked why he went on when the demands were often so unreasonable, Barrett replied, 'Buchman had such infinite expectations of you. It is a kind of compliment when someone inspires you to do more than you can possibly do. You felt his will was really given to God and he expected yours to be, so you did what was necessary without a murmur. Besides, you knew he was doing as much or more himself.' 'Of course,' Barrett added, 'there were occasions when I should have said, "Look, Frank, this is ridiculous!"'

A principal reason why people like Barrett stayed with Buchman year after year was because they believed he was, in a very real sense, in touch with God. 'When you went in to see him in the early morning, the room sometimes seemed electric with the amount of thought he had been putting in,' Barrett says. Some trained observers, coming to him fresh, noticed this quality, and concluded that he was a mystic. Harold Begbie, one of the shrewdest political journalists of his day, commented, 'Fuller acquaintance with F.B. brings to one's mind the knowledge that, in spite of his boyish cheerfulness, he is of the house and lineage of all true mystics from Plotinus to Tolstoy.'[13] Van Dusen, in his critical essay written some years after leaving Buchman's work, remarked on his 'vivid mysticism'.[14] 'It is impossible to understand Frank at all unless he is thought of as always in God's presence, listening for direction and accepting power,' wrote A. J. Russell.[15]

Herbert Grevenius, the Swedish literary critic, came to the same conclusion. Grevenius had written of Buchman, before meeting him, as a 'pocket Caesar issuing his dictates from afar with self-assured power and perfection'. After watching him for some days at an assembly in Sweden, he wrote, 'Well, I never knew Caesar, but I don't think he was in the least like Frank Buchman. It is not his lightning smile that forms his secret. His epigrammatical sayings, his briskness, his ability to hold a meeting in his hand and yet disappear into the background – none of these really tells you anything about the real Buchman. Look closely at a photograph of him, and you will see something in his expression, a sort of listening apart, and for once the camera does not lie. Sit a few days and study his face. You will be amazed how often he appears to be questing, at a loss, not to say helpless. And he does not try to conceal it. His enormously active life is built on one thing only – guidance for which he is on the watch every moment. He is a sail always held to be filled by the wind.'[16]

Buchman never spoke of himself as a mystic, although it seemed obvious to those who saw much of him that he often – even unconsciously – gained pre-knowledge of events and unusual insight into people's characters in his times of listening. He never used big words about himself or his experiences, mainly perhaps because he was so convinced that anyone who was willing to put it to the test could find the same relationship with God as he had. He expressed his relationship with God in terms which anyone could understand, by reducing it to a matter of Speaker and listener. He tried, again and again, to present it in metaphors which were in tune with the age as it developed. Thus, early on, he referred to Edison inventing the light bulb and bringing illumination into every home. Later he used the metaphors of the telephone, of wireless or of the 'electronics of the Spirit'. Yet his claim, for every willing listener, was constant – that 'adequate, accurate information can come from the mind of God to the mind of man. That is normal prayer.' 'Waiting and watching for the Living God to break through the shadows of the night,' he said, 'I came to know the Holy Spirit as the light, guide, teacher and power. What I am able to do, I do through the power that comes in the early hours of morning quiet.'

It was easy for the intellectual to think him over-simple; but behind his words was a hidden depth of experience which the Oxford theologian, B. H. Streeter, for instance, recognised. Streeter once remarked, 'You have got to make Christianity so simple that even an intellectual can understand it.' In a copy of his rewritten Warburton Lectures, *The God Who Speaks*,[17] he wrote: 'To Frank Buchman – apart from you, much herein would be written otherwise.'

Buchman attributed his insight into people to this listening relationship with God. 'I once prayed to be super-sensitive to people, and I often wish I had not. It can be so painful,' he once remarked. Fortunately, he prayed at the same time for an enhanced sense of humour. If his insight became biased by his own personality at this period, it was most often on the side of generosity and vision. 'He understood there are cart-horses and race-horses, and that you must not treat cart-horses like race-horses or vice versa,' says Thornhill. 'He had immense appreciation – realistic diagnosis, but also great vision for people, a great belief in what under God they could do.'

Buchman, in becoming sensitive to others, had not escaped being sensitive about himself. He was far more easily hurt than people realised. He once engaged a housekeeper to help with the domestic side of his life, but she found the comings and goings impossible to understand or to cope with, and left without talking with Buchman personally. He was deeply hurt by this apparent slight. 'Spiritual brush-offs he expected,' said a friend, 'but this was different.'

Once in Newcastle, when we were there together, there was a column report of his work in the newspaper. It was broadly favourable, but contained a critical description of him. 'What do you think of it?' he asked me.

'Pretty good,' I answered.

'Even with what they said about me?' he replied.

On another occasion in the 1930s he asked me what I thought of a speech he had delivered. 'Not one of your best,' I replied. He said nothing at the time. Twenty years later, when some of us were with him, a friend came in and said how delighted a South American labour leader had been when he read that particular speech earlier in the day. 'And Garth said it was no use,' said Buchman.

He undoubtedly found it difficult to take criticism. But it was by no means always rejected. Particularly during the early and mid 1930s, when I saw most of him, he gave me considerable latitude. In Copenhagen he humbly accepted my juvenile views on how he could have done better with a newspaper proprietor – someone, I later discovered, he had known for years. He waited several years before he told me I was 'cocky'. Then he moved in massively and kept up the treatment for some time. His reaction to people was generally conditioned not by their words or even their actions, but by what he felt they needed at the time – or what he sensed they could take, a sound Pauline principle. If he felt they were trying to be led by the Holy Spirit, he would listen with attention; but if he sensed they were determined to make an impression or were motivated by pride, jealousy, ambition or fear, he would say so in the frankest way.

Buchman occasionally had black, despairing days. Lawson Wood has said that on one occasion when a promising situation fell apart because of unjust criticism, he turned his face to the wall and groaned, 'Will these

[172]

people never understand me?' I was part cause of one of these despairing periods in late December 1937. I had gone to the United States to help to produce an American edition of a one-shot magazine called *Rising Tide*, which originated in Britain and was now being brought out in several countries.* Buchman had worked long and lovingly on every line of text, every picture and every lay-out. On arrival I found my American friends had not only inserted certain local pages, as it was agreed they should do, but were making a number of other changes which they felt would make the magazine go better in America. In particular, the original cover – a dramatic picture of young men marching with banners – was eliminated and in its place a picture of a packed mass of smiling young people had been substituted. I acquiesced in this decision, and was proud that the paper created a mild sensation in the New York publishing world – the magazine *Life* reproduced six pages from it and privately offered jobs to some of those working on it – and that a large part of its three-quarter-million printing was sold on the bookstalls.

Buchman hated the changes. He felt that the new cover made the magazine look like a youth publication instead of a paper intending to challenge both Hitler and the leaders of the democracies at the same time. Just before Christmas my American colleagues and I received cables from him. Mine read: 'Keen disappointment failure judgement lack control guiding policy *Rising Tide*, making perfect instrument garish, wasting priceless opportunity secondary substitute. Once bitten twice shy. Guidance was "overreaching". Today's evidence floored me. Glad not present in America. Would be difficult. No excuse. You had perfect instrument. Frank.'[18]

Buchman, I heard later, shut himself up in his room for some days, would not eat and took no interest in the coming Christmas, for which he normally prepared with the greatest care and generosity. Finally, Barrett decided that he must try to lift the gloom. He went to Buchman's room, knelt down and prayed, 'Dear Father, please give Frank a glorious Christmas.' This broke the spell.

'Why am I letting that paper spoil everything?' Buchman said. He got up and hurried out to get a Christmas tree and presents for those with him.

The cable did me no harm, though I see I wrote Buchman that it had 'stunned' me on its arrival. Buchman wrote shortly afterwards, 'Forget the past,' and he never mentioned the matter to me again.

It is true that, in matters artistic in which he had been concerned, Buchman was both sensitive and rigid at the same time. He was an artist and felt he knew what was right. He did not encourage adaptations in the

* It was printed in nine languages and 1,630,000 copies in Europe and America during 1937–8.

style or covers of books in different countries, for example. This may have suppressed local talent from time to time, or even affected sales.

Tournier's diagnosis of this facet of Buchman's character was, 'He never drew people to himself, but he was authoritarian.' Cuthbert Bardsley, a close colleague for some time and one of several who later became bishops, remarked, 'His word went, woe betide you if you crossed swords with him. On the other hand, he kept the Oxford Group together – not an easy thing with such a widely divergent group of people. He had to keep discipline and if you do that you have to exert some pretty heavy authority.' Paul Hodder-Williams' view, on a shorter active acquaintance, was, 'He held together a team of very different people on a very loose rein.'

John Wesley, who was known as 'Pope John' by his foes and not a few of his friends, once said, 'Several gentlemen are much offended at my having so much power. My answer to them is this: I did not seek any part of that power. It came upon me unawares. But when it came, not daring to bury that talent, I used it to the best of my judgement. Yet I was never fond of it. I always did, and do now, bear it as my burden; the burden which God lays upon me; but if you can tell me anyone, or any five men, to whom I may transfer this burden, who can and will do just what I do now, I will heartily thank both them and you.'*

He added, 'To me the preachers have engaged themselves to submit to serve as sons of the Gospel . . . Every preacher and every member may leave me when he pleases; but when he chooses to stay, it is on the same terms that he joined me at first.'[19]

With Buchman the freedom to leave was even more open to all because there was in no case any formal binding to him. If, however, anyone asked to work with him full-time and continued to do so for a considerable period, he did assume that they would work in with the strategy which he felt God had indicated to him and help to fulfil the needs of that strategy. He would suggest, ask or even command people to do this or that or go here or there. If they felt guided by God to do something different, he expected them to say so – and, generally, he would listen and reconsider. As he became older, with numbers growing and health providing other impediments, exceptions to this openness became more frequent. But in the 1930s, and on most occasions throughout his life, the basis of action was the guidance of God as sought by the individual and in groups. 'Guidance,' wrote a Danish advocate, 'meant that this manifold, intelligent fellowship functioned as one force without dictatorship or any compulsion of money or power.'[20]

Buchman's view of the matter was expressed to Alexander Smith, then

---

* Once when the Labour Cabinet Minister, Herbert Morrison, questioned Buchman on his leadership, Buchman made him the same offer.

Executive Secretary of Princeton University: 'I will accept people at any point at which they are willing to arrive, and not urge them to do anything they are not led to do. If I lived on any other basis, or had any other approach, I should be surrounded by a group of parasites rather than people who are taught to rely upon God and let Him direct them individually.'[21]

THE CLOTH AND THE CAP

Ever since the South African bishops and clergy had responded so warmly, Buchman's hope was that the Anglican Church as a whole would rise in a new way to answer the spiritual and moral needs in Britain and further afield. 'God is working through the Groups in a distinctive way to bridge the divergence between the life of the ordinary folk and of the Church,' he had noted enthusiastically as he sailed from Cape Town. While they were in London for the 1930 Lambeth Conference, Bishops Carey, Karney and others bore witness to what had happened in South Africa. Buchman's thought for that conference was equally full-blooded: 'A whole new orientation for Lambeth. An international awakening. A great national advance among the clergy so that England is aflame for vital Christianity.'

As the thirties progressed, the English bishops became aware of the effect of Buchman's work on individuals. They neither wished nor were able to ignore it, but they felt a duty to examine it carefully. The Bishop of London, Dr Winnington-Ingram, for example, asked Sir Lynden Macassey, K.C., an eminent lawyer, who had chaired many government commissions, to investigate the Group privately for him. 'I did so, and I did it thoroughly,' wrote Sir Lynden later. 'My investigation showed there was no foundation in fact for the allegations so often made against Dr Buchman and his work. The Bishop was entirely satisfied. He became a strong supporter of the Group and acclaimed its Christian work to the end of his episcopate.'[1]

The Archbishop of Canterbury, Dr Cosmo Gordon Lang, made even more extensive enquiries. Reading the dozens of reports and letters to him, one is surprised how few of them mention Buchman himself: they usually comment upon the people he has affected or the 'Groups' at large. Bishop James Perry, the Presiding Bishop of the American Episcopal Church, perhaps supplied the explanation when he wrote to Lang that 'Buchman is active in the background providing the mechanics and the direction', but that 'the place of conspicuous leadership . . . is taken now by Clergymen of the Church and laymen of our own and other Congregations.'[2]

Lang had written Perry a 'private and confidential enquiry' because he had 'had recently a great deal of very confidential information about Buchman himself which, I must frankly acknowledge, fills me with considerable disquiet'.[3] Making clear that he had 'the greatest sympathy' for the movement, Lang asked whether Perry had 'any grounds for hesitation as to Buchman's own personality and influence'.

Bishop Perry replied at length saying he had 'made your inquiry the subject of careful thought and of conversation with many who know the Groups intimately, though with very different points of view'. He himself had 'been in close touch with them' for five years, his first contact being 'through a few men and women of Rhode Island, people of intelligence and good standing, who had impressed me by the moral and spiritual change, in some cases complete conversion, which unquestionably they owed to Buchman and his followers'. He had watched the movement carefully and had attended meetings in various parts of America, in Oxford and Cambridge.

Of Buchman himself Bishop Perry wrote, 'I have not heard from even his severest critics, and they are many and outspoken, a breath of suspicion touching his character. I know him personally and I believe that I know his points of strength and weakness. He has a veritable passion for exerting influence upon men and women of social standing, and a genius for accomplishing this purpose. He indulges himself in a sense of moral and spiritual superiority and his followers are imbued with the same "complex". He cannot easily conceive of salvation outside the system that he confessedly has devised, but I believe him to be sincere in his conviction, and in his personal life above reproach.'[4]*

In general, Dr Lang relied upon regular reports from men like Professor Grensted; his own secretary, the Revd A. C. Don (later Dean of Westminster); and Lord Salisbury. Many other letters flowed in. The Revd 'Tubby' Clayton, the founder of Toc H, wrote, with several enclosures, complaining that Buchman had suggested that two men, for whom he himself had plans, should spend six months with the Oxford Group in America to 'learn evangelism'.[5] Canon Arnold Mayhew weighed in with a balanced report, ending with questions less explicitly raised by other Church leaders: 'Will the movement become one more sect – the Salvation Army of the Middle Classes? God forbid! And yet how are we to make use of it? To direct all this energy and enthusiasm into revitalising the Church, which needs it so much. Can any of the new wine be put into our old bottles without a general bust-up?'[6]

---

* Bishop Manning, Perry's successor as Presiding Bishop, gave the opening address at a crowded Oxford Group meeting in the Waldorf Astoria Ballroom, New York, on 15 March 1934.

A large number of letters were full of gratitude. The Bishop of Dover wrote, after attending the Oxford house-party of 1932, 'It is difficult to write dispassionately about something which has been so great a help to one personally.'[7] Prebendary E. C. Rich of St Paul's added, 'Although I went to Oxford frankly out of curiosity to investigate the movement at first hand, within twenty-four hours my whole outlook on life and religion was changed and now I long to share my experience.'[8]

A frequent subject for mention was the fresh reality – and sometimes the cocksureness – of Buchman's young colleagues. This is hardly surprising, for when Buchman was invited by people like Lord William Cecil, the Bishop of Exeter, to meet their friends over a weekend, he took new recruits with him, and tended to get them to do the speaking rather than doing it himself. Sometimes these young people expressed themselves in highly informal ways. Kit Prescott recalled such an occasion:

'I had been "changed" a few months, and had arranged for the local Anglican canon to invite Frank Buchman to speak to some two hundred clergy and the Bishop at a monthly diocesan meeting. After a very formal introduction, Frank was invited to "give an address". He responded by asking me to speak first. At that time part of my message was that I had given my life to God in spite of my cordial dislike of clergymen and that I infinitely preferred the bar parlour to the church pew which, I maintained, smelled of dust. So this I delivered with all the conviction at my command. There was dead silence except that Frank leant back and roared with laughter. After I had occupied most of his time, he then explained why he had asked me to speak first. He believed, he said, that good fishermen would always prefer fresh fish for breakfast. The meeting went on twice as long as usual and the clergy would hardly let us leave.'

Buchman himself was often equally outspoken. On one occasion the editor of the *Church of England Newspaper*, Herbert Upward, got together twelve of the most critical of his clerical readers to meet him. After posing various theological questions, which Buchman answered, one of them upbraided Buchman for talking openly in men's meetings about masturbation. Buchman thought for a moment and then, since the meeting was confidential, asked for a show of hands from any present who were troubled by that problem personally. First one, then two, then eleven hands went up. The meeting turned into a spiritual clinic among fellow sinners. Upward himself said afterwards to Buchman, 'I am with you for life,' and once when another churchman expressed fears about 'the dangers' inherent in Buchman's work, replied, 'Personally, I would rather face whatever risks there may be than be content with the numbing self-complacency existing in the Churches, or at any rate, in the Church of England today.'[9]

The bishops in general seemed inclined to take the same view. At the meeting of Diocesan Bishops of England and Wales in January 1932 Archbishop Lang, 'in summing up' a discussion of the Oxford Group, 'said that there is a gift here of which the Church is manifestly in need',[10] and two years later a further 'informal conference' presided over by Archbishop William Temple of York 'thankfully recognised that various movements, and notably the Oxford Groups, are being used to demonstrate the power of God to change lives and give to personal witness its place in true discipleship'.[11]

Buchman believed in the incalculable impact of people with a fresh experience of God, who expected to change further each day and to pass on their experience to others. He was confirmed in this by his friend Archbishop Söderblom of Uppsala, Sweden, one of the first ecumenists, who wrote that he feared the ecumenical movement was being choked by 'human arrangements . . . in thoughts and plans'. 'There must be, as you write, and as you act, a deeper unity,' he wrote Buchman. '. . . We need that individual renewal and that deepening of our Christian unity to an utmost degree.'[12] In a message written shortly before his death, he added, 'You are concerned with the only thing that matters in religion and life – Christ's absolute ruling in our hearts and words and deeds. A changed life is more eloquent than lots of sermons.'[13]

'No one can guess which way the live cat on the hearthrug will jump,' Buchman used to say. 'No one expects anything of the china cat on the mantelpiece.' He thought no one – himself included – exempt from this need for further change and inspiration. He responded with sympathy to the cleric who told him, 'I have become like a physician who hands out flowers and good cheer to his patients, but never cures anybody,' because he had known the same condition in himself.

He took no one, however eminent, for granted. Thus when Dr Foss Westcott, the Metropolitan of India, Burma and Ceylon, was coming to the 1933 Oxford house-party, he called a few undergraduates together. He did not let on that he had known the Metropolitan since the early 1920s, but asked them about him. Someone who had been in India told of the Metropolitan's saintly life, how he lived mainly in a kind of hut on the roof of his palace, did not smoke or drink or indulge himself in any way, was one of the few Englishmen whom Gandhi trusted, and was famous for his sermons. 'Yes,' said Buchman, 'that's all true. But he cannot diagnose people.'

He then said, 'I want you to see a lot of him. Tell him how you found your way from agnosticism to faith, how you are fishing for men, how you are learning to bring cure to drunks and straighten out an intellectual's living – and thinking. You might even mention that if one is not winning people for Christ, one is sinning somewhere along the line.'

In the next weeks the undergraduates spent much time with the

Metropolitan. He enjoyed their company and played a good game of tennis, but did not altogether like the idea that if one was not winning, one was sinning. After three days he made a speech about how 'the wheels of God grind slowly', how 'some sow and others reap' and how you never could know what effect you were having on people: all of which had truth in it. But Buchman said to the undergraduates, 'Be true friends to him. Carry on.' He also said, 'I had an hour yesterday when I was very much shaken and needed help. So I went to the Metropolitan, and he helped me. I am very grateful he was there and I could go to him.'

On the eighth day the Metropolitan spoke again. 'I've been like a fisherman who came home in the evening and said, "I did not catch any fish, but I influenced a good many."' He told how his own shyness and other people's flattery had diminished his effectiveness. 'There are always five or six dear old ladies to tell me how well I have preached,' he said. Now he wanted to learn more about how to win individuals for Christ. He had been brought up in a Christian home – his father was Bishop Brooke Foss Westcott of Durham – and had been through the finest theological colleges, but no one before had raised with him the subject of diagnosing and, by God's grace, curing people individually.

Before returning to India the Metropolitan stated to the press: 'For myself, these have been weeks of challenge. I have been twenty-eight years a Bishop of the Church of God, and have kept before me the promises made at the time of my consecration, but it was at the House Party of the Oxford Group Movement (sic) at Oxford last July that I realised that one might faithfully endeavour to carry out these promises and yet fail in that which is a fundamental duty, namely to be a life-changer.'[14]

Back in India he wrote to some of the Oxford undergraduates that, whereas on his many previous voyages he had never had a deep personal talk with anyone, this time nineteen people had talked with him and fourteen, including the kind of people he would never have approached before, had given their lives to Christ. Even before he had left Oxford he had found a new understanding with George West, just appointed Bishop of Rangoon, who had come to him admitting he had always been afraid of him: something of which Westcott had been wholly unaware.

It was this kind of contagious change which, Buchman believed, would revitalise the Church. He felt that many in the Church were determined to keep things as they were. This 'religious trust', as he called it, often caused him to feel frustrated. Thus a popular Methodist preacher who, returning from an Oxford house-party, astonished his invariably crowded congregation by telling them he felt a failure. He spoke of the impact on him personally of Christ's standards of absolute honesty, purity, unselfishness and love, and continued, 'You come here each week and always praise my sermons. But we're just like whited sepulchres. None of you change and nor do I.' He said he saw in the congregation people who had also been at the house-party and suggested that anyone who wished could wait afterwards and hear their experiences there. More than 200 did so. For three weeks such groups met after each evening service, and many found a new or deeper commitment there. Then some church officials closed in and spoke of ultimatums. The preacher disbanded the groups rather than divide the church.

A subtler and more pitiable clash of loyalties was voiced to Buchman by a clergyman's wife: 'I know without a shadow of doubt that I have found God through contact with your wonderful fellowship and that I have got a message which I long to pass on. You will be the first to understand that I don't find things very easy with regard to my husband. He is *in no way* hostile to the Group, but I *always* have the feeling he wishes I could have found God and happiness through the Church, and that it must always be the *Church* for him. I love the Church too, where one finds reality and simplicity as one finds it in the Group movement, but it is so *rare*. I do care most desperately how the Church as a whole faces up to the challenge of the Group movement.' Later, her husband was to show his active sympathy when the Oxford Group was attacked.

There is no doubt that Buchman was often impatient with organised religion. He felt that the Church was increasingly out of touch with the gathering dangers. 'No one is more jealous for the Church than I,' he once said. 'But loyalty to the Church demands that we see the Church as she really is, and the Church, as she is today, is not going to change the nation. If the Church crowds are not remade, some dictator will remake them. Communism and Fascism have created the greatest crisis in the history of the Church since the catacombs. What does this entail? A whole new orientation – go out into the streets, the byways and hedges. Not our conception of the Church, but the answer that the world needs. This means the fur will fly, but I am ready to go through with it!'

Such opinions were bound to provoke reactions. In March 1933 the Bishop of Durham, Dr Hensley Henson, devoted a Charge to his diocese to what Owen Chadwick, his biographer, describes as 'a sustained indictment of the Oxford Group'.[15] It was, in effect, an enquiry into whether 'the Group could be domesticated' within the Church of England, and his answer was an emphatic 'No'.[16]

After a scholarly survey of the emergence of sects through the centuries, from which he concluded that the Oxford Group must inevitably become a sect, Henson examined 'Group principles' as he conceived them. Chadwick summarises his attitude as, 'Here was the confessional, exposed to its worst risks and stripped of its protective discipline; here were adolescents acting as father-confessors, the blind leading the blind;

here was the fascination of prurience as well as a moral ideal; here was an idea of guidance as immediate inspiration, taking the place of reasonable discussion and sensible judgement; here was a movement which seemed to have little place for the poor but went for Oxford undergraduates and political leaders and capitalists, its work done in hotels and centres of fashion; here was a movement claiming to be above denominations but like all such movements turning already into another denomination.'[17]

The Bishop, however, had never accepted any invitation to attend any Group house-party, meeting or occasion, or to meet people closely associated with it. He declared he was not 'temperamentally fitted' for such an ordeal, and had an 'almost physical repugnance'[18] against the kind of movement he conceived the Group to be. Chadwick comments: 'He (Henson) was not well fitted for the impartial critique which would have helped, because his inner revulsion from any such movement ran too deep.'[19] His reasons for writing the Charge were, according to Chadwick, his duty to his diocese, his love of Oxford (whose name he considered Buchman to have stolen) and, 'far more emotionally', that 'one of the young men for whom he cared much . . . and thought to be the most promising of *his* ordinands, became a disciple of Dr Buchman' and 'went off to Canada' with him.[20]

The first edition of Henson's Charge made little impact, but he returned to his theme to more effect in the autumn and winter. During the summer a number of prominent Londoners had urged that an Oxford Group campaign should take place in London. The Bishop of London had invited Buchman and his team to be commissioned in St Paul's Cathedral, and the Archbishop of Canterbury had received them at Lambeth Palace. Henson thereupon summarised his objections in a letter to *The Times* on 19 September, and brought out a second edition of his Charge, with a new preface, in December.

After his letter the bishops, according to press summaries of their diocesan conferences, were divided. The Bishops of St Edmundsbury and Ipswich[21] and of Southwark[22] appear to have been more critical than laudatory, while those of Manchester, Oxford and Rochester,[23] although offering advice and caution, had no doubt that the Oxford Group was changing people's lives and making religion more real to many. A typical contribution came from Dr Hewlett Johnson of Canterbury, soon to be christened 'the Red Dean'. While stating that 'the "house-parties" idea smacks of snobbishness' and saying 'the doctrine of guidance gets dangerously near to magic', he continued, 'What, however, outweighs these tendencies – and they can be avoided – is that careless, selfish and even vicious lives, especially among young men and women, are being changed and consecrated to God. There is a new orientation Godward . . .'[24]

One of the points Bishop Henson, too, raised in his letter was that Buchman concerned himself with the upper and middle classes, the 'up and outs', rather than, as was traditional in evangelistic movements, with the 'down and outs'. Prebendary Wilson Carlile, the current Honorary Chief Secretary of the Church Army, was one of those who replied. 'Many of us have tried to deal with the outcast and the criminal,' he wrote, 'but the Groups have aimed at changing the lives of the lazy and dangerous intelligentsia. I admire their pluck. Let us help them all we can.'[25]

In his new preface the Bishop rested his case largely upon the evidence of Martin Kiddle, a young Oxford man who had travelled for five months with Buchman's team in North America and returned to Britain, leaving a letter of profuse thanks. 'I am looking forward to seeing the Bishop of Liverpool and my friends at Oxford, to tell them of the tremendous achievements of the past months,' he had written Buchman. 'Again many thanks for all your training and fellowship. My work in England will not only be richer but radically different as a result of this experience.'[26] He then went to stay with Henson and apparently supplied 'facts' which the Bishop, owing to his policy of avoiding contact with the Oxford Group, was unable to check. In August Kiddle wrote to a mutual friend asking her to tell Buchman that 'unfortunately many misguided people are using my name in their attacks on the Group in a dishonest way. They have attributed to me things I have never said . . . Please tell him that I shall always keep a very warm affection for him.'[27] Yet in September he wrote to *The Times*, 'I have no hesitation in supporting every statement and criticism made by the Bishop of Durham.'[28] Nine years later Kiddle, who had been ordained, was to become a tragic figure, convicted at Bow Street on a morals charge and found dead shortly afterwards from unexplained causes.[29] Though he was frequently quoted by name in Henson's preface, he was omitted from the Bishop's memoirs which were published in the year in which he was convicted.

During the early 1930s the Church of England made at least two official suggestions of closer co-operation. The first proposal was transmitted to Buchman and Loudon Hamilton by Dr Cyril Bardsley, Bishop of Leicester and Chairman of the Archbishop's Committee on Evangelism. Bardsley had attended several house-parties and had written that his 'chief impression was the utter sincerity and humility of the Group's leaders'.[30]

Buchman and Hamilton travelled to Leicester to hear the proposal. 'The idea', noted Hamilton, 'was that the Oxford Group should be recognised officially as a sort of Provisional Wing of the Church of England, recognised and organised accordingly, with Dr Bardsley as Chairman. Dr Bardsley seemed to me as if he did not relish the part he was chosen to play, but loyally expounded the proposal, ending with the suggestion of himself assuming the chairmanship.' There is some doubt whether Bardsley in fact proposed himself or Buchman for that office, as Buchman asserted the latter in a letter to a friend. To whichever proposal it was, Buchman replied, 'Hitherto there has been no chairman except the Holy Spirit,' and he and Hamilton left by the next train for London.

The second suggestion was made by the Bishop of Salisbury and was talked out in January 1935 at Lambeth, in the presence of three other Bishops. The Ecclesiastical Commission had bought Milton Abbey in Dorset, together with its large house and ample grounds. They now offered it, in the words of the Bishop of Salisbury, to be 'a training centre run by the Oxford Group under the aegis of the Church of England'. 'For my own part', he wrote enthusiastically, 'I confess I am fired with the possibility of grounding all that is good in the Group movement in the soil of the Catholic faith and tradition. It is certainly what the Church wants, and I believe would be for the strength and development of the Movement.'[31] The upkeep, which would fall on the Oxford Group, would be about £2,000 a year.

The Bishops' first approach had been made to a number of Church of England clergy and laymen, and took place in early December. The letter quoted above was sent to Kenaston Twitchell in London, as Buchman was in Norway. Those first approached were enthusiastic about Church sponsorship, but Twitchell, noting that it would take twenty mature people to supply adequate leadership, was more cautious. 'It was offered to us free with the understanding that we would take care of the upkeep,' he wrote Buchman. 'It was pointed out that the Group is not an organisation* and therefore could run no establishment as a Group. With this the Bishop, I understand, concurred, but said he hoped it might be possible for us to supply individuals as leaders and make the place a Group centre as a private house.'[32]

Buchman seems to have left the decision to those in Britain, and by the time of the January meeting at Lambeth, all were agreed that the Group was not then able to take on so large an establishment and, more importantly, that its mission was to a wider audience than could be reached through any one Church. Garrett Stearly remembers Buchman saying to him, 'We cannot afford to become the property of any one group.'

One line of the Bishop of Durham's attack which found many sympathetic ears was his reference to what he considered Buchman's 'assuming' the name 'Oxford' – something which he said had done 'yeoman's duty in South Africa and America'. *The Times*, which had frequently used

---

* There was, at that time, no legal body representing the Oxford Group.

the name 'Oxford Group' in previous years and, indeed, used it in the headline over the Bishop's letter, thereafter dropped the prefix 'Oxford' and wrote an editorial underlining its decision. The issue roused strong feelings. Many Oxford men opposed Buchman on this issue in the belief that he had personally invented the name for publicity purposes and that, the Bishop of Durham's account being true, the use of the word 'Oxford' could bring ill-repute to the University. Others felt that he should have renounced the name when it spontaneously came into general usage. A lively correspondence, pro and con, was published in *The Times*.

This question arose on 31 October 1933 at high table at Oriel College, where both Buchman and the Master of University College, Sir Michael Sadler, were dining. Buchman explained how the name had come into being, and said that he himself had no desire for his name to be central in anything God had done through him, that many Oxford men felt the Oxford Group had brought them nearer their University's motto, *Dominus Illuminatio Mea*, than anything else had done, and that the Oxford undergraduate force was the largest in training anywhere.*

When the public controversy was at its height Buchman wrote to Sadler. '*The Times*', he wrote, '. . . imputes dishonest motives to us, and this vitiates the challenge to a new level of honesty in commercial life. You will remember that at dinner that night in Oxford you told us not to yield an inch on the point. . . .'[33]

Sadler's reply was both practical and prophetic: '. . . you and your friends were right in calling yourselves "The Oxford Group" because, at a critical time, your work here was of determinative importance to the future of the movement. The name is not copyright, and nobody can say Yea or Nay to your right of using it. I feel pragmatic about it. If there is anything essentially connected with Oxford in the movement, the name "The Oxford Group" will survive as representing one historical aspect in its growth. If, on the other hand, the Oxford connection is swallowed up in something bigger and more international, the name "Oxford Group" would be instinctively felt by writers all over the world to have become a misnomer. In the meantime I hope you will stick to it. As you know, I am thankful that Oxford has any share in this spiritual awakening.'[34]

Buchman would no more formally disown the name than he could formally have adopted it. He accepted it with its advantages and disadvantages. Whether he was wise to do so has been questioned even by friendly critics. Sir Arnold Lunn, for example, wrote that Buchman and his friends

* Martin reckoned that of the seven men visiting South Africa in 1928 six were from Oxford; of the twenty-one visiting Canada in 1933, thirteen; in 1934, eighteen out of twenty-seven; of 138 British who went to Denmark in 1935, seventy. In 1939, out of fifty-three men devoting their whole time in London, twenty-nine were graduates of the University. (Martin MSS.)

were 'bound to have enough trouble on their hands if they confined themselves to their legitimate objective, the campaign against sin, and it was a great mistake to risk a head-on collision not only with sin but also with Oxford'.[35] Certainly this first clash immediately affected the policy of *The Times* and other newspapers, and later became manifest in various government departments where Oxford men abounded.

The disadvantages, indeed, grew with the years. After 1933 the name 'Oxford' stood in the United States for something known there as the 'Oxford Oath' – a pledge adopted by students of many American universities following the example of the majority in the Oxford Union who had declared they would not fight 'for King and Country'. 'Oxford' from this moment stood for 'pacifist' in America, and the Oxford Group there was suspected of both pacifism and Communism. Nor was it a great advantage in countries where British rule was being challenged by nationalist and independence movements, and at one point even Mahatma Gandhi's friendship was strained by this. It finally became, as Sir Michael Sadler had foreseen, too narrow a term and was eventually to give way to 'Moral Re-Armament'.

The controversy over the name did nothing to diminish the interest aroused by the campaign in London during the winter of 1933–4. Seven thousand crowded into St Paul's Cathedral. The Archbishop of Canterbury, receiving the party at Lambeth Palace, pointed to the pictures of his predecessors and said that though many of them would possibly have shared the fears of certain writers to *The Times*, he for his part was convinced that the Oxford Group was called by God to London.*

The popular response was large and led to further invitations from various sections of the community. The Lord Mayor received a large group at the Mansion House. Sir Walter Windham, a veteran racing-car driver and airways pioneer, somewhat disconcerted the solemnity of the occasion by stepping forward and saying he thanked God for a man like Frank Buchman and did not mind what was said in *The Times* about him. He then called for 'Three cheers for Buchman', which were given with various degrees of enthusiasm by the embarrassed dignitaries. *The Times* reported all this without comment.[36]

The press were taking a great interest. Among the more sensational

---

* In August 1934 Dr Lang told his Diocesan Conference: 'The Oxford Group is most certainly doing what the Church of Christ exists everywhere to do. It is changing human lives, giving them a new joy and freedom, liberating them from faults of temper, of domestic relationships, and the like, which have beset them, and giving them a new ardour to communicate to their fellow creatures what God has given to them.' (*Church of England Newspaper*, 14 September 1934.)

items was a report of the preliminary house-party at Eastbourne, in which Buchman was quoted in a large headline as saying that 'God is a millionaire', the implication of the article being that Buchman was handsomely endowed.[37] Two weeks later he reported that, on verifying Buchman's financial position, he had found that this man was taking 200 people into London with only a few pounds in hand. 'There was no word of reproach about that previous article,' he concluded.[38] At about the same time Lord Southwood, the owner of the Labour paper the *Daily Herald*, rang Buchman and said tersely, 'I hear you're a class movement.' 'That's right,' replied Buchman. 'There are two classes – the changed and the unchanged.'

Invitations came from two other areas of London life. A Member of Parliament, Sir Francis Fremantle, suggested that a small group of MPs meet with Buchman and a few friends. Buchman had the thought, 'Take fifty with you.' This turned out to be wise. The *Evening Standard* reported the 'extraordinary curiosity' which 'emptied smoking rooms and the floor of the House alike. They collected so large an assembly that the first room chosen was packed out and they moved into a larger one.'[39] The chief speaker was a leading figure at the League of Nations, C. J. Hambro, President of the Norwegian Parliament. He gave a vivid outline of what he believed to be the Group's potential, and concluded by inviting Buchman to bring a team to Norway.*

The second invitation came from East London, from the Revd E. G. Legge, a vicar in Poplar, which he said was 'one of the largest and poorest parishes in England'. He described the response: 'On the closing day of 1933 a team of eighty-five people arrived. Nothing seemed to daunt them. They started a programme of visiting every house. As many as could found accommodation in some of the poorest homes in the parish, sharing fully in their life despite one of the worst periods of fog I have ever known in East London. They were to be found eating in odd coffee-houses, gathering around them groups of men eager to know more of their message. They gripped the people from the first meeting, the midnight service on 31 December. The numbers grew and grew. The people had lost heart. To them the Oxford Group brought a real hope.'[40] Buchman was in the pulpit at this midnight service, his sermon eliciting a high degree of good-humoured audience participation.

From Poplar they reached into East Ham and Hackney, and a team 144-strong, mainly from the universities, spent Easter there. Much of this work was pioneered and followed through by a student from Regent's Park College, Bill Jaeger, the only son of a widow with a tiny millinery shop in Stockport. Jaeger conceived a passion to reach the people of East

* For an account of Hambro's first connections with the Oxford Group, see pp. 216-17.

[187]

London. 'I was off there before the rest of the college were awake,' he recalls. 'Within eighteen months we had a team of 500 in the area.' When he left college in 1936 Buchman set him to work in East London full-time on 'faith and prayer', and his mother, Annie, sold her shop for £40 and went to work with him. He got to know some of the gangs who centred in the local 'caffs', and many civic leaders. Bill Rowell, who was to represent 250,000 London unemployed at the Trades Union Congress of 1936, was enlisted by one of Jaeger's team, the son of a peer, six foot four tall, who slept for much of a winter on two chairs in the Rowells' kitchen. 'I can't help thinking of the peace platforms I have spoken on, telling the nation how to live together, and yet going home to a continuous war in my own home,' Rowell wrote. 'After twelve years of married life, I suddenly discovered I'd got a new wife and family. I gave up being a dictator, and immediately new love sprang up between us.'[41]

It was sometimes risky work. Emerging from the house one morning, one of Jaeger's team saw a belligerent little group of men waiting for him. 'You rat! I've half a mind to break your jaw!' said one of them, seizing him by his lapels.

'My friend, if that is going to help you at all and make me less of a rat, go ahead and break it,' said the young man.

The jaw was not broken, and the group dispersed.

Buchman gave Jaeger his head. 'He never told me what to do, but he always wanted to know what I was doing,' Jaeger says. 'He wanted to know who I was seeing and what I'd said to them. Then he might throw in some insight, some word of advice. He would bring business men and titled folk, who had found new motives, down to help me, and I would take my friends up West.'

When, at the end of the London campaign in 1934, Buchman took a major team to America and Canada, the vicar from Poplar went with him. Another who went was George Light, a leader of the unemployed in Warwickshire. Light had come to the Oxford house-party in 1933 full of bitterness at his own unemployment and that of the men he represented. He described his meeting with Buchman there:

'I never met a man who had such faith, or such a genius for turning up at the right moment. One day I ran into him and he asked me to join him in his room. He asked me what I thought about the Oxford Group. I said something polite. Then he asked, "Do you know anything against us? We'd be glad to know."

'I had just been to a socialist conference and one woman had said, "I have just heard on good authority that someone has given Buchman £50,000 to carry on his work."

'I told Frank this and he said, "It is very queer, George. I have heard the same but you look at my bank book." He put it open into my hands. I think there was a balance of £9. "That is my whole bank balance," he said. Then we chatted of other things. "Where are you going now, George?" he said. I said I had a return ticket and a few shillings. Frank looked into his pockets and said, "I have £9 in cash besides what is in the bank. Here's £9. We both have the same amount. That makes us both socialists now."

'This was the second talk I ever had with Frank. He did not know me. I might have been a twister or anything. I went home and told my wife and family. That £9 was very useful, but it was not a fortune. Yet my family was so overjoyed at anyone taking such an interest in us that they just wept. Frank never postponed an act of unselfishness on his own part because a far greater one was needed on the part of society. What he did and what he fought for had in it elements of true revolutionary action.'[42]

On the final day of the London campaign, speaking in the Metropole Hotel in Northumberland Avenue, Buchman commented upon a newspaper's assertion that Oswald Mosley had 100,000 followers in his British Union of Fascists and that two million Britons were 'fascist-minded'. 'Have you got two million people in Britain who are Holy-Spirit-minded?' he challenged. 'You need what Gandhi says he misses in Christians – being "salted with the fire of the discipline".* I had some people to dinner last night,' he added. 'Some were pro-Hitler. Some anti-Hitler. I told them we were pro-change in everyone.'

Amid the welter of letters appearing in the press throughout that autumn was one from the distinguished missionary and ecumenist J. H. Oldham, who noted that a correspondent had suggested 'the Group movement is the expression in the religious sphere of the modern ideas and movements in the political field'. 'I wonder', wrote Oldham, 'whether what the Groups are reaching after, and in their measure discovering, is not something which is the complete antithesis of both Fascism and Communism. May it not be that they are rediscovering the truth that the meaning of life is found in the relations between persons? True community consists, not in the subordination of persons to impersonal ends, as is demanded by both Fascism and Communism, but in the unrelieved and joyfully accepted tension between contrasted and complementary points of view . . .

'This is the real alternative to the philosophies of both Fascism and Communism, provided its implications in the social and economic spheres are fully thought out and faced. In it lies the only spring of hope for the world. It is the contribution of supreme value which this country, if true to what is best in its traditions, might make to the world in its present distress. But this view of the meaning of life can become a real alternative to Fascism and Communism only if it has its roots in the ultimate

* Mark 9, 49. According to Buchman, one of Gandhi's favourite texts.

[189]

constitution of the universe and if we may dare to believe in a living God who is the source, consecration and sustainer of our personal relations with our fellow men.'[43]

A-WO-ZAN-ZAN-TONGA

His work abroad and the backwash from Princeton had not diminished Buchman's activities in his own country. In the first three months of 1929 he held half a dozen house-parties in the United States, the last being in Briarcliff, thirty miles up the Hudson from New York. Indeed, Briarcliff became so well known as a centre of his activities during the next years that when he called on the Governor of New York State, Franklin D. Roosevelt, at Hyde Park in May 1932, Roosevelt's first remark was, 'Hello, Buchman. What's happening at Briarcliff?' Shortly afterwards Buchman was received by President Hoover, who was preoccupied by the Depression, now reaching its deepest point. The realisation that the prosperity of the twenties had gone, perhaps for good, brought with it despair and the threat of violence. *Harper's* magazine carried an article headed 'Are We Going to Have a Revolution?'[1] There were thirty-eight suicides in Detroit in a single weekend.

Buchman had brought a group of twenty to North America on a reconnaissance that year. He held large meetings in the East and Middle West of the United States, arriving in Detroit in June. Here a couple whose marriage had been saved through meeting the Oxford Group introduced him to Mr and Mrs Henry Ford. Ford, noticing that Buchman's watch was not working, offered him the duplicate of his own – a dollar watch on a neat leather cord attached to his coat lapel. Buchman was celebrating his fifty-fourth birthday, and had asked his Penn State friend, Bill Pickle, now eighty-four years old, to join him for the occasion. He introduced Bill Pickle to the Fords. 'Henry Ford showed himself to me as simply a common man,' was Bill's verdict. 'If he was a neighbour of mine, we could just be good friends.'

Buchman had kept in touch with Bill through the years, and had sent him financial help when times were hard. Hearing that his 'benefactor', as he always called Buchman, planned to visit Europe again, Bill had written, 'Hear you are sailing for Oxford, England, on 15 June, which would be my soul's delight in my last days. Now, Frank, you know I have never asked for anything and have no reason to ask, but you don't know how I would like to go with you to Oxford. We are all quite well and spiritually on the mountain top. Yours in fellowship, love and truth, Your brother, W. I. Gilliland.'[2]

On the day the *Berengaria* sailed for England, Buchman wrote to Mrs Ford, 'You may be surprised to hear that I am taking Bill Pickle to England with me tonight. Bill says the last boat he was on was a ferry boat from Philadelphia to Camden, and before that his biggest boat had been a dog raft on a mill pond!'[3]

On his first journey by air, from London to Geneva for a luncheon for League of Nations delegates, Bill Pickle gave one look at the small plane and asked to see the pilot. 'You're going to fly in that contraption?' asked Bill.

'Yes,' replied the veteran pilot.

'If you don't mind,' said Bill, 'I'd feel much easier if we could kneel down and pray before we start.'

The pilot got down on his knees beside the plane, while Bill entrusted their safety to his 'Heavenly Parent' as he, an illegitimate son who never knew his father, always addressed God.

Henry Ford had in the meantime run across Harvey Firestone's son in the course of business, had noticed the change in him and kept him talking in his office for two hours. During this period he invited Bill Pickle, returned from Europe, to meet some of his hard-drinking executives. Bill was asked how he prayed. 'Well,' he said, blowing out his moustaches, 'the first thing is to get down on your knees, as in crap-shooting.' Laughter drowned the rest of the instruction. In Geneva likewise, his directness made a stronger impression than many more polished utterances. Buchman used to say, 'He's genuine. So you can introduce him anywhere.'

In Europe Buchman had now gathered what the Princeton affair had scattered in America – the mobile force of convinced people for which he had worked ever since returning from China. After his preliminary reconnaissance in Canada, he returned there with thirty-two people in October 1932. On the voyage the ship's barber, while shaving Buchman, asked in rather thick tones what his work was. 'My work', Buchman replied with spirit, 'is to help a bull-necked barber, who has been out on the binge the night before, find out how he can get cleaned up and put on the right road.'

Buchman's initial team, which was commissioned by the Bishop of Liverpool, was drawn from Britain, Holland, Germany, South Africa and the United States. It being October, with the University term in full swing, only six from Oxford were in the first party, including Reginald Holme of motor-club fame who had just got a First in theology, and Marie Clarkson, the 'dog girl'. Dr and Mrs Ebenezer Macmillan had come from South Africa, Frau Moni von Cramon from Germany, Vice-Admiral

Sydney Drury-Lowe from London, and Jimmie Watt, a former Communist, from Scotland. As the *Duchess of Bedford* steamed into Quebec harbour, Ruth Bennett[4] remembers Buchman urging the British to forget they were British and remember only that they were Christians. 'Live on a basis of appreciation, not comparison,' he said, and then threw out the thought, 'Each of you may be leading a team of two hundred before this trip is over.'

The team was mostly under twenty-five and certainly needed training. 'We were as green as grass,' recalls Holme. 'I remember telling a Liverpool journalist before leaving that, in view of all the crime we read about in America, some of us might not come back. We had a meeting with the Salvation Army, and one of our American girls was asked to give a benediction. There was a long silence. She knew what a Benedictine was, but had never heard this new word.' The 'dog girl', attacked by a zealous theologian as to why she had not mentioned 'the blood of Christ' in her speech, replied, 'If you'd raised that at my first meeting, I'd have run six blocks.'

Their very freshness proved attractive. After the first meeting a dignified grey-haired man got hold of Holme. He asked how to have a 'quiet time', and, when he tried it, wrote down the one word 'Customs'. A Balliol man, Bernard Hallward was now Vice-President of the *Montreal Star*, and when the team reached Ottawa they were greeted by an eight-column headline bearing the news that he had returned $12,200 to the National Revenue Department for undeclared goods brought through from Europe.[5]

In Ottawa, Prime Minister R. B. Bennett gave a lunch for his Cabinet colleagues to meet the visitors. 'If, as I believe, Wesley saved England from the effects of the French Revolution,' he said on that occasion, 'so it is my abiding faith that the influences you so powerfully represent are the only ones that can save the world.'[6]

Professor Grensted joined the travellers during the Oxford Christmas vacation and embarked on a heavy programme of meeting his fellow theologians and psychologists. He wrote in his diary, 'Toronto – In the afternoon, interviews; one of them well worth all the time and cost of coming. This evening three meetings, and at least 3,000 people to hear our very simple story. Each of us spoke three times, and I, at least, began to know the curious clarity that lies beyond weariness. But what a need there is, and how patiently these people listen and look for help! The lounge of the hotel is full, after meetings, of groups talking on and on . . . At tea I was supposed to meet a few psychologists and found the whole department had arrived. They seemed to know *how* but not *why*. And clearly they thought me an interesting exhibit. . . .

Hamilton, Ontario – Things moved well, as always, with the clergy, where I was led to proclaim with vigour and emphasis against the opinions of the local psychiatrist who had raised his head against us. . . . I write this at 2.00 am, much delayed by letters. Also by the arrival of a leading Church paper full of attacks on the Group. It is curious how these attacks seem to be organised. The editor says he has waited to form a judgement until the arrival of the Group, and then reprints hostile attacks written weeks ago in an English paper. It is queer to read this attack, written by able people too, and then think of the steady stream of sober miracles going on under my very eyes. Just fear, I believe, lest young people should rise up and save the world. And the challenge to older folk who have not saved it. . . .'

Buchman took his team of sixty for Christmas to Lucerne, Quebec. Herman Hagedorn, the poet and biographer of Theodore Roosevelt, noted: 'No time to get presents. Ellie Forde went to the 5- and 10-cent store. Grensted and others wrote poems for each one. Frank got sixty Christmas wreaths, ribbons and tags. At hotel, big six-sided fireplace. Carols. Creche for Frank. Trees, show, etc . . . Next day Grensted fixed exquisite nativity tableau. Frank loved the homeliness. Acute sensitivity to people and things. A good deal of the artist in him. Tremendous sentiment which never gets into sentimentality. But he is gregarious until he can't rest. Every anniversary has tremendous significance.'

On 29 January in Montreal there was, Grensted noted, 'a great service in the Cathedral in the late afternoon. The Bishop spoke with feeling and warmth, a little staggered to find the Cathedral completely full. People were coming for two hours before time. . . .'

There was a house-party in Detroit just before the Montreal visit, and they returned there on the 30th, en route for New York, for a barn dance given for them by Henry Ford. On the Sunday morning, Bill Pickle spoke in the Chapel of Martha and Mary in Ford's Dearborn Village, and Buchman and some of his team had tea with the Fords at their home. Then on to New York where 3,200 people crowded the Waldorf-Astoria ballroom for what Grensted described as 'a special triumph for Frank, who remembers only too well his earlier difficulties in New York, when all the press was against him and friends were few'.*

From Briarcliff Buchman took his team to Washington, where the Secretary of State, Cordell Hull, attended one of the meetings. Another

---

* Grensted reported his doings in North America with considerable enthusiasm at a meeting in Oxford on his return. By the next year, however, he had come to feel that he must be more detached. According to a private memo by Archbishop Lang of 13 July 1934, Grensted had become disturbed by 'the explosive self-confidence of some of the younger whole-time members insisting that their method is practically the only one by which a man can become a Christian', but said that he would 'continue to be in full sympathy with its main purposes'.

was opened by a black choir, for which Buchman was much criticised – a criticism which became still shriller when he transferred the next meeting to a black church where 2,000 people, black and white, mingled happily, at a time when such racial integration was unusual in the capital.

The journey continued through Louisville, Akron and Kansas City – where Buchman first met Judge, later President, Harry Truman – to Arizona and California. In Phoenix he took the whole party to a rodeo, and ended up talking deeply with one of the cowboys on the platform until the train pulled out.

On the West Coast there were large meetings in Los Angeles and three house-parties nearby. The visitors also found themselves speaking in San Quentin prison. A copy of *For Sinners Only* had made its way there and the changes it had effected were so marked that the prison's Director of Social and Religious Services invited them in. The Director himself said the visit gave him a new approach to his work. Other prisons were visited in Canada and the Eastern States, and changes in many inmates were reported by prison authorities.

Buchman, as the tour proceeded, was more and more insisting that those who 'changed' should relate their experience of God to their public lives and the problems of the nation. Personal experience was important, but it was apt to become sentimental unless immediately applied to everyday life. Two business men who took this step were William Manning of San Francisco, who owned a string of coffee houses, and T. P. Loblaw, whose chain of provision stores spanned Canada from coast to coast.

Manning and his family gave up their large house and began to live more simply, rather than dismiss employees. He remarked that he was amused at all the safeguards he had been trying to take against the Depression: 'Once you have your family lined up on this basis, all fear of the future vanishes.'

Loblaw, whose stores were a forerunner of today's supermarkets and whose turn-over that year exceeded $25,000,000, asked Buchman to send one of his team to be his guest. Buchman sent George Wood, Lawson's eighteen-year-old brother, fresh from school in Aberdeen. One day they knelt down together while Loblaw gave his life and business to God. He promptly told his employees and competitors that his business was under new management, and began to reshape it. In this he enlisted the help of the former Communist, Jimmie Watt, who commented, 'He faced the challenge of having his business on a God-guided basis, knowing full well the adjustments and readjustments which had to be made. He made a noble beginning.' Alas, it was only a beginning, for Loblaw died three months later after a brief illness. Others, however, were stimulated by his example, among them the head of a salmon cannery in Vancouver, Richard Bell Irving, whom he introduced to the Oxford Group.

Throughout the trip Buchman took care to keep his green young colleagues from taking themselves too seriously. One of them became somewhat elated by his success as a speaker. At two o'clock one morning in Quebec, Buchman, on the way to bed, rang him up from the lobby of the hotel. 'My name's Walker,' he said in a disguised voice. 'I heard you speak this evening and was deeply impressed. I want you to come downstairs at once and get me started.' The young man jumped out of bed and went down, only to find, after some fruitless waiting, that he had fallen into a Buchman trap against self-importance. The young, however, had their own back at a mock trial of Buchman for chewing gum – something he never did – on a college campus. The skit parodied all his characteristics and mannerisms, and Buchman laughed uproariously.

The trip was overshadowed for at least one of the party by Hitler's rise to power in Germany. Frau Moni von Cramon was from an old Junker family, had been a lady-in-waiting to the last Kaiserin, and was related to the famous German airman of the First World War, Baron Manfred von Richthofen. She herself ran a finishing school for girls in her large home near Breslau, in Silesia. She had left her three children there. 'Both the National Socialists and the Communists hate me because of my link with the Kaiser,' she told Buchman. 'I must go home.' She arrived home just as Hitler was proclaimed Chancellor.

Throughout the trip, as Ruth Bennett remembers, Buchman's people were so inexperienced that he had to handle all the arrangements himself: travel, luggage, laundry, hotel reservations, checking and paying bills, press coverage, and printing. 'The only time I saw him lose his temper,' she says, 'was when we were all sitting peacefully eating our breakfast at the hotel in Montreal when we should have been well on the way to the station.' 'I say, you fellows,' said someone, 'Buchman's turning cartwheels in the lobby because we're not on our way!'

Buchman was often criticised for using large hotels, but his reply was that they alone had the facilities necessary for the team's work – telephones, a ballroom, the use of which for meetings was often thrown in free, and rooms for smaller meetings. Hotel owners frequently made special concessions. One always gave Buchman a suite at the price of a single room in gratitude for a change he saw in his nephew. Another cut $2,000 from the bill because a large amount of silver had been returned to the hotel as a result of Buchman's meetings: principally, the owner alleged, from people who had been there for other religious gatherings.

In one city the hotel into which Buchman had booked had been burnt down and the proprietor of the only alternative demanded absurd rates. In spite of every argument, he would not budge. Finally Buchman said, 'If that is your last word, I will call a press conference and tell how you have treated us.' The proprietor swiftly climbed down. 'When the other fellow plants his feet you just have to plant yours more firmly,' commented Buchman.

The financial basis of the trip amazed those taking part, and caused curiosity, incredulity or shock to the public at large. Buchman never had in hand more than enough for the next week's needs. Shortly before he left Britain, Roger Hicks, a recently recruited whole-time colleague, offered Buchman £10,000, the remains of the capital left him by his father. Buchman refused to take it. 'It's not my job to look after your money for you,' he told Hicks. 'Now that you are free from the false security of money, God will show you how to use it.' Hicks, unable to get him to change his mind, took further thought and returned with £2,000. 'Frank,' he said, 'I've guidance to give you this.' After a few moments' reflection Buchman accepted it.

'Tell me,' Hicks then asked him, 'how will you spend it?'

'I have thirty-two people going to Canada with me next week,' Buchman replied. 'I have reserved the passages, but I haven't the money to pay for them. That will be the first claim.' Hicks soon afterwards joined him in Canada.

Buchman never asked for money on the tour. No collections were taken at the meetings, though people assured him that this would raise all he needed. He believed that people who had been helped would give out of gratitude, and so it turned out. In fact, an average of forty people travelled from end to end of the continent for eight months in the middle of the Depression without any assured means of support, and none of them ever lacked food or shelter.

Numerous instances of how they were provided for could be given. A Scot, George Marjoribanks, and a colleague found themselves alone and penniless in Edmonton. They prayed about it and half an hour later ran into a man in the street who, without being asked, gave Marjoribanks $25. Francis Goulding, in England, had the thought to send someone on the Canadian trip £4. He had not got it. He prayed, 'If You want me to do it, You will have to send me the £4.' In his post that morning came two letters, each containing £2. A registered envelope cost 10 pence: an hour later a man returned 10 pence he owed him.

Not that this way of living came easily. 'One morning', recalls a member of the team, 'we gathered, some fifty strong. Buchman started by asking whether there was anyone with absolutely no money and held up a very small bundle of notes, all that was left in the treasury. One man stood up and said he was penniless. Buchman walked down and gave him $2. He then talked to us about our lack of faith in a way I shall never forget. "Some of you are content to travel on my faith," he said. The outcome was that we

[197]

all went to our rooms to ask God's forgiveness for our faithlessness and to implore His continued support.'

Western Canada gave the party a big public welcome. '30,000 Flock to Hear Oxford Group' was the headline in the *Vancouver News*.[7] James Butterfield, a columnist in the rival *Vancouver Daily Province*, took a sceptical view. For four days he attacked.[8] On the fifth, Buchman spied him at a reception. 'Hello, Butterfield,' he said, 'you're the fellow who has spelt my name right all week.' That started a talk. Next day, Butterfield's column was headed, 'Dr Buchman, You Win!'

In Edmonton, the Premier of Alberta, who had offered to preside at the first meeting, found himself also speaking to three overflow meetings, all packed to the doors. He said the crowds had the sniff of an election meeting but surpassed any election interest he had known.

When Buchman and Hicks got back to their hotel one night, they found a distinguished-looking older man, in full evening dress and a bit drunk, lying on Buchman's bed. Buchman sent Hicks down to ask the manager how he had got in. When Hicks returned, he heard the visitor saying, 'Now, Dr Buchman, please tell me again – what are those four standards?' Buchman told him. 'I sometimes forget by morning what I heard the night before. Please write them on my shirt front,' the man replied. So Buchman wrote on his shirt front: 'Absolute honesty, purity, unselfishness and love. Tea with Buchman, 5 o'clock.' He came, decided to change, and was a transformed person.

The final all-Canadian gathering at the Chateau Frontenac Hotel in Quebec ended on Whit Sunday, and to the astonishment of the hotel staff Buchman asked one Sully Wood, a highly successful car salesman, to read the Whitsun story from the Acts of the Apostles. Wood had stayed at the hotel twenty-seven times, and never remembered how he had left. The manager could never let the rooms to either side of his because of the racket he made. When Sully arrived this time he said, 'This is the wrong place for you, Sully. A lot of religious people have come.' 'I've come with them,' Sully replied. 'Something may happen.'

The manager was sceptical, and the bell-hops had a sweepstake on how long he would stay sober. One night, finding him roaming the kitchen, they thought they had caught him. But he was only after milk. The 'something' happened. Soon his estranged family joined him, and they were reunited. Six weeks later, while a hundred other Canadians sailed to England for the Oxford house-party, Sully led a team from Toronto to some of the neighbouring cities.

G. Ward Price, one of Britain's leading reporters of the period, visited Canada just after the Oxford Group team left. 'I found the whole Dominion, from Vancouver to Quebec, discussing the success of the mission of the Oxford Group,' he wrote in the *Sunday Pictorial*. 'I must admit I was impressed by the hold it has evidently taken on the minds of many Canadians whose education and knowledge of the world would safeguard them against mere emotional methods.'[9]

In March 1934 Buchman led a second, larger expedition to Canada, with side forays into the United States. The trip through Canada was, as to the crowds and official receptions, a repeat of the year before. But Buchman, from the first, had told his team, 'Our aim is not to win new people, but to get everyone to apply their new experience in the life of the nation. Last time we drove in some pylons. Now we must raise the building upon them.'[10] 'The Oxford Group and World Peace' and 'Oxford Group Influence on Racial Strife' were the titles of two editorials in the Toronto *Mail and Empire*,[11] while the *Ottawa Citizen*[12] wrote of the implications of the Group's message for unemployment. *The Colonist* of Victoria, BC, stated: 'The Oxford Group seemed to one observer to have grown in sensitiveness to the needs of humanity . . . The listener need not deduce that the movement has in any way retired from its leading tenets nor is giving up its characteristic modes of religious life . . . But without doubt, it is giving a new emphasis. It is facing up to the social implications of the gospel.'[13]

A just rebuke, however, came from the *Ottawa Evening Journal* when Holme inferred from the case of his friend Hallward in Montreal that 'the people of Canada are beginning to pay their taxes on a basis of "absolute honesty"'. ' "Beginning" is the word used,' commented the paper. 'The inference that Canadians generally have been dishonest in their income tax payments and that it remained for the Oxford Group to convert them to honest practices, is one which touring ladies and gentlemen would find it difficult to maintain.' Nevertheless, the paper added, 'there is room for improvement'. The statement seemed 'to value this evangelical movement according to its measurable cash return,' the editorial concluded. 'We should like to be permitted to think its objectives are on a higher plane.'[14]

An early part of the tour was spent in the Maritimes, unvisited the previous year. From there Buchman planned to move to the prairie provinces, and this time he was determined that he would not do all the preparation work. Rather he saw it as a way to train younger people by throwing them in at the deep end. One of them, Howard Blake, remembers a night of planning as the train took them from the Maritimes to Toronto:

'While most slept peacefully in the darkened sleeping cars, one drawing room glowed with the light as Frank and a group of friends gathered round the table to plan a lightning dash right across the continent. After two days in Toronto, they were to visit in rapid succession Winnipeg and Regina, there divide into two simultaneous visits in Calgary and Edmonton, to meet again in Vancouver, then Victoria and Seattle. After that was to come a final training period at Banff before the force returned for the summer assembly at Oxford.

'During the night advance parties of two for each city were chosen to move ahead on a connecting train the following morning, while the force visited Toronto. Frank had visited these cities just two years before. So far as we knew, he had no expectation of returning in the foreseeable future. As soon as it was clear which two would go to each city, he began dictating letters of introduction to relays of secretaries on through the night, so that the young men would quickly find their way in each city.

'I have never experienced anything like that night's dictation – each letter a personal one to every major hotel owner and every newspaper editor in those cities, and to other leading men. With no notes or diary, Frank dictated from memory, with name and correct spelling, greetings to wives and often to children with their names, letters brimful of news, of what had happened and what was going to happen, with warmth and spontaneity as though he had seen them a week or two before. By morning all was clear. Fourteen men carried on to seven cities, and prepared the way for the big team that followed shortly afterwards, while Frank in full vigour led the rest into the United States.'

This move took the form of a brief visit to New York and Washington, followed by two days at Allentown. 'Fortunately Buchman has not been a prophet without honour in his own country,' wrote the *Allentown Call*. 'Allentown is going to welcome him not only for himself, but for the message he is bringing to millions of people.'[15]

Back in Canada again, Buchman and his team were received by the Premier in each province, Prime Minister Bennett spending five hours with them in Ottawa. In Vancouver they found that one of the worst shipping strikes in North America up to that time was paralysing the Pacific Coast ports from San Francisco to Alaska. Parts of Alaska had already been put on rations. If the strike continued, the year's salmon run – on which the canning industry depended – would be lost. By the time of the Group's arrival complete deadlock had been reached.

Mainly through the intervention of two of Buchman's team – George Light, the Warwickshire Socialist, and Walter Horne, a Californian ship-builder – a fair settlement was reached. It took them seventy-two hours of continuous effort, moving between the men, who had long-standing and justified grievances, the strike committee, union leaders and employers. The resolution was reported at a business men's lunch in Toronto by the salmon-canner from Vancouver, Richard Bell Irving.[16] 'This was accomplished by the application of Christ's principles as advocated by the Group to the problems of both owners and strikers,' he said. 'My company was very seriously affected by the strike and I therefore know whereof I speak.'[17] The *Ottawa Evening Citizen* commented, 'When Christianity is put into practice it is spiritual dynamite. There is no greater force for enduring reform known to mankind.'[18]

The impetus behind this settlement was studied at the house-party in Banff, immediately after the visit to the far West. There Buchman had two main themes. The first was the need for a society totally controlled by God, through the free co-operation of individuals. The second was how a group, in any situation, could set to work to bring this about.

'What agency will save civilisation from suicide?' he asked. 'It is no use patching up old tyres. We need a new car.' This 'car' would be a nation as totally controlled by God as the totalitarian states of the dictators were controlled by men. 'The main thought at Banff was "Totality" – a Church, a University, a City, a Province, a Country, wholly Christian,' stated the house-party report. 'What vision, what imagination, what devotion, what discipline was needed for the realisation of such a great objective – this was the consideration of the house-party.'[19]

Buchman went into his second theme one morning, instancing how a group of seven dedicated people could operate in a city. They could sit down and listen to God so as to get the names of the seven most strategic, or the seven most tempted, or the seven most difficult people in the city. Then they could set out in a 'shoe-leather activity' to change these people. 'God works on difficult people,' he said. 'It's like a triangle. God at the top, you and the other person. To any group short of the basis of life-changing wave goodbye. Have you thought of a gangster changing? How many Communists do we know personally? Some of you will have unexpected companions on this business.'

Both elements were essential to his strategy: the proclaiming of a vision adequate to interest thousands, and the art of the 'fisher of men', who knew how to go patiently after the big and difficult fish with the right fly or bait.

While at Banff the Stoney Indians, a tribe of the Sioux people, made Buchman a blood brother. Only members of the British royal family may be made chiefs of the Stoneys, and up till then only six other whites had been made blood brothers. During the winter the squaws had made the ceremonial costume of soft white leather and beads, with the traditional feather headdress. Buchman's answers to the ritual questions, given on his behalf by Loudon Hamilton resplendent in a kilt, revealed a sad lack of tepees and cattle, made up for by the number of his braves and by the fact that he and they 'worked without money for God'. The Stoneys gave him the name A-Wo-Zan-Zan-Tonga – Great Light in Darkness – which Chief Walking Buffalo said had come to them as a thought from God. They pledged the tribe's help 'in sorrow or sickness, hunger or plenty, by day and by night,' and ended, 'Thus will you grow great in the hearts of those who now adopt you, and the Great Spirit will look with love and compassion on you when He calls you to the Happy Hunting Grounds.'*

'The work you are doing has made the task of government easier,' said Prime Minister Bennett in a farewell message to Buchman and his team. 'Your influence has been felt in every village and city, even in the remotest outpost of the Dominion.'[20]

* Grant MacEwan, in his biography of Chief Walking Buffalo, *Tatanga Mani* (Hurtig, 1969), states that the Chief was introduced to Buchman in Banff by a white Canadian friend, was asked by this friend to make Buchman a blood brother, and thereupon organised an immediate ceremony. However, the present account is taken from contemporary eye-witness reports.

BID FOR GERMANY

When, in early 1933, Moni von Cramon arrived back in Silesia from being with Buchman in America and Canada, she soon found that the local Nazis 'did not want to have me running my school because I was too Christian. They wanted me to run it for them on their lines, but I refused.'[1] The school was closed and she took a house in Breslau, renting her own home to a family. Unknown to her, a daughter of this family was a Nazi informer with instructions to search the house. She found an anti-Nazi pamphlet which had been given to Frau von Cramon by a French woman in Geneva and which she had stuffed into a bookshelf. On its cover was a swastika with its points hacked off by an axe so that a simple cross remained. Correspondence with theologians was also found. News reached Frau von Cramon in Breslau that she was to be arrested.

Just at this moment a leader of the SS in Silesia, a childhood friend, arrived unannounced to ask Frau von Cramon a favour. He wanted to marry her husband's niece. Would she introduce him to the girl's family? Frau von Cramon told him of her predicament, and he took the matter out of the hands of the local officials on the grounds that so serious a case could only be dealt with at Himmler's headquarters, where a friend of his was an adjutant. So, after a nerve-racking 250-mile drive to Berlin, Frau von Cramon suddenly found herself face to face with Himmler.

Himmler received her, standing, in his large study. He kept her standing at the other end of the room, while he consulted a file. Taking out of it a picture of Buchman, he said:

'Is this Dr Buchman, the leader of this movement with which you work, a Jew?'

'I don't know his ancestry, but I don't think so. I'll ask him,' she replied.

'Do you think he will tell you?'

'If he knows, why shouldn't he?'

'What is the relation between the Oxford Group and Jews?'

'I can't give an answer to that because the Oxford Group is not an organisation. It has no rules or statutes.'

'How often have you been in England this past year?' Himmler continued.

'Three times, I think.'

'You're wrong. Four times.'

Then he told her the exact state of her bank account and asked how she had got the money for these journeys. Frau von Cramon replied that she had sold a treasured possession, her grand piano. 'I have faith that God leads people and gives us what we need when we do what He wants us to do,' she added.

'I believe in God, too. I believe in miracles,' remarked Himmler seriously. 'I'm Party Member Number Two. We were seven men who had faith that this National Socialism ideology would win. Now we are the government. Isn't that a miracle?'

He said he would like to know more about what guidance from God meant and that they would talk again. Then he let her go. From that time she suspected that her phone was tapped and her mail opened.

Buchman had first met Moni von Cramon at Doorn, the ex-Kaiser's place of exile in Holland, in October 1931. Kaiser Wilhelm's initial refuge in Holland had been with a branch of the Bentinck family. Buchman was conducting a house-party in a Bentinck house near Doorn. He and four German friends left visiting cards on the ex-Kaiser, and had therefore been invited to tea. The ex-Kaiser decided not to appear for the tea, and sent Frau von Cramon, as a well-known churchwoman, to vet the visitors' theological credentials.

'What kind of people are you?' she asked one of those with Buchman.

'I really don't know,' he replied. ('I took note of that,' commented Frau von Cramon later. 'I knew precisely what I was.') 'Frank, what are we exactly?'

Buchman replied, 'We are very ordinary people, but we want to put into modern language the truths which turned the early Christians into revolutionaries.'

That happened to be exactly what Frau von Cramon was wanting to do in the Church's youth work, so she bore the visitors away to her sitting room. 'There I put Buchman through a full theological examination. I was perfectly sure that my ideas were correct. It followed therefore that anything that differed was out of order. Dr Buchman survived the test, even if only perhaps with a "pass" mark,' she recalled.

Before leaving, Buchman asked her to attend the Oxford house-party in the following June. She at once said it was impossible, for three reasons. She had not the money to do so, her school would be in full session until July, and ('I tried to put this very modestly') she felt she had little to learn from the English or Americans on religious questions.

'Dr Buchman's response was a hearty laugh. He didn't seem to take me very seriously,' related Frau von Cramon. ' "Oh, pardon me," he said. "I thought you were a Christian." Those were the very words this American said – to me! I forgave him immediately. He could not know that I was unusually active in all sections of church work, that I had actually often spoken from the pulpit and gave very good devotional talks. So I asked him, "And how could you know, Doctor, that I am not a Christian?"

' "Any person who already knows in the autumn what God wants him to do the following June is not living under the guidance of God," he replied. "And any person who is not living under God's guidance is no Christian." That hit home. I could think of no suitable reply. His words stayed with me, moving in my heart and mind in ever-growing circles.'

By next June Frau von Cramon's first two objections were unexpectedly removed. In May she was amazed to receive a letter from Buchman enclosing a return ticket to Oxford. Then, at exactly the time she was invited to travel, a scarlet fever epidemic closed her school for two weeks. She was a little ashamed of her third objection, and reasoned that she would at least be able to give those present a grounding in 'sound German-Evangelical pedagogy'.

This she did in a speech lasting an hour and a half, which caused almost all the audience but Buchman to leave the hall. She then told Buchman she must leave for home. 'Has God told you to leave?' he asked. She felt compelled to go to her room and try 'listening'. Only nonsense seemed to come. 'Genf – Geneva – Genève,' she wrote down, twice, and that was all. At tea she told this to Buchman, and repeated that she was leaving for Germany. He laughed and took from his pocket a printed invitation to League of Nations delegates to attend an Oxford Group meeting in Geneva in a week's time. Her name was on the list of those who would be there. 'God told us you would travel with us, but He always lets people do what they want. We'll take your name out,' he said. At that exact moment, Frau von Cramon was being paged with a telegram. It said, 'New case of scarlet fever. School remains closed. Return unnecessary.'

'My knees began to shake,' related Frau von Cramon. 'Could it be true that God really could speak to people? One week later I was standing on the platform in Geneva before the representatives of the League of Nations.'

By the time of her interview with Himmler, Frau von Cramon had worked with Buchman in a number of countries and had come to appreciate his concern for her own. His Swiss-German ancestry and his knowledge of the language – the only one other than English which he spoke – made him feel at home there. His early visit to von Bodelschwingh at Bethel had been one of the influences which led him to found the Overbrook hospice, and he had been in correspondence with the son, also Friedrich, since the father's death in 1910. During the 1914–18 war he had, at Mott's suggestion, visited Germans interned in India and Japan. After the Armistice, he had helped to feed needy students and families impoverished by war. In 1920 he wrote to Mrs Woolverton, 'The children are starving and dying. They have no cows or food to feed them with. I do not know when I have seen anything so pathetic.' This was when he had urged her to send three cows to Bethel.[2]

From 1920 his visits to Germany became almost annual. After one visit in 1923 he wrote, 'I come from the throes of a distrait world. I have sat with poor and rich, privileged and underprivileged. Some who were rich and privileged two years ago have scarcely enough to eat. My physician, who was one of the foremost in Germany, had a pound of sausage for a family of five the week I was there. In some families half the family spend a day in bed, while the others get enough to eat, and they go to bed next day while the others satisfy their hunger.'[3]

Buchman began holding house-parties of a more public nature from the mid-1920s. Loudon Hamilton recalled one in Potsdam in 1924, and after another there in 1927 Buchman wrote to Mrs Tjader, 'We have had a woman at the house-party who had to borrow clothes to come, a cigar maker and the wife of a former ADC to the ex-Kaiser.'[4] In the autumn of 1928 a young German theologian, Ferdinand Laun, who was doing research on a Rockefeller scholarship at Oxford, met Buchman's work there. He gave up his academic career and devoted his full time between 1932 and the outbreak of World War II to establishing the *Gruppen-bewegung* (Group Movement) in Germany.[5] Local groups sprang up all over the country, house-parties became frequent and a number of Germans went to Oxford or Switzerland for training or travelled with Buchman in other countries.

By the late 1920s Germany was slipping increasingly into demoralisation and chaos. Mountainous inflation, unemployment which reached six million, and recurrent regional revolts kept the possibility of a revolution or civil war alive into the early thirties.

Hitler, meanwhile, gathered strength. He promised the people 'order, work and bread'. At first he did not present his ideas as a crude ideology of blood and race, but as a set of beliefs which would restore the German nation and which did not conflict with Christianity. In 1928 Hitler excluded from his party a man who too obviously wanted to replace Christianity by 'a German faith' and publicly declared, 'Our movement is effective Christianity. We shall not tolerate in our ranks anyone who hurts Christian ideas.'[6] He reiterated this pledge on becoming Chancellor.[7]

Powerful groups were therefore prepared in those early years to wait and see how events developed, meanwhile giving Hitler their tacit or explicit support. The Catholic Bishops wrote in their pastoral letter of 10 June 1933: 'Precisely because authority occupies a quite special place in the Catholic Church, Catholics will not find it difficult to appreciate the new powerful movement of authority in the new German state and to subordinate themselves to it.'[8] Karl Barth, who raised his voice at an early stage against Hitler, wrote after the war, 'In the first period of its power National Socialism had the character of a political experiment like others ... It was right and proper for the time being to give the political experiment of National Socialism a trial.'[9]

Buchman took every chance, in the midst of his strenuous action in other parts of the world, to try and assess the new Germany. He first attempted to meet Hitler personally in January 1932. Passing through Munich, he applied for an interview and called at the Brown House to get any news of his appointment. There, on a desk in the office where he was put to wait, he saw an open telegram to Hitler's staff: 'By no means allow Buchman to see the Führer.' It was signed by one of the ex-Kaiser's sons, Prince August Wilhelm ('Auwi'), whom Buchman had befriended, helping him to sell some of his pictures at the depth of the post-war crisis. The interview was refused.

In the summer of 1932, prior to his first campaign in Canada, Buchman took some twenty young men and women to Germany on a brief reconnaissance. This was for many of them their first contact with that country, and especially with the Nazi movement. Garrett Stearly, a thirty-year-old among the younger group, describes how they were impressed, in one town, to see two bands of young men, one working on a big sewerage project, another draining a swamp. 'It was all on a voluntary basis and gave a great sense of dedication,' he recalls. 'Demoralisation seemed to have gone.'

Sixteen of Buchman's party were invited to a big Nazi banquet in Berlin. 'We were welcomed with trumpeters on each side – they really put on dog,' says Stearly. 'About a thousand present, with a leading military man in the chair. Sat down at dinner with fervent young men – alert, patriotic, filled with faith that Germany could overcome her problems. They were very appealing. Outside our own fellowship, I had never met young men with such commitment before. But there was nothing Christian about it. Many arguments developed over dinner, each side fighting for its beliefs. Our question was, was the Germans' commitment to be centred on the Führer or on Christ? None of us spoke publicly or was presented.'

Buchman had put it to his young colleagues that unless they could bring change to such committed people, their work was inadequate. After this occasion, he gathered about 150 Germans, mostly churchmen, at Bad Homburg and put the same challenge to them. 'Frank did not really get through to them,' Stearly adds. 'They were very intellectual, fortified behind an impregnable wall of theology. They looked down on National Socialism as something quite unrelated to the churches, and thought it would wear itself out. Frank was clear that, whether you liked it or not, it was there to stay, and that it was high time to try and win it for Christ. The clergy decided to do nothing. Frank was disappointed, but thought his friend, Professor Fezer of Tübingen,* might do something. We would have to see.'

In June 1933, at the end of the first Canadian campaign, Buchman went straight to Germany at the urgent request of, amongst others, Baron von Maltzan, then in the Foreign Press section of the German Foreign Office. Von Maltzan sought an appointment for him with Hitler. Again no interview took place.

Buchman's aim in trying to meet the German leader was straightforward. He believed not only that Hitler could experience a change of character and motivation, but that it was vital for Germany and the world that he should do so. He felt the same need for such change in the leaders of other nations and thought no one of them was beyond the reach of God's grace. To have attempted to approach Hitler seems in retrospect indiscreet or naïve; but the same might have been said of St Francis when he crossed the Saracen lines to reach the Sultan, an equally sinister figure in medieval eyes.

Buchman's reaction to these first years of the Third Reich was one of intense interest mixed with a growing concern. He had been appalled by the post-war avalanche of immorality, the aimlessness of youth and the millions of able-bodied people without work. Two features of Hitler's movement made sense to him: the demand that all Germans should be responsible for their country, so that the young and unemployed, for example, were considered to be assets, not liabilities; and the conviction that difficulties could be overcome, given a united national purpose. He had also long felt that the Versailles Treaty had been unjust.[10]

On the other hand, he had been told by Frau Hanfstaengl, as early as 1924, of Hitler's hatred of the Jews, and in the summer of 1933 he caught a glimpse of the man, his style and character, when Hitler opened one of the first stretches of autobahn. 'On the way to the opening,' Ruth Bennett recalls, 'Hitler was smiling and amiable, acknowledging the applause of hundreds of thousands along the route as he stood in his Mercedes giving the Nazi salute. On the way back, he was as black as thunder and sat scowling, looking neither to right nor left. After him, in military formation with spades on their shoulders, marched the men who had built the Autobahn. This was long before Germany began to rearm, but Frank's comment was, "I don't like it. It smells of war." '

* Karl Fezer was Professor of Practical Theology at Tübingen University from 1929. Until 1933 he opposed National Socialism but, when once National Socialism was the elected government, he considered it necessary to deal with them. On 27 April 1933 he was unanimously elected by his colleagues in the Evangelical Church to represent them in the negotiations concerning the future of the Church.

Buchman also realised, from the beginning, that the total claim which Hitler put forward for the state, if not modified, must ultimately clash with the total demands of God which he himself insisted on. This attitude was typified in a comment written by Ruth Bennett to Frau von Cramon in June 1933: 'I do hope, for Germany's sake, that God will come first and your country second all the way through. In Los Angeles you reversed the order.'[11]

Reginald Holme was at first greatly taken by the Nazis' flair and efficiency. He travelled with Buchman in Germany in 1934, and writes, 'I remember Buchman telling me, "Be very clear on this. What we see here is not Christian revolution. But why are the Christians still asleep in their beds when the Nazis can get their men marching early on Sunday morning? The trouble is that when you think of religion, you think of a preacher. You have got to think in terms of a whole nation becoming Christian."'

Buchman felt keenly that the German Lutheran Church, the tradition into which he had been born, had failed to give Germany an adequate challenge to live complete Christianity: 'I am convinced that, if it had been living the life and been on the march for Christ, the Lutheran Church would have had an answer for Germany.'

Having failed to reach Hitler directly and aware that the National Socialist movement had pre-empted any attempt he might have made to work for a large-scale Christian awakening through campaigns after the model of South Africa and Canada, Buchman now concentrated, in what time was available to him, on those Lutheran leaders who appeared to have any chance of redirecting the regime and its followers.

The Lutheran Church was already deeply divided, politically and theologically, into two main streams – the traditional Evangelical Church and the 'German Christians' – and many rivulets. Hitler was hoping to gain control of the Church through the 'German Christians', a body organised by the Nazis in 1932 on foundations stretching back into the early 1920s. At the National Conference of the German Christians in April 1933 those who wished to apply Nazi Party tenets to a unified German Church mingled with many moderates who were, in Eberhard Bethge's words, 'less drastic' and 'at bottom inspired by true missionary zeal . . . for example Professor Fezer of Tübingen'.[12] The young Bishop Hossenfelder of Brandenburg was the leader of the German Christians. On 26 April Hitler appointed Ludwig Müller, a hitherto unknown chaplain to the forces in Königsberg, to be his confidential adviser and plenipotentiary in questions concerning the Evangelical Church.

In April, too, the Evangelical Church, in an attempt to retain some initiative, appointed a three-man commission to draft a new constitution and in May elected Pastor von Bodelschwingh, the son of Buchman's old friend, as Reichsbischof (National Bishop), a new position created by the state to unite the Church under one leader, since the state now had one leader. A month later von Bodelschwingh resigned, as he found the position unworkable when a Wiesbaden lawyer, August Jäger, was appointed both State Commissar of Prussia and President of the Supreme Church Council. In July Müller was named Reichsbischof by government decree, and the manner of his appointment was the starting point of an open split in the Lutheran Church. The 'Young Reformers', a group within the Evangelical Church among whom Dietrich Bonhoeffer was prominent, took the lead in this controversy.

That autumn, as Buchman was preparing for the major campaign in London, some of these men, including Dr Fezer and Bishop Rendtorff of Mecklenburg, appealed to him to intervene in Germany. Bishop Rendtorff had previously been one of the leaders of the German Christians. In July 1933 he had attended the Oxford house-party and, after his return to Germany, preached a sermon against the expulsion of Jewish Christians from the National Church. He had subsequently left the German Christians and was demoted from his bishopric.

When the Bishop of London commissioned Buchman and his team in St Paul's Cathedral on 6 October 1933 for their London campaign, four representatives of the German Church flew over to attend. They were Professor Fezer, Baron von Maltzan, Dr Wahl, Chancellor of the National Church, and Frau von Grone, head of the two million women in the Church organisation. The *Church of England Newspaper* commented, 'It does not need much imagination to realise what it will mean to Germany – and therefore to the world – if the vital message of the Oxford Group permeates German thought and action.'[13] Professor Fezer was so impressed that he flew home to Germany to bring the highly controversial Nazi Bishop Hossenfelder back with him to London.

Hossenfelder's visit to Britain was not a success. 'This little, plump, cigar-smoking bishop, with a big cross on his chest, had no discipline,' commented Frau von Cramon, who accompanied him as interpreter. He brushed aside some of the ecclesiastical appointments which Buchman had made for him because 'he was obviously more interested in finding a Bavarian *Bierstube* in which he felt at home with weisswurst, sauerkraut and beer'.[14] Also, recalls another observer, he 'insisted on slapping English bishops on the back'. Buchman received him graciously, introduced him to senior and junior members of Oxford University, but did not allow him to speak at meetings – only to pray. Naturally Buchman had to absorb plenty of criticism both for Hossenfelder's behaviour and for his opinions.

From the reports they made on their return to Germany it is clear that both Hossenfelder and Wahl had journeyed to London mainly with the idea of improving the image both of the German Christians and of Germany generally. They were impressed by the lack of automatic condemnation of things German among Oxford Group people, but, in fact, influenced none of them. On his return journey Hossenfelder told Fezer he had enjoyed his visit except that he did not understand 'all they kept saying about change'.[15]

While in London Hossenfelder appeared at first sight to have taken what looked like an important step by denouncing the exclusion of non-Aryans from the National Church (the so-called 'Aryan paragraph' and a principal 'German Christian' tenet) – a step which his hosts had urged upon him – though, according to the same source, he 'enthusiastically acclaimed it again' back in Germany.[16] The most recent explanation of his conduct is that he had been given 'direct instructions to explain to all official people, especially the British bishops, but also the German Embassy and perhaps other church gatherings, that it was not the official policy of the government of the German Church to enforce the 'Aryan paragraph' in the Evangelical Church'.[17] Ironically, within a month of his return he was forced, for internal Church reasons, to resign all his offices and return to parish life.

Although Buchman was disappointed by the Bishop's visit, Hossenfelder's report from London did have the effect of frustrating the attempt by a Dr Jäger to get the Oxford Group banned in Germany.* A series of invitations to Buchman from Reichsbischof Müller followed, one, in November, being accepted at two hours' notice. Another led to Buchman spending most of two weeks in Müller's home. Buchman was unashamedly working for change in Müller and, through him, in Hitler. In private, he did not pull his punches with Müller. 'Müller could have changed Hitler,' he was to say later, 'but he failed.'** He was also later to admit to Hans Stroh, one of the Group's leaders in Germany and for some time Fezer's assistant at Tübingen, that Müller was the wrong man to rely upon, even though he seemed the only avenue available.

Bonhoeffer and his friends, who were working – fruitlessly as it proved – for a total break between the Church and Hitler, deprecated these and other attempts to reach Hitler. 'We have often – all too often – tried to

---

* This was not the Dr August Jäger who was the State Commissioner of the Church in Prussia, but a clergyman in Hessen related to the head of the German Christians in Frankfurt. In October he attacked the Oxford Group at a church conference, saying that 'it could not fail to bring confusion and division into the national church's work of reconstruction. I shall continue to fight it in other places and by other means.' (*Deutsche Allgemeine Zeitung*, 21 October 1933.)

** Müller did fix an interview with Hitler for Buchman, Professor Fezer and himself for 11 October 1933. It was cancelled because Germany was to leave the League of Nations three days later.

make Hitler realise what is happening,' he wrote on 11 September 1934. 'Maybe we've not gone about it the right way, but then Barth won't go about it the right way either. Hitler must not and cannot hear. He is obdurate and it is he who must compel us to hear – it's that way round. The Oxford Group has been naïve enough to try to convert Hitler – a ridiculous failure to understand what is going on – it is *we* who are to be converted, not Hitler.'[18] Among Bonhoeffer and his friends the scene was set for the heroic rearguard action, a series of protests, draftings, unitings and splittings of factions which finally, in Bonhoeffer's case, led to active plotting, participation in the attempt on Hitler's life and a martyr's death.

Buchman, in spite of many disappointments, still felt it his task to aim straight at the man at the top because he alone could put evil laws into reverse and avoid war. So his speeches and broadcasts at this time were part drafted with Hitler in mind. Where Hitler demanded the 'leadership principle' and 'the dictatorship of the Party', Buchman called for 'God-control' and 'the dictatorship of the living Spirit of God'.

Many of his friends tried to dissuade him from his efforts on the basis that he was endangering the reputation of himself and his work. Among them was Professor Emil Brunner of Zurich, then probably the most influential theologian in the German-speaking world apart from Karl Barth. Brunner, who had frequently acknowledged his debt to Buchman and had seen in the Oxford Group a great hope for revitalising the churches world-wide,* wrote accusing Buchman of wanting to 'mediate in the German Church struggle' and deploring his contact with Hossenfelder.[19] Buchman replied baldly from Germany, 'Your danger is that you are still the Professor thundering from the pulpit and want the theologically perfect. But the German Church crisis will never be solved that way. Just think of your sentence, 'Unfortunately this hopeless fellow Hossenfelder has damaged the reputation of the Groups.' It sounds to me like associating with 'publicans and sinners'.

'Just keep your sense of humour and read the New Testament. The Groups in that sense have no reputation, and for myself, I have nothing to lose. I think it says something about that in the second chapter of Philippians. I would be proud to have Hossenfelder be in touch with such real Christianity that some day he would say, "Well, as a young man of thirty-two I made many mistakes, but I have seen a pattern of real Christianity." It is not a question of this man's past, but of his future. What might it mean for the future of Germany, if by the grace of God he could

---

* Hamilton recalled that at a house-party in Bad Homburg in the early thirties Brunner described seeing a sandwich-board man advertising a restaurant but looking as if he had not eaten a good meal himself for weeks, and added, 'I have been that sandwich-board man. I was advertising a good meal, but I hadn't eaten the meal myself until I met the Oxford Group.'

see a maximum message of Christ incarnate in you; and you might be the human instrument to effect that mighty change . . . Our aim is never to mediate, but to change lives and unite them by making them life-changers – to build a united Christian front.'[20]

To this end Buchman maintained touch with those he could reach in all sections of the Church, not least with von Bodelschwingh. In January 1934 the *Morning Post*[21] reported that the Pastors' Emergency League, founded by the courageous pastor Niemöller, was about to ask Buchman's assistance, but nothing came of it. He himself was planning a house-party in Stuttgart for the first week of January, although in the event he was himself not present at this occasion, which turned out to be the largest since 1931.

Buchman's Swiss friends played a major part, and a participant wrote, 'Brunner gave a very good address and had a good contact with Landesbischof Wurm (of Württemberg) who came several times. Nearly fifty students were there, mostly from Tübingen.'[22] According to Stroh, Bishop Wurm was particularly interested to discuss the responsibility of the Church in a totalitarian state, a situation which he said had not arisen for a thousand years.

In March Buchman visited Stuttgart to meet those most affected by the January occasion. Frau Wurm describes one afternoon, in the diary which she and the Bishop kept jointly and in which she always referred to her husband as 'Father': '3 March: We walked in the shade . . . and came home via Rudolph-Sophien-Stift to rejoin the Groups. It was splendid. Frank Buchman also came, spoke at length, greeted Father warmly. And in the end Father spoke as well and closed with a brief prayer. Father received a strong impulse to do something openly for the Church. It became quite clear to him what he had to do. He is going with Meiser (the Bishop of Bavaria) to Berlin.'[23]

Bishops Wurm and Meiser thereafter took a firm stand against further state control of the Church. Meanwhile, in May at the Barmen Synod, free and legal representatives of all the German regional churches proclaimed a Confession to the fundamental truths of the Gospel in opposition to the 'false doctrines' of the German Christian Government and, in so doing, severed themselves from the 'Brown Church'. They now saw themselves as the one 'Confessing Church' of Germany, and in October, at the Dahlem Confessional Synod, set up their own emergency church government. Müller's delayed consecration as National Bishop, which took place in Berlin Cathedral on 23 September, was not attended by representatives of the ecumenical movement.

August Jäger, the Nazi-appointed President of the Supreme Church Council, chose this moment to extend compulsory centralisation for the first time to the South German Regional Churches. In the first weeks of

October he put first Wurm, then Meiser, under house arrest. This led to spontaneous demonstrations in support of the two bishops in the streets of Stuttgart and Munich. The general clamour, together with the surprising unanimity at Dahlem, even penetrated to Hitler. On 26 October Jäger resigned. The two bishops were released and, together with Bishop Mahrarens of Hanover, were received by Hitler. Hitler then publicly dissociated himself from the Reich Church. It seemed for a time as though a victory had been won. But after some weeks cracks began to appear in the Confessing Church once more. 'It had taken fright at its own daring,' writes Bethge, 'and there was growing criticism of the Dahlem resolution.'[24] As a result, Hitler never needed to take further notice of the emergency organisations set up by the Synod. No further attempt was made, however, to bring the Southern regions and Hanover under central control.

At the Stuttgart gatherings in January 1934 Buchman and his friends received the first intimation that their meetings were being watched by the Gestapo. At one of the early meetings they realised that there was an informer amongst them, and those leading the house-party decided to speak with this man in mind – to give him the fullest information of what God could do in a person's life. He is said to have reported back to his chief, 'Those people have a strange God who can actually help them!' In April Dr Alois Münch, who had begun to have group meetings in his house in Munich, was questioned for two and a half hours by the political police – probably because some Jewish people were attending.[25] When some Germans went to a house-party in Thun, Switzerland, in August of the same year, their statements were known to the Gestapo within a few days. Word reached Frau von Cramon, through her SS source in Silesia, that the Gestapo were about to take action against the Oxford Group as an international spy network. She prepared a memorandum which was sent to headquarters by the Silesian SS officer. This, for the time being, averted the danger of suppression. The original report, however, lay on the files.

'NORWAY ABLAZE – DENMARK SHAKEN'

When Buchman returned from Canada in June 1934, with Hitler in power and his own work in Germany growing too slowly to affect events, he was looking for a way to bring spiritual leverage on Germany – as well as upon Britain – from outside. He knew that the Scandinavian countries possessed a special Nordic prestige in Germany and were respected in Britain. News of a Christian revolution there might carry more weight in both countries than similar tidings from elsewhere. 'The policy of striking in Scandinavia last year,' he wrote to Sir Lynden Macassey in May 1935, 'was with the hope that the whole continent of Europe would be influenced and find a true answer through the dictatorship of the living Spirit of God.'[1]*

Whether this was, in fact, a wholly deliberate plan, as implied in the letter to Macassey, or one which evolved through taking advantage of unexpected developments in certain people and was then perceived in hindsight – or a combination of both – is an open question.

One evening back in the spring of 1931 Buchman had dined beside Mrs Alexander Whyte, the elderly widow of a once-famous Edinburgh preacher. He asked her what was her greatest concern.

'I'm preparing to die,' she replied.

'Why not prepare to live?' he suggested.

They talked of the chaos in the world. She told him how she had first heard of his work in Shanghai and later in South Africa. Then she spoke of her hopes for the League of Nations where her son, Sir Frederick Whyte, was an economic expert.

Some months later, at the Oxford house-party, Mrs Whyte rose to her

---

* The Gestapo themselves thought this a sound strategy. 'Everything Scandinavian has a good name in Germany,' their report of 1936 stated. 'If Oxford (i.e. the Oxford Group) comes with tall blond Scandinavians of the same Lutheran upbringing, the movement will more easily find entry to the neighbouring countries to the south.' (Leitheft *Die Oxford- oder Gruppenbewegung* herausgegeben vom Sicherheitshauptamt, November 1936, Geheim, Numeriertes Exemplar No. 1, Documents Centre, Berlin, p. 10, quoting from *Nordschleswig'sche Korrespondenz*, 19 November 1935.)

feet and said that someone should take a team to Geneva. When she insisted a second time, Buchman said, in a characteristic phrase, 'Fine, you do it!' She booked a hundred rooms in Geneva, and Buchman set about getting together a suitable team. In January 1932 they stayed ten days in Geneva and met a number of delegates and officials; and this led to an invitation to address a luncheon of League personalities in September 1933.

A senior delegate to the league was C. J. Hambro, the President of the Norwegian Parliament and leader of the Conservative party there. It was his custom to use the long journey from Oslo to Geneva to translate books, and he had picked up a copy of *For Sinners Only* on a station bookstall. The book interested him, and when on arrival he heard that Buchman was speaking in Geneva that September, he made sure of attending.* At the end of the luncheon, he rose and declared, extemporaneously, that what he had just heard seemed to him more important than most of the subjects on the League agenda.

In December Buchman invited Hambro to England to speak to British Members of Parliament at Sir Francis Fremantle's meeting, when he concluded his speech with the invitation to Buchman to bring the Oxford Group to Norway. Buchman accepted, carrying Hambro off through a pea-soup fog to a weekend house-party in Eastbourne so that he would understand what he was letting himself in for. So it came about that, through following a series of unforeseen opportunities, Buchman and his team arrived in Norway in October 1934.

Norway was an unexpected country in which to launch a Christian revolution. Most authorities agree that at that time the intellectual climate was more nihilist there than in most European countries. This was in large measure due to the leadership of students and intellectuals influenced by Erling Falk, who had been converted to Communism in America and returned to Oslo to found the Communist-line paper *Mot Dag*. Moral relativism was a recognised part of Falk's ideological outlook.[2]

Carl Hambro was opposed to these trends. He was, perhaps, the most significant Norwegian statesman in the years between the wars, a kind of Churchillian figure. As the Conservatives were a minority party he never had the chance to form a government; but repeatedly he was re-elected President of the Parliament, and he was twice President of the League of Nations Assembly. His successor as President of the Parliament, Oscar Torp, a former Labour Prime Minister, described Hambro on his retirement as 'perhaps the greatest parliamentarian we have had in the

---

* According to the biography by his son Johan, Hambro's initial interest in the Oxford Group was aroused by enthusiastic letters from another son, Cato, who had met them in London. (Johan Hambro: *C. J. Hambro*, Aschehoug, 1984, p. 174).

recent history of Norway' whose 'name and contribution will live in the pages of history'.[3]

Hambro's invitation to Buchman in the early thirties arose from his realisation that political and economic measures were not sufficient to counter nihilism and a totalitarian faith. Yet he knew that any attempt to redirect the national thinking would meet with resistance, from which he naturally shrank. He also feared the financial cost of such an operation.

In August 1934 Buchman wrote to him, 'In all our planning we must think through all of Norway and the Nordic countries and the part they must play in world reconstruction. I do not think we need fear the publicity. You are accustomed to an Opposition and after all it is an opposition that may be won, because unless they see the need of a world-wide spiritual front, they themselves may have an anti-God movement at their doors which will be far more subtle and devastating; while this carries the constructive answer, as you well know, to the problems of the modern world. I beg of you to have no concern about finances and we need not now decide on numbers. We shall see eye-to-eye as things develop, but "Have no thought what we shall eat or what we shall drink." Our Heavenly Father will look after these things for us.'[4]

Hambro invited 120 of his friends to meet Buchman and thirty companions at the Tourist Hotel at Høsbjør in early October.

'What is going to happen up there?' Fredrik Ramm, a renowned editor who had been the only journalist with Amundsen in his flight over the North Pole, asked Reginald Holme as they travelled together.

'Miracles – and you will be one of them,' replied Holme.

Norwegians like plain talking, and Holme's prediction turned out to be true.

'At Høsbjør God extinguished all hatred and all fear in my relations to other people, classes and nations,' Ramm wrote later.[5]

Ronald Fangen, the novelist, brought two bottles of whisky and a crate of books, expecting boredom. He did not find time to open either. His change was immediately visible and long remembered. The lyric poet Alf Larsen, even twenty years later, spoke of the 'hopeless naivety' of the Group's philosophy as compared with his own anthroposophy. It had however completely transformed Fangen, who before that, in his opinion, had been the most unpleasant man in Norway.[6]

Eighty journalists turned up, and as they spread the news of what was happening at Høsbjør, more and more people came until every bed was filled for miles around and some even slept in their cars. By the second weekend, the number of guests had grown to 1,200.

'I don't know when Frank, or any of us, have laughed so much,' Loudon Hamilton wrote to his wife. 'Hambro is a continuous fund of really first-class yarns.' Four days later he added, 'A remarkable feature has been the way individuals and groups have been reconciled. Church divisions are very deep in Norway. But here they have become united. Two leading theologians detested each other. They were put in the same room and are now fast friends! Two party leaders (they were Hambro himself and Johann Mellbye, President of the Farmers' Party) who were well-known enemies were reconciled. Ronald Fangen, 6 ft 2 ins and former Authors' Association Chairman, has lost many enemies and made many friends. Frank says it is like roasting chestnuts before Christmas. You never know who will pop next.'[7]

At the end of the house-party Fredrik Ramm was offered a lift back to Oslo by Halvor Mustad, the son of a business man who had made a fortune by selling horse-shoe nails to both sides during World War I. Young Mustad was near-sighted and cheerfully reckless. Slithering down the snow-covered mountain road at high speed, he piled up in a snow-drift. Ramm emerged with the remark, 'What an excellent chance to have an "Oxford meeting" while we wait for another car,' and duly called the local villagers together to hear 'the miracles of Høsbjør'.[8]

'The Oxford Group Conquers Oslo: President Hambro, Ronald Fangen, editor Ramm and several other well-known men witness to their conversion' was a typical headline[9] about the first of three meetings that took place in one of Oslo's largest halls immediately after Høsbjør. Fourteen thousand people crowded in to them, and thousands more were turned away. Three thousand students attended a meeting at the University, and informal gatherings took place with railwaymen, nurses and doctors, teachers, civil servants and business and professional groups. The Military and Naval Club invited ten ex-officers travelling with Buchman to address them, with the Crown Prince present. Behind the scenes there was a ceaseless stream of personal interviews, informally estimated at 500 a day.

Early in December the visiting team, reinforced by Norwegians, moved on to Bergen. Again there were the same throngs. 'Oxford Conquers Bergen' ran one headline, as sub-editors began to drop the word 'group' in the interests of space.[10] The idea got around that an 'Oxford' man was one who had undergone a transforming spiritual experience – to the embarrassment of a visiting Oxford don.

Helge Wellejus, a Danish journalist whose articles appeared regularly in some twenty Scandinavian papers, described Buchman in action at one of these Bergen meetings: '. . . With Buchman on the rostrum the questions pour over the audience. He describes a situation. Short and crisp. Then a question. It is repeated. Uncomfortably aggressive. But always something which concerns everyone.

'He encourages a reply. But he catches it in the air. Turns it with lightning speed. And the bullet lodges itself in the bark of your brain. He never appeals to emotions. Often people who come from outside are moved. Then the Oxford people are on their guard. They seize the first opportunity for a humorous remark. The hall is filled with laughter. . . You sense the connection. Freud is a mere schoolboy compared to this. But there is nothing the least mystical or psychoanalytical about the whole thing. Everything is brilliantly a matter of course. Because the audence is forced all the time to creative participation. . . .'[11]

In Bergen one of the visitors was put to stay with the City Librarian, a much respected atheist called Smith, whose wife had recently reached the end of a long search for faith through meeting the Oxford Group. The visitor was an ex-atheist lecturer in moral philosophy, and Mrs Smith thought that he would be just the man to convert her husband. No such conversion took place. However, the indomitable Mrs Smith – one son describes her as one who would willingly have been torn to pieces by lions in the Coliseum but found household chores insufferable – herself came to be so different that all four Smith children found the same faith. The eldest son, who although sharing a room with his brother had not spoken to him for two years, apologised to him. All four later travelled with Buchman in various lands, Victor – the younger brother and an artist – once laying down his brush for two years to do so. 'It was in a small hall, with room for barely 100 people that, as a lad of seventeen, I uttered the words, I give my life to God,' he says. 'The meeting was led by a young engineer named Viggo Ullman, the father of the actress Liv Ullman, who can hardly have been born at the time. But the young engineer was typical of that troop of modern, forward-striving people, with no church background, who had now suddenly become leaders of a dynamic religious development.'[12]*

By Christmas it was clear that something out of the ordinary was taking place. While the London *Times*[13] 'Review of the Year' noted the 'astonishing popular success of the Group in Norway', the Oslo daily *Tidens Tegn* commented in its Christmas number,[14] 'A handful of foreigners who neither knew our language, nor understood our ways and customs, came to the country. A few days later the whole country was talking about God, and two months after the thirty foreigners arrived, the mental outlook of the whole country has definitely changed.'

Ronald Fangen's two-page press summary of the past twenty-five years in Norway, published the following May, was headed 'Into Nihilism and Out Again'. He wrote, 'The Oxford Group's decisive significance is that it

---

* At the age of 50, Victor Smith adopted his mother's name of Sparre. He became in later life one of the principal Western contacts of the Russian dissidents, and Solzhenitsyn travelled to Norway to meet him soon after his deportation from the Soviet Union. See his autobiography *The Flame in the Darkness* (Grosvenor, 1979), first published as *Stenene skal rope*. (Tiden Norsk Forlag, 1974.)

has given us back Christianity as simple and clear, as rich in victory and fresh fellowship as it was in the first Christian era. Its mighty mission and power is to my mind the only hope in an age of nihilism. One cannot drive out demons with devils. Only a great experience of Christian power can convince men that there is a meaning in life, a wholeness and unity in circumstances, and that there are eternal laws and values which cannot be broken with impunity. It is this which is now happening.'[15]

After Christmas this issue was tested at the Technical and Engineering College at Trondheim, where most of Norway's engineers and architects were educated. As in Oslo University the most vocal and strategic element there was nihilist. 'At a meeting in the Students' Hall virtually all the 900 students were present,' recalls Svend Major, then studying there. 'We heard some Oxford students, Elizabeth Morris, a vivacious girl from America, and Randulf Haslund who, although officially a fundamentalist theological student, had led the largest drinking party of the year a few weeks before. Then Hamilton said that anyone who wished could stay and meet the speakers. Virtually no one left. Next day and for many days the Oxford Group was the main subject of conversation.' One of those who regained his faith at Trondheim was a son of Bishop Berggrav of Tromsø.

The author Carl Fredrik Engelstad, then a student and later head of the National Theatre in Oslo, says of this period: 'I experienced the climate in the student world changing radically. It did not mean that the Oxford Group was accepted all round – on the contrary. But it became possible to discuss religious issues seriously and on a broad basis.' He described the irruption of the Oxford Group into the cultural life of Norway in the thirties, 'with a wind of revival, a strong and direct challenge, absolute standards and, at the same time, vision, hope and a Christian confidence of faith – a Christian world revolution'.[16]*

Larger social effects of the Oxford Group visit became the subject of observation and discussion. The London *Spectator*'s Special Correspondent stated that ' "converts" claim that religion has now become so much a part of the people's workaday lives that taxes are coming in more promptly, and debtors are more honest about paying tradesmen's bills. The political situation, they say, is less tense; the class war less ominous; a new idealism is breaking through.' The correspondent regarded such claims as 'exaggerated' but concluded, 'If the Groups succeed in imparting new values or new ideals to the political and social life of the country – and it is on this that the "converts" seem to be concentrating – much will have been gained.'[17] Two weeks later a feature article by 'A Bergen

---

* This did not all take place without controversy. The newspaper *Dagbladet* took a consistently opposing view, as did writers like Helge Krogh and Heiberg, and later ten Norwegian and Swedish writers published jointly a book disagreeing with the Oxford Group, called *Oxford and Ourselves*.

Correspondent' added, 'A national awakening has sprung to life in eight weeks in a country where, according to one of the bishops, 90 per cent of the people do not attend the churches. It has come through a challenge to the mind to think and to the will to take action. It has abundantly revealed that social regeneration comes as the fruit of changed lives.'[18]

The Norwegian Income Tax and Customs Departments began receiving an unprecedented number of overdue and unexpected payments. Supreme Court Advocate Erling Wikborg* stated in December 1936, 'It is unofficially learnt from high quarters that amounts paid to the Government between 1934 and 1936 run into seven figures in kroner and the process continues.'[19]**

Hambro seems to have become increasingly a bridge-builder in politics. As early as December 1933 *Drammens Tidende* stated that his London trip had 'lifted Hambro from the ranks of the politicians to the position of a true statesman'. The occasion was a meeting of the leaders of the Conservative Party which Hambro had led 'with his usual outstanding ability. And yet . . . there was a new atmosphere in the whole gathering. Instead of a bitter and stormy post-mortem on the election results, it was a calm consideration of the situation and of what would be most helpful to the nation. It was as though "party tricks" had all been swept away – no outbursts against other parties, no tactical schemings, no upbraidings. It was politics on a higher plane. Some "change" had taken place. And this seemed to reconnect with another "change" of which news had recently come in. The leader of the meeting had just spoken in the House of Commons building in London at a great religious meeting of something known as the "Oxford Group".'[20]

In January 1935, in a major speech, Hambro emphasised absolute values – 'something that transcends parties', 'lays aside wasteful strife' and 'lets us come quietly and modestly together' so that 'the country is led towards better conditions of work and a more spacious understanding between people on the opposite of old party divides which are now crumbling'.[21] He met a genuine response from a leading Labour Member, who was later elected to serve under him as Vice-President of the Parliament. Hambro, moreover, refused to hit back when a little later the leader of the Labour Party, Johan Nygaardsvold, made fun of the Oxford Group; and when, in March, Nygaardsvold became Prime Minister he

* Wikborg was a founder of the Norwegian Christian Democrat Party and served briefly as Foreign Minister in 1963.

** In January 1939 the Norwegian press announced the repayment of half a million kroner by one individual, and in 1939 Wikborg wrote to a friend, 'Since you introduced me to a new life through the Oxford Group in 1935 no single week has passed without my having at least one case on my hands to make the legal arrangements necessary to help someone pay up arrears of evaded taxes. (Erling Wikborg to Basil Yates, undated, 1939.)

remarked that 'a great deal of what Mr Hambro said today was a bouquet to the new Labour Government, even if there were a few thorns, by which I will try not to be pricked, among the flowers'.[22]

King Haakon received Buchman and thanked him for what he had done for the students, as well as, according to Buchman, expressing surprise at the reconciliation between Mellbye and Hambro. The King also told Dean Fjellbu of Trondheim Cathedral – the Westminster Abbey of Norway – that he was delighted at the new note of authority in the preaching in the churches and on the radio.[23]* Four professors of Oslo University wrote to the Oxford Group, 'Your visit will be a deciding factor for the history of Norway. You have come at the strategic moment with the right answer.'[24]

By March 1935 widespread interest among farmers and industrial workers led to further large meetings in the biggest halls in Oslo. In the City Hall, Buchman addressed one of them: 'Five months ago we started in this hall. Think of the wonder-working power of God in those five months . . . Before I landed in Norway it came to me constantly in my quiet times, "Norway ablaze for Christ".' Then he spoke of the two stages that still lay ahead of them – spiritual revolution and renaissance. 'I believe that Norway will take this message to other countries. I believe the revolution will be a renaissance,' he concluded.[25]

Certainly, something very like a renaissance was to take place in the Norwegian Church in the following years. For a quarter of a century it had been deeply divided between Liberals and Conservatives, who tended towards a fundamentalist theology. 'The conflict became personal and bitter,' writes Einar Molland, the Norwegian church historian, 'and the cleft widened . . . The tension between the conservative and liberal wings rose to its greatest heights in the late 1920s and early 1930s, and the general tone of theological argument, became, if possible, even more bitter.'[26] On one occasion when Bishop Berggrav, as Bishop of Tromsø, called a meeting of all his clergy, such a rumpus broke out that he tried to restore order by crying, 'Stop! We are all Christian brothers!' 'No! No! No!' shouted half his clergy.[27] The leader of the Conservatives, Professor Hallesby, sometimes practically forbade his followers to have any contact with the opposing faction, and, when Berggrav was appointed Bishop of Oslo, Hallesby 'wrote in the press that he could not welcome him until he abandoned his liberal past'.[28]

Meanwhile, where argument had failed to bring unity, change in individuals was having some effect. The beginnings noted by Hamilton at

---

* King Haakon told the Dean that he had thanked Buchman but suggested that he urge his followers to be 'careful in any confessions made in public'. The King twice visited the Oxford Group headquarters in London during the Second World War.

Høsbjør continued at all levels. Professor Mowinckel, the leading Norwegian Old Testament scholar of the day, was seen by conservatives as the very incarnation of the Devil, and his books always aggravated dissension within the Church. Primarily a man of science, a sincere seeker after truth wherever it should lead him, he had little vital personal faith. He saw that faith at work in the people at Høsbjør, and decided that he wanted the 'pearl of great price'. With characteristic honesty, he realised that he would not find it unless he was ready to give up everything for it; and he had two great loves, his new country house and the book which, after years of work, he had just finished. In the end he told God that he was willing to give them up if God asked it. Immediately, the thought came: 'Keep the house; burn the book.' He did so. No one knows exactly what the book contained because, having had orders to destroy it, he felt he should not talk of it: but there can be no doubt that it would have increased the disunity of the Church.[29] From this time, the fundamentalists changed their attitude towards Mowinckel.

Speaking at an Oxford Group meeting in Copenhagen on 31 March 1935, Bishop Berggrav explained: 'I must admit that I did not entirely approve of the methods of the Oxford Group to begin with, but when I saw how God had used it in Norway, especially in the life of my own family, I had to change my whole attitude. What is now happening in Norway is the biggest spiritual movement since the Reformation.'*

In the following year Berggrav, in a long article in *Kirke og Kultur*, noted some 'obvious facts' about changes in Norwegian life during the preceding year: '1. A new atmosphere has been born, a change in the whole situation of the spiritual life of the country. Not only is there more room for the eternal, there is also a greater longing for it . . . 2. God's name is mentioned not in a new way, but by new people . . . Now unexpected people have begun to proclaim God's power in their lives. God has become alive. 3. The whole question has changed from being secret and impersonal to becoming open and personal. There has been a "Nicodemus period" with regard to the deepest inner questions. Now they are discussed on the streets . . .'**

---

* *Kristeligt Dagbladet*, 2 April 1935. The last sentence is omitted from the paper's account of the Bishop's speech in the morning session, but is in contemporary typescripts of his speech and was referred to during a meeting later in the day by the chairman, Kenaston Twitchell, reported in the same article.

** Writing in *Kirke og Kultur* (7 August 1984) on *The Oxford Group in Retrospect after 50 Years*, Stephan Tschudi, former Rector of The Practical Theological Seminary of Oslo University, recalled: 'Many of those gripped had very little knowledge of Christianity. But they recognised themselves in the gospel accounts of men and women who followed the Master – without any dogma. And they looked with astonishment at people who seemed to know all about Christianity without it having any visible affect on their lives.'

'Our Christian and Church life,' Berggrav added, 'has been a life of mistrust in all directions. But now I think we have learnt something new about trust between us. It never can be founded on people, but on God . . . I think the Oxford Group has helped me to see this. Speaking openly should be a vehicle for and an expression of trust.'[30]

More progress was needed, and it was on the day that war in Europe broke out, 1 September 1939, that Berggrav received a compelling thought: 'There is war in Europe. There is also war between you and Hallesby. Go and see him.' He did not know how to start, but his wife suggested he might telephone. 'I have been expecting you,' answered Hallesby, and they met.[31] What exactly passed between them is not known, but it was as a result of this meeting that the two men co-operated in the manifesto, 'God's Call to Us Now', which was printed in all the newspapers. Describing these events, Professor Karl Wisløff, in his history of the Norwegian Church, wrote, 'Many were amazed to see those two names together. Hallesby had always refused to take part in any public statement with a man known as a liberal theologian.' Wisløff also describes a larger meeting in Berggrav's house on 25 October 1940, at which Hallesby and some of his colleagues joined with leaders of the liberal wing to create the Kristent Samråd (Christian Council of Collaboration).[32] This was to become 'the general staff of the church's struggle, which worked together excellently for the duration of the war'.[33]

Before Buchman left Norway in March 1935 Hambro wrote to him calling the impact on the country 'a miracle' and 'a return to mental health'.[34] He received a characteristic reply. 'If the present pace continues, and there seems no abatement, you cannot much longer delay the decision which, under God, may not only change the history of Norway, but of Europe,' wrote Buchman. 'I know no secondary issue can claim you, God demands the maximum.'[35] Through the entire campaign Buchman had been challenging Hambro to a more thorough surrender of his life and plans to God, a surrender which Hambro seems to have side-stepped on various occasions.

Norway's neighbours, meanwhile, had been following events there closely. The interest of the Danes had been heightened, in January 1935, by a visit from Fredrik Ramm, well known to them for his passionate antagonism to their country. Ramm had fought bitterly through his newspaper to protect Norwegian fishing rights around Greenland, and when, after a prolonged dispute, the International Court at The Hague pronounced in Denmark's favour, that had only increased his animosity. But at Høsbjør, as he wrote, 'the ice melted in my heart and a new, unknown feeling began to grow, a love of people unfettered by what they could give me'.[36] Now he said on Danish radio, 'The main thing I am here to tell you is that my greatest fault has been my hatred of the Danes. My mind was poisoned with that hatred ... Now I am here to put things straight.'[37] The Copenhagen daily, *Dagens Nyheder*, headlined its story, 'The Oxford Group effaces Norwegian-Danish hatred'.[38]

Where Norway's intellectual atmosphere had been coloured by Marxism, Denmark's comfortable way of life – 'well-buttered', Buchman called it – was flavoured by the sceptical and free-thinking liberalism of Georg Brandes, the Professor of Aesthetics at Hamburg and Copenhagen Universities successively. He had died only eight years earlier, having published his final book, *The Jesus Myth*, in 1925 at the age of eighty-three. Denmark's deep Christian foundations had been strengthened by a revival in the mid-nineteenth century, but the Church now freely admitted that it had lost the confidence of the intellectuals and the workers. What was happening in Norway was a fruitful topic of discussion and witticism, but it was widely assumed that it could not happen in Denmark.

Buchman visited Denmark in January 1935, at the same time as Ramm. He found the interest intense, and there were strong demands that he bring a team there. But he was aware that the Norwegian pattern could not be repeated. For one thing, there was no Danish figure comparable to Hambro willing to initiate a move from within. 'The local forces are not clever enough to handle the situation,' Buchman wrote to Kenaston Twitchell. 'So I have asked them for the moment to refrain from anything that would catch public attention. Everything had been wonderfully prepared, the Bishop favourable, when some old-fashioned Christians started a house-party on old lines and did not know how to handle the press. They had a prayer meeting for reporters and so gave them a splendid chance to get a scoop. We will not be able to start with a house-party, because of the wrong sort they have been having.'

He went on, 'Do not broadcast the fact that Denmark may begin in mid-March because the same kind of people we met in Princeton are certainly in Copenhagen. That crowd moved north from Berlin and we are already feeling their opposition.' It is not clear whether Buchman was referring here to targeted opposition from specific individuals or groups, or to the general confrontation with those who were committed to moral relativism. Berlin at that period was certainly the centre of a decadence which was spreading through Europe, and Buchman's work was bound to come into collision with this force in situations where both were active. In any case, the awareness of possible confrontation with organised evil was never far from Buchman's mind, due in part to his own militant spirit and in part to his experiences. His letter continued, 'What you have got here is the result of spiritual deformity over a long period. Think of gnomes crawling around in darkness in a cave. All of a sudden there comes illumination and things become clear. But unless we do something quickly, this nation will be overripe and the Christian forces will, sensationalize the Groups and people will not have the opportunity to know the real message.'[39] The thought he had had was, 'Denmark will be shaken.'

Buchman decided 'to go to the court of public opinion', as he expressed it, in big public meetings. But there were difficulties. 'I am confidentially told some of the students are trying to stage a discussion in the University to make the work of the Group look ridiculous,' he wrote. 'One of the best ways to kill anything in Denmark is to have people laugh at it.'[40] Meanwhile opponents from other countries were circulating books like that of the Bishop of Durham.

In March 1935, however, all was ready. Buchman gathered an international force of 300 in Copenhagen for three days of training, during which he instructed them on everything from the policies of the five national dailies to the necessity to keep their bowels open in spite of the ample Danish breakfast liable, according to him, to be climaxed by a rich pastry cake.

Everything, he felt, depended on the first meeting, which was to be broadcast on the national radio and at which many workers and intellectuals were expected, including some of the Socialist cabinet. Consequently, he planned that speakers from Labour backgrounds, like George Light and Jimmie Watt, should predominate. Every ticket was taken, and few clerics were visible except for one black-clad row, all of whom appeared to be taking notes. Buchman hit his target. Many of the workers and atheist intellectuals stayed on to talk with the speakers, some deciding to experiment then and there with the ideas they had heard. One of these was a well-known High Court Advocate, Valdemar Hvidt, who got into discussion with a recent Oxford graduate. The lawyer explained that he had no belief in God but then, spying a young business man, who had that week come to him to institute divorce proceedings, in the room with his wife, added, 'If something happened to that pair, I might even think again.' Next day the couple called at his office and said that they wanted to call off the divorce. All three, the couple and the lawyer, ended up working with Buchman for life.

Next day the Bishop of Copenhagen, Dr F. Fuglsang-Damgaard, who had already publicly announced that the Oxford Group had taught him to listen to God, called on Buchman. He said that the row of clerics reported that the name of Christ had only been mentioned ten times in the meeting. Why was that?

'I was at your house for tea last week, Bishop,' replied Buchman, 'and you did not mention that you loved your wife.'

Silence fell. The Bishop saw Buchman's point. Later, the Bishop declared, 'The Oxford Group is teaching us to talk differently to pagans and atheists, sceptics, critics and agnostics. A new road to the old Gospel –

that is my conception of the Oxford Group. It moves from the circumference to the centre. It stands inside the Church and not beside it.'[41]*

Over thirty thousand people attended meetings in the first six days in Copenhagen. The national broadcast had brought a swift response from the countryside and islands as well as from the Danish population across the Schleswig border. When an anti-Oxford Group meeting was held in the University, it was reported to be a 'colossal fiasco'. Planned by a theological student turned Marxist, who was supported by a brilliant array of Brandesque academics, it was invaded by militant factory workers. 'Something happened which had never happened before in Copenhagen,' reported *Dagens Nyheder*. 'Workers stood up one after another and witnessed to Christianity in a hall that consisted primarily of fanatical opponents of all religion.'[42]

Reports of the campaign in the press were at first unenthusiastic. A highly positive report of the first meeting then appeared in *Social-Demokraten*,[43] and *Kristeligt Dagbladet*, the Christian daily, remarked indulgently, 'You can't expect Americans to get it right on the first night.'[44] Emil Blytgen-Petersen, the *Dagens Nyheder* reporter assigned to the Group, returned to his paper saying he had been unable to interview Buchman. The paper's star feature writer and associate editor, Carl Henrik Clemmensen, went down to try personally. A three-hour talk resulted, at which both men asked questions, and each was equally frank.

Clemmensen wrote a little later, 'I cannot understand how any churchman could think it did not matter what millions of men and women are making out of life. I cannot understand any form of Christianity that has any other goal than a revolution of the unchristian world we live in. And that, of course, implies a revolution, a thorough-going and drastic change of the life of the individual.

'I can understand the Oxford Group. I can understand that group of men and women who, in one remarkable way or another, have found themselves brought together in a common work, with the object of producing the kind of Christian revolution I have described. I can understand the Four Absolutes. None of us, perhaps, will completely succeed in living up to them, but they will always be a standard measuring the quality of our lives and marking how far each one of us does reach. I can understand people who refuse to sit with folded hands, watching the world go to ruin, but who are convinced that in their work to save the world they will receive daily inspiration from the one source from which we can

---

* Nearly twenty years later the Bishop said at the World Council of Churches in Evanston, USA, in August 1954: 'The visit of Frank Buchman to Denmark in 1935 was an historic experience in the story of the Danish Church. It will be written in letters of gold in the history of the Church and the nation. Whenever I visit Dr Buchman, our talk is all of the Cross of Christ, which is the centre of his heart, soul and faith.'

hope for inspiration, if only we will become what a Danish author has called "open" people instead of "closed" people . . .

'They spoke to me on an entirely new wavelength. They spoke in a language I could understand. They did not scare me with any theological terminology. They did not make me apprehensive or suspicious by unfolding a vast mystical apparatus.'

And of Buchman he wrote: 'Calm and smiling is the man who started the whole Oxford Group . . . He has strength. He is a quite outstanding psychologist. He deals with people as individuals. He never deals with two people in the same way. He knows all about you when you have talked with him for a few minutes. He is an ambitious man, but I have a living conviction that he is ambitious only that what is good may triumph. I could easily name straight away at least five eminent church leaders who would do well with a considerably larger equipment of that kind of ambition. He is positive. I have never heard him say a single negative sentence. He never replies to attacks. I have never seen him put on an artificial smile. I call him "the laughing apostle". All round the world I have met very few people so completely harmonious and natural in their ordinary pleasures and happiness.'[45]

Meanwhile, two of the papers founded by Brandes, *Politiken* and *Extrabladet*, had begun to treat the visitors seriously, sometimes with a sly humour but sometimes respectfully and at considerable length.

In addition to the public meetings, Buchman was holding meetings of his team each morning to which more and more Danes came. Besides the Bishop and Dean Brodersen of Copenhagen, an amazing cross-section of the population would turn up. Often these meetings were thick with smoke from short Danish cigars. At one of them Buchman called for a time of listening to God. Then he laughed and said, 'There have never been any rules in the Oxford Group up to now, but I think we will have to make our first one here in Denmark. That will be that all ladies must put down their cigars when we decide to have a quiet time together!'

From Copenhagen Buchman went to spend Easter, with all who wanted to come, at Haslev, an educational centre some thirty miles away. Every school was filled to the brim – adults often sleeping in children's beds* – and as farmers, the unemployed, whole villages flocked in, people slept in cars and even in the local prison. 'Last Friday,' Buchman wrote, 'they had to take to the fields in one village because there was no longer room in the church.'[46]

Berlingske Tidende sent a young woman called Gudrun Egebjerg to cover the event. She now recalls her first impressions of Buchman: 'Certainly

---

* Mrs Fog-Petersen, wife of the Dean of Odense, had such a cot. Asked by Buchman if she had slept well, she replied politely, 'Thank you, I slept many times.'

not a "spiritual leader", whatever that was. A quietly well-dressed man with a long pointed nose in a round face, an incongruity. (Years later, when somebody mentioned it I noticed that he did not like *that*! I was surprised. At the time I thought he was way above human vanity; but somehow I liked him for it. . . .) But what you felt, first of all, right away, was that he was interested in the person he met, in this case me, in a friendly, open way. A journalist is so used to being met with caution, "Now be careful what you say" – not Dr Buchman. He knew what he wanted to say and how, and then he had that wonderful sense of humour and that wise, kind, untroubled way of looking at you. I also felt, without I think registering it consciously, a natural authority in him.'

After Haslev, Buchman's team spread out through Själland and Fyn. The most notable occasion was a meeting in Odense, the capital of Fyn and Hans Andersen's birth-place. It took place on Norway's national day, and the last speaker was Fredrik Ramm. He described how his hatred of Denmark had been cured, and then he asked the audience to sing the Danish national anthem. There was a hush, and then, without a word of prompting, 3,000 Danes broke into the Norwegian anthem, so that the walls and room vibrated with the sound. Ramm stood in tears, seeing unity born where he had caused division.

Now that evidence of change on a national scale had emerged in Norway and Denmark, Buchman wished to bring it to bear on the Continent, and especially upon Germany. He conceived a great Scandinavian demonstration, which took place on Whit Sunday at Kronborg (popularly known as 'Hamlet's Castle') at Elsinore. The castle courtyard was filled with ten thousand people, and other thousands listened through loudspeakers on the grassy ramparts outside. Late that night Clemmensen wrote of the endless streams of people, the rise and fall of the music, the people from politics and the Church on the platform and the youth, the farmers, and the workers who spoke of listening to the voice of the Living God and obeying. He sketched Buchman's life, and went on, 'I have never heard of anything like it in our age. This man had the determined vision of the conquest of the world. He came as an unknown soldier from one of Christendom's front-line trenches, and stood today in this Danish Castle as the leader of a modern crusade that spans the world.'[47]

Soon after this demonstration Buchman returned to Britain for an Oxford house-party, which was attended by hundreds from Scandinavia. In September he returned to the Danish province of Jutland with a team of nearly 1,000, which, according to Emil Blytgen-Petersen, 'swept over the peninsula like a sandstorm'[48] and visited practically every town and village.

Alfred Nielsen, manager of a sawmill in North Schleswig, just short of the German border, was living in constant fear of what the slump might do to his business and industry. 'I followed Buchman round Jutland like a dog, because I wanted the answer I saw in him,' he says. 'What he gave me saved me from a mental breakdown. He opened my eyes to my selfish pride towards my wife, my workers and my colleagues – and towards the Germans living with us in North Schleswig.'[49] One result, according to *Scandinavian Review*, was that Nielsen, 'proprietor of the largest sawmill combine in Jutland', who had earlier 'refused to grant his employees a wage increase . . . on the plea that his firm's finances would not stand it, honestly told his men in 1937 that the true reason was that his private pocket would have suffered. He went into the entire finances of the firm with his men and they agreed unitedly upon adequate provision for everyone.'[50]

By late 1935 the Oxford Group in Denmark was working under Danish leaders. On 18 October 1935, less than seven months after Buchman's arrival in Copenhagen, 25,000 assembled in the Forum there and in two overflow halls. Paul Brodersen, Dean of Copenhagen, led the demonstration and the speakers included a carpenter, a nurse, a horse-dealer from an outlying island, the head of an oil refinery and two of his employees, Copenhagen's top band leader, the Director of the National Technological Institute and fifteen students led by the President of the Copenhagen University Student Council. The audience, wrote *Berlingske Tidende*, 'was not of any one class or type or age, but the whole electoral roll from A to Z'.[51]

On the first anniversary of Buchman's arrival in Denmark he spoke at a weekend rally which brought some 20,000 to Ollerup in the Fyn countryside. 'The Oxford Group goes on its victorious way,' commented *Extrabladet* in an editorial. 'We cannot but be grateful for the contribution they have made to the moral betterment of many people's lives. If there is one thing we need it is to become better people, more honest, more upright than we are and with purer thought-life and warmer hearts than we have.'[52]

The effect of this new life was to prepare many Scandinavians, in Denmark as in Norway, for the perils of occupation. In Denmark Clemmensen was assassinated by Danish Nazis – individuals, incidentally, who had opposed Buchman during his visit – while others like Colonel H. A. V. Hansen performed acts of outstanding courage in the Resistance and lived to tell the tale.[53] Bishop Fuglsang-Damgaard was sent to a concentration camp. Before imprisonment he smuggled a message to Buchman that through the Oxford Group he had found a spirit which the Nazis could not break and that he went without fear.[54]

In Norway Fangen was the first of Buchman's colleagues to be arrested,[55] the Oxford Group being banned at the same time. In the years before the war Fangen and Ramm had travelled up and down Scandinavia from the Lofoten Islands to Helsinki weaving a network of people who were morally and spiritually secure. When Norway was occupied Ramm kept links with them by letter and by articles in his newspaper which, under the innocent title of 'What to do in the Blackout', drew historical parallels full of hidden meaning to Norwegian patriots.

When the Nazis discovered what Ramm meant, they arrested him. A month later he was released with a warning, because his influence 'threatened to demoralise the whole prison'. He returned to the fight, was rearrested and deported to Hamburg where, even in solitary confinement, the radiance of his faith permeated the prison. To the only friend he saw in his two years' confinement, he said, 'Tell Eva [his wife] that my letters express the full truth of my experience. Even though I am alone, I do not feel lonely. Everything we have learnt in the Oxford Group is true. I say "rather in prison with God, than outside without Him".'

Ramm developed tuberculosis. Even now he refused the offer of better food and conditions in exchange for making goods for the Germans. He became weaker and weaker, and was released through a compassionate act by the prison Governor, who had come to respect him. The Danish ambulance which was sent for him crossed the frontier just ahead of a Nazi order forbidding his release, and he reached Odense. There he died, a Norwegian flag in his hand placed there by a Danish friend. When Ramm's body arrived in Oslo, crowds thronged the Cathedral Square, ignoring every attempt to coerce them into dispersing, and when the news reached the Norwegian government in exile in London, Foreign Minister Koht said, 'When the history of these times comes to be written, Fredrik Ramm's name will go down as one of Norway's greatest heroes.'[56]

The active Church resistance in Norway was triggered off by Fjellbu, by now a bishop. On 1 February 1942, the day that Quisling took office as Prime Minister, he found Trondheim Cathedral locked against him when he went to celebrate Holy Communion. Nazi soldiers were telling the congregation to go home, but they would not. Fjellbu slipped in by a small side door, robed and started the service from the High Altar. The soldiers did not dare arrest him there, and the choir, having taken their position, began singing 'A Mighty Fortress is Our God'. Soon the congregation, standing in the snow outside, took it up. For that morning's work, Fjellbu was removed from office. At once all the Norwegian bishops, led by Berggrav and followed by the clergy, laid down the secular duties normally prescribed to them as part of the state Church. On Easter Day all Norwegian pastors followed suit, and at the same time Bishop Berggrav was arrested. It was expected that he would be tried and convicted, because he had visited England in 1940; but suddenly he was moved from prison to the mountain hut where he spent three years in lonely house arrest. Berlin had intervened.

The intervention was initiated by the *Abwehr*, and the two emissaries sent by Admiral Canaris, who secretly worked against Hitler and ultimately was executed by him, were Bonhoeffer and Bonhoeffer's friend, von Moltke. So Bonhoeffer saw in action in Norway the very type of resistance he had advocated to the Church in Germany ten years earlier.[57] Comparison between the two situations is impossible, since it was one thing to achieve a united resistance in an occupied country, and another to create it in Germany once Hitler had become established. However, such unity in Norway was achieved in the face of great risks, and would have been impossible without the healing of bitter divisions which had taken place there from 1934 onwards.

On 22 April 1945 Bishop Fjellbu preached in the church of St Martin-in-the-Fields, London. 'I wish to state publicly,' he said, 'that the foundations of the united resistance of Norwegian Churchmen to Nazism were laid by the Oxford Group's work.'[58] In a press interview, the Bishop added, 'The first coming of the Oxford Group to Norway was an intervention of Providence in history, like Dunkirk and the Battle of Britain. They helped to bridge the gap between religion and the people and make it real every day. We have been fighting more than an armed army. We have been fighting godless materialism. The Oxford Group gave us men who helped us to fight for a Christian ideology.'[59]

Hambro, in the previous year, wrote, 'My thoughts go back to that first house-party in Norway in 1934 . . . to Frank Buchman, the catalyst who made possible the united church front in Norway in this war . . .

'The Germans decreed in Norway that the Oxford Group was a part of the British Intelligence Service and should be harshly suppressed – a most flattering and slightly ridiculous compliment to the British Intelligence Service. The Gestapo feared and hated the Oxford Group as they could never fear and hate the British Intelligence Service. They hated them as men hate and fear the ideals they have lost and prostituted, the faith they have betrayed. They feared them because instinctively they knew the Oxford Group was part of God's Intelligence Service preparing the way for an ultimate defeat of the principles of evil.'[60]

HITLER AND THE GESTAPO CLAMP-DOWN

Buchman had known by early 1934 that he could not work in Germany in the same way as elsewhere. House-parties were spied upon, and large public demonstrations like those in the democratic countries were impossible. He counted upon such events in other countries having some effect upon German leaders, and ensured that news of them reached the highest possible quarters in Berlin. He also relied on the written word – sixteen books and booklets were published in Germany in the early 1930s – as well as on his speeches. At the same time, he had not given up the hope of reaching the leaders of Germany personally.

In September 1934 Moni von Cramon was invited by Himmler to the Nazi Party rally at Nuremberg, and arranged for Buchman and a few of his team to be invited too. Some months before, she had found herself one evening unexpectedly sitting next to Himmler at a dinner, and Himmler's questions had once again been about how the guidance of God worked out in her life. Feeling that 'such a chance God gives only once', she had told him in detail what a drastic change in her living and thinking it had entailed for her and had emphasised 'the significance for individuals, nations and the whole world, if God's plan were to be fulfilled'. He had listened quietly. Now, at Nuremberg, she and Buchman sat next to Himmler at an informal lunch. Their talk was once more about seeking the guidance of God, and Buchman spoke of the moral and spiritual pre-conditions involved. In the middle of the meal, Frau von Cramon was called to the telephone. It was her son to tell her of the death of her divorced husband. She returned to the table much distressed because, although her husband had been legally the guilty party, she had by now realised the part her self-righteousness had played in breaking up the marriage. She told Himmler this. 'If only you could hate this man who broke loyalty with you, you would not suffer so much,' he said.

'This brought us back to talking about God's absolute demands,' Frau von Cramon recalled. Then lunch broke up. Buchman's comment at this time was, 'We should have a greater commitment than these fellows.'

Moni von Cramon reported the profound shock which the 'night of the long knives' of June 1934 – when the leaders of the storm-troopers and many of his non-Nazi opponents were eliminated by Hitler – had been to Buchman. 'It took a lot to win him back to any hope for Germany,' she told Hans Stroh. At Oxford house-parties Buchman did not encourage speeches either for or against Germany. This Stroh appreciated. 'We were surprised to find Christians abroad who did not automatically condemn all Germans,' he recalls. 'The diagnosis was the same, but their attitude was different. But our problem back in Germany remained – and I had been aware of it long before meeting Buchman: how to be faith-full and yet sober and realistic, how to keep the distinction between faith for the destiny of a changed Germany and a sober diagnosis of the moral and political reality of the situation.'

In the following year, 1935, Himmler telegraphed to Frau von Cramon from Berlin: 'I expect you on Tuesday at ten o'clock.'

'Mother was very ill,' recalls her daughter, Rosie Haver. 'She had been with Buchman to Norway and then in hospital in Denmark, where they thought – wrongly, as it happened – that she had a brain tumour. She had just been brought home when she got Himmler's telegram. She decided she had no choice but to go, and handed over responsibility for us children to her brother. Before leaving she made her will. She did not think she would return.'

'My brother wanted me to refuse to go,' wrote Frau von Cramon. 'I trembled at what might happen, but I remembered the commission which God had given me to bring a message to the leaders of Germany.'

At the SS headquarters in Prinz Albrechtstrasse, she was kept waiting alone in a room lit only by a window near the ceiling from ten in the morning till seven at night. She thought that either concentration camp or death awaited her. Then, at seven, Himmler came in with his ADC, SS-Obergruppenführer Karl Wolff.

'So you are going to arrest me? Am I going into a concentration camp?' she asked.

'My ADC will take you in my car. The driver knows where,' replied Himmler.

'Where am I being taken?' Frau von Cramon asked Wolff in the car.

'I am not authorised to tell you,' he replied.

In the dark, the car stopped in front of a house guarded by SS men. Out stepped an unknown woman.

'I'm Frau von Cramon. Who are you?'

'I'm Frau Himmler. Didn't my husband tell you? You are to be our guest for a few days.'

It was Whitsun. The first two days passed as though it were an ordinary visit, including party games in the evening. On the third day, Himmler said to Frau von Cramon, 'I wanted to test you,' and offered her the job of initiating social welfare work among their women and children.

Frau von Cramon declined, saying that she was, in Himmler's eyes, three unforgivable things – she was not a member of the National Socialist Party, she was an aristocrat and she was a Christian. Himmler brushed aside these objections. Finally she said, 'I can't give you a definite reply yet, because I am working with Buchman's team, and I wouldn't take any step without letting him know about it.'

Himmler looked perplexed. 'Are you so tied up with this foreigner and his group?'

She replied, 'Yes. I have accepted the total claim of God on my life, and it was these people who showed me the way to that.'

'Well,' said Himmler, 'as far as I am concerned you can ask them.'

During these conversations Himmler, who had been brought up a Catholic, said to her, 'Tell me, who is Christ?' He maintained it was 'Jewish' to push off on to others the responsibility for one's sins. 'I do not need Christ,' he said.

She asked, 'What are you going to do about your sins which no one can take from you and which you cannot put right?'

He replied, 'As an Aryan I must have the courage to take the responsibility for my sins alone.'

She said, 'You cannot do that, because your disobedience to God is robbing Germany of the plan He has for her.'

He concluded, 'I can do without Christ because Christ means the Church and my Church has excommunicated me.' Several times he came back to this topic.

Moni von Cramon did not like Himmler's offer. She and all her family distrusted Hitler. But she continued to feel that it was her duty to maintain contact with the leaders of Germany so that perhaps some of them might change, as she had changed. That, she thought, was the only hope of averting disaster.

After consulting with Buchman, Frau von Cramon agreed to do what she could for the German women, stipulating that she would on no account compromise the basic convictions of her faith or her freedom of operation. This was conceded; but she was speedily neutralised by others in the organisation. She functioned in name for eighteen months, in fact – due to illness – for five months, and exercised some influence in restraining hotheads, but was removed when her enemies found that she had warned an Oxford Group friend who was helping Jews in Berlin. After that she never saw Himmler again. She was finally dismissed when, during an investigation by Frau Scholz-Klink, the national head of the Nazi women, she refused to take the oath of total obedience to the Party.

Buchman used the brief breathing-space provided by the Gestapo's knowledge that he had a friend at Himmler's court to express his message through local meetings, conducted under the eyes of police agents, and through the printed word. As late as 20 May 1937 the North West headquarters of the Gestapo reported that 'the Group is beginning to spread effectively through Germany and is trying, apparently with success, to gain influence in Party circles' and stated that 'the Reichsführer SS has ordered the maintenance of the strictest observation of the movement'.[1]

Buchman was staking his life's work and such reputation as he had on an attempt to present Germany with an alternative to Nazism. He made this the theme of his call to Europe from Kronborg in Denmark, a call delivered that same Whitsun when Frau von Cramon was staying, half-guest, half-prisoner, at the Himmlers' home: 'There must come a spiritual dynamic which will change human nature and remake men and nations. There must come a spiritual authority which will be accepted everywhere by everyone. Only so will order come out of chaos in national and international affairs . . . Some nation must produce a new leadership, free from the bondage of fear, rising above ambition, and flexible to the direction of God's Holy Spirit. Such a nation will be at peace within herself, and a peacemaker in the international family. Will it be your nation?'

This speech was broadcast in several countries, but refused by the German Propaganda Ministry. Buchman knew he would have to find other ways of getting a hearing in Germany.

During the Oxford house-party in the summer of 1935 Buchman seemed uncertain what to do in Germany. He told Hans Stroh he 'feared that Himmler had closed his heart'. Whether Himmler's heart had ever been open – or whether, as was certainly the case later, he merely wanted to use Buchman and his colleagues for his own ends – was harder to assess then than it is to assume now. Buchman knew that Himmler was a lapsed Catholic – in youth he had been an altar boy – and hoped that some remnant of unease at lost faith still lurked in him. On 19 November 1935 *Berlingske Tidende* of Copenhagen printed Himmler's photograph with the headline 'Nazi confesses his faith in living God', and other papers reported that Frau Himmler had been influenced by the Oxford Group. 'Frank always realised what it would mean for the world if Himmler were to be changed,' Frau von Cramon writes; and Buchman said at the time, 'People will say I'm pro-Nazi if I pursue this, but I am not worried.'

In August 1935 he was once again invited to Nuremberg through Frau von Cramon. He took the Oxford theologian, Dr B. H. Streeter, with him.

This was the first Nuremberg Rally in which detachments of the German Army took part, and Buchman and Streeter were struck, as was every visitor, by the massive mobilisation it represented. 'Frank Buchman,' said Frau von Cramon, 'constantly spoke to me about his growing concern at the military development. He said several times that he felt Himmler had, as his power grew, lost any interest in the Group's message.' He also felt a tenser atmosphere surrounding his own work. It came to light that a Dutch girl who had attended some Oxford Group meetings had fallen for an SS officer and made allegations which supported those in the Gestapo who looked on the Oxford Group as a super-subtle spy network of the democracies. This made Buchman apprehensive for his German team, as well as rendering his own task more difficult.

In 1936, the year of the occupation of the Rhineland and of the Berlin Olympic Games, criticisms of Buchman's work began to appear in Nazi publications. In February, General Ludendorff's extremist newspaper *Aryan* lined up the Oxford Group as one of the 'sinister international forces which wage constant underground war against Germany'.[2] *Berlingske Aftenavis* of Copenhagen added, 'His (Ludendorff's) last issue contained the most fearful curses against the movement. He has discovered that the Oxford Group together with the Jews, the Freemasons, the Pope and the League of Nations constitutes a supernatural power which wants to kill the German spirit.'[3] In February, too, the principal article in the confidential paper issued by the ideologist of the Nazi Party, Alfred Rosenberg, was an indictment of the Group Movement in Germany,[4] and on 21 July the Bavarian Political Police ordered all police authorities to send reports on the strength and composition of the Groups in their districts within two weeks.[5] Later, Rosenberg described the movement as 'a second world-wide Freemasonry'.[6] Time was obviously running out.

In April 1936 Countess Ursula Bentinck wrote to Buchman on his return from America, 'I want you to know that I and others feel it is high time you went to see Hitler . . . I cannot write more.'[7] On the back of the letter Buchman wrote, 'There is enough power in the Cross to solve the world's problems, but we Christians have not used it. A vital experience backed by national and international action would startle the world – not in old moulds but in new thought.'

Influential people in Britain and America were also urging him – some tauntingly, some seriously – to see Hitler. With some the attitude was: 'Don't bother us. We're all right. It's Hitler you need to change!' Others, while seeing the difficulties, genuinely thought he might pull something off.

Buchman went to the Olympic Games in August. When he reached Berlin, Moni von Cramon arranged for him to be invited to a lunch party with Himmler at which the hosts were a German diplomat and his wife. Buchman's objective was to get an interview where he could talk more directly to Himmler and through him reach Hitler. He got his appointment for a couple of days later.

By chance an independent witness to the purpose and outcome of this meeting presented himself twenty-six years afterwards. A Danish journalist in Berlin, Jacob Kronika,* wrote in the paper he then edited, the *Flensborg Avis*:

'During the Hitler years Frank Buchman stayed at the Hotel Esplanade in Berlin. One day we ate lunch together. In the afternoon he was to have a conversation with the SS Chief Himmler, who had invited Dr Buchman to come and see him.

'The conversation, of course, became a complete fiasco. Himmler could not, as he intended, exploit the "absolute obedience" of the MRA** people towards God for the benefit of the obedient slaves of the SS and the Nazis.

'Frank Buchman was then much burdened by the development in Germany under Hitler, for he was deeply attached to this land and this people.

'He said during the meal at the Esplanade in Berlin, "Germany has come under the dominion of a terrible demoniac force. A counter-action is urgent. We must ask God for guidance and strength to start an anti-demoniac counter-action under the sign of the Cross of Christ in the democratic countries bordering on Germany, especially in the small neighbouring countries."

'But the Hitler demonism had to spend its rage. Neither Frank Buchman nor any other person could prevent that.'[8]

Confirmation of this account has come from a number of younger colleagues who went with Buchman to the interview. According to them, Himmler came in with some of his henchmen, gave a propagandist account of Nazism and left, without giving Buchman or his friends a chance to speak. Buchman's immediate comment was, 'Here are devilish forces at work. We can't do anything here.' In fact, he never did meet Hitler, nor did he attempt to do so thereafter.

Within three months of Buchman's interview with Himmler, in November 1936, the Central Security Office of the Gestapo produced the first official document warning their network against the Oxford Group as 'a new and dangerous opponent of National Socialism'. The operative

---

* Kronika was the Berlin correspondent of *Nationaltidende*, Copenhagen, and *Svenska Dagbladet*, Stockholm, and was Chairman of the Association of Foreign Journalists in Berlin during the war. He was also the spokesman of the Danish minority in South Schleswig vis à vis the German Government (see his book *Berlins Untergang* (H. Hagerup)).

** The abbreviation of Moral Re-Armament, the name by which Buchman's work became known from 1938 on.

portion of the document ordered the intelligence service to give the closest attention to the work, tendency and influence of the movement, and in particular to infiltrate every gathering and team meeting, to watch the productions of the Leopold Klotz Verlag of Gotha – a firm which had published Oxford Group books and pamphlets – ascertaining who received the firm's literature, and to find out which men and women in public life were interested in the ideas of the Oxford Group.[9]

Buchman sailed for America on 19 August. Arriving in New York he held a press conference at Calvary House, from which a number of journalists sent off routine stories. The reporter of the afternoon paper, the *New York World-Telegram*, arrived late and asked for a special interview. With several of his colleagues in the room, Buchman answered the reporter's questions. Those present were amazed next afternoon to read the front-page banner headline and the lead paragraphs of the story in the paper:[10]

'HITLER OR ANY FASCIST LEADER CONTROLLED BY GOD COULD CURE ALL ILLS OF WORLD, BUCHMAN BELIEVES.

'To Dr Frank Nathan Daniel Buchman, vigorous, outspoken, 58-year-old leader of the revivalist Oxford Group, the Fascist dictatorship of Europe suggests infinite possibilities for remaking the world and putting it under "God Control".

' "I thank heaven for a man like Adolf Hitler, who built a front line of defense against the anti-Christ of Communism," he said today in his book-lined office in the annexe of Calvary Church, Fourth Ave and 21st St.

' "My barber in London told me Hitler saved Europe from Communism. That's how he felt. Of course, I don't condone everything the Nazis do. Anti-Semitism? Bad, naturally. I suppose Hitler sees a Karl Marx in every Jew.

' "But think what it would mean to the world if Hitler surrendered to the control of God." '

The remainder of the interview, extending to a further twenty-two paragraphs, contained a sketch of what Buchman considered a God-controlled country might look like and his assertion that God could make his will known to any man. 'The world won't listen to God, but God has a plan for every person, every nation. Human ingenuity is not enough. That is why the 'isms are pitted against each other and blood flows.'

Finally, speaking directly to the reporter – for his aim in a press interview was always to offer his deepest experience of change to the reporter as well as to answer his questions – he spent much of the time in telling of his own experience of the Cross of Christ, a Power strong enough to remove hatred from his own life, and so, he believed, to change anyone and control even a dictator.

[239]

The legend of this interview which survives – and has been quoted again and again – is that Buchman said, 'Thank God for Hitler.' This phrase was not Buchman's nor printed in the article, nor, according to those present, did it represent the tenor of the interview. For example, Garrett Stearly states, 'I was present at the interview. I was amazed when the story came out. It was so out of key with the interview. This had started with an account of the Oxford Group's work in Europe. Buchman was asked what about Germany. He said that Germany needed a new Christian spirit, yet one had to face the fact that Hitler had been a bulwark against Communism there – and you could at least thank heaven for that. It was a throw-away line. No eulogy of Hitler at all.'

I arrived in New York from Europe on the following day when the paper was on the streets, and lunched with the reporter, William Birnie, the day after. While gleeful, as was natural in any young journalist recently imported from a small country town who found his story leading the paper, Birnie seemed a good deal surprised at its editorial treatment. Thirty years later, when Birnie was a senior editor of the *Reader's Digest*, he told a visitor that he was always 'proud of his interviewee' for not haggling over the interview as printed, which he had expected him to do. 'My memory of our talk is that he was not endorsing or condemning Hitler,' he said.[11]

Buchman's statements were probably condensed or highlighted in the editorial process. It is, however, clear that Buchman said something to the effect that we could be grateful that Hitler had turned back Communism in Germany. Stroh recalls, 'In the summer of 1934, at the Oxford house-party, Buchman gathered all the Germans present together and told us that the greatest danger to the world was that materialism was undermining society. National Socialism had built a temporary wall against Communism, but that was not enough. The real problem was that people were not guided by God. People in Germany needed to change if they were to give inspiration to the world.'

Buchman refused, at the time as later, to be drawn into further public comment, which he believed would only lead to more newspaper controversy and endanger his friends already facing difficulties in Germany. Nor did he ever yield to the frequent demands that he should denounce Hitler. In fact, he never denounced anyone in public, even his most virulent personal defamers.

To a few friends, he made one comment some time in 1937: 'I have been much criticised because I said, "A God-controlled dictator could change the position in a country overnight." That doesn't mean in any sense when I made that statement that I identify myself with and approve of that dictator. I cannot deny the possibility of change in any man.'

Also, on 7 March 1940, Buchman's secretary noted in his diary that

Buchman said to a group of friends, 'Hitler fooled me. I thought it would be a bulwark against Communism.'[12]

This admission is a long way from justifying the charges of pro-Nazism so frequently levelled against him. In the same month as Buchman's press interview, Lloyd George described Hitler as 'the George Washington of Germany',[13] and over two years later Winston Churchill wrote, 'I have always said that if Britain were defeated in war, I hope we would find a Hitler to lead us back to our rightful place among the nations.'[14]

No democrat in the 1920s and 1930s, if he thought at all, wanted to see the whole of Europe from the Urals to the Rhine united under the single totalitarian ideology of Communism, which was, right up to the time that Hitler took over, a likely scenario. Buchman, with many others, feared that this would take place, and in the early Hitler years he saw Communism, avowedly based on atheism and the suppression of religion, as the more dangerous force. In later years, too, he considered Communism, with its power to capture the allegiance of people in every land, as the more universal and long-term threat. He hoped that Hitler would be a temporary bulwark; but he knew that Hitler's fundamental need was to become transformed by an experience of Jesus Christ, and this he had tried with unflagging faith, optimism, naivety – call it what you will – to bring about.

Following the document circulated from Himmler's headquarters in November 1936 the net around the Oxford Group in Germany was systematically tightened. In July 1937 the Gestapo in South-West Germany made official the measures for surveillance of the Oxford Group, its contacts, telephones and travels.[15] At the same time Himmler informed Count John Bentinck that he had definite proof that the Oxford Group comprised a spy organisation. He demanded that Germans in the movement should cut all links with Buchman, but gave Bentinck permission to travel to Utrecht, where Buchman was holding a Dutch demonstration, to inform him personally. Bentinck stayed only two days, in order to show Himmler that he had obeyed.

Stroh, who had travelled up to Utrecht with Buchman, found him deeply concerned for his friends in Germany. Buchman told Stroh that he felt the Germans must now find their own way unassisted. 'He left us completely free, refusing to advise us what to do. He gave me some papers for Bishops Wurm and Meiser and some sandwiches for the journey. We did not see him again till 1946.'

Buchman had had very little contact with Moni von Cramon during this period. But early in 1938 he asked if she could come to Esbjerg in Denmark. Her daughter went with her, and describes the occasion: 'We met Frank on the ship sailing to England. He said to us, "War is coming, and we won't see each other for a very long time. You will go through hard

[241]

times, but never forget, we are not alone." We knelt down and prayed, then we went back down to the quay and the ship went out, and Frank stood on the deck and made the sign of the Cross for us and for Europe, and that was the last we saw of him.' Frau von Cramon's son never returned from Stalingrad, and her son-in-law, Carl Ernst Rahtgens, a nephew of Field-Marshal von Kluge, was executed on Hitler's orders after the 'Generals' Plot'.

During the war the movement in Germany divided into three portions – some, like Bentinck, submitted to Himmler's demands; the majority, under a different name, *Arbeitsgemeinschaft für Seelsorge**, carried on the work of changing people, without becoming involved in politics and always subject to surveillance; a third group could not accept either alternative. Some of these joined the active opposition.

Buchman continued to visit Germany privately during 1937 and the spring of 1938, centring in places like Freudenstadt and Garmisch-Partenkirchen. During this period he made particular use of the German edition of the world-wide pictorial magazine, *Rising Tide (Steigende Flut)*, which had been banned by the Propaganda Ministry[16] but which was smuggled in, mainly by car. He wrote to friends that a Party leader had taken fifty copies, a postman was distributing it and another friend had ordered sixty-six. Bentinck wrote protesting that his 'action with *Steigende Flut* has done great harm',[17] but Buchman seemed unimpressed. 'Thank the Lord for R.T.,' he replied. 'What a lot of good it has released. You find its influence everywhere.'[18]

In 1939 the Gestapo compiled the 126-page report, *Die Oxfordgruppen-bewegung*, in which they stated that the Oxford Group was 'the pace-maker of Anglo-American diplomacy'. 'The Group as a whole', the document stated, 'constitutes an attack upon the nationalism of the state and demands the utmost watchfulness on the part of the state. It preaches revolution against the national state and has quite evidently become its Christian opponent.' It reproduced precisely those arguments against the Christian conceptions of sin and forgiveness which Himmler had used in his talks with Frau von Cramon. This report was circulated by the Gestapo headquarters in 1942 for official use.[19] In this year also the German Army forbade all officers to have anything to do with the Oxford Group under any name.[20] Those who persisted were restricted to front-line units. Many civilians who had worked with the Oxford Group were put in concentration camps.

At an inquiry into the work of the Oxford Group in Germany the Chief of Security in North Württemberg, Reinhold Bässler, said to some of its members, 'We have no fear of the churches. We take the young people

* Working Team for the Care of Souls.

from them and leave them to die out. But you are changing our best young people. You do not engage in abuse, but you are winning the idealists. That makes you the most dangerous enemies of the state.'[21]

A chapter in the 1942 document on the work of the Oxford Group in Germany says that it had been at work there since 1933 but with the greatest caution: 'For tactical reasons, great meetings of the kind that have taken place in other countries have been avoided. The work has been carried forward in conscious secrecy, and public debate has been avoided as much as possible. Even the postal services have been avoided in sending out messages or invitations. Cipher letters have been used.'[22]

The document adds, 'The Oxford Group preaches the equality of all men . . . No other Christian movement has underlined so strongly the character of Christianity as being supernational and independent of all racial barriers . . . It tries fanatically to make all men into brothers.'[23]

Had Hitler been successful in his invasion of Britain, his instructions were that the Oxford Group headquarters in London were to be taken over 'as being used by the British Intelligence Service'. Secret orders to this effect were discovered in Berlin and reported by the Press Association and the BBC on 19 September 1945. 'Moral Re-Armament', the orders stated, 'was used by English politicians for anti-German propaganda. Through this the Oxford Group Movement showed itself more clearly than ever to be a political power and the instrument of English diplomacy.'[24]

When the Dutch Nazis came to suppress the Oxford Group in Holland, they showed plainly that they had understood and were wholly opposed to Buchman's message and strategy for Europe: 'After 1933, when it became more and more evident that the National Socialist revolution of Adolf Hitler was bound to work its way beyond its borders and capture all the Germanic peoples, there was infused into those Germanic peoples a movement aiming to frustrate the German revolution in advance, while breeding an anti-German, universal spirit of love for mankind. This was the Oxford Group, founded and led by the English Jew Frank N. D. Buchman. We all remember the disgusting un-Germanic Oxford demonstration held in our country a few years ago.* It is an eloquent fact that all the world leaders who were anti-National Socialist and against all Germans have adhered to and supported the Oxford Group.'[25] The exaggeration is considerable, but the hostility undoubted.

* See pp. 257–8.

AWAKENING DEMOCRACIES

While increasingly aware of the dangers developing in and from Germany during the middle and late 1930s, Buchman believed, with Solzhenitsyn fifty years later,[1] that the basic cause of the approaching disaster was that 'we have forgotten God'. Some countries were building their entire system on the denial of God and on total moral relativism, and millions of people in the so-called Christian countries had adopted the same basis for their private lives. Their leaders had often become practical atheists in public affairs, whatever their private profession. Of the League of Nations Buchman remarked, 'It is failing because it is not God-arched'; and of certain Church leaders he said sadly, 'Where is the strategy of the Holy Spirit?'

Most of Buchman's time was spent in the democratic countries around Germany, in Britain and in the United States, which involved many crossings of the English Channel and the Atlantic. He was striving, without haste but with urgency, to convince both the people and their leaders that obedience to the will of God was the only adequate basis for the ordering of society. He believed – over-optimistically as it turned out – that the danger would spur enough democrats to change, and that the totalitarians might note this and alter their ways.

In September 1935 Buchman was invited to their country by Swiss who had worked with him in Scandinavia. Switzerland's folksy President, Rudolf Minger, welcomed him and his 250 companions. He asked himself, said Minger, whether there was any way out of 'the world's dilemma'. 'The answer', he went on, 'is a courageous "Yes". What is needed is the changing of lives through a new spiritual power so strong that it reconciles conflicting forces and produces brotherhood and solidarity. It is in attaining this goal that the Oxford Group sees its task.'[2]

The usual wide variety of meetings, large and small, took place. In Geneva they varied from gatherings of doctors, the unemployed, university professors and hoteliers, to the night when Calvin's cathedral and one of the city's largest halls both overflowed. The response was much the same in city after city.

'It is difficult to measure all the results of these great meetings and of the countless personal contacts,' writes Professor Theophil Spoerri, Professor of French and Italian Literature at Zurich University. 'There is no doubt that for many it was the turning point in their lives. It could be described as a change of climate. It was almost as if something new was penetrating between the chinks of the shutters. A business man, alone in his office, would feel a faint sense of unease if he was planning to cheat his fellow citizens. The public conscience became more sensitive. The Director of Finance in one canton reported that after the national day of thanksgiving and repentance, 6,000 tax payments were recorded, something which had never occurred before in the financial history of the Republic.'[3]

The aspect picked out for comment by the Swiss press was the effect of the campaign on the political situation. It was a period of tension between parties and racial population groups, with talk of secession. President Minger, together with other members of the Swiss Federal Council, twice received colleagues of Buchman. *Der Bund* headlined the report of one meeting 'the hour of frankness in Parliament',[4] while *La Suisse*, half humorously, half in earnest, compared the Group's coming to the historic appearance of St Nicolas von Flüe at the Diet of Stans which averted civil war in Switzerland in the fifteenth century.[5]

Fifteen months later, in its review of 1937, the *Neue Zürcher Zeitung* wrote, 'There have been two ideas especially on people's minds. The first is ... strict constitutionality. The other we may perhaps call the wish to reach a common understanding. People have tried to reach out to others and to explore. "Oxfordism" has been introduced into politics. And there have been results. Things are happening. The tendency to division and fragmentation of 1933 and 1934 has given way to an opposite trend.'[6]

To meet the interest aroused among League of Nations delegates, its President, Prime Minister Eduard Benes of Czechoslovakia, invited Buchman and his colleagues to address a luncheon on 23 September 1935. 'Two Prime Ministers, thirty-two Ministers Plenipotentiary and many other representatives of the political wisdom of the world,' reported an observer in *The Spectator*, 'sat down with a band of volunteers who claim the wisdom that God supplies to those who listen for it.'[7] According to *Berlingske Aftenavis*, this luncheon 'filled Ludendorff with rage', especially because it was given by the Czechoslovak Prime Minister.[8]

The League was facing a major crisis. America and the Soviet Union had never participated, and Germany had just walked out. Italy, which invaded Abyssinia thirteen days later, was preparing to follow. Britain and France were showing little intention of giving the League teeth. Many politicians were looking for hope elsewhere.

They listened to Hambro's account of the Oxford Group's impact in Norway with astonishment. Then he added, 'To most politicians there comes a day when they are bound to contrast the result of their work with the vision of their youth, contrast the things they longed to do with the things they thought they had to do. They will understand me when I say that no man who has been in touch with the Group will go back to his international work in the same spirit as before. It has been made impossible for him to be ruled by hate or prejudice.'[9]

At the luncheon, Hambro told Buchman that he was going to America to address the Scandinavian communities there. Buchman saw further possibilities. 'Some feel', he wrote to Hambro with his customary high expectations, 'that you have in your hands the possibility of shaping the spiritual destiny of America, and that you will be doing a service that will heighten all your previous important plans . . . You know that Roosevelt has sent out a questionnaire to all the clergy in America, and I am afraid the answers have not been satisfactory. $Time$[10] carries in its last issue a picture of Minger, the President of Switzerland. Beneath it, speaking of the visit of the Oxford Group, is the line, "He commended his callers' conviction." You remember his statement that "You are showing the world the way out of the present crisis". Now that is what Roosevelt wants to know. America has not given him the answer. Can Carl Hambro, with the background of the last year, give him the answer?'[11]

Hambro accepted Buchman's suggestion. He spoke in many cities, ending with a powerful speech in the New York Metropolitan Opera House. Everywhere he made clear his strong opposition to Nazi Germany and his irritation at the lack of urgency in the democracies in the face of its threat; everywhere, too, he brought the news of what he had seen happening through the Oxford Group. 'Politics', he said, 'must be an effort to render possible tomorrow what is impossible today . . . The Oxford Group is at work stretching the limits of the possible further out, fixing the eye on wider horizons, setting the clear-cut peace of the absolute demands of Christ up against the restlessness of the relative, removing the barriers between man and man, between nation and nation.'[12]* Hambro did not see the President, but consulted at length with the Secretary of State, Cordell Hull, and other politicians. His statements and interviews gave many a new perspective on the Oxford Group, and prepared the way for Buchman's next moves in his own country.

Buchman's conviction that war in Europe was imminent had shown

---

* $The Jewish Advocate$ of 1 November 1935 commented editorially: 'The contribution of the Oxford Movement (sic) is a vision of what might be, a vision of social regeneration through the cultivation of the idealism of mind and spirit. More power to the Oxford Group, which is growing by leaps and bounds and whose objective is . . . to translate the Ten Commandments into the realities of everyday life.'

itself in his insistence, in December 1935, that a 'war clause' be written into the contract with the Oxford colleges for the next summer's house-party. In May 1936 he called an Assembly in Stockbridge, Massachusetts, entitled 'America Awake', to which five thousand people came. It proved nationwide news. *The New York Times* special correspondent wrote a column a day for almost two weeks,[13] movie companies estimated that their newsreels reached 40 million people, and the CBS broadcast a delegate's speech from coast to coast.

Immediately after this, on 19 May, Buchman was summoned to Reading, Pennsylvania, for a personally painful occasion. He was arraigned there before the regional Synod of the Lutheran Church for not having attended a sufficient number of the periodic meetings of his local Ministerium. Having often been abroad at the time of the annual meetings, which he was by statute required to attend, he had always been meticulous in writing an apology for his absence and an account of his activities, not erring on the side of understatement. This may have aggravated, rather than mollified, his principal accuser, Dr Ernst P. Pfatteicher, the President of the Ministerium of Pennsylvania and Adjacent States. He had previously attacked Buchman in a lecture en-titled 'The Man from Oxford' for, amongst other things, travelling the world instead of serving in a Pennsylvanian parish.[14]

Pfatteicher was opposed by Dr Paul Strodach, editor of the United Lutheran Publication House. The matter was referred back for re-study – and forgotten. Buchman did not himself speak and, as he had had to leave immediately after his indictment, did not know for some days that several ministers had spoken for him. 'Your silence was your best defence if any were needed,' wrote the Revd Edward Horn; 'the unhappy and disgrace-ful procedure was checked,' added C. P. Harry, from the Lutheran Church Board of Education.[15] Buchman had been all the more hurt by this occasion because he was 'put up before the whole conference' alongside a minister accused of committing adultery, a very serious charge in such a gathering. It felt to him, he said, like 'a crucifixion'. Next day, however, he took his European visitors to address Senators and Con-gressmen on Capitol Hill and also to meet Cordell Hull.

That year Buchman addressed delegates to the Republican National Convention in Cleveland. The editor of an Ohio newspaper wrote, 'Whether Democrats or Republicans win the election, Buchman came to Cleveland to say, the result will be about equally bad unless his candidate commands. Buchman's candidate for ruler of America is God ... He doesn't plan to have God rule according to instructions from below. He would have men rule under instructions from God as definitely given and understood as if they came by wire.'[16]

From Philadelphia, where the Democrats were gathered, he broadcast nationally, speaking of the vast effort it would take for the democracies to match the march of the dictators: 'Few people today seem to have any definite plans or any idea of what the cost will be for moral and spiritual recovery. They don't seem to have thought through the united disciplined action under God's control necessary to bring it about . . . This is the true patriotism, for the true patriot gives his life for his country's resurrection.'[17]

Buchman returned to Britain in late June 1936. It was the Britain to which Baldwin neither at first cared, nor later dared, to tell the truth about Hitler's Germany, a Britain missing the chance to rearm because it was more comfortable to refuse even to envisage a threat to itself.

Buchman was striving to awaken Britain to what he felt to be at base a moral and spiritual need. Oxford had, the previous year, shown itself too small any longer to accommodate the annual house-party. So in 1936 simultaneous house-parties were staged during July in Oxford, Cambridge, Exeter and Harrogate, as well as camps for young women on Hinksey Hill outside Oxford and for young men near Birmingham.

The response in Harrogate was typical enough. According to the *Leeds Mercury*, the first meeting at the Royal Hall was packed to overflowing with 2,000 people three-quarters of an hour before it was due to start and, when the overflow was directed to the Winter Gardens, its 1,000 seats filled up within ten minutes and another 500 people had to be sent on to the Hydro for a second overflow meeting.[18] Dr Maxwell Telling, a distinguished psychiatrist, remarked of the speakers, 'This is the first time I have seen people with absolutely no fear.'

On 7 July speakers from the various house-parties combined to address a crowded meeting in the Albert Hall, and at the end of the month a three-day demonstration took place at the British Industries Fair building at Castle Bromwich, Birmingham, then said to be the largest covered hall in Europe. To this gathering 21 special trains brought audiences totalling 25,000 from all parts of Britain.

On 9 August Buchman made a coast-to-coast broadcast to America from London, before making visits of a week to Germany and a month to America. To America, he took thirty with him, and it was on his arrival in New York that he gave the interview to the *New York World-Telegram*. While there he took a party to spend a weekend with Henry Ford, where for the first time he met Rear-Admiral Richard E. Byrd, recently returned from a winter alone in the Antarctic.

Ford admired the vigorous way Buchman went to work: 'Leave that fellow Buchman in a forest and he'll start changing the trees,' he said. He sometimes entertained Buchman and his friends at the Dearborn Inn near his home; but he did not give money to Buchman's work. This was typical of his life-long belief that if a thing was worthwhile it should make its own way. 'Every tub must stand on its own bottom,' he would say – and, in fact, the Fords only gave two money gifts to Buchman or his work in twenty years, one of $1,000 from Mr Ford and the other of $2,000 from Mrs Ford. However, he turned to Buchman on personal questions. He consulted him about his will (from which neither Buchman nor his work benefited); and when he was having an operation asked him to look after Mrs Ford while it took place.

On 29 September Buchman sailed for Britain to take part in a weekend house-party being given by Lord Salisbury, the son of the Victorian Prime Minister and himself a former Cabinet Minister and Leader of the House of Lords, at Hatfield House. Salisbury had first been brought into contact with the Oxford Group through an acquaintance named Andrew Charles who had written several times suggesting to him that he should acquaint himself with it. He had finally attended the Oxford house-party in 1935 and another in January 1936 at Bournemouth. In March 1936 he had put forward the essence of Buchman's message in an economic debate in the House of Lords. 'The cause of the world's state', he said on that occasion, 'is not economic; the cause is moral. It is the want of religion which we ought to possess. If I may use a phrase which is common in a great movement which is taking place in this country and elsewhere, what you want is God-guided personalities, which make God-guided nationalities, to make a new world. All other ideas of economic adjustment are too small really to touch the centre of the evil.'[19]

When asked by august friends why he was interested in the Oxford Group, he replied, 'I saw the spirit moving on the waters, and I dare not stand aside.'[20] To his niece, Lady Hardinge of Penshurst, he had said, 'These people have great spiritual knowledge and strength. Go to them and they will help you.'[21] Now he had invited a number of his friends to meet with Buchman and a dozen of his colleagues at Hatfield House. They talked in the library and walked under the centuries-old trees together. Lord Lytton, glad to meet Buchman again after their conversations in India ten years earlier, told him of his son Anthony's death in a flying accident and gave him a copy of his book about him inscribed 'In memory of our talk at Hatfield'. Buchman himself regarded his conversations with Lytton as the high point of the weekend.

Salisbury's own seven-page summary of the weekend began with a list of those present.* Then he went on: 'I think it may be said broadly that the

* 'The members of the Oxford Group consisted of: Lady Gowers, The Revd Cuthbert Bardsley, Dr Frank Buchman, Sir Philip Dundas, Mr Loudon Hamilton, Mr Kenaston Twitchell, The Revd Jack Winslow, M. Faure from France, Mr J. Roots, Mr Wilson and two others who came for the day on the 11th. They were met in conference by Caroline,

Group leaders made a profound impression upon those who had come to meet them, and the general conclusion appeared to be that a great force had become revealed which assuredly had to be reckoned with. I do not think there was anything in the Notes made after the Bournemouth House Party* which seemed to be in need of correction, but the following points should be noted as specially emerging from the Conference. There was abundant testimony by the Group speakers as to the results in their own lives which had been effected by the Group teaching – the peace, happiness and vigour which had followed. Similarly, in describing their experience of others who had been brought under the influence of the Group, they showed how friction in domestic life, unrest between employer and employed, and violent antagonism in politics had been softened or swept away. Lastly, the impression left upon the audience at the Conference was that great numbers of people in Country after Country are waiting, almost panting, for a lead in things spiritual as the only hope to enable Society to stand up against the moral and social degeneration of the time.'

'Group teaching' was discussed, including difficulties and criticisms regarding guidance, sharing, the meaning of change and the relation to institutional religion. 'But these criticisms', Salisbury concluded, 'do not seem to touch the essence of the Movement – a call to men and women including most professed Christians, for a vital, even a revolutionary change in their lives, namely, the acceptance in thought, word and deed of the immediate guidance of God as revealed in Christ and the recognition of a duty by sharing religious experience to help others to the same acceptance.'[22] In a covering note to the Archbishop of Canterbury he concludes, 'I have certainly not overstated it in the case of many that they were *profoundly* impressed – perhaps all of them.'[23]

After the weekend Buchman wrote to his host, 'You must have the sense of "Well done, good and faithful servant." Certainly the hours at Hatfield were God-controlled. I do not know when I have ever felt so absolutely encased by the presence of the unseen, ever-present Christ.

'The influence of that weekend, I am convinced, will go far beyond our ken. With so much happening in thirty-six hours, you can readily understand what the impact must have been on Norway where we met together for ten days. In our contact with these men we ought always to

---

Lady Bridgeman, Lady Gwendolen Cecil, Mrs Alfred Lyttelton, Mr R. H. Bernays MP, Sir John Cadman, Captain V. A. Cazalet MP, Lord Cecil, Sir John Davidson MP, Sir Francis Fremantle MP, Lord Goschen, Lord Grey, Lord Halifax, Lord Lytton, Lord Eustace Percy MP, Mr Francis Rodd, Lord Sankey, Lord Wolmer MP, besides Lord and Lady Salisbury.'

* A thorough and appreciative summary of the Oxford Group principles he had written after his attendance there, of which I have a copy.

keep in the forefront of our minds that we are only at the beginning.

'I think we must say this too: we can never be grateful enough to the good God who led you to plan as you did for men whose insight and creative ability can make a God-controlled England. Laus Deo!'[24]

To which Salisbury replied, 'I have just received your letter. May I tell you how very grateful I am to you for all you arranged and carried out here during the weekend? I have now read with deep reverence the words you have used as to the impression left upon your mind by what passed, and of course I feel that we must wait for the future of the Movement with hope and faith. I will say no more for the present.'[25]

Lord Robert Cecil said during the Hatfield weekend that 'every problem in Europe today could be traced back to the failure of Christianity to influence the Governments of the nations'.[26] According to Kenneth Rose in *The Later Cecils*, he 'congratulated the Group on having "invested the old, simple Christ gospel with a new vividness particularly effective with people who have lost or never knew it". But at the final session he was disturbed by Buchman's apparent readiness to condone the conduct of the Hitler regime: "I rather warmly protested," Bob told his wife, "and he explained that he was far from approving such things as the persecution of the Jews." '[27]

It is likely that Buchman did express himself strongly about Germany in a gathering where some seemed to assume that Germany was totally to blame and Britain had made no errors. 'Buchman always found it very hard to bear the arrogance of certain of us British who felt the British Empire was better than anything else anywhere,' Loudon Hamilton once noted. 'He was very sensitive to national superiority in us. If we criticised other countries, he wouldn't allow it. He was fighting for cure and part of the cure was that we had to begin with ourselves.'

Salisbury's summary of the discussion on Germany reads: 'Nothing like the dazzling Scandinavian results were claimed in Germany, but a good deal of success was described in certain localities and amongst certain individuals – even individuals high in the public life of the Country. It was thought, I think, generally very difficult to reconcile the recent practice of the Government in Germany with the teaching of the New Testament, and the principles of the Group, and obviously any tendency to condone evil even for so signal an object as getting in touch with the German Government would be wholly unworthy. I need not say that any such "doing evil that good may come" was warmly denied.'[28]

Salisbury was one of the severest critics of the Government's appeasement policy. In February he had opened a debate on national defence in the House of Lords and in July he was, with Winston Churchill, to lead a deputation of Privy Councillors which implored Prime Minister Baldwin to face the fact of German re-armament. Kenneth Rose finds it extraordinary that he should have issued the invitations to his Hatfield weekend in between these two events and that he actually had Buchman and his colleagues to meet his friends there six weeks after the *New York World-Telegram* interview.[29] It would indeed have been strange for Salisbury to have done so – and still stranger for him to have supported the Group consistently throughout the war – if he believed that Buchman was in the slightest degree pro-Nazi. But Buchman had told him what he was trying to do in Germany, including his touches with Himmler, at the Oxford house-party a year earlier, and Salisbury's conduct argues that he understood the motives behind Buchman's initiatives.

Rose is also puzzled why Salisbury, who 'displayed only clarity of thought and robustness of will in all other private and public activities', was 'so pliant in the hands of the Oxford Group'.[30] The fact is that far from being pliant, Salisbury, in his work with the Oxford Group, was always his own man. Some of his initiatives were suggested to him by one or other of his Oxford Group friends whom, like its Secretary, Roland Wilson, he had urged 'never to hesitate to come to me when you feel prompted by the Spirit'.[31] But the letters and memos in my possession* – many in his own hand – show that he pondered deeply any such suggestion and made up his own mind whether or not to act. On other occasions – his interventions in the House of Lords in 1936 and 1941, for example – he acted, and the first thing his Oxford Group friends knew about it was from reports in the press or announcements in the House's Order Paper.

From time to time Salisbury had his questions or *caveats* on particular methods of the Oxford Group, and expressed them freely and courteously. A letter to Twitchell, for instance, suggests that, for the sake of Salisbury's friends, 'an associated body deeply convinced of the main principles of the Group but not committed to its methods' might perhaps be formed. He enclosed a list of *caveats*: that 'the Group teaching is a true road to God' but not the only road; that though one 'ought to ask for and to receive God's guidance', it 'is not necessarily to be had on demand'; that it is not true that when people become convinced Christians 'according to Group methods or any other methods . . . the fierce warfare of the Christian soul is over'; and that it is 'a Christian obligation to share those spiritual experiences which are a help to others' but not to treat all such experiences as public property. He added a further warning: 'The fact is that an undue and insecurely founded optimism involves considerable danger. There must be a reaction sooner or later, perilous to the

---

* I have been unable to examine the relevant papers in the Cecil Archives at Hatfield as there is a fifty-year embargo placed upon them by the family. This embargo the Librarian and Archivist to the Marquess of Salisbury informs me has only been waived twice, for Kenneth Rose and for one other.

individual who experiences it, and it may be disastrous to the fellowship and teaching which may be held to be responsible for it.'[32]

Such warnings did not in any way interrupt Salisbury's co-operation with his Group friends. Two days after this letter he saw Lord Halifax, and asked him to sign a letter supporting the Oxford Group[33] which he was assembling and which appeared in *The Times* eight days later.[34] Halifax felt unable to do so; but two years later, when Foreign Secretary, sent a public message of support to Buchman and his friends in America.[35]*

Salisbury accepted Buchman and more particularly his younger British colleagues as friends engaged in a Christian battle in which he wished to have a part. When, in 1942, Buchman suffered a stroke, he asked Roland Wilson to say 'to Dr Buchman that my thoughts are daily with him during these anxious moments through which he is passing and with concern and prayer for the great movement for which he is responsible'.[36] He also attended Wilson's wedding in 1946, although 85 years old, and telephoned him the day before he died in the next year.

Lord Grey came closer than Rose to expressing the hopes which both Salisbury and Buchman held for the Hatfield weekend when he wrote about it to the Archbishop of Canterbury. 'I was at Jem's house party last weekend and like everybody else, I think, very much impressed by what I heard,' he wrote. 'You know much more what he is thinking than I do, but I imagine that he is principally attracted by what might happen if we could get a great release of spiritual forces in Europe within the next two or three years, such a release as could not be expected to be achieved through the ordinary channels.'[37]

Buchman's hope was precisely for such a release of spiritual energy in Europe, not only because it just might avert catastrophe but, more importantly, for its own sake. This is clear from Salisbury's comment that Buchman at Hatfield called for 'a vital, even a revolutionary change' in the lives of those present, whether already 'professed Christians' or not. Buchman felt that such a release of spiritual energy would require the same kind of national response in Britain as he had seen in Norway and Denmark, and he was looking for public figures prepared to take the same

---

* In the spring of 1939, Rose writes (pp. 100, 101), Salisbury began to arrange another house-party at Hatfield 'to consider practical steps for the promoting of Moral Re-Armament in this country'. 'The Archbishop of Canterbury readily agreed to take part . . . Other eminent men . . . sent their regrets . . . The guest list dwindled into mediocrity. As if at a word of command, Buchman's henchmen turned spitefully on Salisbury.' Rose then quotes from two letters, one from a future bishop, the other from the son of a bishop. 'Salisbury replied to these impertinences with Christian meekness,' he concludes. One deplores both the tone and the content of these letters, while admiring the grace of the recipient. They do, however, dispose of Rose's inference that Oxford Group leaders would go to almost any lengths to obtain an influential patron.

whole-hearted leadership as Hambro and others had taken in Norway and Bishop Fuglsang-Damgaard and Dean Brodersen in Denmark.

But, for whatever reason, Buchman did not feel that most of those at Hatfield had accepted this point. Hence the wistful reference in his letter to Salisbury to the ten days' house-party of the Norwegian campaign in contrast to the thirty-six hours at Hatfield, and his insistence that 'we ought always to have it in the forefront of our minds that we are only at the beginning'. To Twitchell in London, he wrote in mid-November, 'I don't think I would count too exclusively on the senior crowd as the salvation of Britain, because they have too many irons in the fire. They have become old and hardened in their processes and ways of doing things and while one must be grateful for their approval of the work, with a few exceptions, I doubt whether we will have much action.'[38]

He was writing from Budapest, where he had found twenty Groups functioning. There, as in Vienna, he had met the country's Chancellor and members of the Cabinet. 'We have failed,' he noted at the time, 'in the articulation so that the scope is adequate to challenge every statesman . . . the sin of not putting a message that is understandable by everyone.' And again, 'Events are hurtling on and the balance is between war and no war within the next three years. Can we be the deciding factor? All the time there comes in these quiet hours the thought, "You will be used to change the world." I sometimes feel it too much to believe that the Oxford Group can be used to change the world, but unless we work with that object we might just as well fold our hands and rest.'

Buchman returned to London a few days before the abdication of Edward VIII. At the height of that crisis, at four o'clock in the morning, he received a telephone call from the home of the Comptroller of the King's Household. It was from a close friend of the King, one of those who had been on the boat to South America in 1931, begging him to do something to help. 'All I could say,' he told a friend next morning, 'was, "There's nothing I can do now."' Justly or unjustly, he felt that those close to the King, particularly his spiritual advisers, had failed to help him to find a stable foundation for his life. 'The reason is because they are not arch-revolutionaries,' he wrote to a Swiss friend on the day after the Abdication. 'They support an archaic system, and no one can read the story of Russia, where the Church was bereft of the Christ it sought to bring, without seeing its significance.' Of the Prime Minister, Stanley Baldwin, he wrote, 'Humanly he has done a good job. But it is certainly God's plan, in a situation like this, that a Prime Minister should have been able to change the King and bring him under the guidance of God.'[39]

A week later he had the chance to talk with Baldwin. It had been arranged by the Prime Minister's right-hand man, Sir John Davidson, who had been present at the Hatfield weekend. Baldwin had often heard news of the Group from his cousin, Mrs J. W. Mackail, and Mrs Baldwin had attended Group luncheons. When Buchman had held a meeting in the Albert Hall in July 1936 the Prime Minister had booked a box, but cancelled it on being asked by a Sunday newspaper whether he had 'joined' the Group.

At Chequers Baldwin told Buchman that his work was done and that he was planning to resign after the coronation of George VI. Buchman replied that the recent crisis had shown that he had an authoritative voice to unite the Empire on a great issue. Now there was something even greater at stake, to become 'the authoritative voice for the spiritual rebirth of the Empire'. Baldwin replied, 'Yes, I know I ought to. But I'm afraid I can't.'

Many of these people first met Buchman in the Chelsea home of the Dowager Countess of Antrim, a former Lady-in-Waiting to Queen Victoria and Queen Alexandra, who gave a weekly lunch for him when he was in town. It was during the late 1930s that she and her sister, Lady Minto, made the two-month journey with Buchman through the Balkans and the Middle East which Michael Barrett had found so demanding. 'Wherever we stopped,' she wrote in her diary, 'Dr Buchman was received not only by small, virile local teams, but by Rulers, Statesmen and business men. Everywhere they demanded interviews and asked for advice, seeming to realise that only by a God-controlled world can the difficulties which confront us be overcome.'

In the last entry in this diary, she noted, 'I was asked if I liked Dr Buchman. It seemed an unnecessary question, for in him I saw above all the realisation of a force which advances the Love of God, and this showed me how human personality is lost sight of in spiritual power.'*

Another of those who worked closely with Buchman in these years was Dr B. H. Streeter. He had flown three times to Denmark to assist in that campaign and reported his conclusions in a letter to *The Times*.[40] Since throwing in his lot with the Oxford Group in 1934 he had begun to be more interested in people and Buchman frequently sent individuals in need of help to him. He wrote to Buchman on one occasion about a talk with an editor who had come to question him in Oxford: 'I gave him my spiritual autobiography. I stressed the Gamaliel point – that Gamaliel did some good by protecting the apostles, but that if he had gone further and identified himself with them, it might have led the best element in the Pharisees to Christianity, and then the Jewish War and destruction of

---

* In July 1935 Lady Antrim's daughter, Lady Sybil Smith (later Lady Bicester), offered to take Buchman to a Buckingham Palace garden party and introduce him to Queen Mary, whom she kept informed about his work. Buchman declined in a letter of 20 July: 'I thought immediately of your husband, who might be bored by having me about or might feel he was committing himself more largely than he wanted to.'

Jerusalem would not have occurred . . . Gamaliel must take the credit not only for the good he did, but for the good he failed to do, the calamity he failed to prevent.'[41]

It was with shock that in September 1937 Buchman heard of the death of Streeter and his wife, Irene, in a plane crash on a mountain-top near Basle. The trip had been a second honeymoon with his wife, who for years had felt herself estranged by his cleverness and his advanced theology, for which she had small sympathy. He never found faith easy; but his years with Buchman put a foundation of experience under the fine structure of his thinking. 'I am sure I have learnt much about methods of presentation,' he had written to Buchman. 'If I had not met the Group, I might have died a distinguished theologian.'[42]

Buchman, who heard the news while visiting Ramsay Macdonald at Lossiemouth, flew immediately to Switzerland for the funeral. There he was given a statement which Streeter had been preparing for use on his return. 'I was drawn to the Oxford Group not primarily by failure to meet personal and family problems, but by my despair of the world situation,' Streeter had written. 'The more I saw of the trend of things, the less grounds I found for hope. . . . I saw how largely the moral energies of Christianity were demobilized, partly through the differences of opinion on points of doctrine or church organisation, but still more by the failure to realise in actual life the religious and moral ideals which Christians are unanimous in professing. The Oxford Group is recalling the churches to their proper task of saving the souls of nations as well as individuals.'

After describing what he had seen in Denmark, Streeter continued: 'History shows that in case of wars, revolutions, strikes and other major conflicts, a relatively small weight of public opinion on the one side or the other, or the presence or absence of moral insight and courage in a few individuals in positions of influence, has often turned the balance between a reasonable settlement and a fight to the finish. Modern civilization can only be saved by a moral revival. But for this it would suffice if every tenth or hundredth person were changed. For each such person raises the level of those whom he touches in the home, in business and in public affairs.

'What I saw happening in Denmark can happen in Britain. It will happen if those who lead Britain learn to find in God their inspiration and direction. And Britain, thus led, would save the world. But the opportunity must be seized during the period of uneasy respite from the major calamity which at the moment appears to lie ahead.'[43]

Buchman missed Streeter greatly. They had first become friends through a mutual interest in the Indian mystic Sadhu Sundar Singh, and Buchman had written in 1922 that Streeter had consulted him on one of his books. He was counting on Streeter to put the insights which he felt God was giving them into words which the intellectual world would read and understand. Of their friendship Julian Thornton-Duesbery, when Master of St Peter's College, Oxford, later wrote: 'Buchman's mind was not academic, but was of quite extraordinary speed and range, and had the quality of piercing immediately to the heart of the matter. It was this which drew great academic minds to him – this, together with his ability, which they envied, to communicate his ideas in simple, direct terms to ordinary people.'[44]

In the early part of 1937 Buchman made several visits to the Netherlands. His Dutch friends were pressing him to bring a team to their country. His own thought, when he conferred with them finally in April, was, 'Tolerate no activity which doesn't have national significance.' 'You have done splendid individual work,' he told them. 'You have had good house-parties. Now you need a new related activity, and it needs to be related to international problems.'

The Dutch responded, slowly at first, but with increasing enthusiasm, and decided that they should hold a national demonstration. The only problem was that Buchman insisted that the demonstration should take place in Utrecht. The Dutch maintained that it was the wrong town: for one thing, there was no large hall there. 'There is something in or near Utrecht which will hold thousands,' Buchman persisted. An indomitable woman, Mrs Charlotte van Beuningen, scoured the city, and eventually came upon the vast vegetable market. There was an absolute rule against hiring it out; but after interviewing each of the board of thirteen in charge of it, she got permission. Four thousand chairs were imported, and thousands of packing cases laid out in rows behind them.

Over Whitsun, audiences totalling 100,000 attended meetings there. 'At ten o'clock at night, with 10,000 present, people were still swooping on any vacant chair they could find,' Buchman wrote to Bill Pickle. 'Hundreds of people were changed, and we arranged interviews just as we did in the old days at Penn State.'[45]

'The greatest surprise in these two Whitsun days was certainly the appearance of Dr J. Patijn, our Ambassador in Brussels,' reported the Socialist paper *Het Volk*.[46] 'Only those who know him as Burgomaster of The Hague, a sound but unapproachable man and averse to any public show, will be able to appreciate fully what it must have cost this curt Zeelander to speak about his inmost self before many thousands in this Vegetable Market. It was no long speech . . . "It is not for everyone," he said, "to speak in public about his faith, and it is not easy for me to do so. Every man, however, must have the courage of his convictions, and it would be ungrateful of me not to acknowledge that through what I have experienced in the Oxford Group I have learnt to see my fellow men, the world and my whole life in a new perspective."'

Not all newspapers were as positive. The *Nieuwe Rotterdamsche Courant* said the vast meeting was 'un-Dutch'. 'The question is not whether it is non-Dutch or American,' Buchman wrote to the head of the News Agency of the Dutch Indies, Herman Salomonson. 'The question is, "Is it Christian?" It seems so absurd. You see 65,000 men at a football match. Surely the outstretched arms of Christ are for everyone?' He added that he 'wished to heaven it were American, but unfortunately it is not'.[47]

The other voice of complaint was from the Dutch Nazi leader Mussert. He had planned a major rally at Utrecht for these same days. It was a complete failure, with very few people attending. It was four years later, after the German occupation, that he banned Buchman's work in the Netherlands.

1937 seemed propitious for Buchman in Britain.* In April Beverley Baxter, writing as 'Atticus' in the *Sunday Times*, went to see him with 'understandable curiosity'. 'His voice is pleasant without trickeries, his ears large and honest, and his nose long and intelligent . . .' he reported. 'It is easy to ridicule the Oxford Group, and many wits have done so . . . The evidence is undeniable that the movement is spreading through the world. Nor would it be gracious or truthful to deny that when I left Dr Buchman I carried away the memory of a man whose spirit is fine and whose bearing is modest and sincere.'[48]

London generally seemed to be opening its doors. Lady Antrim continued her weekly luncheons at which Buchman met members of the Cabinet. He was entertained by the Commander-in-Chief, Portsmouth; attended the Duke of Norfolk's garden party; addressed overflowing crowds in West Ham and Canning Town Halls in East London; and spoke to a large gathering of Members of Parliament in the House of Commons.

But he was not escaping less flattering attention. The Oxford Group were asked by Miss Christina Foyle to present their message at the Foyle's Literary Lunch of 8 July 1937. Seventeen speakers were designated, and accepted by Miss Foyle, to do so. The interest was so great that, having sold 2,500 tickets and filled the salon as well as the ball-room at Grosvenor House, the organisers had to refuse further requests.

Buchman was tipped off the night before by Ivan Menzies, the Gilbert and Sullivan star, that a trap was being planned at the lunch. The occasion had been arranged by some younger Oxford men, and Buchman had been doubtful about it, but felt that for their sakes he should let it go ahead. He

---

* On March 4 the *Daily Mirror* held a competition in which readers nominated their 'perfect Cabinet'. One entry proposed Buchman as Prime Minister, with Winston Churchill and George Bernard Shaw among his Cabinet – a proposal which the paper published, complete with photographs of the nominees.

was not to speak himself. When he arrived at Grosvenor House, he found that an eighteenth guest of honour had been added to the speakers, in the person of the actress Margaret Rawlings. She was seated on the other side of the chairman, next to Loudon Hamilton.

Just before the speaking was due to begin, a hotel employee called Hamilton away to answer the telephone. The operator told him that it was a false alarm and, on his return, he found that his place beside Miss Rawlings had been taken in his absence by Tom Driberg, then the 'William Hickey' columnist at the *Daily Express*. Miss Rawlings spoke last, reading from a prepared text and confining herself to one subject. Exposure of one's soul through public confession was, she said, as shocking as undressing in Piccadilly. Next day the press ignored the other seventeen speakers, who had included a bishop and a leader of East London's unemployed, and shouted Miss Rawlings' message in front-page headlines. The BBC reported her speech only. Driberg gave the whole of his column to the event, admitting in it that he was there to 'give Miss Rawlings moral support'[49] – or, as his friend, Hannen Swaffer, wrote, 'He egged her on.'[50] One paper embellished the story with a picture of Miss Rawlings as she appeared in her current show in the briefest of 1937 bathing costumes under the headline 'Indecency?'[51]

The old story of indecent 'public confession', as originally put out by Driberg nine years earlier, was re-stamped on the public mind. Miss Rawlings, perhaps fearing an action for slander, wrote the *Daily Sketch* that she was 'astonished' at the publicity and asked the paper to correct the impression that she had referred to or criticised any of the other speakers,[52] and Miss Foyle issued a statement that 'Miss Rawlings' remarks bore no possible relation to what was said at the luncheon, which was a reasonable and objective presentation of the case for moral and spiritual renewal at a time of crisis'.[53] A copy was sent to 'William Hickey' by Miss Foyle asking for equal space for an authoritative account of the other speakers, a request which was not granted.

Bunny Austin, the tennis player, was at the lunch, although not then associated with the Oxford Group. 'I went across to greet Dr Buchman as he made his way from the room,' he wrote. 'I greatly admired him at that moment. He gave no outward evidence, as he cheerfully returned my greeting, that he was a man who had just been hit violently below the belt.'[54] Buchman certainly realised how much damage had been done. But his immediate concern was for the other speakers: 'Those good men standing up for their belief in this country and subjected to that. Yet the OP (Order of Persecution) may be better to have than the OM (Order of Merit).' He also knew that it would scare away many of the people upon whom he was relying to rouse the country. He spoke more personally of his barber, whom he had invited to bring his daughter to meet him and

[259]

who cancelled the date. 'That is what hurts me most,' he said. 'It will be some time before they come around again.'*

Fredrik Ramm wrote a letter to the *Morning Post* about the work of the Oxford Group in Scandinavia, in which he commented, 'I have taken part in hundreds of meetings attended by thousands of people and I have never heard anything confessed in public which could not have been said in Piccadilly Circus.'[55]

Prebendary Wilson Carlile, the founder of the Church Army and by then over ninety, sent Buchman a stream of supporting messages in this period: 'I thank God for your prophetic persistence . . . Go ahead. It helps us and the Kingdom of Heaven greatly . . . You are widening my vision. The top dog is more catchy than our bottom dog. Thousands of lazy lives, if they feel our Blessed Lord wants them and can use them, would buck up and be a blessing to the world.'[56]

Many conservative-minded people, like some of those at Hatfield, did turn away from Buchman following the publicity after the Foyle lunch. Lord Salisbury was not among them. On 7 August 1937, he combined with the Minister of Labour, Ernest Brown, Lord Davidson and the recent President of the British Academy, Professor J. W. Mackail, in a letter to *The Times* which read in part:

'The Oxford Group stands out as a challenge to churches of today to be up and doing. The dominating motive which animates these efforts, whether in the Group or elsewhere, is a pledge of loyalty to apply under God's guidance the spirit and principles of Christ to individual conduct and to every department of social, national and supernational life.

'We write this letter to urge the crying need of mankind that this fundamental principle should be emphasised and insistently applied broadcast throughout this and other countries. What nations imperatively require is the development of a sense of personal responsibility to bring men and women of all administrations and governments to the spirit of loyalty to God. This alone can unite a chaotic world.'[57]

---

* A. P. Herbert certainly regarded Miss Rawlings' intervention as a matter of importance. He telegraphed her: 'If anyone writes a history of the "Oxford Group" it will have a pre- and post-Rawlings period.' (Reginald Pound: *A. P. Herbert: A Biography* (Michael Joseph, 1976), p. 155.)

MORAL AND SPIRITUAL RE-ARMAMENT

Buchman entered 1938 with a renewed sense of urgency. 'I am trying to find an approach that will give the message more intelligently to an age that needs it, but is desperately afraid of it,' he wrote at the time. He was looking for a thought that was simple enough for millions to grasp and realistic enough for national leaders to put forward. He also wanted to shake those who, having found a rich personal experience of faith through the Oxford Group, were hugging it to themselves, and to persuade them to enter the struggle to answer the problems of the wider world.

His uneasiness was leading him to another break-out similar to those which had made him stretch beyond the local ministry in Pennsylvania, beyond the care of the students in the American colleges, and beyond the standard missionary field. It was not a new public relations angle which he sought, but a new and larger commitment for himself and any who would go with him.

The seed thought he was seeking came to him from a Swedish Socialist author, Harry Blomberg. The Swedish Labour Party had been the most successful in Europe. Operating in a period of prolonged peace, it had brought prosperity and comfort to all classes. With these had come a sense of self-sufficiency and a general rejection, in intellectual circles, of any need for God. At the same time, some labour leaders there were aware that prosperity by itself had not brought happiness, while the rise of Communism and Nazism was forcing them to reconsider whether they could for ever stay aloof from the conflicts elsewhere. Thus, Dr Alf Ahlberg, principal of the trades-union-owned training school at Brunnsvik, had recently written, 'I would be thought a fool if I were to say to so-called practical politicians, "You talk of rescuing democracy. Excellent. But faith in democracy requires faith in God." Yet I am convinced I am more of a practical politician in this statement than any of those gentlemen realises. History confirms this and I am afraid is going to confirm it in a still more frightful way.'[1]

Harry Blomberg was one of Ahlberg's pupils. He had brought the philosophy of the Oxford Group, which had reached him through his fellow authors in Norway, to the steelworkers among whom he lived in Borlange. His book *Vi måste börja om* (We must begin again)[2] illustrated the dilemma which Ahlberg outlined. His theme was, 'I had come to a dead end, just as democracy had come to a dead end. I, too, had to begin again.' The book was an immediate best-seller. Commenting upon it, and upon Ronald Fangen's two new novels and Hambro's recent book *Modern Mentality*, the Oslo correspondent of the *New York Times Book Review* wrote in his survey of the literary scene in Scandinavia: 'The supremacy of the psychoanalyst, who drew his deductions largely from observations of those who were sick in body and soul, seems to be weakening. The healthy counter-trend is setting in, a challenge to mankind to resist unthinking mass appeals (of dictatorship) and develop the individualism which can counter present-day trends.'[3]

When asked for a theme for the page on Sweden in the pictorial *Rising Tide* published that spring, Blomberg thought of the Swedish steel going to all the nations of Europe for their armaments and wrote, 'Sweden – the reconciler of the nations. We must rearm morally.'

Buchman received the Swedish edition of *Rising Tide* while spending a few days quietly in the Black Forest in Freudenstadt. Walking one afternoon in the Forest and preparing for his next moves in Britain, Blomberg's thought returned repeatedly to him, and with unusual force: 'Moral and spiritual re-armament. Moral and spiritual re-armament. The next great move in the world will be a movement of moral re-armament for all nations.'

Buchman was due to make a speech in East Ham Town Hall in London a few days later. Bill Jaeger's work in East London had been growing and penetrating the civic life of the area, to the point of becoming a steadying factor in districts where Fascists and their opponents were clashing in the streets. The attitude displayed by one Council member resulted in his becoming known in his borough as 'the councillor with the changed face'. He apologised to the Mayor, to whom he had not spoken for twenty years because of bitterness originating in a policy difference. 'Either something's gone radically wrong with him or something's gone positively right,' commented the Mayor, and soon afterwards fifteen Councillors of different parties issued a statement saying, 'An entirely new spirit of co-operation has come into our work as a Local Authority. This has resulted in a considerable saving of time in reaching decisions.'[4]

The effect of the Oxford Group in East London caught the attention of certain national labour leaders. A group of them had met several times to hear about it under the chairmanship of H. H. Elvin, Chairman of the Trades Union Congress in 1937–8. 'Why don't I have the power to change people like this?' the Deputy Speaker of the House of Commons asked on one of these occasions. Now several mayors in the area were hosting a meeting of 3,000 to hear Buchman, who took this opportunity to launch Moral Re-Armament.

'The world's condition', he began, 'cannot but cause disquiet and anxiety. Hostility piles up between nation and nation, labour and capital, class and class. The cost of bitterness and fear mounts daily. Friction and frustration are undermining our homes.

'Is there a remedy that will cure the individual and the nation and give the hope of a speedy and satisfactory recovery?

'The remedy may lie in a return to those simple home truths that some of us learned at our mother's knee, and which many of us have forgotten and neglected – honesty, purity, unselfishness and love.

'The crisis is fundamentally a moral one. The nations must rearm morally . . .

'We can, we must and we will generate a moral and spiritual force that is powerful enough to remake the world.'[5]

Soon after this meeting Tod Sloan, a well-known East London militant who as a boy had canvassed for Keir Hardie when he stood for Parliament for East Ham, and in whose house Ben Tillett, Tom Mann and the 1899 dockers' strike committee sometimes met, saw a poster outside Canning Town Public Hall. It asked 'What is Moral Re-Armament?' and answered:

> It's not an institution,
> It's not a point of view,
> It starts a revolution
> By starting one in you!

He went in to the meeting and, as he later said, 'got a basinful'. He came to realise that his agitations on behalf of the unemployed and homeless, his fights for meals and boots for the school-children, essential activities which had sometimes landed him in gaol, had inadvertently taken a wrong turning. 'I'd always said that I loved my class and family . . . But I saw that the main thing I'd done was to teach them to hate. I'd said I was an idealist, but I'd made materialists out of them,' he said. One of the first things he decided to put to rights was his relationship with his wife.[6] He later wrote to Buchman, 'The words, Moral Re-Armament, are God's property coined for His service and this is what goes into them – there will be no more unmoral bargaining, no more social injustice, no more conflict. Chaos cannot obtain if we work, live and practise Moral Re-Armament. It is a real laughing, living, loving, obedient willingness to restore God to leadership.'[7]

A few days after speaking in East Ham, Buchman visited Sweden. On arrival in Stockholm he told the press that his vision was that Sweden would become 'a reconciler of the nations' – a long step forward, in his view, from mere neutrality. He took part in King Gustav's eightieth birthday celebrations and, with his usual insatiable interest in public occasions and the character of public men, was present at the arrival, by boat or train, of most of the principal guests. The visit was in reality a reconnaissance on his part, as he had for three years been resisting invitations from many quarters to take a team to that country. When, for example, Archbishop Söderblom's son-in-law, Professor Runestam, who attended Hambro's house-party at Høsbjør, had pressed him to go there in 1935, he had answered, 'Are you clear what you want to accomplish? I think those who want to sponsor the work are beset by . . . misimpressions of its true character.'[8] He had written to another friend, 'What I fear so much about Sweden is that what they want is something that will just be a "pick-me-up" for the Church . . . rather than the rebirth of everything in the Church. Men like these . . . bishops and clergy are not willing to go through the pain of rebirth.'[9]

Now that Blomberg and the steelworkers were coming forward, Buchman felt more confident. Even so, not everyone immediately took to him. Sven Stolpe, Blomberg's literary colleague, was 'horrified' when they met. He had first heard of Buchman in Norway 'through that marvellous team of brilliant men, Fangen, Wikborg, Skard, Mowinckel', and was expecting to be deeply impressed by this man to whom they all declared they owed so much. But Stolpe found him 'one hundred per cent American, ugly and so unintellectual'. 'He did not think logically and what he said often seemed to me naive and incoherent. He laughed and laughed and smiled all day. He was never solemn, and we Swedes are always very solemn about holy things.'

To his astonishment, however, Buchman asked him to interpret for him when he returned in August to hold the first Moral Re-Armament Assembly at Visby, on the Baltic island of Gotland.*

Stolpe protested: 'I've never been to England or spoken English or known any English people.'

'Oh, God will help,' replied Buchman, and Stolpe agreed to do it.

The crowds at Visby were all the greater because the visit had been so long delayed. They poured in until there was no building large enough to hold them except the ruins of the old church of St Nikolai. *Stockholms-Tidningen*, then the largest Swedish daily, sent its aeroplane each day for pictures and reports. Yet Buchman believed it would be tough going,

---

* The wife of the Bishop on the island of Gotland, Torsten Ysander, consulted Buchman on the seating of a dinner party. Buchman said, 'Oh, I think we seat the changed and the unchanged alternately.' 'Where should I sit?' asked Mrs Ysander. 'Beside me, of course,' replied Buchman. 'And we both laughed uproariously,' added Mrs Ysander. (*Frank Buchman – Eighty*, p. 192.)

against the complacency of Swedish society and the cynicism among its intellectuals. Stolpe agreed. 'I have never known such hatred as there was towards Buchman from some present and from some who had sent them,' he said. 'This American coming to teach Christianity to good old Swedes!'

Stolpe himself, meanwhile, was beginning to reassess Buchman. He was immediately impressed by the people who accompanied him. 'Buchman had dozens of the finest people you ever saw. Those boys and girls. Incredible! Absolutely convincing! You felt kindness, purity, absolutely clean air around them. They thought of others all the time and had nothing to hide. They never got you into a corner. They had a sort of absolute loyalty to God, a burning conviction, yet laughing all the way,' Stolpe recalled forty years later.

Then he noticed Buchman's attitude to the workers whom Blomberg and he had brought with them. 'They interested him far more than the young lords. He made the two lots meet and like each other, torpedoing the twentieth-century nostrum of anti-class.'

What did all this say about Buchman? After a bit, Stolpe worked out his own explanation: 'I saw he was an inspired man, a kind of poet. Not a charmer, but someone guided by God. Why? I couldn't understand it. Then I remembered the Finnish poet Runeberg saying that if God wants to play a beautiful tune, it doesn't matter if He does it on a poor instrument. Buchman seemed to me the strangest instrument I had ever seen: but God had chosen him.'

The interpreting went well. 'I never heard anyone lead a meeting like him. He always ended at the highest note. He was deeply serious, doing only one thing – and he had to do it. Your impression was, "Here is a man, a genius. There are ten thousand more gifted people in Europe, but he is enough for God to remake the world with." '[10]

The assembly started well. Many people found deep personal spiritual experiences, and there was good press coverage of the public speeches. But Buchman was uneasy. For most of one night he was awake, praying and listening for God's direction. His speech the next morning was made straight from his jotted notes of the night before, wrecked the apparent success of the proceedings, and presented the small-minded and complacent among his hearers with an uncomfortable dilemma.

'I am not interested, nor do I think it adequate,' he said, 'if we are going just to start another revival. Whatever thoughtful statesman you talk with will tell you that every country needs a moral and spiritual awakening. That is the absolutely fundamental essential. But revival is only one level of thought. To stop there is inferior thinking.

'The next step is revolution. It is uncomfortable. A lot of Christians don't like the word. It scares them. It makes them goose-fleshy. That's where some of your critics come from – goose-fleshy Christians with armchair Christianity. What the Oxford Group will give this and every nation is a spiritual revolution.'

'The point is this,' Buchman continued. 'Are the Christians going to build a Christian philosophy that will move Europe? Are you the kind of Christians that can build that revolution? If you are not going on that battlefront, I wish you well. I am not going to quarrel with you or criticise you. You do exactly what you like in the way you like. That's your idea of democracy. I don't say it's true democracy, but it's the popular practice of democracy ... Somewhere on the battlefront we will have the real revolutionaries.'

Beyond revival and revolution, he went on, 'There is a third stage, renaissance. The rebirth of a people, individuals and the rebirth of a nation ... Some people do not like the idea of nations reborn, or of reaching the millions. They deride such a programme by calling it "publicity" ... All the publicity must be for destruction – or must it? Gospel means "good news", front-page news. But people object if it gets on the front page.'

One of the events which had generated this onslaught was an article in the important Stockholm daily, *Dagens Nyheter*, which mentioned 'the movement's loud-mouthed propaganda methods' and 'advertising about world revival'.[11] Buchman felt that many present, including some who had found personal help through the Oxford Group, were sheltering behind the criticism in their desire to have a safe, restricted movement which would avoid public ridicule; and that some were also looking for a movement which would reassure them about their souls while allowing the pattern of their lives to continue much as before.

'I am going to promise you one thing,' he concluded. 'I am not turning back. I am not turning back, no matter who does, no matter what it is going to cost. If you join in this great crusade, you will get the way of the Cross. I am not going to lure you by hopes of material success. I am not going to lure you by saying you are going to be heroes. I am not going to lure you, although I believe that these lands can give a pattern on how to live. It is a personal experience of the Cross. It is not I, but Christ. It is not I at the head, but Christ who leads.'

He then suggested that people should not attend more meetings but should think it out alone. 'The thing you have got to decide is between you and God. Do it alone. Write it down if you want to. It is a deed, like the transfer of property – so you turn over your life to God, for full and complete direction as a fellow-revolutionary.'[12]

As a result of this speech, some decided to cease working with Buchman. Some even decided to kill his work if they could. Nils Gösta Ekman, who later became an editor at *Svenska Dagbladet*, records that some reacted against Buchman's challenge 'as against a personal insult or an espionage into their private defence secrets'.[13]

A large number of Swedes, however, accepted his challenge to themselves and their country. They were a fair cross-section of the nation – teachers, farmers, steelworkers, clergy, students, authors and artists. Waldemar Lorentzon of the well-known Halmstad Group of painters experienced a reconciliation with his wife, and came to believe that 'art can be a powerful spokesman of a new morality'.[14] A number of students at the Music Academy, among them some who were to become distinguished composers and initiators of new musical trends, met daily to learn how to put into practice what they had decided at Visby. Groups flourished from then on for some years in each of Sweden's four universities. Their conference at Undersåker in 1939 was a national event and provided the core of Buchman's Swedish full-time colleagues for the future. The next year 10,000 teachers presented an appeal for moral re-armament to the nation. The ideas summarised in their book, *Ikke för skolam utam för livet* (Not for school but for life),[15] gained a wide influence and were supported by the Minister of Education of the day. The churches also were deeply affected. Sweden's foremost hymn-writer, Anders Frostenson, says that the language used in sermons changed completely after the arrival of the Oxford Group.*

People who went home to other countries also began to tackle practical problems in their nations. Finns who had been at Visby mounted a national assembly at Aulanko in January 1939. Twenty years earlier Finland had been riven by a civil war between Whites and Reds, and intense bitterness lived on among those who had lost relatives in the fighting or been confined to detention camps by one side or the other. Leaders of both sides attended the Aulanko assembly. Bishop Eelis Gulin of Tampere repeatedly stated that reconciliations effected there were a significant factor in uniting the nation in the months immediately before the Soviet invasion later that year. 'God gave us a miracle,' he said in Australia years later. 'Many of us thank God for Frank Buchman as one of those used as His tools.'[16]

In Denmark some of those affected by the Oxford Group three years earlier had been seeking a way to tackle the country's most serious social problem – an unemployment rate of over 20 per cent. Alfred Nielsen, the wood industry employer from Silkeborg, remembers Buchman asking the Danes at Visby whether it was God's will for a fifth of the work force to be unemployed.

---

* Six Nordic bishops summed up the continuing effect of this infusion in a message to Buchman on 10 January 1951: 'With its realistic faith in God, its ethical radicalism, its fellowship and its conquering spirit, Moral Re-Armament has made the original Christian elements of faith come alive in the midst of our modern secularised environment.'

'No,' they replied.

'Then go home and tackle it,' said Buchman. This was also a major theme of his speech in Copenhagen in late August on his way from Sweden to Switzerland.[17] Some experiments had already been made, and Valdemar Hvidt wrote about them in *Politiken*[18] while the Visby assembly was still in progress. The result was a national campaign. It began, according to the *Scandinavian Review*, when 'citizens in many towns, awakened to civic responsibility through the Oxford Group, began to tackle the problem of Denmark's 100,000 unemployed by spontaneous sacrifice'.[19] The paper relates how the Socialist Prime Minister, Thorvald Stauning, 'expressed his own and the nation's gratitude for the surge of voluntary effort' and helped the initiators to gather a National Association for Combating Unemployment composed of fifteen prominent farmers, employers and trades union leaders, with Hvidt as chairman and Nielsen as an executive member. 'Each success in tackling unemployment', adds the *Review*, 'has been the outcome of a new spirit. The joint action of the fifteen is another instance of the putting aside of private and party ends for national service. The chief task, therefore, is to work constantly for that change in the individual throughout the country which calls forth new qualities of selfless national service.'*

Meanwhile, in the international field, some of the politicians who had been influenced by Buchman were among those who created an organisation called 'the Oslo States'. This was an attempt by the smaller countries of Europe to unite to avert war. The originator of the plan was the former Norwegian Prime Minister, J. L. Mowinckel, who had been reconciled to Hambro during Buchman's Norwegian campaign. Another participant was the Finnish Foreign Minister, Rudolf Holsti, who, in July 1938, had told the American press that Buchman and the Oxford Group 'have been able to penetrate the highest political and economic circles, bringing people together'.[20] Another, J. A. E. Patijn, the Dutch Foreign Minister, who had spoken at the Utrecht demonstration, had gone with Buchman to Sweden to prepare the Visby assembly.

The editor of *The Spectator*, Wilson Harris, noted in his personal column that the co-operation of Hambro and Holsti at the League of Nations was due to their association in the Oxford Group. Harris wrote, 'Alike in their relation to Dr Buchman, the Norwegian and Finnish delegates are very different in other respects . . . But both are transparently honest men.'[21]

A few weeks after the Visby assembly, the Foreign Ministers of the seven 'Oslo States' met in Copenhagen. They decided to work towards a

---

* The methods used in this campaign and its social effects are outlined from official documents at the end of this chapter.

more active concept of neutrality than, for example, Switzerland, and hoped to be able to confront Hitler with a united voice. This was accompanied by a rapid re-armament in Sweden; but the Oslo States were thrown into confusion by the Soviet–Nazi Pact and failed to maintain their unity in the pressures of war.

Some groups as well as individuals ceased to work actively with Buchman as a result of the launching of Moral Re-Armament. In Norway, for example, some who had come to rely for personal spiritual comfort on a weekly group meeting split away, calling themselves The Old Oxford Group. This also took place in other countries, sometimes on a considerable scale. Some maintained that Buchman's attention to matters not purely personal involved a change of principle. His own explanation was that if Moral Re-Armament was the car, the Oxford Group was the engine, and that individual change was the basis of both.

Others dissociated themselves because they thought Buchman was 'going into politics'. For Buchman, however, Moral Re-Armament was only the realisation of the aim he had enunciated to his students at Penn State and Hartford, which he redefined in 1921 as 'a programme of life issuing in personal, social, racial, national and supernational change'.[22] 'The Oxford Group', he had often said, 'has nothing to do with politics, yet it has everything to do with politics, because it leads to change in politicians.'[23]

The individual withdrawal which Buchman most regretted was that of his old friend and travelling companion, Sherwood Day, who had worked closely with him for twenty-two years. During the winter of 1936–7, Day had pleurisy followed by pneumonia. During his slow recovery, he found himself increasingly reacting to some of his colleagues, to some attitudes, to some phrases. Was it right to consider that alcoholics were no longer part of their responsibility? Was the word 'moral' in 'Moral Re-Armament' misleading: did it imply self-effort and an end in itself? Was a fellowship becoming an establishment? Day eventually returned to the United States, became minister of a Presbyterian church, and settled to a life of steady usefulness with individuals, consciously leaving aside any attempt at a wider application of spiritual belief. Buchman missed Day personally, but never challenged his right to take a different path.

There were, of course, people who had found a transforming experience through the Oxford Group who felt a specific calling to work other than that undertaken by Buchman. One of these is Paul Tournier, the Swiss psychiatrist and best-selling author.* 'I owe him everything,' he

---

* Since 1938 he has written eighteen books which have sold two million copies.

said in 1982: 'all the spiritual adventure which has been in my life . . . my own transformation, the transformation of our home, of our married life and our family life . . . I owe him all my career, all the new orientation in the understanding of medicine and in our medical thought which I have been able to develop.'[24]

Interviewed in 1978, Tournier said that Buchman was the man 'who has had by far the greatest influence upon me of anyone in my life'. In 1932 he had been a general medical practitioner, an orphan, a very closed man, who found it practically impossible to make personal contact with anyone. Meeting the Oxford Group in Switzerland had eliminated this problem and set him free, along with his wife, to help people spiritually. 'Then in 1937 I went to Oxford, for the only time, to a house-party,' Tournier continued. 'There Frank was interested in our applying our personal experience to our professional life. I had considerable experience of this area, but more like a laboratory experiment – I had started to bring about changes in patients without seeing the consequences for the future of medicine. I got a very clear conviction that God wanted me to devote the rest of my life to showing the effect of spiritual life on the health of people.'

After he returned from Oxford Tournier sent a printed letter to all his patients saying he would no longer function as an ordinary doctor, but would be available to help any person spiritually. 'I lost practically all my patients. Then slowly I built up a completely new clientele, and in 1938 I started to write *Médecine de la Personne*,[25] which I dedicated to Buchman.' Tournier felt so strongly about this dedication that he delayed publication in Britain for fifteen years rather than omit it as his publisher wished.

'My own road went differently, but I have always felt myself an integral part of the spiritual revolution Frank brought to the world. When Frank launched Moral Re-Armament I admired his courage in concerning himself with politicians and the prickly matters they have to handle. I think historians will see in him the man who launched a whole spiritual development of humanity rather than the founder of the movement of Moral Re-Armament. I think he was a prophet. I compare him with Wesley and St Francis. In the purely rational West, he restored the value of irrational human relations. Why was he opposed? For the same reason as Jesus and His disciples were opposed.'

Malcolm Muggeridge writes that for a long time he was puzzled by 'the extraordinary hostility which Buchman's Christian evangelism caused' in Britain. 'Yes, he's an American,' he says, 'but then so is Billy Graham, for instance, and I've never heard people denigrating Billy in quite such vicious terms as they did Buchman and MRA.

'An experience I had some years ago shed light on the conundrum. I had been elected by the students of Edinburgh University to be their

Rector, and when I went to Edinburgh to be installed I had a wonderful reception. Then some months later I was asked by the Students' Union to put in a request to the governing body of the University that contraceptives should be made freely available by the University Medical Unit. I refused to do this, whereupon I was subjected to abuse, to the point that I found it necessary to resign. In a farewell sermon in St Giles' Cathedral, I explained why I had done what I had, and received some private thanks, but none publicly. The conclusion I came to was that in a libertine society any attack on libertinism is anathema . . . Tom Driberg was an inveterate enemy of MRA; readers of his posthumous autobiography will see why.'[26]

Appendix to Chapter 23:

Danish Campaign to Combat Unemployment

The official account of the origins of what was to become a national campaign states, 'During 1938 people in contact with the Oxford Group met and considered whether it was possible to activate private initiative to supplement public efforts.'[27] The idea, in essence, was that it was everyone's responsibility to find work for others. 'When a stone is too heavy to move,' the lawyer Valdemar Hvidt said, 'break it into small pieces and get many to carry it.' Unemployment was a matter of conscience for everyone, where each town and village would take action to find work for its own unemployed.

The first experiment was initiated by Knud Oldenburg of the Department of Forest and Heath. Oldenburg had, for example, formed a flying corps of people from Jutland towns who were once thought unemployable. They thinned the copses which an earlier generation had planted along the Jutland coast to reclaim the land, work which had now become essential but which the peasant proprietors had not the capital to undertake. This enterprise, which reclaimed men, land and what proved in the coming war to be valuable fuel, was at first financed voluntarily, but quite soon the Ministry of Social Affairs, with trade union agreement, guaranteed the men a small wage until the work became self-supporting. 'Oldenburg, once a man of great *personal* ambition, had learnt to transmute this energy into *national* service after his contact with the Oxford Group.'[28]

In December 1938 Hvidt, Nielsen and their friends obtained an interview with the Socialist Prime Minister, Thorvald Stauning. 'We have achieved much in the social field and I had hoped the social changes would make people responsible,' he said. 'What is needed is the change of attitude which you have experienced.' He suggested people – leading farmers, employers and union officials – who, if they worked together, could bring a solution. On 1 August 1939 the National Association for Combating Unemployment (LAB) was founded, with Hvidt as Chairman and Nielsen as an Executive Member. Speaking at the inaugural meeting in Copenhagen, the Prime Minister 'expressed his own and the nation's gratitude for the surge of voluntary effort which had culminated in the Association and which had brought to work together men from all camps and classes who previously found it most difficult to co-operate on anything'.[29]

The German invasion on 9 April 1940 stimulated the Association to wider efforts. Every employed Dane meant one less who could be transported to work in German war industries. Many initiatives were taken. In the town of Vejle, for example, people had been postponing the painting of their houses, while there were twenty-five painters unemployed. All these became employed, and the demand for carpenters and joiners was so great that they were brought in from other towns.[30] In 1944, in preparation for peace, 100,000 farms were visited to see what repairs and land improvements were needed, resulting in a register of 30,000 extra jobs.[31] LAB continued in operation, under the same leadership, until 1965, when, through the improvement of the economy and other factors, the unemployment figure had declined from 20.1 per cent at its formation to 3.7 per cent.[32]

Commenting after the war the economist, Finn Friis, wrote, 'The words "change in mentality" have to be used in connection with this work. It brought a new understanding of the value of the worker and is leaving permanent traces on our post-war economy.'[33]

MORAL RE-ARMAMENT GOES PUBLIC

From Visby Buchman moved on to Interlaken in Switzerland, where he had called an international assembly for Moral Re-Armament. Oxford was now not only too small but also too far away from the centre of events. The assembly covered the first twelve days of September 1938, when Europe seemed to be on the edge of war following Hitler's threats to Czechoslovakia. 'We have set ourselves the difficult task of trying to liquidate the cost of bitterness and fear, which mounts daily,' said Buchman at the outset. 'The odds are seemingly against us, but just as individuals are delivered from their prison cells of doubt and defeat, so it is possible for nations to be delivered from their prison cells of fear, resentment, jealousy and depression. . .'[1]

At every meeting he strove to demonstrate this through living examples. One day Japanese and Chinese spoke side by side; on another French and German, or Sudeten and Czech, Conservative and Marxist, black and white. All described, from their own experience, how fear and greed could be overcome or the gulfs of national and racial hatred bridged. Buchman himself, contrary to his custom, spoke day after day. Whereas normally he had made only one or two major speeches a year, in mid-1938 he delivered twelve in six months.

The most controversial and long-quoted – or misquoted – among them was entitled 'Guidance or Guns'.* 'The world is at the crossroads,' he began. 'The choice is guidance or guns. We must listen to guidance or we shall listen to guns.

'Every man in every land should listen to guidance. In industry, in the workshop, in the nation's life, in Parliament, the normal thing is to listen to God. Each nation expresses it in its own way – but all God-controlled and God-led. Thus, with God leading, all will understand each other. Here in this philosophy is lasting peace, and only here.'[2]

A young Swiss asked him if it would be possible to stop war breaking

* Certain critics misquoted the title as 'Guidance not guns', implying that Buchman was against the democracies rearming; cf. heading to Chapter 5 of Driberg's *The Mystery of Moral Re-Armament.*

[273]

out. 'I don't know,' he replied. 'But if there are fifty men in every country who give themselves wholly, we shall pull through.'[3]

As the crisis deepened, delegates to the Assembly were called into the armed forces of their different nations. Buchman's closing speech dealt with the massive moral mobilisation needed to 'answer the aching hunger of mankind for peace and a new world'.[4] Then other delegates left for home. As Gudrun Egebjerg, the Danish journalist, sat having lunch at the railway station just before her train left to cross Germany to Denmark, a car drove up. 'Buchman walked straight to our table', she recalled later, 'and said to me, "You looked so sad this morning. I just want to leave this with you: 'I can do all things through Christ who strengtheneth me.' Goodbye," and he was gone.'

'I had never seen that side of Frank before,' Miss Egebjerg added. 'The leader, the statesman I knew. The gay, warm laughter, the sharpness and challenge; but never before this simple deep compassion, taking time on a very full day to drive across town to say a last word, just because he remembered a gloomy face.' It was one of many such incidents. Another participant in the Assembly, General C. R. P. Winser, remarked, 'Far from being obsessed by the crisis, Buchman was thinking for everyone and of everyone.'

Buchman took a team to Geneva for a luncheon at the invitation of League delegates, which Hambro had delivered personally at Interlaken. The luncheon was held on 15 September 1938, the day Chamberlain flew to meet Hitler in Berchtesgaden. Buchman's hosts were four leading political delegates to the League,* and diplomats from fifty-three countries were present. Hambro introduced Buchman and his colleagues to his fellow diplomats: 'Where we have failed in changing politics, they have succeeded in changing lives, and giving men and women a new way of living.'[5]

Patijn, now Dutch Foreign Minister, told how tension had grown between his country and Belgium, while he was Ambassador there. The International Court at The Hague had decided against the Netherlands in a vital case, and he himself had been annoyed by the way certain Belgian papers reported the affair, making the Netherlands look ridiculous. 'At that time', he continued, 'I had to speak at an important dinner in Brussels. It was suggested I should talk about the case. I resolutely refused. But just before I was about to respond to the toast, the conviction came to me that I had to refer to the dispute. I complimented my hosts on their success and said that in the future we should be better friends. From that day all bitter comments against my country ceased.' 'The fact that I

* C. J. Hambro, J. A. E. Patijn, N. W. Jordan of New Zealand and V. V. Pella of Roumania.

was able to make such a speech', Patijn added, 'was only because of my deep conviction that it was much more in accord with God's will than the speech which I had previously wished to make.'[6]

The *Journal de Genève* issued a four-page supplement on this occasion and the editor, Jean Martin, sent it to his fellow editors in many countries. 'Whatever happens in Europe,' he wrote them, 'Moral Re-Armament remains the only answer to recurrent crisis and the one foundation for permanent peace.'[7]

Munich, with its attempt to contain Hitler's drive by appeasing it, came and went. Buchman was relieved, as were most people, at the removal of the immediate threat of war, but he did not think anything fundamental had been achieved. He regarded it as a respite in which moral and spiritual re-armament must be pressed ahead in parallel with increased material re-armament.

Buchman's speech in East Ham had, meanwhile, stimulated a series of letters in *The Times*. The first was from thirty-three Members of Parliament of all parties, who pointed to 'the Oxford Group's crusade for Moral Re-Armament' as 'urgently needed'.[8]

On 10 September, as diplomacy became ever more frantic, this letter was followed by one headlined 'Moral Re-Armament – the Need of the Hour', signed by seventeen public figures, including former Prime Minister Lord Baldwin, two Field Marshals, an Admiral of the Fleet and Lord Trenchard, the creator of the Royal Air Force: 'The strength of a nation consists in the vitality of her principles. Policy, foreign as well as domestic, is for every nation ultimately determined by the character of her people and the inspiration of her leaders; by the acceptance in their lives and in their policy of honesty, faith and love as the foundations on which a new world may be built. Without these qualities, the strongest armaments, the most elaborate pacts, only postpone the hour of reckoning . . .

'God's Living Spirit calls each nation, like each individual, to its highest destiny, and breaks down the barriers of fear and greed, of suspicion and hatred. This same Spirit can transcend conflicting political systems, can reconcile order and freedom, can rekindle true patriotism, can unite all citizens in the service of the nation, and all nations in the service of mankind. "Thy Will be done on earth" is not only a prayer for guidance, but a call to action. For His Will is our Peace.'[9]

Lord Salisbury, who both signed and took part in assembling this letter, hoped that 'the German leaders would read it'.[10] So not only were copies sent to Lord Stamp, one of the signatories who was in Germany at the time, but General Winser telephoned Lord Redesdale, currently Hitler's guest in Berlin, who promised to read it to his host. The letter was printed all over the world and was favourably commented upon in some Austrian and Italian newspapers.

[275]

Swiss[11] and Dutch national leaders instigated their own campaigns for moral re-armament. The Dutch call was signed by the Commander-in-Chief of the Army, the Chief of the Naval Staff, the President of the Supreme Court and a number of former Ministers and Governors of the Dutch East Indies.[12] Queen Wilhelmina described this Call to her foreign Minister as 'a campaign against defeatism'.[13] The Queen issued a Personal Word to the Nation three weeks later emphasising that 'our civilisation, even though undergirded by the reinforcement of our military strength', could not avoid destruction without 'the conviction which has been expressed in this call for moral and spiritual re-armament'.[14]* When King Leopold of the Belgians made a state visit to Holland, he spoke of 'the rapprochement and co-operation of our two nations' developing and gaining solidarity and strength 'in the service of this ideal'.[15]

Public support for Moral Re-Armament in Britain was growing. Seventeen national trades union leaders, including the current and three former Chairmen of the Trades Union Congress, wrote that it 'represented the dynamic spirit of the best of the early Labour leaders and it must be recreated'.[16] Groups of civic leaders and journalists, and thirty-seven top sportsmen, followed. Fourteen prominent Scots[17] and the leaders of cities like Liverpool[18] joined in. On Armistice Day the Earl of Athlone and six others** wrote of the readiness of Britain throughout her history 'to meet recurrent crises with the courage each demanded'. 'But the spiritual crisis remains,' they continued. 'Nation and Empire must stand or fall by our response to that call. The choice is moral re-armament or national decay.'[19] The call was taken up by the Governor-General of Australia, Lord Gowrie,[20] and by national leaders and the press in many parts of the Commonwealth. On 10 October Buchman wrote to King George of Greece, 'Moral Re-Armament is becoming a rallying point for the democracies to give an answer to the taunt of the dictators that democracies have no plan.'[21]

The idea of Moral Re-Armament had, in fact, caught the imagination of many leaders, who saw in it the expression of an essential requirement for the preservation of peace. The urgency of the situation impelled many people, known and unknown to Buchman, into action. He had nothing to do with the letters themselves, and Patijn among others thanked him for his readiness to stay in the background.

In Britain Buchman had, after prolonged public pressure, been invited

---

* Whether the Queen realised that this whole campaign had originated in Buchman's speech in East Ham is not clear.

** Admiral of the Fleet Sir Osman Brock, Viscount FitzAlan of Derwent, the author Ian Hay, Lord Howard of Penrith, Major-General Sir Frederick Maurice and Lord Rennell of Rodd.

33. Fredrik Ramm,
Editor of the Oslo
Morgenbladet.

34. Ronald Fangen,
Norwegian novelist.

35. Carl Hambro, President
of the Norwegian
Parliament, invited
Buchman to Norway.

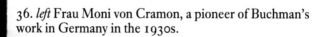

36. *left* Frau Moni von Cramon, a pioneer of Buchman's
work in Germany in the 1930s.

37. *below* 10,000 people fill the courtyard of Kronborg Castle at Elsinore,
Denmark. Buchman's work spread rapidly through the North.

38. *inset* Buchman speaking at a mass demonstration in the British Industries Fair building, Castle Bromwich, Birmingham, in 1936.

39. *above* Part of the crowd drawn from all over Britain and from overseas.

40. *below* Harry Blomberg, Swedish socialist author, with Buchman. Blomberg's book *We Must Begin Again* called for a moral foundation for democracy to meet the threat of totalitarian ideologies. Asked by Buchman for a message of hope, he replied: 'We must re-arm morally'. This gave Buchman the key thought to issue a world-wide call for Moral Re-Armament.

41. *left* Moral Re-Armament in Sweden was launched in the ancient city of Visby.

42. *above* Buchman speaking at Visby, translated by Swedish author Sven Stolpe.

43. *below* Holland's Foreign Minister speaks to League of Nations delegates. Extreme right: Buchman and Carl Hambro.

44. *left* Four searchlights representing the absolute standards of honesty, purity, unselfishness and love, illuminate the sky over a packed assembly for Moral Re-Armament in the Hollywood Bowl, California. Several MRA assemblies were held in the U.S.A. in 1939 and 1940.

46. *below* In spite of the public demand, Buchman withdrew to Tahoe in the Sierra Nevada mountains in September, 1940, with close colleagues, to seek the next moves and find a deeper commitment.

45. *above* H. W. 'Bunny' Austin and his wife with Buchman in America, July 1939.

47. *above* Mackinac Island, Michigan, where a training centre was set up in 1941 in support of the national campaign evolved at Tahoe.

48. *left* Buchman (centre) with Mr. and Mrs. Henry Ford. Buchman asked them where an assembly line of ideas to meet the world's need could be based. Mrs. Ford suggested Mackinac Island.

49. *left below* Buchman with Ray Purdy (centre) and explorer Rear-Admiral Richard E. Byrd.

50. *below* John Riffe, CIO steelworkers' organiser, with Mrs. Thomas Edison, widow of the inventor, both friends of Buchman.

51. *above* Buchman (right), who suffered a stroke in 1941, is examined by an old friend, Dr. Loring Swaim.

52. *above* Staunch supporters: Senator Harry S. Truman and Congressman Wadsworth (right).

53. *below* When General Marshall ordered the early release from the armed forces of some of Buchman's key workers, Buchman was at the airport to meet them.

54. *left* Buchman entering 45 Berkeley Square, 30 April, 1946. This London house was given in 1938 as a centre for his work in Britain.

55. *above* Returning to Britain in 1946, Buchman is welcomed by Wing-Commander Edward Howell, OBE, DFC, at Southampton.

56. *below* Buchman's first major move in Britain was to the coalfields.   57. *right* Buchman leaving the Yorkshire miner's cottage of Reg and Ivy Adams.

58. *above* Mountain House, Caux, Switzerland. Part of the conference centre opened by Swiss friends as a base for Buchman's post-war work in Europe. It rapidly became a world centre.

60. *bottom right* On arrival at Caux Buchman appreciated much, but asked: 'Where are the Germans? You will never rebuild Europe without the Germans.'

59. *below* Hundreds of Germans and French came to Caux in the next few years. Left to right: Dr. Artur Sträter (Germany), Buchman, Madame Irène Laure (France).

for the first time to speak over the BBC,* though the Director of Religion, F. A. Iremonger, tried to retain some control and deprecated the use of the world 'change',[22] to no avail. Lord Salisbury had led the demand, encouraged by Archbishop Lang who was glad he was trying to get the BBC 'to make some sort of reparation for the rather grievous wrong which it did to the Movement by its record of that unfortunate Foyle luncheon'.[23] Buchman sent Salisbury the draft of the talk, which he entitled 'Chaos Against God', for his opinion. 'I admired your speech very much,' Salisbury wrote. 'I may say that I think you put the order of spiritual awakening the right way up – first the individual, then the society and last of all the international relation . . . I think the phrase, "The dictatorship of the Holy Spirit", is a most noteworthy phrase which will persist. Altogether it is a most striking utterance.'[24]

Archbishop Lang had sent a message of congratulation to Buchman for his sixtieth birthday in June 'on the great work he has been able to achieve in bringing multitudes of human lives in all parts of the world under the transforming Power of Christ'.[25] At the beginning of October the Archbishop made a broadcast calling for national repentance and a return to the will of God, in which he referred to the statements calling for moral re-armament: 'All, in one way or another, insist that what is most needed in our personal, civil, industrial and international life is, to quote the letter of the Members of Parliament, "a re-dedication of our people to those elementary virtues of honesty, unselfishness and love which many of us have allowed to take a secondary place; the subjection, as the Foreign Secretary once reminded us, of every part of our being to the service of God". . . . The commonplaces of the pulpit may begin to bear fruit if they become the convictions of men in Parliament, in office and in the factory – of "the man in the street". Companies of men and women united in such loyalty to the leadership of Christ in the midst of the nation would . . . gradually leaven the whole lump. Here is the highest and deepest form of national service.'[26]

That November, Buchman addressed a luncheon at the National Trade Union Club, of which George Light was now Chairman. He sat between Ben Tillett and Tom Mann, the legendary leaders of the 1889 London Dock Strike. Both became firm friends of his, and Tillett later entered the lists when Buchman was criticised in the *Daily Telegraph*.[27] He said of him, 'I like Frank Buchman. . . He is a great man because he is a lover of his fellow men,' and, during his own last illness, sent Buchman a verbal message: 'Tell him to go on fighting. Give him my love and tell him I wish him the best of luck. Tell him: You have a great international

* In a series on 'The Validity of Religious Experience', broadcast on 27 November 1938.

movement. Use it. It is the hope of tomorrow. Your movement will bring sanity back to the world.'[28]

Asked for a New Year message by the Press Association, Buchman tried to put his message in terms understandable to everyone at that particular moment. The initials ARP (Air Raid Precautions) were by now familiar to everyone in Britain, as trenches were dug and shelters installed in parks and back gardens. Someone had suggested that Moral and Spiritual Re-Armament was cumbrous, and might be shortened to MRA. Buchman at once accepted this idea, just as he had taken the original phrase from Blomberg. 'MRA', he began his New Year message, 'is the answer to the dark forebodings and fears for 1939. MRA is as essential as ARP, and takes away the fear. MRA is a commodity for every householder ... It is God's property ... It means God in control personally and nationally. It means the knowledge and exact information that God's guidance brings.'[29]

MRA was also being promoted in Britain by Bunny Austin, Britain's current tennis idol.* Austin had first met Buchman six years before, while playing tennis in the South of France. He became convinced that Buchman's ideas were the best hope of maintaining peace in Europe, something which he had been much concerned about, though unable to find any practical form of action. When he had returned to London, however, he had met determined resistance from his actress wife, Phyllis Konstam. To keep the peace at home he had given way, and apart from their encounter at the Foyle lunch had seen little of Buchman and his friends. He had, however, continued to believe in Buchman's approach and, when the Munich crisis blew up, he had decided that he must follow his conscience, come what may, and throw in his lot with them.

'The full impact of the crisis came home to me when, on 11 September 1938, a warden called with gas masks for us,' he wrote later.[30] 'He said our baby would have to have a gas-proof tent. Suddenly I realised that my forebodings of six years earlier had come true. And what had I done about it? I had been brought in touch with an answer – and had turned away, betraying the best in myself, betraying my wife and betraying my fellow men. For I believe that if the countless Englishmen like myself, who had met the Group in the early thirties, had wholeheartedly accepted its challenge, there could have been such a stiffening of morale that Hitler would never have doubted our willingness to fight. As it was, we in Britain had drifted towards war unwilling to face what Germany was doing, although it was spelt out for us in *Mein Kampf.*'

Austin's first thought was to mobilise sportsmen behind Moral Re-

---

* And still, as I write, the last Englishman to have reached the Men's Final at Wimbledon.

Armament. Hence their letter to *The Times*. With George Eyston, the racing motorist, he spoke to 58,000 spectators at half-time in the Arsenal v Chelsea match, introduced by the Arsenal coach George Allison. Similar action was taken elsewhere in the country. Then Austin produced a book containing the calls for Moral Re-Armament in various countries, together with vivid personal stories by himself, the unemployed leader Bill Rowell, and others. Work on the book began on 1 December; it was printed and on the bookstalls on 14 December. 'I was used to moving with speed on a tennis court,' remarks Austin; 'I was not used to moving with this speed off it! The book sold rapidly. It was advertised on ten thousand posters up and down the country, donated by the advertising agencies. The first edition of 250,000 soon sold out. The second quarter of a million were printed.'[31] To advertise the book, the MRA symbol was printed on millions of milk-bottle tops.

Moral Re-Armament, Archbishop Lang said in his New Year broadcast, had 'caught on across Britain'. But it had not been without its struggles. Bill Jaeger reported from East London: 'Will Jacob (a Labour Party agent), Councillor George Morcara and Councillor Mrs Brignell were brought before their Ward Committee on a motion that they could not be in the Labour Party and the Oxford Group at the same time. . . the motion was defeated by eight votes to six. Tod Sloan was recently waylaid outside his home by three Communist Party leaders and told what they thought of him for an hour and a half.'[32]

Moral Re-Armament was also, according to Buchman, meeting 'persistent opposition from certain conventional religious people'. The opposition was focussed round 'phraseology', the objection being that the letters in the press did not mention the name of Christ sufficiently. To one old friend who raised these criticisms, Buchman wrote, 'I fear your informants have not grasped the truth that lies behind MRA . . . Take the close of the Baldwin letter: who does "His Will" refer to but Christ? After all, who rearms us? We have got to remember, however, that if we are going to reach statesmen, we have got to put our truth in the language of statesmen. The Christian standards of honesty, purity, unselfishness and love – these are the foundation stones of the state . . . Now, for a man to be honest is not all the gospel – that is true – but it is a place where certain people can begin and where certain nations have to begin if they are to challenge the thinking of the world.'[33]

As the campaign strengthened and the weeks passed, the American press took an increasing interest. 'In America, the beginnings of the recognition of the need of moral rearmament are to be noted,' wrote David Lawrence, editor of *United States News*.* 'But in Great Britain the

---

* Later *US News and World Report*.

movement has reached proportions which are truly sensational.'[34] Invitations to launch Moral Re-Armament more widely in America came from many sources. A group of Congressmen cabled: 'Washington responsive to Moral Re-Armament. Growing interest here in British experience with MRA . . .'[35] Later, a staff writer of the *Saturday Evening Post* even wrote that it was 'probably true that, as much as any other agency, Moral Re-Armament had advanced the programme of England's military preparedness on the non-military side. To it is due an important part of the credit that, since Munich, British morale has improved at least as fast as Britain's fighting machine.'[36]

During these months in Britain Buchman's attention was also focussed on two domestic matters. The first was the need to find a new headquarters for his work. When in 1937, the year of King George VI's Coronation, Brown's Hotel could no longer provide the cut rates negotiated in the Depression, temporary offices and a flat nearby were taken. It was not until 1938 that the problem was solved by the purchase of 45 Berkeley Square* as a centre for hospitality and administration. The house had been the home of Lord Clive of India and its reception rooms, designed by Sir William Kent and Sir William Chambers, were ideal for large-scale meetings and entertaining. The Earl of Powys, Lord Clive, agreed to the use of the name 'Clive House', while regretting that, as far as he knew, the tradition that Lord Clive's ghost appeared from time to time was without foundation.

On Buchman's sixtieth birthday in June 1938, while there was still no furniture or carpets in the house and nothing but hessian on the walls, a dinner for 200 was held for him there. It was an occasion which reflected his years in Britain. The white-haired Cockney, Tod Sloan, sat next to Lady Antrim. Sloan was one of the few speakers. 'In Tidal Basin', he said, 'the people are really hungry for this new leadership. There are many homes in West Ham, East Ham, Barking, Ilford and Dagenham where whole families are living this quality of life. We must see its meaning is kept intact, that it stays a living, loving, obedient willingness to restore God to leadership and not merely words to use as a slogan.'

Buchman recalled his first days in Cambridge when he felt that God had promised him a rebirth of Christian living in Britain within ten years. 'There was no Brown's then; only my knees,' he said. Now he was looking forward to using this new house as a 'spiritual embassy' in the middle of London.

The other practical matter also stemmed back to 1937, when an old friend had left a legacy of £500 to the Oxford Group. Previous legacies

---

* A 99-year lease of the house was bought for £35,000 and was the property of the Oxford Group. The sum was given by dozens of people in all parts of Britain and beyond.

had been paid without question, but this time relatives contested the payment, and when it came to court Mr Justice Bennett ruled that the bequest must fail because there existed no body definable at law as 'the Oxford Group'. Hitherto everything had developed informally. Personal links were the basis of the Group's commercial dealings, accounts had been kept by responsible people and the Inland Revenue had recognised the status of volunteer workers. Now it became clear that a legal entity would have to be established.

Buchman regretted the need. When the same issue arose two years later in America, he commented, 'It looks as if we shall have to incorporate. We have always had the joy of being given money and being able to pass it on to anyone who needs exactly that help. But maybe it can't be done in just that way any more. It has still got to be a group affair – each in honour preferring one another.' It seems to have been in this spirit that he accepted the necessity for legal incorporation in Britain, while changing nothing essential in his way of working. Whole-time workers continued, like himself, to receive no salary, but to come forward and function on their own resources, if any, and their own faith and prayer. He continued to countenance no hierarchy, no membership, nothing sectarian; the only membership was in the church of a person's choice, and not in the Oxford Group or Moral Re-Armament.

Having decided on incorporation in the simplest form befitting a non-profit, charitable enterprise, the question of the name arose. Ten years' public usage of the name 'Oxford Group' made it, for Buchman, the only candidate, so a request for incorporation under that name was sent to the Board of Trade. A. P. Herbert, as the University's senior representative in Parliament, presented an official motion of the University's governing body, the Hebdomadal Council, opposing the use of that name. Herbert also had other support. One letter came to him on behalf of the Oxford Union, signed by its President, Edward Heath, while the Warden of New College, H. A. L. Fisher, thought it 'intolerable that Oxford should be saddled with the responsibility for this Salvation Army for snobs'.[37]

Herbert maintained that he had nothing against the Group except its use of the word 'Oxford' – 'I am not saying anything against the Oxford Group: it may be the best thing in the world. But it does not, in any true sense of the word, come from Oxford.'[38] He took the matter to the correspondence columns of *The Times*, supported by Bishop Henson, A. L. Rowse and others. Lord Hugh Cecil, younger brother of Lord Salisbury and Herbert's predecessor as Member of Parliament for the University, however, took a contrary view. 'The Group want a name,' he wrote. 'They want it for purely practical purposes . . . The name "Oxford" is in fact in colloquial and popular use; it should therefore be also in legal use . . . As to the Oxonian sentiments of Mr Herbert and others, I cannot take them very seriously, though I have been connected with Oxford ever since I was an undergraduate and was Burgess for I forget how many years. Are Mr Herbert's feelings outraged when his bootmaker speaks of "Oxford Shoes"? . . .'[39]

The Board of Trade indicated that it would be helpful to have an expression of opinion from members of the University who favoured the use of the name. Buchman welcomed the opportunity, looking upon the controversy, as usual, as a chance to make the work he was trying to do more widely understood. He went to Oxford with a number of his Oxford-trained whole-time workers and directed a canvass, using the themes agreed between him and Sir Michael Sadler four years earlier. Lord Hugh Cecil was an early signatory.* Fellows of twenty colleges, fourteen bishops, the Public Orator, and a hundred more Oxford men prominent in the nation's life followed. A senior member of the Hebdomadal Council withdrew his name from Herbert's motion, saying he had been inadequately informed, and four college heads called for reconsideration. Professor J. W. Mackail answered a complaint at his joining Buchman's list: 'Your letter received. May I ask you to read the Acts of the Apostles?' Nonetheless the Hebdomadal Council maintained its opposition, and undoubtedly carried the majority of senior Oxford with it.

On 17 March 1939 Herbert switched the contest to the House of Commons, but only obtained fifty names for his motion on the Order Paper as against eighty-four who signed Sir Cooper Rawson's contrary motion. Two hundred and thirty-two MPs then sent a petition to the Minister in the Oxford Group's support. On 4 June, after Buchman's departure for America, the President of the Board of Trade, Oliver Stanley, decided in the Group's favour.**

Herbert now launched into what he later described as his 'long, lone and – it must be confessed – losing battle with the Buchmanites'.[40] He attacked Buchman in the press as 'an American crank preacher' and 'an alien who should be banned from Britain as a humbug'.[41] When, in the House of Commons, he called Buchman and his colleagues 'canting

---

* His actions raise a doubt about Kenneth Rose's statement (*The Later Cecils*, p. 95) that because he declined an invitation to a house-party Lord Hugh was 'suspicious' of the Oxford Group. However, as the Hatfield papers are not available for research, I can come to no final conclusion.

** As a non-profit body with charitable purposes, it was given permission to omit the word 'Limited' from its incorporated title. The Articles of Association were drawn up in the then standard form for a Christian charity, but their wording was challenged by the Inland Revenue in 1949 in what became a test case. Charitable status was granted after a slight rewording, and hundreds of other charities, many of which had functioned for decades under the original wording, followed suit. Buchman's work was, in subsequent years, incorporated in many countries.

cheats', he was rebuked by the Speaker.[42] He then announced that he would 'pursue the pirates until they haul down the noble flag they have stolen',[43] a vow which was to lead him on to wider and wider accusations in the following years. How far the humorist gave way to the campaigner is illustrated by a story told by his *Punch* colleague Anthony Armstrong and recorded in Reginald Pound's biography: 'A.P.H. and A.A. had adjourned one afternoon to a club in Covent Garden much frequented by journalists . . . Within minutes of their arrival at the club a mild-mannered man on a bar stool mentioned Buchman. A.P.H. brought the life of the place to a standstill by raging at the man as if he were an offensive heckler at a public meeting. The poor man was utterly subdued by the onslaught which, says Armstrong, was continued for "a good twenty minutes, by which time I left", cheated of his hope of a companionable interlude with an admired contemporary.'[44]

In Britain, the name 'Oxford Group' remains the official name of the incorporated body. But, as Sir Michael Sadler had foreseen, growth was already beginning to make the name too limited. In the nearly two years between the request for incorporation and its confirmation by the Board of Trade, the Group's campaign for Moral Re-Armament had grown so well known across the world that the new phrase became more and more used in day-to-day affairs.

By the time of the Board of Trade's decision, Buchman had been back in America for three months. On 4 March 1939 he had sailed for New York with twenty British colleagues, as well as others from the Continent. 'I love England and am surrounded by faithful friends,' he wrote at the time, 'but I am also eager to obey the call for America, an America that will know her true freedom and democracy. My spirit is still youthful, although sixty and more years have fastened their grip on me! I am still eager for the fray.'[45]

He planned to be back in three months; but it was seven years before he set foot in Britain again.

'AMERICA HAS NO SENSE OF DANGER'

Buchman was shocked by New York. 'America has no sense of danger,' he told his friends. 'She doesn't know what it means to have the front line right in her own backyard. London does. It's right in St James's Park, just a mass of trenches. You talk about peace, but it is a selfish peace, not a battle to rouse the country.' He felt that something dramatic had to be done to awaken a nation so vast and so complacent, and decided to hold mass demonstrations in New York, Washington and Los Angeles.

The Mayor of New York declared 7–14 May 1939 to be 'MRA Week', and the largest hall in the city, Madison Square Gardens, was taken for 14 May. On that night 14,000 people cheered the speakers' procession, headed by kilted Scots pipers. As with most public meetings he held, Buchman had picked out one person who was coming and planned the whole occasion as if he were the only person to be present. He reckoned that if that person was affected, everyone would be. That night his target happened to be the City Commissioner for Drains, with whom he had talked the day before. He thought twelve young Scots – workers, unemployed shipyard men and students – would be particularly effective for him. They spoke early on for a minute each. 'MRA for me means I stop sitting on my machine when the boss isn't looking and I stop driving his car like a fire-engine,' said one of them. Bunny Austin, who had gathered the support of American sportsmen like 'Babe' Ruth and Gene Tunney, was warmly received, and Lord Salisbury, Tod Sloan and three generations of the Antrim family spoke by direct telephone link from London. The newspapers gave the occasion front-page treatment, but tended to miss Buchman's point by calling it, in all good faith, a 'peace meeting'. 'You've got to get a sense of battle,' he told his people afterwards. What effect the meeting had on the Commissioner for Drains is not recorded.

Three weeks later a second demonstration took place in the staider setting of the Constitution Hall, Washington. Two hundred and forty British Members of Parliament had sent a message which read in part: 'Only if founded on moral and spiritual re-armament can democracy fulfil

its promise to mankind and perform its part in creating mutual understanding between nations . . .'*

Buchman spoke briefly. 'America is not without her problems in
business, the home, in industry, in civic and in government life,' he said.
'We need a rededication of our people to the elementary virtues of
honesty, unselfishness and love; and we must have the will again to find
what unites people rather than what divides them . . . The future depends
not only on what a few men may decide to do in Europe, but upon what a
million men decide to be in America.'[1]

Harry Truman, by now a Senator, read out a message from President
Roosevelt: 'The underlying strength of the world must consist in the
moral fibre of her citizens. A programme of moral re-armament, to be
most highly effective, must receive support on a world-wide scale.' All the
Washington papers reported the meeting on the front page, the *Post*'s
headline declaring, 'First Anniversary Finds Moral Re-Armament World
Force'.[2]

Next day Truman read an account of the meeting and messages from
ten Parliaments into the *Congressional Record*, adding, 'It is rare in these
days to find something which will unite men and nations on a plane above
conflict of party, class and political philosophy.' As Buchman sat in the
gallery of the Senate listening to Truman word was brought to him that
the British Board of Trade had granted incorporation of his work under
the name 'Oxford Group'. Elated by these two events, he was aware that
he must keep his feet on the ground. 'When you have a day like this', he
commented that evening, 'you have to live in the midst of the world and
keep direction.'

Roosevelt had several old friends working with Buchman, but a more
immediate reason for his interest perhaps lay in the recent action of one of
his severest press critics. Moved by his contact with Moral Re-Armament,
he had, over a private lunch in Roosevelt's study, apologised for the
bitterness and bias of his writing. The apology was accepted. The writer
remained an independent critic of the Administration but wrote more
constructively, appreciating the President's many difficulties. Roosevelt,
in his personal capacity, lent Moral Re-Armament discreet support.
'Though some at one time may have laughed at MRA,' he told Austin,
'today it commands great respect.'[3]

In the next weeks Buchman addressed the National Press Club in
Washington; received his second honorary doctorate, this time of Laws
from Oglethorpe University in Georgia; spoke with deep emotion at Bill
Pickle's funeral in Pennsylvania; and held a week's training session for

* *The Daily Telegraph* (26 June 1939) headlined its report of the British MPs' message:
'Community of Ideals: Washington and Westminster'.

some hundreds at Stockbridge, Massachusetts. Then he travelled, via Detroit, Chicago and Minneapolis, to Los Angeles, where his third, most publicised blow was struck at a meeting in the Hollywood Bowl on 19 July.

Fifteen thousand people were turned away after 30,000 had packed the arena. The setting was dramatic, with four great fingers of light, to represent the four moral standards, piercing the velvet sky behind the Bowl. 'A preview of a new world' was Buchman's theme. The *Los Angeles Times* reported: 'They came in limousines. They arrived in jalopies that barely chugged along the traffic-jammed roads leading to the Hollywood Bowl. They came afoot, in wheel-chairs, in buses, taxicabs. One and all, they came marvelling. The Bowl rally brought together all the strength of the vast movement – leaders from Burma, London, East Africa, Australia, China and Japan – and showed 30,000 persons how it might work.'[4] Half-way through the meeting twenty burly press and camera men elbowed their way on to the already crowded press seats because William Randolph Hearst, reading of the crowds on his teletype at San Simeon, had seen that his papers were missing a big story.

Louis B. Mayer, who had the week before given a luncheon for Buchman, sent up a note asking if he could speak on behalf of the film industry. A school teacher from a small town in Nebraska, who had never before addressed an audience larger than the pupils in her one-room schoolhouse, described how a new spirit had taken hold of her hard-hit area and how honesty about farm relief cheques had created a new atmosphere in the community. Her story was made the basis for the film *Meet John Doe*, with Gary Cooper.

At the end of the rally Buchman announced the next stage of his strategy – a mobilisation, over the days of 1, 2 and 3 December, of 'one hundred million people listening' – prepared to face personal, national and international issues in the light of God's will for the world. He envisaged speakers from different countries linked by a world-wide radio network. The suggestion first came from 'Manny' Straus, the public relations man from Macy's Departmental Stores, who said, 'Everyone has some MRA in them, even if it is only one per cent. The thing is to increase the per cent.'

But when December came, Europe was at war. The Nazi–Soviet pact in August 1939 took Buchman by surprise. 'The Communists are the strategists!' he exclaimed. 'Look at France. The serpent of Communism has coiled so long in her breast, and the Communists have turned the tables by shaking hands with Hitler. Where is France's future now?'* Just

* Nikolai Tolstoy writes in *Stalin's Secret War* (Jonathan Cape, 1981, p. 114): 'Astonishing as it may seem, the French Communist Party's anti-patriotic campaign was directed by Hitler himself . . . French Communists' support for Stalin's ally played a significant and perhaps crucial role in the destruction of the French will to resist.' Anthony

before war actually broke out, he voiced his distress. 'War means the suicide of nations. Everybody loses. There is no such thing as the winner of a war. As for Hitler – if he starts it, he will repent at leisure.'

As the crisis grew Buchman was particularly concerned about his colleagues in Britain. On 1 September he cabled them: 'You are all in our constant, loving, prayerful thoughts. Guard against unnecessary danger. Ensure Tod Liz Sloan maximum care in home outside London. Remember that in times of difficulty and danger the temptation always is to take the lesser course and do the lesser thing. Regard your work as essential service.'

When the news finally broke that war had been declared, Buchman and others were sitting with a Los Angeles hotel proprietor in his private apartments. At first Buchman was stunned. One Briton broke down in tears. Their years of effort to avert the conflict were over, and they could see nothing ahead in their minds' eye but the cities of Europe lying in ruins.

Then after a time, Buchman looked up and said, 'Someone, some day, is going to have to win the peace.'

Now that war had come Buchman had no doubt that it had to be fought and won. There was no comparison between the 'demoniac force', which he had tried to exorcise, and the democracies, however lacking in God's grace they might be. He had always considered patriotism and nationalism as being as different as health and fever. But he believed there should be an extra dimension to patriotism. 'A true patriot', in his view, 'gives his life to bring his nation under God's control.'[5] He believed that a force of such people had just as particular a part to play in war as in peace – and would also be needed to bring reconciliation after the fighting ended.

Hundreds of MRA men and women enlisted; some were soon to die. But for the moment there followed the 'phoney war' when no bombs fell on Western Europe, and Americans inferred that the war scare was being overplayed. Those months strengthened America's traditional isolationism – Jefferson's policy of 'Friendship with all nations, but entangling alliance with none'. Roosevelt took this tradition into account, for he knew that he could only be re-elected in 1940 as 'the President who kept us out

Cave Brown and Charles Macdonald, in *The Communist International and the Coming of World War II* (Putnam, 1981, pp. 528–9 and 536), state that Comintern propaganda was one of a number of factors which reduced the French Army by the spring of 1940 to 'a nerveless, soulless body, a castle made out of cards'. They write that this was particularly true of the 9th Army, drawn mainly from the 'Red Belt' of Paris, and that this army was placed in an apparently non-crucial sector of the front line, precisely where the German panzer divisions chose to make their major attack.

of the war'. Neither the invasion of France, the Low Countries and Scandinavia, nor Dunkirk, nor the Battle of Britain, altered the basic fact that America as a whole was strongly against becoming involved in Europe's war.

Buchman's announced campaign on the days of 1, 2 and 3 December 1939 took place under these new circumstances, and again emphasised unity between Britain and America. Radio networks covering large areas of the world carried the voices of the Speaker of the House of Representatives, the Democrat W. B. Bankhead, who stated that 'Moral Re-Armament must become the mainspring of our national life and the touchstone of policy at home and abroad'; and of Republican Senator Arthur Capper from the isolationist state of Kansas who urged that America 'read the handwriting on the wall and throw every energy and influence we possess behind this cause'.

Over the BBC Home and Commonwealth Services, the Earl of Athlone replied from London in a speech which was relayed throughout America. Lord Athlone quoted 'A Call to Our Citizens' recently issued by 550 British Mayors and, after outlining the principles of Moral Re-Armament, continued, 'In fresh and whole-hearted acceptance of them now lies our moral strength for these dark days – the answer to our fears and to our griefs, our one sure hope for a new world.'

Lord Athlone had expressed Buchman's view exactly. Buchman was determined that if America came into the war, she should prosecute it with as clean hands as possible; and that, when peace came, she should use her power for the creation of a better world. But this involved working for a new quality throughout American life.

At first the extremes of both left and right in America had a common cause. As Russia was still allied to the Nazis, the American Communist Party opposed America entering the war – and so received the strong, though involuntary, support of right-wing isolationists intent on keeping out of the war for quite different reasons. The Communists' immediate programme was to hinder production in war industries through strikes, especially in the aircraft arsenal of America, the West Coast.

Buchman already had links with labour there through the mass meetings he had held, and Senator Truman's recommendation had opened further doors into the industry. Seattle business men offered to give a lunch for Buchman with a leading banker in the chair, and asked if there was anyone he would like invited. Buchman immediately replied, 'Yes, Dave Beck and the other labour leaders.' Beck, a controversial figure, then West Coast head of the Teamsters' Union, did not normally get asked to lunch by bankers. But he and his colleagues were invited, and they came.

On 29 December 1939 the Seattle *Star*, in a full-page editorial, invited

Buchman to hold a round-table conference of all the elements in their city which, it wrote, had 'come out of the thirties with a black eye'. '*The Star* apologises publicly for the mistakes it has made in the past . . . and offers its hand to competitors and all others who want honestly and consciously to help build a new Seattle,' the newspaper added. The Boeing Aircraft Company, Seattle's major industry, then gearing up to produce the B17 Flying Fortress bomber, was in turmoil, due partly to break-neck expansion and partly to the ideological confusion spread by the Communist leadership of the local branch of the machinists' union. At the round table initiated by *The Star* Buchman met the District President of the Union, Garry Cotton, who invited him to speak to 5,000 of his members. The meeting was crowded, as Cotton assured his guest it would be, since under union rules there was a five-dollar fine on absentees. Buchman introduced workers from Britain's shipyards and factories as well as from other American aircraft plants. From this developed a training programme for the Boeing branch, and shortly afterwards, Cotton's leadership prevented a strike in Boeing which would have halted production of aeroplanes on the whole of the West Coast.[6] At the Lockheed Company in Los Angeles a similar Moral Re-Armament training programme was launched in the largest union local branch in the country, with 35,000 members.[7]

Buchman's influence with these aircraft unions challenged Communist plans for industrial slow-downs. The Communists denounced him for co-operating with their greatest enemy, the armament manufacturers. This continued until Hitler invaded Russia. Then, for the Communists, the war industries and the armament makers became overnight the saviours of democracy and 'the Fascist Churchill' became the heroic friend of the Soviets. Their description of Moral Re-Armament also changed, if not so beneficially. From being a 'militarist pro-British spy network', it became a 'pacifist, anti-union organisation' busily interfering in American war industry and fostering mysterious peace moves.

Buchman's people were, meanwhile, introduced from one industry to another all across America, and found themselves in demand in aircraft and steel plants, and later in shipbuilding yards. His manpower was always at full stretch, and without those he had brought from Britain he could have undertaken little.

The outbreak of war, however, did raise the question of where the Britons' duty lay, and this presented them with a dilemma. Ought they to return to Britain and enlist in the armed forces? Or should they remain in America doing the work which they were doing? In September 1939 they sought the official view upon British subjects in the United States and seem to have been advised by the British Consul-General in San Francisco, Paul Butler, and by the Consul in Seattle, C. G. Hope-Gill, to remain in America.[8] In May 1940 this advice was repeated for Britons generally in America*, but by now Butler and Hope-Gill had reassessed MRA's position and were strongly representing to the Embassy in Washington that Buchman's British colleagues be called home. Their reasons, according to Foreign Office files recently released, were a mixture of representations which had come to them from "local" sources and some fantastic errors of identity.[9]** It is clear that, after much minuting to and fro at the Foreign Office, the Consuls were overruled by the Foreign Secretary, Lord Halifax, though officials took measures to conceal that he had intervened.***

Quite apart from the official view, however, each individual had to decide for himself where his duty lay. 'I support you whatever you decide,' Buchman said. Many of them found it the most difficult decision of their lives. On the one hand there was the natural call to return to family, home and country, and the certainty of being understood. On the other was their conviction that the result of the war would depend upon America, where there was a job to do for which they had been trained in a way that few others had been.

Reginald Hale, the erstwhile *Isis* cartoonist, a British territorial officer of four years' experience and a passionate soldier, writes that by inclination and training he longed to rejoin the colours as fast as he could, but that he came to the conclusion that 'as a Christian, as an Englishman and as a soldier' his duty was to stick with Buchman at all costs. 'I could not expect that all my friends would understand and I did not blame them when they wrote harshly to me. But for me, my course was clear.'[10]

Most of the others made the same decision. The British Government of the day seemed to agree with them. Bunny Austin, who had returned to Britain before war began, and William Jaeger sailed to join Buchman in December, after consulting the Ministries of Labour, Defence and Foreign Affairs. They were granted exit permits and never asked to

---

* *New York Times*, 31 May 1940: 'Britain Gives Mission to Nationals in US – Rejects Service Offer but Bids them Cultivate Good-will.'

** For example, Hope-Gill alleged that the Dutch woman, Charlotte van Beuningen, who was subsequently decorated by Queen Wilhelmina for her heroism in the Resistance, was a 'Nazi agent'. 'It has also been pointed out', he added, 'that Denmark, Norway, Belgium and Holland were the most heavily "morally rearmed" countries in Europe and that the leader of the Movement is probably of German origin.' (A 4219, 21/8/1940.)

*** A 3942/26/45 Public Record Office. In August 1940 William Jaeger applied for a renewal of his passport. It was granted on the grounds that (a) the war effort did not require his return; (b) to deny renewal would be discriminatory and would involve the Foreign Office in controversy in Britain and America. This appears to have been the occasion of Lord Halifax's memo, and a further case referred from Seattle was decided on this precedent. (A 4219, 17/9/1940.)

return. Yet they, like those already with Buchman, were to be chased by reporters and denounced in sections of the British press for many years.*

Certainly they had nothing material to gain from staying. They worked very long hours without pay, and money, even for survival, was often short. Of one period in Seattle, Hale writes, 'I had breakfast one morning with Buchman and he ordered one breakfast, halving with me the poached egg and toast. Another morning five of us English pooled our wealth and found we had fifteen cents. We ordered three cups of coffee and asked for two extra cups. That was breakfast. We lived three miles from where the morning meeting was being held. The other four hitched a lift but I elected to walk. I got lost and arrived late. The leader of the meeting asked me why. I was tired, hungry and fed up. "I'm late because I didn't have the bus fare." About three hundred pairs of eyes came round and stared at me. The leader of the meeting went round all fifty from overseas and asked how much money we had. We couldn't have raised $20 between us. From then on our friends in Seattle knew that MRA was financed by faith and prayer. Until then it was a theory.'[11]

These painful decisions taken by most of Buchman's British colleagues, and a few from Scandinavia and elsewhere, enabled Buchman to continue his nation-wide programme in America. But what kind of programme would arouse Americans? And how could it be presented in a way which would make them ready and anxious to listen?

These questions haunted Buchman during the first months of 1940, constantly on the move between New York, Washington, Florida, Los Angeles and San Francisco. In each place he was spending time with his resident teams and meeting people at all times of the day and night. His secretary, Dr Morris Martin, records him as 'very tired'. 'These are exceptionally heavy days,' he noted on 9 January, 'spent with an at first unresponsive team. Also every lunch and dinner with someone uses a lot of energy.' Always Buchman was struggling to see what to do next. 'I feel as if I were in a thick forest,' he said to a friend one day. 'I don't see the way out.'[12]

Buchman felt dissatisfied, too, with the spiritual progress of many of his closest fellow workers. 'I feel Mike has blinkers,' he once said to a group of them with typical, if infuriating, frankness. 'I wish he would throw them into the sea and shake the nation. John is wonderful – but hopeless if he has to change the children's diapers. He's born to feed on ambrosia. Lovable Jimmy – he's got fears, bundles of fears. Ken is still too smooth –

---

* The assault on Austin was to continue long after the war was over, in spite of his later service in the American Air Force, and untruths about him are still believed by many to this day. He had to wait until 1984 to be restored to membership of the All-England Lawn Tennis Club at Wimbledon.

let's have the rough side of the nutmeg.' 'I wish you had fifteen children,' he said to another. 'It would make you less of a pedant.'

Sometimes his approach was even more abrasive. After a day when some letters had missed the mail, his secretary notes, 'Frank dressed Mike and me down thoroughly. It was one of those occasions when everything brought up in evidence is unjust, wrong and irrelevant, yet the charge is correct and thoroughly deserved. There is a gigantic, Olympian quality in F's wrath that is something to be experienced to be believed. It certainly produces change. When he is most irritated it is with people who he feels should know better. He suffers fools astonishingly gladly, but is intolerant of sloppiness in those around him.'[13]

Gradually Buchman became convinced that an adequate plan for their work in America would only come to birth if his team found deeper spiritual roots. So, in July 1940, he stopped all the diverse activities in which they were engaged and gathered them in a group of holiday cottages and shacks beside Lake Tahoe in the Sierra Nevada mountains. It began, typically, when he was offered a five-room cottage in which to take a few days' rest. Within ten days he had fifty people with him, and as neighbours got to know him and saw the numbers growing they offered more cottages, cabins and beds. A former bootlegger called Globin lent his disused casino for meetings and later a whole floor of his near-empty hotel. Off-duty sailors found themselves in hammocks slung between trees, and Boston and New York ladies slept on camp beds, sometimes five to a garage. It finally turned into a three-month training exercise for several hundred people.

Buchman deliberately set about welding these already committed people into a united force. The perspective of the war in Europe sharpened their thinking and dedication. Alan Thornhill, for instance, although a clergyman and one who had undergone a great enriching of his spiritual experience during ten years with the Oxford Group, had never systematically studied his life in order to allow God to clean out every last corner. 'I had a good friend, a Scot called George Marjoribanks, and felt I should tell him all the murky details. They would not have made a lurid book, but I found it terribly hard on my pride, and it turned out to be very important for me. It was painful and I felt utterly rotten and told George so. It was the death of self. Though I had valued what I had learnt from Buchman, I had never till then felt wholly committed to God and to work at Buchman's side. God focussed it around my longing to return to Britain. The decision to stay in America was the hardest I'd ever taken – but I knew it was God's will.'

'I can't speak for others,' Thornhill adds now, 'but for me there is the clearest connection between personal purity and creativeness. I felt a great sense of peace and clarity.' Within a few weeks he had written a play

– completed in thirty-six hours though he had never written one before –
called *The Forgotten Factor*. The play dealt with the relations between and
within the families of an industrialist and a labour leader at a time of
industrial crisis and suggested the importance of a change of attitude from
'who is right' to 'what is right'. It was to be performed to over a million
people in dozens of countries, often playing a part in settling conflicts of
various kinds.

Buchman held a meeting each morning. They were wholly unpredictable. One day he arrived with a peach in one hand. 'Every woman should
be like this,' he said. 'But some of you are like this,' and he opened his
other hand to disclose a prune. He felt that some of the women in his team
had become dry in spirit because they had not given God unconditional
control of their lives, and were therefore not free personalities. 'It meant
fearlessly tackling some of us dominating American women,' one of them
said later. 'But it was done so delicately, with such hope.'

On occasion Buchman's method was far from delicate. Phyllis Konstam, Bunny Austin's actress wife, had come to the Hollywood Bowl and
had found a measure of personal change during that visit. She returned
home and later came back to Canada on an evacuee ship with their
daughter. She came briefly to Tahoe from there. 'I arrived in a belligerent
mood, furious that Bunny had not crossed the country to meet me on
arrival,' she wrote later. 'The man who focussed my fury was Frank
Buchman. I had been used to getting my own way. If I could not get it by
temper and tantrums, I would get it by charm or tears. None of these had
any effect on Buchman and this increased my anger. I hated everything
about Tahoe and everybody in it. Used to wafting around in glamorous
clothes and expensive restaurants, my fury increased when I was put on a
house-keeping team and found part of my job was cleaning out the
lavatories.

'One day, unable to contain myself any longer, I went to find Buchman
to tell him what I thought of him. He saw me coming and turned his back
on me and walked away. I had never been treated like that in my life. I
raved and berated Bunny.

'One afternoon Buchman sent for me and told me what he thought of
spoiled, selfish, bad-tempered women and the effect they had on their
husbands and children. He looked me straight in the eye, and said: "This
is love and it's going on." That afternoon I went for a walk with Bunny . . .
We were crossing a field. Bunny, wearied by my nagging, lay down on a
plank of wood and flung his arms out. I looked down on him and suddenly
caught my breath. The plank was an old piece of fencing. It had a
cross-piece nailed across the top. Bunny was lying stretched out on a
cross.

'I realised for the first time how I crucified him with my selfishness. I began to realise the courage of a man like Buchman who cared enough to tell me the truth and to cure the things in my nature which made me so difficult to live with. When he said it was love, it was precisely what it was.'[14]

Her husband wrote of another aspect of Buchman's approach: 'Like a true surgeon Frank knew the necessity of bringing healing. I too had been spoilt and selfish. One day the necessity for change was made clear to me by a friend. I deserved the corrective, but healing had not been brought about. I remained in an unhappy state. Frank sent for me. He looked at me with compassion and spoke three words, "Don't stay bleeding." Then he prayed. I wish I could remember that prayer. I only remember the sense of healing and peace which came into my heart. I went out of the room a different man.'[15]

During the time at Tahoe Buchman often brought up in the full morning meeting the personal faults he had observed in his colleagues. Bremer Hofmeyr, the former Rhodes Scholar from South Africa, had borrowed a hammer from a local resident and not returned it. Buchman spent much of one morning underlining the sloppiness of some of the men and what such negligence would do to the confidence of the community. Alan Thornhill, when his turn came to be fireman for the night, vaguely thought his job was to prevent fires – and no fire was lit to make the breakfast porridge the next morning. This hardly called for comment.* A cook for what turned out to be a disastrous dinner for a special guest hardly dared appear next morning. To her astonishment all Buchman could say was, 'That soup!' and dissolve into laughter. But often Buchman felt that these minor mistakes needed serious discussion, for they could be a key to making intelligent but impractical individuals into whole personalities. It was the old Gospel principle of 'He who is faithful in little is faithful in much.'

Hofmeyr, who found such treatment particularly painful, told me why he thought Buchman sometimes handled close friends so roughly. 'He was concerned with training two hundred people. All got the impact, all learnt the lesson. When he was sailing into anyone, you felt it could justly be you.'

But Buchman, now as always, was unpredictable. He shook with rage one day because a cook had once again produced tough meat. The next day he appeared at the kitchen door holding a tiny wild flower for her.

---

* Thornhill's own comment was:

Oh, son of Oxford's dreaming spires,
You really are a smart one.
You thought your job was stopping fires,
When you were meant to start one!

'Here you are,' he said. 'This is "self-heal".'

Most of the lessons of those days were drawn out of simple things. Buchman inspected a cottage which was to be returned to its owner and found an obstinate rim round a bath. 'It was like that when we came,' protested the culprit.

'Always leave things better than you find them,' Buchman replied and got down on his knees and cleaned the bath himself.

In fact, quite apart from spiritual needs, the team with him – many of them university men and women, 'ladies' who had done little housework for themselves and men who had done none – needed a full course in housekeeping and economy. A lorry went down to the towns to buy in the cheapest markets, and every cent was guarded.

The end result of the time at Tahoe, according to Reginald Hale, was 'a force-in-being, like a regular army, capable of fighting anywhere any time'. 'Most of us', he explains, 'had experienced God's power to change our lives. But at Tahoe we had a corporate experience of Christ. Together we accepted the finality of His victory on the Cross to break the power of evil in our lives and in the world. As we became irrevocably committed to Him, we found our petty divisions of nationality, class, language and points of view just dropped off. Committed to Him, we were committed to each other also.'[16]

Workers from West Coast war industries would drive all night to spend a day with Buchman and his friends at Tahoe. Among them was John Riffe, a 250-pound steelworkers' leader from San Francisco, whom his union president called 'the roughest, toughest man in the steelworkers'. Buchman had first met him at a weekend round-table in June, a month before going to Tahoe. On that occasion Riffe had argued hotly with Buchman that he had no need of change. 'That's fine,' Buchman had replied. 'Maybe there's someone else you'd like to see different.' Several names had immediately leapt into Riffe's mind, including a steel industrialist with whom negotiations had broken down, colleagues in his own union, and his wife, Rose. 'That's the point,' Buchman had added, 'to learn to change your enemies and make them into friends.' They had spent the rest of the evening together, and Riffe had gone to bed with the final thought that if he listened to God he could find out how to make people different.

Next morning early there had been a knock at the Riffes' door, and Buchman had appeared with a steaming pot of coffee. 'I thought you might like this before you start your quiet time,' he had said, with a twinkle. 'Quiet time' was a new term to Riffe and he had asked for an explanation. 'A time to let God tell you what to do.' Riffe went back into his room, but not to sleep. The thought of that steel executive and the deadlock between them had kept coming into his mind. 'Take the initiative with him. Get off your high horse. You know his hands are tied. Be honest. Make him a decent offer – and apologise.' Later that week he had tried it, and within forty-eight hours an unexpectedly generous settlement had been reached.

Now the Riffes came to Tahoe, still curious. At dinner they were served by two girls. 'Who are they?' asked Mrs Riffe. When Buchman replied that they were the daughters of Will Manning, owner of the Manning's chain of restaurants on the West Coast, John Riffe exploded, 'Good God! My union is planning to picket that outfit.'

Mrs Riffe added, 'I would never serve the way they're doing.'

'Nobody asked you,' replied Buchman.

Riffe wondered again if he had fallen into an anti-labour plot, but next day at dawn the Manning son took him out fishing. The two men came back with three small fish and an understanding of each other's problems. Next weekend Riffe returned with six of his executive committee including James Thimmes, who later became Vice-President of the United Steelworkers of America and, with Riffe, played a significant part in the settlement of the national steel strike of 1952.[17]

On 23 August Buchman told his friends that he thought a new 'handbook' or manual was needed. A first draft of this new book was written by an Oxford Doctor of Philosophy. The text was then streamlined by a varied group to cut out every unnecessary word. 'It has got to be simple and put pictorially to capture America,' said Buchman. 'It has got to be almost ABC.' The handbook was entitled *You Can Defend America*. It called for 'sound homes – teamwork in industry – a united nation', and for America to become a nation governed by God. The final product, only 32 pages, was simply but vividly illustrated by Hale.

A musical revue, based on the handbook and bearing the same name, followed. This, as so often in Buchman's company, developed almost accidentally, starting from a series of sketches given at a birthday party. A little later Globin, the ex-bootlegger, also had a birthday, and Buchman invited him to come and bring his friends. 'Night clubs are his world,' said Buchman. 'Let's make this a floor show with tables around it in a circle.'

Marion Clayton, who had played in the film *Mutiny on the Bounty*, and Cece Broadhurst, the Canadian radio singer, beat the material from the original birthday party into shape. Globin brought his wife and a group of friends, including the Mayor of Carson City, Nevada's capital. Mrs Globin laughed so much, she said, that she hurt face muscles she had not used for years.

At the end of the evening the Mayor said to Buchman, 'That's the way to put patriotism to our people. You must bring the show to Carson City.'

'Fine. When shall we come?' said Buchman.

'Friday,' said the Mayor.

'We'll be there,' said Buchman. This was Tuesday.

The show played to a full house in Carson City on Friday. At the end, Hale went down to the best bar in town to fetch a telegram. 'Suddenly', he recalls, 'the bat-wing doors of the bar burst open and a big Irish gold-miner burst in. "Boys, have you been up the street?" he bellowed as the bar-stools swivelled. "I don't know what it's all about, but it's terrific! TERRIFIC!"'

From Carson City the show was invited to Reno. This would mean facing a more sophisticated audience, but Buchman, for whom everyone was a potential librettist, musician, actor or producer, saw no difficulties. So, shedding local references, the revue was launched on a career which in the next years took it back and forth across the country, reaching audiences who were perhaps unreachable through any other medium.

In November 1941 *You Can Defend America* was shown at America's two rival trade union conventions – the Congress of Industrial Organisations in Atlantic City and the American Federation of Labor in New Orleans, giving it a powerful send-off into American industry. Civilian Defence Councils of states and cities sponsored it, first on the West Coast and then in an extended tour in 1941 from Maine to Florida. The cast travelled 36,000 miles through 21 states and performed before more than a quarter of a million people. The General of the Armies, John J. Pershing, wrote a foreword* for the handbook in which he said, 'No patriotic citizen can read it without feeling its inspiration. None can fail fully to endorse its ultimate objective – the preservation of our precious heritage.' Army and Air Force bases and Naval shipyards asked for performances of the revue and distributed thousands of the handbook.

On 6 December 1941 a well-known Philadelphian, J. B. Kelly, father of the actress and future Princess Grace of Monaco, saw it in the Philadelphia Academy of Music where the city fathers and the Civilian Defence authorities sponsored it. His remark afterwards was typical of many: 'I thought I had all the patriotism I needed, but as I watched the play I felt here was a group of people who almost looked over my shoulder and read my mind and produced the answer I have been feeling America needs.'[18]

Early the following morning the Japanese attacked Pearl Harbor. America was at war.

---

* General George C. Marshall approached him to write it. In complying, Pershing, who had been American Commander-in-Chief in World War I, said he had broken the custom of a lifetime to do so.

WAR WORK DEBATE

The first casualties of war are often the spiritual values. Buchman believed these to be the basis of freedom, and he and his team had been able to carry them to people and situations seldom reached by the Churches. He therefore felt keenly the importance of keeping his trained, whole-time force intact.

Many American leaders supported this view. Thomas Edison's son, Charles, who was Secretary of the Navy, remarked that in national defence, 'Moral Re-Armament shares equally in importance with material re-armament . . . Without character and a deep-seated moral re-armament bred in the fibre of our citizens . . . there will be little worth defending.'[1]

The two agencies mainly concerned to ensure the allocation of American manpower in war-time – the Department of Justice and the Selective Service – agreed that the Moral Re-Armament programme had a particular relevance to the war effort. In October 1940 the Justice Department approved the stay of 28 British MRA workers in the country as performing an essential service, and the Selective Service deferred the call-up of Americans, and later British, working with Moral Re-Armament as an essential element in the national defence programme. During 1941 a few of Buchman's American workers were classified as available for military service by local draft boards, but in each case the Presidential Appeals Board intervened and granted them deferment.

Soon after the attack on Pearl Harbor the Chairman of the Presidential Appeals Board, Colonel John Langston, wrote to Buchman, 'I am firmly convinced that as our emergency grows more acute, the need for buildling the moral stamina of our people will correspondingly grow. The weaknesses of France did not show themselves as pronouncedly in the beginning. I get afraid of the smug complacency of many of our people who have softened to the point that they think they see straight when it is only a mirage. It will take all the morale-building that you and others who are giving their lives to this work can furnish to keep us on an even keel. Already I see efforts to unsettle and confuse Civilian Defence. It is hard to determine when such efforts are the natural, misguided efforts and confused thinking of patriots, or inspired work of subversive groups.

'Moral Re-Armament has demonstrated its value to national defence. The President has so held. But the individual worker needs to make his necessary connection clear and certain as to the quality and type of his training and the actual things he is doing, because there is need not only to have his status proved but to satisfy the public that it is justified and thereby sustain selective service morale.'[2]

The issue Buchman was beginning to face in America had already become a matter of controversy in Britain. By the summer of 1940 twelve whole-time workers and 240 of MRA's most experienced part-timers had already voluntarily enlisted in the services, leaving only twenty-nine men of military age available to carry on. These twenty-nine were directing a nation-wide campaign sponsored by 360 Mayors and Provosts, concentrating particularly in heavily bombed areas. Their efforts had been widely welcomed,[3] except by a section of the London press. In three weeks that August the Communist *Daily Worker* attacked them eight times and Tom Driberg in the *Daily Express* six times.[4] Their complaint was that the MRA campaign mingled Christianity with morale, while Hannen Swaffer in the *Daily Herald* resurrected Buchman's alleged statement of 1936 to infer that MRA was pro-Nazi.

Peter Howard, also of Express Newspapers, whom many considered the toughest columnist of all, decided to investigate Moral Re-Armament personally. To his surprise he found his colleagues' accusations groundless, and when the editor of the *Express* refused to print his answer to Driberg's charges, he wrote a book, *Innocent Men*,*[5] which both gave the facts about Moral Re-Armament as he saw them and described the unexpected change that it was bringing to his own life. The book sold 155,000 copies, and led to his resignation from his highly paid job, since Dick Plummer, the Assistant Manager, in the absence of Lord Beaverbrook and the paper's Managing Director, E. J. Robertson, forbade him to publish it.

Buchman's personality and mission were, from the first, made central to the controversy. Soon after Howard associated himself with Moral Re-Armament, his editor, John Gordon, and Brendan Bracken, then Minister of Information, took him out to lunch and told him categorically that Buchman would be arrested immediately America entered the war. Howard asked them for their evidence. 'Impossible to tell you, Peter,' they said. 'It comes from too high and secret a source.' Knowing of the support which Roosevelt and others had given his new friends in America,

---

* The title echoed *Guilty Men*, the book he had written with Michael Foot and Frank Owen under the pen-name 'Cato' the previous year.

Howard discounted their statement. 'Come back when you can show me real evidence,' he said.

The novelist Daphne du Maurier had meanwhile published *Come Wind, Come Weather*,[6] in which she told stories of how ordinary people, affected by Moral Re-Armament, were facing up to war-time conditions. She dedicated the book to 'An American, Dr Frank N. D. Buchman, whose initial vision made possible the work of the living characters in these stories', and added, 'What they are doing up and down the country in helping men and women solve their problems, and prepare them for whatever lies ahead, will prove to be of national importance in the days to come.' Her book sold 650,000 copies in Britain alone.

In the middle of the war of words about Buchman Ernest Bevin, General Secretary of the Transport and General Workers, became Minister of Labour*. According to his biographer, Professor Alan Bullock, he was characterised on arrival as 'a bad mixer, a good hater, respected by all'. 'His ability, his strength of character and determination were obvious,' writes Bullock, but 'his unusual confidence was combined with a marked sensitivity to criticism, which he always inclined to take as a personal attack and with a strong suspicion which, once aroused, put a brick wall of distrust between him and anyone who took against him.'[7] In the dire situation of 1940 none of these characteristics seemed to matter compared to the fact that he had the qualities of toughness and courage needed to stand up to the crisis, but they were to have a profound effect upon the fate of Buchman's workers.

On assuming office Bevin found that his predecessor, Ernest Brown, had inserted into the Conscription Act a clause granting occupational deferment to 'lay evangelists', a category in which he included the MRA workers, whose work he knew and valued. Brown was a man of faith, where Bevin was a sincere atheist who discounted any spiritual factor in the war effort. In December 1940 he wrote to the Oxford Group saying the position of its workers was being reviewed and asking for comments. Full documentation was sent to him and, in February 1941, a delegation of Members of Parliament presented Moral Re-Armament's case to Bevin's deputy on manpower, Sir William Beveridge.

A. P. Herbert regarded this as a suitable moment to put down a motion on the House of Commons order paper on 27 February asking the new President of the Board of Trade, Oliver Lyttelton, to deprive the Oxford Group of the name and privileges granted them by Stanley, on the ground that Buchman had never denounced Hitler, that his work was 'harmful to the British cause' and that 'he was occupying in the United States young

---

* In May 1940, when Churchill's Government was formed. He entered the War Cabinet in September.

British citizens who might be better employed in their own country'. Herbert's motion gathered forty-nine supporters, while Sir Robert Gower's counter-motion, put down on the same day, was signed by seventy-six Members.

On 14 March, before the Oxford Group had received any reply from Bevin, the *Daily Express* Labour Correspondent in an exclusive story announced that the Oxford Group's twenty-nine workers would soon be liable for call-up. This caused an immediate public outcry. The Archbishops of Canterbury and York, the Moderator of the Church of Scotland and the heads of all the Free Churches wrote to Bevin affirming that the MRA men were in fact 'lay evangelists' and therefore protected in their work by the Conscription Act. They were supported by a petition signed by over 2,500 clergy and ministers, as well as by civic, industrial and trades union leaders. Bevin, true to his biographer's characterisation, took this opposition as a personal affront and expressed resentment at what he called 'pressure'.[8]

On 19 March Oliver Lyttelton summoned the Secretary of the Oxford Group, Roland Wilson, to his office. 'Lyttelton said they had enquired fully into the Group's work and found it to be of value to the country,' says Wilson. 'He said he was empowered to offer us the full endorsement of the government, if we would disavow Buchman "just for the period of the war" since "doubts had been raised about his attitude to Nazi Germany". "After the war," he added, "the link could be restored." When I said that the answer was "No", Lyttelton replied that that was the reply he had expected.' Soon after, Lyttelton attended the current MRA play and congratulated the cast on their work.

On 11 September, in reply to a question from A. P. Herbert, Bevin confirmed officially in the Commons that he intended to call up the men. One hundred and seventy-four Members then put down a motion opposing this course, and their spokesman, George Mathers, demanded a debate on the subject, which took place on 7 October. A few days before the debate Herbert issued a long statement to the press reiterating his belief that 'Buchman is no friend of Britain' and announcing that he had sent a 'secret letter' to Bevin with damning evidence. The Minister, meanwhile, let it be known that he would resign from the Government if he did not win his point,[9] and the Government, mindful of Bevin's great importance to the war effort, put a three-line whip upon its supporters, compelling them to attend and vote with him. This course was, in fact, unnecessary as Mathers and his colleagues had announced that they would not call for a vote, but relied on the Minister to recognise the justice of their case – a traditional practice with 'debates on the adjournment', in which category this debate fell.

On the night, everyone expected Herbert to produce his 'secret letter'.

In fact, he only produced three letters from unnamed individuals who alleged that other unnamed persons whom they had met were connected with the Oxford Group and had made remarks not unfavourable to Hitler. The debate was scrappy and angry. Trivial issues prevented any intelligent discussion of the basic questions of whether one set of Christians should be treated differently from all others and what, in fact, is 'national service'. Bevin rode out the storm, implying among other things that the men were all conscientious objectors. None, in fact, was.

In his biography of Herbert, Reginald Pound writes: 'APH was comforted in his opposition by a letter marked "Secret" from an intelligence department in Whitehall: "You will be interested to know that everybody I have seen who has had opportunity of watching Buchman, in this country, on the Continent and in the United States, is of the opinion that he is working for Germany. A number believe that he has been subsidised by Dr Goebbels. At the moment proof is lacking." '[10] This may have been the 'secret letter' which Herbert sent to Bevin. It could also have been the source of Bracken's suspicions and Lyttelton's suggestion on behalf of the Government. It may or may not be relevant that Driberg was at this time working on supplying information on people and movements for a branch of MI5.*

The debate next day in the House of Lords, initiated by Lord Salisbury, was calmer. Concern was expressed that the Moral Re-Armament workers had been treated hardly less arbitrarily than they would have been in a totalitarian state. Every speaker, except the Government spokesman and one other, deplored Bevin's decision. *The Times* stated in its editorial next morning, 'It is impossible to think that the Minister has handled wisely or prudently a case which, rejected out of hand, was bound to arouse deep and sincere feeling going far beyond its immediate bounds.'[11]

---

* Chapman Pincher states that Driberg was enlisted by MI5 while a schoolboy and instructed to infiltrate the Communist Party, from which he was expelled in 1941 when Harry Pollitt, the Party's General Secretary, discovered his duplicity. After his election as MP for Maldon, Essex, in 1942, however, Pollitt approached him to work for the KGB. For the rest of his life he worked for both organisations, to the knowledge of both. His job was, in each case, to provide information and misinformation and report on the private lives of leading politicians, including close friends, and of any others of interest. Inquiries after his death, writes Pincher, 'convinced MI5 that he had been controlled primarily by the KGB since the end of the war'. It was, according to Pincher, Driberg's 'long relationship with MI5' which 'solves the mystery of why such a notorious homosexual, who was repeatedly caught in the act publicly by the police, was never successfully prosecuted'. (*Their Trade Is Treachery*, Sidgwick and Jackson, 1981, pp. 198–206.) See also *Dictionary of Espionage* by Christopher Dobson and Ronald Payne (Harrap, 1985, p. 40), where he is described as 'a double agent working on behalf of both MI5 and the KGB'. 'The KGB', they add, 'always had it in reserve to produce pictures of his homosexual affairs . . . and threaten to shatter his public career if he failed to do their bidding.' See also *The Man Who Was M* by Anthony Masters (Blackwell, 1984), pp. 168–79.

Bevin's decision, however, was not reversed. The men now remaining were taken into the armed forces, though because of the need for firemen during the blitz some were able to opt for the National Fire Service in London, permitting them to continue their MRA work in their hours off duty.

Gusts from the Parliamentary storm crossed the Atlantic and epithets like 'pro-Nazi' used in the Commons debate now made their appearance there. So did Driberg, who spent six months that summer and autumn touring America, during which he prosecuted his campaign against Buchman with the newspaper editors who were his hosts. A fresh crop of rumours spread through the country. In particular, a nationally circulated news sheet, *In Fact*, reprinted many attacks on Moral Re-Armament and so spread them to the major American newspapers.

The Selective Service headquarters asked what lay behind these rumours. A memorandum submitted by Moral Re-Armament in answer read in part: 'We have known for some time that attempts were being made to influence adversely high Washington officials. In November (1941) we were told that a British newspaperman long unfriendly to us had been in this country and was gaining the ear of important officials to prejudice them against Moral Re-Armament. Our informant told us that while he personally had been able to counter successfully this man's efforts in the case of one important official, the newspaperman's strategy was to get the ear of the President, but that, as far as he knew, he only got as far as the President's Press Secretary, Stephen Early.'[12]

Early had been sent a telegram by the editor of the *Bangor Daily News*, asking whether Roosevelt had 'specifically endorsed' Moral Re-Armament, to which he had replied that there had been no 'specific endorsement'. When he heard of the use the paper had made of this telegram, Early again telegraphed the editor, 'I exceedingly regret that this telegram has been used to impugn the motives of those associated with the Oxford Group for Moral Re-Armament. Had I believed my telegram would have been used in this way, I certainly would not have answered the telegraphic enquiry I received from you to which my message was in acknowledgement.'[13] Similarly, an official of the New York Selective Service was reprimanded by Washington when he passed on to the American press, in his official capacity, statements derived from the London *Daily Mirror* which had now begun to accuse the British men working with Moral Re-Armament in America of being 'draft dodgers'.

In fact, the British Embassy had once again reaffirmed on 1 May 1941 that all these British workers were in America with the knowledge and permission of the British government. After Pearl Harbor the British Ambassador ordered that no further statements should be made by any member of the Embassy staff as, by agreement between the Allied partners, the status of all British citizens in the United States was now an American matter. The American administration continued its policy of support for the Moral Re-Armament workers after this date.[14]

Elements in the press, however, reiterated charges back and forth across the Atlantic. Denials were ignored. When Rudolf Hess, Hitler's deputy, made a surprise parachute visit to Britain, the American and Canadian press reported a 'confident announcement' by William Hillman, European editor of *Collier's*, that Hess was a follower of Buchman and had flown to England to make contact with the Oxford Group for the purpose of negotiating peace.[15] Buchman was as surprised to read this as anyone else. Only the *Allentown Morning Call* printed his statement that he did not even know Hess.[16]

In the midst of these battles came a public statement by Sam Shoemaker, whose large parish house, attached to Calvary Church in New York, had been for fifteen years the home and office of Buchman's work in America. Shoemaker announced to the American[17] and British press that he had decided to end his association with Buchman 'because certain policies and points of view have arisen in the development of moral re-armament about which we have had increasing misgivings'. He would not, according to the *Daily Telegraph*, say what these 'policies and points of view' were, but added, 'When the Oxford Group was, on its own definition, "a movement of vital personal religion working within the churches to make the principles of the New Testament practical as a working force today", we fully identified ourselves with it.'[18] Shoemaker concluded by asking Buchman to remove all personal and Oxford Group material and personnel from Calvary House.

Logan Roots, the retired Primate of China, now working full-time with Buchman, gave his own explanation of this development. 'The simple issue', he said, 'is that Shoemaker has initiated a new parish policy whereby he felt the parish was the prime objective. Buchman, true to his twenty-year-old definition of the Oxford Group as a programme of life issuing in personal, social, racial, national and supernational change, felt the work could not be limited to the confines of a parish but must give itself and its work to every parish and every denomination, and that if the parish would rightly see it the Church could really be a focal centre to save the world.'[19]

Neither statement, it seems today, quite embodied the whole truth. Buchman had not changed his aims, nor did Shoemaker wish to confine his influence to a single parish. But Shoemaker had, as early as 1925, decided to work within a traditional church framework, while Buchman was convinced that he himself, and also the Church, must reach out into every corner of life, and that this would require a new and revolutionary attitude. The same issue had arisen between them whenever Buchman took a new, cocoon-breaking step.

Behind these differences were the characters and aims of the two men. The friendship between them had been long-lasting and genuine, and Buchman appreciated Shoemaker's skill in helping individuals. But they were both strong personalities and, although Shoemaker was a good deal younger than Buchman, he had never willingly accepted tutelage, and seems to have sometimes chosen to interpret Buchman's directness on personal matters as an attempt to dominate.

For Buchman the rupture was a personal sorrow. He had seen it coming, as personal recriminations against him within the Calvary House community had begun to surface during the spring. These difficulties caused his health to deteriorate, and his doctor had him moved from Calvary House into the country. 'His great concern', writes the doctor, 'was not his health but his friend . . . which caused him great agony of spirit, yet without any word of bitterness or resentment. One day I found him relaxed, and his face shone. It was apparent something tremendous had happened to him. He said he had prayed all night for his friend . . . "I will live unity," he said to me. "Tell everyone that." '[20]

When the public statement came he discussed it for the first and last time with a few friends: 'They say there has been a split between us. Not a split, but there's always been a splinter . . . I can't raise any feeling against him. My temperature does not rise an inch.' To one friend in Calvary Church who wrote asking whether he should cut his association with Shoemaker, Buchman replied that he must certainly not do so, as Shoemaker would need his support more than ever.[21] Indeed, Buchman's calm and kindness are evident in every mention of Shoemaker at this period. He also seems to have felt that part of the blame was his. 'I made an idol of Calvary,' he said, 'and it was a mistake.'[22]

Various solutions were found to the practical problem of where Buchman and his friends would take their belongings. In reality, this development had been inevitable: a world action was difficult to run from a parish house, and a parish difficult to run from what had become a world centre.

The event was used by some of Buchman's critics to try and drive a wedge between him and his considerable support in the Church – and, in some cases, this succeeded. It also gave any who found the current press campaign against Buchman hard to bear an easy way of dropping their connection with him, even if that was not Shoemaker's intention. It did not alter Buchman's own relationship with the Church in any way. 'I believe with all my heart in the Church, the Church aflame, on fire with revolution,' he said two years later.[23]

The battles being fought round Buchman and Moral Re-Armament embarrassed but did not prevent the progress of the *You Can Defend America* programme across America. The play had made a long tour through the South and up through the Middle West to Detroit via Cleveland, Ohio, where it was shown for the Annual Convention of the Steelworkers of America. Philip Murray, the craggy, Scots-born leader of the CIO, spoke after the performance there: 'It exemplifies the spirit and the kind of unity for which America is looking.'[24]

In Detroit it played to 5,000 people a night. The first rush of patriotic response after Pearl Harbor, resulting in increased industrial production, was dying down. The brunt of the war burden was falling upon industry, which was divided by deep ideological disputes. Nearly every major union meeting was a pitched battle between the Communists demanding a Second Front in Europe at once and trying thereby to obtain control of the union, and the Socialists trying to prevent this and restrict discussions to industrial matters.

Buchman believed that 'total victory means we must win the war of arms and also the war of ideas'. 'Both', he remarked, 'are being fought right here in Detroit. The war can be lost or won in Detroit.' Henry Ford was his host in the city over Buchman's birthday in June. He had Buchman and a number of his colleagues staying as his guests at the Dearborn Inn, and he and Mrs Ford were at a large birthday lunch in the Ford Museum at Greenfield Village and several times saw *You Can Defend America*. Having finally decided to go into the production of aeroplanes, Ford was building up his vast Willow Run plant. Buchman wondered how such organising genius could become equally effective in the war of ideas. 'How can we set up an assembly line to produce men who know how to work together, who can cure bitterness, increase production and supply the imagination for a new world to be born?' he wrote to Ford. 'Where can we find the place to build the Willow Run to produce the ideas that will answer the "isms"? We have re-tooled our industries to meet a national emergency. With the same speed and thoroughness we must re-tool our thinking and living to meet a changing world.'[25]

The hint which eventually led to the place Buchman was seeking came not from Henry Ford but from his wife. At the birthday party she had remarked that Buchman looked unwell and should take a rest. The heat was oppressive, and she spoke of the cool climate of Mackinac Island, in the Great Lakes where Lakes Huron and Michigan meet. Buchman had already heard that war restrictions had left the island empty, and went to make a brief reconnaissance. Mrs Ford established his *bona fides* with the proprietor of the Grand Hotel there, Stewart Woodfill, and when a member of the island's Park Commission offered the use of an historic but dilapidated hotel, the Island House, for a dollar for a year, Buchman felt he had found his equivalent of Willow Run. The Island House was in a state of hardly describable filth – with two-year-old food still in the pots on the wood stove – but there was, he noticed, a barn behind the main building, where meetings could be held and plays performed.

An advance party was immediately despatched to make the Island House habitable. Hale was one of them. 'Frankly, the place was such a wreck I thought we were being overcharged,' he writes. 'When I woke up the first morning I found 79 bed-bug bites speckling my body. We scoured and scrubbed and bit by bit got the place de-bugged, de-stinked and de-grimed. But there was still much to do when the main force arrived from Detroit.'[26] Nevertheless, the Island House opened as the first training centre for Moral Re-Armament on 9 July.

Buchman and most of his team had meanwhile remained in the Detroit area, and this had irritated the 78-year-old Ford. He grumbled to Charles Lindbergh, who was assisting him in the setting up of Willow Run, that Buchman's force had overstayed their welcome and also that they had asked him to an evening party and kept him up much too long.[27] Indeed Buchman and he seldom met after that. However, James Newton and Eleanor Forde, now married, were always welcome, and when Bill Jaeger's mother, Annie, contracted cancer and spent a year at the Henry Ford Hospital, Mrs Ford, who was devoted to her, paid the bills.

Mackinac Island, situated near the border between the United States and Canada, a short plane flight from Chicago and Detroit but forbidden to all motor traffic, accustomed itself by degrees to receiving delegations first from the Mid-West industries and later from all over the world. Stewart Woodfill, whose Grand Hotel was a massive wooden structure of the last century looking like an ocean liner stranded on a green hill, had moved intimately among the industrial tycoons of the past forty years. He described later his first meeting with Buchman: 'I was curious about what was going on at the Island House. As he explained matters, I was impressed with his dedication to very big goals but my business mind could not grasp how such an organisation could successfully function without membership dues, without fixed income and seemingly without working capital. I invited Dr Buchman to be my guest in my hotel. It was the beginning of an amazing documentation of Moral Re-Armament, to which something was added every year I knew him.'[28]

Over the Labor Day weekend in early September, this year and in 1943, the Mackinac training centre was visited by labour and management from many parts of America. One of the labour leaders was William Schaffer from the Cramp Shipbuilding Company in Philadelphia, where *You Can Defend America* had been shown the previous year. He was twenty-nine and his wife, 'Dynamite', and he had already agreed upon a divorce, which meant separation from his two daughters. He met Buchman. 'My first impression was, "What's this bird want from me?" Much to my amazement, I found he wanted nothing. In his own quiet way, without saying much about it, he gave me a great sense of feeling that there was something wrong within myself.'[29] Schaffer left Mackinac after four days, thinking furiously. He had been amazed to find Henry Sanger, Ford's banker, sweeping out the porch in his shirt-sleeves; and on his homeward journey he discovered that a former President of the Los Angeles Chamber of Commerce, George Eastman, whom he had regarded with deep suspicion at the conference simply because of the position he held, had sat up in the train all night so that he could have a sleeping berth. 'I knew then, whatever anyone might say, that this was the greatest revolution in existence,' said Schaffer.[30] Later, when *The Forgotten Factor* was shown at his shipyard, he realised that Buchman had 'the only answer that was going to save my home, my union and the Cramp Shipbuilding Company'. In 1958 he wrote 'the Schaffer family will always be grateful'.[31]

Denis Foss, a young British Merchant Navy officer who had been torpedoed twice in twenty-four hours and was now resting between voyages, visited Mackinac that year and noted the beginning of change in another union leader: 'There were maybe a hundred children there with their parents. Just as the Sunday session was starting, Buchman moved from the back of the barn-theatre on to the platform. He sat down and waited for everyone to settle. A little girl walked up and climbed on his knee. Buchman asked her if she wanted to tell the crowded meeting anything. "No," she said, "I just want to be with you." Almost immediately two other children were on the platform, and then the grown-ups discreetly withdrew as twenty others followed. "Well, children," said Buchman. "This is a working session. What are we going to say to these people?" One by one some of the children told us what they had been learning at Mackinac. In front of me sat a man called Nick Dragon with his wife. He was Regional Director of the United Automobile Workers – CIO in Detroit. I noticed that he had tears slowly coursing down his cheeks and heard him say to his wife, "Here I am trying to control thousands of workers and I can't control my own children. Look at them with Buchman. What has he got that we haven't?" '

Foss also describes how Buchman enlisted him in getting his own work more shipshape. As they sat in two deck chairs by the lakeside, he handed Foss the day's *New York Herald Tribune*. 'I expect you're like me', he said, 'and have got into the habit of doing two things at once. While we talk about England you read the *Herald Tribune* and I'll read the *New York Times*. You tell me if you see anything I ought to know about, and I'll do the same for you.'

Then Buchman said, 'Now, Denis, I want you to tell me where we are going wrong here.' Foss, embarrassed, replied that three things struck him: an extremely untidy front lobby, the absence of people in uniform, and a certain stiffness between the men and women. In subsequent days Foss was approached first by a group of women who informed him that Buchman had said that he had some revolutionary ideas about house-keeping and that they should ask him about them; and then by a posse of journalists accompanied by a cartoonist and a secretary, requesting advice on how to get some of his service colleagues to Mackinac. Foss, having no advice whatever to offer on either matter, suggested listening to God. The results were a sketch written by the housekeepers which produced a transformation of living habits all over the building; and a duplicated newspaper, with cartoons, telling Foss's own experience of the guidance of God under battle conditions, which was sent out in thousands and brought a group of servicemen to Mackinac. On the subject of re-lationships, Buchman's only comment was, 'Sometimes I am sad I never had guidance from God to get married – I might have been able to help more.'[32]

Despite the growing tensions over the question of the call-up Buchman said at this time, 'I am living in a zone of calm.' But events were taking their physical toll, and his health was far from good. The summer had brought him no rest. Nevertheless, on 16 September he decided to go to California 'to make the speech of my life', and left Mackinac that day. He arrived in Los Angeles suffering from fatigue and a sore throat, but started his first day there with a phone call at 4 am, and ended it with a scolding to his team, busy performing *You Can Defend America*, for 'selling a show instead of the philosophy' and consequently not speaking convincingly from the platform or selling books to the audience afterwards.

After a week in Los Angeles he felt that he should go to San Francisco, then to Seattle and back to Mackinac. Again, he left on the day the decision was made. These days were a mixture of fatigue, minor pains, travel, and seeing many people, individually and in groups. Once back at Mackinac, he conferred with his team; encouraged them to cook better, write better, 'talk well and accurately', 'take time to be holy'; made plans for their next moves; followed the battle in Washington over the call-up of his younger colleagues; had Victor Reuther, Walter Reuther's brother and, like him, a leader in the Automobile Workers' Union, to see *The Forgotten Factor*; walked in the island and spotted blueberries which were picked for the next day's lunch; sent books over to Woodfill at the Grand Hotel; and battled with pain and fatigue. 'I can't think,' he said to a doctor one day. 'It's no good. I never thought my sixties would treat me like this. Do you think I shall be like this to the end?'

The urgent question of manpower still remained. With increased demands for the services of his trained men, he still could not plan far ahead until he knew whether they would be available. The Selective Service Administration continued to defer them for six months at a time, but it was now becoming a highly explosive political as well as administrative decision. In Washington, as in Westminster, there were those who believed that what these men were doing was of vital importance. A group of senior public figures headed by Senator Truman* in April 1942 wrote President Roosevelt a letter in which they said, 'We feel it would be nothing short of a contradiction of the spirit of the Selective Service Act, should these men be assigned to any other type of war-service than that in which heretofore they have been so usefully engaged.'[33]

President Roosevelt's official response was to acknowledge the letter and pass it to the Selective Service Director for consideration. His personal conviction was reflected in a letter written to his old headmaster, Dr Endicott Peabody, who had been impressed by *You Can Defend America*, play and book. The President wrote, 'We need more things like that to maintain and strengthen the national morale. From all accounts they are making a splendid contribution to patriotism and I hope a large number of communities will have the benefit of witnessing a performance.'[34]

But personal conviction and political pressures do not always coincide. The issue was becoming as hot for the legislators in Washington as it had been in Westminster, and was stoked to roasting heat by a section of the press.

The beginnings at Mackinac had been fruitful, but for Buchman it had been a tough summer. As so often he was dissatisfied, feeling the need of a new depth of spiritual experience and a new way of reaching the mind of the country. 'We need the medium to give a richer spiritual life to America,' he said. 'I want to go away and find a whole new vision, an expression of what we need to bring to the nation.'

He decided to go for a few days' rest to a small hotel in Saratoga Springs in New York State, a place where he had spent a holiday in his student years. He arrived a weary man, with no clear idea of what he should do or what resources he would be left to deploy. 'I don't know what the future holds,' he told some friends quietly. 'I have a sense I am going to be attacked physically. I have no fear about it, but I want you to know what I feel may happen.'

---

* Truman, a Democrat, was now Chairman of the Congressional 'watch-dog' Committee on War Contracts. His co-signatories were Congressman Wadsworth, a Republican, who had introduced the Bill setting up the Selective Service Administration, and the Presidents of the two national labour organisations, William Green of the AFL and Philip Murray of the CIO.

NEAR DEATH

Buchman arrived in Saratoga Springs in late November 1942. On 20 November he had news of the death of two friends, one the son of the London business man Austin Reed, killed in action, the other a notable suffragette and Republican *grande dame*, Mrs Charles Sumner Bird, who with her granddaughter, Ann, had played a major part in putting on *You Can Defend America* in Boston in August 1941. Buchman was devoted to them and had just written the granddaughter encouraging her to get to know the women leaders of the Garment Workers' Union in her city: 'I think this development is akin to that which came to your grandmother through the suffragette movement. Some people here are dying on their feet because their only goal seems to be the end of a cigarette and the next cocktail. You are truly doing what happened in the New Testament. I remember some lines when I was a boy:

> Dare to be a Daniel, dare to stand alone,
> Dare to have a purpose true, and dare to make it known!

For Daniel you have only to put in the name "Ann". There are people who won't understand, but I would rather have the appreciation of those four hundred Garment Workers than all the modern tittle-tattle which all of us have to listen to, but not always agree to.'[1]

That evening in Saratoga Springs, in a relaxed and radiant mood which brought the sense of eternity into the room, he talked with a few friends about the two who had died: ' "The memory of just men made perfect!" Many funerals are so unnatural and inadequate. They should breathe what is necessary into the next generation. What a joy to have people who will give you a setting at your passing which will make others rise up and take on your work.'

He said the benediction which he loved most: 'The Lord bless thee and keep thee; the Lord make his face to shine upon thee and be gracious unto thee; the Lord lift up the light of his countenance upon thee, and give thee peace.' Then he went to his room. 'He was', recorded his secretary, 'supremely happy with a deep sense of the triumph of death in Christ.'

Next day, walking down the hotel corridor to go out, he suddenly collapsed. The local doctor, Dr Carl Comstock, was there within ten minutes and found he had had a stroke, which had impaired his speech and paralysed the right side of his body. However, half an hour later Buchman was speaking a little. Shortly afterwards, he sat up, and then, with his younger colleagues too astonished to stop him, he got up and walked to the bathroom and returned to bed unaided. Comstock, told of it later, said he had never heard of anything like it. But the prognosis was bad, and with local nurses away at the war and an influenza epidemic in the town, nursing would be difficult.

Without knowing anything about the emergency a New York doctor who was a friend of Buchman, Irene Gates, had had a strong inner compulsion to visit him that day. A few hours after his stroke, she walked in. Paul Campbell, a rising young physician from the Henry Ford Hospital in Detroit who had resigned his job to work with Buchman, arrived to join her. In the next days he and Dr Gates nursed their patient through successive crises, supported by the prayers of thousands to whom the press had carried the news. Several times Buchman's pulse disappeared almost entirely, as his friends watched hour by hour. Each time they prayed, either by his bed or in an adjacent room, and each time he pulled through.

Three days after the stroke Buchman sent for the friends who had come to stay nearby. Campbell's diary reads: '11 pm 24 Tuesday: Evidence of circulatory collapse. Frank felt approaching death. Asked for Communion Service. Had everyone come in. Called, "John, John – he is always with me." "You mean Mike?" "Mike! Yes, Mike, Mike, Mike." Mike came in. Frank looked at him, said quietly, "Sit down for a while," and broke into tears. "How long, four years?" Mike answered, "Eight years, eight good years." Frank then asked for his wallet. Went through every item of it with Mike, distributing the money, designating some cheques to be sent back. Then he called us all in. Standing around the bed in this order – Ken, John, Grace, Enid, Garrett, Elsa, me, Mike, Ray, Irene, Ellie, Laura, Morris. "I feel death close." "Funeral Allentown, Sunday or Monday." Ken: "We will go on fighting". Frank broke into tears again. Then he looked at Garrett and said, "Pray." Garrett led us all in the Lord's Prayer. . .'

Another of those present recalls that after they finished the Lord's Prayer, Buchman 'slowly and with difficulty repeated, "Thine is the kingdom, the power and the glory." "I want to say goodbye. But I hate to leave you." He asked that the two hotel maids who looked after the room come in so that he could thank them. Then he slept.'

Some of his friends spent the night in prayer. Others worked through the night handling press enquiries and considering urgent decisions. Again next morning he was at his weakest and felt he was going. 'I'm sixty-four. I'm ready; but perhaps the Lord won't take me yet. But you must get to work.'

The following day was Thanksgiving Day. Again he asked his friends to come, and prayed, 'Oh, sweet Jesus, wilt Thou use us, and bless us, and own us.' He paused between each phrase and then opened his eyes. 'I saw the outstretched arms. It was wonderful. I have been waiting a long time for this. I am ready.'

Later, however, he was a little stronger and was able to be given news of friends who had enquired after him. When he heard that Henry Ford had telephoned, a twinkle came back: 'He doesn't like using the telephone.' The ex-bootlegger from Tahoe had been enquiring after him, and cables had come from William Temple, who had become Archbishop of Canterbury that year, and Lord Lang of Lambeth. Friends in Britain had made a chain of continuous prayers throughout the country. 'Perhaps God will give me ten days or so more,' he thought that night. But from that Thanksgiving Day he began very slowly to improve.

Some time later he spoke of this experience: 'The old doctor was there. He expected me to go, but I had the experience of a glorious victory. I saw the glory of the other world. I saw the outstretched arms of Christ and they were marvellous. It was better than anything I have ever seen, the vision of the life beyond . . . I'm going to stick to that vision. The unfathomable riches of Christ. It was glory. I knew I was on the rocks out there in Saratoga. But after a time it came clear, "The time is not yet. Your work is not finished. You have other things to do." I'm glad I stayed.'

To Ray Purdy one day Buchman added, 'I saw Jesus. He showed me where I was going wrong. I have been organising a movement. But a movement should be the outcome of changed lives, not the means of changing them. From now on I am going to ask God to make me into a great life-changer.'

This dilemma in Buchman's life was crystallised for him by his illness; but it was perpetual, and inherent in the undertaking of doing personal work with individuals on as wide a scale as possible. The temptation to movement-mindedness may also have been usually more obvious to him in his colleagues than in himself.

Slowly, to the amazement of Dr Comstock, Buchman pulled back to convalescence, handicapped only in his right hand and leg. On 11 December, he first sat out of bed in a chair. On 9 February he paid his first visit to the bathroom. On 11 March he went downstairs for the first time, and on 18 March departed by car and train for New York and, next day, on to Washington to see five of his colleagues off to the army. 'He was still desperately sick but insisted on risking the journey,' writes Hale. 'As he was carried in, he looked paper frail, but his eyes were combative.'[2]

When Dr Comstock came to say goodbye he told Buchman that watching him during those weeks had restored the faith he had long abandoned. He refused to submit an account, but simply said, 'I am your debtor.' Later in the war when his own son was seriously wounded he wrote to Buchman that, without this refound faith, he would at that moment have despaired of life.[3]

Buchman's recovery was slowed down by a long-term heart condition, of which he had first been warned by a German doctor in the late 1930s. Campbell's notes for the summer preceding the stroke sometimes show his pulse shooting up to a rate of 130 or 140. He also suffered chronic and often acute pain from haemorrhoids. All these symptoms were to persist for the next twenty years and Campbell cared for him almost the whole time, only taking a break when he was needed for MRA work elsewhere and when another doctor could take his place. He believes this stroke saved Buchman's life, for otherwise he would have killed himself through overwork.

His friends did not find Buchman an easy patient. He had always maintained there was a right way and a wrong way of doing everything, a belief partly inherited from his mother. Now what he had applied for years to his world-wide activities all seemed concentrated into his one room. The curtains had to be just right and every other detail correct. His friends could see he wanted or felt about something intensely; but often he could not speak or only used Pennsylvania German. 'Food?' they would say. It wasn't that. 'Drink?' No. 'You got to longing to find the right thing, which seemed so obvious to him,' one of them recorded.

Campbell says, however, that, throughout his long convalescence, which was such a traumatic change from the crowded activities of his former life, Buchman showed no signs of frustration. Once early on, when he found that Campbell had been discussing with Dr Comstock whether 'anxiety' was aggravating his situation, Buchman said to him, 'You don't understand me yet, do you?' Comstock wrote later of his 'calm, unperturbed attitude with no evidence of fear for the future, either here or there, so to speak'.[4]

His prayers at this time were short and simple. 'Cure me,' he prayed on 30 March, 'and I promise to be a good boy,' and on 17 April, 'You know I am far from well. Grant me wisdom for the sight I need for today, and tomorrow and the next day. I am just a poor, weak, helpless child of Thine coming to Thee for aid.' But most of his prayers were for others, and especially for those being drafted into the services.

[314]

For New Year's Day 1943, a matter of five weeks after his stroke, Buchman dictated a message for the friends and colleagues who were carrying on his work in America, which reveals something of his style of leadership. It reads in part:

'The call of God is to spiritual leadership, the rarest, the most precious and the most urgently needed commodity in the world. The need for it is universal, its possibilities infinite – and it remains unrationed. Our task as a fellowship is to provide that leadership . . .

'New Year is the time to take stock. Don't miss it. May the call of God take precedence over every other call . . . Everyone longs in their hearts to play some part, however humble, in the remaking of our world. They will respond when given a chance to see how . . . Build up in every way you can, and build in to every situation, every home, every person, all you can of this life-giving spirit. Never hesitate, never be inferior . . .

'Don't let the failures of 1942 get you down – learn from them and march on. Don't go by them but by the call of God and the power of God. They never fail. Remember this especially under attack. There is no power on earth can stop you, or even divide you, if you live in humble dependence on Almighty God, in simple obedience to His Holy Spirit, and in fellowship with Him and with one another.

'Always be ready to change, in whatever way you are shown. Never be proud or obstinate, but give all you've got. If feelings dominate guidance, be sure there's selfishness somewhere. Let all that go at once. God alone can satisfy . . .'

During the early weeks of his illness a fierce campaign against Buchman was being carried on in certain newspapers in New York, where the decisions about his overseas full-time colleagues had to be made by the local Draft Board since it had been their port of entry. These decisions sometimes became available to enquiring newspapermen even before they had been officially taken, or the person concerned interviewed. One British newspaper published in the morning the decisions of a meeting to be held in New York twelve hours later.[5] General Hershey, National Director of Selective Service, publicly condemned such practices as 'unjust', and was attacked for exercising influence from Washington.

On 4 January 1943 the *New York World-Telegram* carried a headline right across its front page accusing Washington of 'protecting draft-dodgers'. It was the toughest blow so far and with Buchman still seriously ill in Saratoga Springs his friends hesitated at first to show the paper to him. When they did, he looked it over and commented, 'Well, we've certainly made the front page this time!' Alongside the story he saw the pictures of the Washington men accused of exercising 'influence', among them Congressman Wadsworth, Admiral Byrd, and Senators Truman, Thomas and Capper. 'That's a team I'd be proud of anywhere,' he said. 'Thank God for them. God's truth goes marching on.' And he laid the newspaper aside.

Buchman's allies in Washington stood firm. Admiral Byrd told the press, 'These men are working long hours without pay in an effort to show all people that everyone has got to do his part to win the war.'[6] Congressman Wadsworth wrote, 'Moral Re-Armament is not only helping us immensely in the war effort, but we shall need it just as much in the aftermath of this war as we do during the actual fighting of it.'[7]

The American attacks, but not these replies, were reported in parts of the British press, stimulating more attacks in Britain which were in turn given wide publicity in New York and Washington. Hale, who was in New York, states that 'for five whole weeks we were on the front pages of the more sensational papers every day'.[8] This left the New York State Director of Selective Service, whose decision regarding Buchman's last twenty-two men was final, facing a political rather than an administrative problem. On 12 January he decided to forbid any further appeal by Moral Re-Armament to Washington, as he was by law entitled to do. Buchman received the decision lying, still very weak, in his room in Saratoga. 'I'd be a fool if I didn't recognise what this means. But I can't take it out of the realm of the Almighty. I hate like sin to lose these men, but now others must take off their shirts. I probably made a mistake or two in these cases, but I don't think I'll be a politician. Let's have guidance.' With his left hand, for the first time since his stroke he wrote, 'Change – Unite – Fight! Probably my battle is over – for six months at least.' 'It will mean a maturing for you,' he added. 'Now you take on.'

Then looking out of his window, he added, 'It's beautiful out there. It's all I've got – about three or four miles. But I accept it. Whatever comes, tempest or peace, you've got to accept it. It's a torn world and it's going to be more torn still.' He turned towards the small group of men bound for the armed forces and prayed, 'Father, these men are going out into the wide world. May they be able to bind together a group of men to be like-minded men. Keep this old country together. Thou hast a better idea for it than we. Guide, guard and keep us all from danger of body and soul, through Christ our Lord.' His farewell was, 'I wish I could come with you. It's a geat battle.'

Buchman was left with those above military age, several who were rejected on medical grounds and some who were ministers of religion. An attempt by the New York Board to induct these last was ruled to be illegal by Washington. The loss of key personnel meant, among other things, that it was no longer possible to show *You Can Defend America* in the

United States, although the follow-up programme in industry and else-where continued apace.

In June 1943 William Jaeger wrote Buchman, 'We now have something like 1,500 labour allies in this country . . . We have stayed in the homes of a good many.' In September he wrote that eighty-six labour leaders and their wives had been at Mackinac that summer. By January 1944 he estimated the 'labour allies' at nearly two thousand. Similar work was going on with management.

During the spring and early summer Buchman steadily recovered strength, staying with different friends in the warmer states of the East. Though from this time he was never robust physically, he was mentally and spiritually as active as ever. He followed the activities of his colleagues, which included adaptations of *You Can Defend America* in Canada, Britain and Australia, with the keenest interest. In Australia the Prime Minister, John Curtin, adjourned Parliament early so that the revue *Battle for Australia* could be seen in the Members' dining room, which was converted into a theatre for the occasion. The Minister of Navy and Munitions cabled Buchman, 'There is new light coming to Parliament through your vision.'[9]

Buchman was particularly interested by the findings of an intelligence analysis for the Selective Service Administration. It noted that Moral Re-Armament drew the fire equally of Nazis and Communists, of the extreme right and extreme left in politics, of aggressive atheists and narrow ecclesiastics. It had been charged by radicals with being militaristic and by warmongers with being pacifistic. Certain elements in labour denounced it as anti-union: certain elements in management as pro-union.

In Britain, the report went on, MRA was accused by some of being a brilliantly clever front for Fascism: in Germany and Japan of being a super-intelligent arm of the British and American Secret Service. One day a section of the press would announce that MRA was defunct: and the next that it numbered nearly the entire membership of the British Cabinet at the time of Munich, and was responsible for engineering Hitler's attack upon Russia.

'Nothing', concluded this analysis, 'but a potentially vast moral and spiritual reformation of global proportions could possibly be honoured by antagonisms so venomous and contradictory in character, and so world-wide in scope.'[10]

Meanwhile Buchman was grateful to have time to think of the meaning of his struggle and of life itself. Carl Hambro and his wife Gudrun were now in the United States, and he wrote from Florida to her, 'We have come to the Southland to recuperate. The warm balm of summer is on us and we are enjoying a wealth of honeysuckle, laurel, iris, dogwood and roses, and it is real country like your own Norway. It brings us closer to eternal truth – the thing that matters. There are so many real truths we want to learn for which we never seem to have time. Since this illness one has more time.

> Thou, O Christ, art all I want;
>   More than all in Thee I find;
> Raise the fallen, cheer the faint,
>   Heal the sick, and lead the blind.
> Just and holy is Thy Name,
>   I am all unrighteousness;
> False and full of sin I am,
>   Thou art full of truth and grace.

These lines come with a great life-giving experience. I remember all the good times we have had in life together. Will they ever come back? The day in Interlaken with you and Carl and your daughter: and in Geneva, and all that you and Carl made possible.

'Now you have come by mercy protected and your life has been miraculously spared to carry on further your good work. Rest assured I follow you and yours in God's loving care and keeping.'[11]

In July came news of her sudden death. 'Gudrun loved you dearly', wrote Carl Hambro, 'and you were often in her thoughts. She was intensely grateful for all you had given her – and us. And so am I. I send you her love.'[12]

By then Buchman was back in Mackinac with his team. En route from the South he had stopped in the quiet North Carolina countryside at Tryon where he attended the wedding of George West, the Anglican Bishop of Rangoon, to his own former secretary, Grace Hay. Sensing some agitation that the principals were a little late, he remarked, 'Think of the wedding in Cana. That wasn't just ten minutes and then all over. Christ made it something greater. The point about a wedding is not whether it's at five or a minute past five, but whether God is there.'

At Tryon, too, he celebrated his sixty-fifth birthday. 'It has been an amazing year,' he said on that occasion. 'I feel God has a great plan for the future. I am marching forth with certainty because I believe something bigger is coming. We have got to prepare. My job is not to worry about anything. I go to bed at night. I go to sleep. I wake up in the morning. This morning I was awake at half-past three, the time I was born. Since the first week of my illness certain things have become fixed. New things have become important. Things I once thought important no longer are. The Lord gave me a thrombosis because I wouldn't learn to go more slowly. I thank Him for the past six months, and the next. It would be wonderful to be well again, but maybe, if I go to work again, I'll change some more. If I had my life to live again, I would only do the things that really matter.'

IDEOLOGY

During his period of convalescence in 1943 – the year of the Casablanca, Quebec, Cairo and Teheran conferences on the future of Europe – Buchman had time to think about and talk over what lay ahead for the world and for his work. The Soviet Union, it seemed to him, had an aggressive belief about how the earth should be run, a faith which had shown itself capable of winning adherents in every country. America, too, was originally a nation founded in a faith with a universal appeal. Yet that faith was seldom now related to practical affairs or politics, and seemed unlikely to be prominent in the public mind when it came to shaping the world after the war. How could this factor be brought home to the American people, and what should be done about it?

Michael Hutchinson, a thirty-year-old former Scholar of Balliol College, Oxford, who was working with Buchman in North America, had talked to him about 'ideology'. 'I don't think I'd use that word,' Buchman had replied. 'I would rather say "a big idea".' In fact, up to this point, Buchman had only used the word 'ideology' in a negative context, as something to be combated or overcome. But the more he pondered the matter, the more it seemed clear to him that any idea with a world-wide outlook and programme, and which made a total demand on a person, could properly be called an ideology. Christianity, as Christ preached it, was such an idea. Where it differed from the materialist ideologies of the day was that it prescribed a total obedience not to any person, but to God.

The word 'ideology', in fact, was neutral. It had acquired a bad name because it was being used almost exclusively by those materialist brands which, in practice, meant tyranny. Yet the word implied a degree and breadth of commitment which the word 'religion', through the half-heartedness of many religious people, had lost. Why should not America live out her original faith with such fire and thoroughness that it would offer an attractive and universally-recognised alternative to the materialist ideologies?

With such thoughts developing in his mind Buchman arrived back at Mackinac at the end of June. As he boarded the boat for the crossing he was, according to one of those with him, tired but gleeful. 'He sang what he imagined to be the "Mackinac Song" and looked long and lovingly across the waters as the island came in sight. It was an effort to get off the boat and to climb into the carriage which took him off to Island House.'[1]

On 18 July, still looking frail, he talked informally to several hundred people at the Assembly about the thoughts he had been maturing. 'Today', he began, 'I want to talk about great forces at work in the world.' He spoke of Karl Marx and how, gradually, Communism had become 'a tremendous force'. Then of Mussolini and Hitler and how their ideas had, at first, brought 'a seeming order'. 'So we have Communism and Fascism – two world forces,' he continued. 'Where do they come from? From materialism, which is the mother of all the "isms". It is the spirit of anti-Christ which breeds corruption, anarchy and revolution. It under-mines our homes, it sets class against class, it divides the nation. Materialism is democracy's greatest enemy.'

Then he spoke of the concept of Moral Re-Armament as an ideology with a different origin 'where the moral and spiritual would have the emphasis'. 'Communism and Fascism are built on a *negative* something – on divisive materialism and confusion. Wherever Moral Re-Armament goes, there springs up a *positive* message. Its aim is to restore God to leadership as the directing force in the life of the nation . . . America must discover her rightful ideology. It springs from her Christian heritage, and is her only adequate answer in the battle against materialism and all the other "isms" . . .

'People get confused as to whether it is a question of being Rightist or Leftist. But the one thing we really need is to be guided by God's Holy Spirit. That is the Force we ought to study . . . The Holy Spirit will teach us how to think and live, and provide a working basis for our national service . . .

'The true battle-line in the world today is not between class and class, not between race and race. The battle is between Christ and anti-Christ. "Choose ye this day whom ye will serve." '[2]

The young Norwegian artist Signe Lund[3] was there. 'I was riveted,' she recalled later. 'The speech came out of his guts. He knew that by launching out as an ideology, he was sending us as well as himself out into a dangerous world.' This was further clarification of the thought he had been reaching for at Visby, the understanding of the particular role of his work at a particular stage in the world's history and of the direction in which he must be ready to go. It was a realisation that the war for the world would in future be fought out not between countries, economies or armies but between sets of ideas: that the basic divide was between materialist ideas of right and left on the one hand, and the moral and spiritual ideas at the heart of the world's great faiths on the other. It was a vision of the battle between good and evil within the individual soul being reflected in the affairs of the world, and the acceptance that he and his small band of colleagues had a particular role to play in that battle.

This step forward was not to make him or his ideas any more popular among the complacent or the relative moralists; but it was to give an impetus to his thinking and his operations during the coming years. Conscious acceptance by a group of people of the role of an 'ideology' did entail temptations to self-importance and self-effort. To Buchman it remained simple: 'The whole gospel of Jesus Christ – that is your ideology.' But he would have to carry with him a group of people not all of whom yet had his grasp of the root experience of this ideology, an undertaking demanding courage and wisdom of no ordinary kind and the extent of which he may or may not have comprehended during those summer days among his friends.

The previous day he had led his first meeting since his illness. But although he spent much time talking with individuals and small groups, he took little public part in the summer-long Assembly that year. He first went off the island – for a dentist appointment during which he did 'quite a lot of walking and stair-climbing' – on 13 September. The next morning he called in two friends to write down thoughts which were coming to him, 'the first time for some weeks and flowing just like the old days'. 'Thoughts came for the next steps for the fight,' one of them recorded. 'He felt again at grips with the problem. He hates more than anything to feel that there is no place where we can get on the attack.'[4]

Buchman spent the winter quietly in Sarasota, Florida, the guest of a hotelier who had been to Mackinac and who put a small hotel near the Gulf of Mexico at his disposal as, in the usual way, the number of people round him grew. Here he cultivated many friendships, old and new. Artur Rodzinski, the newly appointed conductor of the New York Philharmonic Orchestra, and his wife Halina spent Christmas with him. Cissie Patterson, the proprietor of the Washington *Times-Herald*, had evenings where she invited Adlai Stevenson and the Chicago composer, John Alden Carpenter, and her editors to meet him. He also became fast friends with many of the famous Ringling Circus troupe whose winter headquarters were in Sarasota, and was much taken by the family life, the integrity and the sheer courage of the circus people.* But he refused to do anything public in the community. This baffled some of those around him.

Then, one day he surprised them still more by announcing that he was taking his whole party, about twenty strong, to the local playhouse. The play was to start at 8.30, but for some inexplicable reason he insisted they

---

* Asked whether he would prefer to see Mr Ringling's famous horses or the Fat Woman, he immediately opted for the latter.

should all be there by 7.30. He was met by a distraught manager. The second lead, he told Buchman, had had a heart attack. He had no understudy. The play could not go on.

'Oh, don't worry,' said Buchman confidently. 'My friend Cecil Broadhurst will be delighted to play for you.'

An astonished Broadhurst was rushed backstage and given a script. One or two scenes were quickly rehearsed and Broadhurst, a talented actor, got through the performance with script in hand. The manager was delighted and said he hoped Broadhurst could play for the rest of the week. Broadhurst was sorry, but he had to go to New York to see his draft board the very next day. Once more the manager was in despair.

'Oh, don't worry,' said Buchman again. 'My friend Robert Anderson will be glad to play for you.'

The week went off triumphantly, and all Sarasota heard of it. Indeed, it was said that the occasion healed a breach between the playhouse and the local newspaper, which for the first time for months printed a notice about the theatre.

Arthur Strong, the English photographer, who had come to Sarasota a little before the theatre party, had been greatly puzzled not only by Buchman's inactivity but by his insistence that all the party should rest and not take any local initiatives. 'Most evenings Buchman would have the whole party in for supper, and we would sit on for hours over the table, while he drew people out, one by one,' says Strong. 'It was the first time I had been with him since his stroke, and I noticed a real change. More listening and waiting. Less attacking. A much greater sense of humour. I think he wanted to show us that God had a better way to approach Sarasota than our activism.'

'The stroke, maybe, took some of the self-effort out of him,' Barrett once commented.

Alan Thornhill adds, 'Frank at Sarasota was truly remarkable. He seemed to vary from extreme weakness and illness, often only speaking in his brand of German, to these surprising exploits with people. I think his life-changing there must have been a direct outcome of his prayer to be a great life-changer. In all my times with Frank, I never knew him so mellow, so sensitive.'

Early in 1944 Buchman was variously rumoured by certain American papers to be in Germany, in prison in England, or in hiding in America. A national publication, entitled *Cross and Doublecross*, appeared on American newsstands at this time. It accused Buchman of seeking a 'soft peace', and claimed that he had been responsible, among other things, for the abdication of King Edward VIII and the Munich Pact; had been at the heart of the appeasement-oriented 'Cliveden Set' in Britain before the war; had, during the war, tried to engineer peace through arranging

Hess's flight to Scotland; and, finally, had been responsible for turning the war against Russia by inducing Hitler to attack the Soviets.

Buchman kept in touch with his friends in Washington. Truman, in his position as chairman of the Senate Committee investigating war contracts, had during the past four years demanded and obtained a high standard of honesty which had saved the nation billions of dollars. In 1943 he, Admiral Byrd, Congressman Wadsworth and other political, business and labour figures signed the foreword to a report on the industrial work of Moral Re-Armament.* Truman told a Washington press conference, 'Suspicions, rivalries, apathy, greed lie behind most of the bottlenecks . . . these problems, to which the Moral Re-Armament programme is finding an effective solution, are the most urgent of any in our whole production picture . . . What we now need is a fighting faith which will last twenty-four hours a day, seven days a week and fifty-two weeks a year . . . This is where the Moral Re-Armament group comes in. Where others have stood back and criticised, they have rolled up their sleeves and gone to work. They have already achieved remarkable results in bringing teamwork into industry, on the principles not of "who's right" but of "what's right".'[5]

Truman, with Congressman Wadsworth, attended a showing of *The Forgotten Factor* at Philadelphia in April 1944. There he added, 'If America does not catch this spirit, we shall be lucky to win the war and certain to lose the peace. With it there is no limit to what we can do for America and America for the world.'[6]

Truman and Wadsworth had sent a thousand personal letters inviting the political and military leadership of America to a showing of *The Forgotten Factor* at the National Theater in Washington on 14 May. After the Philadelphia showing Buchman went to Washington. He concentrated now on getting all the arrangements for this performance perfect, including the play itself, every detail of which interested him. As he was watching a late rehearsal on the afternoon of the performance word was brought to him that the father of one of the backstage crew, Jim Cooper from Scotland, had died. He immediately met Cooper in a room in the theatre and told him the news. He asked him how his mother would manage financially, and told him about the death of his own father and the certainty of life after death which it had confirmed in him. He then abandoned the much-anticipated public event, took Cooper home for supper and spent the evening with him.

Truman also failed to appear. Shortly before the showing he had said to two of Buchman's colleagues, 'They are trying to get me to agree to be

* *The Fight to Serve* (Moral Re-Armament, 1943). Other signatories included the Vice-President of Cramp Shipbuilding, Vice-Presidents of the AFL and CIO, and the previous year's President of the American Society of Newspaper Editors.

nominated as Vice-President, but I think I could do more by staying in the Senate. Please let me know what you think.' When they returned the next day Truman had accepted the nomination, one condition of which was that he drop all connection with any other groups, however worthwhile. They were told that Truman was 'in conference', and a large man, unknown to them, added, 'From now on, we're arranging the appointments and strategy for Mr Truman. He'll have no opportunity to see you in future.' This proved to be true. There is no evidence, however, that Truman changed his view on Buchman and his work, and during his Presidency some of Buchman's colleagues maintained close contact with his chief labour negotiator, John Steelman, Director of the US Conciliation Service.

Buchman spent his birthday that year with Charles and Margery Haines at their historic Wyck House in Germantown, Philadelphia, and next day took a large party to Pennsburg and Allentown, giving a running commentary all the way. Here he used to fish with Daddy Shiep; there his old headmaster was buried; that was the place where he took twelve girls to a dance. Fifty-six people had lunch in his old home in Allentown, and, with the neighbours dropping in, it was eighty-five for tea. One of them was Arthur Keller with whom he had gone to Montreal when they were sixteen. Buchman stayed the night. Next day just eleven sat down to a lunch of chops, mashed potatoes, dandelion greens and pie.

Buchman was at his most relaxed when he was back in his boyhood surroundings, entertaining people in his own home, visiting his old friends in theirs, never mentioning his work unless he was asked about it – 'an old friend in an old tweed jacket'. He loved to return there, and to show off the beautiful countryside to his overseas friends. But it was no more than his cradle. Alan Thornhill once said to him, 'I can't think how you ever tore yourself away from this place.' Buchman replied, 'I couldn't wait another minute to get away.'

From Allentown Buchman moved on to New York and then to Boston, where he paid a visit to his old friend Mrs Tjader. At that time he could still only walk short distances, and he arrived before her house in a wheelchair. Mrs Tjader came out of her front door and looked down at him from the top of a flight of twenty stone steps. 'Oh, Frank, you're ill!' she exclaimed. 'Ill!' retorted Buchman, got out of the wheelchair and stumped, unaided, up the twenty steps.

From Boston he returned via Detroit to Mackinac. 'Brevity, sincerity, hilarity! In that spirit we will get to know each other this morning,' was his opening to one of the only two meetings he led at the three-month Assembly that summer. At the end of Mackinac he decided to spend the autumn and winter quietly in Southern California and then to take part in a full-scale action programme on the West Coast with *The Forgotten Factor* and other plays in the spring. He was invited to spend the winter months in the Los Angeles home of Miss Lucy Clark, which he equipped with Mackinac-trained cooks to cater for a household of a dozen and many visitors. Meanwhile, theatres were being booked all up the coast for the spring campaign.

For the rest of 1944 and the first half of 1945 Buchman seems to have left most things to his lieutenants – and to have been well-pleased to do so. 'The work is in competent hands,' he remarked on 3 April. And later that month: 'An absolutely perfect evening and I didn't have to do a darned thing about it.' His health was steadily improving, though occasions when he could manage a full day without a rest are mentioned as noteworthy in his secretary's diary, and sometimes he spent the whole day in bed. 'The Lord has given me a wonderful peace,' he said in January, and by June he wrote to a friend, 'You will be interested to know I am my old self again. At a reception yesterday, a reporter, who interviewed me fifteen years ago in Seattle, came over and said, "You don't look a day older." So I have recaptured the blush of youth and am storing up masses of energy for some visits I hope to pay very soon.'[7]

That letter was written from San Francisco where the United Nations Conference on International Organization was in progress. On 12 March, at the Yalta Conference, Roosevelt, Stalin and Churchill had decided to hold the San Francisco Conference in April, precisely when Buchman had a theatre booked there. 'It looks as if you had been guided to the right part of the world three or four months before Churchill, Roosevelt and Stalin knew anything about it,' wrote a member of the British delegation.[8]

Buchman had already given thought to the quality needed in any new international organisation. At Mackinac the previous summer, when the first delegates came from Europe, he told them, 'I had a vision early this morning of your cities – Stockholm, Copenhagen, Berne and London – their rulers learning to be guided by God. Then there would be less confused thinking. Any new League of Nations must have that atmosphere. But then the task will still lie ahead – to build men who so live in the councils of nations that "Thy will be done on earth as it is in heaven" is a practical purpose, not a pious hope.'

The Yalta Conference had been officially hailed in America as a triumph of co-operation between wartime allies now uniting for the purposes of peace, which this new international organisation would safeguard. Russia's aims had not been clear to an ageing Roosevelt, who felt that he could easily handle Stalin. The dividing up of great areas of Europe, which followed Yalta, was not foreseen. One of Roosevelt's chief aides, Admiral Leahy, later wrote in his memoirs, 'The ink was hardly dry on the Yalta Protocol before serious difficulties of interpretation arose.'[9]

On 12 April 1945, a few days before the San Francisco conference opened, President Roosevelt died. President Truman took over. On 25 April Buchman attended the opening ceremony of the Conference, which Truman began by saying, 'Let us not fail to grasp this supreme chance to establish a world-wide rule of reason, to create an enduring peace under the guidance of God.'

Six days later came the end of war in Europe. Buchman listened to the radio announcements early in the morning by Truman in Washington and Churchill in London. Relief that the conflict there had ceased was tempered by the thought of the suffering and destruction it had left behind, and by the fact that a real peace still needed to be created.

The San Francisco Conference ran into difficulties before it began. Molotov would not attend until the West had given the Soviet Union its way on Poland. When he arrived Halifax described him as 'smiling granite'. And Halifax was driven to lose his temper – a rare occurrence – by Gromyko's immobility. Gradually, however, the Charter of the United Nations was painfully evolved, with damaging concessions. The central issue was the extent of the veto to be held by the Great Powers. The smaller powers distrusted it altogether, while the Soviet wished it to be available to stop any matter being even discussed in the Security Council. In the end a compromise was reached. Another main issue was the fate of non-self-governing territories, for which the theory of 'trusteeship' was, not without a good deal of conflict, worked out. Field Marshal Smuts,* in the end, 'thought the whole world could reasonably look forward to an era of security from war, in so far as the three Great Powers were all, broadly speaking, satisfied Powers'.[10]

Two of Buchman's friends offered to entertain any of the delegates who wanted to meet with him. Over lunches and dinners in their home, or in the Fairmont Hotel, where he would watch and meet the delegates, Buchman heard many contradictory views aired. One day he lunched with Bishop Bell of Chichester and John Foster Dulles, who told him that the Russians had only temporarily put aside the concept of world revolution. That night at dinner he heard that a leading British diplomat was equally convinced the Russians would not return to world revolution, but wanted to work loyally through whatever organisation was set up by the Conference, an opinion which Halifax shared.[11] Sitting in the Fairmont Hotel he watched Molotov with his bodyguard of eight move with a wedge-like unity through the lobby; he also saw the diplomats for whom social contacts and the autograph hunters had the biggest attraction.

Out of one private dinner party came a request from a group of delegates for a special performance of *The Forgotten Factor*. A committee

---

* Prime Minister of South Africa and a member of the British War Cabinet.

drawn from ten countries asked for it to be put on the official programme, and this was arranged for 3 June.

General Carlos Romulo of the Philippines, chairman of his country's delegation, who had for weeks been a thorn in the side of the British delegation because of his attitude on trusteeship, headed the committee with the British diplomat, A. R. K. Mackenzie. In introducing the play to the audience, General Romulo said, 'I see many of my fellow-delegates here, and that fills me with joy because what you see on the stage tonight is something that can be transferred to our conference rooms.' Many agreed with him. Adlai Stevenson told one of Buchman's friends how 'Scotty' Reston of the *New York Times* had said to him afterwards, 'This is what your old conference needs. You could do with some of it up in the "Penthouse"' (where Secretary of State Stettinius, Eden, Molotov and others met for private bargaining sessions).[12]

Romulo himself was as good as his word. After seeing *The Forgotten Factor* at its first showing, he completely changed the tone of his next speech on trusteeship. When he had finished speaking, he passed a note to Mackenzie with the words, '*The Forgotten Factor?*' Alistair Cooke reported that, as the conference dragged on, journalists had been listing the unsolved issues which were preventing them from going home. 'The list last night was formidable, but now to the astonishment of delegates and press alike, it would seem that Dr Evatt* has undergone a personality change and General Romulo has unaccountably fallen in love with the British.'[13]

From friendships made during the three months in San Francisco came invitations to Buchman to visit Saudi Arabia, Syria, Lebanon, Iraq and India. Field Marshal Smuts, however, had picked up a rumour in London and warned his secretary, Henry Cooper, an old friend of Buchman's, 'not to get in too deep as he was told MRA had fascist leanings'. Cooper, unshaken, took answering information back to his master.

When Buchman celebrated his sixty-seventh birthday in the Century Club at the beginning of June, Indian, Chinese, Middle Eastern, South American, Greek, Yugoslav, British and French delegates came to greet him. Carl Hambro had left to accompany his King back to Norway, but Rudolf Holsti, again Foreign Minister of Finland, had just arrived and was present. Rear-Admiral Sir Edward Cochrane presented a pledge on behalf of a thousand servicemen to raise, in the next six months, $50,000 for Buchman's use 'in memory of those who have given their lives' on many battlefronts. Their message to Buchman read in part: 'In the war of arms your vision of Moral Re-Armament has shown us what we are

---

* Australian Minister of External Affairs.

fighting for. In the war of ideas MRA has spearheaded the battle to restore moral standards and the guidance of God to men and nations. On the beaches of Dunkirk and Normandy, on the shell-swept mountains of Italy, on the coral shores of Pacific isles, on the war-torn soil of Asia, through stormy seas and flak-filled skies, your promise not to turn back has given us the steel to advance to victory.' Buchman was moved to tears.

The San Francisco Conference ended. After being warmly welcomed by President Truman at the final session reception on 26 June, Buchman left for Mackinac.

En route, he and his party called on 'Poppa' Globin, the ex-bootlegger who had lent them his casino at Lake Tahoe five years earlier. '"Poppa" wept when he saw Frank,' recorded one of the party. 'Then he put on a large steak dinner for us all.' 'All complimentary!' Buchman insisted in telling the story.

Further adventures ensued when they boarded their train. Buchman had wired a friend's grandmother to meet them during their stop at Omaha, Nebraska, if she would like to do so. 'Frank and I ventured on to the platform,' notes Martin. 'His policy was to send me to every likely looking lady over seventy – and then just to every lady over seventy. Drawing a number of blanks he reduced the age to sixty and despatched me to do the rounds again. The expression of some of the attendant husbands, as I ignored them and inquired if their wives were Mrs Thomas Hunter, had to be seen to be believed. Finally, Frank pointed out one more lady, but as I approached I recognised her as someone we had already tried. Only then Frank was satisfied and we retired to the train again.'[14]

Next day, in Chicago, Martin continues, Buchman went on 'one of his gigantic handkerchief shopping benders'. 'Once every two years or so he buys them in bulk for birthday gifts for the team. He begins by asking for a few handkerchiefs, and goes through the whole stock rejecting until he finds one he likes. Then he says, "How many do you have of this?" The answer invariably is, "How many can you use?" To which he says, "Oh, about ten or twelve dozen." The attendant either faints or does business. The price goes down, the obsequiousness mounts and Frank leaves, generally with two gross of handkerchiefs. "What do you need so many for?" asked the girl today. "Oh, I have a lot of poor people I give them to as presents!" replies Frank blandly – and accurately.'[15]

INTO THE POST-WAR WORLD

The 1945 Mackinac assembly lasted from 1 July to the end of the first week in November. On arrival Buchman was greeted by a large company of teenagers who had come back from a nationwide tour with two plays which they had written and produced. He wanted Artur Rodzinski, who was there with his wife Halina, to meet them, as he realised that they could probably get through to him when no one else could. Rodzinski was reluctant because, as he told everyone there later, he had, in spite of decisions made at the time when Halina and his son had been 'miraculously saved' in childbirth, 'got confused about all four standards'. Two of the youngsters came to invite him to their play. He told them he was unwell. 'Popski, you're all right. We've got your number,' one of them said.

'They were right,' Rodzinski told the assembly next morning. 'They had my number. I was ashamed not to go. The readiness of those youngers to lead a God-guided life, to do without what older people call the spice of life. I had had it, so I admired them. This morning I had clear guidance. My disobedience. God talks to me all the time, but I don't obey. We had a quiet time after breakfast. Frank walked in just as we were finishing. He smiled, and I knew he knew everything which had happened.'[1]

It was also while the Rodzinskis were at Mackinac that the newly formed Mackinac Singers gave their first performance. Rodzinski's comments encouraged Buchman to make wide use of this chorus, singing its own songs, as part of the growing array of productions and publications being deployed by his team.

Various Allied officers now found that their duties somehow led through Mackinac. One of them was Edward Howell, a Wing Commander in the Royal Air Force. After being seriously wounded in Crete, he had been imprisoned in Athens, and, although gravely ill and without the use of either arm, had escaped over the walls and covered the length of Greece on foot. This escape plan had started in hospital when he recalled his brother David's belief that people could be guided by God and experimented with listening. On his return to London, Churchill had had him to dinner to hear about it and he told Churchill how he was guided from point to point, at one stage following a star. 'That was how I escaped from the Boers,' commented the Prime Minister. Howell told his story at Mackinac, where he was meeting Buchman for the first time.*

During a birthday dinner for Bernard Hallward, the Canadian who had repaid $12,000 to the Customs in 1932, the end of hostilities in the Pacific was reported on the radio. Buchman, his voice shaking, announced simply, 'The war is ended.' Then everyone at table said the Lord's Prayer together. In the evening they met in the barn. 'There is only one war left now – the war of ideas against materialism,' Buchman said. 'Now let us ask God to show us together our part in world reconstruction.' Then he prayed: 'We pray for the entire world, especially for Japan. Hold them in the hollow of Thy hand, and give them Thy peace and freedom. May future years be undimmed in God's Holy Spirit in Germany. Give her the answer of sound homes, teamwork in industry and a united nation. For the Allies we pray that they may be kept by Thy Holy Spirit pure and unsullied in victory. May the Lord bless and keep them all, and all of you, and give His peace, now and for ever.'

More and more friends and colleagues from Europe began to arrive. Swiss and French were the first, followed by Dutch, Danes and Norwegians. They brought news of heroism under Nazi occupation and in the Resistance. Buchman was keen as well to see some of his British friends, but travel from there was still strictly controlled by the Government. On 21 July word came of a Foreign Office cable to the Washington Embassy that a Member of Parliament, Sir George Courthope, had requested that a group might join Buchman in the States: 'In view of President Truman's well-known interest in this work, does the Ambassador see any reason why they should not come?' A cable had gone back from Lord Halifax, now Ambassador in Washington, that there was no objection at the American end, and permission had been given. Foreign Office minutes now available show that this was the conclusion of a rather devious delaying action in some sections of the Foreign Office. Halifax had, in fact, strongly supported a similar request made by Lord Salisbury to Anthony Eden the previous year. Eden had written across Salisbury's letter in red ink, 'Surely these are deplorable people? and it is staggering that Lord S should wish them well.' A minute of 3 August 1944 recording Eden's view added that since travel restrictions had been mitigated, 'the delegates would probably obtain exit permits if they applied for them' but 'there is no need to inform Lord Salisbury of that'. Permission had

* Howell tells his story in *Escape to Live* (Longmans, 1947, Grosvenor, 1981).

[331]

been refused.[2] This time the weight of favourable American opinion evidently determined the Foreign Office to grant permits for a delegation of five.[3]

They arrived at Mackinac on 13 September. They were Roland Wilson who, at the age of 32, had been left as Secretary of the Oxford Group in Britain when Buchman went to America six years earlier; Buchman's old friend Arthur Baker, chief of *The Times* parliamentary staff; Peter Howard, whom he had never met; George Light; and Andrew Strang, a whole-time worker with MRA who had been caught by German armies in Scandinavia and spent the war in detention camp. Buchman was ready an hour ahead to go and meet them. On the dock, sitting in his ramshackle carriage with Brookes, a friend's black chauffeur, beside him, he waited patiently, a curiously unpretentious figure. When finally the British arrived, Buchman introduced each to the head of the local ferry service before greeting them himself with tears in his eyes. The next day turned into a combined meeting and large family party.

Another visitor from Europe was a Dutch Catholic priest, sent by his Archbishop to 'observe' Buchman's work. On his way he had allowed himself to be trapped by a reporter into making some rather sweeping statements about Moral Re-Armament, and some of those at Mackinac regarded him with veiled suspicion. After he had been there about a week Buchman called in a few of his friends and said that he felt Father Frits should lead the morning meeting. They all raised objections. Would he *want* to speak? What would he say? Who would he get to speak with him? But Buchman held to his thought, and in the end a number of his colleagues met with Father Frits and suggested he might speak.

'Yes,' said the Father, 'I have things I would like to say.'

'We thought you might lead the meeting,' they added.

'Well, I don't know about that, but we can ask God.'

So, after a song from the Mackinac Singers, Father Frits began: 'I thought I would say things just out of my heart, very simple things. My heart tells me to, and my reason tells me not to. As I am trained to let reason prevail, it is difficult for me.

'When the bishop speaks we obey. I assure you it was not in a very nice spirit that I agreed to come. On first coming I tried to be an honest Catholic onlooker. You simply can't look on here. Soon I felt utterly humble and ashamed. For my impression is that this is a great school of love. You cannot resist it. The first thing I did when I went to confession on Sunday was to make a resolution to imitate the quality of life I had seen.

'I am convinced people like you can play an immense part in the unification of all Christians. Charity always unites. Never have I seen it more clearly than in this place. I had expected, maybe, not to hear Christ's name mentioned as it should be. But it was not true. I found here the real living of the mystery of Christ.'[4]*

The Swiss who had come over made what was perhaps to prove the most far-reaching decision of all. Their time at Mackinac crystallised in their minds the idea that Europe needed a similar centre where some of the wounds of the continent might be healed. And where better than in Switzerland? This idea had originated, the previous year, with Philippe Mottu, who was working in the Swiss Foreign Office. It worked powerfully in two young engineers, Robert Hahnloser and Erich Peyer, who accompanied Mottu on this, his second visit. The three of them went back to Switzerland to start turning dream into reality.

From Mackinac Buchman and two hundred others, including many from Europe, returned through Minnesota to Seattle. En route Buchman took his friends to see the home and grave of his uncle, Aaron Greenwalt, who died in the Civil War. Then he obtained special permission to take them through Yellowstone Park in winter, where they saw elk, deer, buffalo and mountain sheep. Buchman was, as ever, an eager sightseer, and spotted the sheep before the forest ranger with whom he was driving.

In Seattle it was probably a sign of his returning strength that Buchman was seized with impatience at what seemed to him inadequate and unimaginative planning. True, Dave Beck of the Teamsters was putting Buchman and others of the party up at the Olympic Hotel**, but there were no plans to see Beck or to 'personalise' the city. 'It was one of those days when everything went wrong or felt as if it did,' reads his secretary's diary. 'One by one we were mowed down by his wrath . . . Frank moved quietly like an avenging thunder cloud among the faithful.' Next day, 'A few rifts appeared in the clouds of yesterday, but they swiftly passed and Frank was greatly dissatisfied. We all walked, like Agag, delicately . . . The fight to meet the Governor, Mayor and Dave Beck began to be carried to a successful issue. The Mayor agreed to see twenty of the team tomorrow, but Frank forcibly pointed out that there were 200 and he should see all of them.'[5]

Buchman was now using six plays, ringing the changes at will. They had been raised to a high standard of performance through the participation of professionals, now turned whole-time workers, like Phyllis Konstam, Marion Clayton and her husband Bob Anderson, Cece Broadhurst, Howard Reynolds and others. They were accompanied by the Mackinac Singers under the leadership of the Edinburgh musician, George Fraser.

* Father Frits, Frederic van der Meer, later dedicated his book *Augustine the Bishop* (Sheed and Ward, 1961) to Bernard Hallward.

** Beck had asked the hotel manager for ten double rooms. 'Very difficult, Mr Beck,' the manager replied. 'I wouldn't ask you personally unless it was very difficult; if it was easy I'd get someone else to do it,' said Beck. He got them.

Peter Howard often introduced the plays, and sometimes there were speakers afterwards. In one city, under Buchman's personal drilling, twenty-seven spoke in twenty-two minutes.

So a versatile and trained force moved through Detroit, St Paul, Seattle, Vancouver, Victoria, Salem, San Francisco and down to Los Angeles for Christmas. Meanwhile, word had come that General George Marshall had decided to release all MRA full-time men from the armed forces immediately so that they could resume their life's work. On 26 December, the first six arrived together at Los Angeles airport. Buchman, in tears, greeted them in silence. Then he turned towards the cars saying, 'Well, you're home. And now let's get into the fight.'

According to Reginald Hale, Buchman told them sadly that he could never return to Europe. 'He was nearing seventy, his health was frail and his right hand paralysed. But it was not that which made him hesitate,' he writes. 'All too clearly he saw the immense task of reawakening faith in a hate-fragmented Europe ... Then the Servicemen had come home bringing stories of bridgeheads which MRA-trained soldiers had built in country after liberated country. Within a week he was planning to move to Europe.'[6]

Another element which influenced him was the publication of the salient points of the Gestapo report of 1942, *Die Oxford-Gruppenbewegung*, in the British press. A letter in *The Times* in December from a distinguished all-party group* gave details of the report and commented, 'The whole report throws an interesting light on the Nazi mind, as well as finally dispelling the widespread misrepresentations which have been circulated about this Christian movement.' The letter concluded, 'It is vital that we should understand the spiritual foundations of democracy as clearly as did our enemies, and that we should sustain with all our strength what they feared and hoped to destroy.'[7] DeWitt Mackenzie, the leading foreign affairs columnist of the Associated Press, had been in London that December, had obtained a sight of the original report and wrote a column in a similar vein which was carried widely in North America.[8]

To many reasonable people this disposed of a misrepresentation which had followed Buchman and his people on both sides of the Atlantic. But the lie did not die easily. It became known that copies of the Gestapo document had been in the hands of British Intelligence for at least a year before *The Times* letter appeared. An intelligence report, dated 7 January 1945, came to light in which the writer had stated that it would be better if

---

* Lord Ammon, Deputy Leader of the House of Commons; Harold E. Clay, Chairman of the London Labour Party; Lord Courthope, President of the National Union of Conservative Associations; the Bishop of Lichfield; Sir Lynden Macassey, Chairman of Reuters; Sir Cyril Norwood, President of St John's College, Oxford; Sir David Ross, Provost of Oriel College, Oxford.

the Gestapo report did not fall into the hands of Moral Re-Armament, as it would destroy the allegations made against them. However, a copy of the report was found in the offices of the Haut-Rhin hydro-electric works, which had been used by Gestapo officers between 1940 and 1944, and was sent by an engineer in the company, Pierre Koechlin, to Paris and finally to MRA's London headquarters. Hence the letter in *The Times*.

As late as February 1947 *Time* was questioning the authenticity of the document. At this point I took the copy which had reached London through Alsace to Lieutenant-General Sir Frederick Browning, then the Military Secretary at the War Office, and asked him to check its reliability. He promised to pass it on to General Templar, then head of Military Intelligence, and a few days later I received Browning's official reply.

'The enclosed document is authentic,' he wrote. 'It only goes up, in its historical survey, till 1939. It was published by the German Secret Service Agency who were responsible for SS publications. You can rest assured there is nothing phoney about this document.'[9]

During March Buchman and his team spent time together preparing to return to Europe. One day, on a friend's country ranch near Los Angeles, amid the orange groves with the distant snows of Mount Baldy as backdrop, they talked together of the needs and challenge of that devastated continent which many of them called home. The seven years together in America had altered them. All, Americans and Europeans alike, were more mature. They had been through times of personal testing and had seen many tough situations tackled. Now they were determined, God helping them, to do what they could to prevent the post-war world from being drawn into the cycle of chaos and revenge which had followed the First World War. Buchman put to them his highest hopes. 'You have crossed the divide. You are going back to change the policy of governments with the statesmen. You will upturn the philosophy of government with a practical message simply applied.' They must think in terms of the nation: that was the statesman's responsibility and the Churches were not yet sounding that note.

He could not see far into the future, he said, but of one thing he was sure: 'Labour led by God must lead the world, otherwise Marx's materialism will take over.' Then he added, 'But Marxism may capture the spirit of Christ. Some of you may be working in Moscow one day. We must be ready.'

Buchman decided to sail for Southampton on the *Queen Mary* in late April 1946. Passages were extremely hard to come by but in March he told

[335]

John Vickers, who looked after Moral Re-Armament's travel arrangements in America throughout the war, to go to New York and get 100 berths. 'I have only got six places at the moment,' Buchman said, 'and I want to see who I can invite.' Vickers approached the shipping company on arrival in New York with this outrageous request. 'Certainly,' replied the company's representative. 'The ship has been de-requisitioned this morning.'

In the end a party of a hundred and ten sailed on April 24. Their fares were paid by a New York stockbroker, by no means a millionaire, who said he wanted to try and match the sacrifice of those who had contributed so much to America through the war. To them and those who had come to bid them farewell in New York, Buchman said, 'We have learned much. We are in a global effort to win the world to our Lord and Saviour Jesus Christ. There is your ideology. It is the whole message of the Gospel of Jesus Christ. That message in its entirety is the only last hope.'

Then he spoke the lines which meant so much to him:

> Oh, Thou best Gift of Heaven,
> Thou who Thyself has given,
> For Thou hast died:
> This hast Thou done for me –
> What have I done for Thee,
> Thou Crucified?

'WHERE ARE THE GERMANS?'

Buchman was returning to a Britain much altered both by war and by its aftermath of austerity. The circumstances of his own work in that country had altered too. Now he was coming into a headquarters where both administration and entertainment were being wholly handled by his full-time colleagues. He first set foot in 45 Berkeley Square as a fully furnished house on the afternoon of 30 April 1946. In the war years, its cellars had been used as air-raid shelters, its ball-room converted into a small theatre and the rest of the house sparsely furnished. In the last month, gifts and loans of carpets, pictures and furniture had flowed in from all over the country. On arrival, Buchman sat in the hall beneath the stair-well, while friends who had not seen him for seven years crowded the hall, stairs and landings up to the fourth floor.

Some were shocked at his appearance – he had arrived walking with a stick, instead of with his old, vigorous stride – but he did not behave like an invalid then or in the weeks ahead. For two hours that afternoon he greeted people individually and then spoke to all those gathered to meet him. Next day he lunched with Lord Hardinge, had tea with the Courthopes and dinner with Henry Martin, editor of the Press Association. In the following days he saw Percy Cudlipp, editor of the *Daily Herald*, Lord Lytton, Tod Sloan and Lady Antrim, attended a party in East London, had two lunches with groups of Members of Parliament, and entertained the Indian cricket team to supper.

The first weekend he spent at Peter Howard's farm in Suffolk. He much enjoyed his visit to this 'wholesome place', and insisted on visiting some of Howard's friends and farm-workers in their homes in Lavenham. To attend seven weddings among his full-time colleagues he travelled to the Cotswolds, Cheshire, Edinburgh, Glasgow and Worcester, and on one occasion agreed to take the whole service, after he had incautiously told the pair that he would do anything they liked. Their Methodist service was unfamiliar to him, so that the happy couple had to prompt him on the questions he was to ask them, but he came through strongly with the words, 'Whom God has joined together, let no *man* set asunder.' At the reception he told them, 'That is what comes of asking an old man to marry you!' When the new wife phoned that night and said life was 'wonderful', his earthy retort was, 'See it stays wonderful.' While he was in Glasgow he paid a visit to Henry Drummond's grave at Stirling. All this activity, however, was punctuated by days of rest, and planning sessions often took place around his bed.

Before leaving for a campaign in Northern Ireland with *The Forgotten Factor* Buchman also visited Cambridge and Oxford, where he heard the Master of St Peter's Hall state in the University Sermon, 'During the last twenty-five years there has been going out from Oxford not only a Christian ideology, but men and women fired with the conception of remaking the world.'[1] The student magazine, *Isis*, had already produced an editorial for the twenty-fifth anniversary of Buchman's first coming to Oxford. 'Our interest in the Oxford Group is aroused', it said, 'because we feel their opponents, so vitriolic and yet so vague, have held the floor too long and failed to substantiate their charges . . . Certainly Oxford has no need to be ashamed of any real spiritual crusade that she fosters – she has nursed many in her time and, indeed, what could be more fitting for a University with the motto *Dominus Illuminatio Mea*?'[2]

The old opponents, Tom Driberg and A. P. (now Sir Alan) Herbert, were soon in the field. Two days after Buchman's arrival Driberg, speaking in the House of Commons, criticised the Home Secretary, Chuter Ede, for permitting 'this man, who has never repudiated his expressed admiration of Hitler and deceived the public by putting false entries into *Who's Who*,* to enter the country. This was dismissed by the Home Secretary with the words, ' "The wind bloweth where it listeth"; I am not prepared to put any obstruction in the way.' Driberg then gave notice that he would raise the matter 'on the adjournment'.[3]

The adjournment debate, strictly limited in time, took place two months later, on 5 July. Driberg deployed his argument at such length that only a few minutes remained for other comment. In this time Herbert briefly stated his accusation that Buchman had falsified his entries to *Who's Who*, while Quintin Hogg (later Lord Hailsham) ridiculed both

---

* Buchman's alleged falsification of *Who's Who* is examined in detail in J. P. Thornton-Duesbery's *The Open Secret of MRA*, pp. 82–3. The main charge was that Buchman had stated that he studied at Cambridge University, 1921–22, and that this was inaccurate, because Westminster College, where Buchman was received at that time as a guest in the Senior Common Room, was not technically a part of the University but an independent Presbyterian theological college. 'Even so,' Driberg later stated, 'the entry might have been justifiable if Buchman attended University lectures: Herbert ascertained from the University authorities that he never asked permission to do so.' (Driberg: *The Mystery of Moral Re-Armament*, p. 51.) This was, of course, because Buchman was invited personally by Professor Oman to attend his lectures at the request of Principal Mackenzie of Hartford Seminary. Buchman did attend Oman's lectures (see p. 91).

Driberg's and Herbert's arguments as 'tittle-tattle which would not do credit to the senior common room of a girls' school'. 'What are we coming to in this country if we act on such grounds?' he asked. The Home Secretary stood firm, and censured Driberg for 'taking so long to develop his case that it was impossible for other Members to intervene'.[4]

This was the last public attack which Herbert made on Buchman. Acknowledging his lack of success, he remarked in his autobiography, 'Like Mr Churchill, I cannot maintain my hatreds for ever.'[5] Driberg, on the other hand, continued his onslaughts until Buchman's death and after.

In his first weeks back in Britain Buchman was particularly interested to talk with two whole-time MRA workers who, during the war, had enlisted to serve in the coal-mines. While still in America he had heard from another former miner, Will Locke, who had entertained him in 1937 when he was Lord Mayor of Newcastle upon Tyne. Locke had been spending the previous months travelling the coalfields by bus and on foot, and had written, 'The industry is not in a healthy state. There is discontent which is above man's power to alter, but we must try and reach the rank and file as best we can. The MRA spirit is needed. There is great promise in the Doncaster area where a group of six mines, each employing 1,500–2,000 men, have got hold of the subject quite correctly, and men at the coal-face and the officials are working finely together. We are fighting fit and going on: no rusting for us. And what about yourself, young man? We hope your health is equal to the foraging that must go on . . .'[6]

Britain had many problems – one-third of her dwellings destroyed or damaged; industrial plant run down and overseas assets of four billion pounds credit in 1939 transformed into a debt of nearly three billion; the impossibility of increasing exports quickly to the necessary seventy-five per cent above pre-war; the need, as the Soviet Union's stance became clear, to maintain a million and a half people under arms. Yet Buchman's thought, after receiving Locke's letter, was, 'Coal is the key.'

Here, unconsciously, he was in tune with Ernest Bevin, the Foreign Minister in the new Labour Government, who told the miners, 'Give me thirty million tons of coal for export and I will give you a foreign policy.' The national miners' leaders were also appealing for increased production. But exhortation does not dig coal. Absenteeism, for example, had risen from 6.4 per cent in 1939 to 16.3 per cent in 1945. 'It is my duty to warn the House', said the Minister of Fuel and Power, Emmanuel Shinwell, in the Commons in January, 'that the existing position contains the elements of industrial disaster.'[7]

Buchman believed that he had, in the play *The Forgotten Factor*, a weapon which could be useful in this situation. On 13 May he put it on in

[339]

the City of London at the Cripplegate Theatre, which stood unharmed amid the ruins around St Paul's Cathedral. To it came miners from several coalfields, among them four from the Doncaster area. These men convinced their colleagues to invite the play to the mining village of Carcroft, where six weeks later two thousand people connected with the industry came to see it.

One Doncaster miner wrote to Buchman, 'This play has been the main topic of conversation at our colliery this week despite the fact that it was Doncaster races on Friday and Saturday,' and added, '. . . miners at our colliery . . . agree that if the spirit of the play is put into practice, teamwork in the Doncaster mines will become the pattern for the country. Therefore if it can make tough miners feel like that, it ought to be shown to every miner in the country, both management and men.'[8] Another miner and his wife wrote to thank Buchman for his visit to their home.[9]

The *Doncaster Free Press* commented, 'Somebody last week threw a pebble in the pond that is industrial England, and the ripples will reach far.'[10] The very next week one of the largest pits reported that production had risen from 10,000 to 16,000 tons. The secret, apparently, was the change in a dictatorial manager, commonly called 'the pocket battleship', who had apologised to the men after seeing *The Forgotten Factor*. The colliery agent at Brodsworth Main, who showed Buchman around the workings for an hour, commented, 'The play raised the finer feelings of all sections.'[11]

Buchman felt *The Forgotten Factor* should be staged in London, where the Westminster Theatre, an elegant building with 600 seats, had for some time been the property of a Moral Re-Armament trust. It had been bought, as a living memorial to the men and women of Moral Re-Armament who had died in war service, for £132,500. In April, while Buchman was still in America, Roland Wilson wrote to him, 'The theatre is ours and is paid for, all but a very small sum. A soldier came in yesterday from Wales. His father, a miner, had saved £200 to send his son to college. The soldier asked if it might be given to the Fund to buy the theatre. A number of servicemen have given their gratuities, and gifts have come from all kinds of people, including trades union leaders, dockers and miners.'[12] Altogether 2,857 people contributed. It was to become available in October, at which point, Buchman felt, people from all sides of the coal industry should be invited.

In Switzerland, at the same time, another building was being bought which was to play an even larger part in Buchman's life and planning. True to their thought the previous summer Philippe Mottu and Robert Hahnloser, with their colleague Erich Peyer and others, had been looking for a place where people from the divided countries of Europe could meet in an atmosphere similar to Mackinac. After a prolonged search, they came upon the near-derelict Caux Palace Hotel, 3,000 feet above Montreux, which Buchman had visited during his trip to Europe forty years before. Now it was no longer an economic proposition and was due for demolition. Some sixty Swiss families took counsel together and, in a notable leap of faith, decided that they would buy the hotel – which had cost six million Swiss francs to build – for 1,050,000 francs (then around £130,000), the first instalment of 450,000 francs to be paid within a matter of weeks. By prodigious sacrifice – some sold their homes, others put in all their savings – they succeeded in meeting the deadline. Buchman left London for Caux on 15 July.

In the first nineteen days of July a hundred Swiss backed by international volunteers set to work to refurbish the building, with its 500-bed capacity and magnificent reception rooms. During the war the hotel had at first been inhabited by Royal Air Force and other Allied personnel who had escaped into Switzerland, and later by families of refugees. The kitchens were black with smoke, the lift wells clogged with rubbish and most of the locks broken. Every wall had to be washed.

Typical of the voluntary effort was that of a retired locksmith. After ten days he announced to Hahnloser's reconstruction team that he had so far mended 640 locks, but there were 1,220 more to do. 'It's impossible. I just can't do it in the time.'

'All we can do', said Hahnloser, 'is to listen to God and let Him show us the way out.' After a few minutes' silence, the old locksmith suddenly said, 'Take me to a phone.' He telephoned his home, and his sons and grandsons shut the family business for a fortnight, came to Caux and finished the job.

When Buchman entered the front hall it was shining with some of the pristine beauty which he remembered. With him were a party from Britain and America. Gathered in the hall were old friends from France, Scandinavia, Holland, Italy and Switzerland, many of whom had fought against or lost relatives at the hands of the Germans.

Buchman stood in the door looking from face to face in the ring of welcome, deeply moved. Then he said, 'Where are the Germans? You will never rebuild Europe without the Germans.'

'The effect was stunning,' writes Reginald Hale. 'Shock, outrage, anger showed on many faces. Frank passed on to his room leaving consternation behind him. Supper that night was a subdued meal and many were strangely silent.'[13]

People had been brought face to face with Christ's command, 'Love your enemies.' Many found the power to do so. Then the technical difficulties had to be faced and overcome. No Germans were allowed to leave their country without Allied permission, and few, if any, had the means to do so if permitted. Work with the Allied authorities was immediately initiated, and sixteen Germans, including Moni von Cramon and the widows of two men executed for taking part in the plot to kill Hitler, arrived that first year.

The inherent difficulties of this operation were revealed even in the attitude of some of Moni von Cramon's non-German friends from the pre-war years, who went so far as to ask Buchman to send her away from Caux as she was 'no longer trustworthy'. Instead he took her with him to Locarno when he went there from Caux for a rest, as always with a group of colleagues. 'There,' according to Frau von Cramon's daughter, 'everything blew up. Frank listened to it all, and then sat silent. Then he said, "Feed her, clothe her, love her." And a Swiss friend took her home and took care of her.'

All the rooms at Caux were full for two months, many of the visitors being workers and their leaders, most numerous among them British coal-miners who had established a special fund for the purpose.

On 22 October *The Forgotten Factor* opened at the Westminster Theatre. To begin with, Buchman sat in a box each evening, watching not the play but the audience. Busloads of miners came from several coalfields, as well as managers and, after the nationalisation of the mines at the beginning of 1947, Coal Board officials. That winter in Britain was the coldest for sixty years and 8,000,000 extra tons of coal were needed. Acknowledgements of the effect of the play began to flow in. Tom Collier, the Coal Board's Area Labour Officer for North Staffordshire, said at a meeting in the Westminster Theatre on 11 May, 'If the Coal Board would send this play round the country, their problems would be at an end. A week ago I told our people that with the help of the spirit of this play the five-day week* would succeed . . . Now, in five days, more coal has come from the pits than in any other week for many years.'** Speaking with Collier was Harold Heath, Union Committee member at Chatterley Whitfield Pit, the fifth largest in Britain. 'We hit our six-day target in four and a half days,' he said. 'A thousand of our men saw *The Forgotten Factor* last week.'

The ensuing campaign in the coalfields, initiated both by management and trade unionists, centred on performances of *The Forgotten Factor*, was to continue for the next four years. Independent evaluations of its effect were numerous. For example, the editor of *The Spectator* wrote in his column, 'Tribute should be paid where tribute is due. I heard this week of a striking impetus to coal production. . . . Some 300 miners from a pit went to London to see *The Forgotten Factor*. The result, I am assured, is

* An experimental replacement for the six-day week.
** cf. *Birmingham Post*, 12 May 1947: 'Five-Day Week Brings More Coal in Four Areas: North Staffordshire Pits Lead the Coalfields'.

that the pit regularly tops production for its region. The story comes to me from no MRA quarter, but from someone who knows the pit and pitmen particularly well.'[14]

After a year *The Birmingham Post*, writing of the West Midlands, stated, 'The new spirit is so revealing itself in increased output that, according to one computation based on recent figures, if the same results were obtained in all Britain's coalfields, the target of 200,000,000 tons a year would be exceeded by 30,000,000 tons.'[15] Tom Beecham, Area Production Manager for the Rhondda, where 15,000 miners saw the play, said in April 1949, 'Production in this area rose seven per cent, while it rose two per cent in the whole Welsh coal-field. It has had a real effect on relationships, which is showing itself in negotiations between the Board and the Union. There is not the acrimony that there was. Men are quick to see any change in management.'[16]

Buchman prized the resulting practical changes for their own sake – for the increased wages for the miners and the lessening of hardship to the country at large. But as he insisted to his team, 'Remember, whatever I do, I am out to teach the soul.' By this he meant that he regarded the maturing of the individual as basic, first for its own sake and as the essential raw material of larger improvements. He realised that it was often in a time of crisis that people were ready to open their hearts to the Holy Spirit and, also, that busy public figures often only paid sufficient attention to the possibility of change in themselves when they saw results of a practical kind in their own spheres of interest. *The Forgotten Factor* led to many crucial personal talks. Christ was not mentioned in the script but Dr Edward Woods, Bishop of Lichfield, commented after a performance, 'I saw Christ on the stage and thank God no one had to say so.'[17]

After the first two months of the run at the Westminster, Buchman, on medical advice, started to travel south in search of a warmer climate. On 16 December, at Folkestone, he was met by an obliging dockside official with a wheel-chair. Buchman waved it aside, insisting that John Caulfeild – a robust ex-captain from the US Air Force – was the invalid, so that the unfortunate Caulfeild was pushed to the passport officer, through the customs, and on to the dock. The passage was rough, and though Buchman, with his Pennsylvania Dutch stubbornness, insisted on sitting upright in a chair, he was obviously glad when it was over.

In Switzerland, where he spent Christmas, he met Philippe Etter, who was to be the next President and Home Minister. Etter promised to visit Caux officially the following summer. 'Europe has lost its soul,' he said, 'and it was its soul which gave it the leadership among the nations. Caux is going to be a great centre of spiritual strength.'

Christmas was spent peacefully in Berne. A sparsely decorated, candlelit tree was put up in his hotel sitting-room, and he and his friends sat quietly around it in the evenings. 'One of my earliest memories – I must have been one or two – is being carried into a room where there was a lighted tree,' Buchman said. On Christmas night Buchman's thoughts, as they listened for guidance together, were, 'You will be spoken to in no uncertain way this next year. Caux a miracle of the first order. Germany will come into her own. Go to Ganda with the lightest touch. Make our way slowly and gradually.'

For, in spite of the bitter weather, Buchman was not to reach the sunny south. He had accepted the invitation of Eugene von Teuber and his aged parents to spend the next months at their medieval castle, Castel Ganda, in Appiano near Bolzano. Gene, an ebullient character whose family had deep roots in Austria and Italy, had emigrated to America twenty-five years before and there become a full-time colleague of Buchman. His parents had just been released from a Communist prison camp in Czechoslovakia, and opened their old home for the occasion. The Tyrolean countryside, which Buchman had long known and loved, was in deep snow when he and his party arrived, and remained so for many months. His doctor and friends were anxious for his health, but in fact he kept well and stayed at Ganda, apart from two visits to Rome, until early May. The senior von Teubers described these weeks as 'coming out of hell into heaven'.[18]

The Tyrol was bitterly split between the Austrian and Italian elements of the population, a bitterness which had been endemic since the Treaty of Versailles had transferred the territory from Austria to Italy. Then, more recently, there had been the German war-time occupation, and a number of German soldiers were still hiding in the mountains. The Italian military authorities still retained British liaison officers on their staff. The area was a minefield of delicate feelings. In particular, the old Austrian families and the Italian officials and military were hardly on speaking terms.

All parties, however, came to see Buchman, beginning with the Austrian families who naturally called upon the von Teubers, and going on to the Italian mayor and the regional commander, General Negroni, who turned out to have on his staff a British major who had seen *The Forgotten Factor* in London and a sergeant major who had been concerned with Buchman's trip to Amman with Lady Minto in 1938. Inevitably the day came when all sides were invited to a party together. An atmosphere was created in which Buchman was able to tell how, forty years before, he had passed through that country, his heart consumed with bitterness against the managing committee of the hostel in Philadelphia and how, after going over the Simplon in a horse-drawn carriage and on to England, he had, at Keswick, been freed from his hatreds. The Mayor never forgot it and, when he later came to Caux, said he traced the new friendliness in the area to that day.

Buchman's first visit to Rome from Ganda began in mid-January. His thought, once again, was to move quietly: 'Let people come to you. No hint of pressure or suggestion to anyone. This is not the time to see the Pope.' He did want to see, among others, Count Lovera di Castiglione, a Papal Chamberlain who had written understanding articles about his work before the war, and the Foreign Minister, Count Sforza. Count Lovera was one of the first to see him, and during the conversation talked of Moral Re-Armament as 'the gateway to modern man'. One morning Buchman spent an hour with Giuseppe Saragat, the Vice-President of the Parliament and later President of Italy, who described their talk as 'the most important I have ever had because it dealt with fundamentals'. 'Yours is the real struggle for Europe – to give democracy a faith that will outlive the ideologies,' added the Socialist leader. Saragat's family remained in touch with Buchman until his death.

Randolfo Paccardi, the leader of the party to which Sforza belonged, asked Buchman what he could do for him. Buchman made no suggestion. Paccardi volunteered that he wanted him to meet Sforza, and this accordingly took place. Buchman had read Sforza's recent book with its references to 'Christian democracy', and the conversation turned on how this could be created in Europe.

Several Catholics in Buchman's party, which had now expanded to thirty, were received by Pope Pius XII. They mentioned their work to him and eagerly reported to Buchman that the Pope had blessed it. This pleased Buchman, who mistakenly believed that if enough loyal Catholics told the Pope that they worked with him, it would favourably influence the Church's attitude. He himself, however, politely refused suggestions from a number of well-placed persons who wanted to arrange for him to see the Holy Father. The *Manchester Guardian*[19] and the *Daily Worker*[20] reported from Rome that Buchman was holding a convention there and was trying to see the Pope. But the nearest thing to Buchman which entered the papal chambers was, in fact, his top hat, in the hand of Gene von Teuber, whose brown trilby Buchman considered inadequate for the occasion.

He did well to move cautiously. True, he had always had good relations with Catholic priests with whom he had been in contact. Far from taking anyone away from the Catholic Church, he had helped many to return to it. In the pre-war years, his work was mainly in Protestant countries, and Rome looked with sympathy on his activities there. The great Catholic countries were only marginally affected, and Bishops had been left to decide their attitudes according to how their local situations appeared to them. Some reacted negatively, but most were neutral or mildly favourable. *L'Osservatore Romano*, the organ of the Vatican, reporting a Moral Re-Armament meeting in Lausanne in 1937, had underlined the value of silent listening for God's will and the importance of people of all classes putting their faith into practice unitedly.[21] On the first anniversary of the launching of Moral Re-Armament, it headlined its report 'The supremacy of spiritual and moral values for the peace of the world'.[22]

Now, however, a new situation was about to arise. As, from the new centre at Caux, Buchman bent his energies to the reconciliation of Europe, and that trio of Catholic statesmen – Schuman of France, Adenauer of Germany and de Gasperi of Italy, together with their mentor the Italian priest, Don Sturzo – increasingly saw in Moral Re-Armament an idea which could supplement their efforts, the hierarchy in Rome began to feel the need to take up a definite attitude. The sight of a Lutheran drawing the faithful to Caux aroused suspicion – or at least caution – in the Holy Office, the institution which guarded the integrity of the faith. In the next few years, they were to come to conclusions which were to puzzle many Catholics who had found in Caux a new impetus to their faith, conclusions which were to take nearly two decades to reverse.

That, however, was in the future, and Buchman's next visit to Rome, five weeks after his return to Ganda, was at the invitation of Monsignor François Charrière, Bishop of Fribourg, Lausanne and Geneva, in whose diocese Caux was situated. He was taking 8,000 Swiss to Rome to attend the canonisation of the Swiss saint, Nicolas von Flüe, and invited Buchman and a party of his colleagues to be present. They were placed in excellent seats near the High Altar in St Peter's, and Buchman was fascinated by the story of the Saint and by the colour of the ceremony. In June, over Swiss radio, he spoke of the significance of the occasion, recalling how Saint Nicolas had become 'the most sought-after arbiter in affairs of state' and had saved Switzerland 'when the bitter quarrels of the cantons brought his country to the verge of civil war'. 'Truly he is a saint for our times, a model for the United Nations,' Buchman commented.[23]

The whole year had been a revelation to his European team of the difference between this post-war period and the days of the physically quicksilver Buchman they had known. Then, he had been in the lead of each campaign, moving from situation to situation and country to country 'with compact vigour – quietly like an express train', as one of his younger colleagues remarked. Now he was often to initiate some idea – like the work among coal-miners in Britain or the struggle to bring the German nation out into the world again – but to leave its execution to others. He had always professed that it was more important to teach ten people to do the work than to try to do ten people's work yourself. Now more than ever he had to learn to practise this, for his work, unrestricted by war, was breaking out in countries all across the world.

His trained people scattered to work in Japan, South Africa, the Middle East, and although they kept in touch by letter, they were out on their own and he seldom intervened. He himself never moved without a team; but it was one of many mobile units throughout the world, who would meet, annually or more often, at assemblies at Caux, Mackinac or elsewhere.

RECONCILIATION FROM CAUX

Five thousand people from some fifty countries went to Caux for the summer assembly in 1947. President Etter of Switzerland fulfilled his promise to make an official visit, and General Guisan, war-time commander of the Swiss Army, came three times. Others included the Prime Ministers of Denmark and Indonesia, Count Bernadotte of Sweden, the Smith-Mundt Committee of the United States Congress, and two hundred Italians, including twenty-six Members of Parliament and eight senior editors, representing all the major democratic parties.

The crowds were so great that another large hotel, the Grand Hotel, had to be bought to accommodate them. The unusual pattern of work at Caux attracted as much press attention as the numbers. Guests were encouraged to help in the running of the assembly – and Ministers and workers could end up preparing the vegetables or washing up together. Cartoonists and photographers had a field-day; but the Prior of the monastery of Kremsmünster found it natural. 'We Benedictines', he said, 'know that working together is the best way of tilling the soil of each other's minds.' A French anarchist declared with enthusiasm, 'I have seen anarchy actually lived out here!'

Asian visitors included G. L. Nanda, Labour Minister in Bombay state and later twice stop-gap Prime Minister of India, and U Tin Tut, the first Foreign Minister of independent Burma. Nanda went on from Caux to the British coalfields to verify what he had heard from miners there, and was much impressed by what he found.

However, the country most on Buchman's mind in that summer of 1947 was Germany. What was its future to be? How could any worthwhile future be brought about?

These questions had long been the subject of urgent, and often acrimonious, discussion among Allied statesmen. In September 1944 Churchill had been surprised, on arrival at the Quebec Conference, to find that President Roosevelt was accompanied not by his Secretary of State but by the Secretary of the Treasury, Henry Morgenthau, and that the main issue on their minds was how to treat Germany after victory.[1]

Morgenthau, it turned out, had been outraged by the 'soft' treatment proposed for Germany in a US War Department paper sent to General Eisenhower in August, and had won the President's support for his so-called 'Morgenthau Plan' whereby Germany would be reduced to a pastoral nation, with her industry removed, her standard of living reduced and segments of her population shifted to other parts of the country. Churchill disapproved, but let the matter pass for the time being. In the end, less extreme counsels prevailed, but the fear of the 'Morgenthau mentality' remained to plague German relations with America for some years.

The honeymoon period following the Yalta Conference of the great powers in February 1945 had lasted less than two months. Already on 2 April the US Secretary of State was advising of a 'serious deterioration' in relations with the Soviet Union. At the Potsdam Conference, the division of Germany into four zones was confirmed and the Soviet desire to gain control of Germany's industrial might became ever clearer.

James Forrestal, US Secretary of the Navy, noted in his diary for 14 May, that the Communists had one great advantage, a clear-cut philosophy 'amounting almost to a religion in which they believe is the only solution to the government of men'. 'There is no use fooling ourselves about the depth or the extent of the problem,' he added. 'I have no answers, but we had better try to get an answer.'[2]

This diagnosis echoed Buchman's two years earlier at Mackinac. Since that time he and his colleagues had been making a conscious effort to express their beliefs in terms of 'an ideology for democracy' which could give moral and spiritual content to the freedom of the so-called free world. They had seen it applied in various situations in war-time America and since then in the British coalfields. Now Buchman felt that the crucial test was whether this philosophy would be adequate to meet the needs of post-war Germany. The vacuum in Germany after the collapse of the Nazi ideology and his own failure to counteract that ideology before the war made him the more eager.

Preparations for getting significant numbers of Germans to Caux had been going forward ever since Buchman's remark on arrival there the previous year. In the same week in which General Marshall, now Secretary of State, made his proposals for the economic rehabilitation of Europe,[3] Senator Alexander Smith had arranged for his son-in-law, Kenaston Twitchell, to see him. This interview, in which Twitchell and his colleagues outlined Buchman's plan to bring the future leadership of Germany to Caux, led to a further interview with Robert Patterson, the Secretary of War. Patterson promised to remove the many obstacles to Germans who wanted to travel abroad and sent his visitors on to see General Lucius Clay, Commander in the American zone of Germany, and his political adviser, Robert Murphy. In London, meanwhile, Lord Pakenham, Minister in charge of the British zone, also gave his blessing. 'Along with food,' he said, 'the kind of work you are doing is the only thing which will do any good in Germany now.'[4] A list of fifty-five Germans in the British zone began to be screened, and Pakenham subsequently telephoned General Sir Brian Robertson, Commander of the British zone, to ask him to give Moral Re-Armament every facility.

General Clay was equally responsive, and arranged an occasion in Stuttgart where Twitchell and his colleagues could meet political leaders of the states in the American zone. Clay gave them no hint of what was in store for them, and the invitation to Caux as guests, with their wives and children, was completely unexpected. Most of them had not been out of Germany since 1933, and many had been in prison. 'Their bewilderment gradually brightened into surprise and appreciation, as they glimpsed the chance of visiting a free country with good food and friends ready to receive them,' says Twitchell,[5] noting that the Minister of Labour of North Rhine-Westphalia had been making do with 'two narrow slices of stale bread for breakfast and a few potatoes and decaying cabbage for lunch'. One of Buchman's Swiss colleagues, who did much of the pioneering work in Germany, told Buchman that, according to the Minister of Education in Hesse, infant mortality had risen to 20%, 10% of the youth had TB, 52% had one pair of shoes, while 11% had none, 23% had no bed of their own and output per working man had gone back to half the pre-war standard.[6]

In the event, 150 Germans were to attend Caux that year, and nearly 4,000 more between 1948 and 1951.*

Their arrival at Caux made an indelible impression on those first Germans. One of them, Peter Petersen, who had been indoctrinated at a special Nazi school from the age of twelve and had emerged from the army cynical and bitter, described his reactions: 'We were met by a French chorus with a German song ... We were already past masters at defending ourselves when we were attacked. But here the doors were wide open for us and we were completely disarmed.'[7] 'On one point especially the German guests agreed,' wrote the Berlin daily *Tagespiegel*. 'Nowhere in the world at the present time would Germans find such a warm welcome awaiting us as at Caux.'[8]

---

* Dr Gabriele Müller-List, a German historian, gives the numbers as 150 in 1947, 414 in 1948, 1,364 in 1949, 1,111 in 1950 and 941 in 1951, ('Eine neue Moral für Deutschland? Die Bewegung für Moralische Aufrustung und ihre Bedeutung beim Wiederaufbau 1947–52'. In *Das Parlament*, 31 October 1981.) David J. Price, whose London University MA Dissertation is perhaps the most thorough academic study of the subject in English, states that 'most of the Minister-Presidents and leaders in industry and education' attended during these years. (*The Moral Re-Armament Movement and Post-War European Reconstruction*, p. 29.)

Buchman insisted that the emphasis at Caux must be upon Germany's future rather than her past, her potential rather than her guilt. Whether dealing with an individual or a nation he was only interested in reviewing past mistakes as a basis for discovering a new way forward. He simply treated the Germans exactly like everyone else.

This enabled Germans to consider both past and future as they had never done before. 'For years we German people praised, supported, and defended an illusion,' wrote Dr Erwin Stein, Minister of Education for Hesse, on his return from Caux. 'As a result, endless suffering befell many of the nations of Europe and the world because of Germany. Our task, as responsible Germans, is, once and for all, to build up a democracy inspired by God. Only on this basis will it endure, and Moral Re-Armament shows us clearly how this is to be done.'[9]

Another of these early visitors to Caux was Baron Hans Herwarth von Bittenfeld, then Director of the Bavarian Chancellery and later the first post-war German Ambassador in London, who has written of his part in the Resistance to Hitler in his book, *Against Two Evils 1931–45*.[10] 'It is one thing to fight an ideology,' he wrote at the time. 'The real answer is a superior ideology. At Caux we found democracy at work and, in the light of what we saw, we faced ourselves and our nation. It was personal and national repentance. Many of us Germans who were anti-Nazi made the mistake in putting the whole blame on Hitler. We learned at Caux that we, too, were responsible. Our lack of a positive ideology contributed to the rise of Hitler.'[11]

Reinhold Maier, Minister-President of Württemberg-Baden, was also at Caux in 1947. One night he saw a play about the heroic Norwegian journalist Frederik Ramm, *And Still They Fight*. He slipped away from the theatre and threw himself on his bed 'completely shattered' with shame at what his country had done. 'It was a presentation without hatred or complaint and therefore could hardly have been more powerful in its effect,' he wrote.[12]

Not all the German guests responded like Stein, Herwarth and Maier. The *Neue Zürcher Zeitung* correspondent wrote that some were unconvinced by the 'terrible simplification' of the Christian ethic,[13] while Terence Prittie, then the *Manchester Guardian* man in Germany, wrote in 1979, 'To be honest, I think some politicians climbed on the bandwagon in order to get a free trip to Switzerland and to be treated like ordinary human beings.'[14] But according to Professor Carlo Schmid, a leading Socialist, 'although some were disappointed and complained of too much activity, nearly all came home feeling fulfilled and even former Nazis made real inner changes'.[15]

Many of the German leaders, whose experience of democracy before the war had been so disappointing, were greatly taken by Buchman's conception of 'inspired democracy'. Hans Peters, Professor of Constitutional Law at Berlin University, not only spoke much of it at Caux that year but published a book in 1948[16] in which he analysed the various types of democracy through the ages and described 'inspired democracy', as conceived by Buchman, as the best form to answer the failures of the twentieth century.[17]

Buchman himself seldom led the plenary sessions during this period. He sometimes slipped in at the back, or took an armchair on the floor to the left of the speakers' platform where he could watch the audience. But most of his time was spent in his two rooms – a bedroom and a sitting room – on the same floor as the meeting hall. There he frequently took part in the preparation of meetings and saw a stream of individuals and small groups privately.

One of his most fruitful contacts that year was with Mme Irène Laure, the Secretary-General of the national organisation of socialist women and a recent Member of Parliament for Marseilles. A friend and disciple of Léon Blum, Irène Laure had tried to build friendship with pre-Hitler Germany. Thereafter she was disillusioned, and the experience of the Occupation, when she was a leader of the Resistance in Marseilles and her son was ill-treated by the Gestapo, turned this disillusionment to hatred. After the war she had witnessed the opening of a mass grave containing the mutilated bodies of some of her comrades.

Irène Laure came to Caux expecting a capitalist trap, and her suspicion turned to revulsion when she found there were Germans present. That some were the widows of men executed by Hitler after the July plot made no difference: whenever a German spoke, she left the hall. On one such occasion she met Buchman in the corridor. 'What kind of unity do you want for Europe?' he asked her. The question plagued her and, though her bags were packed to leave, she decided to stay on. Through sleepless nights, she struggled with her hatred. Finally, she decided that she must give it up. She asked to speak at a meeting.

The preparation for the meeting next morning could hardly have been less propitious. It was to be a German-speaking session, and Buchman, from his bed, around which the possible speakers were gathered, suggested that an Austrian Minister should speak. He refused. 'I was in a concentration camp for four years. I cannot speak with Germans,' he said. A young German said that if the Germans were guilty, the Austrians were no less so. A heated argument broke out. 'The young man is right,' interrupted Buchman. The preparation meeting broke up in some confusion, and those who expected to run the public session moved uncertainly towards the meeting hall. Just as they were about to start, Buchman, now fully dressed, climbed on the speaker's platform and took over.

After a little, Mme Laure, a small quietly dressed woman whose

[352]

dynamism went unnoticed until she spoke, walked up to the front. Peter Petersen knew of her history and had been waiting with some compatriots ready, if she denounced Germany, to reply with stories of French 'atrocities' in the Black Forest. Instead Irène Laure said, 'I have so hated Germany that I wanted to see her erased from the map of Europe. But I have seen here that my hatred is wrong. I wish to ask the forgiveness of all the Germans present.'[18]

The effect on the Germans was electric. 'I was dumbfounded,' said Petersen later. 'For several nights it was impossible for me to sleep. All my past rose up in revolt against the courage of the woman. But we knew, my friends and I, that she had shown us the only way open to Germany if we wanted to join in the reconstruction of Europe.'[19]

The key moment, Mme Laure told me in 1982, was Buchman's question in the corridor. 'If at that moment he had pitied me or sympathised with me, I would have left. He gave me a challenge in love. It was the quality in him which arrested me – above all the tranquil look in his eyes. One felt his life corresponded exactly to his belief. He transmitted the feeling of certainty to you, that if you accepted change, you could have a part in the transformation of the world.'

'I was not interested in the Oxford Group as previously presented to me,' she explained. 'The ideology I saw at Caux involved giving mind, heart and body. Like Marxism in a way, but this was superior because the motive power was love.'*

It was the same all-inclusive philosophy which appealed to the Germans, and while at Caux they distilled its essence into a booklet entitled *Es Muss Alles Anders Werden* (Everything Must be Different), which they determined to spread throughout Germany. But where would they get the paper in post-war Europe? A Swedish paper-maker in Caux provided enough for an edition of one and a half million copies, and the booklet was distributed in all four zones of Germany, including 450,000 in the Soviet zone. The Soviet police confiscated the stock of an Eisenach bookseller, mainly, it appears, because they read ideological significance into a picture of wolves coming, they thought, from the East; but the stocks were later restored to him. In Leipzig, too, it was removed from the bookstalls for a time, but returned. Lord Pakenham's estimate was: 'I applaud the spirit of co-operative Christianity that has produced the booklet. It shows the kind of spirit that Germany, and indeed all nations, require . . . in these difficult times,'[20] while General Clay wrote, 'I was pleased indeed to

---

* On her return from Caux Irène Laure visited Léon Blum, who had been imprisoned in Dachau during the war. 'He told me that he had met Frank Buchman on a ship to America,' she recalls. 'He had a great respect for him.' Blum promised to help Mme Laure to free herself from her official responsibilities so that she could work fully with Moral Re-Armament.

see representative Germans . . . return to Germany refreshed and invigo-rated in spirit. I was equally impressed with a pamphlet which is now being published in Germany by these German visitors to Caux which explains democracy in simple and moving terms.'[21]

Some others in the Foreign Office and the British Control Commission in Germany took an opposite view. In December 1947 a member of the Political Division in Germany was transferred to other work because of his support of Moral Re-Armament. His superior informed him, 'The attitude of HM Government to Moral Re-Armament in Germany is a strictly negative one . . . and it is not really possible for you to keep that detached (call it cynical if you like) attitude which is so important for sizing up and dealing with old foxes like Adenauer.' The recipient protested to General Robertson, who assured him that 'it is quite wrong to say that the policy of His Majesty's Government is a negative one; it is not'. The same division is apparent in the Foreign Office files. London-based officials frequently took a doubting, or even a hostile, line, but these were countered in memos by Lord Pakenham and another Under-Secretary of State, Christopher Mayhew.[22]

Leaving strong teams to follow up in Germany, in the British coalfields and in the French industrial North, where Irène Laure and industrialists she had met at Caux held an industrial assembly for a thousand at Le Touquet, Buchman sailed for New York on 10 October 1947, ten days after the Caux assembly ended. He had again been advised that he should seek a warmer climate for the winter but he did not, in fact, reach California until 16 January.

Buchman wanted to return to the United States to encourage his countrymen to become aware that the practical aid being provided by the Marshall Plan would be inadequate without a moral and spiritual infra-structure. He also wanted to offer Congressmen and Senators first-hand information, rare at that period, on the current European scene. In Mackinac, during his absence, the theatrical team which had been developed during the war had been at work. They had written a musical show which, when combined with the thoughts and talents of the young Europeans whom Buchman brought with him, became known as *The Good Road*. It dramatised the spiritual heritage of the West, tracing its Christian roots back to personalities in European and American history and applying their principles to the circumstances of the post-war world. This musical was presented in New York, Boston, Montreal, Ottawa and Washington, where it was seen by a third of all Senators and Congress-men.

Meanwhile Buchman and his colleagues saw many friends and public figures in the Eastern states of America. News of what had been happening through his work in Europe had already reached many of them. 'New hope for the moral and spiritual regeneration of the German people is held out to the world and to Germans themselves by the Moral Re-Armament movement, as a result of experience during its summer-long conference at Caux,' the *New York Times* correspondent had written.[23]

Buchman spent the late winter and spring in California. There he decided to mark his seventieth birthday, 4 June 1948, which was also the tenth anniversary of the launching of Moral Re-Armament, with a full-scale assembly to articulate the need for an ideology for democracy in the Americas. During this winter, too, a former residential club in Los Angeles was bought as a base for operations on the West Coast. The assembly itself was held at Riverside, some fifty miles outside the city.

Eighty-one Senators and Congressmen signed the invitation to the assembly, and a group of Dutch business men chartered a KLM plane to transport the European delegates. From Italy, France and Austria and from various German provinces came politicians from government and opposition who had been at Caux. Others included Denmark's 1947 Prime Minister, a British peer, the President of a regional Miners' Union in Britain and a Papal Chamberlain. From Asia came distinguished Indians, a Buddhist scholar and the former Japanese Ambassador to the United States, Kensuke Horinouchi, recalled before the war because he disagreed with the war party at home, but now re-established as President of the Foreign Training Institute, which was creating Japan's new diplomatic service.

The visitors were welcomed by a message of support from Paul Hoffman, the administrator of the Marshall Plan, who stated, 'You are giving the world the ideological counterpart of the Marshall Plan.'[24] After the assembly the European delegates lunched with Secretary of State Marshall and Paul Hoffman in Washington. Marshall told the guests that, while Hoffman's work concerned material things and was an obvious necessity, a spiritual regeneration throughout the world was absolutely vital.[25]

Buchman stayed on in California after the assembly and then travelled back to Europe. In Paris on 6 August, between trains, he for the first time met Robert Schuman, who had been Prime Minister till the month before. Of this occasion Schuman said, 'Unhappily I had not enough time with Dr Buchman, barely twenty minutes, but he is a personality who made a deep impression on me.'

A Lille industrialist, Louis Boucquey, had first interested Schuman in Moral Re-Armament. He had met the then Prime Minister during a train journey and told him that industry in Northern France was working better, with closer relationships between labour and management, an improvement which he attributed to the change at Caux in Irène Laure and Robert Tilge, the Secretary of the regional employers, and the Moral Re-Armament assembly they had held at Le Touquet the previous autumn. At the end of the journey, Schuman said, 'Keep me in touch. I would like to meet this Dr Buchman.'

When he met Buchman, Schuman was Foreign Minister and involved in an extremely tense European situation. In protest against the reform of the German currency, Russia had blockaded Berlin. The Western Allies were replying with an airlift of food, fuel and all necessary supplies – a demonstration of their joint determination to carry through the economic rehabilitation of Germany – which lasted nearly ten months. During the early days of the blockade, Buchman wrote to Schuman, 'The country is safe in your hands. I do covet the opportunity of your coming to us at Caux.'[26]

Instead of Schuman there came to Caux on 11 September a man still comparatively unknown outside Germany, Dr Konrad Adenauer, who had recently become President of the Parliamentary Council of the three Western zones. Invited by one of his Christian Democrat party colleagues who had been at Caux in 1947, Adenauer arrived with most of his family and two secretaries. He listened, met many delegates and saw *The Forgotten Factor*. After the play he spoke to an audience which included President Enrico Celio of Switzerland. 'I have been here two days. I have attended meetings. I have spoken to people. I have observed very carefully and pondered my impressions,' he said. 'I admit that I came with some degree of scepticism, but I now gladly admit that, after two days and after consideration of my impressions, I have been completely convinced of the great value of Caux. I consider it a notable act in a time when evil so openly rules the world, that people have the courage to stand for good, for God, and that each one begins with himself. I believe, as do all who have come here from Germany, and it is my dearest wish, that the ideas of Caux will bear rich fruit a thousandfold.'[27]

Adenauer privately urged that *The Forgotten Factor* and *The Good Road* should go to Germany, as did Major-General Bishop, the British Commissioner for North Rhine-Westphalia – including the industrial Ruhr – who was at Caux that month. At the same time invitations arrived for *The Good Road* from the cabinets of North Rhine-Westphalia and Württemberg-Baden, headed by Minister-Presidents Karl Arnold and Reinhold Maier, and from Minister-President Ehard of Bavaria. The British, American and French administrations offered such facilities as were available, with the result that what was described as 'a most welcome invasion' began, the largest non-military operation in Germany since the war.[28]

RETURN TO GERMANY

On 9 October 1948, at 7.30 am, Buchman and a team of 260 rolled out of Zürich for Munich in a cavalcade of cars and buses. As they entered Ulm some hours later the bells of the cathedral welcomed them for their first official reception. They reached Munich that night, and gave the first performance of *The Good Road* in the damaged Opera House two days later. Here, as elsewhere on the tour, they had to give several performances a day to accommodate even some portion of those wishing to attend. For many Germans it was, as one said, 'the reopening of our windows to the world'. Even when the words of the play were not understood – it was played in English, and the supply of headphones for simultaneous translation was limited – the symbolic effect was significant. Bergrat Knepper, a mine manager who spoke no English, called the play 'the great experience of my life' because 'it meant we were accepted again by the international community'.

Buchman was happy. In 1937 he had said, 'This is not the time in Germany, but that time will come.' Now, while saddened by the devastation on every hand, he felt that he was for the first time entering Germany with an adequately trained team, with appropriate tools in the plays, and with the freedom to work. He was happiest of all at reunions with old friends. En route from Munich to Stuttgart the whole party took a detour to Freudenstadt, the place where the idea of moral and spiritual rearmament had borne in on him in May 1938. The little town had suffered severely from the shelling, and the Waldlust Hotel, in which he had often stayed, had only just ceased being used as a hospital and looked drab. But the proprietors, the Luz family, were back and the old mother, her son and daughters and Rosa, the cook, had worked much of the night baking with their last supplies. There were songs and memories and promises for the future. Rosa went on a ride with Buchman down the valley. 'I've made coffee for thousands of people in this hotel, for kings, princes and a lot of famous people. Not one of them thanked me. But today', she said, 'I am able to sit in the best seat and drive in this car with this gentleman.' Before leaving Buchman replenished the Luzes' store of coffee and flour, as he did when he visited Princess Margaret of Hesse a few days later in the three poorly-heated rooms which the occupation forces had allowed her. He had been sending her food parcels for months, and there was, his colleague John Cotton Wood recalls, 'a tenderness about his visits as though visiting an old aunt'.

The cavalcade rolled on and *The Good Road* was played to over-full houses in Stuttgart, Frankfurt, Düsseldorf and Essen. Twenty thousand Germans got in to see it, and many more talked with the travellers outside the theatre and in the streets. Many meetings took place, including one where 'we addressed 1,500 men who ran the entire coal industry here'.[1] In each place the German and Allied authorities worked together to overcome the tremendous difficulties of receiving so large a body of people, and the London *News Chronicle* quoted a Military Government official as saying, 'You (Moral Re-Armament) have done more in two days to interpret democracy to the German people than we have been able to do in three years.'[2]

When, on 26 October, the time came for *The Good Road* to move on to The Hague, the Minister-President of North-Rhine Westphalia, Karl Arnold, and his Ministers, Heinrich Lübke, August Halbfell and Walter Menzel, pleaded with Buchman to continue a major action in the Ruhr, where eighty per cent of German heavy industry was then located. 'On every lip', said Halbfell, the Minister of Labour, 'is the question whether the ideas of Washington or Moscow will dominate this region.' A Cominform document, *Protocol M*, issued in January, had stated, 'The centres of mass-struggle in Germany will be (i) the Ruhr and its industrial capacity, and (ii) the means of transport in West and North Germany.' 'The coming winter', it added, 'will be the decisive period in the history of the German working class.'[3]*

Halbfell did not want the Russian or the American ideas to become dominant. He had begun to see a third way: 'Moral Re-Armament', he said, 'is our one big hope.'[4]

Buchman was ready. *The Forgotten Factor*, at Halbfell's request, had been translated into German at Caux. A cast had rehearsed under the direction of Phyllis Austin. Her French relatives had been murdered in Nazi gas chambers, and when she was asked to direct the play she 'felt physically sick'. But she decided to do it, and wrote later that in the doing of it 'a deep love of Germany was born in me'.[5] Buchman was prepared to

---

* James Byrnes, the US Secretary of State, described how he had had a few drinks late one night with Molotov during the Potsdam conference. After the third highball, he asked Molotov, 'I would like to know what you would *really* like in Europe.' Molotov's reply was that he would be ready to give up almost anything to obtain Russian representation on the Control Council for the Ruhr. (*Forrestal Diaries*, p. 347.)

leave this production and a team of fifty behind him in the Ruhr while he went on to The Hague.

During a dinner given for him by the North Rhine-Westphalian Government, Buchman was approached by Dr Heinrich Kost, the head of the German Coal Board and Chairman of Directors of a mining company centred in Moers. 'Dr Buchman,' said Kost, 'your idea is right. We need it urgently. What do we do now? When Hitler was around, he told us what to do. If the Russians come, they will tell us what to do. What do you say we should do?'

'I can't tell you what to do, nor would it be right for me to do so,' replied Buchman. 'But I can tell you how to find out for yourself.' He told Kost that God would speak to anyone who committed himself to find and follow His plan.

Next day Buchman and Kost spent four hours together. They talked further about God's guidance, and listened together. Kost had one thought: 'Invite a German cast of *The Forgotten Factor* into the coal mines at Moers.' He asked how Moral Re-Armament was financed, and was amazed to find that there were no government subsidies or large industrial backers. It was all a matter of individual courage and sacrifice, Buchman explained. Kost was especially impressed that an American doctor in Virginia had cashed in his insurance policies and sent $40,000 towards *The Good Road*'s tour in Germany, and that Allied servicemen had given their demobilization gratuities to help their former enemies.

The first performance of *The Forgotten Factor* took place on 23 November under the shadow of the ruined Krupps works at Essen and was introduced by the Lord Mayor, Dr Gustav Heinemann*, and Minister-President Arnold. Arnold's government had voted 60,000 marks – about £3,000 – to the venture, but this was soon used up, and the play could only proceed from place to place as each town provided transport, accommodation and an inviting committee of labour and management. Many individuals gave generously, and not only in money. The wife of one of Arnold's cabinet ministers sang in the chorus accompanying the play. A dozen young Germans, some like Petersen new to Moral Re-Armament and others the children of people who had met Buchman in the thirties, took part as actors, scene-shifters and in visiting the miners in their homes. One man who had narrowly escaped death on the Eastern Front said that nothing in the army or the Allied prisoner-of-war camps had been as tough as his first months with *The Forgotten Factor* in that freezing winter of 1948. Meanwhile Dr Kost issued his invitation to Moers for late January 1949, jointly with his works council representatives, most of whom were Communists.

---

* President of the German Federal Republic, 1969–74.

In its first two years 120,000 people, mostly from the coal and steel industries, saw the play in the Ruhr. Buchman was only occasionally in Germany during those years, but he was in constant, often daily, touch with what was going on. Whereas before the war he would have been present throughout such campaigns, he now had to concentrate on thinking strategically about the work going on in many countries simultaneously. He tried to deploy to each area those best equipped by background and experience for it. To the Ruhr, for example, went a relay of British miners and of capitalists whose motives and practice had changed. Irène Laure and her husband Victor, a merchant seaman who had been a Marxist for forty-seven years, addressed two hundred meetings in Germany in eleven weeks, including ten of the eleven state parliaments. With them went two Frenchmen, one of whom had lost fifteen, the other twenty-two, relatives in Nazi concentration camps.

Much of the continuing work was done by two young Norwegians, one of the British wartime coal-miners and an upper-class Oxford graduate. Each at times lived with the miners in their homes. In all, Buchman sustained a team of over a hundred people, mostly under thirty years of age, in the Ruhr for several years – all working without pay, generally sixteen hours a day and living on food and in conditions far inferior to those obtainable in their own countries. Buchman's own contacts with German workers and industrialists were mainly during the long summer assemblies at Caux.

The battle for the Ruhr was, from the outset, a hot one. Not only Communists but many Socialists were suspicious. A Danish journalist with Buchman's travelling force wrote him, 'Very warm greetings from your friends Minister-Presidents Arnold and Maier, who quietly solved a ministerial crisis between them, as Maier said, "in the spirit of Caux".' She told how the SPD (Socialist Party) Executive had passed a resolution at this time warning their members against Moral Re-Armament. 'The Board Member who proposed it told us many members had protested against the resolution,' she continued, 'but he himself is at present an enemy . . . He was a political emigrant since 1933, first in Prague and, during the war, in London. He said he got his strong antipathy against MRA from "political circles in London who hated the Oxford Group during the war"!'[6]

More and more Socialists sought the opinion of Dr Hans Böckler, the President of the new unified German Trades Union Federation. He had been convinced enough by the reports of those returning from Caux in 1947 to join Minister-President Arnold and others in sending *Es Muss Alles Anders Werden* to over a thousand leading people in North Rhine-Westphalia, with the request that they think out 'how and where you can use this weapon in trade union circles, with management and in town and country districts'. But as the controversy hotted up with the tour of *The Forgotten Factor*, he decided he must investigate the matter more closely.

In the spring of 1949 Kost summoned a meeting of 190 leading industrialists to hear a panel of Moral Re-Armament speakers at the Kaiserhof Hotel in Essen. Böckler and a Marxist lecturer from Düsseldorf named Heinz Grohs decided to attend. When they arrived and saw so many capitalists together, Grohs decided he could not stomach the sight and went out for a drink. But he returned, and Böckler told the speakers after the meeting, 'What impresses us is that you people say the same things and put the same challenges to management as you have to us.' They were also impressed by Kost's opening words to his fellow industrialists. 'Gentlemen,' he had begun, 'it is not a question of whether we change, but how we change. It is not for us to wait for Labour to change. Change is demanded of us.'[7]

Böckler asked for a further talk in his home, of which a Clydeside shipyard worker, by now working full-time with Moral Re-Armament, wrote to Buchman: 'Fresh from Kost's meeting and the way the changed management with us tackled the Ruhr barons, Böckler spoke from his heart. He spoke of the sacrifices of the people leaving jobs and home. He said, "Some people hold the doctrine that you have to change the system in order to change society. That is, of course, true, but it is only half the truth. People must change drastically like those men who spoke to us at Kost's meeting. Both must be done, and you fight for both, I am convinced of that." He added, "I want to make a statement that you can use." '[8]

At Caux, a few months later, Böckler met Buchman, and they became friends. It was after this that he produced his carefully weighed statement: 'If men are to be free from the old and the out-moded, it can happen only as they set themselves new goals and place humanity and moral values in the forefront. I believe that Moral Re-Armament can bring about a definite improvement for mankind in many areas of life. When men change, the structure of society changes, and when the structure of society changes, men change. Both go together and both are necessary. The goal which Moral Re-Armament strives to reach is the same as that for which I am fighting as a trade unionist.'[9]*

When Böckler was forced by a stroke to retire some years later,

* Other German trades union leaders who went to Caux at this time included Lorenz Hagen and Gustav Schiefer, President and Vice-President of the Bavarian Trades Unions; Otto Franke, Secretary of the Trades Unions in the French Zone; Ernst Scharnowski, President of the Free Trades Union Organisation of Greater Berlin; Erich Galle, Chairman of the Metal Workers; and Hans Frenz, Chairman of the Post Office Workers.

Buchman visited him in his home in the outskirts of Cologne and found him depressed and fretful at his disability. Buchman told him of his own months of inactivity and how he had learnt not to worry, and to go at a slower pace. Böckler shook his head. 'But you have all your friends around you who carry on your work, so you can take the time to come and see me. Our people are not so friendly.'

The intensive work of the Moral Re-Armament team in the Ruhr seems to have contributed to a severe set-back to Communist plans there. Already in January 1948, under *Protocol M*, the Communists had decided that their expected take-over of the Ruhr would be won not in Parliament but in the factories and at the pithead. The exclusion of the Russians from the International Authority for the area, set up the following December, had confirmed them in this strategy. They concentrated on the election for the works councils in each mine, and, before the arrival of *The Forgotten Factor*, were said to hold 72 per cent of the works councils seats in the coal and steel industries. The British authorities recognised the situation. 'Much the most serious aspect – more than the possibility of sabotage – is the Communist penetration of works councils and trades unions,' concludes a minute based on a top secret Foreign Office report at the time.[10] By 1950, however, the percentage of Communist representation had declined from 72 per cent to 25 per cent and, according to Hubert Stein, an executive member of the German miners' union, this decline was 'to a great extent due to Moral Re-Armament'.[11] The Minister of Economics for North Rhine-Westphalia, Artur Sträter, said at a public meeting in the Parliament building, 'We are battling with great difficulties in coal production. It is no exaggeration to say that through this ideology of Caux a great bottleneck has been broken.'[12]

Exactly how much the improved industrial relations and decline of Communist influence in the Ruhr should be attributed to Moral Re-Armament is impossible to assess accurately. Other obvious influences were the improving material position of the workers in the wake of both the Marshall Plan and the currency reform, the introduction of new technology, the news of conditions in the East brought back by prisoners of war and millions of refugees, and the progress of other political parties as they rebuilt their party machines. But it is hard to ignore the factor which both Stein and Sträter emphasise.

Many of the workers were interested not so much by *The Forgotten Factor* as by the meetings which took place, in those early years, in miners' halls, at union meetings and in beer halls where long, and sometimes fierce, discussions developed between workers and the MRA visitors. These visitors were not presenting any particular political or economic point of view. They gave evidence of an experience which, they believed, could free individuals from personal difficulties and unite homes, trade unions and industries to rebuild the country. An occasion at Moers was typical.

One cold evening in February 1949 Max Bladeck, the chairman of the works council representing 2,500 miners at No 2 mine of the Rheinpreussen Coal Company, called a meeting at the Heier Tavern on the outskirts of Moers. A member of the Communist Party for twenty-four years, he was a small man, every inch a fighter, with sharp eyes, an intellectual forehead and a chest racked by silicosis. He had brought with him some of the keenest debaters in the Party. 'Their aim', writes Leif Hovelsen,[13] who was one of a small Moral Re-Armament team at the meeting, 'was to sink us with all hands, and six of them opened fire, one after another. Their basic theme was: "The West European countries are preparing for a new war. Every capitalist is a fascist at heart. The system must be changed. For 2,000 years Christianity has tried to build a new world – and failed. There is no ideology above class." The "blitz" went on for an hour.'

'Then', continues Hovelsen, 'it was our turn. A Clydeside shipworker, a small, solidly built, energetic man, got up. "The working class has never been so powerful as today, yet it has never been so divided," he said. "We have learned to split the atom but we have not learned to unite men. People must be changed all over the world. Only so will a classless society come. But we don't have to wait for it till we are in our graves."

'A worker from East London followed. "If we British had lived up to what we talked about after the First World War, you men would have been spared the suffering you have gone through," he said. "God help the party or the nation which does not change these conditions. But we need a full dimension of change – new social relations, new economic relations, new international relations, all based on personal change. To have any lesser aim is reactionary."'

'The next speaker', continues Hovelsen, 'was a Canadian employer (Bernard Hallward). "What has created injustices in the Western world is selfishness and moral compromise in men like me," he said. "I can see how the hard-boiled materialism of the right wing is reflected in the bitterness of the left wing." As the tall, slim employer, with many humorous touches, told the story of his own change, of his two factories, his workers and their hopes, his wife and his two sons, he carried everyone with him. The meeting lasted four hours; when it broke up all were agreed to meet again. The Germans came to see *The Forgotten Factor* and we noticed its ideas gripped them.'

As the Heier Tavern meeting ended, Bladeck said, 'Capitalism is the thesis, Communism the anti-thesis; what you have brought may be the synthesis.'[14] After seeing *The Forgotten Factor*, he began to realise implications for himself. The process was precipitated by his daughter pointing out that although he spoke a lot about freedom and democracy from platforms, he was a dictator at home. This cut him to the quick, and soon afterwards he asked a young Norwegian MRA man to stay in his house. In the summer of 1949 he went to Caux, accompanied by his friend Paul Kurowski who, with twenty-five years of Communist Party experience, was conducting the training of Party functionaries in the district. At Caux, they had many conversations with Buchman.

'The atmosphere that surrounded this man was something completely new for me,' Kurowski recalled later. 'It was like a revelation. There was a peace, a love, a caring and a great humility. I had not met a man like this before. We talked about great forces that were moving in the world and he listened very patiently to my ideas. He never tried to convert me. He never tried to answer my anti-religious points of view. He just had faith in the best in me.'[15] What struck Bladeck most was 'Buchman's freedom from himself. I felt that here was a man who really subjected his will to a higher Authority. . . . If Lenin were still alive, he would have found the answer to a question he once put to a bishop: "Bring me one man in the whole of Christendom who lives today as Paul lived, and I will have faith!" '[16]

Rumours of the change in Bladeck and Kurowski reached the Party hierarchy in the Ruhr, who then sent Willy Benedens, a Party secretary in Moers, to Caux to bring them home. He too was convinced by what he saw. All three echoed Kurowski's verdict: 'For twenty-six years I have sung the Internationale with all my heart, but this is the first time I have seen it lived.'[17]

When Bladeck, Kurowski and Benedens returned together to the Ruhr, they were called to the Communist headquarters for North Rhine-Westphalia. There they recommended that the Party should make itself acquainted with 'Moral Re-Armament's world-revolutionising idea'. They supported their contention with quotations from Marx and Engels and made it clear they had decided to live a new life 'for logical and realistic reasons'. They did not want to leave the Party; they wanted the Party to take its next step of development, by facing up to the moral standards of absolute honesty, purity, unselfishness and love. Their approach was rejected and they were expelled from the Party at a meeting attended by the chairman of the North Rhine-Westphalia executive, Hugo Paul.

On 6 October 1949 *Freies Volk*, the Communist paper in Düsseldorf, carried an article by Paul headed 'Unmoral Disarmament' which stated, 'The dangerous activities of the MRA apostles have up to now been underestimated by the district executives, yes, even by our Party provincial executive . . . MRA's work has created ideological uncertainty and confusion in some units of the Party, for example in the Meerbeck-Moers district, in the Rheinpreussen pit groups and in the Ford plant in

Cologne.' The article outlined the case against Bladeck and his friends, and complained that when officials reasoned with them, they only kept trying to pass on this 'new ideology'. Finally, Paul stated, 'It is resolved that all comrades who seek contact with these men shall be expelled from the Party and unmasked as traitors to the workers' interests.'

Hugo Paul's article was part of a desperate attempt to maintain Communist influence in the forthcoming works council elections. On 31 October Bladeck wrote to Buchman describing the campaign and reporting the election results in the Rheinpreussen pits. 'My deepest thanks for everything,' he wrote. 'Our silver wedding went off well and we had the delightful surprise of a gift from Caux. Then came the battle with the Communist Party and at the time of the union elections in the mine there was the pamphlet distributed against us and against Generaldirektor Kost. It smeared us and MRA in the dirtiest way. So I put up a statement at the pithead which said why I went to Caux and what Caux was out for. The important thing is that, in spite of the bitter campaign against me, I got the biggest vote at the poll.

'In the other pits where Benedens, Burckhardt and Kurowski are union officials, they too increased their majorities and have all been re-elected officers of the union in spite of all the propaganda against them. The ideology of MRA has carried the day in the Rheinpreussen pits . . . I am entrusted with many warm greetings from Generaldirektor Kost to you, dear fatherly friend. He told me that in his opinion this ideology is the most effective way of breaking through all the barriers which create national and international unhappiness today.'[18]

Similar developments were taking place around men in other parts of the Ruhr. In Alten-Essen, for example, the Communist chairman of the Hoesch pits began working with Moral Re-Armament after seeing *The Forgotten Factor* in 1948, which brought him into conflict with the town's Party chairman, Johann Holzhäuser. In 1948, however, Holzhäuser himself went to Caux and underwent the same change as Bladeck and Kurowski. Through him, change spread to a member of the provincial executive of the Party, Hermann Stoffmehl, who was Town Clerk of Alten-Essen. Stoffmehl announced that he now believed Moral Re-Armament was the uniting ideology needed by the world. If the Party would not accept it, he would not only leave the Party but take a third of the local membership with him.

When, two weeks later, the issue of Moral Re-Armament was put to a meeting chaired by the Vice-Chairman of the West German Communist Party, Heinz Renner, Paul and Stoffmehl faced each other. Each proposed a motion diametrically opposed to the other. When Renner put both to the vote, Stoffmehl won 400 votes and Paul 407. Finally, on 8 January 1950, at a special conference in Düsseldorf, the West German executive of the Party decided to reorganize the entire executive and secretariat in the Ruhr because it was 'tainted with an ideology inimical to the Party'. The *Manchester Guardian*, under the headline 'A New Communist Heresy: Moral Re-Armament', described the purge which had been carried out in the North Rhine-Westphalian Party and quoted the new chairman of the provincial Party, Josef Ledwohn, as saying that 'one of the most dangerous symptoms was the growing connections between Party members and Moral Re-Armament'.[19] But the reorganisation of the Party executive did not stop the spread of the spirit of Moral Re-Armament through the Ruhr.

Over Whitsun 1950 miners and management in the coal industry decided to hold an MRA demonstration at Hans Sachs House in Gelsenkirchen to coincide with the World Youth Festival in East Berlin. Karl Arnold wrote to Buchman asking him to be there and Adenauer, now Chancellor of the Federal Republic, also wrote to him. His hand-written message began, ' "Start with yourself" – that is the essence of your message,' and then referred to 'the great success which the team of Moral Re-Armament had achieved in the Ruhr'. He added, 'Moral Re-Armament has become a household word in Germany. I believe that, in view of the offensive of totalitarian ideas in the East of Germany, the Federal Republic and, within it, the Ruhr is the right platform for a demonstration of the idea of Moral Re-Armament.'[20] Buchman accepted these invitations, and went to stay with Hans Dütting, the Director of the Gelsenkirchen Coal-Mining Company.

His speech in Gelsenkirchen was broadcast throughout Germany, reaching over the borders into the East. 'Marxists are finding a new thinking in a day of crisis,' he declared. 'The class struggle is being superseded. Management and labour are beginning to live the positive alternative to the class war. . . Is change for all the one basis of unity for all? Can Marxists pave the way for a greater ideology? Why not? They have always been open to new things. They have been forerunners. They will go to prison for their belief. They will die for their belief. Why should they not be the ones to live for this superior thinking?'[21]

They were remarkable words from an American of 72 and were authenticated for the audience of three thousand by the presence on the platform of Bladeck, Kurowski, Benedens, Stoffmehl and a dozen of their friends.* Few realised that the vision of Marxists pioneering a new thinking had first come to Buchman amid the orange groves of California before ever he returned to Europe after the war. Its immediate relevance was caught by the *Essener Allgemeine Zeitung*, which headed its stories of

---

* Also on the platform were the Vice-Chancellor of Germany, Franz Blücher, and sons of Chancellor Adenauer and of Minister-President Arnold.

the day's demonstrations: 'Berlin a Wash-out' and 'Moral Re-Armament the final remedy'.[22]

The battle was not, however, won by headlines. Every week, every day, much personal work and sustained friendship were required. In the winter of 1951, for example, when Buchman was again in California, Bladeck's ex-colleagues went after him. They knew that he had a weakness for alcohol, and they managed one evening to get him drinking. They then sat him next to a particular woman on a bus on his way home and he publicly embraced her. At once, all over the Ruhr, the Party said, 'See what hypocrites these Caux men are.' They threatened to publicize the incident if Bladeck did not leave Moral Re-Armament. He was so bitterly ashamed that he wrote Buchman asking that none of his friends should call on him again. 'I have betrayed you,' he said.

Buchman cabled back:

> Man-like it is to fall in sin;
> Fiend-like it is to dwell therein;
> Christ-like it is from sin to rise.

' "The blood of Jesus Christ His Son cleanseth us from all sin." The biggest sinner can become the greatest saint. I have faith in the new Max. Sincerely, Frank.'

'I had expected anything else, but not that,' Max told his friends later. 'I felt ashamed, but it gave me inner strength. I felt Frank's faith in my change, and also the challenge to me. I also felt in the sentence he sent me, "The Blood of Jesus Christ, God's Son, cleans us from all sin", the deepest message of Christianity, and it came at the right time.'[23]

Up to that time Bladeck had experienced something of moral change. His thinking had become different and he had experienced on occasions the direction of a higher authority in his life. But he had resisted surrendering his will to God. He had thought he could alter his own life by himself; he began to discover that he needed Christ.

When the next works council elections came around Heinz Renner, now the West German Party Chairman, told an old comrade who had left the Party to work with MRA: 'We are determined to destroy Moral Re-Armament's power in the works councils and reduce it to a sect and nothing else.'[24] In fact Bladeck and his friends in pits all across the Ruhr were returned with increased majorities. In 1951 Walther Ulbricht, the East German Party boss, took the West German Party to task at the Party Conference at Weimar for losses in the elections, especially in the Gelsenkirchen area. However, in 1953 the pattern was repeated even more dramatically in Nordstern, the pit of which miners used to say, 'When Stalin has a cold, we all sneeze.' Of the eight men listed by name in the Communist leaflets as MRA men seven were elected, and the Communist representation fell from eleven out of thirteen in 1951 to three out of twenty in 1953. That year the works council sent a birthday telegram not to Stalin but to Buchman.

In these next years hundreds of Communists left the Party. Scores of Marxists discovered, in their own words, 'a superior ideology', and many who had been without faith found one. These miners – 'men full of songs and dreams and poetry and a deep longing for a world in which brotherhood and peace would become realities in everyday life', as Hovelsen describes them – were to move out from the pit galleries to take their new discoveries to their fellow workers in the mills of Italy, the mines of Northern Sweden, the factories of the 'Red Belt' in Paris, the docks of London and Rotterdam, to Cyprus, India, Africa, Japan, Australia and America; and to challenge the policy-makers of Washington and the bankers of Wall Street to open their minds and hearts to the needs of the whole world. This was the new Germany of Buchman's dreams.

The battle for the Ruhr went on year by year, but it became increasingly clear that the Communist Party had lost. By July 1959 the Managing Director of the Nordstern mine, Fritz-Günter von Velsen, was able to say, 'Following the training and change of heart that many of us found in Moral Re-Armament, Communist influence has gone down and the power of the Party on a mass scale has been broken. In my own mine, where the men formerly elected 90 per cent Communist representatives, the atmosphere has so changed that people come from many countries to see what has happened.'[25]

Again, it must be stressed that by 1959 many factors besides Moral Re-Armament had been in operation, but Buchman's vision and the work of his teams were important enough for Adenauer to repeat then, as many times before, that for him the 'great success' of that work in the Ruhr was 'the test of MRA's effectiveness'.[26]

The changes in many of the hundreds of industrialists who went to Caux between 1947 and 1952 played a major part, as they revealed an alternative to class war and the Marxist view that no capitalist could rise above his material self-interest. Von Velsen was a case in point. A Prussian, with duelling scars on his face from his student encounters, he was a tough master. After a talk with Buchman at Caux he decided to take an objective look at his life. He remembered a young executive whom he disliked and whose removal he had engineered by going behind his back to head office. He apologised to this man, brought him back, and they became trusting colleagues. Von Velsen said to his secretary, 'If you see or hear me doing anything which offends the absolute standards of honesty, purity, unselfishness and love, please tell me.' The change in him was a major factor in creating the new atmosphere at Nordstern.

Similarly, the alteration in Kost himself had affected many, not least his employees at Moers. When he introduced the first showing of *The Forgotten Factor* there, Bladeck and the others were amazed to hear him say, 'We need to put people first in our business and then build the business around them. In this way we can unite as human beings so that something happens not only in the business, but in the community and in the nation . . . If, in addition, we let the forgotten factor of God shine in our plant and rule there, then we shall see that not the bookkeeper's pen nor the adding machine nor reason alone governs the undertaking, but that the hearts of men must beat for each other.'[27]

Hans Dütting, the Director of the Gelsenkirchen Coal-Mining Company, with whom Buchman stayed for the Hans Sachs House meetings, employed 27,000 men. He had gone to Caux in 1949 with the idea of getting a holiday and doing some mountain climbing, but when he returned he completely altered his business methods: 'We began to conduct our operations in such a way that we no longer had the slightest thing to hide. We began quite spontaneously to give our workers' representatives more information. The result was an extraordinary growth in trust between work force and management. Every month I have a special meeting with all chairmen of works councils, some twenty-five in all. Absolute honesty prevails. Each side knows that no one in that gathering is telling an untruth.'[28] 'Perhaps I myself gave the strongest push towards a change in our mutual attitudes when I spoke openly about a wrong decision I had made, which I then put straight with the help of the works councillors,' Dütting added.[29]

Paul Dikus, the works council chairman for Dütting's 27,000 workers, confirmed the change as early as 1950: 'A year ago, I believe both of us would have said we were mad if I had said that Mine-Manager Dütting and I would speak together on the same platform.' Then he referred to a meeting where Dütting told the works councillors the full figures of the financial situation of the firm and took them completely into his confidence. 'That was the meeting of my life,' said Dikus. 'Dütting told us things we have always wanted to know. He laid all his cards on the table. It was something entirely new. And look at all the other things that have happened – all the houses that are being built, all the new social amenities for the workers. I tell you it is the practical application of Moral Re-Armament.'[30]

The first employer in the Ruhr actually to provide for the chairman of his company's works council to 'sit on the Board as a member with full and equal rights' was Ernst Kuss, the head of the Duisburg Kupferhütte. He took this action, according to Müller-List, 'under the influence of Buchman' following his visit to Caux in 1949. His example inspired Dr Peter Wilhelm Haurand, who had attended Caux in 1948, to frame a crucial resolution in favour of co-determination which he brought before the Annual Congress of the Catholic Church in Germany at Bochum in September 1949.* This resolution was accepted by the Congress after some 'clarification' by Cardinal Frings, which strengthened Adenauer's hand as Catholics were so influential in his party.

At this time there were discussions between Adenauer and his old colleague on the Cologne City Council, Hans Böckler, about whether the trades unions would be willing to renounce public ownership in favour of *Mitbestimmung* – co-partnership or co-determination between labour and capital in industry. Böckler and his colleagues agreed. There was much controversy over the resulting legislation which, amongst other things, would give the workers equal representation on the supervisory boards of all large companies.[31] This turned out to be 'one of the most serious tests not only for the government coalition but for the new-born Republic as a whole'.[32] On the management side were many 'Ruhr Barons', dictatorial employers who had retained their positions throughout all the changes of regime. On the other side were workers' representatives who had suffered greatly under the Nazis or who had turned to Communism. Both groups were opposed to *Mitbestimmung*.

Men like Dütting and Dikus, in their new relationship, saw co-determination as a natural development. 'We find that on the basis of the same ideology we understand each other better and better,' said Dütting. 'As a result we are not worried about the working out of the . . . law . . . An employer who really applies the four absolute basic demands gives his workers more than any law could insist upon.'[33] 'We don't need to have any fear about the fight over the co-partnership law,' added Dikus.[34]

And so it turned out. 'When recently a new Labour Director for the Gelsenkirchen Coal-Mining Company had to be chosen under the new law of co-determination,'** Sydney Cook, one of Buchman's experienced colleagues in Germany, reported to him, 'the men's representatives, of their own accord, came to Dütting and asked him to choose the candidate jointly with them. When this was done, they presented their united proposition to August Schmidt, the national miners' President, who at once accepted it. When the new Labour Director – a worker – was himself told the news, he said to Dütting, "The first thing I want to do is to go to Caux. And secondly, I want you to help me choose the right subordinates."'[35] Max Bladeck, then vice-chairman of the works councils of the Rheinpreussen mines, also asserted that long before the

---

* Confirmed by Herbert J. Spiro in his authoritative treatise *The Politics of German Co-determination* (Harvard University Press, 1958, p. 59).

** The Co-determination Law for the mining, iron and steel industries was passed on 21 May 1951, and similar provisions were enacted for most other industries, except family businesses with less than 500 workers, on 11 October 1952.

new law was introduced 'we had already partially introduced it at Rheinpreussen'.[36]

So, both in the easing of relations between management and labour and also in preparing people to take a lead towards co-determination, Buchman can be said to have played some part in creating preconditions for Germany's 'economic miracle'.

In a different sphere, Buchman also had a part in the post-war resumption of the Oberammergau Passion Play. Early in 1949 he received a letter from the President of the Bavarian Parliament, Dr Michael Horlacher, who had been in Caux, asking him to become chairman of an International Committee of the Friends of the Oberammergau Passion Play for its fresh start in 1950. He had attended the first performance of the play after World War I, taking a number of Oxford and Cambridge students with him, and had been greatly impressed by it. The Bavarian State Tourist Committee had now heard rumours of vast financial resources available to Buchman as an American. When he met with the local committee in a smoke-filled room in a picturesque Oberammergau inn, the question seemed to be whether he would supply one million dollars or two.

Buchman looked around this roomful of solid, beer-drinking villagers. He told them how important he believed their play to be. Then he dropped his bombshell. 'Silver and gold have I none, but such as I have give I unto you,' he quoted, and went on to ask, 'Did this village take an oath to put on this play?'

They agreed.

'Is that oath still binding?'

'Yes,' they replied.

'Then is it God's will you put it on again?'

Less enthusiastically they agreed again.

'Then you must do it. If you rely on money, Oberammergau will be another outpost of materialism. If you rely on your oath and your courage and readiness to work together, you will succeed.'

The producer of the play, Georg Lang, was there together with his son, a Munich architect who had been to Caux. There was a long silence when Buchman had finished talking. Then the younger Lang said, 'That is true. I saw it in Caux. I have seen it work out at home. We must be true to our oath and trust God.'

The next day the Mayor came over to see Buchman. 'I am sorry we spent so much time on the business side of the play,' he said. 'I am convinced that what we need is one-twentieth of the spirit of Caux and we shall be successful.'

They set to work. The producer later told Buchman, 'Since the war many young men have come back disillusioned and unwilling to take their part in the play, because it demands so much of them spiritually and morally if it is to be done right. We owe you a great deal. We had come near to selling our birthright.' When the play opened, Buchman and nine friends were among the honoured guests.[37]

Perhaps Buchman's greatest service to Germany during these years was to stimulate responsible people in many spheres to take leadership and to represent a new Germany to the world. This drew people of character back into public life and gave the average German faith in the country's future, as well as gradually convincing Germany's neighbours that this future could benefit Europe as a whole.

As, according to Dr Hermann Katzenberger, Secretary of the Bundesrat, half the German Cabinet in 1951 were 'firm MRA believers',[38] the effect was felt in many areas. Dr Hans Lukaschek, Minister of Refugees, for instance, stated that he was encouraged by his visits to Caux to have faith in the future and look on every person who came from the East, not as another mouth to feed but as an asset for the rebuilding of Germany. Consequently, he did not set up permanent camps for refugees, but integrated the millions of refugees from the East as rapidly as possible into the community. Dr Alfred Hartman, the first Director of Finance for the Anglo-American zones and later Secretary of State in the Ministry of Finance, also spoke at Caux of this need and of the inspiration they had received to tackle it.[39] So did other important leaders. 'We stand before the task of solving the issue of "burden sharing" so that justice is done for all, and it must be done in such a way as to exercise a powerful magnetic power upon Germans in the East,' said Thomas Wimmer, the Socialist Lord Mayor of Munich,[40] while Wolfgang Jaenicke, Secretary of State for Refugees in Bavaria, declared, 'I am leaving here with the firm conviction of spreading the ideas of Caux between the resident population and the displaced persons.'[41]

The work of such men and many others, under the leadership of Lukaschek, who was Minister from 1948 to 1951, and his successor, who also visited Caux frequently, led to the 'law of equalization of burdens' (*Lastenausgleichsgesetz*), passed in its final form on 14 August 1952. This provided that those in West Germany who still had capital or property paid a special tax amounting to half their wealth, after a tax-free minimum, so that the refugees could receive regular payments as well as some compensation. Such a massive redistribution of wealth, as Joseph Beyerle, Minister of Justice in Württemberg-Baden, had stressed at Caux, 'demands high moral standards from our population'.[42] It had also required a group of leaders courageous enough to propose it and to enforce it.

Dr Otto Schmidt, Reconstruction Minister for North Rhine-Westphalia, wrestling with 'house-building, building policies, town planning, rehousing projects and so on – all of which fall within my portfolio', found 'the divine object of his task' in 'what Buchman says and practises again and again about the solving of social issues – that "when everyone cares enough and everyone shares enough, everyone has enough".' 'We cannot evaluate in detail what it means that since 1947 thousands of people in public life have been to Caux,' he added. 'If I look back on myself and my personal experiences of reorientation and the new vision for the whole of public life which I have found here, I believe I can say a great force has been at work on many people to give positive shape to the conditions of the free nations.'[43]

SCHUMAN AND ADENAUER

Six weeks after the French and German cabinets had, at their dramatic meetings of 9 May 1950, agreed on the essentials of the Schuman Plan for pooling the French and German coal and steel industries, Buchman was gazetted a Chevalier of the Legion of Honour for his 'contribution to better understanding between France and Germany'.[1] Two years later, the German Government awarded him the Grand Cross of the Order of Merit 'in recognition of his significant work for peace and understanding between nations'.[2]

From the first this led to speculation in the British press. Robert Schuman, because of the decoration's special link with Germany, arranged for the French Senator, Madame Eugénie Eboué, to present it at Gelsenkirchen during Buchman's visit for the Moral Re-Armament demonstration in early June – a week before it was officially gazetted. The *Evening Standard* questioned on 10 June, quite reasonably, whether the honour had actually been conferred.[3] It went on, however, to state that Buchman had never met Schuman. Meanwhile the *New Statesman* attributed the Schuman Plan as a whole to 'Buchman's pious anti-Socialism'.[4] Neither report was high in accuracy. Nor were the assertions made by some enthusiasts in after years that Buchman had been almost solely responsible for the Franco-German reconciliation after the war. What was, in fact, his part?

Obviously, Buchman had nothing to do with the details of the Plan to bring the coal and steel industries of Europe under a single authority. That had been the work, over a long period, of Jean Monnet and a small team of dedicated experts who only presented it to Schuman himself in April 1950. Nor had Buchman been responsible for putting the idea of a closer European unity into the mind of either Schuman or Adenauer. Schuman had believed in the need to bring France and Germany together in some such way since the 1920s,[5] while Adenauer was considering the possibility of linking the steel industries of the two countries as far back as 1923.[6]

Nor would it be accurate to infer, as some have, that Buchman was in any way responsible for planting in either Schuman or Adenauer the concern to rebuild Europe on a Christian basis. Both were devout Catholics and had long cherished that hope.

Schuman once seriously thought of entering the priesthood but, in his own words, 'chose to aid atheists to live rather than Christians to die'.[7] Some of his friends regarded him as a 'saint in a jacket', but he thought of himself as 'a very imperfect instrument of a Providence which makes use of us in accomplishing designs which go far beyond ourselves'.[8] He believed in the individual direction of God. 'Often he tacked about, delayed a decision, tried to dodge the call which was making itself heard in the depths of his conscience,' wrote his close collaborator, the Socialist leader André Philip. 'Then, when he was sure what the inner voice was demanding, he took the boldest initiative and pushed it to its conclusion, equally oblivious of attacks as of threats.'[9]

Adenauer, too, was deeply rooted in his faith. When Hitler hounded him out of office as Lord Mayor of Cologne in 1933, he sought refuge at Maria Laach Monastery, which was presided over by an old school friend, Ildefons Herwegen; and when Hitler was overthrown he, like Schuman, was convinced that Germany and Europe could only be rebuilt on Christian foundations. He regarded the uniting of Europe as 'not only a political and economic aim worth striving for, but as a real Christian obligation'.[10] He too sought God's direction in affairs – often, according to one biographer, while shaving.

The carrying through of the Schuman Plan was made possible by the pressure of outside events – the determination to avoid yet another war between France and Germany, and the emergence of an aggressive Soviet Union – and by the convergence of an unusual group of men who were 'kindred spirits'. Professor Henri Rieben, Director of the Jean Monnet Institute in Lausanne, used that phrase to describe Monnet and Buchman, who never, in fact, met. Buchman, he said, had 'geo-political diagnosis plus inspiration', and did on a spiritual level what Monnet did on a political level.[11] The same phrase can be used even more certainly to describe Buchman, Schuman and Adenauer,[12] despite the fact that the last two sometimes doubted each other. Each played an essential part, sometimes together, often independently. As far as Buchman was concerned, he had once more been led to people whom he could assist, by word and action, to make their highest hopes come true.

Adenauer had first been attracted by Buchman's open-hearted reception of the Germans at Caux which, in Reinhold Maier's words, 'ended the moral outlawry of Germany'.[13] At Caux itself, Adenauer was impressed that 'people have the courage to stand for good and for God and that each begins with himself'[14] – a point he was to reiterate. Finally, 'the great success' of Buchman's work in the Ruhr was to convince him of Moral

Re-Armament's effectiveness. That work, too, was a prerequisite of Franco-German rapprochement. As the *Neue Zürcher Zeitung* wrote in 1959: 'The Ruhr, instead of being the apple of discord for Europe, has become the growing point of international agreement... Without the Ruhr, no High Authority*; without the High Authority, no Common Market and no far-reaching plan for European integration.'[15]

In March 1949 in Bern, in one of his early political speeches outside Germany, he mentioned the promising attitude of some French leaders and the new outlook in the Benelux countries. He concluded, 'In large sectors of the German public, there is a profound conviction that only a union of the countries of Western Europe can save this old continent. If France behaves wisely and generously towards Germany, she will render historic service to Europe.'[16]

In the same month Robert Schuman, now France's Foreign Minister, dined with Louis Boucquey and two of Buchman's close colleagues, Philippe Mottu and John Caulfeild. According to their reports, Schuman talked at length about the Atlantic Pact, which was about to be signed, describing it as a defective diplomatic instrument if confined to the political and military spheres: 'We must reach the masses so that the Pact will be sustained not only by the atom bomb, but by a change in the way of life of the Western world. In the economic field we have the Marshall Plan; in the political and military field the Atlantic Pact. Now we need to give fresh ideological content to the life of the millions of Europe.' Then he added, 'The Germans need a lot of courage to work with the French. It is no good being sentimental about these things. We all need to reach a deep inner change in order to find the solutions to our major problems.'[17]

This so closely coincided with Buchman's own thought that Boucquey asked Schuman if he would write a foreword to the French edition of Buchman's speeches, which had appeared in English under the title *Remaking the World*. Schuman accepted, although he remarked, 'I have not yet crossed the Rubicon.'[18] The opportunity to write the foreword came when a mild attack of 'flu gave him a brief respite in February 1950. By that time he had met Buchman again, and he was later to say that reading the book gave him 'a glimpse of the meaning of Frank Buchman's life, past and present'.[19] Certainly, his foreword expressed Buchman's aims and methods during these years with extraordinary accuracy. After stating that 'thus far statesmen have only been moderately successful in "remaking the world"', he wrote that if Buchman had presented some new scheme for public welfare or just another theory he would have remained sceptical, but that, on the contrary, 'What Moral Re-Armament brings us is a philosophy of life applied in action'. Then in three succinct

---

* The governing body set up under the Schuman Plan.

sentences he outlined Buchman's programme: 'To begin by creating a moral climate in which true brotherly unity can flourish, overarching all that today tears the world apart – that is the immediate goal. The acquisition of wisdom about men and affairs by bringing people together in public assemblies and public encounters – that is the means employed. To provide teams of trained people, ready for the service of the state, apostles of reconciliation and builders of a new world – that is the beginning of a far-reaching transformation of society in which, during fifteen war-ravaged years, the first steps have already been made.'

'It is not a question of a change in policy: it is a question of changing people,' Schuman added. 'Democracy and her freedoms can be saved only by the quality of the people who speak in her name.'[20]

Schuman wrote these words at a time when his efforts towards Franco-German agreement seemed likely to be frustrated. 'I had a sort of intuition that came to me through that book,' he recalled three years later. 'I saw new perspectives opening before me.'[21]

Western defence, then, had been secured by the signing in April 1949 of the Atlantic Pact. The larger task, as Schuman saw it, of 'giving ideological content to the lives of the masses', remained. Buchman was making this a main theme at Caux in the summer of 1949 and, with Schuman's agreement, printed the essence of what Schuman had said at Boucquey's dinner in the invitation. He also asked Schuman and Adenauer to come to Caux and help him. Schuman agreed and suggested dates in June which suited Adenauer. 'Your desire to dedicate a week at Caux is of major importance for the pressing problems of France and Germany,'[22] Buchman replied. He also wrote to Minister-President Arnold that if the leaders could 'get together and have a common mind under the guidance of God, then He can give the answer to the extremely difficult and seemingly insoluble problems that present themselves'.[23]

In the event, Schuman was tied up throughout June at the fruitless Paris meeting on German reunification and asked Georges Villiers, President of the French Employers' Federation, to represent him at Caux. Adenauer, too, wrote, 'I am extremely sorry that, contrary to my original intentions, I could not get to Caux last week. Now that we have decided on the elections and choice of government I have been completely taken up with the preparations, but I hope to come later to Caux and to have the pleasure of seeing you again. I would like to express my thanks once more for the help you have shown us Germans in making it possible for us to meet people from other countries again and so to bridge the gulf which, alas, still separates us from the rest of the world.'[24]

Over 1,300 other Germans, however, did come to Caux that year, including Alfred Hartman, the financial director of the British and American zones, Hans Böckler, the head of the German trades unions, and many other key figures, including twelve state cabinet ministers. From North Rhine-Wesphalia, for example, came seventeen politicians, eleven newspaper editors, fifty-nine industrialists and eighty-one members of works councils. The problem of Franco-German relations was, according to L'Aube, Schuman's MRP party paper, dealt with frankly and courageously.[25]

One day Villiers sat at table beside Böckler, whose part in creating the new Germany some historians consider second only to Adenauer's.[26] Böckler said, 'We ought to be enemies on two counts – I am a German, you are French; you are the head of the employers, I am a trade union leader.'

Villiers replied, 'Yes, and there's a third count. Your countrymen condemned me to death; I was in a political concentration camp; I saw most of my comrades die around me. But that is all past. We must forget it. And personally, I would like to shake your hand.'[27]

Countless similar encounters took place at Caux, not only between the Germans and the smaller but influential French delegation,* but also between them and former enemies from other countries. As Price concludes: 'It was not merely the personal trust relationship between Adenauer and Schuman that had been built (and Schuman had a deep distrust of the Germans). It was between hundreds and thousands of men and women – opinion formers at all levels and occupations at Caux – which gave a decisive impetus to European unity at a critical time.'[28]

On 25 October 1949 Boucquey invited Buchman and Schuman to dine together in his home, where they talked freely through a long evening. It had been a frustrating summer for Schuman, and he felt discouraged by his inability to move his colleagues and his nation forward along the road to a new Europe. Prime Minister Georges Bidault, for example, was at first indifferent, if not opposed, to any such proposition. When Boucquey spoke of the honour of having the two men at his table Schuman replied, 'If I have contributed anything to mankind, I must also admit that much of my work has been destroyed and frustrated. But Dr Buchman, because he has concentrated his efforts on one section of human life – the most important one – has the joy of seeing them succeed and spread all over the

---

* Among other French to attend Caux in the first years were Paul Bacon, Vice-President of the Provisional Assembly and then Minister of Labour in several governments, business men like Pierre Carteron, President of the French Association of Insurance Companies, and Robert Carmichael, President of the Jute Industry, and trades unionists such as Yves Fournis, General Secretary of the Foremen, Technicians and Engineers' Association, and Maurice Mercier, one of the founders of the Force Ouvrière. Henri Lespès, a Deputy and later a member of the French High Court of Justice, had been one of those to urge Irène Laure to go to Caux. His assessment was: 'At Caux is the centre of international renaissance which all have been longing for.' (Manchester Guardian, 26 August 1946.)

world. Statesmen can propose far-reaching plans, but they cannot put them into effect without far-reaching changes in the hearts of people – that is your work, and it is the kind of work I would like to do for the rest of my life.'

Then turning to Buchman, he said, 'I need your advice. For years I have wanted to get out of politics and write about the lessons of my life. I have no family or dependents. There is a monastery where I would be welcome. It has a library. It is quiet. I feel I could do my best work there. Will you advise me? What should I do?'

Buchman looked at him. 'Monsieur Schuman, what do you think in your own heart you should do?' he asked.

Schuman threw up his hands and a broad smile creased his expressive face. 'You shouldn't have asked me. Of course, I know I must stay where I am.'

Then very seriously he added, 'There is one thing I must do. I feel it in my bones and it has led me as far as I have gone recently, but I am afraid of it. I am from Lorraine, and I was brought up as a German. Then Lorraine returned to France and I became a Frenchman and served in the French army. I know the problems and mentality of both countries. I have known for a long time that I have a big part in ending the hatred between us. I have talked about it with de Gasperi.* He is in the same situation – born Austrian and served in the Austrian army, then Italian, and understanding both. We know that something can and must be done and that we are the men to do it. But I shrink from it.'

'Yes, you must stay where you are,' Buchman said. 'Under God that is your place.'

'One difficulty', Schuman went on, 'is that I do not know whom to trust in the new Germany. Adenauer, for instance, I have only just met.'

Buchman replied, 'We have had some excellent men in Caux and I can give you a dozen names.' He gave Schuman a list.

'I am going officially to Germany in the next weeks', Schuman said, 'and I will look them up.'

In Boucquey's guest book Schuman wrote, 'This evening spent with Dr Buchman and the close friends in his great work has been a treasured first step which will lead me, I very much hope, to Caux.'[29]

How often Schuman and Adenauer had already met by this time is disputed. Schuman says that a meeting in Koblenz in August 1949 was their first encounter.[30] Adenauer, in his memoirs, writes of an earlier meeting in October 1948,[31] while another source speaks of them spending a day together, sometime in 1949, at the monastery of Maria Laach.[32]

---

* Then Prime Minister of Italy. De Gasperi was a pupil of the priest, Don Luigi Sturzo, whom he succeeded as leader of the Popular Party in 1923, only to be imprisoned when the party was dissolved in 1926.

The important point seems to have been not how often they had met, but that neither of them fully trusted the other at this time. Schuman might recognise intellectually, as he said to Boucquey, that 'Germans would need a lot of courage to work with the French', but he still had deep suspicions of his own about the Germans. Adenauer's meeting with him in October 1948, for which there is independent evidence, seems to have been rather unsuccessful, not least because Adenauer had had to listen to Schuman's 'personal theory' that Germany should be divided up into Rhine, Elbe and Danube states.[33] It is difficult today to remember how deep a chasm seventy years of enmity had left between even the most sympathetic French and German minds. What part, if any, the evening with Buchman played in determining Schuman to continue his European mission it is hard to assess. Another influence upon him at this time must have been Dean Acheson's encouragement during the NATO Council in September 1949 that he should take initiative towards Germany, perhaps in concert with America and Britain; and Stalin's continued aggressiveness was a constant spur to action. However, Christopher (now Lord) Mayhew spoke of conversations in which Schuman said that Buchman had helped him to continue with the Germans.[34]

In December 1949 Buchman was in Bonn. A lunch in his honour was given by President Heuss and a number of Ministers. Afterwards he went to the Palais Schaumburg where Chancellor Adenauer was waiting in high spirits. He had just listened to seven professors each make a half-hour speech, and it had, he said, given him time for peaceful reflection. He thanked Buchman for what he had done for Germany, and asked warmly after Schuman and his concern for a new relationship between France and Germany. The conversation passed to news of Moral Re-Armament. The Chancellor, who had a strong sense of the practical, maintained that his son Georg was studying better since his visit to Caux. Buchman disclaimed all responsibility and laughingly said it must be due to his father's good influence. The Chancellor countered that his two secretaries who had been in Caux were also working better. When he offered to show Buchman the Palais Schaumburg Buchman surprised him by saying, 'I believe I know it very well already. I used to stay here when it was Princess Victoria's home.'

Less than a month later, on 13 January 1950, Schuman made his promised call on the Chancellor. When he arrived Bonn station was almost empty except for Adenauer, who hurried him to a waiting car as, he explained, he feared an attack on Schuman 'because you French are on the way to absorbing the Saar'.[35] Schuman's opening statement was full of faith that Germany and France could co-operate in future, and the two men moved closer together. However, nothing was settled about the Saar, though Adenauer seems to have got the impression that Schuman thought that, one day, the Saar might be returned to Germany: an impression he had also carried away from their previous talk in October 1948. Things, however, did not work out so smoothly. On 3 March the French Government took steps to integrate the Saar into France.[36] So, when three of Buchman's friends called on Adenauer on 7 April, they found him greatly incensed with Schuman. 'He is a liar,' Adenauer told them. 'Even Bidault lets me call Schuman a lying Alsatian peasant.' His visitors suggested that, if this were true, Adenauer himself should think how to change Schuman. 'I also need to change more myself,' Adenauer replied, reiterating the impression that the thought of each starting with himself had made upon him at Caux.[37]

At all events there was a moment when it looked as if the great opportunity might be missed. Jean Monnet noted that there was 'une atmosphère glacée' at the January meeting in Bonn[38] and remarked to Schuman, 'We are on the brink of making the same mistake as in 1919,'[39] even though Adenauer describes their last two-hour session of the meetings as 'characterised by mutual trust'.[40] By April there was no doubt about the danger of breakdown. 'We were in an impasse in almost whatever direction we turned . . . we were surrounded by walls,' Schuman said later. 'In order to advance we had to open a breach. First of all we had to get rid of the terrible mortgage of fate – fear. We felt the need of some psychological leap forward. . .'[41]

Monnet provided that leap by producing his plan for the coal and steel pool which had hurriedly been completed. On 20 April he gave a copy to Bidault who ignored it. On 28 April he passed a copy through his *chef de cabinet* to Schuman who realised that time was running perilously short if there was to be an agreement by 11 May, when a crucial foreign ministers' conference was to take place. Schuman studied it over a weekend, and said on his return, 'I'll use it.'[42] At a lunch with Monnet in the first week of May he suggested that the plan should be introduced in a sudden and dramatic way. They agreed that only two French Ministers, Mayer and Pleven, should be told the details before the Cabinet of 9 May, while Bidault (who dismissed the project as 'a soap bubble – just one more international body') was only told in general terms.[43]

On 9 May the German Cabinet too was in session. Adenauer, while at the Cabinet table, was handed a letter from Schuman containing an outline of the plan. Recognising, as he said later, that this was 'a magnanimous step . . . of extraordinary importance for the peace of Europe and of the entire world', Adenauer replied, accepting, within the hour. 'Because a personal relationship of trust had been formed,' comments Price, 'the opportunity was not lost.'[44] So when Schuman brought the proposal before his Cabinet an hour later, with the strong support of Mayer and Pleven, it was approved.[45]

In 1951, two months after the Schuman Plan agreement was finally signed, Adenauer sent to Buchman in America a message which was reported in the *New York Herald-Tribune* under the headline 'Moral Re-Armament is Credited for Role in Schuman Plan Talks'.[46] Adenauer wrote, 'In recent months we have seen the conclusion, after some difficult negotiations, of important international agreements. Here Moral Re-Armament has played an invisible but effective part in bridging differences of opinion between negotiating parties, and has kept before them the object of peaceful agreement in the search for the common good which is the true purpose of human life . . . It is my conviction too that men and nations cannot outwardly enjoy stable relationships until they have been inwardly prepared for them. In this respect, Moral Re-Armament has rendered great and lasting service.'[47] The presentation of the German Order of Merit to Buchman followed in the next year.

It was not until 1953 that Schuman was able to fulfil his promise to visit Caux. After attending every meeting during his brief stay and seeing two plays, he asked if he might speak. 'I leave in a spirit noticeably different from the one in which I came here,' he said. 'I have been in politics for thirty-four years, and during that length of time one learns to be sceptical. I am leaving with much less scepticism than when I came, and at my age that is a considerable advance.' What had impressed him more than anything else, he said, was how Moral Re-Armament could be translated in terms of international relations between countries. 'Thank you for giving me that hope,' he concluded. 'From now on we will never give up.' As he left Caux he added, 'This has been one of the greatest experiences of my life.'[48]

Schuman continued to give regular support until Buchman's death in 1961. There has been speculation why Adenauer did not mention Buchman in his *Memoirs*. Similarly, although his name headed a list inviting a Moral Re-Armament mission to Germany in 1956, he does not seem to have attended its theatre production in Bonn. The latter is easily understandable in a busy statesman; but the former might seem to leave his attitude equivocal. However, he was continually in touch with Buchman through the years, asking his help.

In 1958, for example, when de Gaulle assumed power, Adenauer sent Buchman two personally signed messages, one for publication in the official government *Bulletin*, the other in a personal letter. The latter read in part: 'I share the conviction that now is the time more strongly than ever for European unity through Moral Re-Armament. You have given most valuable stimulus to the great work of unifying Europe. I am convinced with you that unless this work is carried forward, peace in the world cannot be maintained. Therefore, I would be extremely happy if you yourself could give your personal attention to it in the coming months, which are decisive for developments in Europe.'[49] And when, in 1960, Adenauer visited Los Angeles, he specially asked Buchman to meet him there. It was their last meeting. 'I want to tell you with all the emphasis at my command how highly I value your work,' he told Buchman. 'It is essential for world peace.'[50]

Many Germans have confirmed this evaluation. For example, in 1960, when Dr Hasso von Etzdorf, Deputy Under Secretary of State at the German Foreign Office (formerly Ambassador to Canada and later, from 1961 to 1965, Ambassador to the United Kingdom), was asked by journalists in Atlanta, 'What is the most significant development since World War II?', he replied, 'The new accord between Germany and France, which I believe is permanent. For this the work of Moral Re-Armament is largely responsible.'[51] 'Dr von Etzdorf seems to have expressed this view in similar words in 1959.[52] And it is a view to which he still subscribes,' Price concludes.[53]

When Buchman died in 1961 the German Government's official *Bulletin* wrote, 'Since 1947 Caux has been the symbol of Dr Buchman's work for the German people. Through it he brought Germany back into the circle of civilised nations, after Hitler had forbidden his movement in Germany and had earned for our country the distrust and disdain of other nations. At Caux every kind of German – politicians, scientists, industrialists and workers – met those who had been their bitter enemies during the war. So Caux became one of the great moral forces to which we owe our new standing in the world. For this Dr Buchman will never be forgotten. His name also stands for ever linked with the understanding between Germany and France, the foundations of which were laid by the first meetings between Germans and French at Caux.' Nor have these services been forgotten. In September 1982 the President of the German Federal Republic, Professor Dr Karl Carstens, received Moral Re-Armament delegates from twenty-two countries and said to them, 'During the post-war years, when we Germans regained acceptance in the international community and rebuilt relations with France, it was to a large extend due to Moral Re-Armament.'[54]

How then can Buchman's contribution to the reconciliation between Germany and France be summarised? First, it appears to be beyond dispute that, as the official *Bulletin* stated, he 'brought Germany back into the circle of civilised nations' – and, in so doing, reconciled German leaders with their opposite numbers in France and other European countries. Secondly, the work of Moral Re-Armament in the Ruhr and in French industry was an essential prerequisite to the uniting of the French and German coal and steel industries. Thirdly, Buchman's friendship with Adenauer, Schuman and other leading figures played a real, if unquantifiable, part in easing the negotiating process.

[383]

Yet, for Buchman himself, all this was a by-product of the work which he felt that God had laid upon him with individuals. When, on one occasion, a letter of praise reached him from Adenauer, he said to his friends, 'I am dumb-struck', and when he was decorated with the Order of Merit he accepted it 'mindful that it is an honour shared by every man and woman who played a part'.[55]

JAPAN

The first country for which Buchman prayed on that evening in Mackinac when he heard that the Second World War was over was Japan. Nearly thirty years earlier he had visited that country seven times, although he only twice stayed as much as a month. He did not go back there until 1956. Yet by then he was a national figure on whom the government wished to confer Japan's highest decoration.

In November 1935 Buchman had whole-heartedly backed the decision of a young Oxford graduate, Basil Entwistle, to accompany Bishop Roots and his family on their return from the Oxford house-party to China. They passed through Tokyo and Entwistle took up the introduction of the Washington columnist, George Sokolsky, to meet Kensuke Horinouchi, then head of the American desk at the Japanese Foreign Office. This meeting led to a renewal of the Christian faith of Horinouchi and his wife. A year later Horinouchi, now Vice-Minister for Foreign Affairs, gave a reception for his friends to meet Entwistle on a return visit. By then a serious power struggle was in progress between the young military and Horinouchi and his moderate friends at the Foreign Office. For a time those in the Foreign Office who wanted peace held their own, though always in danger of assassination. In 1937 Horinouchi was appointed Ambassador in Washington, where he met Buchman. When in 1940 it became clear that he was being forced to pass untrue messages to the Americans, he asked to be recalled. 'I don't know when we will meet again,' he told Buchman and Entwistle in San Francisco before leaving. 'We face difficult times. Maybe we shall not be able to be in touch. But, whatever happens, we are so grateful to God for the peace we have found inside us. We will be faithful to everything you have taught us.'[1] Back in Tokyo he had been dismissed from the diplomatic corps and during the war he lived under close surveillance. But he kept his promise.

Other Japanese, who had met Buchman and his friends abroad, had also returned home. Among them was Takasumi Mitsui – brother of the head of Japan's most powerful business house – who had studied under Streeter and Thornhill at Oxford. There he, his wife Hideko and their children were baptised. They worked with Buchman in Europe until 1938, when they returned to Japan. Through the war he and Hideko, too, kept faith through many difficulties. They lost their two Tokyo houses in one night through fire-bombs, and lived for the rest of the war in a concrete store-house. Like all Japanese they had little to eat – one of their children died of malnutrition – and they were watched by the police because of their identification with Moral Re-Armament. But, as members of the powerful Mitsui family, they were not arrested.

Horinouchi and the Mitsuis were among ten Japanese to attend Buchman's Riverside conference in California in June 1948. This group, the first other than a few technicians to travel abroad since the war, also included Yasutane and Yukika Sohma, who had met Moral Re-Armament in Japan. Yasutane was the head of a noble family with estates in central Japan who had been stripped of his title and most of his land under the new Constitution. A whimsical, charming *bon viveur*, he had married the brilliant daughter of Yukio Ozaki, 'the father of the Japanese Diet', who as Mayor of Tokyo presented the cherry trees to Washington which have ever since been a spring tourist attraction. Yukika had not only shared occasions when her father narrowly missed assassination because of his democratic principles, but herself flouted tradition at every turn, and had met Yasutane while she was riding a motorcycle, an unheard-of activity for a Japanese woman at that time. Only the change brought to both of them through another friend of Buchman's, an American diplomat, had converted a difficult marriage into a creative partnership.

At Riverside one of the Japanese said to Buchman, 'We have this new Constitution the Americans have given us. It is like an empty basket. What shall we put in it?' The United States government, realising the vacuum created by the destruction of Japanese militarism, had acted quickly to reorganise the country on a democratic basis, but the forms introduced did not of themselves fill the vacuum. Buchman saw that this question was as urgent as those facing Germany.

The distinguished German delegation at Riverside gave the Japanese the hope that what the Germans had found at Caux could also fill the vacuum in Japan. The Sohmas asked the Entwistles to come to Japan, bringing their baby daughter. 'In Japan, right now, with everything in ruins?' said Entwistle. 'Maybe not immediately. We'll work on it,' replied Yukika.

The next summer thirty-seven Japanese went to Caux, including a delegation centring round the recent Socialist Prime Minister, Tetsu Katayama, and his wife. They arrived in America en route just when Jean Entwistle was in hospital for the birth of her second child, Fred. Entwistle cabled Buchman the news of his son's arrival, and received a reply welcoming Fred into the world and asking his father to accompany this

Japanese party to Europe. 'Never had I felt less inclined to leave Jean,' writes Entwistle. 'I felt rebellious . . . but I regarded the request as a soldier viewed his travel orders. Jean, still in hospital, was more resolute than I as I bade her farewell at her bedside.'[2]

The trip lasted ten weeks. After a month at Caux, Katayama's party was received by the German, French and British governments and Socialist parties. At an official lunch given by Christopher Mayhew in London Entwistle sat next to Denis Healey.* 'Moral Re-Armament must be an extremely powerful world organisation,' said Healey. 'It has succeeded in doing what the British Labour Party has failed to do in the last two years – secure permission for Japanese Socialists to visit Britain.'[3]

In January 1950, back in America, Entwistle received a cable from Buchman asking him to go to Japan to stand by some of the Japanese who had been at Riverside and Caux. 'Take Ken with you,' the cable added. 'Ken Twitchell was even more startled than I was,' writes Entwistle. 'Neither of us considered for a moment not responding, although I was loath to leave my family for what looked like a long period.'[4]

Their only commission from Buchman had been to give thought and care to particular Japanese families. They had also heard from the Mitsuis and Sohmas that there was a division in the ranks of Moral Re-Armament in Tokyo. Some were determined to confine Moral Re-Armament to a narrow Christian practice which stressed moral standards and the need for the guidance of God, but only as they applied to personal matters, and demanded immediate acceptance by all of particular doctrines. Others, like the Mitsuis, Sohmas and Horinouchis, saw it as a moral and spiritual force to reshape Japan into a united, democratic, responsible nation.

The travellers realised they were entering a non-Christian nation, and one whose conception of Christianity was shaped by the long-experienced superiority and doctrinaire theology of some Christians in Japan, as well as by what many felt were hostile policies of the 'Christian' countries of the West. Buchman had said from the beginning that 'the outstretched arms of Christ are for everyone', Christian and non-Christian alike. Thus he had taught his team to talk about moral and spiritual change in terms which the non- or anti-Christian – the Communists in the British coalfields and the Ruhr, for example – could understand, and not to place any doctrinal obstacle in their way.

At the appropriate moment he would always give those at his gatherings, whatever their faith or lack of it, the deepest Christian truths he knew, often centred round the story of how he had himself been washed

---

* Mayhew at that time was an Under-Secretary of State at the Foreign Office, Healey was Secretary of the International Department of the Labour Party.

clean from his hatreds by his experience of the Cross at Keswick and how Christ had become his nearest friend. This was done with the utmost urgency – that everyone must face the reality of their sin, and find change and forgiveness. But he never added that those in his audience must break with their traditions, or join this or that church. He felt that his task was to bring people into vital touch with the Holy Spirit who would lead them each personally, and, in the process, would help them to live by the will of God. His purpose was to enlist everyone in the moral and spiritual revolution which he held to be vital if the nations were to be remade and become instruments in the hands of God for the benefit of one another. In this he was a pioneer of what was to become an increasingly held open and inclusive position towards those of other faiths.

Thus in two speeches in America and Germany at about this time he made what were, to him, two entirely consistent statements. 'MRA is the good road of an ideology inspired by God upon which all can unite,' he said in 1948. 'Catholic, Jew and Protestant, Hindu, Muslim, Buddhist and Confucianist – all find they can change, where needed, and travel along this good road together.'[5] In 1951 he said, 'It needs this stronger dose . . . "The blood of Jesus Christ His Son cleanseth us from all sin." That is the discovery everyone is looking for. That is the answer.'[6]

How could Entwistle and Twitchell apply these principles in Japan? That first Sunday they met with the strict 'Christian' group, the dominant spirit in which was a woman missionary, reminiscent of some Buchman had met in China years before. She was, records Entwistle, 'elderly, emphatic, very British and very sentimental'.[7] She had independent means, but lived in the humblest circumstances, surrounding herself with impoverished Japanese Christians – some dedicated like herself and some free-loaders. She insisted that those like the Mitsuis, the Horinouchis and the Sohmas must, in effect, join her particular circle and concentrate on their personal lives. Entwistle and Twitchell, while respecting her faithfulness and self-sacrifice, felt that they must back these three couples in taking the change they had found to the centre of the nation.

This they had already begun to do. In the next ten days they took their visitors to see Prime Minister Shigeru Yoshida, the outstanding politician of the day, and also to the two men commonly known as 'The Pope' and 'The Emperor'. The 'Pope' was Hisato Ichimada, Governor of the Bank of Japan; the 'Emperor' was Chikao Honda, President of the *Mainichi* communications conglomerate. They also saw Yukika's father, the veteran parliamentarian, and were given receptions by the three leading newspapers, the directors of the Bank of Japan and the Speaker of the Upper House of the Diet.

Out of all this came the idea that a special planeload of seventy-six, the most representative group to leave Japan since the war, should go to Caux in the summer of 1950. General Douglas MacArthur, the US supremo in Japan, warmly endorsed the venture, and one June evening the DC-4 lifted off over a moonlit Tokyo Bay, taking a delegation which included Members of Parliament from all the main parties, seven Governors of Prefectures, the Mayors of Hiroshima and Nagasaki, and leaders of industry, finance and labour. Prime Minister Yoshida offered them a vivid conception of their mission at a luncheon for leaders of the delegation. 'In 1870', he said, 'a group of Japanese travelled to the West. On their return they changed the course of Japanese life. I believe that when this delegation returns you too will open a new page in our history.'[8]

The Japanese arrived at Caux full of apprehension about how they would be received by the people from many countries, including recent enemies. Buchman had anticipated their fears. He was at the door of Mountain House to greet each one personally, and had made sure that the Japanese flag was flying alongside those of the other nations. Under American occupation the flag could not be flown, and at the sight of it tears came to the visitors' eyes.

Buchman also took care to observe the niceties of Japanese manners – bowing instead of shaking hands, paying attention to their rules of seniority, and providing them with Japanese food perfectly cooked. One of the labour leaders in the party, Daiji Ioka, chairman of the Municipal Workers of Osaka, told the assembly, 'Our nation took a road to war which has caused tremendous suffering to the world. When my colleagues and I left Tokyo we fully expected to be treated as enemies, even to the point of segregation, but we were overwhelmed by the warmth of the welcome we received.'[9]

During their stay Buchman planned the meetings so that they heard French and Germans promising to rebuild a ruined Europe together, management and labour undertaking to help industry to meet the needs of people, and rival political leaders seeking ways to unite their countries. He met with the delegation and with individuals privately, alert to draw out their aspirations and reinforce their new decisions. Such decisions were numerous. For example, the Governor of Nagano province and the Mayor of its capital publicly forsook their well-known antagonism to each other; and a militant labour leader, Katsuji Nakajima, and his 'public enemy number one', the regional police chief, Eiji Suzuki, were reconciled.

The youngest of the six Diet Members in the party, Yasuhiru Nakasone, who was to become Prime Minister of Japan in 1983, wrote from Caux to a Japanese paper: 'People who spoke at the assembly were largely representatives of labour and management . . . The Japanese representatives who heard these witnesses had many doubts and conflicts within their hearts. Some of the excuses they made were: "The workers of Japan are up against a far more serious problem of living which will not permit such sweet compromises; we have to solve first the problem of our inadequate national resources." However, the ice in the Japanese hearts was melted by the international harmony that transcends race and class in this great current of world history moving through the continents of America and Europe.'[10]

When the Japanese were due to go home via Bonn, Paris, London and the United States, Buchman put it to them to demonstrate a change of heart which would affect the leaders and peoples they would meet. While they had been at Caux the Korean war had broken out, and it was only after considering the mission which Buchman put up to them that they decided to continue as planned rather than return direct home. According to Morris Martin, they expressed doubts to Buchman whether to continue to America, partly because of expense and partly because of the strong antagonism they expected to find there. 'Of course you must go to America,' Buchman said. 'You have your biggest job to do there.' 'Then', continues Martin, 'Buchman asked for an envelope to be brought to him. Inside were some cheques. "I have had a birthday and some American friends were good to me. My thought is to turn the money over to you. Count the cheques." A Japanese banker obliged, and found nearly $9,000. "Is it enough?" asked Buchman. "Not quite," said an American who was present. "But I will make up the difference." The Japanese were deeply touched and now looked on their journey as a sacred mission.'[11]

They were well received throughout Europe, and as they left Britain for America *The Observer* printed the delegation's farewell message on its front page. It expressed the group's reaction to the news from Korea. 'We hope in future as a nation to show by our deeds that we have found a change of heart and that we can make our contribution to the remaking of the world,' they said. 'Russia has advanced in Asia because the Soviet Government understands the art of ideological war. It fights for the minds of men. We appeal to the Governments and peoples of the West to do the same – to make themselves expert in the philosophy and practice of moral re-armament, which is the ideology of the future. Then all Asia will listen.'[12]

Buchman made a deep impression on most of the Japanese and during their travels and on their return home they frequently quoted words he had said to them. Mayor Hamai of Hiroshima, speaking on a nation-wide radio programme in the United States on the anniversary of the dropping of the atom bomb, stated, 'Dr Buchman has said, "Peace is people becoming different." This hits the nail on the head. I for one intend to start this effort from Hiroshima. The one dream and hope left to our surviving citizens is to re-establish the city as a pattern for peace.'

When they visited the United States Senate Vice-President Alben

Barkley greeted each of the delegation personally, conducted the Diet members to seats in the chamber and expressed the hope that the long friendship between Japan and America, broken by the war, might be resumed. The senior Japanese representative, Chorijuo Kurijama, said, 'We are sincerely sorry for Japan's big mistake. We broke almost a century-old friendship between the two countries. We ask your forgiveness and help. We have found in Caux the true content of democracy.'[13] The Senate gave him a standing ovation. The House of Representatives next day was equally responsive.

A *New York Times* editorial on this occasion noted that it was less than five years since the atomic bombs had fallen on Japan, and wrote, 'The Mayors of Hiroshima and Nagasaki were among yesterday's visitors . . . For a moment one could see out of the present darkness into the years when all men may be brothers.'[14] The *Saturday Evening Post* more colloquially wrote, 'The idea of a nation admitting that it could be mistaken has a refreshing impact . . . Perhaps even Americans could think up a few past occasions of which it could safely be said, "We certainly fouled things up that time." '[15]

On their return home the Japanese initiated fresh approaches between management and workers which bore rich fruit in the years ahead. They also influenced some turbulent debates in the Diet by their moderation and the underlying unity between members of different parties created at Caux.

In July 1951, when the Korean war was still raging and the United States trying to create the mutual defence pact which later became SEATO, an Asian delegation from Japan, China, Malaya, Burma, Ceylon and India formed the nucleus of a conference which Buchman called in Los Angeles with the theme of the reconstruction of Pacific relations. Here he gave the Asians a platform from which to talk to America, and particularly to Washington. Their stories showed how different these lands were, how each had its own pride in its traditions and aspirations, and how, by implication, it would be necessary to respect these if any pact was to function. Anti-Communism and pro-Americanism, the Asians made clear, were not broad enough philosophies to hold together such divergent peoples. Nor was the mere provision of 'hardware' and dollars by the United States adequate. Something positive was needed – an idea which could be lived out by both Americans and Asians, but which Americans would need to experience before they could export it to others. Buchman believed that America's blindness to this ideological factor was America's greatest weakness in her approach to the world, just as the understanding of it was Soviet Russia's greatest strength. He insisted that a new book by Peter Howard and Paul Campbell should be called *America Needs an Ideology*.

The unexpected news that the Japanese Peace Treaty would be signed in September 1951 in San Francisco was suddenly announced. Once more, as in 1945, Buchman had unknowingly anticipated the event. Months earlier Buchman had engaged a theatre in that city for that period to show a musical, *Jotham Valley*, which illustrated, through the true story of two feuding brothers in Nevada, how deep divisions could be overcome and hatreds healed. When the plenipotentiaries arrived, it became clear that much healing still needed to take place. The United States had convinced most of her World War II allies that the time was ripe to sign a treaty, which would be followed in eight months by Japan's full independence. But Russia boycotted the conference and, among the participants, Australia, New Zealand and others expressed serious reservations about the integrity of an independent Japan. So the delegates met in an atmosphere of tension, the Japanese finding themselves almost totally segregated except during the official business of the conference.

Buchman, Twitchell and Entwistle knew five of the six official Japanese delegates, as well as a number of the alternative delegates. Much of their work was done around a table for twelve at the Mark Hopkins Hotel which Buchman booked for lunch nearly every day, and often for breakfast and dinner as well. There delegates from most of the other nations met the Japanese, while in the evening large groups of them attended *Jotham Valley*. On his return to Japan, Hisato Ichimada, the Governor of the Bank of Japan and a principal delegate, told Mitsui and Entwistle that Buchman's efforts had been the one means of bridging the gulf with the delegates of other nations at the conference.[16]

On the eve of the official signing five of the Japanese signatories dined with Buchman, and at the signing itself Buchman introduced them to Robert Schuman. A week later Schuman was in Ottawa for a NATO conference. Buchman was in Ottawa too, and Schuman and the Danish Foreign Minister, Ole Bjørn Kraft, came to tea with him at the MRA centre there. As they left, Schuman said to his host, 'The world is not big enough for you. You made peace with Japan before we did.' Back in the house Buchman, according to one present, 'led his friends in a spirited, if discordant, rendering of a favourite song, "After the ball is over".'[17]

During these years Buchman's name was often put forward as a candidate for the Nobel Peace Prize. In 1951 he was nominated by groups of parliamentarians from Britain, France, Sweden, Denmark and Greece, as well as by many individuals such as Walter Nash, leader of the Opposition in New Zealand, and Ahmed Yalman, the editor of *Vatan* in Turkey. He was short-listed but the Prize went elsewhere, as it did in 1952 when parliamentary groups from Japan, the United States, Italy, Holland

and Switzerland added their voices to the others. Buchman's comment on one occasion was, 'But I haven't made peace between nations. Let's get on with the work.'

THE PRIVATE BUCHMAN

The writer Hannah More said of William Wilberforce that he lived in a 'kind of domestic publicity': 'in such retirement', she added with gentle irony, 'that he does not see above three and thirty people at breakfast'.

With Buchman, in the days before his stroke, the figure would often be a couple of hundred; and afterwards, at Caux or Mackinac, the numbers constantly around him were even larger. Moreover, for the last twenty years of his life, all his immediate colleagues would come in and out of his room, without knocking, at any time of the day or night. On a 'holiday', as in Ganda in 1946, his party might start with five or a dozen, but would generally increase before long to at least thirty or forty. For him, as he said, a holiday was 'a change of location not vocation'. It was made easier because he genuinely liked people. Yet at heart he was a very private man. He once said what a wrench it was when finally he had to let others pack his bags for him.

This bias towards privacy was masked by the intertwining of his two roles, as an individual and as a symbol of the work he represented. It was this which bewildered Peter Howard when, during their first meeting in America, it was agreed that he should write a book to be called *That Man Frank Buchman*. Straight from *Daily Express* journalism, which had taught him the value of the personal angle, he was amazed to hear Buchman add, 'Of course, there must be nothing about me in the book.' Buchman meant that the book should be about his work and must not go into 'irrelevant' matters like his tastes and habits, his likes and dislikes, his looks and dress – the very stuff of Fleet Street writing. This avoidance of all personal information may not have been well-judged for, where there is a vacuum, rumours soon fill it. It may be one reason why this much discussed man was so little known and so little understood. Once, when I talked with Buchman about this, he said, 'When I am dead, everything must be told.'

The practice of privacy went deeper than his public attitudes. Buchman very seldom spoke of himself in private conversation – and then only to a few. Part of this his doctor, Paul Campbell, believes, went back to a decision Buchman once made 'never to think of himself again'. If taken literally, it is a decision which sounds impossible. It could perhaps be translated as 'never to put himself first again'. But at the least it meant that he spent much more time thinking of others than of himself.

Another reason for this reticence may have been a consideration which faces any leader of a moral and spiritual crusade. Although it was accepted that the final reference-point for the thousands working with him should be God, not Buchman himself, he did not care to unload his own unhappinesses on others, who might as yet be spiritually immature. He said frequently that he was not without sin, and sometimes publicly specified that he was fearful or had done an injustice or lost his temper. But he was often forced to take up King Alfred's attitude: 'If thou hast a woe, tell it not to the weakling; tell it to thy saddle-bow, and ride singing forth.' Buchman had often to bear his burdens alone, as few had the courage or insight to ask him how he was getting along. He said on one occasion, 'I am surrounded by people with great faith, but they lack love.' He was, by nature, an ebullient person and too many believed that the exterior was the whole man.

Oliver Corderoy, Stella Belden's younger brother, who began to work with Buchman soon after the war, remembers walking on the lawn at Caux with Buchman one evening in the late 1940s. 'Are you depressed?' Corderoy asked him, putting his hand on his shoulder. 'Does it show?' replied Buchman. Then for a quarter of an hour Corderoy listened. He said nothing in reply. At midnight the buzzer went in Corderoy's room. Buchman wanted some mint tea. It was full moon, and the mountains across the lake looked like black velvet. 'There are many people more committed to God's plan than you,' Buchman said. 'But not so many who do for me what you did this afternoon. You didn't say a blooming thing. I felt your peace.'

Buchman, in fact, was not only a private, but often a lonely man. The few who did take the risk of breaking through his reserve found a man who was informal, relaxed, often groping his way uncertainly, on occasion as lost as he sometimes looked. At one point Bunny and Phyllis Austin felt that they should return to Australia, leaving Buchman in Europe. 'Oh, no, no,' said Buchman. The Austins, after reflection, still thought that this was what they should do, and told him so once more. 'Come back and see me tomorrow morning,' said Buchman. The next morning, he said to them, 'Yes, go to Australia. The truth is I just didn't want you to leave me.'

His own answer to the natural question of why he never married was invariably, 'Because I have never been guided to.' In his early twenties he had, like most young men, his list of 'possibles', and seems a little later to have taken more than a friendly interest in Edith Randall during their encounters in Europe. But he wrote to his mother from Seoul in 1918, 'It may relieve you to know that I am still single, and expect to remain single for the rest of my life.'[1] Whether, as his cousin Fred Fetherolf believed, he, like Bacon, regarded wife and children as 'impediments to great enterprises' we do not know, though it is clear that Buchman always and increasingly felt called to such enterprises. Mrs Adams, his hostess in Kuling and long-time friend, wrote to his mother in 1922, 'Our prayers and love will mean more to him as the years go by, especially if it does not seem God's purpose to bestow upon him the companionship of a wife – though he deserves one of the very best.'[2] There was no lack, until far on in his life, of women who would cheerfully have risked marrying him; but he seems to have accepted, equally cheerfully, that his life was destined to be a single one.

The home-making instinct never left him. He put it to use wherever he went, always making sure that his friends and visitors were properly looked after in every respect. 'This is outrageous,' he said in the middle of a large international conference. 'This is not the way we are meant to live.' He had spotted dirty water in a flower vase; so all the flower vases had to be cleaned and refilled. Meals, too, had to be served properly: 'My mother never stacked.' But he did long at times for his own surroundings. Once, standing outside his home in Allentown when it was let to other people, he said, 'You know, the thing I would really like to do would be to live in that house and run it perfectly.' Whether this would have satisfied him for long is doubtful; but the constant journeying was not without its unseen cost.

What then was Buchman's private life like? What did he enjoy doing, apart from following his vocation which he undoubtedly relished?

He did not smoke or drink alcohol. Coming from a home where wine appeared on the table as a matter of course, he gave up alcohol while at Overbrook in order to help his dipsomaniac cook, Mary Hemphill. But here, as elsewhere, he was not iron-clad in rules. When entertained by a modest French family, Buchman accepted naturally the quite ordinary wine which they served. Next day, when offered a fine vintage by a prominent French couple, he refused. When a Swiss cigar manufacturer asked him what he should do about his business, he replied, 'Make the best cigars in Switzerland,' and to an English brewer who wanted to help to remake the world, 'Make better beer.'

Buchman did enjoy eating. 'His stroke was not only due to worries about his men being taken into the army,' Campbell once said. 'He did love rich food – thick soups, nice creamy desserts, roast duck, vacherins – all the things which modern doctors abhor. In his mind, these foods were a source of energy.' Needless to say, this diet had to be modified thereafter, though he continued to provide such food for his guests, in accordance with the Pennsylvanian motto, 'Good food and good Christianity go together.' In later life he was not a big eater, and he may never have been, in quantity, up to the Pennsylvania-Dutch norm. He needed, however, to keep an eye on his weight and did not always welcome his doctor's comments. Lacking, or taking less and less time for, exercise did not help.

In the days before his stroke he walked in the country whenever he could, and he also loved horse-riding. His last ride seems to have been in December 1940. With half a dozen others he had spent ten days in Mexico. On their way back north they stayed at a hacienda which took guests. 'We breakfasted at a magnificent huge oak table,' recalls John Cotton Wood, who was one of the party, 'and then Frank took us outside where horses were waiting for us. We climbed into our saddles, and off we rode around the ranch with Frank in the lead.'

Even after his stroke he enjoyed walking, when he could be got to do it. 'He took delight in the world of nature around him,' writes Wood. 'He noticed the fine tracery of twigs and branches of a tree. He noticed the birds. Whether he was walking in a lovely park overlooking San Francisco's Golden Gate or in an orchard in the Tyrolean hills of northern Italy, he would often be lost in wonder at what his eyes and senses took in. He would sometimes simply stand and stare with his mouth open.'

'He was very fastidious in his living, without being demanding on those round him,' writes Loudon Hamilton. 'He spotted, and preferred, quality.'[3] This instinct for the genuine encompassed both people and objects. 'What an awful man that is,' he remarked once after a visitor had left. 'He makes conversation.'

He did love beautiful things. Sir Neil Cochran-Patrick had in his Ayrshire home some fine pieces of china which had long been in the family. He was astonished when Buchman could tell him where each piece originated. When my wife and I gave him a crystal bowl full of wild Swiss flowers, his eyes lit up with genuine appreciation. But his judgement could be overruled by the desire to encourage an individual. A certain lady presented him with an imposing Italian marble statue of one of the Muses, to be put in 45 Berkeley Square. Some of his friends thought it a little overwhelming and Mrs Nell Glover, the talented Yorkshirewoman who was blending the furnishing of the house into a harmonious whole, told him so. 'That is great art, and *I know*,' he replied. 'It stays.' And it did, in a corner of the front hall.*

He never bought any picture, china or work of art for himself. Indeed, he seldom bought anything except to give to others. People who attended the Oxford house-parties remember him best in flannels and a grey herringbone tweed sports jacket. In Caux it was more usually a suit. His wardrobe, according to Campbell, generally consisted of two suits – one blue, one grey – a sports jacket and flannels, plus dress and morning

---

* He was right. When 45 Berkeley Square was sold the statue was bought by the Fitzwilliam Museum, Cambridge.

clothes for rare official occasions. There was also a much-prized old jersey and an ancient dressing-gown. The only time anyone remembers him weeping about his disabilities was once when he struggled to get his paralysed hand into that dressing-gown. 'Oh, this *thing!*' he cried in frustration. 'I'm a cripple.'

Many times in his life he wore other people's cast-offs, and he urged his friends not to be too proud to do so. 'Your trouble is that you refuse to be one of the deserving poor,' he once said to a Scottish colleague. Yet he always managed to keep that spick-and-span look which Begbie and Russell noted in the twenties and thirties.

He lived, according to Campbell, mainly on gifts which came to him at Christmas or on his birthday – or sometimes personal gifts given to him during a conference. The money was apt to pass through his hands quickly. 'He'd look at you and say, "You need a new suit." Or if someone gave him $500 at Christmas, he would call in the team with him and give them $10 each.' Campbell adds that never, through all the years he served him, did Buchman give him any money except such a small gift at Christmas. 'He paid the bills where we had to stay with him. But he knew we served on the same free basis as himself.' In later years, his birthday gifts could amount to sizeable sums. In 1958, for example, gifts from 138 people are listed amounting to just under $67,000, ranging from two gifts of $5,000 to one of $5.00 from Brooks Onley, a friend's black chauffeur, and $1.00 from Martha Lambert.

Campbell states that Buchman 'never worried about money'. Corderoy says he sometimes did. The nearest I heard him to expressing such worry was at Caux, when, in the face of one crisis, he said, 'I know I should have no fear, but I do wonder how we'll make it.' However, he never confined his enterprises to the cash, if any, which he had in hand or could reasonably expect.

Buchman's favourite reading was the newspapers. He read *The Times* whenever he could get it, always starting with the obituaries. His favourite books were biographies. The diaries and letters of Queen Victoria fascinated him. He loved inside information about public figures – including gossip – although he did not pass it on. He was interested in anything which gave him the feel of a country, a government or a community. Countries, for him, were the people he knew in them. Sometimes this gave him a lop-sided view, but generally news gleaned from many angles kept him very well-informed.

What John Wood chiefly recalls is Buchman's 'delight in life, a delight in parties; a delight in towns and cafes, a delight in what was happening'. He could never resist a parade, a band or a procession. He had to go and see, and took everyone who would go along. He also liked public lunches or dinners, because they helped him to sniff the atmosphere of a country or a community, besides giving him a chance to meet people. Not that he wanted to meet everyone, however 'distinguished'. When his host wanted to introduce him to Anthony Eden, at the height of Eden's popularity, he was not interested. 'It's not our job to help lame dogs over stiles,' he said.

Public occasions and places also gave him a welcome break from a team life in which he was always surrounded by people wanting to consult him. One night in early 1946 he told Corderoy he had to get out of 45 Berkeley Square. 'I feel cooped up here. In Brown's there were always new people coming and going.' They went to the Berkeley Grill, where Lord Bossom bowled up and asked them to join him at dinner. Bossom was very worried about coal, and said he had seen the Prime Minister, Clement Attlee, who was worried too. Buchman mentioned *The Forgotten Factor*. Wherever could he put it on in ruined London? 'The Cripplegate, near St Paul's. It's still standing among the rubble and it's empty,' said Bossom. 'Now, that was a well-spent evening,' said Buchman as he hobbled back into Berkeley Square. Then looking across at the lighted windows of the house, he said, 'Only history will show whether we were right or wrong to take that place.' In the next twenty years other centres in other countries were given or acquired, and Buchman welcomed, even initiated, them. But he never lost an element of nostalgia for the freer life of a hotel, where he could meet unexpected people and see the world go by. 'You will never understand him', an early associate said, 'unless you remember he was brought up in a hotel right on the railway tracks.'

In America in the 1940s and 1950s he would never miss the Charlie McCarthy show on the radio if he could help it. What he liked, according to Campbell, was the irreverent treatment of the great by Edgar Bergen's dummy. Indeed, he would take extreme measures to hear it – slipping out of an important meeting, cutting short an interview with a movie mogul, disappearing with the nearest imitation he could manage to his invisible quicksilver motion of the thirties. One day he listened to both the programme and its repeat, and then remarked, 'Charlie must come to Caux!'

Three of his friends, Campbell, Cece Broadhust and Charles Haines, often put on their own 'McCarthy show' at parties, mocking him and other colleagues with affectionate or pointed cheek. Broadhurst and Richard Hadden,* a gifted pianist in everything from Chopin to jazz, also had a topical patter act which delighted him. Evenings full of hilarious and often brilliant humour were a feature of the life around him, and a frequent element in house-parties and conferences. Buchman would laugh and laugh, the tears rolling down his face, while people feared he might fall off

* Hadden and his wife, Frances Roots, were the first Western pianists to give concerts in Communist China.

his chair. 'That was sheer worship,' he remarked after one such evening.

By contrast he also loved to sit in complete silence with friends. One of his French colleagues, Michel Sentis, remembers one evening at Caux when they sat for an hour looking out as the sun went down over the lake and tinged the mountains opposite, 'saying nothing, just enjoying the silence. There was no need to say anything, because we were aware of the third Person above the two of us who was keeping the conversation going.' Sitting with some friends on one occasion, he mused, "God be in my head." As long as God is in my head, I can have a good laugh.'[4] On another, with Campbell, Austin and Martin, he said, 'I'm an old man of 72 and I'm glad to have you with me. Not many old men have friends like you.'

He was unmusical, and did not enjoy serious concerts. He would only go for the sake of some guest or more often some musician friend, like Artur Rodzinski. He liked something with a beat and a tune. 'That's beautiful music,' he said when a Souza march came on the radio. 'That's music I understand.' After a concert by Gracie Fields, which he enjoyed to the full, Buchman remarked thoughtfully, 'I don't think I'd be a success as a concert singer.' That night he prayed for Gracie Fields and that Capri, where she lived, might be 'cleaned up'.

He used vocal music a great deal in his work, both a chorus and various trios and quartets, especially the three Californian Colwell Brothers with their witty topical songs. One day a diplomat came to lunch with Buchman and was duly entertained by the chorus with various uplifting songs about his country. 'He woke up when the yodelling began,' relates one of the party. 'When he had left, Frank took on the training of the chorus. They had learnt "Stars in My Crown" which they sang slowly and dully. So Frank waved his arms around to great effect and trained them how to sing it. Also he insisted on the words of "The Longest Porch" being audible. For one who claims not to appreciate music he did a wonderful job with them.'[5]

The theatre he always loved. His letters home from Philadelphia in the 1890s announced that he had seen Henry Irving and Ellen Terry in *Robespierre* and Bernhardt as Ophelia – 'Think of it, the most noted actress in the world.'[6] Later in life he was to use plays as a main, often the main, expression of his message – probably the first spiritual leader to do it on such a scale since the Middle Ages. The idea struck him when, in 1937, he made a trip from a Brighton house-party to London to see William Douglas-Home's play *Great Possessions*, in which the Oxford Group was treated with not unkindly humour. He took a young Oxford graduate with him and on the return journey startled him by saying, 'You will write the plays which the world and we need.' That man has never written a play, but he later introduced Peter Howard to Moral Re-Armament, who subsequently wrote many. The other principal playwright among Buchman's colleagues was Alan Thornhill, to whom he had talked about theatre when they first met in the twenties.

Phyllis Austin, who had worked under some of the major directors of stage and screen, was of the opinion that he would have made a great director. 'His timing was impeccable, and all his suggestions were to the point,' she said. He could never understand, however, the need for rehearsal. 'Where have you been?' he would indignantly ask Campbell, who often acted in addition to his doctoring, when he returned from a gruelling session. For him a play was ready to go on stage the moment it was written, just as his secretaries had found that he often seemed to expect a letter, once dictated, to be already typed. Cece Broadhurst told him one morning that he had an idea for a musical. 'Fine,' said Buchman, 'can we have it tonight?'

To have a holiday or take time off would not have occurred to Buchman. He did go away to quieter environments when his health demanded it: Bunny and Phyllis Austin describe one such 'rest' in Italy when Buchman was 78. For once, the party was small – Buchman, the Austins, Paul Campbell and Jim Baynard-Smith, one of his personal assistants. They stayed in a hotel. Buchman was low in strength, but wanted to be in touch with his friends in other parts of the world. Austin rashly mentioned that he could type a little. Instantly, Buchman started: 'Then take this down – "Dear . . ." '. And for days Austin and Campbell struggled with the typewriter, Buchman dictating practically non-stop to prime ministers, presidents, the priest on Mackinac Island, the cook on the island ferry, and a myriad others.

While following this method of doing nothing, Buchman was also making friends with the hotel management and staff. Mario, the waiter who brought his breakfast each morning, arrived one day in tears. His father had died. Buchman had himself driven to Mario's village and carried up the wooden steps into the sitting room, and spent two hours with Mario and his family. Another waiter had escaped three times from the gas chambers during the war, had lived on roots and grass for weeks, and joined the Communist Party after the war. He and Buchman had long talks and one day he said to Phyllis Austin, 'I would be willing to die for that man.' The manager and his mother of ninety, the maid, all became friends.

As Buchman's strength returned other friends began coming in to see him, and by the time the Christmas tree and the crèche were in place, Communists, royalty, old ladies, small boys, gathered round them with Buchman and his party. The chamber-maid, meeting one of the royal family later, said joyfully, 'Hullo, Mrs Queen!'[7]

It was during this 'holiday' that Buchman met King Michael of

Roumania again. They had, of course, known each other since his childhood when Buchman visited his grandmother, Queen Marie, in Bucharest. Since then he had twice been King, first from 1927 to 1930 in the absence of his father and then from 1940 to 1947, after his father's death. In the latter period he had overthrown the Fascist dictatorship of Antonesco, but had been forced into exile by the Communists in 1947. Now, on 23 December 1955, he came to tea with Buchman, together with his mother, Queen Helen, and his wife, Queen Anne. Of this time King Michael writes: 'One thing I remember so well of Frank's caring was my own experience after meeting him again in 1955. With my sadness and unhappiness at having lost my country, my bitterness had grown because of a feeling of not belonging. After our meeting, I felt this great load was taken off my mind and soul. I realised that no problem was too great or too small for him. The greatest or the smallest problem in someone else's life received the same loving care from him.'[8] After that he and his wife paid frequent visits to Caux from their home in Geneva and took part in various MRA activities both during Buchman's life and thereafter.

To sit by a crèche at Christmas was one of Buchman's great delights. He would sometimes sit for long periods looking at it, living into an experience beyond the senses, remarking to himself occasionally, 'Isn't it wonderful? Isn't it wonderful?' Spiritual experience never ceased to fill him with this sense of wonder. He always prolonged 'Christmas' as long as possible, sometimes leaving the tree up for weeks. And New Year's Eve was part of the mingled celebration and reflection. 'I used to go to church with my mother for the watch-night service,' he said once. 'We called it "heart-searching". We used to think of the past year, and of the future. It was a solemn night.'

The strength of Buchman's effect on people may have arisen in part from his ability to concentrate on the present moment and the present person. Friends say that wherever in the world one was with him, he lived as though he would be there for ever and treated each friendship as if it were permanent, despite the fact that he might not have been in that place for years and might never return again. In terms of people too, he created his home around him, wherever he might be.

Buchman enjoyed the company of children, and took them seriously. He told one mother who was very anxious that her daughter should behave well to stop repressing the child, and insisted on letting the small girl chatter all during a long car drive he was taking with the family. He sat down with a twelve-year-old who was feeling overworked and in forty-five minutes told her the history of the trade union movement, covering the Tolpuddle Martyrs, workers' rights, hours of work, and then said, 'Goodbye, have a good term.' 'I was so glad he treated me like an adult,' she now says. One small girl, attending a conference with her parents, broke her toy horse, and immediately set off to find 'Uncle Frank – he's the strongest man here'. Children sent him letters and Christmas cards and their pocket-money, and each one received a personal reply.

Along with the warm heart and the retentive mind went a quick temper. Sometimes he was right, sometimes he was wrong. Sometimes he apologised, sometimes he did not. People found him at times an uncomfortable person to be with, because he was unpredictable. But temper, or even anger, were often the sign of friendship and concern. I asked Campbell, who saw more of him than perhaps anyone, how often Buchman lost his temper. 'Very seldom, really,' he replied. 'And he was a hard man to be angry with because you felt his motive was generally selfless,' he added. 'You didn't like it, but you didn't get mad.'

According to Corderoy, Buchman's unpredictability was not caprice, but was quite often mischief. Certainly he had a lively sense of humour. 'You will get more people changed by pulling their legs than by kicking their bottoms,' he said. And he did not take himself over-seriously. He remarked of one portrait which had been painted of him, 'Oh, it's in some cellar now, and every now and again the rats come out and have a look at it!'

Buchman did, however, take his work seriously. One of his major dislikes was 'understatement'. I remember him taking some of us British aside on our first visit to America and saying that unless we said things loud and plain, no one would listen to us. It was not that he wished us to exaggerate – Russell remarks in *For Sinners Only* that he many times heard Buchman tell the same stories but never heard him alter them in the smallest way for effect – but that he felt we dishonoured God if we at any point understated what He had done in our lives or in any situation. 'Speak right up to, but never beyond your experience,' he used to say.

His exhortations could, however, lead to overstatement by colleagues trying to please him, and sometimes by Buchman himself when he repeated the evaluations of others without having them researched. Something which was an important factor in the solution of a problem became, in common speech, the answer to the whole affair. In his speeches he was careful seldom or never to make a personal claim about such situations, but quoted the public opinions of politicians, newspapers or other authorities on the spot. But in his later speeches, drafted by others though always read to and altered by him, inaccuracies did at times get through. In one speech, for example, it was said that the *Times of India* had 'carried a full page' of MRA news when in fact Moral Re-Armament had inserted it as a paid full-page advertisement. The editor of the *Times of India* quite properly pointed this out in a letter to the London *Times*.[9] It became almost an international incident. When I next met the drafter of the speech I asked him how such a silly mistake had been made.

'Mistake?' he said. 'It *was* carried by the paper. That's what they say in America.'

Upon small incidents like this Buchman's opponents, with a near monopoly of the press in some countries, built up an illusion that all the achievements attributed to Buchman – and which he attributed to God – were exaggerations if not plain lies. What made this particularly ironic was the fact that, at the deepest level, such 'results' meant little to Buchman personally. He felt a tremendous urgency to get the potency and relevance of God through to everyone, and that many were so secularised that they would only pay attention to practical results – but this very urgency sometimes provided ammunition which defeated his own intentions.

There were times when Buchman felt shaken in his belief, that God had left him. 'I'm lost,' he said at one such period. 'I'd be surprised if you weren't sometimes,' the person with him replied. This feeling is well known to anyone who tries to orientate his or her life towards God. In Buchman's case he was also very often on unfamiliar ground, reaching out for the next step for some person or some large group of people. As well as feeling lost, he was frequently fearful. 'No fear' recurs constantly in his written or dictated thoughts. Once in the middle of a meeting he suddenly said, 'Oh, no fear, it's so stupid,' and stood up and shook himself to be rid of it. It seems to have been a mixture of ordinary human fears – of making mistakes, getting plans wrong, missing God's direction – and a more mystical fear. 'Do you fear the love of God?' a friend once asked him. 'Yes,' he replied, with emphasis. This is a fear presumably only known to those who have come close enough to the love of God to understand its power. And there is no doubt that the relationship with God was the one which Buchman most assiduously cultivated for himself and most urgently wanted to share with other people.

He was willing to feel, and look at a loss. 'Wakeful, like the bird on the bough, with mouth open, eyes and ears wide open, looking absolutely gaga in a crowd sometimes, but deeply at peace, listening to catch the faintest whisper of God,' Baynard-Smith describes him at cocktail parties or diplomatic receptions. 'Then, like the sail filling, he was off on a fresh tack, mind and body bending to the prevailing breeze of guidance, full-running, free. That was the impression he made, totally careless of what others might be thinking of him.'

What satisfied Buchman most deeply was to sit quietly and search for the mind of God. He liked to do it with others but also spent much time doing it alone. Thoughts often came to him during wakeful periods in the night. After his stroke, when he could not write, he always had a bell by his bed. 'The buzzer would go at two or three in the morning,' says Campbell. 'Often his first words would be, "What's your guidance?", when you couldn't even see straight. He'd been listening to God and he assumed you'd been doing the same. I used to get so annoyed. Then he would dictate – usually general thoughts about plans or thoughts to go ahead with or stop some activity. He never dictated to me thoughts he had for other people. Those he would tell direct to the person concerned next day or by letter. There might just be a note, "See X".'

Then he would go to sleep again, sometimes waking to plan the day with a largish group of colleagues at seven or seven-thirty, sometimes waking only at nine with the words, 'Now let's have breakfast.' It all depended on what he had been doing the evening before. 'But', says Campbell, 'he might equally call for a few colleagues at five in the morning and start work. In the last years night and day began to lose their significance. But every day of his life he would want you to read him the Bible, first thing – always a psalm and often the New Testament too.* He always wanted you to pray with him at bed-time. He didn't often pray then himself. He was too exhausted. He'd get you to. He'd pray at other times, for his country or for his people, but he was more of a listening man. "A very great day, underlined three times" was a common thought. He had great expectations.' 'I get it in my American way,' he said one day to a friend: '69 times a very great day of power.'

Buchman's communing with God, his 'guidance', was not, of course, just a matter of early mornings. He did not chop life up into times of listening and other times. He tried to be aware constantly, any moment expecting 'a new disclosure'. On a big decision, according to Campbell, he would often include large numbers of people, listening to what came to everyone, especially the youngest and the newest, weighing each contribution carefully, even if he made the ultimate decision. Then too there was that lost, seeking look which Grevenius observed in Sweden and Baynard-Smith remarked at public receptions. Many experienced this searching process more intimately as they consulted him on personal matters.

Mrs van Beuningen, who was in America during 1939 and early 1940, wanted to return to Holland immediately Norway and Denmark were invaded on 9 April 1940. He pointed out to her that the particular things she had had direction to try and do had not been completed; they listened, and she stayed. Meeting Buchman again in New York a little later, she told him that she now felt she should go home. He was silent. Then he said, 'Yes, it is time to go.' She wanted to go back via Rome and see the Pope, to whom she had excellent introductions. 'No. Not this time. Go straight home,' responded Buchman. She did so, and reached Holland on 9 May, the day the country was invaded. Her war-time work saved the lives of hundreds of prisoners of war.[10]

---

* Favourites were Psalms 23, 32, 103 and 121, 2 Timothy 2 and John 17.

An American friend with him in Europe heard that her mother was ill but that there was no hurry to return. She talked it over with Buchman, and they listened together. 'Go,' said Buchman. 'Go immediately.' She did not go immediately, and she was too late.

Corderoy describes Buchman as 'a growing person – not perfect, but always growing'. The man who refused to be confined by his much-loved Pennsylvania Dutch origins and the traditional methods of the American missionary establishment in China, who did not arrive in Oxford until he was in his forties, launch Moral Re-Armament until he was sixty or speak in terms of a moral and spiritual ideology until he was sixty-five, was always looking for new insights and new impetus. 'We have not yet tapped the great creative sources in the Mind of God,' he said launching Moral Re-Armament at East Ham, and in the last year of his life he told a friend, 'I am learning more about moral re-armament every day.'

Most people thought of the Oxford Group and Moral Re-Armament as movements he had founded – a notion he strenuously denied. Of the Oxford Group, he used to say, 'You can't join it and you can't resign. You are in or out according to the quality of life you are living at any moment. Sometimes I am right outside it myself.'

When in 1948 the film star, Joel McCrae, asked, 'Well, Frank, how is MRA doing?' he replied thoughtfully, 'Oh, I think we are occasionally illustrating it.'

One of those with him remarked to him as they drove home, 'I seem to have a different conception of Moral Re-Armament from you. I thought you founded it.'

'No, discovered it – discovered it,' Buchman replied immediately. 'All can be co-discoverers.'

'I suppose the future of Moral Re-Armament, as you conceive it, is in its future illustrations,' said this companion later that day.

'Of course,' said Buchman. 'It's God's property, not mine.'

In Garmisch-Partenkirchen, a few months later, he told several colleagues a little more of how he saw it: 'At Keswick I experienced the recuperative and restorative processes of God. Moral Re-Armament is such a moment in the life of anyone. Its future is in such moments occurring in the future in different lives, in different countries, the outcome being illustrated in national circumstances. It is the continuity of such moments in the lives of all sorts of people, the outcome sometimes affecting governments ... The fellowship can look with zest to the adventure of receiving further disclosures.

'The Kingdom of God is symbolic of a definiteness of experience directly observable by someone else, but not easily described. What is observable is a peace, a confidence, a recovery of freedom, and spontaneity of thought, of will and of nerve. This is not joinable. You have to experience it for yourself.'

'With the world still in the making,' he added, 'what does Moral Re-Armament aim to remake? Remaking what is wrong? It is more than that. It is adding to what is right. It is being originative of relevant alternatives to evil in economics, in government policy and so on. It is seeking God's experience for the human race, and is open to everyone.'

A year before his death, ill and exhausted, he complained one day, 'I'm not going to last.' Then he cheered up and said, 'It was here before I came. I guess it'll be here after I've gone.'

'BUCHMAN KI JAI!'

Through the years Buchman kept in touch with Mahatma Gandhi. When he was in London for the 1931 Round Table Conference he came to tea with Buchman at Brown's with his son Devadas. 'Frank realised that my father never carried any money with him, indeed he could not because he was dressed in his dhoti which had no receptacle for it,' Devadas told Michael Barrett years later. 'When we arrived at Brown's Hotel, Frank was waiting on the pavement with the money for the taxi, plus a tip for the driver. After tea he put my father in another taxi and paid the driver the fare to the East End of London plus tip. That is why I always send my car to the airport for him when he passes through India.'

Buchman and Gandhi also conducted a correspondence at various times.* In the main, however, Buchman maintained his touch through mutual friends like Charles F. Andrews and Metropolitan Foss Westcott, and colleagues like Roger Hicks, Bishop West, and the Burmese school-mistress, Ma Nyein Tha, who visited Gandhi in his ashram. On occasion Gandhi made criticisms of Buchman's work. However, Hicks – who spent many years in India and stayed at the ashram for weeks at a time – told Gandhi of the character changes in certain British officials, notably Lionel Jardine, then Revenue Commissioner in the North-West Frontier Province, and the effect of this change in bringing peace between Hindus and Muslims. Hicks writes that when they next met in May 1940, 'Gandhi reminded me of the stories I had told him about Jardine and said that he had had Khan Sahib, the Chief Minister of the Province, investigate them and "they were all true". He considered that this was the most important thing coming out of the West today. . . . If men's motives and conduct could be changed, then the chess board was upset and anything could happen. He bade me go and see the Viceroy and tell him that if this spirit prevailed India and Britain would be able to come to terms at once.'[1]

Buchman had a natural sympathy with the newly independent countries of Asia, and in 1952 he accepted invitations to take an international team

* This correspondence is referred to in other papers, but is lost.

to India, Ceylon and Pakistan. The Indian invitation had come in September 1950 from eighteen distinguished personalities headed by G. L. Nanda, by then Minister of Planning in Delhi.* The Prime Minister of Ceylon, Dudley Senanayake, and members of his government and the opposition had sent a similar invitation, and Pakistani ministers had repeated one given to Buchman personally by Mohammad Ali Jinnah – and accepted by him – during the Independence talks in London.

Just when Buchman's acceptance of these invitations became known to his colleagues is not easy to ascertain. At any rate, news leaked out at Caux during August 1952 that Buchman intended to leave on 10 October. Meanwhile, discussions had been going on with various Indian 'experts' about the scale of the venture. Some suggested to Buchman that a couple of dozen people were the most who could be accommodated. Hicks, returning from two years on the sub-continent, advocated fifty, and received the reply, 'We're taking two hundred people and five plays.' In the event, only three MRA plays were taken, but these involved eight tons of equipment.

Things now began to happen fast. KLM offered a DC6, and the Dutch who were at Caux pledged the charter fare. The first planeload became largely a matter of 'spokesmen' and advance stage crew, and people who could answer in the affirmative the question, 'Have you been inoculated and can you leave on Saturday?' Thirty-five nations were represented.

The night before leaving Buchman gave a dinner party for the workers employed at Caux and their wives – masons, plasterers and cleaners – together with the postman, the station-master and an Egyptian cabinet minister who was still there. 'Buchman's speech characteristic,' Morris Martin noted. 'Humour, appreciation of the workers, more humour, the world outreach from Caux, plus a measure of personal challenge and leg-pulling.' Then he announced that he was giving presents to 'the good children', who turned out to be four recently married couples among his full-time workers. After that he called for 'the soon marrieds'. This provoked even more enthusiasm, as two couples had become engaged that day. Then Buchman said another couple were in the offing but that 'the young man is still upstairs proposing'. When the beaming pair arrived the applause was terrific.[2]

It had been a long day, full of decisions and ending after midnight, but

* Others on the invitation committee included R. K. Patil and G. L. Mehta, members of the National Planning Commission; Khandubhai Desai, President of the Indian National Trade Union Congress; Sir Lakhshmanaswami Mudaliar, Vice-Chancellor of Madras University; Dr B. C. Roy, Chief Minister of West Bengal; K. M. Patnaik, Speaker of the Legislative Assembly of Orissa; Dr Sampuranand, Minister of Education in the United Provinces; A. N. Sinha, Minister of Labour in Bihar; J. R. D. Tata, Chairman of Tata Industries.

Buchman left his room for the airport at 6.30 next morning. On the way to the front door, he suddenly exclaimed, 'Clutterbuck. He's coming this week. Don't forget Clutterbuck!' Speedy detective work revealed that he meant a Mr Puttkammer from Mackinac Island, and the car moved off.

The first stop was Cairo. At the airport Buchman was met by an official who said that the Prime Minister, General Neguib, would like to receive him at 8.30 that evening. Meanwhile Dr Abdel Khalek Hassouna, former Foreign Minister and later Secretary General of the Arab League, called on Buchman in the hour between returning from Gaza and flying on to the United Nations in New York.

Neguib was anxious to hear the recent news of Moral Re-Armament. After half an hour he asked, 'Will you do me the honour of dining with me? If it is more convenient for you, I will arrange it at your hotel.' So began a long evening during which the General met many of Buchman's colleagues. After dinner he asked, 'What would you do, Dr Buchman, about a small boy who is not a problem child but has lots of vitality and doesn't like books – and I want him to like books?'

'Let him read the books he wants, not the ones you think he ought to read,' replied Buchman. 'You must get his interest. Then get him to change others. The average boy doesn't have enough to do. Don't do things for him. Shoot him out into the lives of others. I've got a Foreign Minister's* son with me. His father runs NATO, but he had difficulty in running his son.' At this Neguib threw his head back and gave a loud guffaw. Next morning he was at the airport at 8.00 to see Buchman off.

Once more it had been a long day for one whose health was as precariously balanced as Buchman's. Some days that summer he had been recorded by Campbell as 'full of energy'. On others he could only lie in bed, and Campbell had diagnosed 'a danger of heart failure whenever he is not lying down'. Two days before he left Caux a woman cleaning his sitting-room had heard him saying aloud next door, 'Lord, I can't do it. I can't do it.' Jim Baynard-Smith, a former army officer and ADC to the Governor of Sudan, who began his five-year stint of caring for Buchman's personal needs on this trip, was astonished at his resilience. 'Sometimes he seemed completely done for,' he says, 'but two hours later he suddenly revived. I think it had something to do with his liking people.' 'Unlike some of us', Baynard-Smith added, 'he never just retired into himself when he was tired. He had the sense to go to bed. He would say, "Oh, you fellows must do it. You've got the energy. I hate like sin to go to bed, but I'm going."'

After a quiet night in Karachi the party landed in Colombo to an airport welcome. Buchman and Baynard-Smith found that they were being cared

* Ole Bjørn Kraft, Foreign Minister of Denmark, Chairman of NATO 1952–3.

for at their hotel by the bearer who had always looked after Baynard-Smith's father when he visited Colombo from his tea plantation. From the talk which ensued Buchman conceived the idea of going into the hills to visit the holy city of Kandy and to meet the Baynard-Smiths' planter friends. Their way of life interested and amused him. 'If they had real morning risers, they'd have fewer sundowners,' he commented. He also saw their quality and potential. 'Nothing would have greater power here than a humble Englishman who admitted his mistakes,' he added. After four days he returned, relaxed if a little dilapidated-looking, announcing that he had begun to get the feel of the country.

His team, meanwhile, were entering into Colombo life at many levels, from the Stalinist and Trotskyite factions in the dockers' unions to the dignitaries of the invitation committee. They told Buchman on his return, however, that the plays were to be given in the Young Men's Buddhist Association Hall although the best place would have been the Regal Theatre, now a cinema and booked solid. ' "Dear Lord and shall we ever live at this poor dying rate!" ' exploded Buchman. 'Things must be best, absolute best, BEST!' A party was despatched to find the heavyweights of the invitation committee, who were all discovered at Sir John Kotelawala's birthday party. A letter from them secured the release of the cinema – at a price. They were left haggling about it with the manager, while Buchman rejoiced that they were now getting into action. Surya Sena, the well-known singer of Sinhalese folk music, who was secretary of the invitation committee, had earlier told Buchman of the committee's plan to charge from 3 to 20 rupees for seats at the plays. 'No, no,' Buchman had replied. 'There will be no charge anywhere in the theatre . . . I've not come to Asia to get but to give.'

'How on earth can we meet the expenses of two hundred people for ten days?' protested Surya.

'The Lord will provide,' said Buchman, and, in his autobiography, Surya Sena notes, 'Every cent of expense was met.'[3]

The plays themselves – *The Forgotten Factor*, *Jotham Valley* and *Annie the Valiant** – were put on in repertory, and were an enormous success. The Prime Minister and six of the cabinet, with forty-three MPs and diplomats to match, came on the first night. The populace besieged the threatre, one man walking twenty-six miles and queueing six hours in hot sun to get in. Every seat was taken, and the police estimated that 500 stood in the aisles and at the back for each performance. No one was turned away.

The talk of the hour was the barter agreement just negotiated by the Minister of Trade, R. G. Senanayake – known as 'China Dick' – whereby Ceylon was to exchange her rubber for Chinese rice. Ceylon had always

---

* A play about the life of Annie Jaeger.

been an exporter, not an importer, of rice. But rice lands had been put down to more profitable crops like tea and rubber, and besides, to save labour, rice seed was being broadcast instead of planted in the old way, thus sometimes reducing the crop to around a quarter of the old yield.

One day the Minister of Food invited Buchman to see a demonstration of the old method by a thousand women in the lush green paddy fields sixty miles out of town. Buchman took off his shoes and socks, rolled up his trousers and planted the first shoot – for him a painful exercise. Paul Kurowski, the German miner, and many of the other visitors followed suit. When asked to address the workers Buchman said, 'What you are doing today is most significant. There is enough rice in the world for everyone's need, but not for everyone's greed.* And there is another great truth I want to utter. If everyone cares enough and everyone shares enough, won't everyone have enough?'

The Prime Minister gave a reception in the garden of his residence, Temple Trees, and Kotelawala, who was soon to succeed him, did likewise. The sessions of the conference with which the visit ended were attended by cabinet ministers, opposition leaders, diplomats from East and West, Buddhist priests, Christian missionaries, tea-planters and workers, dockers and the dock superintendent, school children – a lively and unpredictable mixture. In Bombay Buchman received a cable from the Prime Minister and the leader of the Opposition, S.W.R.D. Bandaranaike, expressing 'deep gratitude'. 'We feel the hour calls for the continuance of this work in Asia in the interests of unity, security and peace,' it said.[4] But the message which pleased him most was from 'China Dick', who said, 'You have definitely brought an easing of the tension, even in the Cabinet.'[5]

The voyage to Bombay was a blissful rest, especially for the stage crew who had been working for forty-eight hours virtually without sleep. But it was not all holiday. The first evening Buchman said to one of the chorus, 'On our last night at sea we will give a concert for everyone,' and seemed surprised when it was pointed out that tomorrow would be the last night. However, the concert took place, preceded by a reiteration of the health rules for the trip. No fruit must be eaten unless protected by a skin, and no salads at all. Other precautions clearly stemmed back to Buchman's Indian experience thirty years before: everyone had to wear a topee – and a belly-band. 'That goes for you too, Emily,' interjected Buchman, pointing to the venerable Mrs John Henry Hammond, née Vanderbilt. Buchman's science may have been somewhat outdated, but at the end of the

* This phrase has been widely attributed to Gandhi. In fact, it appeared first in Buchman's East Ham Town Hall speech on 4 June 1938.

eight-month tour the group of two hundred had travelled the length and breadth of the sub-continent with hardly any serious illness.

As the *SS Strathmara* steamed into Bombay harbour a large notice, 'Welcome! MRA Reception', became visible, and standing below it could be seen the Mayor of Bombay and most of the Bombay inviting committee. On the day after arrival a two-hour press conference resolved itself into a violent debate on Moral Re-Armament between the journalists present, with Buchman, according to his secretary, 'in one of his smiling, silent frames of mind, sitting happily in the cross-fire'.[6]

The opinions being expressed mirrored India's condition, five years after Independence and four since Gandhi's assassination. The unity achieved in the freedom struggle and around the personality of Gandhi had disappeared, and the spirit of Gandhism was waning. Nehru was his political heir; but no one had inherited his moral mantle. A Congress Party leader told Buchman, 'We have not ten men in Parliament with the old idealism. Independence hasn't solved our problems. No one wants to go back, but we don't know how to go forward.' Communism had attracted many intellectuals, if only because it was what those they considered their age-old exploiters disliked most: some wrote off Buchman and his colleagues as 'anti-Communists', others simply felt opposed to all 'Western ideas', good or bad.

Buchman gave his views in private: 'In a materialist ideology the ultimate authority is a man or a party line, a human will, and the ultimate basis for change is force. In a moral ideology the ultimate authority is God's will and the basis for change is consent.' But at this press conference he said little, because he felt that, at that moment, only the plays he had brought could convey what he wanted to say to Indian hearts and minds. The first night of *Jotham Valley* started the ball rolling. Morarji Desai, then Chief Minister of Bombay State, surprised everyone by admitting from the stage after it that he had seen a likeness between himself and the self-righteous elder brother in the play. Next day a journalist, who had been violently critical of him, thanked him and asked if they could meet.

Socialists like J. P. Narayan, who had separated from Gandhi to follow a Marxist path but were now looking for new ideas, talked at length with the visitors. In co-operation with Socialist trades union leaders like Purshottam Tricumdas, the founder of the Socialist Party, and Congress-inclined unions like H. N. Trivedi's cement workers, they called huge meetings to hear Buchman and other speakers.

After four weeks of plays and meetings, S. A. Sabavala reflected in the *Bombay Chronicle*, 'So far no one has tried to analyse the reasons for the very obvious resentment to its (MRA's) simple philosophy. We pride ourselves as the sons of Mahatma Gandhi, the man who lived the teachings of Christ and the Buddha. Since Independence we have developed a superiority complex about our spiritualism and an exalted sense and understanding of non-materialistic values. Now along comes a band of men and women, non-Indians, who are practising what we preach. They are encroaching on what we thought was our exclusive preserve and many of us do not like this at all. I think much of the hostility and exhibition of bad manners at Dr Buchman's press conference springs from this particular resentment ... The truth is that we, the heirs of Gandhi, are a little ashamed that others are doing what he told us to do and which we say we are doing ... I think MRA will catch on in post-freedom India. It represents a challenge just as Gandhiji did many years ago.'[7]

Not everyone agreed with Sabavala. In particular, the widely circulated far-left weekly, *Blitz*, carried adverse reports of the whole tour. Nevertheless, the departure from Bombay came near to an ovation. Crowds blocked the railway platform and groups from three trade unions – dockers, cement workers and textile workers – arrived with banners and loud cries of 'Buchman ki jai!' Garlands multiplied. Many called for the international chorus to sing the national anthem, as they had done in the theatre each night. Buchman was moved to tears: 'They are a great people. Some of them said, "God be with you." I thought, "If that can be a reality, then India could lead the nations."'

Many superlatives were to come Buchman's way during this tour. The Ceylon Minister to the United Nations classed his visit as of equal importance to the coming of Independence, while the Thai Ambassador referred to him as a 'second Buddha'. 'When the history of the century is written, we will think of FDR, of Stalin, of Churchill, Hitler, Mussolini, Gandhi,' declared the President of the Bombay Rotary Club. 'But if the creed of "what is right and not who is right" should succeed in permanency, then we shall see Frank Buchman's name there.'[8]

Buchman was not unduly impressed. At one point he dictated these thoughts to Baynard-Smith: 'Be calm, prudent, not caring what men say nor held in their wiles by their ill-considered praise. Be a simple man of God, and then God will love you. A loyal band about you. Ties of deep affection. Willing to give their all, or will be as you work together.'

One of his main personal sources of poise throughout the tour was old hymns, which Baynard-Smith would hear him repeating to himself again and again. 'Nothing in my hand I bring, Simply to Thy Cross I cling'; 'Jesus, I my cross have taken'; 'Jesus, lover of my soul'; 'At the Cross, at the Cross where I first saw the light . . .'; 'Perverse and foolish, oft I strayed, and yet in love He sought me . . .'; 'O for a passionate passion for souls'; and many more. At bedtime, he often repeated,

Jesus, I my cross have taken,
All to leave and follow Thee;
Destitute, despised, forsaken,
Thou from hence my all shalt be.

The cavalcade proceeded to Delhi via Ahmedabad and Agra. In Ahmedabad they visited Gandhi's ashram and were entertained by officials of the textile union he had founded; at Agra they saw the Taj Mahal by moonlight. While an Indian train journey was a new experience for most, Buchman enjoyed this renewed view of an ageless land after twenty-six years' absence. On arrival in Delhi he gave 100 rupees to his sleeping car attendant. When an old India hand in the party protested that this was far too much, he replied testily, 'He looked after me. I'm looking after him.'

In recent weeks his thoughts had turned more and more to Pandit Nehru. Nehru relates in his autobiography that Buchman gave him a book – it was Begbie's *Life Changers* – when they first met at Belgaum in 1924 and that he read it 'with amazement' as the 'sudden conversions and confessions ... seemed to me to go ill with intellectuality'.[9] They met again eighteen months later in Switzerland, where Nehru had brought his wife for her health and where he was taking the chance to view Indian politics in a wider setting, a process which led to his adoption of his own particular brand of Marxism. 'I had long been drawn to socialism and communism,' he writes. '... While the rest of the world was in the grip of the depression and going backward in some ways, in the Soviet country a great new world was being built up before our eyes ... Russia apart, the theory and philosophy of Marxism lightened up many a dark corner of my mind.'[10]

In the middle of this process Buchman invited him to a house-party in Holland, and Nehru wrote regretting that he could not leave his wife to attend. He said that he had been 'very interested' in *Life Changers*: 'I well remember the description in the book of the weekend in Cambridge. At the time I did not quite appreciate the significance of the sudden changes brought about in the lives of individuals ... I can understand the value of absolute frankness ... But somehow the idea of faith cures does not appeal to me much ... And this is so in spite of the fact that Mr Gandhi, for whom I have great respect, lays the greatest stress on faith. Perhaps my early scientific training as well as the general irreverence of the modern age are partly responsible for this.'

'I am still obsessed by the Indian problem,' Nehru went on, 'both in its narrower nationalistic aspect and in its relation to the rest of the world, but doubts arise and no obvious solution seems to one (sic). I welcomed therefore the chance of withdrawing for a while from an active participation in public movements and looking at them if possible from the view point of an outsider. And now, far from India, many questions occur to me – of the general drift of western culture and civilisation, of industrialism and the like – and there are few answers. But the question which affects and troubles me more than any other,' he added, 'is: what is my duty to India and how can I serve her best and reconcile that duty with my other responsibilities.'

Of the weekend in Holland he wrote, 'I feel very much tempted to come. I am not at all sure that I shall be helpful in the friendly discussions and talks that will take place there, but the company of earnest and thoughtful people is always attractive and so I should like to come. I am tied up here for some time and cannot leave my wife. But later I may be able to do so.'[11]

In September 1926 the two men met for lunch in Geneva at Nehru's request, with the Swedish Archbishop Söderblom as an unlikely third, clearly included by Buchman. Nehru and Buchman lunched once more together, this time after his wife's death in 1936. 'He has had a sad life,' Buchman often said of him.

Nehru had been consulted about the present visit. He had gone through the original invitation committee with Hicks, eliminating six whom he thought too close to the administration but leaving his Minister of Planning, G. L. Nanda. He had sent a message that he looked forward to seeing Buchman again, and had assigned Jaipur House, the former home of the Maharajahs of Jaipur, as a base for Buchman's force while in Delhi. His attitude was polite, even generous, rather than enthusiastic.

Buchman, according to Baynard-Smith, seems to have felt that he had in some way failed Nehru during their earlier meetings. Now he had another chance, and he would not have been Buchman if his expectations had been anything but high. 'Nehru will realise that this philosophy is his best bet', 'Nehru will turn to you more and more' and 'Nehru sees the importance of this work' are the kind of phrases which recur in the notes he dictated. At the same time, he felt he should make no approach to the Prime Minister. 'Make haste slowly . . . He will come your way.'

On their first day in Delhi Buchman and his full team laid a wreath at Raj Ghat, the place where Gandhi was cremated, and later Buchman addressed a large number of Members of both Houses of Parliament presided over by the Deputy Speaker. He was also officially welcomed by the city. Then he was content to rest until the plays had done their work. As in Bombay the crowds were large and enthusiastic. A Cabinet Minister arrived to find his seat taken. An usher spoke strong words to the occupant, who replied, 'Who do you think I am? I'm a Minister too!' Both were fitted in somehow.

Soon invitations were reaching Buchman thick and fast. President

Rajendra Prasad, an old colleague of Gandhi, received him and his team at the former Viceregal Palace where this simple man, by virtue of his office, had to live. His face lit up when he heard of the times spent with workers in Bombay, Ahmedabad and elsewhere. 'Ah, you are taking it to the people,' he said.

Another day the Vice-President (later President) Dr S. Radhakrishnan had Buchman to tea. He had known something of Buchman's work from his time as Professor of Oriental Religion and Philosophy at Oxford. Later he had been Ambassador in Moscow, and now he asked Buchman how Communists could be changed. On his farewell visit to Stalin, he related, he had told the dictator about the Indian Emperor Asoka who, after wading through blood to his throne, had renounced war and promoted religion and was now much revered throughout Asia. It was an example, he had suggested, which other dictators might follow. 'Well, I spent five years at a theological seminary,' replied Stalin. 'It might happen, but I don't think so.'*

At a function presided over by India's President, to celebrate the nineteenth centenary of the arrival of St Thomas in India, Buchman was offered a seat at the front with the diplomats and other dignitaries. He chose instead a seat in the fifth row. Nehru spotted Buchman and went to spend several minutes talking with him before joining the platform party. At the end of the occasion the person Buchman singled out to talk to was John R. Mott, his old friend and mentor.

Nehru suggested that he might come to tea with Buchman at Jaipur House on 3 January. Buchman took great care in planning the occasion so that Nehru should meet those who would be of most interest to him, and also so that he should feel treated not as a public figure but as a human being. He talked for half an hour with Buchman, and was then much moved when the chorus sang the national anthem and other songs. After their 'Song of India' there was a long silence and those near the Prime Minister noticed that there were tears in his eyes. Buchman was delighted with the occasion. 'We did the unusual and no one asked him to speak,' he said. Nehru told his sister, Mrs Vijaya Lakshmi Pandit, how much he had enjoyed the afternoon. He had, too, been represented earlier at a ceremony in New Delhi when the German Minister had presented Buchman with the Grand Cross of his country's Order of Merit. But there was scant sign that the Prime Minister was turning to Buchman in the way he had hoped.

Christmas was a busy time. Each night, including Christmas Day, a play was given and, beforehand, the most varied dinner parties took place at

---

* In 1951, a Los Angeles *Evening Herald Express* reporter asked Buchman if he could change Stalin. 'I couldn't,' replied Buchman. 'But God could.' (13 March 1951.)

Jaipur House. The chorus – many of whom had to combine singing to the guests with changing in time to take part in the play – sang carols, closing with an exquisite tableau of the Mother and Child. Christians, Muslims, Hindus, Sikhs, Buddhists sat spell-bound. 'I used to think of Christmas as a drunken orgy,' one distinguished Indian told the Austins. 'I begin to understand what it is all about.'[12]

On 6 January Radio Tashkent, beamed to India and Pakistan, fired the first in a series of Soviet broadsides against Buchman's tour of India. It was followed on 8 January by a prominently displayed article in *Pravda*, under a Delhi dateline, and a talk on Moscow Radio's home service entitled 'Buchmanism is the Ideological Weapon of the Warmongers'. Next day the same commentator, Georgi Arbatov, repeated his allegations on Moscow Radio's overseas service. The four reports covered similar ground – the 'Hitlerite' Buchman and his colleagues aimed to 'penetrate into the sphere of India's political life' on behalf of 'American imperialism'. Moral Re-Armament's financial backers, according to the 9 January broadcast, were 'kept a secret' but were known to include Firestone, Rockefeller, the *Los Angeles Times*, the 'US West Coast Shipping Company and other representatives of the US monopolistic capital'.

Arbatov's home service broadcast was a revised repeat of a talk he had given on the same station on 21 November 1952, stimulated by the publication of Peter Howard's book *The World Rebuilt* the year before. Arbatov described Moral Re-Armament as 'a universal ideology' and quoted a statement that 'it has the power to attract radical revolutionary minds'. 'Moral Re-Armament', he said, 'supplants the inevitable class war by the "permanent struggle between good and evil" . . . Moral Re-Armament, in addition to building bridgeheads on each continent and training cadres who would be capable of spreading the Buchmanite ideology among the masses, has now started on its decisive task, the total expansion of Buchmanism throughout the world.' In this revised version he added a description of the current Indian visit. 'The American press in India has raised a great to-do, glamourising Buchman and propagating his ideas,' Arbatov remarked, while the 'Indian democratic press', in which connection he quoted *Blitz*, 'reacted differently'.

This attack had, at first, little impact. The musical *Jotham Valley* was given for 20,000 party workers at the All-India Congress Party Conference at Hyderabad, as they prepared for their public meetings of 200,000. The Nizam of Hyderabad sponsored a special showing solely for his family, household and government. His Chief Minister, who was host to the visitors, invited some to stay on to cope with the interest among his people.

In Madras students picketed the theatre with placards and leaflets, using slogans taken direct from the Tashkent and Moscow talks and linking Moral Re-Armament with 'monopoly capitalists like Rockefeller, Henry Ford and Paul Hoffman' and 'enemies of the European working-class like Léon Blum, Kurt Schumacher and Giuseppe Saragat', then the Democratic Socialist leaders in France, Germany and Italy respectively. But the general enthusiasm about the plays soon lured the protesters inside the theatre and the agitation faded away.

Here in the South, Communism had many adherents in the universities and elsewhere. Neither Christianity – which was stronger here than elsewhere in India – nor Gandhism, as they had been lived out, seemed to be providing an adequate alternative.

One afternoon Buchman asked a prominent Gandhian, 'What would Gandhi say to the South being gripped by an ideology foreign to India?'

The Gandhian replied, 'Gandhi's sentiments are slowly dying. It has become an individualistic thing, not a social factor any more. Gandhi fought for the oppressed, the poor, the frustrated. But after he went, things have changed. There are new problems and we haven't found new answers.'

'Maybe you'll have to get down to the real trouble,' said Buchman. 'You will have to create a lot of men who will live what Gandhi lived, and you may have to be one of them.'

The Gandhian's reply was honest. 'I lived and worked with Gandhi for thirty years, but I never wanted to be left alone with him,' he said. 'I ran away from him. I clasped my weakness to myself because I did not want it to be taken away from me.'

The public interest in Madras was so overwhelming that no theatre was large enough, and the city's film industry took over. First one and then another company provided space to put on the plays. Finally, the Vahini studio constructed the largest stage in India for them. On the final day three performances had to be given to accommodate the crowds. By now Buchman had decided that his force must stay longer on the sub-continent, and wires went off to Burma, Thailand and Japan cancelling any immediate visit.

Phyllis Austin had one particularly vivid memory from the time in Madras. She was walking down a hotel corridor with Buchman, the corridor so long and the heat so intense that it was almost too much for him. 'Out of one of the rooms came a bedraggled, bent old sweeper, an "untouchable". Frank bowed low, took off his hat and said, with great warmth of feeling, "So nice, so nice to meet you." The old man was startled, then looked at Frank, who obviously meant what he said. The man hesitated, then drew himself up till he stood quite straight, and a big smile spread over his face. Suddenly he seemed for one moment to regain his dignity.'

[419]

Buchman summed up his hopes for India in a New Year message, widely published: 'Men are hungry for bread, for peace, and for the hope of a new world order. Before a God-led unity every last problem will be solved. Hands will be filled with work, stomachs with food and empty hearts with an ideology that really satisfies.'[13]

In Calcutta, perhaps more than in any other city, the contrast of rich and poor and the clash of class war were strongly apparent. The labour men and the group of employers travelling with Buchman found their way into the homes of labour leaders, some not long back from Moscow or Peking. Rajani Mukherjee, Vice-President of the West Bengal Socialist Trade Unions Congress (Hind Mazdoor Sabha), commented, 'Asian workers have been suspicious of the West. Moral Re-Armament does not come from the West to the East, nor from the East to the West. It comes from man to man. When I saw your plays, I thought, "You are not against Communism or any other 'isms'. You are way beyond Communism. You are reassessing Marxism in relation to modern problems and moral values." '[14]

One day in Calcutta Buchman was sitting listening to God with a largish group, when an unknown man came in and sat down at the back. After some minutes Buchman said, 'The only thought I had was, "Stop stealing." I don't know what that means. It may mean my watch that someone stole the other day. It may refer to myself, though it is some years since I stole anything. I just don't know what it means.' At this point the unknown man slipped out. 'Who was that?' asked Buchman. No one knew. Next day, however, he returned. He was a rich Marwari business man. 'I am amazed how Buchman knew my problem,' he said. 'I have been cheating on my taxes for years.' He had sent a cheque to the tax department for many thousands of rupees that morning. Later he had Buchman and two hundred of his colleagues to meet a group of business men whom he told that he had decided to be honest in future.[15]

Buchman went from Calcutta to Darjeeling to see Metropolitan Foss Westcott's grave at St Paul's School, 800 feet above the town. He told the boys there, 'I am thinking about the Metro. He used to sit in the Bishop's chair, but he had one of these little black books. He listened every morning . . . He had a big house, but he lived up in that little hut on the roof. It was in his house I met Gandhi. One met everybody there.'

'At seventeen I was a rascal,' he continued. 'I had all sorts of problems . . . I used to go to a chapel like this. A good old fellow, the salt of the earth, used to preach, but he never touched my problems. And school is the time when you meet your problems . . . Did you cheat at school? I did. I got caught once. I used to take money, too, and buy candy for the girls. I was always thoughtful for other people!' His audience were enthralled.

The following weekend he was asked to return to unveil a bust of

Westcott and again spent time talking to the boys. This time he told them about his own experience of change – the resentment which had driven him to Europe, the discovery in the small chapel in Keswick: 'I had never experienced the Cross. It just didn't mean anything to me. I had seven people I didn't like. But in this chapel I actually saw Christ on the Cross. It was a vision. I left that place a different man.' He then asked one of the boys to read the inscription on the memorial tablet to Westcott. On it are the words, 'A great saint, yet the friend of sinners and loved by so many of them.' 'That's the important thing to me,' said Buchman. 'And if you want to put something on my tombstone I hope it will be something like this: "Here's one who understood." '[16]

Back in Calcutta Foss Westcott's successor, Metropolitan Mukerjee, summed up the visit there: 'If even a hundred British in India had lived out their Christianity as these people do, India would have been a very different country.'[17]

A journey to Kashmir to rest the team in the cool after six months' intensely hard work was greatly appreciated. However, after ten days the local demand for the plays became irresistible, and Buchman decided to give way. Kashmir was one of the main bones of contention between India and Pakistan, an important and an intensely sensitive area. The Prime Minister, Sheikh Abdullah – a Muslim who had sided with Gandhi on national issues and who was partly responsible for Kashmir adhering to India instead of Pakistan at Independence – came to the plays and meetings, one after the other, at first on the insistence of his two sons. One of them made a deep impression upon him by admitting that it had been he who had led a student strike when his father was Minister of Education. Sheikh Abdullah told Buchman, 'You have here the answer for India and Pakistan. It takes patience. I saw the answer in the plays, and it is God.' His wife added, 'When I saw the plays, I knew the Spirit of God was there. It is something you don't run into much in the world today, and we are grateful.'

The time came to move on to Pakistan, a journey only possible then by going back via Amritsar and that with difficulty, as no large group of foreigners had made it since Partition. Most of the party of 150 took off by a round-about surface route for Karachi, while Buchman flew with an advance party of five, stopping in Delhi en route. 'It was heartening,' records a contemporary diary, 'to be met by many new faces, mostly students who had changed in recent weeks, and including a member of the staff of Nehru who, ever curious, had questioned him about his change for so long that he was half-an-hour late for Parliament.'[18]

One of these students remembered, years later, the impression Buchman made on him: 'The first time I saw him it was winter in Delhi. He was wearing a tweed suit and a red and black striped tie. He was walking with a stick and had a flabby, round face, and I thought he was a total dud and wondered how the hell he got these people to do all these things for him. The second time I saw him was after a meeting. I didn't know he was there – he was sitting at the back. "Oh, I remember you," he said – and there was something in his eyes which was challenging and penetrating and straight. Then I went to see him off from the airport. He took hold of my hand and said, "India is a great country. Keep at it. You will be greatly used. God bless you." And I knew that man was trying to convey something to me, and almost praying that it would penetrate into my heart. He was not a man of words – that left a deep impression on me – but a man who wanted to go beyond words to something far deeper in my soul and spirit.'

The visit to Pakistan was in fulfilment of the promise which Buchman had made to Mohammed Ali Jinnah in December 1946. The London talks over Independence had deadlocked. Jinnah and all his delegation went to see *The Forgotten Factor*. The portrayal of the tough employer as a man who 'would not budge' tickled him and he laughed loudly – the first time, his companions commented, that they had even seen him smile since arriving in London. At supper afterwards he urged Buchman to bring the play to Pakistan as soon as the nation was created. 'It shows the answer to the hates of the world,' he said. 'Honest apology – that is the golden key.' 'But who will put that key into the lock of history and open the gates of the future?' commented Buchman later. Neither Jinnah, Nehru, nor the British did so on this occasion. The Scotland Yard man attached to Jinnah told Buchman, 'The Viceroy, Nehru and Jinnah should have seen this play the first night they were in London!'[19]

Standing now in front of Jinnah's tomb, Buchman repeated Jinnah's words to him in London seven years before and recalled their first meeting in 1924 at Belgaum. 'May Pakistan rise and live as an answer,' was his prayer. Later, dining with the Cabinet, he found himself seated next to a son-in-law of another of his Belgaum acquaintances, one of the Ali brothers, and told him of his conversation with Lord Reading about them.

Buchman went on to Teheran, leaving the plays to be shown in Karachi. He had been invited there by another earlier guest at Caux, Dr Matine-Daftary, the son-in-law of Prime Minister Mossadegh. More than half of Buchman's party were British, and tension over Mossadegh's nationalization of the Persian oilfields was high between the two countries; but an assurance was given that, if they came with Buchman, the British would be welcomed as government guests. Mossadegh and Buchman met, both in high spirits, each surprised and relieved to find the other unlike the press reports. Buchman told a series of stories of difficult people who had become different and, with Mossadegh's son standing by, included among them tales of difficult fathers and sons.

'How do you get these results?' said Mossadegh. 'I hope you won't have the same difficulty with me.'

Buchman told him one more story – and ended up, 'That's all I do. You see, I do simple things, but that is what the world needs.'[20]

It may be worthwhile, in attempting to understand Buchman, to transcribe more fully here some of the thoughts that he called Baynard-Smith to write down during the nights in India, and try to see what they consisted of.

During one of the first nights in Bombay, Buchman dictated, 'You will be guided beyond your wildest dreams. God has a unique part for you and your work in India. The tops of a thousand hills are yours. India politically will have a large place in the future.'

Shortly before going to Delhi, he dictated, 'I will lead you forth in Delhi as I led you years ago, and I will work through you mightily. My will and way, not yours. Men will know it is the will of God and not any work. I am going to speak to you. Make no moves with Nehru. He will come to you. Alone in the mountains, away from others, I will give you the mighty secret that will win India back to her rightful place. Be alert, sympathetic, constant. Greater days are yours.'

On another occasion, later on: 'You are needed in India. You can create an organism here which will decide the future of the world. Keep close to Delhi and Nehru . . . He will commit his strong right arm. He will come your way . . . He will select his own plan. The days in Hyderabad will be monumental. Stay in the background but you will be in the foreground, too. Stay in this country for the present. Strifes and rumours of wars. Your team has the skill to meet the situation . . . Build up constructive personalities who can handle the situation everywhere . . . Lucknow will help. The Munshis will be great assets . . . You will not go to Burma now. No Japan this year. It will resound to Japan from Delhi.'

On the morning of his interview with President Prasad he dictated, 'The President is as worried as anybody that Gandhiji's philosophy will not be carried out and will grasp eagerly at what we can give.'

What are we to think of such thoughts, written down in the night some decades ago?

I asked Michael Barrett once about the seemingly fantastic ideas which he wrote down for Buchman on such occasions. What were their purpose? 'Assurance,' he replied, and, indeed, many of those large visions could have come to him – or have welled up from within him – to give him courage to tackle the immense tasks he had taken on with such meagre resources. Also, perhaps, they were thoughts emerging through the spirit

[423]

of an American bred in the era of expansion, a man who, in Loudon Hamilton's words, 'had not a negative bone in his body'. They were an indication of attitude rather than action; and when it came to action, the tests of common sense and spiritual integrity were there to be applied. Baynard-Smith's summary of Buchman's attitude in India is 'a persistent search for the will of God'.

Clearly, in the passages quoted above, there are many unfulfilled promises, or hopes. On the one hand the President of India was concerned in exactly the way Buchman foresaw and, after their interview, was a friend of Moral Re-Armament to the day of his death. The Munshis were a great help and kept in touch through the years. And Moral Re-Armament has, ever since, had a permanent place in India, represented more particularly by the outreach of the conference centre built at Panchgani, near Pune. On the other hand, 'an organism which will decide the future of the world' did not become visible in India. Nor did Nehru 'turn more and more' to Buchman.

On the last point, however, it is arguable that something did happen to Nehru in the last years of his life which brought his thinking nearer to Buchman's, greatly to his colleagues' surprise. Many of them – T. T. Krishnamachari, one of his cabinet, and Sanjiva Reddi, a future President of India, for example – remarked how much more frequently from late 1955 he spoke of the importance to the individual and the nation of moral and spiritual standards. Nehru himself said to his biographer, Michael Brecher, in June 1956, 'If they (moral and spiritual standards) fade away, I think that all the material advancement you may have will lead to nothing worthwhile.'[21]

After Nehru's death Reddi described in a public speech in London the excitement when he had first spoken of such values at a rally in the state of Andhra. 'Congress Party leaders who had so often heard the Prime Minister say that the steel mills and factories were the real temples of India crowded round him and said, "What has happened to you, Panditji?"' Reddi reported. '"Yes," Nehru had replied, "I have changed. I believe the human mind is hungry for something deeper in terms of moral and spiritual development, without which the material advance is not worthwhile."'[22] It is even possible that someone influenced by Buchman may have been a contributory factor to his change of thinking. Appadorai Aaron, a YMCA Secretary in Glasgow, returned to India in 1955, after being at Caux, and started to spend time in quiet each morning. When he told Vice-President Radhakrishnan, an old school friend, about it, Radhakrishnan remarked, 'You must meet Nehru. I will arrange it.' They met and Panditji said, 'People flatter me. They don't tell me the truth and I feel out of touch with the country.' Aaron told him that a daily time of quiet meditation would help him to 'read men's characters'. 'That sounds like Moral Re-Armament,' said Nehru. 'It doesn't matter what you call it. The thing is to try it,' Aaron replied. Some days later they met at a Delhi reception. 'I've been trying what you suggested,' Nehru said. 'I find it a real help.'[23]

How did Buchman finance the expedition to Ceylon, India and Pakistan – and the other even larger ventures of the years ahead?

During the Asian expedition invitation committees in the different countries and regions took on certain responsibilities – the Ceylonese and Bombay committees, for example, paying all expenses while the group was with them. As usual, no one travelling with Buchman took a salary. But there were heavy transport and other costs and, with India, as with many post-war operations, money came from the most varied quarters. Buchman never issued public appeals of the kind usual with most charities or made by many American TV evangelists today. Sometimes a Sunday morning collection at an assembly at Caux or Mackinac was devoted to a particular purpose, but usually it became known informally that a certain venture had been decided upon and people then came forward with gifts according to their means, desires and inner direction. Sometimes these were large amounts, as when the group of Dutch people financed the first of the three planes to India. Also, just at this time an Englishwoman received a large family inheritance and gave £50,000 of it for the Asian journey.

To other ventures and for the general conduct of Buchman's work there were, as well as small givers, other large donors, rather in the fashion of Mrs Tjader long before. Like her they were usually motivated by some specific help which Buchman had given them or members of their families. Bernard Hallward of Montreal, who had restored a large sum to the Canadian Customs in 1932, and his wife Alice, were consistently generous.

Another couple who gave frequently were Mr and Mrs Albert H. Ely of Washington, DC. 'Dear Frank,' they wrote on his birthday in 1951, 'You have given us a sound home, many happy years and a chance to fight with you in the greatest revolution of all time. Our birthday gift this year is ten thousand blessings, with symbols thereof, and the prayer God may give you ten thousand more happy, joyous days.'[24] In June 1949 the Elys had written that a number of couples had taken responsibility for raising the monthly payments for the purchase of the Los Angeles centre, and enclosed $25,000 to cover the June payment.[21]

In October 1951 Gilbert Harris, who had given up his job after seventeen years with the Chase National Bank to be the Treasurer of Buchman's work in America, wrote, 'At last the "miracle" cheque arrived.

[425]

It was for $124,843.75 and came from T. Henry Williams. It was the more welcome as we were in a pretty tough spot financially.'[26]

Whether it was a 'miracle' cheque because money had been so much needed and prayed for or because the donor, T. Henry Williams, the inventor of the tyre mould machinery from Akron, had been having difficulty in realising money which he had long wanted to give, is not known. It is known that Williams had previously written of his efforts to free money from a business in which he had partners and various commitments.

Mrs John Henry Hammond, who took part in the Asian journey, was another frequent and generous donor. On 5 January 1957 she wrote, 'This is the guidance that came to me early this morning: "Whoever does the will of God, that is my brother and sister and mother . . . Your money belongs to God . . . Give a million of your capital. Have $100,000 of it go to the work in Africa . . . This gift will help my family to see why I feel MRA is the only hope for the world . . .

"This is a critical time. God has work for me to do. I want to be available. Why count on the Fords and Rockefellers when I am committed to remaking the world? . . . Freely as you have received, so must you give. . . . Your grateful friend, Emily.'[27]

There was certainly no point in waiting for Ford or Rockefeller. The former had been generous with hospitality and had made one small gift. The latter had never given anything. Neither had ever been asked for a cent, and Buchman was determined to keep it that way. He did, however, feel badly when large companies or unions to which Moral Re-Armament, as a by-product of its spiritual work, had been of service gave little practical help in return. His secretary wrote in his diary for 18 January 1951, 'Frank full of energy began to feel the wrongness of our friends who had benefited so by MRA not giving more generously. Patterson was sending $10,000 personally, but F had expected something big from the company.'

W. A. Patterson was president of United Airlines, based in Chicago. Fifteen days previously, as reported in the *New York Herald-Tribune*, he had spoken at an MRA assembly in Washington along with officials of the Airlines Pilots Association: 'Mr Patterson said that when a pilot strike seemed inevitable four months ago because negotiations were deadlocked over 119 union demands, he was informed that Lawrence Shapiro, chairman of the pilots' grievance committee, wanted to see him about MRA.

' "I knew nothing about MRA, but plenty about Larry Shapiro – and it wasn't good," said Mr Patterson. "He was rated our toughest negotiator – a man who wouldn't give an inch. Imagine my surprise when he began his conference by suggesting that we use 'absolute honesty, purity, love and

unselfishness' as a basis for reopening labor management discussions. He
... convinced me of his sincerity. So we called a meeting in Denver, Oct
26."

'At the end of five days around a conference table, Mr Patterson said,
management and labour had "openly and frankly and entirely without
rancour, reduced the original 119 demands to thirteen". Eight of the
thirteen demands have been entirely settled and the rest will be concluded
within the next weeks, Mr Patterson said.

' "If anyone had told me sixty days ago that we weren't headed into a
knock-down and drag-out strike, I would have said they were dreaming,"
Mr Patterson said. "We had been trying for sixteen months to avoid a
strike, which I knew was going to cost our company at least $12,000,000
and also be a possible threat to national security. But there isn't going to be
a strike – and what is much more important, a new spirit of trust and
confidence has been born." '[28]

In fact, neither in America or Britain did industrial concerns give large
sums to Buchman's work. In the financial year which included Buchman's
death the contribution of industrial firms in Britain was a fraction more
than 1% of the total received, as it was also in the following year. In
America industry's contribution in 1962 and 1963 was approximately
0.5% of the total received.

Indeed, an analysis of any year shows that large gifts were exceptional.
In the year of Buchman's death, 84.9% of contributors in Britain gave less
than £10 and 0.4% £1000 or more, while in America 85.2% gave less
than $100 and 14.8% more than $100.[29]

TWO ATTACKS AND A WARNING

Buchman's last call on his journey back from India was at Istanbul and his last date there was with the Ecumenical Patriarch of the Orthodox Church, Athenagoras of Constantinople. The Patriarch was a towering figure, six feet seven inches and topped by a tall mitre. He had spent thirteen years in America and was, in fact, an American citizen.

'I welcome you as the new apostle,' were his first words to Buchman. He seated his guests and then continued with a smile, 'I follow you, Dr Buchman, on my own personal "television" everywhere you go. I read all you write. I receive your inspiration. Many more people than you know are your followers and belong to your brotherhood and army. I belong whole-heartedly to your programme, not only because of my office, but because I personally believe in it. Something told me you would come, but your stay is much too short.'

The Patriarch had, he explained, been impressed by a move made towards him by Ahmed Emin Yalman, the editor of the major Turkish newspaper *Vatan*, after his visit to Caux in 1946. Yalman had first become reconciled with his old enemy, the then Prime Minister, and started to work for better understanding with Greece. Then he had approached the Patriarch. Together they had entered a mosque, a former Christian cathedral. 'Here I am moved to pray,' the Patriarch had said, casting the unity of faith in one God over the divided group which accompanied them.

'It is all so simple,' Buchman commented when Athenagoras had finished his story.

'Truth is simple,' replied the Patriach, 'but unfortunately people don't like simple things. They want them complicated. At the Last Supper there were no creeds and no doctrines, but one commandment – unity in love.'

When Buchman left an hour later to catch his plane, the Patriarch looked at him severely: 'I would like to keep you here as a prisoner, but you are a free bird and you fly away. God bless you. You are a modern St Paul.'

'No, no,' said Buchman. 'I am a very simple man.'[1]

It was perhaps ironic that this interview should have taken place just as Buchman was returning to Europe to face severe attacks. In India, soon after the strongest yet propaganda offensive from Moscow against his work had begun, he had heard rumours that two dissimilar bodies in the West – the Secretariat of the International Confederation of Free Trade Unions (ICFTU)* and the Social and Industrial Council of the Church of England – were producing reports on his activities.

Both these reports were focussing upon Moral Re-Armament's work in industry, one of its major emphases since World War II. Buchman's vision for industry had, from the first, been both simple and exalted. It was meant to 'produce enough for the needs of all'.[2] The basic need was a new motivation in people at all levels. 'Suppose everybody cared enough, everybody shared enough, wouldn't everybody have enough?' he had said in East Ham Town Hall in 1938. '. . . Only a new spirit in men can bring a new spirit in industry. Industry can be the pioneer of a new order, where service replaces selfishness, and where industrial planning is based upon the guidance of God.'[3]

He felt management and labour could 'work together, like the fingers on the hand',[4] and in order to make that possible he aimed to answer 'the self-will in management and labour who are both so right, and so wrong'.[5]

This philosophy was in Buchman's view the answer to the class war which was being wastefully fought by people on both sides. He did not see Moral Re-Armament's function as taking sides on economic nostrums – private enterprise versus nationalisation, for instance – nor as working out detailed solutions for particular factories or industries. That was the task of the people involved in each situation. Moral Re-Armament's role was to offer the experience which would free those people's hearts and minds from the motivations or prejudices which prevent just solutions. Buchman believed that if 'the forgotten factor' of God's plan and purpose became a reality to people in any situation, they would be free to find solutions which had previously eluded them. It would take hard work and detailed negotiations. Everything would not be solved automatically just by people changing, but often the way to creative thought was blocked until someone did change – and, in the world at large, that was the last thing people thought possible.

However, by 1953 numerous business men and industrialists in many parts of the world were trying to conduct their affairs on these principles and, according to William Grogan, an International Vice-President of the American Transport Workers' Union, 'between 1946 and 1953 national

* Created in 1944 as a breakaway from the Communist-led World Federation of Trade Unions.

union leaders, local union officials, shop stewards and rank and file union members from seventy-five countries had received training' in them 'at Caux and Mackinac Island, or in their own countries'.[6] Not all of these, of course, had applied MRA principles when they got home, nor did all those who did have startling results to report; but Evert Kupers, for twenty years President of the Dutch Confederation of Trades Unions, stated that 'the thousands who have visited Caux have been deeply impressed by its message for our age and by the real comradeship they found there'.[7]

Teams equipped with plays had been at work in most of the advanced industrial countries as well as in many developing countries. They had used much the same methods as in the Ruhr and the British coalfields. In Britain this work had spread to many situations in the docks, the motor industry and elsewhere. For example, at Mackinac in 1951, Buchman had been presented with a model of a tractor, symbolising the end of a personality clash in the Ford Motor Company's Dagenham plant between a shop steward convenor responsible for 16,000 men and the superintendent of the assembly building. The results were reflected in productivity and pay charts. The superintendent, H. W. Whatham, speaking with the convenor, Arthur Morrell, at his side, said, 'Production efficiency has reached 100.4 per cent, the highest it has ever been since the war. Not a single grievance has left the assembly line unsolved since we started on moral re-armament. We have cut out overtime in the export shipping department and the men are receiving pay increases.'[8] Buchman always chaffed Whatham on his figures. 'My standard is 100 per cent,' he would say. 'How do you get 100.4 per cent?'*

A more far-reaching development had taken place in the French textile industry through the initiative of Maurice Mercier, Secretary-General of the textile unions within the Force Ouvrière, and French textile employers whom he met at Caux. On an initial visit to Caux in 1949, Mercier 'observed that the employers of almost all countries, transported into this atmosphere, were reconsidering their original, outdated points of view and were more easily becoming conscious of their responsibility as men and as employers'.[9] He himself had left the Communist Party when he saw the Resistance movement degenerate into petty jealousies and obscure intrigues after the war. The conference at Caux and a subsequent meeting with Buchman brought him a new perspective. 'Class war today', he said, 'means one half of humanity against the other half, each possessing a powerful arsenal of destruction... Not one cry of hatred, not one hour of work lost, not one drop of blood shed – that is the revolution to which Moral Re-Armament calls bosses and workers.'[10]

* Buchman refused to quote this figure in his next broadcast, contenting himself with the previous month's figure of 99.43 per cent, which was already better than anything since the war.

On the initiative of those who had met at Caux, certain textile managers and workers signed a national agreement on 1 February 1951 – the first in France since the war. It was also the first to guarantee to employees a share in the benefits of higher productivity. Six hundred thousand workers were immediately given large wage rises. The same year, on Mercier's initiative, eighty textile factory delegations made up of employers, workers and staff met at Moral Re-Armament conferences.

Two years later, on 9 June 1953, the textile employers and trades unions – except the Communist CGT – signed a solemn agreement 'in complete openness, in the common interests of workers, firms and country', which was the foundation-stone of a policy of co-operation for the next twenty years. Under it, textile workers were also the first in France to benefit from, among other things, a retirement pension scheme and partial unemployment benefit. A subsequent anti-inflation agreement was called by Prime Minister Antoine Pinay 'one of the first solid achievements on the road of the change which is indispensable to the economic survival of the country'.[11] It was not until 1968 that employers at a national level in other industries were obliged to grant their workers the same level of social benefits as the textile workers had been given voluntarily.

Buchman's part in helping towards such transformations generally came when people in industry met him at Caux, Mackinac or elsewhere. These were often people who were at the heart of major industrial battles in their countries. Thus in the summer of 1950 Dan Hurley, the Chairman of the National Amalgamated Stevedores and Dockers' Union in Britain, came to Caux. It had been he who had initiated the British dock strike in 1949 by declaring the Canadian ship *Beaverbrae* 'black' – a strike which was said to have cost the British economy the equivalent of the entire Marshall Aid received from America that year.

Hurley wrote to Buchman after getting home, 'My outlook has certainly adopted an entirely new aspect, and how much easier it has become to see the other fellow's point of view, and not to be for ever prepared to ram home the very aggressive doctrine which has been part of my policy for such a long time. . . . Well, Frank, no matter how long it may be until we meet next, I shall always recall you as I last saw you, in your room, not infirm, but resting after a very hard day's work, which I suppose was a replica of your days since Caux opened. What a strain it must be teaching mankind an ideology, which by a great many like myself is approached with a good deal of suspicion, and yet with all that amount of strain that we fools impose upon you, you are able to look the most serene person I ever met.'[12]

Hurley was one of many dockers who met Buchman and his colleagues. When *The Forgotten Factor* was shown in Poplar, East London, in November 1951 ten present and past officials of three rival dock unions sent invitations to every Member of Parliament, as well as to dockers and dock employers.

Similar effects could be quoted from many countries. Some were reported in the local or national press,* while others were recorded in various Moral Re-Armament Information Services. Indeed, it was upon such accounts in MRA publications that the compiler of the ICFTU report relied for what turned out to be an uncompromising attack on Moral Re-Armament.

The existence of this report was first revealed in a daily bulletin issued by the ICFTU Secretariat during the Confederation's Third World Congress at Stockholm in July 1953. It stated that 'a report was presented on the Moral Re-Armament Movement, headed by Dr Buchman, with particular reference to its attempted incursions into the field of industrial relations' and added that 'free trades unions would be well advised to guard against any interference from quarters whose financial backing is in any case dubious'. The world press naturally concluded that, as the *New York World-Telegram and Sun* reported, 'The ICFTU meeting in Stockholm has passed a resolution condemning MRA for "anti-Trade Union efforts".'[13]

This was not so. A draft report did exist, which was presented to the Executive by the Secretariat at Stockholm. But neither at the Stockholm meeting, nor at any other time, was this report or any resolution concerning it presented to or voted on by the Congress itself, the only body entitled to make policy statements on the Confederation's behalf. The report was nevertheless issued the following September as a supplement to the Secretariat's *Information Bulletin*.[14] Again there was world-wide publicity.

The report declared that it had been prepared at the request of the Socialist Trade Unions of India, Hind Mazdoor Sabha (HMS). The HMS's President, Sibnath Banerjee, promptly denied that either he or his executive had made such a request. Later it emerged that an individual HMS official had made a personal, unofficial inquiry as a result of the wide response to Moral Re-Armament in India. An official of the ICFTU Secretariat had thereupon suggested that he put his inquiry in writing, which would enable a report to be made.

The theme of the report was that 'MRA interfered with Trade Union activities' and was engaged in 'anti-union efforts, even to the extent of trying to found "yellow unions"'. It also stated that 'MRA's results in industry are illusory' and that its 'dubious financial sources . . . mean that

---

* For example *Miami Herald* (25 March 1950): 'National Airlines. Pilots Union Settle Grievances. Philosophy of Moral Re-Armament Ushers in Era of Understanding.'

the movement has to make concessions scarcely in keeping with the original Buchman programme'. By this last statement the report presumably meant that MRA received large sums from industry and was therefore biased in favour of management. No inquiry was directed by the ICFTU to Moral Re-Armament before this allegation was made. The American Federation of Labour and the Congress of Industrial Organisations (AFL and CIO) did make such inquiries and were shown that, in the relevant year, no contributions were received from the larger industrial organisations or companies in America, and that in Britain gifts from all industrial sources had been less than three per cent of the whole.

The evidence presented to substantiate the main charges consisted of nine quotations from MRA publications and nine opinions from members of the ICFTU's Executive Board or of affiliated organisations, who had been sent a questionnaire. The nine quotations from MRA literature were presented under the subhead 'MRA provided the Proofs'. But, on examination against the original texts, it became apparent that seven of them had been so edited as completely to alter their meaning, while the other two, even in their truncated forms, had little to do with the charges made.*

The nine 'opinions' printed in the report were correctly so described, as only one of them contained a factual statement of any kind – a statement which was, incidentally, declared to be misinformed by one of the men referred to who had since become the Branch Chairman of the complaining official's own union in the area. Seven of the opinions were hostile to Moral Re-Armament, one neutral and one favourable. Whether this was a representative sample of the replies to the questionnaire sent out by the ICFTU's Secretariat is not known. Other answers favourable to Moral Re-Armament were subsequently found to have been sent to the editor and ignored. The favourable reply of the Executive Vice-President of the American CIO, John Riffe, was included in the original July draft of the report but omitted in the final September version.

No national trade union bodies, to my knowledge, adopted the ICFTU report. In Britain, the Trades Union Congress and the Labour Party expressly dissociated themselves from it on the basis of freedom of

---

* Julian Thornton-Duesbery, then Master of St Peter's College, Oxford, in *The Open Secret of MRA* (Blandford, 1964, pp. 96–119), printed the original texts of the items quoted and the ICFTU versions side by side. 'The purpose of this "highly prejudiced" editing was to try to prove that MRA "interferes in Trade Union matters",' he commented. 'The original, unedited texts prove exactly the opposite . . . Study of the unedited texts, also, makes it clear that the author of the report has been unable to produce a single instance of any attempt to found a "yellow union".' Thornton-Duesbery also printed beneath each item the comments of trade union officials in the situation concerned, comments which contradicted the report's interpretations. These statements had been sent to the ICFTU, but had never been published by that body.

conscience for their members.[15] Monitors of East European broadcasts and press remarked, however, on the use made in them of the draft report even before its publication, and the world media, unable swiftly to check on the report's sources, gave it wide publicity when it appeared. Later some editors, discovering its defects, began to wonder why the ICFTU had acted so precipitately. *Der Bund* of Berne hazarded the possibility that the report might be 'a cuckoo's egg laid by Moscow in its opponents' nest to bring suspicion both on them and on Moral Re-Armament, to create confusion'.[16] Dr William Bohn, editor of the New York Social Democrat weekly, *The New Leader*, was more cautious as to the report's origin, but clear about its falsity: 'These charges, apparently launched with the backing of so respected an organisation (as the ICFTU), created a great impression in many parts of the world. But as time wore on and new facts came to light, their impact has tended to fade... It seems to me that, on the whole, the men and women of MRA have come out of the conflict with colours flying ... It is disturbing to note that the charges made against MRA by the Secretariat of the anti-Communist ICFTU have been picked up by Moscow.'[17]

Buchman was convinced that the ICFTU report was 'only the opening round of a world offensive', but he did not commit himself as to its source. He seems to have been mainly interested to see how opposition would affect people. 'Persecution is the fire which forges prophets – and quitters,' he used to say. He was particularly delighted by John Riffe's forthright action when the matter was raised at the 1953 CIO Convention, where, coincidentally, Riffe's position as Executive Vice-President was up for ratification.

Challenged by prominent members on his relation to Moral Re-Armament, Riffe said, 'Some of you have met people in Moral Re-Armament; some of you haven't. Well, you're looking at one now... Nobody can object to John Riffe quitting whisky and poker and a lot of other things he shouldn't have been doing. Now if contact with MRA makes a union man like me honest and decent and with an unselfish love for his fellow men, is that interfering with labour? If it gives me a happy home life again, and makes me do my job with greater responsibility, is that hurting labour?

'Millions of our members believe in these principles. There isn't a man in this room that wouldn't say they are right. But do we all live them? ... I'm in your hands. No matter what you decide, I won't harbour any bitterness.'

Out of the silence, one member rose: 'We've heard the Executive Vice-President. We know the way he has lived. I only wish I could live that way myself.' When the full Convention met and Riffe came up for confirmation in his post, no one stood against him and he was elected by acclamation. The Chairman of the International Committee also made it clear that no constitutionally sound ICFTU report had been authorized and that the AFL had also refused to condemn Moral Re-Armament.[18] Buchman's comment was, 'Grateful for an intelligently thoughtful friend like John.'

Meanwhile James Haworth, President of the Transport Salaried Staffs' Association in Britain, a former MP and member of the Labour Party Executive, had gone to Brussels to confront the ICFTU Secretariat with their report's inaccuracies. He had an interview with the Secretary-General and the officer who had compiled the report. 'We went through the Report in detail, and when I left, I was under the impression it would be withdrawn,' Haworth wrote.[19] It was – but not until twelve years later, on 18 August 1966, when the ICFTU Secretary-General, Omer Bécu, wrote to Moral Re-Armament in London confirming the ICFTU's 'attitude of strict neutrality' to Moral Re-Armament, and released his letter to the media.[20]

Whatever the motive of the compiler of the 'ICFTU report', most trade unionists who, without examining it closely, lent to it the authority of the ICFTU Bulletin, were probably moved by a quite simple human emotion – the feeling that an outside body was poaching on their preserves. This same feeling seems to have been at least one factor behind the launching of the report of the Church of England's Social and Industrial Council.

During the spring and summer of 1952 *The Forgotten Factor* was performed in a series of British industrial centres at the invitation of local management and trade union leaders. In each city the cast and accompanying team were welcomed by Church leaders who found that the play stimulated interest in spiritual matters among people who had little touch with organised religion. That, for example, was the theme of the Provost of Portsmouth's sermon at a service of thanksgiving for their visit in Portsmouth Cathedral,[21] and the thought behind a letter of support from the Bishop of Coventry to that city's daily newspaper.[22] The Moderator of the Church of Scotland, the Revd G. Johnson Jeffrey, wrote to 1,560 Scots Ministers announcing the play's visit to Glasgow as 'a venture of faith which deserves the closest attention of all Church leaders'.[23]

In Sheffield, however, the play encountered a different reception from one influential group of churchmen. A prestigious industrial mission, led by the Bishop's industrial chaplain, Canon E. R. Wickham, was already at work there, and it soon became apparent that Wickham and those close to him disapproved of Moral Re-Armament's intervention and regarded *The Forgotten Factor* as a hindrance, rather than a help, to the work they were doing. The Bishop of Sheffield himself, the Rt Revd L. S. Hunter, expressed this view when, addressing the Convocation of York shortly after the visit of *The Forgotten Factor*, he dismissed the play, which he had not himself seen, as 'glib emotionalism and shallow psychology' and added, 'It is frightening how easily some industrialists and others fall for the salesmanship of MRA.'*

The Bishop was Vice-Chairman of the newly founded Social and Industrial Council of the Church of England, and at its fourth meeting on 26 February 1953, which he chaired, the Council decided it 'should consider publishing a report on Moral Re-Armament'. Three months earlier the Council[24] had asked Gerald Steel, Managing Director of the Sheffield-based United Steel Company and a member of the Council, to produce a short factual account of Moral Re-Armament's work in industry, which he now presented. In introducing it, he said 'he knew a number of people who were extremely critical of the Church who were saying MRA was first-class and that the Church, as far as they could make out, was sneering at it, and they did not think very much of the Church on that score.' He thought the Church should make its position clear. This was generally agreed and the matter was passed to the Council's Standing Committee.[25]

The Standing Committee set up a Working Party. Canon Cyril Hudson of St Albans, who undertook to be both Convenor and Secretary, selected as Chairman, 'acting on his own initiative',[26] the Bishop of Colchester, the Rt Revd F. D. V. Narborough, who had been a consistent critic of Buchman's work since the 1920s. Canon Wickham was co-opted. Another of those co-opted had shortly before expressed strong disapproval of Buchman's work in a conversation with MRA workers. None of those suggested in the Council or the Standing Committee who had recent association with Moral Re-Armament was included or consulted. The Revd Dennis Nineham** and Bishop Geoffrey Allen*** were invited to draft the theological and psychological chapters of the report, while Canon Wickham was to be entrusted with the third and last chapter, 'The Social Thinking of MRA'.[27]

The Council of Management of the Oxford Group only heard that the Working Party was in operation when three individuals who had been helped by Moral Re-Armament – the Mayor of Folkestone, a lecturer in history at Greenwich Naval College and a young East End clergyman –

---

* 14 May 1952. Reprinted in *Sheffield Diocesan Review*, August 1952. Observers were all the more surprised at the Bishop's speech because of the broadly sympathetic description of Buchman's work given in his book, *A Parson's Job* (SCM Press, 1931, pp. 86–8) written when Archdeacon of Northumberland.

** Professor of Biblical and Historical Theology, King's College, London, 1954–1958.

*** Then Principal of Ripon Hall, Oxford, and later Bishop of Derby. In the early thirties as Chaplain of Lincoln College, Oxford, he had worked closely with the Oxford Group but by then, in his own words, 'had had no active association for many years'.

61. *left* Ruins at Essen, Germany, 1948.

62. *below* In 1948 Buchman, aided by the Allied authorities, took a mobile force into Germany, with plays, photo displays and literature, to present an ideology for democracy.

63. *above* Radio Stuttgart intercepts and interviews the mobile MRA force on the autobahn from Munich.

64. *left* In the Ruhr many Marxists were won by Buchman's message. Here, talking with him, are Max Bladeck (left) and Paul Kurowski (right), both of them miners and Communist Party activists.

65. *right* Konrad Adenauer (centre) at the Caux assembly, September 1948, where he asked Buchman to work in Germany. On the right is Oskar Leimgruber, Chancellor of the Swiss Confederation.

66. *left* Robert Schuman (left), Foreign Minister of France 1948–1953, takes leave of Buchman after attending the 1953 Caux conference.

67. *below* A Japanese delegation of seventy-six flew to the Caux assembly in 1950. Among them were the Mayors of Hiroshima and Nagasaki, and representatives of the Democratic, Liberal and Socialist Parties.

3. Buchman planting rice in 1952 in
eylon (Sri Lanka), at the beginning of
tour of Asian countries.

69. Buchman addressing members of both
houses of India's Parliament.

). Buchman renews acquaintance with
andit Nehru in Delhi.

71. Buchman (left) with J. P. Narayan,
leader of the Praja Socialist Party of India.

72. *left* Ahmed Guessous of the Moroccan undergr[ound]
with Pierre Chavanne (right), a French settler.

73. *above* Buchman with William Nkomo, a founde[r of]
the ANC Youth League of South Africa, and his wi[fe]

74. *centre left* Buchman with delegates at
Caux from Nigeria, Kenya and South
Africa, in 1952.
75. *above* The Tolon Na, President of the
Northern Territories Council of Ghana, at
Caux.
76. *left* Jomo Kenyatta introduces MRA
speakers at his teacher-training school in
Kenya.

77. *above left* Dr. Jamali, Foreign Minister of Iraq, at the
1955 Bandung Conference of non-aligned countries,
called for 'a great moral force for ideological disarmament
and moral re-armament'.

78. *above* Rajmohan Gandhi, grandson of Mahatma
Gandhi and of Rajagopalachari.

79. *above left* Hans Bjerkholt,
pioneer Norwegian Communist.

80. *above* Victor Sparre, Norwegian
painter.

81. *left* Peter Howard (centre),
farmer, author and columnist, to
whom Buchman entrusted his
work shortly before he died.

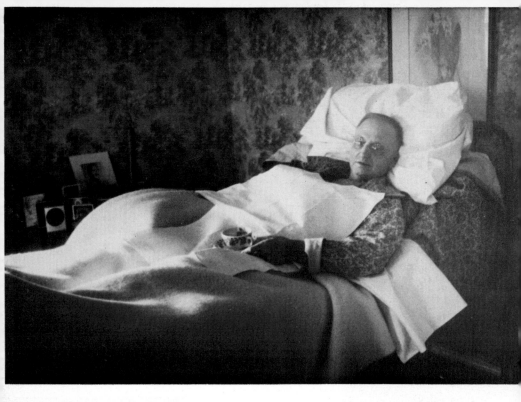

82. *above* By the end of the 1950s the world-wide demand for the work of Moral Re-Armament was mounting. 'Sitting up in bed, where he was increasingly confined whether in Caux, Oxford or London, Paris, Milan or Rome, his mind was constantly at work on how to meet the crisis of manpower which was confronting him from every continent.'

83. *below* Nobusuke Kishi, the Prime Minister of Japan, maintained close links with Buchman.

84. *below* The Broadway actresses, Muriel Smith (right) and Ann Buckles, played the leads in the musical *The Crowning Experience*, which spearheaded Buchman's work for racial reconciliation in the U.S. 1957–58.

85. *above* In 1960 Chancellor Adenauer asked Buchman to meet him in Los Angeles. He said to Buchman: 'Your work is absolutely essential for the peace of the world.'

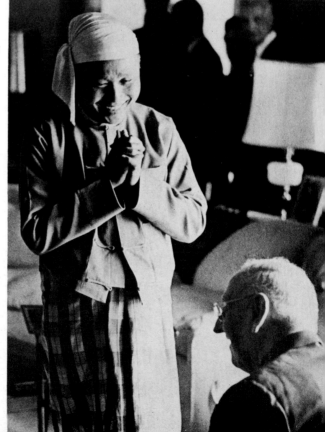

86. *right* U Nu, Prime Minister of Burma, visits Buchman at Tucson, Arizona, in 1960.

87. *above* View from the room in Freudenstadt where Buchman spent his last days.

88. *below* August, 1961. Europe's last farewell, with Ruhr miners standing guard.

were informally approached to give evidence to it by Bishop Narborough or Canon Hudson, neither of whom, according to these individuals, concealed their hostility towards Moral Re-Armament. These three felt incompetent to give evidence of MRA's national and world-wide work, but were willing to give their personal experience provided some of those centrally responsible for the whole work were also invited. This condition was not accepted, so they declined.

Throughout 1953 there was practically no contact between the Working Party and people identified with Moral Re-Armament. Canon Wickham spent a few hours at Caux. Canon Hudson had dinner with R. C. Mowat, the history lecturer, and three friends, at Mowat's invitation. Finally, on Mowat's insistence, a meeting between the Working Party and the Oxford Group Council of Management seemed about to take place, Bishop Narborough suggesting 27 January 1954 as a convenient date.

Two weeks before that date events took place which destroyed that opportunity. The *Daily Telegraph* printed letters from Canon Wickham and Bishop Narborough strongly criticising Moral Re-Armament.[28]* Sir Lynden Macassey, who had chaired numerous government tribunals and was advising the Oxford Group, was scandalised that the chairman and a member of a body 'preparing what must be assumed to have been intended to be a fair and impartial report . . .' should 'write partisan letters to the public press condemnatory of what they had to inquire into. . .' 'It would be difficult if not impossible', he added, 'to imagine a parallel action . . . in the case of any committee or tribunal which was engaged in forming a judgement on an important controversy . . .'[29] The Archbishop of Canterbury, Dr Geoffrey Fisher, opined, 'One must suppose that this Working Party was not meant to consist entirely of impartial people', but a week later assured his correspondent, the Mayor of Folkestone, 'May I just underline that no kind of report from this Working Party will reach the press or be made public at all . . .'[30]

When it met on 28 January 1954 the parent Council at first seemed almost as shocked as Sir Lynden. It minuted that the letters were 'not only ill-advised but improper', while a senior member, the Bishop of Birmingham, regarded them as 'vitiating the whole work of the sub-committee'. In the end, however, the Council agreed that the Working Party should not

---

* Canon Wickham's letter of 13 January was answered by a strong statement by the Moderator of the Church of Scotland and leaders of all the Free Churches on 15 January. Others who wrote in protest as the controversy developed included the Metropolitan of India, the Most Revd Arabindo Nath Mukerjee, nine Swedish bishops, and Dr Toyohiko Kagawa and Bishop Augustine Takasa of Japan. These and other statements, some of which appeared in British newspapers, are collected in *Report on Moral Re-Armament*, edited by R. C. Mowat (Blandford, 1955). None of these are quoted in the report.

be dismissed, but that the Council itself should write the Oxford Group and invite two or three representatives to meet with it.[31] Next day its Secretary sent this invitation – the first communication received by the Oxford Group from either the Council or the Working Party.

In spite of all that had passed the Oxford Group decided that they should still be prepared to meet the Council. In accepting the invitation they made two conditions, common in such cases: first, that the Council should supply them with a list of matters on which information was required so that they could have it available, and second, that they might bring a competent shorthand writer so that a verbatim note of the discussions could be made.[32] The council replied that if the Group felt discussions had to be 'invested with so much formality', it would be better to 'defer any meeting for the time being'.[33] The Oxford Group twice officially repeated their willingness to meet the Council. On both occasions the Council refused.[34]

So on 28 January 1955 the report was given to the press, before it had been seen by the Church Assembly and without any meeting having taken place between the Council or its Working Party and anyone responsible for the work on which they were reporting. Prominent stories were carried next day in all British newspapers and many abroad. Typical headlines were 'Utopian and Escapist' (*The Times*), 'Psychologically dangerous: Two Dissentients' (*Daily Telegraph*), and 'Buchmanites should use more thought: Church lacks vigour' (*News Chronicle*).

It is not known on what grounds Dr Fisher had given assurances to Alderman Moncrieff – and also, it appears, to Lord Hardinge of Penshurst – that 'no kind of report will . . . be made public', for it is clear from their minutes that the Council and the Working Party had long had publication in mind. On 9 November, however, in what looks like an undignified scramble, the Archbishop wrote to the Council's Secretary insisting that any report must be issued by the Council 'on its own authority as its own report' and not, as the Council intended, by the Working Party. 'Providing that is done,' he said, 'my answer (to Lord Hardinge) holds good.' The Council thereupon obligingly reversed its decision.[35]

The two dissentients mentioned in the *Daily Telegraph* headline were General Sir Colin Jardine and Gerald Steel, the industrialist who had written the original outline of Moral Re-Armament's work in industry. They were only permitted to make brief formal statements in the report. In the Church Assembly debate Jardine protested amid 'cheers' at the impropriety which led Bishop Narborough and Canon Wickham to write to the press,[36] while Steel wrote to the Secretary of the Council, 'Sentences (in the report) will be quoted out of their context – and certain derisory sentences in the report are the very stuff of which headlines are made.* Idealism and goodwill, on the other hand, are not "news", and references to the sincerity, courage and self-abnegation of the adherents of MRA are likely to appear in very small print if at all. I believe the publication will result in causing much distress to those men and women of goodwill, will be a set-back to their work and reflect little credit on the Church.'[37]

As far as publicity was concerned he proved a true prophet. Even though, following a spirited two-day debate, the report was not adopted but only 'received' by the Assembly, and then only with the proviso that 'this Assembly does not wish to record any judgement upon the merits or demerits of MRA',[38] the effect of the initial publicity was not washed away. The world-wide impression had been given that Moral Re-Armament had been condemned by the whole Church of England.

This impression, not perhaps unnaturally, was self-defeating for those in the Council who genuinely hoped to improve Moral Re-Armament's work. People who had sustained such universal public attack tended to feel beleaguered and not only to ignore the occasional praise within the report, but also to become disinclined to pay attention to any helpful advice. For example, Bishop Allen's chapter on the 'Psychology of Group Revival' (which he specifically stated was 'not intended as a description of MRA in its present form') was a helpful discussion of the dangers of any association of people becoming dependent on each other. He rightly emphasised that in the relations of parents and children, of priest or teacher and disciple, psychologist and patient, the junior partner must not remain dependent on the senior or he will not 'grow into the maturity and power of his own free personality'. The present book will have shown how keenly Buchman felt this danger and what drastic steps he took to try and avoid it. He did not always succeed: but the strictures on Moral Re-Armament as 'psychologically dangerous' – added to Bishop Allen's theme, it would seem, by another hand – would surely never have appeared if the Working Party had contained anyone with up-to-date knowledge of the inner life of the Moral Re-Armament fellowship, or even, perhaps, if the Council had accepted the Oxford Group's repeated invitation to meet its responsible representatives.

This lack of contact threw the writers of the report back on a study of MRA literature: and it was for some reason a selective study. None of the writings by theologians, such as Streeter or Thornton-Duesbery or the German Professors Karl Adam or Werner Schöllgen, for example, are mentioned, and Buchman's own speeches are only referred to once. The

---

* Some of these 'derisory sentences' do not seem to have been in the original text, but to have been added by a small editing committee. The Bishop of Sheffield in the Council meeting of 9 December 1954 tried to get two of them removed against Canon Hudson's successful defence.

literature which was referred to seldom gave any account of the devotional life of the individual or the corporate life of those working with Moral Re-Armament, but was concerned mainly with giving good news of God's power at work in society. Here again adequate personal contact would have been helpful for an informed appraisal.

Professor Nineham in his chapter, 'The Theology of MRA', wanted MRA to produce precise theological definitions for doctrines such as Sin, the Atonement, the Incarnation and the Resurrection. This showed a lack of understanding of the function of Moral Re-Armament, which was not to define doctrine. Any attempt to do so would have altered its nature from an organism to a sect, the antithesis of what Buchman intended.

Buchman was outside Britain for all except a couple of months during the years when this report was being planned, prepared, published and debated, but he was kept broadly informed of the different incidents. As he became aware of the methods being employed by the Social and Industrial Council, it seemed to him that, however well-meaning the majority of its members might be, its Working Party had an active core who wished, for whatever reason, to make his work more difficult. One night in Morocco in the spring of 1954 – after the letters to the *Daily Telegraph* and the renewed refusal of the Council to meet with representatives of the Oxford Group – he expressed to Baynard-Smith the thought that Tom Driberg was involved somewhere behind the scenes: 'The mature politician knows Driberg and assesses him. The Church people are duped by his position. He is a clever article.'

Buchman may have been right or wrong in deducing a Driberg connection with the Church of England report. Nothing overt has appeared to prove it. It may be coincidental that he lived, had his constituency and was a church warden within the diocese in which Bishop Narborough served, and was prominent in the Christian Socialist movement with which both the Bishop and Canon Wickham sympathised. They, of course, would have been unaware of his KGB connections, of which Buchman and his colleagues had been warned by sources as varied as Walton Cole, when Editor-in-Chief of Reuters, and a member of the Central Committee of the Communist Party of Great Britain. What is clear is that he had never, since 1928, been absent from any major British move against Buchman, and that he made extensive use of the report both at the time and in a book published after Buchman's death.

As with the ICFTU report, however, Buchman's main interest was with those who spoke up for his work in the Church Assembly. They included the Archdeacon of Halifax, who asked that the Assembly pass on to other business; Sir Cyril Atkinson who wished the Assembly to declare

that the report was 'harmful and unjust to a great religious movement';
Lord Selborne who said he read it 'with profound regret and not a little
resentment', and the Dean of Exeter who made a last-minute attempt to
have the report withdrawn. Buchman was particularly interested in the
intervention of the Dean of Westminster, Dr A. C. Don, who, as
Archbishop Lang's Chaplain, had conducted the earlier and far more
thorough investigation into Buchman and his work. In the debate he
stated that 'the report gave him an impression of a lack of open-
mindedness in one or two cases. He felt that no good would accrue to the
MRA or the Church of England by continuing the debate . . .' The
Assembly, he went on, 'should guard against saying things that might be
untrue and uncharitable, and thereby alienate from the Church of
England many good and high-principled people who – whether the
Assembly liked it or not – had found in MRA something that they had
failed to find elsewhere.'[39]

Neither the report nor the debate did any good to either party. The
Church's supposed condemnation was used by the enemies of Moral Re-
Armament, and naturally made many Christians cautious or even con-
temptuous in their attitude. Those associated with Moral Re-Armament
who were members of the Church of England continued to go to their
churches, where alone they could receive the sacraments, but it did
reinforce in many an impatience at the 'ineffectiveness' of the Church, as
admitted in the report, and in some an unwarranted sense of superiority.

Apart from these disparate public attacks on his work Buchman had a
more long-term and constant concern: the attitude of Rome. Hundreds
of Catholics were coming to Caux each year, and he encountered many in
the London docks and in the factories of France, Italy and America. He
himself held to the attitude he had expressed to a leading English Jesuit as
early as 1933, when he wrote, 'Our principle has always been to send all
Roman Catholics back to their Fathers for confession . . .'[40] As for those
non-believers who had come to an experience of God through his work,
he had added in the same letter, 'Our whole policy is to let each individual
decide to what church he is guided to go. Many have become convinced
Roman Catholics.' He felt that any renewal of faith which God used him
to bring to anyone should enhance, not weaken, their primary loyalties.

It was only in the summer of 1951 that Buchman became aware that a
new situation was developing. In August of that year the Holy Office
formulated a three-point warning to Catholics, which was not issued to
the press or sent immediately to the Nunciatures round the world but
which became known at Caux. It read:

[441]

1. It is not proper that priests of the diocesan or regular clergy, or, *a fortiori*, religious women, should take part in meetings of Moral Re-Armament.
2. If special circumstances render such participation desirable, let permission be asked in advance of the Sacred Congregation of the Holy Office; it will be granted only to learned and experienced priests.
3. Finally, it is not proper for the faithful to accept any office of responsibility in the Moral Re-Armament movement, and much less to take part in the so-called 'policy teams'.

This was a great surprise to Buchman, as the friendly relations he had maintained since 1948 with the Bishop of the Caux area, Monsignor Charrière, had led him to believe that the Catholic Church was taking a positive attitude to his action. But Charrière made it clear that the warning was a serious matter, although he arranged for priests to serve the Catholic chapel which is a part of the Caux assembly buildings.

As is its custom the Holy Office did not give any reasons for its action. Those of Buchman's many Catholic friends who made enquiries in Rome brought back a confirmation that the statement came from the highest authority on dogmatic matters and that there was no possibility of discussion. At the same time it was made clear to them that the warning did not amount to a condemnation, and, in fact, a stream of Catholics continued to arrive at Caux. Among them were distinguished theologians like Karl Adam, the Professor of Dogmatic Theology at Tübingen University, and Werner Schöllgen, Professor of Catholic Theology at the University of Bonn, both of whom recorded their favourable impressions. Professor Adam wrote in the Tübingen *Theological Quarterly*: 'It is not mere dreamers who have followed the movement which within thirty years has grown into a great world offensive, but prominent intellectuals, world-famous statesmen and politicians, big industrialists and workers' leaders, trade unionists, dockers and miners, men of all conditions from cabinet ministers to cooks. They all have one aim, to solve the toughest political, economic, social and cultural questions in the light of the Gospel. And it is amazing, it is wonderful, how, time after time, it is the simple, clear concepts of the Sermon on the Mount which throw light on the most involved political and economic problems. The four absolutes, the challenge to complete surrender to God, faith in the power of the Cross of Christ and the "quiet time" which Buchman urges, are basic elements of the Christian life, they are Christianity lived out. That is why Buchman's message is in its very core a Christian message. One can understand why the Catholic finds no new truths in Caux. But shaken to his roots, he has to admit that in Caux, Christianity has been more deeply understood and lived out than in many Catholic communities. In answer to the question "What has Caux to give Catholics?" Monsignor Eugène Fischer, Dean of the Cathedral of Strasbourg, replied, "The first thing that strikes us in Caux is the nagging of our conscience. I believe that outside the religious orders, there is no place on the face of the earth where so much prayer goes up." '[41]

Dr Adam wrote in 1952, while Professor Schöllgen devoted a chapter to Moral Re-Armament in his book *Aktuelle Moralprobleme* in 1955.[42] And during this period Father Riccardo Lombardi, a Jesuit, felt free to invite Buchman to address a gathering of a hundred priests in Rome when he was launching his movement 'Per Il Mondo Migliore'. But the Holy Office eventually sent its warning to Nunciatures throughout the world and in December 1957 it was published in prime position on the front page of *L'Osservatore Romano*.[43]

The warning was a great embarrassment to Buchman. Although many Italians came to Caux, for example, he was not free to work in Italy for European reconciliation in the way he had done in France and Germany. De Gasperi, when Prime Minister, was prevented from visiting Caux by the doubts then dominant in the Holy Office. Also, some of the Roman Catholics who had worked closely with Buchman left him, although others were encouraged by their spiritual advisers to continue the work which had been their personal calling. Several cardinals and bishops who knew Buchman personally and had developed a trust in him let him know that they still trusted him. But he and his colleagues were perplexed by the Holy Office's ruling and still ignorant of the reasons behind it.

Count Lovera di Castiglione made strong representations to the Holy Office, with no effect. He also gave advice to Buchman and his colleagues which was heeded less than it should have been. For instance, he voiced cautions on the use of language. People in Moral Re-Armament sometimes lapsed into 'generalisations which make it seem as if MRA had started an activity which had never existed before and exists nowhere else today', he wrote. 'I know well the men of MRA and their pure intentions. Others, however, find their affirmations excessive, not quite just, and a demonstration of inborn presumption.'[44]

The reasons for the Holy Office's decision did finally become clear to Buchman, but only gradually. They were a combination of understandable pastoral concerns and one profound 'misunderstanding' – a word which Cardinal Alfredo Ottaviani, then Prefect of the Holy Office, himself later used.[45]

The Holy Office's concern in 1951, nearly a decade before Vatican II, was whether it might be dangerous to let Catholics and non-Catholics participate jointly in an action which drew upon the spiritual heritage of each. There was a fear that the differences between the heritages might be obliterated, leading to 'indifferentism', meaning 'the affirmation of the

[443]

equal value of the various religious confessions which claim to originate from Christ'. 'We do not say that Moral Re-Armament teaches this equality of value,' wrote an observer in Rome, 'it breathes and lives it, which may be a more discreet method but is also a more effective way of unintentionally spreading it.'[46] It therefore appeared dangerous to allow Catholics to participate.

'My friends and I offered facts which might allay this natural pastoral concern,' says Michel Sentis, a French Catholic working with Buchman. 'In practice, we said, Moral Re-Armament did not cause people to deny their spiritual heritage; on the contrary, it often led individuals to renew their loosened ties with their own church. The "conversions" of which Moral Re-Armament was the instrument were conversions within the religious confessions of the people concerned, or conversions from atheism. These facts were listened to with sympathy, but we were told that the Church would judge in the long term whether our optimistic view was justified.'

'There were a number of other criticisms, which could be summarised as concluding that non-Catholics in Moral Re-Armament had a mode of thought and spiritual conception which differed from the Catholic tradition,' continues Sentis. 'These criticisms, which were, of course, justified, seemed to us to reveal a lack of realism about the necessary dialogue between different Christian confessions. Rather than discouraging the Catholics working with Moral Re-Armament, we thought that the Church should try to clarify the issues for them, as certain bishops were already doing for members of their own dioceses.'

The 'misunderstanding' was more serious. As a result of distorted information, the Holy Office at that time had an inexact, indeed a totally mistaken, impression of the actual structure of Moral Re-Armament. It was convinced that behind the lack of organised framework which Buchman had always encouraged, there was a carefully concealed hierarchy similar to that of various secret societies it had encountered in the past. This view lay behind the prohibition against Catholics holding positions of responsibility; and it also gave rise to suspicions of duplicity which meant that all information proffered from Moral Re-Armament sources was received with distrust. Hence, for example, the evidence of Count Lovera di Castiglione was disregarded, since he was thought to have been duped.

The notion of Moral Re-Armament being a secret society with a hidden hierarchy had first been mooted, in a comparatively simple form, by a pamphlet issued in Paris in 1949 by a certain 'Michel Rovers', but had since become elaborated, on the evidence of an informant whom one official later described as having 'the soul of a traitor', into a more complicated form. It had grown to the point where the Holy Office believed that Moral Re-Armament was strictly organized into seven grades, ranging from 'the Founder' alone in grade one, 'the Policy Team of fourteen members' in grade two, 'the Central Team (sixty-two members') in grade three, 'the full-time workers (more than a thousand)' in grade four, 'the friends', 'the supporters' and 'the contacts' in grades five, six and seven respectively.

The existence of this misunderstanding only became known to Buchman and his friends after one of their number, a Catholic, summoned by an official of the Holy Office, was suddenly confronted with the question to which MRA 'grade' he belonged. Mystified, but remembering the example of St Paul, whom he tried limpingly to follow, he replied, 'The least of the least.' He was therefore classed as a mere 'contact' and encouraged to maintain his touch with Moral Re-Armament. He gathered from this talk a hint or two of where the misunderstanding lay, but the full meaning of his interview only became clear to him in 1958 when the fantastic story was set forth in one of five articles in the Jesuit fortnightly review, *Civiltà Cattolica*,[47] by Father Prudenzio Damboriena, who had attacked Moral Re-Armament in the influential *Monitor Ecclesiasticus*[48] during the previous year.

The difficulty experienced by sincere officials, who had only second-hand information, was to find a pigeon-hole into which the organism created by Buchman could be placed. Some priests, no doubt wishing to help, tried to identify it with purely secular bodies like Rotary or the Scout movement, and insisted that if Buchman promised never again to use religious language – the name of Christ, the Holy Spirit and the Cross of Christ, for example – all would be well. In Buchman's absence, conversations were held with Peter Howard. The record of one such conversation shows clearly that their attempt could not have led anywhere. One priest urged Howard to drop all religious terminology from Moral Re-Armament's statements. Howard said, 'If somebody comes to me and asks the places where I have changed, can I tell him?' 'Yes,' was the reply. 'If he then asks me where I find the power to break habits of sin, can I tell him "Christ"?' continued Howard. 'No, you are on no account to mention Christ. That is the point we are discussing.' Such a course was obviously out of the question.

At the same time as the Holy Office was making public its attitude in *L'Osservatore Romano*, a current of sympathy towards Moral Re-Armament was developing in some circles in Rome, which made itself felt very discreetly in order not to undermine the authority of the Holy Office. In particular the people working around Monsignor Giovanni Battista Montini, Pro-Secretary of State to Pius XII who was himself to become Pope Paul VI, always welcomed news of Moral Re-Armament actions, and were eager to be kept informed.

FREEDOM

As Robert Schuman left Caux on 13 September 1953 he turned to Buchman and said, 'Will you help us in Morocco?'

'Gladly,' said Buchman, 'but I don't speak Arabic.'

'That doesn't matter,' replied Schuman. 'Use French.'

Buchman explained that he had gone to Grenoble when young to try and learn French,* but 'I have only two words left – "mauvais garçon"!'

'That will carry you a long way,' laughed Schuman, 'and besides, you get along without language. You speak the language of the heart.'

Two weeks later Buchman's attention was again drawn forcibly to the problems of French North Africa when the French socialist journalist, Jean Rous,** brought two nationalists, one Moroccan and the other Tunisian, to Caux.

The Tunisian was Mohammed Masmoudi, the senior representative of Néo-Destour, the illegal nationalist party, at liberty in France. Its leader, Habib Bourguiba, had been arrested in 1952 and Masmoudi, having no identity papers, crossed the frontier into Switzerland secretly at Saint-Gingolph on the opposite side of the Lake of Geneva from Caux. He had reason to hate the French. He had himself been for some days in a condemned cell and, while at Caux, heard that his brother had been arrested.

The Moroccan was Si Bekkai, who had just resigned as Pasha of Sefrou. A colonel in the army of France during World War II, he had lost a leg in her defence. But when, that August, the French had deposed Sultan Sidi Mohammed Ben Youssef and deported him to Madagascar, Si Bekkai had resigned his office and exiled himself to Paris. The Sultan had been deposed because of his sympathy with the independence movement, and replaced by his uncle Ben Arafa. The powerful Pasha of Marrakesh, El Glaoui, feeling that the Sultan had been promoting too precipitate a move to independence, had encouraged the French in his deposition. Si Bekkai came to Caux perplexed and bitter.

* This was in July 1912, during a vacation from Penn State College.
** Then working for *Franc-Tireur*, Paris.

Buchman met both Masmoudi and Si Bekkai, and learnt much about the situation in their countries. He also introduced them to his French colleagues, who astonished them by their open admission of French mistakes. Above all, he saw that they heard the inside story of the reconciliations wrought at Caux between French and Germans. Masmoudi was particularly affected. 'I said to myself', he wrote later, 'that, after all, relations between France and Tunisia had never been so bad as those between France and Germany.' When he received a letter from his eighty-year-old mother ending, 'God bless you, my son. God curse the French', he had replied that she should indeed continue to ask God to bless him, but should cease cursing the French.[1] On his third day at Caux, he declared publicly that he was prepared to meet any representative of the colonial authorities and believed that 'in the spirit of the four principles of Moral Re-Armament' they, like the Germans and French, might be able to come to an understanding.

Si Bekkai also spoke. 'I have been trying to find a formula which will enable my country and France to break the present deadlock and preserve Franco-Moroccan friendship,' he said. 'Caux has miraculously provided the answer to the questions I have been asking, without any hatred or bitterness. I hereby undertake to put into practice the four moral standards of Moral Re-Armament, for I know that in order to change my country, which needs to change, I have to change myself. If I have had doubts about France, I apologize to my French friends here and elsewhere.'[2]

Buchman heard from Si Bekkai much about the Moroccan impasse and particularly about the part played by El Glaoui, whose support had been decisive to the French.

From Caux Buchman went back to Italy, and then in early February set out for Marrakesh with Paul Campbell, John Wood, Morris and Enid Martin, and Jim Baynard-Smith. Before leaving Caux he had told these colleagues his thought that El Glaoui would be affected. He also knew that General Antoine Béthouart, the former French High Commissioner in Austria who had been to Caux in 1951, would be there, and hoped that he and Pierre Lyautey, nephew of the Marshal who had created French Morocco, would help them to meet the relevant people.

In Marrakesh the Béthouarts were already ensconced in Buchman's hotel when he arrived. To begin with he spent most of his time in bed, resting and thinking. The Pasha, El Glaoui, and his family occupied much of his mind. Physical inactivity renewed his strength; but as it returned, he maintained a deliberate social inactivity which allowed others to take the initiative. He had the recurring thought, 'Our job is to mine for men, to quarry out leadership.'

After some days Buchman and his party dined with the Béthouarts, who then arranged for them to meet the French authorities. Then M and Mme Lyautey gave a tea-party for them, at which they met international visitors like Prince William of Sweden and his son, Count Bernadotte, and also the lawyer son of El Glaoui, Si Abdessadeq, president of the Chereefian Tribunal in Marrakesh, whose political views differed from his father's.

Soon afterwards Abdessadeq came in for the evening. Buchman's thoughts beforehand were: 'A free, natural, open-hearted time. He will set much of the pace with his lively intelligence. He is starved of the fellowship he needs here. He will step out into a whole new leadership.' As Buchman reflected on the occasion at bedtime, he said, 'A very great evening – new horizons are breaking. He was profoundly gripped beneath his shell of politeness.' Their guest asked them to dinner the following Saturday.

The following week the new Sultan was to make his first official visit to Marrakesh. On the Friday three bombs were thrown at El Glaoui, his host, while at prayer in the mosque. Two people were killed and twenty-six wounded by the first two, the third rolling to El Glaoui's feet but not exploding. Abdessadeq's dinner was the next day. It was a noble banquet, Moroccan style, the guests sitting on divans at a round table, the host poking the fire with a long, curved dagger from his belt. There were ten courses and ten different words to describe each dish – a whole roast lamb and a dozen chickens; cous-cous; a pastilla like a small cartwheel filled with pigeon, almonds and eggs; fish; honey cakes, yoghurt, oranges, coffee, almond milk, mint tea. Everything was eaten with the right hand, and the host picked the choice piece of meat from the central platter and proffered it to the guest of honour. For the Western guests it was an exotic evening.

Back at the hotel Buchman remarked to Baynard-Smith, 'Sadeq sees the challenge already clear. He has the stature to lead the nation to sanity, when the time comes.' Following this evening Buchman's colleagues played tennis with him and had many talks. Buchman met four of his brothers, but not his father, the Pasha.

When the Sultan arrived a few days later he was met by a thousand of El Glaoui's tribesmen, mounted on magnificent Arab horses with brightly coloured saddle-clothes and carrying muskets of fearsome length. Buchman's love of processions took him to the roof of the hotel to see them pass. Abdessadeq then had the party escorted to a place of honour on the city walls to see his father greet the Sultan with the traditional gifts of dates and milk. Beneath the pageantry, however, Moroccan nationalist fervour against the French puppet continued to simmer. The Sultan was wounded by hand grenades thrown at him during prayers the following Friday. The 84-year-old Pasha took the Sultan to his palace and then immediately returned and personally shot the Sultan's assailant.

Buchman, meanwhile, was in detailed contact with his forces all over the world through his enormous mail. He kept in the front of his mind the continuing work in India and the attacks on Moral Re-Armament in the ICFTU report and the report being prepared by the Social and Industrial Council of the Church of England. He rejoiced at the news of time spent with Mahatma Gandhi's son, Manilal, in South Africa; of new openings in Italy and France, and of the reception of a delegation by the King of Saudi Arabia. However, a thought came to him one morning, upon which he made his own comment: 'Intelligently pray for an experience of the Cross of Christ and how to present it to each one of our workers. It is wonderful that they write and say they pray for me every day, but I wish that everyone had an experience of the Cross of Christ so that he could present it intelligently to anyone.'

Among the French, official and unofficial, whom Buchman's party met was Pierre Chavanne, a young second-generation French settler who farmed 300 hectares – two-thirds grain, one-third fruit – twelve miles outside Marrakesh. His name had been given to Buchman in Caux by an aunt of his. He was concentrating on his own personal and commercial success, an agnostic with Marxist leanings who held liberal views on Moroccan politics. These views, however, had been formed without any personal contact with Moroccans – a not uncommon attitude which created much resentment among educated Moroccans, who felt that even the liberal French were merely exploiting their country. Some of Buchman's party also met a friend of Chavanne, Philippe Lobstein, an inspector of schools at Marrakesh. Like Chavanne a leftist in politics he was, however, a semi-practising Protestant. His wife was Orthodox, and they had emigrated from Alsace in 1948.

Both couples were intrigued, although not convinced, by Buchman's friends. Chavanne only met Buchman himself once in Morocco, outside a hall where both had been attending a lecture on the local situation. 'He was not the kind of great man I was looking for,' says Chavanne. 'I wasn't very impressed with him.' The Chavannes and Lobsteins agreed, however, to meet at Caux the following summer, and there they all decided to experiment with applying Moral Re-Armament in their private and professional lives. This caused them to review not only their personal relationships but also their attitude to Moroccans, and to become as concerned for the future of the country as the Moroccans themselves. Chavanne says, 'I discovered that I was no longer afraid of the Moroccans, and I realised that I had been a liberal out of fear as well as care – the same fear which had made other French become reactionary.'

In the autumn of 1954, soon after their return from Caux, an invasion of locusts threatened to ravage the farmlands around Marrakesh. The Moroccan agricultural services took the necessary action and the danger was averted. Chavanne thanked Ahmed Guessous, the head of the provincial agricultural department, something he says he would never have done without the change he had experienced in Caux. 'You are the first Frenchman who has ever thanked me for anything,' replied Guessous. Chavanne went on, 'I want to apologise for the selfish way I have lived in your country and for my attitude to your people.' He talked of his visit to Caux, and added, 'I have decided now to serve your country on the basis of the standards of Moral Re-Armament.'

Guessous was interested, but suspicious. He was able to discover, through his staff, the details of life on all the farms in the regions. He found out that the Chavannes, out of respect for their Muslim workers, had decided to give up drinking alcohol themselves, later making their decision final by throwing out their remaining bottles. Guessous also discovered that working relationships on the Chavannes' farm were better than on others. This helped to convince him that Chavanne had meant what he said.

That same autumn one of Guessous's daughters was refused admission to a French kindergarten. He was convinced that the decision had been based on racial discrimnation. He took the matter to Lobstein, who recalls, 'My heart went out to him. I remembered the brotherhood I had seen at Caux, and I felt impelled to do something.' He went to the relevant authority and got the decision – made, it turned out, because the child was a little too young – reversed. 'Guessous was very touched by this, and invited us to his home,' continues Lobstein. 'There was wine on the table and when we said we did not drink it out of respect for Islam, Guessous replied, "I am thankful. If you had taken it, politeness would have obliged us to drink it too."'

The Chavannes, Lobsteins and Guessouses became firm friends, and often visited each other. Only now did the Frenchmen discover that Guessous was one of the regional underground leaders of the nationalist movement, Istiqlal, which was determined to shake off the French yoke by every possible means. The three men decided to go to Caux together in 1955, and only his new French friends' intervention with the authorities made Guessous' trip possible. His motive in going was chiefly to counter-act the conciliatory statements made there by his friend Si Bekkai the previous year. He himself arrived on the second anniversary of the Sultan's exile. That day there were violent riots at Oued-Zem in the centre of Morocco, during which many French were killed and the French Army took terrible reprisals. Guessous was much upset by this but, at the same time, gripped by the size and outreach of the assembly at Caux. He was particularly moved that the Moroccan flag was flown in his honour, a rare courtesy before independence.

To welcome Guessous, Buchman asked Campbell to chair the first meeting. Campbell gave an enthusiastic account of their stay in Morocco and a glowing description of Moroccan hospitality, taking as an example the way they had been received at a Glaoua castle. He described El Glaoui as 'a powerful leader of South Morocco'.

At the end of the meeting, Guessous, pale with anger, tackled Campbell: 'I regard Caux as a holy place; but by speaking here of our worst enemy, El Glaoui, you have spoken of the devil incarnate. I shall not stay at Caux if his name is mentioned again.' Campbell invited Guessous, Chavanne and Lobstein to lunch. Chavanne declined. 'We told Campbell he hadn't a clue about the situation in Morocco or he would never have made such a gaffe, and Guessous poured out his hatred of El Glaoui as the traitor who had sold out to the French,' recalls Lobstein. Campbell listened quietly. Then, at the end of the meal, he said, 'I too have known hatred of people. My own experience is that I am as close to God as to the person I am most divided from.' There was silence. 'I'm a good Muslim,' said Guessous, 'but if I'm as close to God as I am to El Glaoui, I have a long way to go.'

Soon afterwards Guessous departed to take a cure at Plombière. 'Everywhere Campbell's phrase kept pursuing me,' he said later. 'Being a Muslim, the thought that I was not really submitted to God was terrible. I decided that I couldn't rest till I had got it straight.'

Back in Morocco Guessous got in touch with Abdessadeq, El Glaoui's son, whom he already knew. They discussed the critical situation in the country, and Guessous suggested that he should meet El Glaoui to try and find some common ground.

Abdessadeq had earlier asked Guessous to meet his father, but had always received a polite refusal. By now he was sceptical about such a meeting, as he thought his father was locked into an irreversible position.[3]

Abdessadeq was facing a real dilemma. On the one hand he had a certain sympathy for the nationalist movement, and on the other he retained considerable respect for the personality and opinions of his father – and the political positions of the Istiqlal and El Glaoui were diametrically opposed. In spite of his doubts, however, he felt it valuable to continue seeing Guessous and to try to prepare his father to meet him.

The French, meanwhile, faced with Ben Arafa's non-acceptance by the population and his chronic desire to abdicate, had on 15 October set up a four-man Council of the Throne as an interim solution which they hoped would calm the situation. The Istiqlal had refused to accept its members as representative of the country. 'By now', writes Gavin Maxwell in his history of the Glaoua family, 'the Berber Tribes of the Middle Atlas and the Rif mountains were in a state of open rebellion,'[4] and there was danger of guerrilla war breaking out between the growing nationalist forces and the French army of occupation and its supporters.

It was on 25 October that, thanks to concerted action by Guessous and Abdessadeq, a series of events took place which had unforeseen consequences.

That morning Guessous was received in Rabat by the Executive Committee of the Istiqlal. He told them of his plan to meet El Glaoui, that the way had been prepared by Abdessadeq, and that the aim was to induce El Glaoui to change his attitude towards the Council of the Throne and the Sultan. The Executive, initially both surprised and sceptical, finally authorised Guessous and two of their number to undertake the mission. Abdessadeq had been waiting outside in the hall, and, on being informed of the Executive's decision, immediately took the three nationalists to meet his father.

This took place on the very day when El Glaoui was expected in Rabat to recognise the Council of the Throne. Old and ill, the Pasha had left Marrakesh that morning and was by then at his palace in Casablanca, en route for Rabat. There he received the delegation.

After introductions by Abdessadeq, Guessous opened the dialogue by telling El Glaoui that he regretted all the bitterness he had harboured against him for many years. This honesty and humility touched the old man deeply, and he embraced Guessous. The onlookers found tears coming to their eyes.

The Pasha then asked his visitors to stay for lunch. It was during this meal that Guessous, supported by his colleagues and by Abdessadeq, presented their plan for national reconciliation, based on a reconciliation between El Glaoui himself and Sultan Sidi Mohammed Ben Youssef. They worked hard and managed to formulate, little by little, the five points on which a settlement could be based. El Glaoui then wanted to give his visitors a large sum of money in gratitude. They refused, saying that they were activated only by concern with what was best for all parties and for the country as a whole. At 3.15 in the afternoon El Glaoui left for Rabat.

In Rabat the Council of the Throne awaited him. Its president received him and asked him if he wished to make any declaration. Then in Maxwell's words, El Glaoui 'entered the throne room, and before the Council made the speech that set his whole life's work at naught: "I identify myself with the will of the Moroccan people for the restoration of the rightful Sultan Mohammed Ben Youssef and for his immediate return from Madagascar." The brief session closed with scenes of incredulous jubilation. [El Glaoui] and his retinue left the Palace to find a vast throng awaiting them outside, among them clamorous journalists of all nations. They pressed round him as he entered his car, saying, "Excellency, show us your declaration!" but the old man was now showing signs of acute fatigue and replied, "Address yourselves to my son Si Abdessadeq." '[5] This declaration became known as 'the Pasha's Bombshell'.

The extent and unexpectedness of the explosion are reflected in the front-page story of *L'Express* next day, under the headline 'El Glaoui Recalls Ben Youssef!' 'General Latour, Resident General in Morocco, arrived by plane in Paris last night. During his journey, the most astonishing *coup de théâtre* of recent years was taking place in Rabat,' wrote the paper's special correspondent. 'El Glaoui, the declared enemy of the former Sultan, publicly issued a statement at the Imperial Palace calling for the return of Sidi Mohammed Ben Youssef to the throne. Neither M. Edgar Faure nor M. Pinay nor General Latour had been told of El Glaoui's intentions ... It was after meeting the Council of the Throne that he got one of his sons, who had long favoured the nationalists, to read the declaration which rather ironically blended his "gratitude" for France with his desire, along with the mass of the Moroccan people, to put himself under the authority of Ben Youssef... the French Government is now faced with an unbelievable situation in Morocco.'[6] The paper went on to say that this action by the exiled Sultan's chief opponent had made his return to power inevitable.

On his return from Madagascar the Sultan had set up his headquarters in St Germain-en-Laye. There El Glaoui, accompanied by Abdessadeq, came to pay him homage. He knelt before the Sultan and, almost in a whisper, begged his mercy on one who had lost the road and gone astray. According to *The Times*, 'The Sultan endeavoured several times to interrupt this declaration – exclaiming, "Do not speak of the past: the past is forgotten," – and to raise El Glaoui from his knees, where, however, he remained throughout the interview. In his reply, Ben Yussef (sic) declared, "The future is what counts. We are all sons of Morocco: you, too, are a son of Morocco and it is on your actions in the future that you will be judged."'

'By any standards', commented the paper, 'it seems to mark a final reconciliation between the two adversaries, and El Glaoui's gesture had a nobility and grandeur lacking in some of the professions of loyalty which reach St Germain daily from other erstwhile supporters of Ben Arafa.'[7]

Buchman's part in these events was not forgotten in Morocco. When the first government of independent Morocco was formed, Si Bekkai, the 1953 visitor to Caux, was its Prime Minister. While negotiating with the French at Aix-les-Bains, he had written to Buchman, 'In these negotiations I assure you I have not lost sight of the four standards of Moral Re-Armament. More than ever I am looking to you and all in MRA to help us in every way to solve the Franco-Moroccan crisis.'[8] Once in office, he sent Buchman a message saying, 'We are determined to make Moral Re-Armament the philosophy and practice of our government.'[9]

In June 1956 the Sultan, now King Mohammed V, received the Chavannes, Lobsteins, Guessous and others who had taken part in these events. He likewise sent a message to Buchman: 'I thank you for all you have done for Morocco, the Moroccans and myself in the course of these last testing years. Moral Re-Armament must become for us Muslims just as much an incentive as it is for you Christians and for all nations. Material re-armament alone has proved a failure. Moral re-armament remains the essential. My desire is that your message, which is founded upon the essential moral values and the Will of God, should reach the masses of this country. We have complete confidence in the work which you are doing.'[10]

Mohammed Masmoudi, the Tunisian revolutionary, had returned to Paris after his visit to Caux in 1953. At the MRA centre in Paris he met some of the French most concerned with Tunisia, among them Jean Basdevant, then responsible for Tunisian affairs at the Quai d'Orsay. He also met Robert Schuman, then Foreign Minister, who was moved by the story of his experience at Caux. Pierre Mendès-France had earlier offered to defend Masmoudi when he was arrested, and when he became Prime Minister in 1954 the two men talked. Mendès-France's historic journey to Tunis, when he promised Tunisia internal self-government, followed. Though still under thirty, Masmoudi was appointed one of the three Ministers of State to negotiate independence with the French government. After nine months of hard talking, independence was granted, and Masmoudi became the first Ambassador to France.

Throughout this period Masmoudi was in close touch with Buchman. At a difficult moment in the negotiations with France he heard that Buchman was passing through Paris and hurried to the Gare de Lyon to see him. 'You will be the William Pitt of Tunisia,' Buchman told him. In December 1956, while leading the first Tunisian delegation to the United Nations in New York, President Bourguiba declared, 'The world must be told what Moral Re-Armament has done for our country.'[11]

To say that Buchman or Moral Re-Armament brought independence to Morocco or Tunisia would, of course, be nonsense. The tides of the times and the determination of the people would eventually have achieved that in any case. But it was Robert Schuman who wrote to Buchman, 'There can be no doubt that the history of Tunisia and Morocco would have been different if it had not been for Moral Re-Armament.'[12]

In the case of Algeria, significant people from both sides met at Caux; but this approach failed, and it took a terrible war and the intervention of de Gaulle to bring independence there.

Buchman's Moroccan visit was his second, and last, trip to Africa. His meetings with Africans took place either at the summer assemblies in Caux or Mackinac, or in European capitals like London and Paris, and his understanding of the issues had to be built on these.

An outstanding example took place in Caux in 1955 when a group of Africans from several countries, among them members of new Parliaments, students, trade union leaders and powerful market women, were present. They seemed happy at first, but after a week began to come to Henry Macnicol, a Scot who had accompanied them from Africa, and say, 'We've enjoyed Caux. Now will you please arrange for us to see more of Europe?' It was a perfectly natural request, but one which worried Macnicol as he felt they had not yet taken full advantage of what Caux had to offer. He went to see Buchman and poured out his anxieties. Buchman looked at him and said, 'You're all screwed up. Go to bed! The Africans are all immortal souls.' 'I went to bed,' says Macnicol, 'but I didn't stop worrying. What on earth would happen to my delegation without me?'

Next morning Buchman called the Africans together. 'I spent much of last night in Africa in my thoughts,' he said. 'I understand some of you are bitter. I can understand that. But if I were you I would shed it. It'll only give you ulcers!' Then he went on, 'Africa is not meant to be torn apart between East and West, but to speak to both East and West with an answer. I think that it may come in the form of a play. Do you think you could write a play?'

Ifoghale Amata, then a young graduate from Ibadan University in Western Nigeria, recalls, 'Thirty of us Africans met after lunch, and soon we started quarrelling about what should go into the play. Then someone called for a time of silence. When we all pooled our thoughts, I noted them down, and I noticed that Manasseh Moerane* was doing so too. They all fitted together in a strange way. When this finished, I said, "I have the first act here." "And I've got the second," said Manasseh. Dr Karbo, a Ghanaian, said he would try the third. I went away and worked straight through tea and dinner till three the next morning. So did Manasseh, and in the morning Karbo, Manasseh and I read what we had written to the thirty. We spent the next hours fitting the acts together, and at five o'clock we told Frank we had the finished play.'

The play told the story of an African country emerging into independence, vividly recording the insensitive reactions of the colonial Governor and the intrigues and counter-intrigues of politicians representing different tribes and factions. Freedom is achieved when a

---

* Then Vice-President of the black teachers of South Africa, and later editor of *The World*, Johannesburg.

change of heart comes both to the Governor and to some of the African leaders.

All that was missing was the title. Buchman had already thought that it should be *Freedom*, but he did not want to impose his ideas. After some discussion among the Africans produced no clear idea, he suggested, 'Why not see which word comes most often in the text?' They counted, and found that 'freedom' appeared forty-eight times. It was adopted unanimously.

Amata continues, 'Then Frank said, "Fine. We'll have it tomorrow night." Somehow we managed it. After the performance he announced, "This play will go on at the Westminster Theatre in London a week today." ' That, too, took place.

Those Africans stayed together and took their play round the world. Later it was made into a full-length colour film, the first made by Africans, and was adopted by a number of countries as their national film for showing on state occasions. It is still being shown in many languages.

Kenya in the years immediately before independence felt its effect. Some of Buchman's colleagues in Kenya had known Jomo Kenyatta and the British leaders involved long before Mau Mau broke out in 1952, but little discernible impression was being made upon the situation there. Then in 1954 the colonel in charge of the Mau Mau rehabilitation camp at Athi River took the unusual step of admitting to the detainees that he felt that arrogance and selfishness in people like himself had helped to create the atmosphere which gave rise to Mau Mau. He offered from now on to work with anyone, black or white, who wished to rebuild Kenya on the basis of Moral Re-Armament. By July 1954 *The Times*[13] was reporting that 270 hard-core detainees at that camp had severed their connections with Mau Mau. By 1955 the number was 600. Two of them wrote to Buchman, 'If Moral Re-Armament can change hard-core Mau Mau like ourselves who were full of hatred . . . it can change any sort of hard-core hearts.'[14]

It was two of these men who, with the permission of the British authorities, took the film of *Freeedom* to Kenyatta in his lonely imprisonment. They showed it to him in English, but it had already been translated into Swahili, and now Kenyatta asked that a Swahili version should be made and used in Kenya. Stanley Kinga, one of the former Mau Mau, had gone to Buchman earlier, saying. 'We have had guidance from God to translate *Freedom* into Swahili but we don't know where to get the money.' 'Well,' Buchman had replied, 'you have had guidance to translate the film, now you can have guidance where to get the money from.' The money was raised, *Freedom* was dubbed into Swahili, and it was shown to a million Kenyans in the months before the first elections, in the open air, in cinemas, and in homes. *The Reporter* of Nairobi wrote in the spring of

1961, 'MRA has done a great deal to stabilise our recent election campaign.'[15] That summer Kenyatta sent his daughter Margaret, recently elected Mayor of Nairobi, to Caux.

Gabriel Marcel, the French Catholic philosopher, who went to Caux in a sceptical mood in 1956, was particularly interested in these events in Africa. 'What seems to me absolutely marvellous and providential,' he wrote, 'is the confluence that has come about between Moral Re-Armament and the young nations which are being born into freedom. In this, as in other ways, Frank Buchman has shown a truly prophetic sense.'[16]

As an example of Buchman's own impact upon African leaders, Marcel quotes the experience of the Tolon Na, a distinguished Muslim, then President of the Northern Territories Council of Ghana and later High Commissioner in Lagos. 'It was at one of the morning meetings at Caux,' the Tolon Na related. 'Frank was there, and someone spoke about stealing and what it cost the nation. Then turning to me, as I was standing close to him, with a smile on his face, Frank quietly asked, "When did you last steal?"'

'This struck me like a depth charge. My heart leapt into my mouth. I retired to my room and prayed to Allah to take me into His loving care, repenting for all the evils I had done since childhood. As I lay there by myself I felt God was still waiting for a reply to Frank's question. It was the greatest challenge that I had ever faced in my life. I thought and thought. At last relief came when I decided to write down the number of times (as far as I could remember) that I had stolen since my infancy. I made a note to return all the textbooks that I had brought home from the schools in which I had taught; I also noted all the persons to whom I owed apologies for wrongs I had done them. I decided to live Frank's way of life.'[17] Buchman himself had a profound respect for this man. He said once, 'If Jesus Christ came to earth now, he would look like the Tolon Na.'

Buchman knew that the intense moral, ideological and psychological pressures upon African leaders would grow stronger. As early as 1949 Dr Nnamdi Azikiwe, President of the National Council of Nigeria and the Cameroons, was brought by a friend to a Moral Re-Armament home at a time when he had come to London to negotiate progress towards freedom, but was being vilified in the tabloid press as 'Black Mischief'. 'This is the first evening in England when I have ever been treated as an equal and expected to enjoy music and discuss things on an equal level with white men,' he commented. To the surprise of certain of his backers in Britain, including the Communist *Daily Worker*[18], which wrongly suspected the Colonial Office of having a hand in it, he went on to Caux instead of to the Party-line Civil Rights Conference in Prague, from where he had been due to proceed to Moscow.*

Speaking three years later to Nigerian students, he said, "I know it was a bombshell when the news was given out that I was going to Caux. Accusations were made against me, but I did not mind because my conscience told me it was the right thing when I saw what was being done there to salvage humanity. I became attracted to Moral Re-Armament because I felt those who were preaching it were also living it. . ."[19]

Azikiwe became the first Governor-General, and then President of independent Nigeria. After his initial visit to Caux he several times called on Buchman. When he saw him in London on 19 May 1960 he said that, while he could not claim to have lived up to Moral Re-Armament standards, his visit to Caux had given him a new perspective. He had always wanted to be the first Prime Minister of Nigeria. He was, when Independence was declared, Premier of the Eastern Region. He had been offered the Prime Ministership of Nigeria if he would combine with the West against the North, but had refused, as he felt it would mean the eventual break-up of Nigeria. Instead he accepted the figure-head position of President, while a Northerner became Prime Minister.

Buchman also made a considerable impact on one of the men at the heart of the black nationalist movement in South Africa. William Nkomo had been first President of the Youth League of the African National Congress, a group of younger men who felt that the main body was moving too slowly and peaceably. In 1953 he went to a Moral Re-Armament conference in Lusaka, capital of what was then Northern Rhodesia, and was deeply affected by hearing and meeting George Daneel, the Afrikaner sportsman and Dominee who had met Buchman in 1929. The following year Nkomo came to Caux where Buchman made friends with him and, for reasons best known to himself, dubbed him 'Diamond Dick'. 'Diamond Dick', a robust figure sporting the small pointed beard which was the badge of nationalism, felt thoroughly at home in the atmosphere of Caux and responded to a view wider than only his own country and people.

Buchman, with his combination of realism and optimism, expected such men to understand his aims, and as the years went by there was a steady flow of revolutionary leaders from Africa to Caux and Mackinac. Nkomo describes Buchman speaking one evening at Mackinac after the first performance of a new play which he and his African colleagues had

---

* I once told this story to Bjørne Hallström, who had been at that time editor of the Communist newspaper in Northern Sweden but had since left the Party. 'You don't need to tell me this story,' he interrupted. 'I was the man delegated to sit next to Zik on the plane to Prague. I had in my pocket a speech which we expected him to make which would be the signal for a prepared massacre of the British in Nigeria. But Zik never came, and when I got to Prague I was arrested for failing to bring him.'

recently written, *The Next Phase*. 'He said to the audience, "You have been listening to saints of Africa." He called us saints even though he knew us to be rascals. That challenged us more than anything could do. None of us had a restful sleep that night. We went through our own lives and saw the places where we needed to be different.'[20]

That same night Buchman had said to these Africans, 'Ninety-seven per cent of Africa belongs to you. Take it.' Nkomo's interpretation of this was interesting: 'He did not mean that we should take over Africa by subversion, etc, but that through change we could right the wrongs in Africa and play our rightful role.'[21] While never relinquishing his political aims, Nkomo's methods of working towards them altered considerably over the years. His own verdict was: 'I am no less a revolutionary because I believe in God. I am now fighting with greater passion for a hate-free, fear-free, greed-free Africa, peopled by free men and women.'[22] Two months before his death the *Rand Daily Mail* called him 'the father of all blacks'.[23] In the context of Southern Africa the commitment to spiritual warfare of people like Nkomo and Daneel and many others of all races was tested to breaking point, and held, even as contrary pressures mounted over the years.

Buchman's Christmas message for 1956 reflected his abundant hopes for Africa: 'At the first Christmas wise men came from Arabia and Africa to acknowledge the hope of the world. Today Arabia and Africa may be the unexpected source that gives the answer to chaos . . . It is the moment for a miracle. A Moor came to worship the Babe; Egypt sheltered the Child Jesus and an African carried the Cross to Calvary. The voice of this Africa can speak to every humble heart everywhere.'

Four years later the Belgian Congo was in its pre-independence throes. Numerous conflicts developed, among them a struggle between the Lulua and Baluba tribes in which hundreds were killed. Buchman received a letter from a chief of the Luluas, who had seen the film *Freedom* at a conference in Brussels and had been moved by it to seek an understanding with a Baluba leader who was also there. Leaders of both tribes then travelled together to Caux to ask for Moral Re-Armament's help in their country. One of these was the Grand Chief Kalumba of the Luluas. He talked about the situation to Buchman, who promised him that there would be peace between the two tribes before he himself died.

Fifteen volunteers from eight countries left Caux at once. 'I wish it were fifteen hundred,' said Buchman, 'but we must do what we can.' The group included former Mau Mau men, white South Africans, and the Colwell Brothers. They visited every provincial capital, and through some of the darkest days were directly responsible for averting bloodshed in certain places. The Colwell Brothers made four hundred broadcasts over Radio

Léopoldville, containing songs and stories in French and the indigenous languages.

The Auxiliary Bishop of Léopoldville, Monsignor Malula, described these broadcasts as the 'one voice of sanity to the nation'. The Catholic communities were hard-pressed, as bitterness against whites in general was often avenged on the white priests who did not now desert the Congolese. The Archbishop of Stanleyville, Monsignor Kinsch, said to the Moral Re-Armament force, 'I can't tell you what it means to me to hear the things you are saying. This is the message of the Gospel, and it comes with more force from your lips than it ever could from mine.' He insisted on their coming to stay with him, and when he heard that Moral Re-Armament was financed by the sacrificial giving of thousands of people around the world he went to his safe and offered a gift in the same spirit.[24]

Buchman, meanwhile, was playing his part in Caux. 'Four men from the Congo met in my room on Sunday morning,' he wrote to Robert Schuman. 'They were four men with different and opposing ideas. Two were Belgians, one a governor of twenty-seven years' experience, the other a banker. The banker said, "There is no hatred in the Congo."

'The other two were Congolese. One dropped his head. Finally he said, "I feel I must tell you that there is a black list of the white men to be liquidated after its independence. I was one of those who drew it up." "But," he added, "here at Caux I have seen how wrong I was. We must learn to change men, both white and black. Otherwise we shall destroy Africa." An hour later he told this to the public Assembly meeting, from the same platform from which you once spoke to us.

'The Belgian governor added, "We Belgians have been superior and so we are responsible for the hatred that is in the country. Now we must bring an answer and create a real basis for freedom." Two days later all Belgium read this in *Le Soir*. The significant thing is that the Congolese who made this courageous statement is the right-hand man of Prime Minister Lumumba in Brussels.'[25]

The Moral Re-Armament force in the Congo were everywhere implored to stay longer, and remained for over three years through the coming of independence. They were often in considerable personal danger: one of the white South Africans, for instance, was saved from attack only by the timely appearance of one of his ex-Mau Mau colleagues.

A year after Buchman's conversation with Grand Chief Kalumba – on the day of Buchman's death – a cable arrived at Caux from Kalumba saying that a peace treaty between the Luluas and Balubas had been signed in the presence of President Kasavubu.[26]

'I HAVE ALWAYS LIKED PEOPLE'

How did Buchman, without forming a sect or order, without binding anyone by vow, contract or financial guarantee, gather so many full-time and part-time colleagues of the most various kinds, who stayed with him for his lifetime and with each other afterwards?

It was certainly not eloquence or any of the usual charisma of a popular religious or political leader. There was nothing flamboyant or emotion-rousing about him. No one called him handsome; some indeed thought him ugly. 'God knew what he was doing when he gave me this nose,' he said. 'He didn't want people to be drawn to me personally.'

His own explanation, when asked in the early 1950s, was, 'I have always liked people.' And while some cordially disliked him, widely differing people liked him in return. For example, one of the founders of the Norwegian Communist Party, Hans Bjerkholt, writes, 'My first meeting with Frank Buchman showed me a very humble man, a man gifted with exceptional affection and understanding of other people, a man who did not think of himself. Once when I met him he looked at me and said, "I feel there is something left in you of your old life." That was a very tactful way of putting it. The truth was that there was still left in me a great deal of my old life.'[1]

Bjerkholt took such concern as a sign of friendship. So did an international businessman, a Dane, whom Buchman told bluntly that he needed three things: 'Humility, humility and humility.' The Dane was grateful and, over the years, developed accordingly. But not everyone took it that way. A British industrialist and politician had shown increasing interest in Buchman's work in industry and promised to open many doors. He visited Caux in the late forties and expressed a wish to talk with some of the miners there.

Paul Campbell, who was present at the conversation, told Buchman about it later in the day: 'He walked in and assumed immediate charge, without being introduced. He took a large packet of cigarettes from his pocket and handed them round. Almost everyone turned them down, which rather unsettled him, but he sat down, puffing away, and dominated the discussion.' Buchman, knowing that some of the miners had silicosis and had, to the relief of their wives, just given up smoking, was angry. 'Go and tell that man what he has done,' he said to Campbell.

Campbell did so. The industrialist was furious. 'I'm a managing director,' he said. 'I know how to make contact with men and that's the way to do it.' Campbell replied that he might also destroy them. The industrialist went down the mountain by the next train, en route for Britain.

'All right,' said Buchman. 'You chase him down the hill, chase him down the hill, keep at it.' Campbell had been relieved that the fight was over, but down the hill he went and tackled the industrialist again on the main-line platform. The industrialist never came near Moral Re-Armament again, and put off many others. Buchman did not mind. He was thinking of the miners and of helping the industrialist to realise his arrogant attitude to them and to workers generally.

Buchman took similar risks with people far more important to his daily life and comfort than a visiting industrialist. While he was convalescing from his stroke, he was completely dependent on Campbell who tended him day and night, seldom getting more than two hours' unbroken sleep. According to Campbell, Buchman sensed at one period that he was relying too much on his medical expertise and too little on his contact with God. One day there was something wrong with Buchman's stomach. Campbell gave him his diagnosis.

'You don't know anything about stomachs, do you?' asked Buchman. Campbell, who had studied stomachs in one of the best hospitals in America, was outraged.

Two days later, Buchman said, 'I don't think we'll call you "doctor" any more.'

'Just single sentences, but what sentences for a proud young doctor,' says Campbell. He was deeply hurt. He seemed suddenly to be able to do nothing right in Buchman's eyes. He said to Barrett, 'Doctors are meant to be helpful. I seem to be making Frank worse. I think I'd better go home.'

'What do you want from him?' asked Barrett.

'To be appreciated from time to time. Not always to be under criticism. To be able to tell my family I am doing something worthwhile.'

'Would going back to Canada cure that lust for appreciation?' asked Barrett.

Campbell saw the point and decided that he would do whatever God wanted, however he was treated by Buchman or anyone else. 'Buchman could not have known anything about that midnight decision. But from the first moment the next morning his whole attitude was different. He could not have been more appreciative,' Campbell adds.

Another instance was Peter Howard, the *Express* journalist who had thrown in his lot with Buchman's British friends during the war. By the time he met Buchman in America in 1946 his own life had greatly changed. He had also resigned his highly-paid job and risked the enmity of powerful friends to announce in three widely-read books that he believed Buchman's way was the best hope for the world.

Immediately they met Buchman and he felt at one. Buchman said within the first few days that he thought Howard could be the 'Henry Drummond of his generation'. He put him on to speak before the best audiences he could muster in America and introduced him to all his friends. They worked together closely for a couple of years. Buchman greatly enjoyed having near him so lively and contemporary a mind, a man who had for seven years been a prominent political journalist and before that captain of England at rugby football.

Howard's rugby career had displayed his iron will. At birth his left leg was very thin and its heel was attached to the knee. He had had to have his Achilles tendon cut, and for years he walked and ran and played games in irons. Twice in boyhood he broke his thin leg – a leg which was little more than a pillar of bone and an inch shorter than the other. 'Keep off football, my boy,' the doctors said; but that had made him all the keener to excel at rugby. He reached the very top. His time in the rough and tumble of Fleet Street, working closely with his mercurial proprietor, Lord Beaverbrook, had toughened him further.

Buchman noticed these things. He also felt that there was 'something of his old life left in him'. He saw, as well, that Howard was becoming dependent on him – that he wanted to please Buchman as he had once wanted to please Beaverbrook, which he felt was an inadequate reference point.

Buchman's unease about Howard coincided, quite unknown to him, with Howard's receiving two thoughts in a time of listening: 'Live absolute purity for My sake. The heart of this revolution will be your permanent home for the rest of your life.' The possible implications of these thoughts staggered him. He told no one about them, but secretly resolved that he was unwilling to go so far and 'in order to make up for that compromise began to pay particular attention to Buchman, to flatter and to praise him'.

Buchman decided – whether by thought, 'guidance' or instinct, one does not know – that he must now risk everything with Howard. 'From one day to the next,' Howard wrote later, 'Buchman bolted and barred every door and window in our relationship. Nothing I could do was right. Publicly and privately, in and out of season, I was rebuked and assailed. Buchman was determined that I should turn to God alone and to no human authority for my foundation in life. Once at a meal to which many important guests were invited I was asked to sit at Buchman's table. When

Buchman arrived and saw me there he at once and in a loud voice said, "Take him away. I will not sit down at table with him. I do not want him among these people." The incident was typical of our relationship at that time, and things continued so for nearly four years.'

It was a real risk. Few people, perhaps, would have endured those years and remained faithful to their calling, particularly as Beaverbrook was assiduous in his offers of renewed employment which would, he hinted, lead to an editorship. Howard could have done with the money, but he felt that his work with the Moral Re-Armament team in Germany and elsewhere was the place for him, whatever his place with Buchman.

Once or twice through those years, Buchman and Howard sat and listened for guidance together. Each time Buchman's thought for Howard came in the verse of Augustus Toplady's hymn:

> Nothing in my hand I bring,
> Simply to Thy Cross I cling;
> Naked, come to Thee for dress;
> Helpless, look to Thee for grace;
> Foul, I to the fountain fly;
> Wash me, Saviour, or I die.

Once Howard asked him, 'How long shall I go on in this state of darkness and despair?' Buchman replied. 'I just don't know. It's your decision, not mine.'

At last, one day in Berlin, Howard decided that, no matter what it meant, he was going to do what God asked of him. He told his friends in Berlin that he wanted to make this decision before God, and did so, on his knees, with them.

This decision was at once put to the test. A telegram arrived from Buchman inviting all those in Berlin except Howard to join him in Switzerland. Howard returned to spend the summer at his farm in Suffolk with his family, and he found himself able to help people spiritually more effectively than before.

'After two months,' writes Howard, 'an invitation came to join Buchman. He was polite, but no more than that. The barriers were still up. He wanted to see whether I really meant my decision or whether I still depended on any living man's favour. Then, after some weeks, as I walked along the passage, I felt an arm through mine and heard Buchman's voice beside me: "Just like old times, isn't it?" That was all.'

One day in Rome the two men talked over those difficult years and Howard apologized for 'running away from Buchman'. 'Yes, I felt you did that,' said Buchman. 'I think it has been all as much my fault. I could have made things easier for you. I could have talked to you early on, but I lacked the strength, or maybe it was not the time.' Howard said that one came to the place where, without conscious sin, one just did not know where or how to turn. 'I understand that,' said Buchman, 'and I felt it in you, but always and always I knew you would change.' 'You know,' he added, 'I have had to be ready to risk every relationship in life, seven days a week, for the last forty years. Otherwise our work would not be where it is in the world today.'[2]

During his days in the wilderness, Howard sometimes wondered whether there were other, less altruistic, motives in Buchman's treatment of him. 'I remember the idea crossed my foolish heart', he wrote to Roger Hicks, 'that Frank might be piqued by the attention then paid to my writings and so wanted to keep me down or limit my field of action . . . But the plain truth and the real point is that for a long, long time I did not want to be like Jesus in my heart, I wanted to go on being like Howard in my heart, in my heart as well as in many other parts of my anatomy. And the atmosphere Frank creates around him is the hardest place in which my way can have its right of way. That is what folk really get up against.'[3]

Although probably it could and should have all ended sooner, it is hard to find any adequate explanation except Howard's final one. He was fairly new to Moral Re-Armament and there was no possibility of his supplant- ing Buchman, and the tremendous scope he was given in the next eleven years, when he became Buchman's most trusted companion, argues against any desire to keep the younger man down.

Howard's daughter, Anne Wolrige Gordon, concludes: 'The apparent harshness with which Buchman dealt with Howard at this period was, in reality, a measure of his trust in him . . . He saw in Howard the possibility of great leadership, coupled with weaknesses of pride, conceit and a dependence upon man's approval. Buchman was out to produce a man whose blade was sharpened and whose life was freed from every human attachment.'[4]*

Howard was not the only person to be held at arm's length for a shorter or longer time. Austin, on the other hand, once said he never remembered Buchman saying a harsh word to him. Buchman, in fact, tried to give each

---

* A bishop who read Howard's daughter's book told me he could not understand Buchman's treatment of Howard in this period. I reminded him of Ignatius Loyola's harsh treatment of his successor, Diego Laynez, as described by Pedro Ribadeneira, the friend and first biographer of both men. Ribadeneira was astonished by it, particularly as Ignatius had assured him 'that there was no man in the Society to whom it owed more and he had told the Father that he designed him to be his successor'. 'Yet during the year before he died he showed so much severity towards this Father that at times it made him completely miserable , . . .', he continues. 'The reason was that the Blessed Father desired to make Father Laynez into a saint, and to inure him to hardship with a view to his being General, so that, from what he himself had gone through, he might learn to govern others.' (Quoted in James Broderick: *The Origin of the Jesuits* (Longmans Green, 1940), pp. 259–60.)

person what would help them most to greater maturity at each particular moment. Thus he waited twenty years before pointing out to one artist that he had transferred his affection for his father, who had rejected him, to himself. This man's wife, who sometimes experienced sterner treatment, says that her dominant impression of Buchman in the 1940s was of his tenderness: 'We knew that it was not out of spleen or spite that he sometimes said something very sharp. He never held it against one. There was not one of us who could not go to him and discuss anything, including plans, problems or thoughts we had had, and have his full interest and attention.'

Buchman's attitude often depended on the other person's attitude. 'He was a friend of sinners, but hated hypocrisy,' another Englishman says. This man, nationally known in his sphere, enlisted with Buchman but several times went off and did things which brought temporary discredit to Buchman's work. On the first occasion Buchman's only comment was, 'Well, I thought you were going to get away with it! Come along with me. We'll have a chance to talk.'

On a second, more calamitous occasion, the man could only say, 'Can you forgive me, Frank?'

'Forgive you!' was the answer. 'I did that long ago.'

On a third occasion this man said, 'I don't know what I can say except that I know you're my friend.'

'Eh,' Buchman replied, 'there'd be something pretty wrong with old Frankie if he wasn't.'

'No word of reproach,' this man comments. 'Reproaches were not in his make-up. Only encouragement and a forward look. Recreative repentance, not stultifying remorse.'

Buchman once said to me in the late 1930s, 'I have never withdrawn my love from anyone.'

Immediately after Buchman's brief conversation with Howard in the passage, he began asking Howard whether actions he was taking or had taken were right or wrong. 'You will always give me the correction I need, won't you?' he said. 'I'm just like everyone else. I need correction every day of my life, but too few people have the care or the common sense to give it to me.' According to his daughter, Howard faithfully did this in the years that followed. Campbell, and Phyllis Austin, on whose judgements Buchman greatly relied, have told of occasions when they challenged his decisions and when he admitted he was wrong. Most of his colleagues had such experiences from time to time, but too few had the courage consistently to speak up when they disagreed. He did not always make it easy to do so. He once said to Corderoy, 'Follow Him not me.' 'You make it bloody difficult,' replied Corderoy.

Austin says that he feels he should have been firmer with Buchman at times. In 1948, for instance, Buchman was convinced that *The Good Road* should be filmed. 'We showed it in Hollywood and got a tremendous response,' says Austin. 'At one point we had a studio that had offered to film it, a man ready to direct it and Technicolor prepared to give us the film – all for nothing. So we went to see Frank. He said, "No, no, no. Darryl Zanuck is going to make this film." Zanuck never did anything, and we left America without anything being done. The following summer, at Buchman's behest, we took a large building in Lausanne and spent a lot of time and money trying to do it ourselves. It was a colossal fiasco. In the end, Frank gave us hell for the fiasco, and then, too late, some of us told him that he had been wrong and that Zanuck had never intended to do the film. Frank said, "I made a mistake – and when I make mistakes I make big ones! We'll have to write it off to experience." He'd have respected us if we'd been honest and passionate in the first place.'

Michel Sentis, at this time in his middle twenties, was often Buchman's go-between with Robert Schuman. Being a Catholic, he was asked his advice on matters concerning the Church, about which Buchman's understanding was limited, though he did not always recognise the fact. 'Buchman was a very strong character, and it was a challenge for everyone who tried to work with him not to submit to that strong character, but to stand on an equal footing,' Sentis says. 'He had a forceful way of saying things, he was very clear, and he had a lot of things to decide and not much time to do it in. If you disagreed you had to say bluntly that you thought he was on the wrong track. You had to take issue. Then, if you were right, he was quick to see it. A lot of people got a wrong impression of Buchman because they submitted to him.'

Sentis was one of hundreds of young people whom Buchman trained by helping them to take initiative. One year he sent Sentis to Rome. 'How much money will you need?' he asked. Sentis made a rough calculation and Buchman gave him the money. 'Life was far more expensive than I had thought. It was a week's job, and by the end of three days I ran out of money. What was I going to do? I phoned Frank. "How are you doing, Michel?" he said. I told him, not mentioning money, as I felt guilty because my calculations had been so inaccurate. Suddenly he asked me, "How are you getting along with money?" "Frank, I am almost out of it," I said. "That's what I thought," he replied. "So I have sent you some more by cable." Instead of correcting my wrong calculations, he had let me go to Rome and find out for myself. He taught me a lesson without giving me one.'

But, with Sentis too, Buchman could be sharp. 'My last contact with him was in July 1961, just a month before he died. Frank was quite weak, now blind, and had been in bed almost all day. I had just come back from Tunisia, where I had seen President Bourguiba. I went into his room, feeling very important, and gave a big account of my visit. "Fine, fine," he said. Next day I again found myself in his room with others, planning the day, and made a suggestion for the morning meeting. "Who's that?" he said. I gave my name. "You came to see me yesterday, Michel," he said. "You were so full of yourself that I couldn't make out a single thing you said. All you were interested in was what you had done. If you want to work like that, you'd better go away." I felt extremely miserable because it was true.

'I never felt any embarrassment with Frank,' Sentis concludes. 'He expected every person to bring him something new. And not just great spiritual truths, but simple things. Once I drove some American friends of his across France. "Where did you have lunch?" "What did you eat?" He wanted to know all the details. We had eaten snails. "I'll never travel with you in France," he said. "I like French people but not snails!"'

Rajmohan Gandhi, the grandson of the Mahatma and of Rajagopalachari,* was another young man whom Buchman trained. His father, Devadas, who was the editor of the *Hindustan Times*, had been helpful to Buchman in India in 1952 and 1953. He and Rajmohan met Buchman in Europe in 1956 and, while learning journalism at *The Scotsman* in Edinburgh, Rajmohan stayed with a doctor friend of Buchman's. In 1957 he turned up in Mackinac where he first saw Buchman over a period, although Buchman took no particular notice of him at that time.

Later, however, Buchman sent Gandhi on a number of missions. In early 1959 he sent him to an Asian Prime Minister to warn him that one of his closest advisers was disloyal and had serious moral weaknesses. Gandhi was 24, and Buchman, in America, gave him $250, told him to put them into travellers' cheques and to get on his way. 'First I had to find my fare, which was one of my earliest experiences of "faith and prayer",' says Gandhi. 'Then I asked Buchman how I should get to see the Prime Minister.

'"I don't know," said Buchman. "You'll be guided."

'I got an appointment with the Prime Minister within a day or two of arrival in his capital. I told him to be careful about this man, feeling that what I said was perhaps true, but I was not sure. The Prime Minister was not as angry as I had feared, saying without heat that there was not much in the allegations.' Later there was a coup. The Prime Minister was ousted; the adviser was not. 'Buchman saw the whole venture as a good way to train a young man to do difficult things,' comments Gandhi.

On another occasion Buchman sent Gandhi to the United States with an older American, because he was unhappy about aspects of Moral Re-Armament's work there. 'At first I fought to put right anything I felt

* See p. 115.

[468]

was not the best,' says Gandhi, 'and I had pleasing reports that Buchman was interested in my work. Then I am afraid I settled down to comfortable relationships and became anxious about the opinions about me among the people I was with.

'After some months I rejoined Buchman at Caux. The next day I was asked to speak. Buchman was not present, but heard it over the loud-speaker in his room. He sent for me. "Are you in top form?" he asked.

' "Frank, I – er – arrived yesterday," I replied, trying to convey that any weakness might be put down to tiredness.

' "Something is wrong with you. I could feel it in your voice. What is it?" said Buchman.

'Suddenly I thought of the comfortable relationships. "I think I tried to please people," I said.

' "Shocking," said Buchman. "Shocking, I didn't expect this. Shock-ing, I am ashamed." This went on for several minutes. Finally a number of people, mostly Africans, started trickling into the room. Buchman started to greet them. Then he turned to me and said, "Tell these men what is happening in our work in Africa." I thought it hardly fair of him, after giving me such a lashing, to get me to tell about Africa, but I did. Then he got me to talk about another part of the world. I learned from this that he expected to tackle you firmly and resolutely, and trusted you to continue to fight instantly and never demand a holiday in which to recover.'

'Buchman', writes Howard, 'fought strongly, with a fierceness that seemed unreasonable, against the weakness in those who tried to put their trust in him as a man.' He was battling against the wish to please which so easily creeps into any group of people, whether a cabinet or a company or a trade union, where there is a forceful leader or leaders, and others who would rather be dependent or fear that speaking up would affect their careers. Particularly in the late 1950s – when he was confined to his room for days at a time and his contacts were limited to those who looked after him and those who came to see him – this became a danger among his colleagues. For example, if he sensed a character weakness in someone and challenged it, that person sometimes passed on the heat to others, and a point meant for an individual could become a general rule. He hated this 'parroting', which he also called 'man-pleasing', but more often 'homosexuality'.

He may have used this word to shock people into reality, but it certainly led to confusion. Once in Los Angeles, when he was sitting with Lord Hardinge and Oliver Corderoy, someone came in and told him of such an incident. 'Shocking homosexuality!' he burst out. Lord Hardinge was startled. 'Does Buchman have much trouble with his people on that kind of thing?' he asked Corderoy, assuming that Buchman was dealing with a case of physical homosex. Corderoy later told Buchman of the confusion he had caused and asked him what he meant by 'homosexuality'. 'Same-ness,' said Buchman. 'Are we going to have this sameness all around? Parroting to please. Sameness. Yes, that's it.'

'To him,' concludes Corderoy, 'the worship of people, including himself, was a kind of spiritual homosexuality. It brought a sameness instead of the diversity which comes when God is the reference point. If he raised some issue, he always expected people to seek divine guidance for themselves, but often we did not.'

Shut off in his later years from the mass of his force by illness, informed – and sometimes misinformed – only by those who looked after him or came to see him, Buchman's view of an individual or a situation some-times became distorted. But in the early fifties, when he was compara-tively well and everyone was stretched on tasks far bigger than they could tackle, tasks which threw them back upon God, this was largely in the future.

Sometimes, not infrequently as time went on, Buchman used to shout at his colleagues. Austin points out that people do sometimes have such tough hides of self-esteem or hypocrisy that it may be the only way to get through, yet admits that 'Frank, especially when in pain, was too violent in his rebuke'. Dr Irene Gates, who could be stern with him, warned him sometime in 1941, after he had dressed down some of his colleagues with a considerable burst of temper, that, if he wished to live, he would have to forego that kind of explosion.

There are, of course, different kinds of anger. There is the anger that stems from hatred of evil and is a part of the capacity to love good, and there is the anger which comes from hurt pride, a wounded ego or simple irritation. Buchman exhibited both. His rage was usually curative, and people seldom experienced it without being given the lifting hand of humour or compassion soon after the point had been made. Sometimes, too, he queried people's ideas sharply, to test how deeply they were held. He feared, and with reason, their being expressed to try and please him; but, if the conviction was genuine and the person would do battle for it, his response would generally turn into enthusiasm.

One person who was never afraid to clash with Buchman was Irène Laure, the French Resistance leader whom he had helped to overcome her hatred of the Germans. 'He was in his bed in his room at Caux, and there were a number of us there,' she recalls. 'He wanted me to visit – no, he had guidance from God that I should visit – a certain monsignor in Rome. "I'm sorry, Frank, but I can't do it," I said. "I have nothing to say to the Vatican." But he had had guidance that I was the person to go, so there was at once a battle. "Yes." "No." "Yes." "No." It went on for some time. Beside him, at the head of his bed, was his stick. Exasperated, he picked it up and hit me. Everyone was stupefied. "Oh là là," said my husband,

Victor, "what is going to happen now?" What happened was that the good God made me laugh. "It is lucky for you that you are Frank Buchman," I said. "Otherwise I would have scratched your eyes out!" The atmosphere relaxed. And it was true that I was the right person for the job. I went and did it.' 'He was impossible – *insupportable*,' she adds with a smile. 'He got you to do things you thought you couldn't do.'

Later on, Mme Laure was passing Buchman's room at Caux when Campbell emerged saying that Buchman was refusing to take his medicine. Mme Laure, a nurse by profession, took the bottle and marched in. 'Do you think you could be reasonable for once in your life and take your medicine?' she demanded. Buchman took it.

Irène Laure often tells how Buchman sent her son, Louis, and a French friend to develop his work in Brazil. It was at an MRA assembly in 1952, during which Laure and his friend devoted more time to the city and the beach than to the sessions. Buchman sent for them.

'God has told me to put into your hands the changing of Brazil – a country several times the size of France,' he announced as they came in. They were flabbergasted and asked whatever they would do down there. 'It's quite simple,' he said. 'When you get there, you plant a post in the ground at the airport and then another some way away from it. Then you tie a rope between the posts and suspend yourselves from the rope. Go whichever way the Holy Spirit blows you.' They left his room little the wiser – but he had caught their imaginations.

They went to Brazil, and some of the first people they contacted were the dockers of Santos, who led them on to the dockers of Rio de Janeiro. Such changes took place in the port of Rio that the film *Men of Brazil* was made about it and shown all over the world. The dockers took Buchman's work throughout Brazil and to many other South American countries.

Buchman's personal relationships with women were as varied as the women themselves. He treated Eleanor Forde, the first woman to travel with the Oxford Group, as a close and trusted companion. Women often led meetings at house-parties in the thirties, and many of the larger initiatives came through them. 'What shall we do next?' Buchman asked a roomful of colleagues at the end of the 1931 Oxford house-party. Out of the silence, Eleanor Forde piped up from the back row, 'I think we should go to Canada.' 'That's it,' said Buchman. 'You go and get it ready.' She did, the campaign starting just a year later. Similarly, Mrs Alexander Whyte, nearly three times Eleanor Forde's age, first led him to Geneva. Dozens of other instances could be given, both before his stroke and afterwards.

'Frank responded to the *spark* in people, regardless of gender,' writes Signe Strong, the Norwegian artist who was with him as a young woman during the war. 'He respected the courage and trust displayed by the women, whether lettered or unlettered, who came out in public, opened their homes, introduced us to their friends, risked their reputations.'[5] One of those he loved and respected most was Annie Jaeger, the tiny shopkeeper from Stockport. When she spoke at a meeting of Oxford students in the thirties and some looked bored, he said, 'You listen – she has more of Christ in her little finger than most of you have in your whole bodies.'

With women as with men, Buchman was unpredictable. To one girl who left a conference to chase a man who proved rather different from what she had imagined, he simply said on her return, 'Never mind. There are plenty of better fish in the sea.' To another, who made a habit of such expeditions, he said, 'Look out. One day you'll do it once too often.' And one day she did – though many years later she turned up again, saying, 'It's marvellous to be back.'

He was delighted with a dashing young Swedish journalist who told a meeting at Caux that she thought she would in future use her lipstick to polish her red shoes. A couple of heavily-painted princesses happened to be sitting near him, and he remarked to them, not too softly, 'Do you hear? Do you hear?'

Buchman asked this journalist to look after a strikingly beautiful Swedish blonde – a girl who had done everything and been everywhere but who had changed dramatically after meeting him at Caux. 'She was very real,' says the journalist. 'That's why she was never afraid of Frank, and he loved meeting this very real, beautiful girl. There was a complete miracle. The outer light went off, the inner light went on. She started helping people. She went at it with real Swedish energy, fire surging like a river through Caux – a marvellous gift of God which cut through unreality whenever she met it.

'Then one day she collapsed, and wept and wanted to see Frank again. We were both invited to tea. She said, there among the teacups, "Frank, I'm empty. I have nothing more to give," and burst into tears.

' "You say you're empty," Frank said.

' "Yes."

' "Nothing more to give?"

' "No, Frank."

' "Wonderful," said Frank – and gave her a handkerchief to dry her tears.

'She stared at him amazed, with those wide, blue eyes.

'Then he said, "That's it. That is as it should be. 'Nothing in my hand I bring, Simply to Thy Cross I cling . . .' ", and he went through the whole verse. "You see, you give everything and then it is Jesus who will do it for you. Jesus has done it and Jesus will do it."

'She sat back in her chair and said, "How wonderful." '

Buchman believed there was a definite connection between sexual purity and the extent to which people were available to be used by the Holy Spirit. Absolute purity, he maintained, referred to a wider realm than sex, but the way people handled that powerful instinct was important. It was not a question of rules or prohibitions, but of the fullest use of the energies of the affections. Kenaston Twitchell, a married man with three children, enunciated Buchman's philosophy on the subject: 'A single man or woman finds in the discipline and freedom of absolute purity complete satisfaction and the free use of every energy and affection. The married man and woman find exactly the same freedom in this redirection of instinct, along with whatever natural use of it God may direct . . . In that renaissance of character there comes a burning love for people that gives without demanding in return.'[6]

In the thirties and war-time forties, those working most closely with Buchman, with the exception of older people like the Twitchells and Hamiltons, were mostly single. It is probable that the foundations of Buchman's world-wide work could not have been laid without a core of 'footloose' people, not tied by young children and the homes they would require. Whether that was in Buchman's mind, one does not know, but it was not the primary consideration of the young people themselves. In giving their lives to God for the remaking of the world, they had given into His hand their affections, their careers and their futures, including the question of whether or not they would marry. The criterion was not their personal desires, but whether they could, at that moment, be best used by Him married or single, and although many were already in love with the person they ultimately married, most felt that the time was not yet.

They were virile, often attractive, young people. Signe Strong writes of that time: 'There was great freedom between the sexes, in the sense that there was no 'angling'. Friendships could flourish; but they were never exclusive . . . Great insight and strength came from those years – which were not always easy, but full of creative work.'[7]

After the war there was a spate of marriages, which Buchman greeted with joy. To one couple who had waited twelve years before getting engaged he said, 'It's been too long.' Throughout his life he took an active and sympathetic interest in his colleagues' marriages – and was not above prodding some of the more cautious to take the plunge. To one young man, whom Buchman felt unduly hesitant, he sent an embroidered tablecloth. On the other hand, he did sometimes, rightly or wrongly, wish couples to delay their marriages, possibly because he felt that the people concerned were not yet mature enough to cope with each other as well as with the demands of their calling. Many continued to travel with Buchman after they were married; others settled down with their families to man the centres which by then were opening up all over the world; some set up private homes and used them as a base for the expansion of Buchman's work in their communities.

Buchman thought that discipline in marriage was no less necessary than discipline out of it. Nor did he think that married people should necessarily be any less mobile than when they were single. This sometimes led to long partings between husbands and wives, and even between parents and children. On occasion the partings were either wrong or too long. At the same time, if Buchman heard of illness, death in the family or some other domestic crisis, he would send word and finance to get a child, parent or partner on to the first plane home.

One of Buchman's closest colleagues relates how Buchman helped him to grow closer to his wife. 'I've been thinking of you,' Buchman told him one day. 'Aren't you still ruled by your mother's ideas?'

'Frank, she died ten years ago,' replied the man.

'I know that,' Buchman said. 'But her ideas of duty, a cramping something still holds you. It doesn't help your wife.'

The man goes on, 'We talked for an hour and next morning I told my wife about it. She broke into a paroxysm of tears. I couldn't comfort her. "I've known and felt it for years," she said finally. "It's blighted our marriage. Always comparing me with your mother, I always felt I was playing second place to her." It marked a new day for us.'

Buchman could be particularly vigorous towards strong women if he felt that they were trying to dominate other people or his work. He was apt, if one of his married male colleagues seemed subdued, to blame his wife, sometimes unjustly. In some cases these wives felt unable to approach him – and as he got older and more confined, this difficulty increased, leaving some uncertain where they stood and what to do.

Questions of relationships, inside and outside marriage, often came up at Buchman's training sessions with his teams, whether in the early days in Oxford, during the wartime stay in Tahoe, or later at Caux or Mackinac or elsewhere. Of one such occasion in Kashmir in 1953, Victor Sparre, the Norwegian artist, writes, 'For a whole week Buchman gave himself the task of opening our eyes to human nature. The essence of this teaching was that beneath our passions lies the will to control the world and dominate our fellow men. Even in our love life this will lies hidden. Through grace the act of love can be a creative act. But when self-gratification pushes aside the creative element, that love is only used for self-satisfaction and violence against others. The dictator states can be seen as the mass organisation of these perverted passions in individuals.'[8]

During these days in Kashmir Buchman spoke of the prerequisites of finding an openness to the spirit of God and of the joy of having it. 'He had noticed that some of us grew a little slack and flirtatious in those hard-working months in a hot, romantic country,' says Virginia Crary[9] from California. 'He was sharp about it, knowing how such things could absorb one and make one insensitive to others – but he was understanding.' 'You girls on the whole are pretty fine,' he said to his young friends one morning. 'I would trust you anywhere. But when the boys are about . . .' 'You need something', he added, 'if you are going to change society.' Then he went on. 'You know, we have a wonderful Saviour. He has that amazing quality – he understands. He gets rid of every spot, no matter what it is.'

Back in Oslo Sparre, who had put down his paint brush for two years in order to travel with Buchman, told of his travels in India. A Bohemian friend of his spoke enviously about them and asked, with a bit of a sneer, 'Can't you get me a job like that?' 'I explained', Sparre writes, 'that on such journeys you lived very much like a medieval begging monk: owning nothing, living on what you were given, staying where you were offered a bed, totally abstaining from alcohol, tobacco and womanising. In those days, too, it was *de rigueur* to dress neatly like an Englishman in every detail down to the polished shoes. My friend's interest cooled off . . .

'I had not joined a movement or organisation. I had found a new life, as an artist and as a man; basically it was an anarchistic way of life, since rules are superfluous when people live openly and care totally for one another. It was a free life led by an invisible mysterious force, the Holy Spirit; each and all followed the inner voice, with no fixed jobs, no salaries, no chains of command.'

'Idealistic movements have a typical pattern of development,' Sparre adds. 'What begins as something liberatingly new and alive becomes rigid and dead behind the prison bars of theory and organisation. Frank Buchman used to shake his head when anyone wanted to state too definitely what MRA was. Let it be a lake where the elephant can swim and the lamb can wade, he said. Of course, there were always a few would-be sergeant-majors who wanted to drill us in what they took to be MRA's ideology, but even they helped the individual to find his own way, through learning to withstand them. For me MRA was always a school for standing on one's own feet, not for leaning on other people, but for reaching out to the firm reality that transcends us all.'[10]

Most – and the number still increases – came through to this independent freedom under God. But it is all too easy in any large association of people, civil or spiritual, to become a 'sergeant-major' or, which is equally wrong, to become dependent on a 'sergeant-major' and conform to a decision taken by others, not because so commissioned by God but in order to take a momentarily fashionable step. When this happens, life and divine guidance dry up. Some couples, after the time in Kashmir for instance, felt called to take a resolution of abstinence in marriage, somewhat similar to that undertaken by Mahatma Gandhi. To those who took this – and other steps of self-denial – out of genuine calling, it brought not strain but greater freedom. Buchman's aim was always that of which Sparre writes: that Moral Re-Armament should be 'a school for standing on one's own feet, not for leaning on other people but for reaching out to the firm reality that transcends us all'.

WORLD JOURNEYS

Buchman had spent much of the middle period of his life outside his own country. During his last twenty years, an era when America became progressively more dominant in world affairs, he spent more time based there, and was glad to do so, for he loved it deeply.

In the mid 1950s Buchman was critical of America's mentality vis à vis Russia and China. He did not believe that Communism was the right way for the world. But he feared the shallowness which was, he felt, making America redouble her military, political and material efforts without defining an alternative philosophy – and, above all, the complacency which made her unable to perceive the thoughts and feelings of other nations.

At a Moral Re-Armament assembly in Washington at the New Year, 1955, Buchman had listened to cabinet ministers, bankers, military and cultural leaders from Asia and Africa. What they told him convinced him the time was ripe for a new initiative on a world scale. The Bandung Conference of non-aligned states in April that year confirmed this conviction. The Foreign Minister of Iraq, Dr Fadhil Jamali, had spoken to Buchman in San Francisco in 1945 of a world caught 'between materialist revolution and materialist reaction', and now at Bandung, in the presence of Chou En-lai and Nehru, he said, 'We must work on the basis of moral re-armament, whereby men of all races and nations with clean hearts and with no rancour or hatred approach each other with humility, admit our own mistakes and work for mutual harmony and peace. The world would then turn into one integral camp, with no Eastern or Western camps.'

With Jamali in Bandung were men whom Buchman had known: Prince (later King) Faisal of Saudi Arabia, who had also met him in San Francisco in 1945; Dr Abdel Khalek Hassouna, Secretary-General of the Arab League; El Azhari, Prime Minister of the Sudan, who had visited him in London; Dr Luang Vichien, Director-General of the Ministry of Culture of Thailand; Sir John Kotelawala, Prime Minister of Ceylon; U Nu, Prime Minister of Burma; Mohammed Ali, Prime Minister of Pakistan, and General Romulo, who became the Philippines' Ambassa-

[477]

dor to the US in 1955. It was of these men that Buchman was thinking as he planned.

Ole Bjørn Kraft, the former Danish Foreign Minister, had already proposed that he and nine other members or past members of European governments might go in a private capacity to talk with governments about Moral Re-Armament. When this proposal reached Buchman in Santa Barbara, California, he gathered a dozen of his friends. He felt the plan was good, but inadequate: he wanted to tackle the course of events more directly.

Peter Howard had been working on an idea for a full-scale musical play on the theme of a divided world. The group were quiet for a while. Then with great force Buchman said, 'We have got to reach a billion people in Asia. Let these men go there and let them take this play with them. Make it a "world mission".' The play was not yet finished. The cast would be large. The venture would cost at least a quarter of a million dollars, of which none was in sight. Transport would be needed for two hundred people and much baggage. But the size of the project set people in motion. The European politicians accepted this expansion of their plans and joined in.

Howard's play, *The Vanishing Island*, portrayed two countries. One, the land of Eiluph'mei (I Love Me) had a faith but did not live it; she turned liberty into licence. The other, Weiheitu (We Hate You) had a faith which she lived fully and passionately – the drive and discipline of hate to conquer the world. The tone was one of sharp satire but also compassion, for it recognised the human roots of the conditions on each side. The aim was to show the futility of both 'materialist revolution' and 'materialist reaction' – taking up Jamali's alternatives at Bandung – and to put flesh and bones on the answering concept he expressed there. 'This play', wrote the author, 'is not, of course, the story of any one country. It is the story of every country and every human heart in the world today.'

Some of Buchman's Hollywood friends caught the idea of what he was aiming to do. Lewis Allen, the film director, cancelled engagements to produce the show. Herbert Weiskof trained the chorus, Nico Charisse gave them their choreography, Thomas Peluso sat up three nights running arranging the musical score, and Reginald Owen and Ivan Menzies offered to play leading parts without salary. Thomas Peluso said to the cast, 'This is the greatest thing I ever have done ... the most unique thing of my forty-two years as a conductor.'

The cast and public figures from various countries gathered at Mackinac Island in May 1955. During June, July and August 244 people of twenty-eight nationalities were to visit eighteen countries on four continents. In eleven countries they were to be government guests. Asia and Africa were to be the first continents visited. But preliminary showings were given in the National Theater in Washington, each performance concluded by brief speeches from the national spokesmen. One of the most effective of these was Mohammed Masmoudi. Now a member of the Tunisian Cabinet, he stood with the French Secretary of State for Air in the Mendès-France Government, Diomède Catroux, and said, 'Without Moral Re-Armament, we would be involved today in Tunisia in a war to the death against France ... Tunisia would now be a second Indo-China.'[3]

Some others who took part in the Mission are worth listing, as they indicate the calibre of those Buchman expected to 'remake the world' with him, and many were his personal friends. William Nkomo, the founder and first President of the African National Congress Youth League, went from South Africa; the Tolon Na, then a Member of Parliament, from Ghana; and Basil Okwu, a member of the Eastern Region House of Assembly, from Nigeria. James Haworth and Lady Dollan, recent members of the British Labour Party National Executive, went with a group of senior British servicemen including Air Vice-Marshal T. C. Traill, Rear-Admiral Sir Edward Cochrane, Rear-Admiral O. W. Phillips and Major-General G. O. De R. Channer. Ole Bjørn Kraft, Danish Foreign Minister from 1950 to 1953 and Chairman of NATO during his last year of office, Dr Oskar Leimgruber, a recent Chancellor of the Swiss Confederation, and Eugène Claudius-Petit, a member of ten post-war French governments, were among the politicians from the continent of Europe. Major Kahi Harawira represented the Maori people of New Zealand, and Majid Movaghar, a newspaper publisher, represented the Shah of Iran. From Japan came Kanju Kato, the post-war Minister of Labour, with his wife, Shidzue, who was a Senator in the opposing wing of the Socialist party, and Niro Hoshijima, a Member of the Diet; and from Taiwan, Daniel Lew, technical counsellor to the Chinese UN delegation. Charles Deane, a Congressman from North Carolina, was among the Americans on the Mission.

The World Mission was launched. One important factor, however, was lacking: the transport to carry the Mission round the world. Charter planes were elusive and costly. In the audience in Washington was the chairman of an airline flying charter planes for the United States government, ferrying soldiers from Japan. His planes went empty from the States, and, if official permission were given, would be available. A group of Congressional leaders sought an emergency meeting with the Secretary of the Army, and while the cast were giving one last performance in Los Angeles word was flashed to them that the planes were freed and the whole party could take off on schedule. The chairman of the airline himself settled the bill for the planes as far as Tokyo. Faith – severely tested up to the last moment – was justified.

Meanwhile, in Washington, a counter-attack developed. At the first performance, a 'government investigator', armed with a tape recorder, had made recordings of certain sections of the musical, from which isolated quotations were distributed to various Members of Congress. Taken out of context these seemed to show that the play was a damaging attack upon 'American democracy' and had 'pro-Communist' leanings. A portrayal of a visit from a dictator to the free world was considered preposterous (this was before Krushchev, with his shoe-banging tactics, visited the United States). A reference to stuffing ballot-boxes, and a presentation of business men 'busy with their business' in a society cheerfully unaware of its own irrelevance, were taken to be an exclusive attack upon America – though other countries later visited equally thought they were being depicted. A chorus of journalists, for whom everything negative was 'news' and everything positive 'propaganda', was resented by some of the press. The chief offence of the play was that it was, as events proved, only too prophetic. But the rumour that it was 'pro-Communist' spread among highly placed members of the Eisenhower administration who had not themselves seen it.

When the World Mission arrived a few days later in Japan there was a coolness in Americans' reception of the play which contrasted with the enthusiasm of local audiences. A chance conversation revealed that a telegram from the State Department had been sent to all Embassies on the route of the Mission stating that the play 'ridiculed Western democracy, emphasized neutralism and represented an overall gain for the Soviet concept'.

Enquiries showed that the telegram had been signed with Secretary of State Dulles's initials, as were many other communications from his office which he had not personally seen. But before the people actually responsible for the drafting and sending of the directive were identified, a further major storm blew up in Washington. Other Senators and Congressmen, convinced of the value of the World Mission, requested the use of three American Military Air Transport Service planes to carry the group from Manila to Geneva – a two-month journey carefully planned, paid for by Moral Re-Armament at the approved charter rate. The planes were made available, but *Time* magazine attacked this move, and some Washington newspapers gave public utterance to the private gossip that *The Vanishing Island* was 'pro-Communist'.[4]

When an attempt was made from the same quarters in Washington to prevent the Cairo–Nairobi leg of the journey, Admiral Byrd intervened to have the extension approved. Later, on the return of the Mission, he went over the sequence of events. Kenaston Twitchell wrote Buchman, who had been directing the Washington battle from the West Coast, that 'Byrd checked up on information about the cable and intimated that it had been sent by the State Department forty-eight hours after the force left. He was deeply disturbed by the fact that the only opposition, in addition to that from the Communists, was from American Consulates and Embassies.'[5] Byrd also confirmed that the 'government' investigator at the Washington performance was operating unofficially and not under his own name;* and that the man who had drafted the State Department message had given false information about Moral Re-Armament to a leading Congressman.

Meanwhile the World Mission had been moving from country to country, first through Asia, then to East Africa. In Taiwan, Peter Howard upset American officials by speaking on the radio about the wrongs inflicted on China by the West, as well as the wrongs of Peking; in Madras an extremist group tried to stop the American planes from landing as violating India's neutrality, but a stronger body of Indian opinion insisted on welcoming the Mission; in Cairo the orders from Washington withdrawing the planes' further use were awaiting them, and it took Herbert Hoover Jr as well as Byrd to get them rescinded. But in Rangoon one Asian Ambassador stated publicly, 'I have looked down on the West with contempt. I thought the West with the hydrogen bomb was drawing us all to destruction . . . When I saw *The Vanishing Island* and saw . . . all the nations on the stage – particularly the Americans – all my prejudices vanished and my bitterness for the West went with them.'[6]

Russian diplomats on the route were just as disturbed as the Americans. The Russian First Secretary in Cairo felt the second act was an attack on the Soviets, but added, 'The future is either your way or our way. I don't believe you will ever change the motive of a capitalist, but I appreciate how strongly you believe you are doing it.'

What they felt to be a one-sided reporting of the journey in the United States press prompted a group of American business men to buy space in *Time* magazine and in daily newspapers to supplement and correct their stories. This inaugurated a stream of pages in the next years which appeared, sometimes as the gift of the newspaper, but more often paid for by individuals in different cities, and which were soon copied in other lands. These carried the news at a time when some sections of the press were adopting a boycott. Sir Beverley Baxter, MP, took up this point in his review of *The Vanishing Island* when it came to London: 'Apparently only two London newspapers saw fit to record this event,' he wrote. 'The long-established boycott continues. In my opinion this was not good journalism. If a musical comedy is presented in London, no matter from

---

* Several years later the investigator wrote a letter of apology to Peter Howard saying that he had been 'sold a bill of goods' about Moral Re-Armament and regretted very much having misrepresented it. (Martin MSS.)

what source, the drama critics should have reported on its qualities. If, in the view of Fleet Street, the show was propaganda, it could still be dealt with on its professional merits, which were many. And why should not Dr Buchman use the theatre for propaganda? Bernard Shaw never did it for anything else, and Shakespeare was by no means guiltless of the charge.'[7]

Caux, when the World Mission arrived there, was at full stretch with 931 people from thirty-seven nations attending the assembly at the time. Buchman, who had seen the Mission off from Mackinac Island, had followed their reports with intense interest and moved to Europe to greet them on their arrival at Caux. He had not been surprised at the attempts made to prevent the completion of the task. 'This backwash is to be expected. It is an expression of our materialistic philosophy and we have to accept it. But that is America!' he commented sadly.

Immediately afterwards, in early September, Buchman left for Italy where he spent the autumn, while *The Vanishing Island* was played first in the main Swiss cities and then, during November and December, in the four Scandinavian capitals. In Helsinki, U Nu, who had just come from Moscow, accompanied President Kekkonen to the show and at the first night in Stockholm, the King, who was present with Prime Minister Erlander, led a standing ovation in the packed Royal Opera House. Then the cast followed Buchman to Italy, giving their first performance there on 27 December in Sesto San Giovanni, a Communist-dominated suburb of Milan. They were accompanied by the African cast of *Freedom*, and in the front row at their performance sat the Communist mayor and his council.

One unexpected result was that Luigi Rossi, the proprietor of the local Communist paper, apologised to the priest in charge of the Sesto parish, whom he had maligned, and found his way back to his faith.[8] Monsignor Montini, who had recently become Archbishop of Milan, had, on arrival, paid special attention to the Communist strongholds in and around the city, and he was kept informed of these developments. On New Year's Day 1956, when he celebrated the solemn mass in Milan Cathedral, Buchman was invited to sit in the choir while his two hundred colleagues were given front row seats in the nave. Montini referred to them in his homily, and received Buchman and a few of his friends in the courtyard of his palace after the ceremony.

Buchman, meanwhile, was about to set out for Australia. He had received an invitation from five Melbourne-based politicians, headed by the Federal Minister of the Interior, Sir Wilfrid Kent-Hughes, whom he had last met in 1921 in Loudon Hamilton's rooms in Oxford. He took with him some thirty people, including Hamilton; George West, who had been Bishop of Rangoon; Colonel Malise Hore-Ruthven, brother of the previous Governor-General of Australia, and his family; Bunny and Phyllis Austin; the three Colwell Brothers from America with their

[482]

western songs; Paul Campbell, Jim Baynard-Smith, and Prince Richard of Hesse, whom he had invited to go with him to Australia thirty years before, but who had then been unable, or unwilling, to go.

The party sailed on 5 January 1956 from Genoa in an Italian emigrant ship. The first stop was Palermo, where hundreds of Sicilians on their way to cut sugar cane in Queensland came on board. The captain was a cavalier type, fiercely proud and patriotic. When the ship passed Italian Somaliland, the only remaining Italian colony, he was determined that his international visitors should see the forts still manned by Italian troops, and took the ship so close in that he had to do a ninety-degree turn at the last minute to avoid the rocks. 'We could see the sharks swimming around, as he ran up flags, hooted and sent signals,' says Baynard-Smith.

Two weeks later, as they neared Perth, where the captain knew that Buchman had engagements planned, a fog descended. Should he proceed at eighteen knots with the fog-horn blasting every ten seconds, or play safe and have Buchman miss his appointments? He chose the former. 'It was a calculated risk,' he told Baynard-Smith, 'but I knew it was right to get Dr Buchman in on time.'

'Frank hugely enjoyed the ship and the reckless foibles of the captain,' adds Baynard-Smith. A week later, however, on arrival in Melbourne, the confidence of some of the party was somewhat shaken. After they had disembarked the Australian authorities called for a life-boat inspection and exercise. The signal was given – and every life-boat except one was rusted to the davits and would not move. The one which did reach the water promptly sank.

Buchman was given an enthusiastic welcome. But the temperature in Perth on his arrival was 105 degrees and his Australian friends kept apologising to him about it. 'I haven't come all this way to talk about the weather!' he finally burst out. He talked later of 'the easy-going, pleasure-loving nature of the people. Don't spare yourselves, your health or anything else. The hour is late indeed.' 'Australia's heart is sound,' he added, 'it is only overgrown with indiscipline.'

He did not spare himself. He was often unwell and in pain on this trip, and his friends were alarmed to see that his eyesight was failing. 'I'm dimming out,' he told George Wood, whom he had taken to Canada when he was eighteen and who was now living in Melbourne. It was first noticed here that Buchman increasingly formed his assessment of people by their voices.

This assessment was too discerning by half for the comfort of one Australian. After a reception given for him Buchman asked this young man whether he knew a certain public figure, who had been present and had been flirting rather outrageously. 'When I said I did,' this Australian writes, 'he asked me whether I prayed for the man and whether I would like to do so now. We did. Then Frank suggested that, although it was quite a late hour, I should go and see this man and bring him an answer to his problem, adding, "If I were him, I would be lying awake hoping somebody would come to help me." While I thought this was an unlikely scenario, I went to see him, on the strength of Frank's faith. I was not much surprised when it turned out to be a stormy session and I was shown the door. Two days later, however, the man invited me to lunch and was completely honest about the flirtation which Frank had noticed. That talk freed him and led to years of happy marriage and effective service to the country. Frank was not in the least surprised at the eventually happy outcome of his suggestion.'

Buchman only stayed ten days in Melbourne. There seems to have been some misunderstanding with those who asked him there as to what he had in mind. 'They had thought they were going to be witnesses to some kind of evangelistic crusade and were quite upset at Buchman's sudden departure for Canberra,' says James Coulter, the man who had planned the invitation. 'Actually he was quite unwell, and Melbourne did not suit him. Buchman just said, "Let's go to Canberra."'

'Buchman did not seek to meet politicians,' according to one Canberra journalist, 'but his door was open. He was not success-orientated in any way. If he had been he'd have lowered the hurdles, made it easier.'[9] He in fact saw Dr Evatt, the leader of the Opposition, the Speaker and numerous MPs including Kim Beazley, who had been at Caux in 1953 and was to become a reforming Labour Minister of Education. He was warmly received by the Governor-General, Field Marshal Sir William Slim, who remembered an MRA visit to the Imperial Defence College in Britain. Prime Minister Menzies was not interested to meet him.

Though Buchman was sleeping in a hotel he made his Canberra base with four up-and-coming young men, two journalists and two government employees, who lived together in a quiet suburban bungalow. They attended one of Buchman's first gatherings in the capital and Buchman got them talking. According to one of them, John Farquharson, then a reporter with a national news agency, his first question was what they felt about each other. 'Having told him quite honestly, we found we had established a new relationship between each other, and I was deputed to ask him to a meal in our establishment. He replied, "Why, I'd be delighted. Thank you very much."'

The other journalist, Peter Barnett, then political correspondent of *The West Australian*, says of that first meeting, 'I can never forget the feeling of peace that filled the room that morning, like light.' The quartet, he recalls, regarded their invitation to lunch as something of a risk. 'The dining room was small; the house was clean but none too tidy; and in the kitchen we had a funny old electric stove and the oven door wouldn't stay shut. Frank arrived. And with him were eight people. We were astounded to see so many in our small dining-room – in fact the guests had to walk sideways to get to their places. Frank enjoyed himself immensely. So much so that for the next six weeks he came at least once a day to our home for a meal.

'His tastes were simple, and just as well because the kitchen stove wouldn't have coped with anything difficult. Frank's diet was more or less standard – corn soup, roast lamb with mint jelly, and a milky rice pudding, finishing off with Earl Grey tea. During these days our home was used to entertain some of the most distinguished people in the national capital. Fortunately an American lady travelling with Frank came in and helped to cook.'

Farquharson's mother was staying with them at the time, a shy person who felt her place was in the kitchen. Buchman insisted that she sat at his right at table, says Barnett. 'In a few minutes she was relaxed, and she and Frank were talking like old friends.'

'These were the most privileged days of our lives,' Barnett reflected years later when he was the Australian Broadcasting Corporation's correspondent in Washington. 'We got to know Frank as a man. He was a gentle, affectionate, humorous father to us all. No matter how he felt, what time of the day it was, he was always the same. He radiated a joyous peace. The harsh Australian light affected his eyes. But whether in pain or not, Frank was always quietly happy. Though he was partly paralysed, he fed himself, with his superb, expressive, sensitive long fingers. He never assumed he was boss, but always behaved as a guest in the house.'

'We found him fascinating,' writes Oliver Warin, a government geologist. 'What would he say next? He was utterly unpredictable and possessed of a great sense of fun. When someone reminded him of an incident from the previous day he said, "I know. I woke up laughing about that this morning." He was also simply a very interesting person; he had done so much, been to so many places, and had met and talked deep and long with so many people.'

'One evening and a follow-up the next day I particularly remember,' continues Warin. 'Frank spoke of someone he was seeing that evening and invited his dinner guests to go along. He did not particularly invite me and I didn't go, nor feel left out. To tell you the truth, I commonly thought of myself as something of an also-ran in Frank's sort of company . . . Next day I got a call at the office. Could I possibly get away to lunch with Frank? When I got home Frank, who one always felt was such a robust, impish, vital spirit held captive in a frail body, was bobbing about on the front step waiting to greet me. "I am *so* sorry I did not invite you to join me last evening," he said. "And I just want you to know that I am the kind of fellow who makes those kind of mistakes." '[10]

The fourth of the quartet, Allan Griffith, was a junior member of the

Prime Minister's office. One day Buchman came in to find his hosts in conversation. 'How are things?' he asked. 'Fine,' said one. 'Fine be damned,' said Griffith. 'We've just had a monumental row.' Buchman was much amused. 'You needn't think I didn't know,' he said, and it was all dissolved in laughter.

Griffith remembers best that Buchman was constantly thinking into the future. The racial discrimination in the Southern states of America was much on his mind. 'People want me to go there, but it isn't the time yet,' he told Griffith. 'I haven't the right means of going or the right people or weapons to take.' 'He was always wrestling with situations all over the world, as well as living intensely in the present,' says Griffith.

'I'd say he's the most impressive man I've met,' said Barnett in his office in Washington. 'He was a sick, weak old man, but he had tremendous inner strength and spiritual undergirding. I've rarely seen anyone at such an age with such courage and discipline, with such a combination of compassion and almost ruthlessness against anything which prevented the progress of God's work as he saw it. He could be very tough with his experienced team. Sometimes I have seen them stunned by the fire of his wrath. There was no sense of continuing petulance. It was an instant flame and then it was over. And above it all was his abounding sense of humour and his kindly, but outrageous, leg-pulling.'

'And then came my last day in Canberra,' Barnett concluded. 'Before lunch the last day he spoke to me like a father. "What you need is a faith," he told me. "Faint not nor fear, faint not nor fear." Then with a twinkle in his eye he mimicked an old man with a high shaky voice and added, "You'll have this until you're an old man like me and your legs won't carry you any more and they take you off to the grave!"

'After lunch, I walked slowly with him across the lawn, in the brilliant sunshine of a golden autumn day, to the car waiting at the kerb. Half-way across, he stopped and his face was radiantly happy – an image for ever etched in my mind. And then he laughed freely like a boy, and said, "My, Peter, hasn't it been fun!" At seventy-seven that's what life was for him, and it's just what he made it for the four of us who got to know him for the first time.'

Farquharson said that all four of them had had a faith before Buchman came. 'Through his visit', he says, 'we saw how it could be applied in our work and in the formulation of policy.'

Buchman's own evaluation was, 'So much has taken place in Canberra that will never be undone.' Certainly it was true of these young men, who all went on to take large responsibilities. Barnett, at the time of writing, is head of Radio Australia, the country's overseas broadcasting network; Farquharson is Associate Editor of the *Canberra Times*; Warin is Director of Exploration for the Utah Company based in San Francisco and an internationally known geologist; while Griffith spent thirty-one years in the Prime Minister's department till his retirement in 1982. When Griffith retired the *Sydney Morning Herald* headed a half-page appraisal, 'Griffo's going: Fraser loses a third leg'. Describing him as 'an untidy dresser with an immaculately tidy intellect' who 'manages to get on with people who can't get on with each other', the article named him as 'the anonymous power behind Australia's biggest policy thrusts'[11].

During the whole Australian trip, and in New Zealand which was his next stop, Buchman was much troubled over the growing crisis in the Middle East. In Perth he had heard of the death of El Glaoui and cabled Abdessadeq, 'Deeply grieved. Your father's recent historic reconciliations were his most significant acts of statesmanship, turning the key for his country and opening new chapters on Morocco's nationhood. Loving messages to your brothers Mohamed, Abdullah and Ahmed.'[12]

The knowledge, from his personal contact with North Africa, that there was a ready response from the Muslim world on a basis of moral values, created in Buchman a growing uneasiness about the attitude of Western politicians at this time. Six months before the disastrous Franco-British expedition to the Suez Canal, he remarked, 'Eden and company don't know how to handle people so they have to try and get rid of them. This makes martyrs of them and inflames a nation's feelings.' One day he said that he sometimes imagined a Muslim leader rising from prayer and having to say to himself, 'Communism wants to take over my country to make the world different. America wants to buy my country to enable her to stay as she is.' His own hope was that the Muslim countries should become 'a belt of sanity to bind East and West and bring moral rebirth'. To Baynard-Smith he added, 'If Britain and America were to defeat Communism today, the world would be in a worse state than it is. Because the other man is wrong doesn't make me right.'

On arrival in New Zealand he was touched to hear that Sir Willoughby Norris, the Governor-General, had rung up personally to ask whether he would like to bring his party to tea. Among politicians he got to know best the Minister of Agriculture, Keith Holyoake, who was to become Prime Minister in 1960. He also spent time with the Maori people, and as the guest of King Koroki at Ngaruawahia he challenged the Maori people to become spokesmen for New Zealand. Seldom in his lifetime or afterwards did a major Moral Re-Armament force travel anywhere in the world without Maori representation.

Christchurch, when he visited it, was full of self-righteous comment about a sensational trial in which two girls had been sentenced to imprisonment for the murder of the mother of one of them, who had tried to break up their lesbian attachment. One girl was the daughter of a university president; the mother had been head of the local marriage guidance council and was separated from her husband. One afternoon Buchman disappeared from the house where he was staying. He came back late, thoughtful and silent. He had asked to be driven to the prison where the girls had originally been detained, and had sat outside in the car. 'I was so tired of all the gossip about them from people who had done nothing to help; it came to me that I could go and pray for them,' he said. Next day he sent a married couple who were travelling with him to Wellington to see the Chief of Prisons, who gave permission for them to visit one of the girls who had been moved to Auckland. This and other visits, together with the fact that Buchman had cared enough to pray for her outside the prison, finally led to the restoration of faith and hope in the girl, who was released not long afterwards and took up useful work in life.

It was while in Christchurch that Buchman made a startling alteration in his plans. On arrival in New Zealand he had announced, to the dismay of some of his companions, that he was going to stay in the area for two years. This may have been a device, conscious or unconscious, to get them to take the kind of responsibility there which they would expect to take in their own countries. One afternoon while resting, however, after only two weeks in the country, he was startled by the thought: 'Hell is breaking loose in Britain. Your whole work will be demolished unless you are at the helm. Hurry, hurry back.'

What prompted this thought we do not know. According to Campbell, Buchman was disturbed that the reports he received from *The Vanishing Island* tour concentrated on speeches and crowds and said little of changes in people. It does seem likely, from odd notes, that he had the sense that the cast of the musical, who had so brilliantly concluded their round-the-world mission, were becoming preoccupied with public success and neglecting the needs of individual people, to the point of arrogance. He evidently feared that in particular this would mean another clash with Peter Howard, who, in the years since their reconciliation in Caux, had become his most trusted colleague and one whom he held responsible for the conduct of those with him. 'No appeasement. The selflessness to live without another's approval. Care enough to clash,' run some of his thoughts at the time. 'I want to live as nearly as possible the way He said,' he noted a few days later. 'Thirty-three years from cradle to Cross, and not one moment wasted on self.'

Buchman did not go straight back to Britain, but decided to pay shortened visits to Japan, Taiwan, the Philippines, Thailand and Burma. He may have thought that he could thereby supplement what *The Vanishing Island* had achieved in these countries by spending time with certain individuals. He cabled his prospective hosts, revising his plans, and within a fortnight was in Tokyo.

The week in Tokyo was a tumultuous series of engagements with individuals and groups of all kinds. Some six hundred Japanese from all walks of life had attended assemblies in Caux or Mackinac since that first party seven years before and they wanted to see Buchman and have him meet their friends. At the airport alone a couple of hundred were waiting, including leaders from the chief political parties, who had come from a violent debate but seemed strangely at one in Buchman's presence. At the ninety-minute press conference, indeed, when Buchman mentioned that in one parliament he had visited recently an opposition leader had called the Prime Minister a 'quack', 'a slight shock seemed to shake' the Socialist Senator Togano and the Prime Minister's daughter, Mrs Furusawa, who were standing one each side of him. Amid some laughter, the Senator then told how he had said much the same about Prime Minister Hatoyama recently and that he now regretted it.

The next day was supposed to be a rest day for Buchman. But, after an official lunch, a series of individuals arrived seeking personal talks – first Taizo Ishizaka, head of the Toshiba company, whom Buchman congratulated on his economic leadership, adding, 'In the clamour of business you must take time to ponder deeper issues, to give the moral and spiritual emphasis without which we shall never meet our countries', or our families', needs.'

'I am just like the "busy, busy business men" in *The Vanishing Island*,' Ishizaka replied, 'always thinking of the next thing I must do, and that is wrong.'* He was followed by the President of Toyo Rayon, the editor of *Mainichi*, and the Governor of the Bank of Japan.

There were receptions by the Governor of Tokyo and Finance Minister Ichimada, and then leaders of the Seinendan, a four-million-strong youth organisation, called on Buchman. He asked them to come to Mackinac next summer.

On the fifth day, the Emperor's birthday, Buchman and all his team took breakfast with the Prime Minister and a flock of his children and grandchildren. Like Buchman he moved with difficulty after a stroke but

---

* Under Ishizaka, Toshiba was a pioneer of Japan's economic miracle. Entwistle describes the role of management and trade unionists influenced by Moral Re-Armament in creating the improved industrial relations within Toshiba and other electrical firms, as well as the textile, shipbuilding and steel industries, which was an important factor in this recovery. In a foreword to the book, Toshiwo Doko, Honorary Chairman of the Keidanren, the Japanese Federation of Economic Organisations, writes, 'Moral Re-Armament helped the political, financial and labour leadership of Japan to realise that a sound society must be based on universal moral standards. As President of Ishikawajima Harima Heavy Industries I had personal experience of a full scale change brought to the company through this influence.' (Entwistle, *Japan's Decisive Decade*, xv.)

[489]

did not allow it to interfere with his activity or good humour. He thanked Buchman particularly for what Moral Re-Armament had done for his daughter and her husband. He had been asked to write for the Japanese edition of the *Reader's Digest* in the series 'The most unforgettable man I have known'. In it he described Buchman's visit, ending with the words, 'We Japanese must not betray his conviction that Japan can be the lighthouse and the powerhouse of Asia. As I face the scene in the Diet I cannot but long that the spirit of MRA would permeate the lives of every single member. When the people of Japan and of the world live the spirit of MRA real peace will come.'[13]

When Buchman appeared in the distinguished visitors' gallery of the Upper House two days later he was accorded an ovation, which apparently had never been previously given to anyone other than a state guest or a senior parliamentarian. Passing on to the Lower House he found a bitter fight in progress. The Government was trying to press through an electoral reform bill which the Socialists thought would deprive them of fifty seats. The Socialists had already forced two all-night sessions and were planning to use the next day, which happened to be 1 May, to create riots in the streets. The Conservatives, meanwhile, were thinking of using police powers inside the Diet, a move reminiscent of the old repressive days.

Over luncheon and at a packed meeting afterwards, Buchman brought a mood of gaiety and relaxation into this heavily-charged situation. The senior members of the two main parties, Niro Hoshijima and Tetsu Katayama, both of whom knew Buchman well, welcomed him, each stressing the timeliness of his visit. 'To welcome this man of peace at this moment of crisis gives me hope that we shall find an answer to the deadlock between our parties,' said Katayama, the former Socialist Prime Minister. Buchman then told in colourful detail the stories of the recent reconciliations in Tunisia and Morocco. That evening, at a meeting elsewhere in Tokyo, Hoshijima suddenly mounted the platform and announced that he had just come from the Diet where a special meeting between the parties had agreed that the offensive Bill should be sent back to committee. 'Violence has been averted and we owe it to Dr Buchman,' he said, a verdict soon endorsed by Socialist Senators Togano and Kato.

When Minister of Finance Ichimada and Hoshijima had first heard of Buchman's intended visit they felt that the country should honour him, and that the appropriate decoration would be the Order of the Rising Sun, First Class, which was seldom awarded. When this decoration was given to a foreigner, three bodies were involved – the Cabinet, the Ministry of the Imperial Household, and the appropriate embassy. With the Prime and Foreign Ministers and other colleagues convinced of Buchman's importance to their nation, they encountered no difficulty with the

Cabinet or the Imperial Household. To their astonishment, they met bitter and determined resistance from the American Ambassador, who, echoing the cable from Washington at the time of *The Vanishing Island*, stated that Moral Re-Armament followed the Communist Party line, and that Buchman was a self-seeker who was *persona non grata* at the Embassy. Before a delegation of Senators he maintained this attitude. In face of this opposition some of the more cautious members of the Cabinet, mindful of the need to maintain goodwill with their powerful American ally, wanted to draw back, but Ichimada let fly at such hypocrisy. 'You all know Buchman deserves this honour,' he declared, pouring scorn on their timidity. In the end Buchman was awarded the honour – Second Class, since protocol prevented bestowing the first degree without ambassadorial recommendation.

In Taiwan he received a decoration and saw many old friends of forty years before. They sped him on his way to Manila. Here he made the acquaintance of President Magsaysay. At breakfast in the Malacañang Palace Buchman said only one sentence, conveying to Magsaysay the greetings of Monsignor Paul Yu-pin, Archbishop of Nanking. For the rest he let the different personalities with him make their impact. Magsaysay remarked later to his aide, Major Palaypay, 'I have just met a unique and fascinating group of people, that has brought us answers instead of loading us down with problems.' Palaypay visited Mackinac the following summer and experienced a profound change of attitude towards the Japanese, who had condemned him to death during the war. When Prime Minister Kishi visited Manila in December 1957 Palaypay was assigned as his aide by President Garcia, who had succeeded after Magsaysay's death in March in a plane disaster.[14]

In Vietnam Buchman was received by President Ngo Dinh Diem and his Cabinet. The war between North and South was in its early stages, but the basic dilemma of Western intervention was already evident. The President was much interested in Moral Re-Armament's approach to his people. 'The people of Asia can welcome Moral Re-Armament only with enthusiasm, as for a long time they have been awaiting from the West a change of heart,' he said. To Buchman personally he said, 'When faith and hope pass away, love will always remain and for that I thank you, from the bottom of my heart.'[15]

In Thailand Prime Minister Pibulsonggram, who had been in Caux, was Buchman's host and conferred a decoration upon him in the name of the King. Buchman also met the Foreign Minister, Prince Wan, then President of the Assembly of the United Nations.

In Burma Prime Minister U Nu flew down from the hills to Rangoon to save his guest the difficult trip to him. It was the month of the twenty-five-hundredth anniversary of the enlightenment of the Buddha.

'This new era', said Buchman, 'can open a door to a new world. . . Every man can be illumined by God.' Then Buchman spoke of the guidance he had had to take this journey.

U Nu commented, 'And you heard it clearly?'

'Why, yes,' said Buchman. 'I wrote it down. God gave a man two ears and one mouth; why don't we listen twice as much as we talk?'

U Nu told how he had just once had a similar experience – on a matter concerning his family – and of his longing to find some way of finding such direction for his wider responsibilities. Joining in this long conversation was U Nu's right-hand, U Thant, later Secretary General of the United Nations.

Buchman flew to Rome, from where he travelled by train. In Milan there was an eleven-minute interval between trains, and there occurred what Buchman called 'the most wonderful thing that I saw in the whole trip'. A group of his friends had come to meet him, among them a one-legged Communist revolutionary called Rolanda Biotello, who had been in Caux and whose life had changed. Buchman immediately asked her about her brother, Remo, a Communist leader of the tramway workers of Milan.

'Why, he's here,' she said.

Buchman, putting his arm round Remo, saw that he was a very sick man. But he had come to tell Buchman he had married his wife in church the day before. She was a Roman Catholic and had always begged him to marry her. When Remo died, two months later, Buchman was in Caux and had Mass said for him in the Catholic chapel there.

In London, too, Buchman received his fourth decoration of the tour, this time from the Philippines Government. While appreciating the spirit behind these honours, he commented wryly, 'They certainly weigh me down.'

Back in London Buchman's emphasis, according to Campbell, was 'to restore a commitment to the changing of individuals as the primary expression of Moral Re-Armament'. Roland Wilson writes, 'It was at this time that Buchman dealt faithfully with my own sense of satisfaction at large-scale results. I went to his room and described to him the theatre queues for *The Vanishing Island* and the enthusiastic response. "Yes," he said "that is a good reconnaissance work. But remember our work is founded on the handful of men with whom I spent seven years at Penn State."'[16]

HEALING – FAR EAST AND DEEP SOUTH

'I was brought up to be property-poor,' Buchman said. 'People first; bricks and mortar later.' But the growth of Moral Re-Armament in America made larger provision inevitable. In 1952 Mrs John Henry Hammond offered her country home, Dellwood, in Mount Kisco outside New York, as a new centre – the equivalent in the East to the former residential club in Los Angeles, bought in 1948.

Mackinac Island continued to be the main meeting place for American assemblies but the available accommodation was still inadequate. From time to time Buchman would engage the whole of the Grand Hotel, and other buildings on the island were rented, leased or bought, but the islanders lived from the tourist trade, and some claimed that their livelihood was threatened by MRA's expansion. To meet this Buchman began to think of building a permanent centre of his own and to plan its construction in the way most helpful economically to the island.

Buchman had many friends among the islanders. When their fortunes were at zero during the war through the ban on tourism, his conferences kept them going and brought the island good and needed publicity. He helped by providing work in the difficult times after the war, especially in the hard winters when, with the lake frozen and the snows deep, there was normally no work. He also concerned himself with the health service, and doctors from his team took over the year-round medical care of the island.

In the middle of the island there lived Indians descended from the original tribes of the area, alongside Americans of English, French and black extraction. Buchman befriended them especially. He would invite them to meals and, when he heard one or other of them was ill, would send one of his busy young men up into the woods with a hot meal for the sufferer. He was proud of his own association with the Indians as a blood brother of the Stoney tribe. Some of the Mackinac Island Indians, ashamed of their ancestry, called themselves French. Meeting some of them one day, he said, 'I hear you are French.'

'Yes,' they replied.

'That's very interesting,' said Buchman. 'I'm an Indian myself.'

Once when about to leave the island for Europe with a hundred people Buchman surprised Kenaston Twitchell, who was engaged with a thousand details of the departure, by asking him to drop everything and come with him. He had had the sudden thought to 'go to Gladys Hubbard's house'. Mrs Hubbard was a black woman who often helped with the cooking for the conferences. After several months in hospital she had just returned to her home at the centre of the island. They found she had been praying to see Buchman. She was carried out into the sun to greet him. 'I only wanted one thing,' she said, 'that you pray with me before you go.'

In 1954 land on the south-east corner of the island became available and was purchased by a group of business men who gave it to Moral Re-Armament. Buchman's dream of a properly designed centre began to take shape. Characteristically, the first building he erected was not a residence, nor even a conference hall, but a theatre. The foundations were blasted out of the rock, the construction done in the bitter winter, and the first play performed in it was *The Vanishing Island* before it left for Washington and Asia.

The response to the World Mission with *The Vanishing Island* brought still greater demands on Mackinac Island as a training centre. A complex of buildings was designed to harmonise with traditional island style and materials, and during the winter of 1955 large-scale construction was begun. Buchman was in Europe and was soon to leave for Australasia and Asia. Before he sailed from Genoa he received a letter from Gilbert Harris who was administering the financing of the building. Money had been coming in – a Canadian industrialist had sold his business and made a sum of money available – gifts of timber, building materials, promises of furnishings, but it was not enough. One hundred and fifteen paid islanders were hard at work, as well as forty-five volunteers from Moral Re-Armament, and the weekly wage bill was heavy. Harris urged a more cautious tempo in construction.

Buchman replied, 'I know how many difficulties there are in getting money for that stupendous work at Mackinac but God has many ready helpers. I assure you He has people who will make it possible. I greatly sympathize with you and feel at times the burden is too much for anyone; then the unexpected happens. It is by faith and prayer our money comes. . . . I am grateful for your business caution but I want you to move with me and the people of America in the dimension of what needs to be done, not what we think we can do. I want you to help me always to live at the place where I rely not on what I have, but on what God gives. It is such freedom and it works.'[1]

At each stage in the building, accommodation was no sooner up than it was filled. When Buchman had met leaders of the Seinendan in Tokyo in 1956, he had invited them to his assemblies abroad. Early in the spring of 1957 Sontuku Ninomiya, the Director of the 4,300,000-strong youth organisation, told Buchman's friends in Tokyo that he had received an invitation to send 500 delegates to the International Youth Festival in Moscow that summer. His organisation, which was officially non-political, its aim being to promote the cultural life of Japan, had become an arena of ideological conflict, and the Communists on the National Executive had seized on the invitation as a chance to influence much of the movement's leadership. Ninomiya wanted to know whether Moral Re-Armament could make a counter-proposal. Soon a letter was on its way to Buchman suggesting that one hundred of the prefectural leaders be invited to Mackinac. Buchman immediately replied guaranteeing return travel and a month's stay although, at the time, he did not know where the money would come from.

This invitation raised a storm in the Seinendan's Central Executive, but it was accepted at a special meeting by 85 votes to 65. So, while a handful went to Moscow, 104 set off for Mackinac, along with fifty other Japanese, thirty from the Philippines and twenty from Korea.

The Seinendan delegation were the bones and sinews of Japan. They had all shown leadership qualities, but their horizons had been limited to their farms, villages, towns and prefectures. Entwistle, when he arrived in Mackinac some two weeks after them, found them very insecure. 'They were surrounded by strange people, strange language and food, and a very different style of life,' he writes. 'They were also faced with a challenge to take a look at themselves in the light of absolute moral standards and in the perspective of a world struggle of ideas. . . Some plunged into arguments to blunt the moral challenges with which they were confronted. Some retreated into their own world; they left their watches on Tokyo time . . . and tried to eat and sleep according to their home time. . . A number were soon making decisions about their lives, facing such basic problems as stealing, marital infidelity, bribery and hatred, and were experimenting in straightening out what they had done wrong and how to live in the future.'[2]

Prime Minister Kishi was paying a visit to President Eisenhower at the same moment, and some of the senior Japanese like Niro Hoshijima and Senator Shidzue Kato, with a number of the Seinendan leaders, went from Mackinac to Washington to meet him on his arrival. He spent an hour with them before seeing Eisenhower, and they told him of Buchman's initiative. He regretted that he could not squeeze in a visit to Mackinac but proposed a talk with Buchman on the phone. The hour-long conversation between the two men next morning was amplified so that the thousand people at the assembly could hear. Kishi asked how the young Japanese were doing, to which Buchman replied, 'We are teaching them to go not to the right, nor to the left, but to go straight.' At one point, the Prime Minister said directly to the young Japanese, 'I hope you are fully understanding Moral Re-Armament and will get its spirit into your whole being and take it back to Japan.'[3]

'A few evenings later', relates Entwistle, 'the Japanese electrified the conference by mounting a production of songs, dances and skits. The performance was both a flowering of their personal changes and growing maturity and an interpretation of the best of their distinctive culture. It combined grace, beauty and a good deal of candid humour. Frank Buchman was so delighted with it all that he got to his feet about midnight and said they must give their presentation in the cities they were due to visit, leaving in a couple of days. To any other group the idea would have seemed madness, but somehow, with the aid of round-the-clock work, a stage crew was assembled, a portable stage set was made, halls were booked and invitations rushed out to friends in Detroit, Washington and New York.'[4] The party of two hundred interviewed management and labour at Ford's and the leaders of the NAACP* convention in Detroit, were entertained in the House and Senate at Washington and given lunch by delegates to the United Nations in New York. They then returned to Mackinac, bringing with them the Japanese Ambassador to the UN. Soon after, half of the Seinendan delegates had to leave for home, while the others stayed for further training.

Those who had remained decided to develop their skits into a play through which they could portray their new ideas on their return. One of them, a small-town business man with a farming background, named Yoshinori Yamamoto, came up with a story of family life, down-to-earth and moving because it was based on the real-life experiences of many of them. They called it *Road to Tomorrow*, and performed it in the following months in many parts of Japan.

Kishi decided to visit Japan's South-East Asian neighbours in that autumn of 1957, in the hope of revitalising economic relations with them. Before he left Tokyo he was visited by Senator Kato, who offered him the support of the Opposition if, before discussing trade relations in these countries, he would first express the sincere apologies of the Japanese people for the wrongs of the past. Senator Kato told Kishi about *The Vanishing Island*'s visit to Manila. She described the indrawn hiss of breath when Hoshijima began to speak to a thousand Filipinos in the hated Japanese tongue, and the thunderous applause when his apology and the Government's promise of reparations, which he had been empowered to announce, had been translated.

---

* National Association for the Advancement of Colored People.

Kishi heeded Mrs Kato's advice when he went to the Philippines, Korea, Burma and finally Australia. The *Sydney Morning Herald* wrote editorially, 'We cannot afford the luxury of living in the bitter past... Kishi handled a delicate mission with skilful tact. His ice-breaking tour ... could hardly have been a pleasant experience. But no one could have gone further in making official amends for the sins of his country.'

The *Washington Evening Star* commented, 'Premier Kishi is now back in Tokyo after having completed one of the most unusual missions ever undertaken by a statesman of his rank. Over the past three weeks he has visited no fewer than nine nations that Japan occupied or threatened with conquest... and in each of these lands he has publicly apologized for his country's actions during the war.'[6]

On Kishi's return to Tokyo he told the press, 'I have been impressed by the effectiveness of Moral Re-Armament in creating unity between peoples who have been divided. I have myself experienced the power of honest apology in healing the hurts of the past. This idea is most needed at this critical time in our history.'[7]

Among other issues Kishi also reopened the question of relations with Korea, along lines first suggested at a Moral Re-Armament conference at Baguio in the Philippines in March 1957, and emphasised by Senator Kato in the Foreign Affairs Committee on 30 April. After a second conference in Baguio, during which the Seinendan's play *Road to Tomorrow* was shown in Manila with much the same effect as *The Vanishing Island*, Kishi decided to give a reception in his official residence on 12 April 1958 to acknowledge the part Moral Re-Armament had played in helping Japan to regain the respect of other nations. On 10 April one of his brothers died, so he was unable to attend, but he asked the Parliamentary Vice-Minister of Foreign Affairs, Takizo Matsumoto, to speak for him. Matsumoto reviewed the successive steps:

1. In the late 1940s the first Japanese allowed to travel overseas were welcomed at Moral Re-Armament conferences in the United States.
2. The historic 'Mission to the West' in 1950 – the visit to Caux, Europe and the United States – re-established contact with Europeans and enabled Diet Members to address the United States Congress.
3. The good offices of Buchman and his colleagues provided the only means for Japanese delegates to the San Francisco Peace Treaty in 1951 to meet Asian, American and European delegates personally.
4. The inclusion of Japanese in the World Mission in 1955 was the first occasion for them to visit other Asian countries.
5. Kensuke Horinouchi, as Ambassador to Taiwan, had prevented a

serious rupture with the Nationalist Chinese Government, the one close diplomatic ally Japan had in Asia at that time.

6. The two MRA conferences in Baguio gave Japanese opportunities to establish wide contacts with their former Asian enemies and led directly to the diplomatic breakthroughs in negotiations with both the Korean and the Philippine governments.

Summing up this record Matsumoto stated, 'I speak in the name of the Government, and especially of the Foreign Office, when I say that at each critical turn we have been aided by the services of Moral Re-Armament.'[8]

Matsumoto also spoke for himself. During the reception he drew Entwistle aside and said that he had decided to run his election campaign for the Diet on MRA principles: he had gone through his speeches and eliminated the bitter references to opposition candidates.

The policies initiated by Kishi were carried to fruition by his successor, Takeo Fukuda, whom he had in the meantime brought to Caux.

In 1958 President Garcia of the Philippines paid an official visit to Japan. His host in the Diet was Niro Hoshijima, and the President stated, 'The bitterness of former years is being washed away by compassion and forgiveness.'[9]

Another of Buchman's long-cherished aims – to make some contribution to better race relations in the United States – began to become both possible and more urgent during that summer of 1957. He had, as he had told Griffith in Australia the year before, previously refused invitations to intervene in the Southern states because he lacked the people and the means to make such intervention effective. The initiative finally began in an unusual way.

While the Seinendan delegation was at Mackinac, two actresses arrived there independently in the course of a single week. One was Muriel Smith, the mezzo-soprano who had created the role of *Carmen Jones* on Broadway, and in London sang *Carmen* at Covent Garden and played for five consecutive years at the Drury Lane Theatre, first in *South Pacific* and then in *The King and I*. The other was Ann Buckles, who had been appearing in *Pajama Game* in New York. Muriel Smith met the young Japanese, and was particularly moved by the honesty of one of them who had faced the implications of terrible things he had done during the war. Ann Buckles, who was, she now says, so heavily made-up that if the wind blew parts of her face would blow away, felt that some of the Americans present disapproved of her. She was struck, however, by the warmth and reality of the German miners, Max Bladeck and Paul Kurowski. They took her to see Buchman. She was on the point of separating from her husband, but had told nobody. 'We had three-quarters of an hour together and I talked all the time, trying to impress him,' she recalls. 'Buchman just gave me a long, quiet look and said one sentence: "Divorce is old-fashioned." I felt stunned. I was trying to pretend the divorce didn't matter, but I felt all wrong inside. He saw it. He said nothing else. He just looked.'

Both women were fascinated by the creative atmosphere at Mackinac – the writing, music, theatre – and above all by the idea that their talents could be used constructively. They stayed and stayed, in spite of long-distance calls from their agents. Buchman saw in them what at first they would not see in themselves, a dramatisation of the answer to America's racial problems. Muriel Smith, a black American, had been brought up in Harlem and she and her mother had known real deprivation. Mrs Smith often talked of the red-letter day when she could finally afford to buy her daughter a pair of stockings. Ann Buckles was a striking blonde at the beginning of her career and came from the Southern state of Tennessee. As the weeks went on they began to sort out the many factors which divided them and to become friends.

Alan Thornhill and Cece Broadhurst decided to write a musical for them. It was based on the life story of Mary McLeod Bethune, the daughter of slaves who, starting with only one dollar in her purse and a determination that her people should have the chance of a good education, founded the first black college in America and finally became a special adviser to President Roosevelt. Meeting Moral Re-Armament some years earlier she had said to Buchman, 'To be a part of this great uniting force is the crowning experience of my life.' So they called the play *The Crowning Experience*.

Another long-term drama ran concurrently, in the lives of the two actresses. Once, when some recording with a symphony orchestra was being done for the subsequent film, they were sharing a hotel room together, exactly opposite Buchman's. 'Muriel has this glorious voice,' says Ann Buckles. 'When she sang the orchestra lit up, but when I sang they looked glum, as if to say, "Who's this?" Then I would go back to the hotel, and have to listen to Muriel humming and singing all night long. One night I finally screamed, "Shut up!" I was terrified at what I had done. Muriel just said, "You didn't have to say it like that." That was the end of conversation that night. Next morning Frank sent for us, and we were petrified because we had been yelling. He said, "We have a South African judge and a black African leader returning to South Africa to get *Freedom* through the Board of Censors. Will you come to lunch and tell us how you found unity?" Muriel and I retired shamefaced and began to be honest.'

When *The Crowning Experience* opened in Atlanta, Georgia, in January

1958 11,000 people saw it during the first weekend. After the first night the local radio announced, as though astonished, 'There were no incidents in the Civic Auditorium.' During the first performances plain-clothes police had formed part of the audience, but they soon realised that their presence was unnecessary and stopped coming. Then the play moved from the Civic Auditorium to the Tower Theater, where the manager provided equal seating for white and black, something which had never happened before in Atlanta. 'I came in trepidation and left in exaltation,' he said after the first performance. The wife of a white minister commented, 'For years we have been listening to the tick of a bomb waiting for it to explode in our city. Now we are listening to the tick of the Holy Spirit. You have come at the right time.'[10]

The play ran for five months in Atlanta. A leading black lawyer, Colonel A. T. Walden, remarked, 'After the visit of *The Crowning Experience*, Atlanta will never be the same again.'[11] It is a fact that integration was calmly and wisely achieved there in the next years, and John Kennedy, after he became President, sent for Walden to hear the story behind it.

When *The Crowning Experience* had a seven-week run in Washington that summer it drew 80,000 people, more than any play in the 123-year history of the National Theater. In September Drew Pearson's syndicated newspaper column described its effect in Atlanta, and added, 'Behind what happened in Georgia is an even more amazing story of how dedicated people from all walks of life are organizing to find a solution to a problem that our political leaders have been unable to resolve – the explosive challenge of Little Rock.'[12]

The explosion of violence in Little Rock, Arkansas, over the integration of black and white children in the schools, had made world news in the autumn of 1957, and it was one of the events which had stimulated the writing and production of *The Crowning Experience*. Buchman, who had had a group of black and white Africans with him in America at the time, urged them to take the film *Freedom* to Little Rock. They showed it first to the leaders of the white community, then to the Federal troops who had been despatched there, to the school authorities and to the leaders of the black integration committees. Among the latter was Mrs L. C. Bates, then President of the Arkansas NAACP. She had risked her life taking to a white school each morning the group of black children over whose presence there the riots had broken out. After seeing *Freedom*, Mrs Bates came with a party of both races from Little Rock to Mackinac. She there decided to visit the Governor of Arkansas, Orval Faubus, who, unknown to her, had also seen *Freedom*. The resulting interview was described by a CBS radio news commentator, summing up the principal events of 1959, as 'possibly the most significant news event of the year which marks the end of a hundred years' civil war in the United States of America'.[13]

The story behind this event was told by the black weekly, the *Pittsburgh Courier*,[14] under the banner headline, 'Bates Stresses Role MRA Played in "Miracle" of Little Rock'. The paper quotes Mrs Bates's husband, L. C. Bates, as saying, 'This week Mrs Bates, a strong foe of Governor Faubus, met the Governor for more than two hours. It was her experience with MRA that gave her the courage to ask for this appointment. It was probably something of Moral Re-Armament in him which made him accept. It is hard to evaluate now, but it may be a turning point. If we instil MRA into the people of Little Rock, it will turn the city from chaos into happiness.'

Six years later the London *Observer* reported, 'Governor Faubus now seems to be leading a movement to bring about integration in his State . . . Whatever the motivations, the results are remarkable. In school integration, better jobs for Negroes and the desegregation of restaurants and hotels, Arkansas has made more progress than any other state, according to the Governor's old adversary, Mrs L. C. Bates, field secretary of the National Association for the Advancement of Colored People in Arkansas.'[15]

Buchman, because of age and increasing ill-health, was not always able to participate in these adventures, but no one doubted who was behind the initiatives. In 1958 the National Association of Colored Women's Clubs, at their convention in Detroit, awarded him a permanent trophy as 'the greatest humanitarian of them all'.

The Seinendan delegation and those who accompanied them from Korea and the Philippines were only a fraction of those who came to Mackinac Island in the summer of 1957. Further delegations arrived during the five-month assembly from Thailand, Vietnam, Burma, India, Cambodia and Taiwan. Two special planes arrived from Europe, in addition to other parties from Italy and Germany, the latter including fifty-five students. Fifty-three arrived from Iceland in mid-August, and towards the end Buchman lunched with an influential group of Sudanese, brought by Ahmed el Mahdi, the grandson of the Mahdi, then studying at Oxford.* Another visitor was Charles Assalé, the leader of one of the parties striving for independence in the Cameroons. 'I have eaten the bread of bitterness all my life,' he told Buchman. On his return he became reconciled to Ahmadu Ahidjo, his keenest rival, and together they were able, three years later, to achieve a peaceful agreement with France. Ahidjo subsequently became President, and appointed Assalé Prime Minister. A number of these groups wrote plays to be performed at home,

* He later held a number of cabinet posts in several governments.

while a party of MPs and others from Ghana and Nigeria took theirs, *The Next Phase*, to Washington. In addition, individuals and groups were coming from all over America and Canada.

All this would have been impossible if the new centre had not been built, and the building continued during the next years. Finally, during the filming of *The Crowning Experience*, much of which was done on the island, a Canadian movie director, impressed by the expertise and dedication of some of the young people doing the technical work, suggested to Buchman that he build a studio to make films rather than remain dependent on commercial studios. Buchman responded with characteristic enthusiasm. 'Next year it will be producing one MRA film each week to reach the millions,' he wrote in a letter.[16] The studio was built during the winter of 1959–60, in sub-zero temperatures, by two hundred or more MRA volunteers. Two planeloads of Buchman's Hollywood friends – actresses and actors, directors and technicians, led by the veteran Western actor Joel McCrea and his family – came up the next summer to inspect the building. They were all greatly impressed by the quality of the building and by its facilities, but raised major doubts as to its location. How could it be adequately employed on an island which was isolated by frozen lakes and bitter winds from early winter until late spring?

Buchman, now eighty, and never at his best at grasping the practicalities of technical operations, had let his vision outrun his common sense. There had been doubters among his colleagues, but he would not listen to them. He preferred to listen to the enthusiasts whose views matched his own. The studio was used occasionally in the following years, but never on any scale to justify the costs of its creation in money and manpower.

BEATING A PATH TO HIS DOOR

In June 1958 Buchman celebrated an eightieth birthday which, a few months earlier, neither he nor his friends had expected him to see. In the previous two years his health had stood up to the strenuous six-month journey to Australia and Asia, after which he had conducted a large assembly in Mackinac and launched *The Crowning Experience* in the Southern states of America. In the winter of 1957, however, his health declined seriously, Campbell diagnosing the main trouble as cardiac. He was advised to seek a warmer climate and accepted an invitation to a family home in Miami.

His arrival coincided with a period of damp, oppressive weather and he did not respond to rest, as he generally did. On occasion he was extremely irritable with those around him, his anger partly originating from frustration at his own inability to do what he saw needed to be done. His repentance, according to his secretary, was prompt. 'Why don't you tell me to go to blazes?' he said once with a smile. 'I would.' He recalled that his father had suffered from arterio-sclerosis and had become continuously difficult and even violent in his last years. 'If ever you see me getting like that, shoot me!' said Buchman. That he never became. But there is no doubt that his arteries had been hardening for a number of years and that his temper – and judgement – were at times affected.

That winter he was listless. His mail, though as varied and fascinating as ever, failed to interest him. One day he asked how much money he had in the two accounts he personally controlled. One contained seven hundred dollars, the other three hundred. He emptied both with four cheques to workers' families in Europe to whom he sent gifts from time to time. 'If I could help it', he once said, 'I would be ashamed to die with any money in the bank.'

In April he developed pneumonia. For two weeks he knew little of what went on around him. One day he decided where his funeral would be and asked to have an obituary notice drafted and read to him. Then he looked up and announced with a twinkle that he thought he would live till he was 94. Gradually he overcame his weariness. On 5 May he wrote to Peter

Howard, 'My present plan is to lie low and play Brer Rabbit. I have not the strength for more.' Yet two weeks later he travelled to New York by train, carried through various duties there, and on 2 June arrived in Mackinac, ready for the birthday celebrations.

Buchman's birthdays were always important to him and he enjoyed this one in particular, as the friends around him helped him to celebrate and messages reached him from all parts of the world. An editorial in the *Frankfurter Allgemeine Zeitung* read, '. . . Frank Buchman puts a moral diplomacy . . . alongside the political diplomacy of the nations . . . As a moral ambassador Frank Buchman enjoys, far beyond all national borders, almost unlimited trust. His selfless role of mediator, mostly unseen by the public, is again and again called upon. This man who without sentimentality, without dramatic oratorical gifts, nevertheless fascinates his hearers, has become more and more the conscience of the world.'[1]

This new illness, however, still further restricted him, and the access which his growing whole-time force had to him. More and more information was filtered through several minds both on its way to him and back, and sometimes got distorted en route. A first reaction to a report about someone's actions, perhaps incomplete, might be passed on with a harshness which he would not necessarily have displayed if he had seen the person himself. Perhaps the shielding by those near him was overdone; or in his weakness he himself ordered it. One whole-time worker of twenty years' standing, wanting to discuss sincere disagreements, left his work because he failed eight times to get through the protective screen. A young woman who believed that her ill mother needed her in another country received a long letter signed in his name telling her in strong terms that her place was to care for certain Asian girls at an assembly and she should trust her mother to God. Yet when, two weeks later, she eventually got in to see him personally, he said, 'Go at once,' and clearly did not recall any such letter being sent. Whether this was his forgetfulness, or whether a letter was written for him on a first, unconsidered response, is not clear. A real problem of communication, difficult for all concerned, developed. In the days before his stroke, every contact had been personal and straightforward; in the intervening years such contact had become more limited; now it was even more sparse, and some of his old friends at times felt cut off.

This difficulty was magnified by a great increase in the numbers of whole-time workers in the late fifties. Buchman still originated many fruitful initiatives, and was as effective and compassionate as ever when meeting people – especially people new to him – face to face. But it was impossible for him to know the personal situation of his many hundreds of whole-time colleagues throughout the world, and mistakes regarding them became more frequent.

As winter drew near he was again urged to find a warmer climate, and his doctors suggested the dry South-Western desert. Friends in Tucson, Arizona, rented a house around which the cactus, sage and cottonwood stretched for miles up through the foothills of the Santa Catalina Mountains. Below, the ground dropped away to a night-time view of the desert studded with the thousands of lights of the fast-growing city of Tucson.

Here he could restore his strength while keeping in touch with developments around the world and receiving a stream of visitors. He wrote to one friend, 'I wish you could see the scene, as on one side I look upon an expanse of cacti – some are two hundred years old – and on the other upon an orange, lemon and kumquat grove . . . Beside the house there are cypress trees, and beyond all, the mountains with a look of the most beautiful parts of Greece. It is an ample place and I have thirty people staying with me. I never felt weary for one moment, and day after day there is sunshine galore.'[2] He enjoyed his first months there so much that generous friends bought it to be his winter home.

The house at Tucson gave Buchman scope for the hospitality he loved to offer. As in the old days he created an atmosphere of concentrated concern for individuals, starting with the Mexican gardener, an embittered young man whom he took on with the house. From time to time he would be absent for a day or two. Buchman accurately diagnosed a drinking problem and said that if the young man, Arnold, was to do the gardening he would have to stop drinking. This produced an absence of several weeks during which, instead of hiring another man, the household looked after the garden as best they might. Buchman was more interested in Arnold than in the fate of the roses and citrus trees.

Arnold eventually returned. Buchman had him in for coffee and cake and told him about his own work. At the end Buchman gave him a notebook. 'What will I do with this?' asked Arnold. Someone told him that the change in his own life had started with writing down everything that did not match up to the four absolute moral standards. 'Well, then,' said Arnold, 'I'd better have two notebooks.'

Arnold told his father about these discoveries, and his father's even more acute drinking problem was cured. When he brought his wife to lunch, she said, 'I hope we act properly – my husband and I haven't been out to a meal together for twenty years.' After that the father came regularly to prune the hundred rose trees round the house and later got a job as gardener at the city hospital.

One night the local plumber, an agnostic, brought his rebellious teenage son to dinner and held forth about his agnosticism. When the meal was over Buchman said to the son, 'I usually thank God for a meal after we've eaten it. However, today I think we'll all sing "For he's a jolly good fellow".' The son became a frequent visitor.

At one tea party the milkman said he wanted to talk. They sat down and the milkman broke out, 'I've been married for nearly thirty years. A few months ago my wife got on a Greyhound bus, and she met a man half her age and has never come back.'

'Have you always been honest with your wife?' said Buchman.

The milkman began to weep: the day his eldest boy had been born she had made him promise not to drink, but he had drunk and got into trouble with a woman and never told her. He went home and wrote to his wife. After that, he often brought milk free to the household.

A local meat producer offered Buchman all the meat his household needed, provided he had a deep-freeze. A farmer delivering fruit and vegetables heard of this offer, went off immediately and bought one. The cowboy who brought the regular supplies of meat through the winter always stayed to lunch and nearly always brought another cowboy with him – the greatest experience of their lives, they said.

Soon the Sheriff and the Mayor and the General commanding the local air base started coming. The General said to his friends, 'You must go and meet Frank Buchman. You get the best food and meet the most interesting people in the world.' After six months Buchman's barber commented, 'You've only been downtown a few times, Doctor, but the whole town's been up to see you, and seemingly the whole world.'

This became increasingly true. One winter when there was an MRA conference concerned mainly with Asia in Los Angeles, people attending it followed each other to Tucson in twos and threes. Koreans and Japanese, Chinese from Hong Kong and Taiwan, Malays and Papuans, Australians and New Zealanders predominated for a while. Then there was a wave from Hollywood, then parties returning to Europe and Africa.

Among those from Japan was Saburo Chiba, then Chairman of the Security Committee of the Diet, who came for the inside of a day. Someone said, 'He's had a long journey. Let's give him a good room and let him rest.'

'Rest?' replied Buchman. 'Here is a man who can affect the life of a nation. Let's use every minute to give him a maximum experience of change.'

Chiba was an agnostic, friendly but cautious. He sat down to breakfast with Buchman and his friends at a quarter to eight. Stories were told of how racial differences were being ameliorated in America and elsewhere through change in people, and how Communists in various countries were saying they had found a better idea. Breakfast lasted till twenty to twelve.

Lunch was a Japanese meal so perfectly cooked that Chiba insisted on meeting the cooks. 'If you have an idea that turns a Wall Street banker's daughter into as good a cook as that one and she does it without being paid, your idea must be a very big one,' Chiba said to Buchman afterwards.

At the end of the afternoon, as Chiba was preparing to leave, Buchman said, 'I had one thought for you early this morning.'

'What was that?'

'The whole world will walk into your heart. You will let the whole world walk into your heart.'

As he said goodbye at the airport, Chiba said, 'Today, for the first time in my life, I have found God.' Soon after, Buchman heard that the atmosphere of the Chibas' family life had fundamentally altered.

U Nu, still Prime Minister of Burma, suddenly announced himself on a journey through America. He wanted to finish the talk he had begun with Buchman two years before in Rangoon. Shortly after that talk U Nu had made a speech to his party, telling of his own youthful dishonesties and calling for an end to moral corruption in his party and in the nation. When a little later he had retired from office the people had demanded his return to lead the nation. Now he wanted to know how to unite his country. Over a fine Burmese curry – the cooks had rehearsed it the day before – Buchman got twenty people to tell U Nu in a few sentences their experience of divine guidance. Then he took U Nu aside privately and warned him of one man close to him whom he believed to have subversive designs on the country.

'You must learn to read people like a book,' he said to the Prime Minister.

'How can I?' asked U Nu.

'You have to know yourself and be absolutely honest with yourself. Listen, and you will know. The thing that makes men and women blind to others is that they allow themselves the same weaknesses.'

At the airport U Nu said, 'Without Moral Re-Armament my country is going into the camp of dictatorship.' He stood on the ramp and said, 'Come soon to Burma, come soon, come soon.' U Nu said of Buchman after his death, 'Surely there has been no other person in our times with such an infinite capacity for friendship and trust.'[3]

Threads from other world events led back to Tucson. Dr Abdel Khalek Hassouna, Secretary-General of the Arab League, told Buchman how, during the Lebanon crisis of that autumn, when American marines had landed in Beirut, he had had a clear conviction one evening in Cairo to fly immediately to New York. With the Egyptian government's backing he brought the Arab delegates together, keeping them in session until they found a unanimous formula. Gromyko, the Soviet Foreign Minister, withdrew his opposition and the United Nations voted to accept the Arab resolution by eighty votes to nil – an almost unprecedented event. 'Overnight', wrote *The Times*,[4] 'an almost magical transformation has come over the scene.' *The Washington Post*[5] described it as a 'triumph' for Dr Hassouna. The Sudanese Prime Minister was quoted to the same effect in an article headed: 'Survival Clue? Arab Nations Display Spirit of Moral Re-Armament at UN.'[6]

In Tucson, too, Buchman continued the training of his team. His first concern was the quality of life within his own home – 'everything under God's guidance and not what we think is good form'. 'I've got a household here that works as one and no one gets a cent,' he said. But this unity did not come by chance. Working together in the kitchen, for example, meant long hours and considerable skill. Once when the two girls working there fell out he stopped having guests for two weeks. One of the girls was American, the other Swiss. Each was sure her way of doing things was best. Buchman said he tasted the tension in the food. 'You're scratchy with each other,' he said to them. 'You're hard-headed people who want to do everything your own way, when you need to rise to something high and noble.' Both girls changed and began to enjoy life again. Buchman then resumed his customary hospitality.

Buchman also prepared bands of people to return to their countries. Eight Japanese came to see him at Tucson before leaving for home. As soon as they sat down to lunch, Buchman asked, 'What is your plan for Japan?' There was silence.

'Are you united?' he asked. Again there was silence.

'I know you have done some good work in Japan,' Buchman went on, 'but what's happening to your nation? What's its real problem?'

'Communism,' someone replied.

'No, no, no,' said Buchman. 'It's corruption and mistresses in high places. Will you tackle these issues? I love Japan, and I'm concerned about what's happening.'

The Japanese left the room. They were honest with each other about the jealousy and bitterness between them, and were then able to work out what needed to be done.

Within three days one of them, Masahide Shibusawa, had written a play, *Shaft of Light*. It was so direct in its picturing of prominent people in Japan that they were afraid of what might happen to them and their children if they put it on. They read it to Buchman. 'Go where the stones are rough,' he said. 'People may want to shoot you, but you will save your nation and future generations will be grateful.'

A month later the play was staged in Tokyo, 400 yards from the Diet building. It caused a sensation. A top security officer, watching the portrayal of bribery in high places and a mistress, who was a spy, attached to a Cabinet Minister, said, 'It is exaggerated. You can't keep this play on. It is dangerous.' A few days later he came back to them. 'I was wrong,' he said. 'I have had it investigated and it is all true.' The Prime Minister sent for the people who had been visiting Buchman. They told him the facts, as they saw them, about his own Cabinet.

'You are the only people who love our country enough to tell me the truth,' he said. 'Go on talking to me like this. The door is always open to you.'

Meanwhile, Buchman had to fight as hard a battle much nearer home. After his return from Asia in 1956 he had talked to Peter Howard about the aftermath of the *Vanishing Island* tour. Though he recognised the immense task which Howard and his colleagues had undertaken, he had considered them responsible for the wrong attitude which had got into the travelling force. Buchman nevertheless did not lose faith in and for Howard. But certain of those who had suffered from his sharp tongue, or were jealous of his apparent position, had set about prejudicing Buchman's mind against him. Weak, increasingly in bed for days at a time, and constantly under the pressure of decisions to be made, Buchman often did not know what to think.

This came to a head in 1957 at Mackinac, where some people shunned and pressured Howard and his family. Howard asked Buchman what he should do. 'Go on doing what you have been doing,' said Buchman. Yet, at a certain point, Howard felt he had to move his family out of Mackinac. He returned to Britain with them and lived on his farm. He kept to his commitment.

After some months Howard had what he believed to be divine guidance to join Buchman in Tucson. He went, taking his wife, Doë, and his daughter, Anne, with him. He had a full, frank talk with Buchman, but kept a low profile. Then one day he had the thought that he should speak after a public showing of a film, as he had so often done before. He mentioned this at a planning meeting. Immediately, fury broke loose among some of those present who were determined that Howard should never resume his former prominence. The noise was so loud that it reached Buchman upstairs. He asked someone what was going on. When he heard, he bellowed down the stairs, 'Come here, every one of you!' Then he startled them all. 'Here am I, an old man in bed,' he said. 'I have relied on you to tell me the truth. But you've misled me about Peter. You've told me stories about him. I've talked them out with him point by point, and they are not true.'

He had sensed a new quality in Howard since his return. The process of becoming freed from other people's opinion which had begun in their earlier tussle, had been taken a step further during Howard's days of rest and thought in England. Now they began once again to work as close colleagues. 'I want to pay a tribute to Peter,' Buchman said some time later. 'I have worked with him night and day these past weeks. He comes at 4.45 in the morning to help write letters to people all over the world. He changes people; he guards the life of the force. He reads his Bible every day and has something pungent to bring out of it. You have a matchless time when people move with you selflessly like that.'

Though from then on the younger man spent much of his time travelling the world and carried the detailed day-to-day responsibilities of the work, while the older man often had to be stationary, they were never again parted in spirit.

From Tucson Buchman returned to Mackinac for the summer of 1959. Here, on his eighty-first birthday a musical called *Pickle Hill*, written by Howard during the weeks in Tucson, had its premiere. It was the story of Bill Pickle, the bootlegger, and Buchman's first experiments at Penn State College. The third man in that story, Blair Buck, was with Buchman in the audience on the opening night. Buchman was so caught up in the drama that at times he answered from the front row himself when questions were put to his stage persona. 'That's the way to do it,' he said afterwards. 'What a strategy God gave – it was people, people, people. You had to be alert all the time.'

The visitors at Mackinac that summer were as varied as ever. Among them were the French Catholic philosopher, Gabriel Marcel; Rajmohan Gandhi; chiefs of North American Indian tribes from Western Canada; U Narada, Secretary of the Presiding Abbots' Association of Burma; the Muslim President of the Sudanese Parliament, Sayed Shingetti; the Catholic Archbishop of Beirut, Mgr Naba'a; military delegations from the Pentagon, groups of Japanese farmers from California, and a representative of the Government of Iran who came to confer a decoration. A group of revolutionary Rastafarians arrived from Jamaica. Bitterly anti-white, they owed allegiance to the Emperor of Ethiopia, and listened with amazement when Buchman told them of his friendship with him during his lonely years of exile, when Brown's Hotel was his London base. A Hollywood film executive, at the end of his first twenty-four hours at Mackinac, compared the conference to a baseball World Series, a world championship fight and the Olympic Games, all compressed into one day and accompanied by the Philharmonic Orchestra.

While this conference was in progress at Mackinac a parallel assembly was going on at Caux, with which Buchman was in almost daily touch. To it came a delegation from the South Indian state of Kerala, which had just experienced a period of Communist rule – the first state anywhere to become Communist by the ballot box. Earlier that year, faced with a threat to impose Communist indoctrination in the schools, the Christian and

Hindu communities had united sufficiently to oust the government; but there was confusion as to what to do next. The delegation to Caux included members of both religious factions, among them the veteran Hindu leader Mannath Padmanabhan, a life-long enemy of Christianity in Kerala. He and the Christian leaders did not talk to each other en route.

At Caux Padmanabhan, who spoke only Malayalam, was a keen observer of everything. After three days he remarked that there was a strange atmosphere at Caux. 'What is that?' he was asked. 'It's a sense of purity,' he said. 'The extraordinary thing is that it can exist in a place where there are so many Christians.' 'You see, a Christian to us', he added, 'is a fat Englishman with a cigar in his mouth, one of our girls on his arm and a bottle of whisky in his pocket.'

One evening the Kerala delegation saw *Pickle Hill* in the Caux theatre. Their reaction was, 'This play has been written for us.' A Catholic leader went directly to Padmanabhan and apologised for his bitterness against him. A few months later the Catholic Archbishop of Trivandrum described the outcome in a message to Buchman: 'History will record our permanent gratitude to Mannath Padmanabhan . . . for creating the unity of all the communities following his return from Caux.'[7]

Throughout that summer in Mackinac, despite the success of the assembly, Buchman seems to have been deeply uneasy about his team. This unease can, indeed, be traced back much further, certainly to 1957. While preparing for Mackinac that year, he had said to some of the Americans and Europeans with him, 'Are we all actually changing people? Some of you are so starched and boiled and ironed – we just need to change and put on clean clothes. Only one person can cancel sin, and that's Jesus.'

He was to return to the attack more forcibly at various times during the 1959 assembly. 'I get the impression you think things can be achieved without changing people,' he said in May. 'We are here to renew our commitment and to free ourselves of debris. A man is either alive or dead. Either changing people or not. Feathery men – we've got some in the fellowship. Bossy women make cowards of men. Impure men make bossy women. Have any of you refused to take on the basic needs of nations? Countries easily become fields in which we work rather than becoming forces to remake the world . . . Whatever I have done hasn't been me. I got up early and there was always the divine thought. It must be *your* secret. The Holy Spirit just dropping His truth. That's Christ's promise: "He that cometh to me I will in no wise cast out." '

This unease was still with him in October. He seems to have felt that many of his colleagues had become dependent on each other and had lost the infectious spirit that changes lives, and that this was leading, as numbers grew, to an institutionalism which he had always aimed to avoid – what he called a 'movement-mindedness'. 'Some of us', he said at this time, 'may have bluffed too long now to be genuine enough to save our nations. Judas felt tremendous remorse. But Peter repented. Judas was in love with his interpretation of the message Christ proclaimed. To love the idea of Moral Re-Armament is no substitute for the love of God who washes us, sets us free and sets us to work.'

After resting one afternoon he told some friends of an experience which had been very vivid to him: 'It was just like something coming down from heaven. I had a conscious sense of what we have to do. I saw that Caux and Mackinac would have to unite and we would learn together to present a world answer.' The scope and cost of the proposition are an indication of the urgency he felt. Three weeks later the main elements of the Caux conference were transferred to Mackinac, which meant that Buchman had the bulk of his full-time force with him in one place – for the last time, it turned out, on such a scale.

It would seem that his remark on seeing *Pickle Hill* earlier in the summer – 'it was people, people, people' – was not just an enthusiastic recollection, but a hint to others and a challenge to himself. On the day that he left Mackinac at the end of the session, he gathered everyone in the buildings and recalled for them and for himself the personal experience which had been at the root of his work through the years:

'I was awake a lot of the night, and I had an ominous sense that we have done well, by and large, but that there are still areas to be possessed,' he said. 'I read the ninth chapter of Acts. Read it and be sure it is your experience. I know a time in my life when I didn't have it, and I thought I was doing pretty well. There are still some people I feel have not reached this experience. They have not been commissioned by the Living God to take this message to the nations. I would not want to go today if I had not a clear sense of what is promised in that chapter.

'There was a time in my life when I was just like some of you. I was in the North of England. I had a good time. One afternoon I had the desire to go and hear a service. I went; there were only seventeen people there. That speaker did for me what no one had ever done. She talked straight to me about the Cross of Christ . . . I realised that God our Father cared for us so much that He gave His only Son. It had never touched me before. But that speaker that day had the wind of the Spirit. I gave my life wholly and completely. I learnt the thing I had never known before, to listen. I heard the still small voice say to me, "Repent." I had had a fairly good education but I needed something very simple and real. And it happened. I reached the experience of St Paul. I heard the wind of heaven and it passed over me and through me and I walked out of that place a different man. The old man was gone. I felt happy again . . . Whether it is Jew or Gentile, democrat or Communist, it is an experience all can have.

'Then I went out and I met a young man, just a young blade. He said, "How about a walk?" We walked by Derwentwater. I told him of my experience, that revelation of the Cross of Christ which met my instant need. And before we reached the end of that walk, he, too, had the same experience.'

'We need a passionate pursuit of the individual,' he continued. 'It is those who are for God and those against Him. If you are in the mainstream of God's will for you, you don't depend on results. It is God who gives the results.'

Some sincere Christians have wondered how Buchman could return again and again to his Keswick experience, and at the same time help men like U Nu and Abdel Khalek Hassouna in their personal and public lives without demanding that they join the Christian Church. It was certainly not because his faith in or dependence on Christ lessened with the years – quite the contrary.

The key seems to have been that Buchman was dedicated to help the people he met to take the next step which God was revealing to them. His friends of other religions knew what he believed and what he tried to live – and were attracted by it. He respected their sincere beliefs, and knew that they had often absorbed a distorted idea of Christianity from the way they had seen people from so-called Christian countries live. He saw his part as demonstrating the beauty and relevance of Christ's living presence in a person or a community – and leaving the Holy Spirit room to work in their hearts as He wished. He was sure that God could make His will known to anyone, just as He did to the Jews in the Old Testament, and that He did not enquire first whether the person seeking Him was a Christian, a person of some different faith or, like the Ruhr Communists, of no faith at all. So, in the deepest sense, he did not aspire to proselytize, but to put people in touch with the Spirit which 'blows where it likes'.

So, with U Nu, he concentrated on helping him to believe he could receive guidance. To the Ghanaian Muslim leader, the Tolon Na, he had simply remarked, 'When did you last steal?' When he emerged, still a good Muslim, from the violent reappraisal of his life into which this one remark had pitched him, the Tolon Na had put right everything in his life which he could see that he had done wrong. He often explained that the Cross meant to him that when God's will crossed his will, he must choose God's will.

'The genius of Moral Re-Armament,' writes the German theologian, Professor Klaus Bockmühl, 'is to bring the central spiritual substance of

Christianity (which often it demonstrates in a fresher and more powerful way than do the Churches) in a secular and accessible form. Hence the emphasis on absolute moral standards. But the direction of the Holy Spirit is just as essential.' 'The genius', adds Bockmühl, 'is in the balance of the two.'[8]

BLIND MAN'S BATTLE

One far-reaching product of this 1959 assembly was a 32-page pamphlet *entitled Ideology and Co-Existence*. After 1956, when Krushchev had denounced Stalin, it seemed to many lovers of democracy and peace that the Soviet Union's old aggressiveness was giving way to a milder competition. The phrase 'peaceful co-existence', which Krushchev popularised, led to the hope that the world was emerging into a less dangerous rivalry between the democracies and the Communist dictatorships.

Buchman did not subscribe to this view. He had been proclaiming for more than a dozen years that democracy without a moral and spiritual ideology at its heart was no match for totalitarians of Right or Left. In his opening address at the assembly in 1959 he had quoted with approval the words of a former American Chief of Naval Operations and Ambassador in Moscow, Admiral William Standley, that 'the choice for America is moral re-armament or communism'.[1] Both Standley and Buchman were referring to the ideologies rather than the organisations. Neither would have said that the choice was between the Oxford Group and the Communist Party. Buchman was aiming for a revolution through which the Cross of Christ could change Communists and non-Communists alike.

The pamphlet, on the other hand, spent much of its space alerting people to the strategies and tactics of Communism. It quoted from Russian, Chinese and other ideologists of the day to show that the long-term aim of revolutionary Communism was still world domination, and warned Western leaders that if they were to meet Communists on equal terms they needed an equally passionately-held philosophy and plan and a more disciplined way of life. The word 'ideology' was defined as 'an idea that dominates the whole person – his motives, his thinking, his living – and fights with a strategy to get everybody else to live the same way'.

Buchman was quoted to the effect that 'the battle for America is the battle for the mind of America'. 'A nation's thinking is in ruins before a nation is in ruins,' the quotation continued. 'People get confused as to whether it is a question of being rightist or leftist, but the one thing we really need is to be guided by God's Holy Spirit . . . America does not have much of her great moral heritage left. Just think, if we fail to give the emphasis to a moral climate, where will our democracy go? Some of us have been so busy looking after our own affairs that we have forgotten to look after the nation . . . The true battle-line in the world today is not between class and class, not between race and race. The battle is between Christ and anti-Christ. "Choose ye this day whom ye will serve." '[2]

During the next months Moral Re-Armament teams in many parts of the world got to work translating, printing and distributing millions of copies of the booklet, and when Buchman opened the summer conference at Caux in June 1960 he stated that 73 million copies had gone into the homes of the United States, Canada and Western Europe, as well as of India, Latin America, Australia and Japan.[3] It was translated into twenty-four languages, and became the most widely distributed publication Moral Re-Armament has ever produced.

It was also the most controversial. In Finland, for example, President Kekkonen sent for Lennart Segerstraale, the reputed painter, who was the chairman of Moral Re-Armament's legal body there, and severely reprimanded him for arranging its distribution to millions of Finnish homes. On the other hand, the grand old man of Finnish Socialism, Väinö Tanner, said it was just what was needed to clarify people's minds.

In retrospect, many people within Moral Re-Armament have doubted the wisdom of the move, since it created an anti-Communist image which was a gross over-simplification of Moral Re-Armament philosophy. Buchman was, however, heart and soul behind the venture. He simply felt that a warning and a challenge were urgently needed and, as usual, cared little about public images or the reputation of his work. Characteristically, he did what seemed to him to be right, sometimes with the minimum of consultation, and let the sparks fall where they would.

While his friends were at work with *Ideology and Co-Existence*, Buchman left Mackinac and returned to the beauty of Tucson. On the way he made two visits – the first to the island's priest, Father Ling, who lay ill in St Ignace hospital just across the water from Mackinac. He had spent forty years on the island and had come to see Buchman about once a fortnight whenever he was there. Now the old priest was slowly dying. He came from his bed to talk to Buchman, who had, the previous year, got one of his own friends to care for the Father's closest companion, his dog Max. The two men said goodbye, each knowing it was for the last time.

The second visit was to Anoka, Minnesota, to the home of his uncle who had died in the Civil War. He and his companions heard once more how the uncle had gone to war leaving his wife and a young baby with only a fifty-cent piece, a coin which was again respectfully passed round.

At Tucson the cables, telexes and telephone calls came incessantly. He worked hard from his bed in the early morning, and over lunch and dinner with his guests. Some were public figures, some old friends; some both. As he got older he dispensed more and more with formality and said bluntly what he thought. One prominent Republican Committeewoman talked non-stop while her silent husband sat resignedly eating. Finally Buchman saw an opening and said, 'Madam, you need to listen twice as much as you talk!' Her husband looked up with delight, and made his first remark of the meal. The wife began to listen and the lunch conversation continued until afternoon tea was served.

By the early months of 1960 Buchman was often thinking of a group of German miners who were setting out on a world tour with their play *Hoffnung (Hope)*. It was playing in Rome on 20 February, and he dispatched Howard to join them there. It was then to proceed to Cyprus and Kerala. One of Buchman's keenest sympathisers in Rome was Cardinal Eugène Tisserant, then Dean of the College of Cardinals. Fifteen months earlier, just two weeks after the election of Pope John XXIII, he had let Buchman know through a friend that he believed a new attitude to his work was on the way. 'The new Pope will take a broad view of this question,' he had told one of Buchman's colleagues in Rome. 'I know him. I know Dr Buchman. He understands. He puts Catholics to look after Catholics at Caux. All my information is positive and favourable. He never takes anyone from their Church . . . I believe you have trouble with some bishops . . . I have spoken to Suenens. He was against. His views are not the last word. I assure you again that something is going to be done.'[4]

The Cardinal had until recently been Prefect of the Congregation of Oriental Churches and was particularly interested in Kerala, where he knew the situation intimately as well as many of the personalities involved. So when, in February 1960, he received an invitation to a private performance of *Hoffnung*, he immediately accepted. At the last moment, however, he decided not to attend in response to a pressing request from an official of the Holy Office. Four days later he was seeing Pope John XXIII, and raised the subject of Moral Re-Armament with him. He described their conversation to two of Buchman's friends two days afterwards. 'It was a long time, I had two volumes to deliver to him, but we did not mention them at all,' he said. 'The whole audience was about Moral Re-Armament . . . The Pope seems to have heard little about your work, except when he was in France. . . I told him that because of the visit of this play to Kerala I was eager to see it. I told him of what had already taken place in Kerala through Moral Re-Armament – how the Hindu leadership and the Catholic leadership became united at Caux and how this had been reported to me by Rajmohan Gandhi. I told him about the excellent work done at Mackinac and Caux, and how Catholics who came there were never put under spiritual direction of non-Catholics. I then told him of the importance of the work in Asia as reported to me. I then told him about the support of Cardinal Liénart and the strong support of Cardinal Cushing.'*

'The Pope', continued Tisserant, 'was very interested and remarked I had probably done the right thing in not going to the play.' Tisserant summed up the occasion as 'a very valuable time'.[5]

For Buchman this news was particularly welcome. It seemed like a light at the end of a dark tunnel. For ten years he had found it difficult to understand why his work was judged harshly by some authorities in the Roman Church. Non-Catholics in Moral Re-Armament had begun to understand the Church better and to realise that in naively insisting on their own ideas and methods they had at times been offensive. This had stopped but it had seemed to make little difference. It was not, in fact, till some years after Buchman's death that it became clear that Tisserant's report was the beginning of a new situation. The ecumenical spirit of the Vatican Council had still to do its work, and personal contacts with Cardinal Ottaviani, the head of the Holy Office at the time of its warning, were nearly ten years ahead. Gabriel Marcel reported that Ottaviani then said, 'There was once a misunderstanding, but that is all over.'[6]

Two weeks after receiving news of Tisserant's action in Rome, Buchman was asked by Konrad Adenauer to meet him in Los Angeles where he was being given an honorary degree by the University of California. The previous December Buchman had had a mock exchange of letters with the Chancellor's eighteenth grandchild, Sven-Georg, the first son of Georg Adenauer. Buchman had written to the three-month-old baby how much he disagreed with Krushchev's statement that the grandchildren of today's statesmen would be Communists. A long letter of news from all around the world followed to support his contention that those children would be Christian revolutionaries who would be changing the Communists. He was amused by the reply which arrived by return: 'Dear kind Uncle Frank,

---

* Cardinal Achille Liénart had remained a faithful friend of Moral Re-Armament since his visit to Caux in 1946, occasioned by what he had seen take place in industry in his diocese of Lille, and once described Moral Re-Armament as 'a crack of the whip to Christians who have forgotten their mission.' (Arnold Lunn: *Catholics and MRA*, unpublished memorandum, September 1953.) Cardinal Cushing of Boston had given many indications of his support. He wrote to Eugene von Teuber at this time, 'I myself and many others have been inspired by Catholics and non-Catholics who are affiliated with this movement . . . MRA does a tremendous amount of good. I don't know of any Catholic who was ever identified with it who did not become a better Catholic . . . Keep up the good fight: you are on the side of the angels.' (Cushing to von Teuber, 12 November 1960.)

'Thank you very much, also on behalf of my parents and my grand-father, for your kind and touching letter which I got today. It is the first letter of my young life and because of its importance, I shall want to keep it safe.

'I am very well, only sometimes at night when I get hungry I have to cry for an hour or so.

'I know my parents follow your work with great interest and we thank you for all the trouble you take and the help you are giving our world. My parents and I send you in America our best greetings for Christmas and the New Year, but most of all we wish you and those working with you health, success and happiness in the year ahead.

'So thank you again very much for your kind letter. Very many loving greetings from your friend, Sven-Georg Adenauer.'[7]

An echo from this correspondence can be seen in an article which the Chancellor agreed to have published in the *New York Journal-American*[8] prior to his visit to America. It was not a literary masterpiece, being a summary of his many previous messages to Buchman and public state-ments about Moral Re-Armament. However, he commented that, for his part, he was 'convinced that Krushchev's grandchildren will not be Communists', and paid unstinted tribute to Buchman's own contribution to the rehabilitation of Germany after the war, to his work for peace over the fifteen post-war years and the continuing need of his message in the years ahead. 'At this time of confusion in Europe we need, and especially in divided Germany, an ideology that brings clarity and moral power into the shaping of international relations,' he began. 'A nation with an ideology is always on the offensive. A nation without an ideology is self-satisfied and dead.' 'Begin with yourself – that, in my opinion, is the basic challenge of MRA,' he concluded. 'May this challenge ring out far and wide across the whole world and into all nations.'

Buchman sat with the Chancellor's party at the degree ceremony and attended three other occasions where Adenauer spoke, including a small luncheon on 19 March. At the civic dinner the Chancellor said to Buchman, 'I must tell you how much I value you and your work. It is absolutely essential for the peace of the world.'[9]

Buchman was now finding it increasingly difficult to move about. He was generally moved in a wheelchair, his strength was strictly limited, and his eyesight continuing to fail. On the way to consult a Tucson eye specialist, his companions noticed that he was striving to distinguish the mountains, trees and buildings. Waiting in the consulting room he sat eager, alert, testing his vision on the crack of light coming through the door of the dimly lit room and the lamp on the doctor's desk. He had brought a book for him, already inscribed, 'To Dr Sherwood Burr, who is helping me to see again, with gratitude.'

As Burr examined him, he asked, 'Where do you come from?'

'Pennsburg, Pennsylvania,' said Buchman.

'Do the people back home know how famous you are?'

'Oh, no,' chuckled Buchman.

'What do you see on the screen?'

'Nothing.' A pause. 'I can just make out a patch of light.'

On the screen was a huge 'E'. A lens enabled him to see it. But nothing could help him to make out anything smaller, despite the specialist's patient experiments and Buchman's concentrated efforts.

'How long has it been since you were able to read?'

'About a year.'

Burr straightened up and looked down at Buchman. 'Doctor,' he said slowly, 'I am afraid that there is no optical device now made that can improve your sight.'

'You mean there is no hope. I suppose this will lead to total blindness?'

'That is the sensible way of looking at it,' said Burr, 'but you may keep what you have, as long as you need it; and only the Lord knows how long you will need it, and He doesn't speak.'

'Yes, that's right, only the Lord knows.' Buchman smiled. 'He doesn't speak . . . but we must get Him to speak.' Then he handed Burr the book with its inscription.

In the same buoyant spirit he was gathering his team, 150 strong, to accompany him on what proved to be his last journey across the Atlantic. He invited a number of his American colleagues to go with him, each with a personal letter.

On 1 April he left Tucson, saying that the two winters he had spent there were among the happiest of his life. During the last week the house was thronged with friends of the most varied kind. A building contractor and his partner – one of the wives came from Italy – prepared a Neapolitan farewell supper of vast proportions in the kitchen. The guests included city, county and business officials, the ice-cream supplier with his family, a banker, overseas students; all sides of the city's life seemed to be there.

Buchman, however, was not looking back. 'We need something new, something absolutely new,' he said to those setting out with him. 'May the grace of God rest upon us to enable us to be different without end – constantly renewed. We are being lifted into spheres we have not worked in up to now. Everything must be different. Our nations must be different.

'Are we ready for the ideological battle? No, we are not. We have done a little, but we need to do much more.'[10]

FINDING TIME TO DIE

As the *SS America* moved down the Hudson River past the glittering skyscrapers Buchman told his party of twenty-four, 'During this journey we will reach every person on board.' Something like that happened, although he himself seldom left his cabin. The purser put on the film *The Crowning Experience* twice because of public demand. The captain gave a reception for the party, and the head of the National Maritime Union on board asked them to speak to a special union meeting at ten o'clock one night. The meeting-place was packed, and after the agreed hour of speaking was over the audience called for more. Some were up talking till three in the morning. One burly man from the engine-room commented, 'That was the best union meeting we've ever had. The whole ship is talking about it. Every time I have a row at home I go to sea. A big row means Asia, a small one means the Caribbean. This was a medium-sized row. I decided to write the old woman tomorrow.'

Among Buchman's party was Eudocio Ravines from Peru. He had been the South American delegate to the Comintern, and responsible for bringing about the first popular-front government on the continent. He had been trained by Mao Tse-tung in what he called the 'Yenan Way' of Communist takeover which concentrated on exploiting the moral weaknesses of the bourgeois world.[1] Disillusioned with Communism he had then found a wider aim through Moral Re-Armament. When he, his wife and daughter spoke together to the shipboard union meeting, the audience, many from Cuba and Latin America, were thunderstruck. Buchman's cabin steward came to Ravines and said, 'I'm also from Peru. My uncle put you in prison. Tell me what has changed you.' When Buchman offered a tip at the voyage's end, the steward refused it. 'You don't owe me anything,' he said, and added to a bystander, 'That man Frank Buchman is a marvel. Three or four men like him would turn the world upside down.'

Passing through Paris at the time of the abortive Summit Conference of May 1960 Buchman entertained General Speidel, Commander of the Ground Forces of NATO. 'Our weakest point in NATO is the ideological sphere,' the General said. 'We have done almost nothing. . . Moral

Re-Armament has been pioneering what Europe really needs to do to reach out positively to other continents.' He instanced the action of the German miners who had taken their play *Hoffnung* not only to Britain, France and Italy, but as well to Cyprus, Kerala and Tokyo. 'That is the type of initiative that NATO is incapable of, but it must be done if freedom is to grow in the world,' Speidel said.[2]

The Chief of Police in Paris gave a deferential bow on being introduced to Buchman at a reception. 'Ah,' said Buchman, 'we are colleagues.' And out of a pocket he fished a card which stated, much to the Parisian's amusement, that Buchman was 'Hon. Sheriff of the City of Tucson, Arizona'.

During these months Buchman was increasingly confined to bed, whether in Paris, Caux, London, Milan or Rome, but his mind was constantly at work on how to meet the demands for manpower which were confronting him from every continent. His imaginative planning would have been remarkable in a much younger man. Some of the revolutionary Japanese youth, members of the Zengakuren organisation whose demonstrations in spring 1960 had prevented President Eisenhower's visit to Japan,* had subsequently been affected by Moral Re-Armament. Buchman invited them to Caux and encouraged them to write a play, *The Tiger*, which went through Europe and, in America, was brought to the former President's attention. Eisenhower listened to their story for an hour. 'This is the last act of the June riots', he said, 'and it has a happy ending.'

Leaders in Brazil, Peru, Argentina and other Latin American countries invited these Japanese to their countries and, during the last months of his life, Buchman sent them and a group from thirty other nations to South America. In Manaus, far up the Amazon River in Brazil, ninety thousand turned out one evening to see *The Tiger*. In Recife, at the heart of the poverty-racked North-East, *Fidelistas* flocked to the performances. Some changed, and were instrumental in diminishing the graft, exploitation, drunkenness and corruption in the port.

The air forces of Brazil and Peru flew the whole party into remote areas. North American Indians, headed by Chief Walking Buffalo in his ninetieth year, went to meet their South American brothers, fulfilling a promise made to Buchman a year previously in Mackinac. In Cuzco, where thirty years before Buchman had seen the students in revolt, thousands turned out to see *The Tiger* and hear the Indians. In Macchu Piccu, the 'lost city' of the Incas, twenty-five thousand Indians poured in from the countryside to meet them and to see the play, perched in huge masses on the gigantic hillsides of the natural amphitheatre.

* The refusal of the Seinendan to join in the riots, together with the support of Social Democrats led by Senator Kato, did much to hold the nation together at this time. (cf. Entwistle, *Japan's Decisive Decade*, pp. 181–6.)

One of those who came to Caux that summer was Dr Bernardus Kaelin, who had from 1947 till the previous year been Abbot Primate of the Benedictine Order. He had come because during the previous winter he had seen the effect of *Hoffnung* in a number of Catholic schools in Switzerland. After several days he asked to be allowed to speak and issued his speech to the press. 'Moral Re-Armament', he began, 'can win all men because its standards are universally valid. It is not a religion nor a substitute for religion. It is not a sect. It has four mighty pillars upon which human living must be based. Every man must accept these ideas if he is honest with himself.'

Abbot Kaelin went on to say that 'Benedict also wants the four standards of absolute honesty, purity, unselfishness and love' and 'enjoins the abbot and the monk really to shape their lives according to the guidance of God'. 'There are so many people who are very familiar with religion, but for whom it is unemployed capital,' he added. 'That is why it is such a great satisfaction to me that so many people in Moral Re-Armament live out their ideology seriously and consistently . . . During the serious world situation of the fifth and sixth centuries, Benedict taught through his life and his rule what nations must do in order to become and remain sound. So, by the eleventh century, he had become a founder of Western civilization. I mention this fact to encourage Moral Re-Armament today . . . It is a new way designed to forestall a false ideology.'[3]

Buchman warmed greatly to the Abbot's personality and vision. He saw in him many of the qualities he had loved in B. H. Streeter twenty-five years before. 'He is a great-hearted prelate, forthright and a fighter,' he wrote to Father Ling.[4] Kaelin accompanied him to St Gallen when the Cantonal Government gave a dinner reception for him there in October, and later joined Buchman in Italy, after the ancestral town of the Buchmans, Bischofszell, had given Buchman a similar welcome.

With the exception of three weeks at Caux over Christmas, Buchman spent the next four months in Italy. He took the plays he had been using in Switzerland, Howard's *The Hurricane* and *The Ladder*, together with the film *Men of Brazil*, to Milan. The response was great, not least in the suburb of Sesto San Giovanni. Abbot Kaelin, like Streeter long before, was delighted at being received in the homes of Communist workers – old friends from previous Moral Re-Armament visits – and having the fresh joy of bringing individuals back to God and the Church. Receiving over Christmas a caution from the Holy Office he obediently stopped speaking in public about Moral Re-Armament, but in November travelled to Rome to tell his many friends, among them Cardinals Tisserant and Bea, of his experiences.

Buchman was unusually active in his three weeks at Caux that Christmas. He took the morning meetings on 20 and 21 December, as well as giving tea-parties for the main guests. 'Here we had a powerful Christmas Day,' he wrote to a friend in America. 'The Greeks and the Turks from Cyprus brought messages from Archbishop Makarios and Dr Kuçuk.* An African, who when he was here earlier was so possessed with hatred of the white man that he could not finish a speech from the platform, stood up a free man ready to take a very responsible position in his country.'⁵ He only spent eight of the twenty-one days entirely in bed, and appeared in the entrance hall to greet his main guests and talked with many over meals.

After Caux, Buchman and a party of over thirty returned to Rome. He stayed till 6 March, and it was again a busy time, combining many individual meetings with private showings of the film of *The Crowning Experience*. Among his visitors were the widow of Signor Marconi, and the widow and daughter of former Prime Minister de Gasperi. On 7 February Don Luigi Sturzo's physician came to tea and said how much his patient had spoken of Buchman's work during his last weeks, referring to it as 'fire from heaven'.** Buchman prepared a dossier at Cardinal Tisserant's request, and entertained a number of bishops including Archbishop Gregorius who brought the latest news from Kerala. One afternoon he also gave tea to Father Damboriena, the man who in 1957 had written the articles in the *Civiltà Cattolica* and *Monitor Ecclesiasticus* which had spread the more fantastic misconceptions about his work.

On his return to Caux Buchman received news of successful premieres of *The Crowning Experience* in Rome and Milan. A Milan critic had written, 'It transcends the theatre. A film of the greatest moral and spiritual force ever to come out of the industry.'⁶ This exactly confirmed Buchman's own view of the film, which did not raise his opinion of the press or his colleagues in America and Britain where commercial audiences were less enthusiastic.

Throughout all this year Buchman was possessed with a tremendous sense of urgency. It was partly caused by the advances which he believed world Communism to be making – though he told his colleagues that they would live to see Communism a spent force. On occasion – particularly in America where to be 'against Communism' seemed to him many people's cheap way of avoiding the need to face their own sins – he would forbid his team even to mention the word. He always maintained that the message of Moral Re-Armament would have been necessary if Communism had never existed, and would still be needed if it vanished from the earth. His

---

* President and Vice-President respectively. In 1960, in recognition of MRA's help, they had jointly sent the first flag of independent Cyprus to Buchman at Caux.

** Sturzo, in old age, drew encouragement from Moral Re-Armament. When he heard from Irène and Victor Laure how they had found faith in God, he remarked, 'I thank God that I have found allies in the fight for the moral re-armament of the world.' His last book was entitled *Riarmo morale*.

chief concern now, therefore, was with what he saw as the growing decadence in nations, and particularly among their leaders.

This sense of urgency caused him to produce three major public pronouncements in three months that summer. All were reproduced in dozens of newspapers throughout the world, as full-page paid advertisements. He chafed at what he regarded as a press boycott, and felt that this was the only way to get his message through.

The first of Buchman's three statements, in April 1961, was headed 'All the Moral Fences are Down'. It had been stimulated by a talk, at which I was present, between him and Sir Richard Livingstone, a one-time Vice-Chancellor of Oxford University. Livingstone had said to him, 'When you and I were young there were moral fences. We did not always keep to them, but we always knew when we had crossed them. Today all the fences are down.' Buchman gave vivid instances of how people all over the world were starting to rebuild the moral foundations of their nations by starting with themselves. He ended by quoting the answer of an American admiral when queried by cynical colleagues why he had three times attended assemblies of Moral Re-Armament. 'I learned', the admiral had said, 'what an ideology means – to start doing what we should have been doing all along and to do it all day, every day, for the rest of our lives.'

Solid Rock and Shifting Sand, in May, was a report of a widespread series of initiatives. Beginning with what *El País* of Montevideo described as 'the greatest ideological offensive undertaken on the Latin American Continent', led by the Japanese play *The Tiger*, he ranged through similar campaigns in Asian and African countries and concluded with his own challenge, 'The world is on the knife-edge of decision. We must go all out to save our nations.'

On 4 June 1961 he gave what turned out to be his final call – an autobiography and testament in one, entitled *Brave Men Choose*. It concluded: 'This is the word of a man on his eighty-third birthday who has spent a long life up and down the world, meeting and knowing men, who has seen the development of two materialist ideologies and the devastation of two world wars, the retreat of freedom and now the advance of a mighty answer . . . There is no neutrality in the battle between good and evil. No nation can be saved on the cheap. It will take the best of our lives and the flower of our nations to save humanity. If we go all out for God we will win.'[7]

Buchman was addressing his challenge not only to the world at large, but also to himself and his closest friends. 'I feel keenly the crucial point we have reached in our lives personally and as a force,' he wrote to two of them. 'We face a desperate moment in the world and we cannot go on living as we have lived.'[8] More particularly, the unease he had felt for some years about some of his longest-standing colleagues came to a head. He was in an agony of spirit at what he regarded as his failure to transmit to them the depth of his own experience. Would they be able to tackle the future without him, a situation which could not now be long delayed?

His unease, at this point, focussed on his American colleagues, although it might equally well have been upon the British, Swiss or other national groups, as it had at different times. 'How terribly they have missed God's truth, those Americans who are the apple of my eye,' he dictated early on 18 July. 'I felt this so strongly this morning that I hoped to come and tell you this, but I am weary.' He got Howard to read these words to a meeting of all his American colleagues in Caux that afternoon. 'But God marches on', he added, 'and all those who know the truth shall be made free. It is my consummate wish for you all.'

The meeting was one of a series which took place every afternoon for a month. Garrett Stearly writes that they were 'an endeavour by every possible means to engender in his closest colleagues a more profound and liberating experience of the Holy Spirit. Buchman showed himself thoroughly dissatisfied with our quality of leadership, finding us move-ment-minded, imitative of himself rather than God-led, encased in an ideological form instead of having freedom to follow the Spirit's new ways . . . Daily he tried to bring alive the inward experience of Christ which he had seen in the past in us.'

Buchman's aim was impeccable, but it is doubtful whether repeated meetings were the most effective method of remedying the situation, particularly as Buchman was often too weak to be there himself and had to relay his thinking and his criticisms at second hand. Some of these were inaccurate and others became distorted in transmission. Many of his old friends were left bewildered. In private, when individuals got through to him, Buchman was as helpful as ever. The Stearlys were two of those who went and talked it out with him. They told him of something which had been stopping their spiritual effectiveness. 'Immediately a living affection was reborn.' Others tried but found him too weak to receive them.

The assembly, meanwhile, was hurtling on at its usual pace. By mid-July the six Buddhist abbots who had been sent by the Presiding Abbots' Association of Burma to celebrate the birthday of the man who, they said, 'comes only once in a thousand years', had flown back home. A special plane arrived from South America, and 129 people returned there to reinforce that campaign. Delegations came from Laos and Kenya, and special planes and trains arrived from around Europe. A cable had been received from Prime Minister Kishi, on behalf of a number of Japanese leaders in various fields, announcing their intention to 'create this year an MRA Asian Centre in Odawara where the statesmen of East and West can meet and develop a strategy to save our continents'.[9] The Prime

Minister also announced that he would visit Caux in August, as did Prime Minister U Nu of Burma.

Buchman was forced to spend almost the whole of the summer in bed, coming from his room as often as he could to greet his guests or to see them in his sitting-room. He would wake early and plan for them, or talk over the news with colleagues, decide on action to be taken, have telegrams read to him, and always, morning and evening, asked for the Bible. 'I'm an old horse', he told some guests cheerfully one day, 'and there isn't much left of me. My right side is paralysed and I can't be left alone. I need someone with me all the time. It's an awful job. But I can still keep at it!'

In late July he decided that he needed a break from Caux. Undoubtedly, what he regarded as the unsuccessful time with his American colleagues was still weighing heavily with him. He said to Campbell, 'We must leave these people here and withdraw to a place where we can think through what we are going to do next.' And he reflected to someone else, 'Perhaps I have come to the end of my usefulness for the Group.' But meanwhile the planning for Kishi's and U Nu's visits was at the front of his thinking. Irène Laure, who saw him several times, found his mind as sharp and forward-looking as ever.

On 22 July he wrote to Maria Luz, the daughter of his first host, thirty-three years before, at the Waldlust Hotel in Freudenstadt: 'My heart turns to Freudenstadt and I plan to visit you very shortly. I am very tired and need a real rest, and I want to come back to the old haunts which are always such a fragrant memory. There would be four of us in the party.

'I would like a room with that wonderful view as I have to spend all day resting, and someone has to be on call in the next room all the time.

'What a joy it will be to be with you again.'

On his last morning in Caux he invited a number of friends to his sitting-room. To one he wrote, 'I am going away, tired out, and must have this rest, but God has been very good. I will see you at 2.45 to say goodbye.'

A vase of roses stood on the table beside him, and as each came in he or she was given one. He took his leave, encouraging them in what they were doing – Muriel Smith and Ann Buckles, one of the Swiss who cooked in his kitchen, two friends just arrived from America, Peter and Doë Howard, and a dozen others who would carry forward the daily programme with the thousand guests in Caux. Then, punctual as ever, he left for Freudenstadt.

The wide vistas of countryside, the healthy air of the pine forest, the sense of a leading hand that had brought him back to Freudenstadt, began their refreshing work. Early on the second morning he had the thoughts: 'This is where God first talked to you about the picture of the world's problems. You will be mightily used. First you must get well.'

Two days' rest, and then on the third day the first guest arrived – Prince Richard of Hesse, driving through to spend the weekend at Caux. That morning Buchman had been awake at three. To Paul Campbell he had dictated thoughts that came to him: 'Here God first spoke to you. He will speak again. Make this a centre for the world work. Here you will lay down your life and die. You can see large vistas from here. All Germany will rise up. The winter plans will develop. These three days you are marking time. Prince Richard will be a great help. This *Frank Buchmanweg* will be a marking point to the whole world. People will come here in droves.'

The *Frank Buchmanweg* was the path leading up from the Waldlust Hotel into the forest, along which he had walked in 1938 when he had the thought of a 'moral and spiritual re-armament for all nations'. It had been officially named on 17 April 1956 by the Mayor and City Council of Freudenstadt. Buchman had not set foot upon it since that May day in 1938. On 4 August, a glorious summer day, Miss Luz sent him a message that the weather was so perfect he must not miss the sunshine. He came down, to be greeted unexpectedly from a neighbouring lunch table by the Governor of East Pakistan, General Azam Khan, and his Ambassador from Bonn. The Governor wanted to thank him for what he had done for his country, and Buchman gave him a book.

Buchman was pushed the length of the *Frank Buchmanweg* in his wheelchair and, though he could not read, looked at the signs that mark it for the visitor. Happy but tired he returned to his room. The next day he worked on a message to Caux, and had read to him a letter from Howard there: ' "His purposes will ripen fast, Unfolding every hour." Yesterday as some of us were telling the latest news to our guests at table, an overwhelming sense of the marvel of what God is doing in the world shook me to my boots. It is an amazing thing to have the chance of living at this time in history and to be concerned with what God is doing through the nations.

'It is joyful to hear your voice so strong and clear on the telephone and I do hope the food and air and strength of the place you are in is refreshing you mightily.'

Buchman was thinking particularly of Kishi's visit to Caux to discuss the Japanese Moral Re-Armament assembly centre. On the morning of Sunday 6 August he felt it urgent to send a cable to Kishi giving him a wide perspective on his visit to Europe. He told him of plans being made for him to meet British leaders in London, and offered him the hospitality of 45 Berkeley Square. He quoted a letter from Eisenhower congratulating the Japanese with *The Tiger* on their 'splendid crusade', and told him that Attorney-General Robert Kennedy had received members of the cast on his visit to Lima. Then he invited Kishi to bring all his party to Caux with him.

The cable was discussed with Howard in Caux by telephone and dispatched. Buchman was happy in his mind, but weary. 'How are my Americans?' was his final question. The thought that he might die in Freudenstadt had not weighed on him or those with him. There was no sense of imminence. Then at 2 pm he had a sharp pain in his chest. The local specialist, who came immediately, turned out to have paid a visit to Caux on his vacation a few days earlier. He eased the pain. From time to time Buchman became unconscious, but each time he recovered consciousness he wanted to know what news had come in. It was his first question the next morning after a restless night. That afternoon came a further shock, and the doctor's verdict was 'deadly serious'. Friends around the world were notified. Prince Richard came from Kronberg, Howard started immediately from Caux.

As Buchman hovered between life and death his favourite passages from the Bible were read. When Prince Richard read Psalm 23, Buchman caught the sound of his voice and smiled. Then not long after he slipped into complete unconsciousness. At 9.45 in the evening the last breath left him like a sigh.

There was shock and sorrow in the hotel, as in the world beyond. The Luz family, the hotel staff, friends from the town bearing a profusion of roses and garden flowers, filed into the room for a last farewell. One of the hotel maids who had looked after his bedroom was found on her knees beside his bed, and she told of the brief conversation with him which had made her life different.

On Friday 11 August the town of Freudenstadt gave itself to the memory of Buchman. It was host to the hundreds from many countries who poured in, to the official representatives of the German federal and provincial governments, to the black-uniformed Ruhr miners who stood as a guard of honour around the coffin below the 14th-century crucifix in the church. They flocked to the church service in the morning and the public meeting in the Kursaal in the afternoon, and as evening began to fall many walked along the *Frank Buchmanweg*.

During the last morning of his life, as Buchman lay between two worlds, he took half an hour, interrupted by moments of pain, to say, 'I want Britain to be governed by men governed by God. I want to see the world governed by men governed by God. Why not let God run the whole world?'

ASSESSMENTS

Buchman's funeral service took place in Allentown and he was buried in the quiet family plot beside his parents. The occasion brought people from many countries, as had his other visits home through the years. With exceptions like David Miller, the editor of the *Morning Call*, and his class-mates Arthur Keller and Nimson Eckhart, his fellow townsfolk had often not known what to make of the people he used to bring home – among them strange exotic creatures clothed in the national costumes of Switzerland, India or Japan for some public occasion. His college, Muhlenberg, had given him an honorary doctorate in his late forties, but he was 80 before he was thought worthy of the Muhlenberg 'Mule' which was reserved for those considered to have rendered really distinguished service to the community. Now, however, the people of Allentown packed the church and an adjacent hall for the service.

The messages to his funeral, no less than those who attended it, showed the volume and variety of his friendships. The boy who sat next to him at high school, the hall porter in Utrecht to whom he gave a book in 1936, the captain of the ship which took him to Australia in 1956, and the spokesmen of the Stoney Indians who cabled, 'The whole world is an orphan as we felt when we heard of his death', were among the thousands who sent cables and letters. There were messages from Carl Hambro, Adenauer, Schuman, U Nu, Kishi, the King of Morocco, the rival chiefs of the Lulua and Baluba tribes of the Congo, and the President and Vice-President of Cyprus. Saragat expressed 'the deep sorrow of the Italian Social Democrats and my family', and former President René Coty of France called Buchman 'the perfect apostle of moral revolution'. The hundreds of newspaper obituaries varied from generous appreciation through measured comment to Driberg's article which concluded that history would remember him, if at all, 'by his egregious statement, "I thank God for a man like Adolf Hitler"'.[1]

Buchman's will was as simple as his possessions. He only owned the title of his family home in Allentown and two bank accounts: a personal one containing a few hundred dollars which he had not had time to give away, and another holding some thousands given to him on his recent birthday to be used, at his discretion, for Moral Re-Armament. His will read: 'I wish I had silver and gold for each one, but since my resources are so strictly limited, I give, devise and bequeath all my estate, whatsoever and wheresoever it may be, unto "Moral Re-Armament" absolutely. There are many I should like to have included in a will like this, but I want all to feel they have a share as they partake of the priceless boon which has come to them and to me through the Oxford Group and Moral Re-Armament. They can best perpetuate this gift by carrying forward a philosophy that is adequate for a world crisis and that will, at last, bring the nations to the long-looked-for Golden Age ushered in by the greatest revolution of all time whereby the Cross of Christ shall transform the world.'

It was his final declaration: the Oxford Group and Moral Re-Armament were not his creations, but God's gift to him and everyone prepared to receive them; they were, and must remain, God's property, not organisations but instruments of the Holy Spirit; he relied on those he left behind to be sensitive enough to God's spirit to find His plan for each new situation. Behind it was the same vision – faith-filled, optimistic, at times over-optimistic – which had animated him all his life.

How is one to describe Frank Buchman two decades and more after his death? Many referred to him as a statesman, a complete misnomer if the Oxford Dictionary definition – 'a person skilled or taking a leading part in the management of state affairs' – is accurate. Yet Kishi, in his last message, called him 'one of Asia's great statesmen', an even more striking description in view of the very limited time he spent in Asia, but one which illustrates the sense in which the word could justly be used. For, while never managing state affairs, Buchman was undoubtedly a catalyst of reconciliation between the states of Asia as he was elsewhere.

Some of his closer colleagues – and some like Brother Roger of Taizé who never met him – have spoken of him as a saint. Donald Attwater in his introduction to *The Penguin Dictionary of Saints* writes, 'A saint is not faultless: he does not always think or behave well or wisely: one who has occasion to oppose him is not always wrong or foolish . . . He, or she, is canonized because his personal daily life was lived, not merely well, but at an heroic level of Christian faithfulness and integrity . . .'[2] If such heroic living is a qualification, it is hard to deny Buchman some degree of sainthood – a notion, incidentally, which he would not only have denied but rejected, as it would tend to set him apart and contradict his contention that the way he tried to live was merely 'normal living', open to anyone. For a man trying to change the world the appellation would, as Dietmar Lamprecht points out in his biography of St Francis, carry a double disadvantage: 'Just as one can avoid the challenge of an exemplary

[531]

life by belittling it, seeking weaknesses and finally consoling oneself by saying "it is really nothing special",' he writes, 'so too can one turn from the call of a saint by raising him to something extraordinary, up among the altars and the stained-glass windows, blunting the challenge of his life by declaring it to be unattainable.'[3]

Personally, I prefer to think of Buchman as a prophet set in an apocalyptic age, an era when God is being pushed into a private ghetto and where moral standards are slipping, a time when civilisations show signs of disintegration and the world itself feels in danger of extinction.

Like prophets through the ages he brought to his day a diagnosis which cut across contemporary fashion. Not all his prophecies of doom or of deliverance have been fulfilled, but his thought had an accuracy and a universality about it which pierced through to people of all kinds in every continent. He said little that was new, but he made old forgotten truths suddenly seem relevant to successive generations. For example, Dr Karl Wick, editor of the Swiss daily *Vaterland*, wrote that he had 'brought silence out of the monastery into the home, the marketplace and the board room.'[4]

In answering my startled enquiry whether he *really* thought, as he had said to me, that 'Buchman was a turning-point in the history of the modern world', Cardinal König* wrote: 'In the last century, there was a feeling among intellectuals that we could build a better world without God. Then came the First World War, and many felt that many things had gone wrong. Buchman was among them, and he began to think what could be done. His great idea was to show that the teaching of Jesus Christ is not just a private affair but has the great force to change the whole structure of the social orders of economics, of political ideas, if we combine the changing of structures with a change of heart. In that sense he opened a completely new approach to religion, to the teachings of Jesus Christ, and to the life of modern man.'[5]

König, who never met Buchman, based his assessment on his own observations in recent years: 'Wherever Moral Re-Armament is active there emerges a new world – in small circles first, but the activity shows how great the force is . . . If I consider the information which comes to me from all over the world, I see changes which are visible and social effects which are tangible. This must come from the faith of the man who was at the beginning, otherwise I could not explain what has happened since in so many places. "By their fruits you shall know them." From the fruit you go back to the root.'[6]

* Cardinal Franz König, Archbishop of Vienna, is a leading authority on Eastern Europe and on the relationship of Christianity to other faiths. According to Mary Craig (*Man from a Far Country*, Hodder and Stoughton, 1979, p. 175), he was the general choice for Pope at one point during the Conclave of October 1978, but declined.

It is too early to come to any final conclusion about Buchman's place in history, but König's observations illustrate what was, perhaps, his greatest achievement – the creation of a world-wide network of people committed to carry on the same work, 'a group of people', in the words of the former Archbishop of York, Lord Blanch, 'who will go anywhere and do anything if they are called by God to do it'.[7]

Of the multitudes whom Buchman reached in one way or another during his life, many reacted hostilely or were indifferent. A very large number, however, were influenced for good in at least some particular, and often the effect was permanent. A Dutch academic whom I recently met by chance is typical. When he heard Buchman's name, he exclaimed, 'He completely changed my life when I was nineteen. I have not kept up listening to God each day, but a foundation was laid and it has always remained.' Thousands went further and pledged themselves to work together to alter the moral and spiritual climate of the world. It is this dedicated fellowship which men like König and Blanch have observed in action.

At various times through his life many of those helped by Buchman gave up working closely with him, sometimes abandoning some of the principles he advocated but more often going on to apply what they had learnt in their individual careers, lay or ecclesiastical, and in some cases creating such 'spin-offs' as Alcoholics Anonymous, Shoemaker's Faith-at-Work Movement and dozens of others which could be cited. This was also to happen after his death, and more particularly after the death of his successor, Peter Howard – when, incidentally, a number of premature obituaries of Moral Re-Armament appeared in the press.

Buchman would say at different times that he wanted 'all my fine horses to run all out together, neck and neck'. At breakfast one morning in 1960 he added, 'When I am gone, the work will be run by a cabinet of like-minded friends around the world. But you are not ready for that yet. First there will be one man.' So it turned out. In the years since Howard's untimely death in 1965, after considerable travail, that collective leadership has come into being. Under its informal direction all are thrown back onto their independent relationship with God, as Buchman had always intended, since there is no single human authority to whom to refer. Whether or not Buchman's aims are carried actively through into the next century will depend on whether all who benefited from his life – a far wider cross-section of humanity than those who ever acknowledged their debt – run their lives and institutions in the spirit of which, in the last year of his life, he spoke to Jean Rey, the President of the European Commission.

Rey, a frequent visitor to Caux, was congratulating Buchman on various achievements which he had observed and attributed to his influence. 'You must feel very proud of all this,' he said.[8]

'I don't feel that way at all,' Buchman replied. 'I have had nothing to do with it. God does everything. I only obey and do what He says.'

It was a reassertion of his earlier estimate of his life, 'I have been wonderfully led to those who were ready.'

SOURCE REFERENCES

NOTE ON SOURCE REFERENCES

Where references in the following list are attributed to Buchman they come from the book of his speeches, *Remaking the World* (Blandford, 1961). Quotes from Buchman which are not attributed were noted by friends at the time or in later recollections.

Dr Morris H. Martin, who was Buchman's secretary for the last twenty-five years of his life, has made available to me an unpublished biography in various drafts, as well as his private diaries for certain years and various occasional records of particular journeys or events. These are referred to as 'Martin MSS', 'Martin diaries' and 'Martin account' respectively.

The other main sources, apart from the various books and unpublished autobiographies hereunder noted, are interviews with people who knew Frank Buchman, conducted by Ailsa Hamilton, Graham Turner, Pierre Spoerri or the author.

Chapter 2

1   The City Archives Department of St Gallen states: 'In spite of the fact that the name of both is Buchman and that both were citizens of Bischofszell, we do not know whether the two families were really related to each other or not. The descendants of Bibliander who kept the family name seem to have disappeared at the end of the sixteenth century' (letter to author, 25 May 1983).
2   The name was variously spelt Greenwald, Greenawalt, Greenwalt. As Buchman always used the last, this version is adopted here.
3   William F. Day, Sellersville, Pennsylvania; note dated 4 August 1927.
4   Mrs Flora Longehacker, 28 November 1933.
5   Press cutting, undated, probably 29 December 1897.
6   William F. Day.
7   Buchman to mother, 14 July 1898.
8   ibid., 12 July 1898.
9   ibid., 14 July 1898.

10   Francis Bacon: *Essays*, VIII, 'Of Marriage and Single Life' (Everyman's Library), p. 22.
11   Bishop Joseph Butler, *Analogy of Religion* (London, 1736).

Chapter 3

1   Buchman to mother, 30 October 1899.
2   ibid., undated (early November 1899).
3   ibid., 8 February 1900.
4   ibid., 4 March 1900.
5   Buchman to parents, 28 October 1899.
6   ibid., 29 October 1899.
7   Buchman to mother, 30 October 1899.
8   ibid., 31 October 1899.
9   ibid., undated (early November 1899).
10   Buchman to parents, 8 November 1899.
11   ibid., September and October 1899.
12   ibid., 12 November 1899.
13   ibid., 8 February 1900.
14   ibid., undated (probably 1899).
15   ibid., 'First Monday in Lent', 1901.
16   ibid.
17   Buchman to mother, 25 January 1901.
18   ibid., October 1899 and 15 November 1899.
19   Buchman to parents, 18 March 1901.
20   Buchman to mother, (undated).
21   Buchman to parents, undated, (early 1901).
22   ibid., 18 March 1901.
23   Buchman to parents, 18 March 1901.
24   ibid., (undated) November 1901.
25   ibid., 1 and 6 July 1901.
26   See A. J. Russell: *For Sinners Only* (Hodder & Stoughton, 1932), pp. 148–50.
27   Buchman to parents, 10 December 1901.
28   ibid., 28 January 1902.
29   Buchman to parents, 15 October 1902.
30   ibid.
31   Quoted in Martin MSS. For her adventurous life see Genevieve Caulfeild: *The Kingdom Within* (Hodder and Stoughton, 1961).
32   Edith Randall to Buchman, 21 December 1910.
33   Quoted in Martin MSS.
34   Interview with Buchman in *Daily Item*, Allentown, 7 February 1906.
35   Letter to Buchman datelined Philadelphia, 2 June 1905, from the Board of Managers of the Inner Mission Society of the Evangelical Lutheran Church, signed by the President, the English Secretary and the German Secretary.

36 J. F. Ohl to Buchman, 15 August 1905.
37 Martin MSS.
38 'Some early recollections of Frank Buchman' by the Revd John D. Wood-cock (unpublished), p. 1.
39 *Daily Item*, Allentown, 7 February 1906.
40 'Hospice Incidents', report by Buchman, May 1906.
41 Buchman to Inner Mission Society of the Evangelical Lutheran Church, 8 October 1907.
42 Woodcock, p. 2.
43 Buchman to parents, June 1907.

Chapter 4

1 To Prince Richard of Hesse (Princess Sophie's nephew), July 1961.
2 Mrs Buchman to Buchman, 17 June 1908.
3 Account taken from Russell, and from Buchman's own verbal accounts in the author's hearing.
4 Buchman to J. F. Ohl, 27 July 1908.
5 Mrs Buchman to Buchman, 7 August 1908.
6 John Woodcock to Buchman, 3 June 1958.

Chapter 5

1 Woodcock, p. 2.
2 H. P. Anderson to J. M. Willard, 2 November 1908.
3 Irving L. Foster to Buchman, 21 December 1908.
4 Dr Mahlon Hellerich, when Archivist to the Lehigh Historical Association. Much of the information on Pennsylvania Dutch society used in this book has come from Dr Hellerich.
5 Mrs Buchman to Buchman, 23 February 1909.
6 Robert Reed, *North American Student*, April 1914.
7 Quoted by Mae Phyllis Kaplan in MA thesis at Pennsylvania State Graduate School, Department of Economics and Sociology, 1934, p. 109.
8 Buchman to Dan Buchman, 29 March 1909.
9 See President Sparks' report for 1911, when he put the YMCA membership at 1,287.
10 *North American Student*; first part of article by Robert Reed, second part by Lloyd C. Douglas.
11 For a fuller account of these events as related by Buchman, see Buchman, pp. 330–46.
12 *North American Student*.
13 Fred Lewis Pattee, *Recollections* (unpublished).
14 Quoted in George Stewart Jr: *The Life of Henry B. Wright* (Association Press, New York, 1925), p. 76.
15 William T. Ellis to Buchman, 5 April 1912.

16   Pattee.
17   Buchman to Hollis Wilbur, 12 September 1918.
18   Dr Schäfer to Buchman, (undated) 1911.
19   Buchman to Paul H. Krauss, 29 November 1911.
20   Buchman to H. W. Mitchell, a director of the Intercollegiate YMCA, sent with his report of the years 1912–13.
21   Edwin Sparks to Buchman, February/March 1912.
22   Mrs Edwin Sparks to Herman Hagedorn, 28 November 1933.
23   Buchman to Sparks, draft, on Canton Christian College paper (undated). It is not known if Buchman sent this letter. It would have been wholly in character had he done so.
24   Buchman's official report for 1914.
25   Kaplan, p. 193.
26   Martin MSS.
27   Buchman to Morgan Noyes, 19 October 1916.
28   Blair Buck to Herman Hagedorn, 9 December 1933.

Chapter 6

1   John R. Mott to Buchman, 21 April 1915. Buchman wrote accepting 23 April 1915.
2   *Chinese Recorder*, August 1916.
3   Buchman to E. C. Carter, 9 November 1915.
4   Buchman to John R. Mott, 10 November 1915.
5   Buchman to Sherwood Eddy, 27 March 1917.
6   K. T. Paul to E. C. Carter, date unknown. A subsequent letter from Carter to Buchman is dated 16 August 1915.
7   Quoted in Theophil Spoerri: *Dynamic Out of Silence* (Grosvenor, 1976), p. 79.
8   Bishop Pakenham-Walsh to Buchman, 3 July 1916.
9   See Russell, pp. 76–81.
10   Buchman to mother, 6 November 1915.
11   Buchman to Sherwood Eddy, early 1917.
12   Sherwood Eddy to Buchman, 13 January 1916.
13   George Lerrigo to Sherwood Eddy, March 1916.
14   W. W. Lockwood to Buchman, 7 June 1916.
15   Buchman to mother, 2 July 1915.
16   Buchman to Dan, 8 November 1915.
17   ibid. 13 November 1915.
18   Buchman at Kuling, July 1918 (see note 5, Chapter 7).
19   Notes by Edward Perry on Buchman's Lectures at Hartford Theological Seminary, November 1921–March 1922.
20   Howard Walter to Buchman, 26 December 1916.
21   Buchman to Douglas Mackenzie, February 1917.
22   George Paloczi-Horvath: *Emperor of the Blue Ants* (Secker and Warburg, 1962), p. 49.

23 Buchman to Dan, 27 September 1917.
24 Sherwood Day, Memorandum of 1933.
25 Howard Walter to Sherwood Eddy, 4 October 1917.
26 See Russell, pp. 70–75.
27 Buchman at Kuling, August 1918.
28 *Chinese Recorder*, September and November 1917, February and March 1918.
29 ibid., December 1917.
30 Buchman to Sherwood Eddy, 25 October 1917.
31 Buchman to parents, 25 October 1917.
32 Buchman to Sherwood Eddy, 20 November 1917.
33 Irving Harris: *The Breeze of the Spirit* (Seabury Press, 1978), pp. 2–6.
34 R. S. Sun, writing as instructed by Sun Yat-sen, to Buchman, 1 March 1918.
35 Hsu Ch'ien to Buchman, 29 April 1918.
36 ibid.
37 Emily Hahn: *The Soong Sisters* (Cedric Chivers, 1974), pp. 82–3.
38 Buchman to Hsu Ch'ien, 3 July 1918.
39 Sherwood Eddy to K. T. Paul (Martin MSS, April 1918).

Chapter 7

1 Buchman to E. G. Tewksbury, 21 June 1918.
2 Buchman to Harry Blackstone, 25 April 1918.
3 Buchman to E. G. Tewksbury, 18 July 1918.
4 Buchman to Mrs Harry Blackstone, 6 August 1918.
5 Quotations from Buchman and others at Kuling are taken from verbatim transcripts of the meetings.
6 Buchman to Bishop Logan Roots, 16 August 1918.
7 Letters in this paragraph quoted in Mrs Adams to Buchman, 23 August 1918.
8 Harry Blackstone to Bishop Roots, 24 August 1918.
9 From unpublished memorandum by Frances Roots Hadden, daughter of Bishop Roots.
10 Bishop Roots to Harry Blackstone, 30 August 1918.
11 Buchman to Harry Blackstone, 12 September 1918.
12 Harry Blackstone to Buchman, 18 September 1918.
13 Martin MSS.
14 Buchman to E. G. Tewksbury and Ruth Paxson, enclosed in letter to Harry Blackstone, 12 September 1918.
15 Buchman to Howard Walter, 12 September 1918.
16 ibid., 1 October 1918.
17 Buchman to Bishop Roots, 8 October 1918.
18 Buchman to Harry Blackstone, 18 October 1918.
19 Mrs Buchman to Buchman, 17 December 1917.
20 ibid., 27 June 1918.

21 Laura E. Heiner to Buchman, 29 July 1918.
22 Mrs Buchman to Buchman, 17 August 1918.
23 Buchman to mother, 23 August 1918.
24 ibid., 10 September 1918.
25 Buchman to Howard Walter, 1 October 1918.
26 Harry Blackstone to Buchman, foreshadowed in letter of 1 January 1924; confirmed in Maxwell Chaplin to Buchman, 20 April 1924.
27 Buchman to Harry Blackstone, 3 April 1924.
28 Bishop Roots to Buchman, 20 December 1942.
29 Hsu Ch'ien to Buchman, 26 February 1920.
30 Holly Hsu to Frances Roots Hadden, quoted in Hadden MS.
31 Arthur Holcome: *The Spirit of the Chinese Revolution*, The Lowell Institute Lectures 1930 (Knopf), p. 87 ff.
32 Buchman to Douglas Mackenzie, 21 May 1919.
33 Buchman to Sherwood Day, 21 April 1919.

Chapter 8

1 Henry B. Wright: *The Will of God and a Man's Lifework* (YMCA Press, 1909).
2 Quotations from Buchman in China are taken from verbatim transcripts of his talks at Kuling.
3 Buchman to Samuel Shoemaker, 26 April 1920.
4 Robert E. Speer: *The Principles of Jesus* (Fleming Revell, 1902), pp. 35–6.
5 Wright, p. 173. Wright listed his sources for these standards as follows: 'Purity – Matthew 5, 27–32; Honesty – John 8, 44–46; Unselfishness – Luke 14, 33; Love – John 15, 12' (p. 169).
6 William Ernest Hocking: *The Coming World Civilization* (George Allen and Unwin, 1958), pp. 166–7.
7 C. H. Dodd: *The Meaning of St Paul for Today* (Fount, 1978), pp. 146–7; first published 1920.
8 Henry P. Van Dusen, *Atlantic Monthly*, August 1934.
9 Thomas à Kempis: *Of the Imitation of Christ*, Book 1, ch. 13, paragraph 5.
10 Buchman to Revd T. S. Hughes, 2 July 1918.
11 Buchman to Shoemaker, 28 September 1918.
12 John R. Mott: *The Evangelisation of the World in This Generation* (London, 1901), p. 16.
13 R. S. Churchill and Martin Gilbert, companion volume IV, pp. 913–14, to *Winston S. Churchill*. Note jotted on a sheet of War Office paper.
14 Paul Johnson: *A History of the Modern World from 1917 to the 1980s* (Weidenfeld and Nicolson, 1983), p. 4.

Chapter 9

1 Buchman to Mott, July 1919.
2 ibid., 2 June 1919.

3   Buchman to Sherwood Day, 21 April 1919.
4   Edward Perry, January 1958, unpublished MS. Perry went to Hartford in the autumn of 1921.
5   Buchman to Shoemaker, 24 November 1922.
6   Douglas Mackenzie to Herman Hagedorn, 10 April 1934.
7   Perry, Hartford notes, pp. 3, 7.
8   Alistair Cooke, *America* (BBC, 1973), p. 305.
9   Loudon Hamilton, unpublished MS.
10 See Henry P. Van Dusen, 'Apostle to the Twentieth Century', *Atlantic Monthly*, July 1934, pp. 1–2.
11 Douglas Mackenzie to Buchman, 5 March 1920.
12 Ray Foote Purdy, unpublished MS, who states the movement was to be called 'The Interchurch World Movement'.
13 Buchman to Sherwood Day, 14 June 1920.
14 Buchman to Douglas Mackenzie, winter 1919.
15 H.S., written from Princeton Theological Seminary, 1 November 1922.
16 Shoemaker to Buchman, 14 January 1920.
17 Van Dusen to Buchman, 11 June 1920.
18 Van Dusen, *Atlantic Monthly*, July 1934.
19 Van Dusen to Buchman, 13 January 1920.
20 Shoemaker to Buchman, 21 November 1919.
21 Prince Richard of Hesse, 'Recollections of Dr Frank Buchman', February 1958, unpublished.
22 Buchman to unknown Yale student, 19 August 1920.
23 Buchman to Dan, 3 July 1920.
24 Buchman to Shoemaker et al., 27 October 1920.
25 Buchman to Dean Jacobus, 15 November 1920.
26 Douglas Mackenzie to Buchman, 23 November 1920.
27 Buchman to mother, 8 March 1921.
28 Buchman to Miss Angélique Contostavlos, 24 March 1921.
29 Katharine Makower: *Follow My Leader*: a biography of Murray Webb-Peploe (Kingsway, 1984), p. 59.
30 ibid., p. 62.
31 ibid., p. 59.
32 Buchman to mother, 5 May 1921.
33 Robert Collis: *The Silver Fleece* (Nelson, 1936), p. 107.
34 ibid., pp. 108–110.
35 Perry, unpublished MS.

Chapter 10

1   Buchman to Mrs J. Finlay Shepard, 3 November 1922.
2   Buchman to Shoemaker, October/November 1923.
3   Buchman to Harry P. Davison Jr, 4 June 1923.
4   Shoemaker to Buchman, 16 March 1922.
5   Buchman to Shoemaker, 26 January 1924.

6   ibid., 26 April 1920.
7   Buchman to Alexander Smith, 26 January 1928.
8   Buchman to mother, 24 May 1922.
9   Charles Haines to Buchman, 7 December 1921.
10 Buchman to Charles Haines, 25 January 1922.
11 Shoemaker to Buchman, 5 May 1922.
12 ibid., 18 April 1923.
13 Account given by Revd A. C. Zabriski to Revd Percy G. Kammerer of Pittsburgh, 20 April 1926. Zabriski writes that these facts were given to him by Irving Harris, former editor of the Princeton *Alumni Weekly*.
14 Shoemaker to A. C. Zabriski, 23 April 1926.
15 Buchman to Arthur Johnson, 3 June 1932.
16 Dr Donald Sinclair to Buchman, 1 and 8 November 1926.
17 John Hibben to Buchman, 24 December 1923.
18 ibid., 2 January 1924; written in answer to letter from Buchman, 27 December 1923.
19 Harold Begbie: *Life Changers* (Mills and Boon, 1923), p. vii.
20 ibid., pp. 15–16.
21 Siegfried Sassoon to Buchman, 15 August 1924.

Chapter 11

1   Buchman to mother, 19 March 1924.
2   ibid., 28 May 1924.
3   Mrs Buchman to Buchman, 9 June 1924.
4   Buchman to Mrs J. Finlay Shepard, 9 May 1924.
5   Revd George Moissides, March 1958; then of the American Academy, Larnaca, Cyprus.
6   Moissides, 21 March 1974.
7   Harris, p. 8.
8   Buchman to Shoemaker, 26 January 1924.
9   Shoemaker to Mrs Tjader, 28 December 1924.
10 Buchman to Mrs Tjader, 11 January 1925.
11 Makower, p. 129.
12 Buchman to Maharajah of Gwalior, 26 March 1925.
13 Martin MSS.
14 Circular letter from Buchman, Singapore, 12 October 1925.
15 Buchman to Mrs Tjader, 20 May 1925.
16 Buchman to mother, 22 April 1903.
17 Buchman to Bishop of Beirut, 15 August 1960.
18 Mrs Buchman to Buchman, 18 April 1925.
19 An account of the months in Australia is given in Buchman's circular letter from Singapore, 12 October 1925, and, in more detail, in regular letters to Mrs Tjader.
20 *Frank Buchman – Eighty* (Blandford, 1958), pp. 162–4.
21 Frank Russell introducing Buchman on radio in Melbourne, 10 July 1926.

22 Buchman to Eleanor Forde, 14 January 1926.
23 Martin MSS.
24 Buchman to Mrs Tjader, 18 February 1926: 'Queen Marie has just wired "The sooner you come the more happy we shall be," and so I am off tonight.'
25 Hannah Pakula: *The Last Romantic* (Weidenfeld and Nicolson, 1985), p. 337
26 Buchman to Sherwood Day, 2 September 1926.
27 Jawaharlal Nehru to Buchman, 1 May 1926.
28 Buchman to Benito Mussolini, 6 February 1926.
29 Acknowledged by Mussolini's secretary, 24 February 1926.
30 Buchman to Mrs Tjader, 6 October 1926.
31 Buchman to 'WRYDRUDGE NEW YORK', October 1926 (undated draft in files).

Chapter 12

1 Martin MSS. Signatories included Sherwood Eddy, the Episcopal chaplain of Harvard and faculty members of Union and General Theological Seminaries.
2 *New York Herald Tribune*, 29 October 1926.
3 *Time*, 1 November 1926.
4 *New York-American*, 30 October 1926.
5 Letter to investigating committee and *The Daily Princetonian* from Donald B. Sinclair, 6 November 1926.
6 *Time*, 1 November 1926, quoted in Ernest Gordon, *The Princeton Group*.
7 Dean A. Clark to investigating committee, November 1926.
8 *Life*, 18 November 1926, p. 18.
9 Howard Blake to Loudon Hamilton, 14 September 1975.
10 Report to President Hibben of Special Committee appointed to study the activities and scope of the Philadelphian Society, 31 December 1926.
11 Dr George Stewart Jr to Ray Purdy, 15 January 1927.
12 Buchman to Ray Purdy, 17 January 1927.
13 Ray Purdy to John Hibben, 4 February 1927.
14 *Daily Princetonian*, 28 January 1927.
15 ibid.
16 *Princeton History*, 1977, p. 39.
17 *Time*, 18 July 1927.
18 *Princeton Alumni Weekly*, 22 September 1961.
19 Alexander Leitch: *A Princeton Companion* (Princeton University Press, 1978), p. 87.
20 Pakula, pp. 345–6, 350.
21 Buchman to Queen Marie of Roumania, 15 April 1927.
22 Buchman to Dr George Stewart Jr, 3 December 1926.
23 Van Dusen, *Atlantic Monthly*, July 1934.

Chapter 13

1   Now Eleanor Newton.
2   *Daily Express*, 27 February 1928.
3   ibid.
4   ibid., 28 February 1928.
5   ibid., 1 March 1928.
6   ibid., 5 March 1928.
7   Anon. to Buchman, 5 March 1928 and later (Martin MSS).
8   Tom Driberg: *Ruling Passions* (Jonathan Cape, 1977), p. 98.
9   *Church Times*, 15 June 1928.
10 *Punch*, 14 March 1928.
11 *Isis*, 16 May 1928.
12 *Time*, 28 May 1928.
13 *New York Times*, 17 May 1928.
14 *Daily Express*, 5 March 1928.
15 See James Lang, Letter 5, Christmas 1928. Also Letter 7, April 1930, pp. 10–12.
16 *Pretoria News*, 10 September 1928.
17 Buchman to Mrs Tjader, September 1927.
18 'A Religious House Party', *Outlook*, 7 January 1925.
19 A. Graham Baldwin, 'A critical study of the movement called Buchmanism' – Yale University Divinity Thesis, 1928.
20 *Plain Talk* (New York), December 1927.
21 Buchman to John Roots, 23 July 1928.
22 *Church of England Newspaper*, 6 December 1929.
23 *Johannesburg Star*, 22 August 1929.
24 Bloemfontein house-party, 28 September–8 October 1929.
25 Albert Luthuli: *Let My People Go* (Collins, 1962), p. 42.
26 *The New Witness*, Montreal, 25 August 1936.
27 *British Weekly*, 6 July 1932.

Chapter 14

1   Duke of Windsor: *A King's Story* (Cassell, 1951), pp. 226–7.
2   Buchman to Baroness van Wassenaer (Martin MSS).
3   Contemporary manuscript account shown to author by Alan Thornhill.
4   Quoted by Loudon Hamilton, who was with Jim Driberg when he telephoned Tom.
5   Quoted in Buchman to Humphrey Butler, 7 April 1932.
6   Butler to Buchman, 7 April 1932.
7   Quoted in letter from Garrett Stearly in London to Buchman in America, 27 April 1932.
8   Jim Driberg to Buchman, 9 June 1932.
9   Driberg, pp. 38–42, 100.
10 Buchman to Brigadier-General C. R. P. Winser, 18 January 1938.

11 Willard Hunter, unpublished MS, 1978.
12 Leaflet published by AA World Services, Inc., 1972.
13 *Alcoholics Anonymous Comes of Age* (AA World Services, Inc., 1957), p. 39.
14 *Plain talk about Mutual Help Groups*, issued by National Institute of Mental Health, printed by US Dept of Health and Human Services.
15 *The Times*, 10 June 1985.
16 Notes by Willard Hunter of Claremont, California, on lecture by Howard Clinebell (Hunter to author, 15 July 1985); also Dr George Wilson of Kogarah Bay, New South Wales, in conversation with author.

Chapter 15

1 Cecil Day Lewis: *The Buried Day* (Chatto and Windus, 1960), pp. 208–11.
2 James McGibbon, *Sunday Times*, 22 July 1984.
3 George Orwell: *Inside the Whales and Other Essays* (Gollancz, 1940), p. 163.
4 Neal Wood: *Communism and British Intellectuals* (Gollancz, 1959), pp. 31, 96–121.
5 Arthur Koestler: *The God That Failed* (Hamish Hamilton, 1930), pp. 29–30.
6 Day Lewis, p. 209.
7 John 9.
8 John 4, 7–12.
9 Acts 8, 26–39.
10 Reginald Hale, unpublished memoirs, Vol. 1, p. 53.
11 Later Margot Lean.
12 Koestler, p. 30.
13 Buchman to Eleanor Forde, 17 June 1930.
14 ibid., 27 June 1930.
15 *British Weekly* supplement, 6 July 1933.
16 Martin MSS.
17 *Oxford Mail*, 12 July 1934.
18 John Guise: *Those Two Imposters* (1985, privately published), pp. 64–5.
19 Malcolm Muggeridge: *The Thirties* (Hamish Hamilton, 1940), p. 20.
20 Van Dusen, *Atlantic Monthly*, July 1934.

Chapter 16

1 Angus Wilson: *Rudyard Kipling* (Secker and Warburg, 1977), p. 200.
2 Sir Henry Lunn to Buchman, 14 September 1932.
3 Buchman to Sir Henry Lunn, 15 September 1932.
4 From *Cross Road*, produced at the Westminster Theatre, London, in 1972.
5 Later Miss Hunter of Hunterston.
6 *Frank Buchman – Eighty*, pp. 153–7.
7 Buchman to Eleanor Forde, 1 July 1925.
8 ibid., undated.
9 Hale, Vol. 1, p. 58.

10   Roger Hicks, unpublished MS.
11   *Frank Buchman – Eighty*, p. 153.
12   Now Stella Belden.
13   Begbie, p. 16.
14   Van Dusen, *Atlantic Monthly*, July 1934.
15   Russell, p. 163.
16   *Stockholms Tidningen*, 19 August 1938.
17   B. H. Streeter: *The God Who Speaks*, Warburton Lectures 1933–5 (Macmillan, 1936).
18   Buchman to author, 23 December 1937.
19   John Wesley speaking at Conference, 1766, quoted in Garth Lean: *Strangely Warmed* (Tyndale House, Wheaton, 1980), pp. 119–20.
20   Valdemar Hvidt to author, 1982.
21   Buchman to H. Alexander Smith, 1 April 1927.

Chapter 17

1   *The Times*, 16 August 1961. Sir Lynden later became Chairman of Reuters.
2   Bishop Perry to Archbishop Lang, 14 September 1932.
3   Archbishop Lang to Bishop Perry, 9 August 1932.
4   Bishop Perry to Archbishop Lang, 14 September 1932.
5   Revd P. T. B. Clayton to Archbishop Lang, 9 August 1932.
6   Canon Arnold Mayhew, six-page memo to Archbishop Lang, after attending Oxford house-party 27–30 June 1932.
7   Bishop of Dover to Archbishop Lang, 19 July 1932.
8   Prebendary E. C. Rich to Archbishop Lang, 15 December 1931.
9   Herbert Upward to Vernon Bartlett, 1 December 1931.
10   Item 12, minutes of meeting of Diocesan Bishops, Church House, Westminster, 18 and 19 January 1932.
11   Minutes of meeting, Church House, Westminster, 5 February 1934.
12   Archbishop Söderblom to Buchman, 10 February 1931.
13   Telegram from Archbishop Söderblom to Buchman, 20 May 1931.
14   *Morning Post*, 4 November 1933.
15   Owen Chadwick: *Hensley Henson* (Chaucer Press, 1983), p. 213.
16   Hensley Henson: *The Group Movement* (Oxford University Press, 1933), pp. 44–5.
17   Chadwick, p. 214.
18   Hensley Henson: *Retrospective of an Unimportant Life* (Oxford University Press, 1943), Vol. III, p. 282.
19   Chadwick, p. 214.
20   ibid., p. 213.
21   *The Times*, 10 November 1933.
22   *Daily Mail*, 23 October 1933.
23   *The Times*, 3 November 1933.
24   *Daily Sketch*, 29 September 1933.
25   *The Times*, 29 September 1933.

26 Martin Kiddle to Buchman, 28 February 1933.
27 Martin Kiddle to Lady Newsom, 20 August 1933.
28 *The Times*, 23 September 1933.
29 *Daily Express*, 19 February 1943.
30 *Church of England Newspaper*, 17 July 1931.
31 Bishop of Salisbury to H. Kenaston Twitchell, 2 January 1935.
32 H. Kenaston Twitchell to Buchman, 7 January 1935.
33 Buchman to Sir Michael Sadler, 14 December 1933.
34 Sir Michael Sadler to Buchman, 15 December 1933.
35 Arnold Lunn: *Enigma* (Longmans, 1957), p. 97.
36 *The Times*, 27 September 1933.
37 *Sunday Dispatch*, 24 September 1933.
38 ibid., 8 October 1933.
39 *Evening Standard*, 8 December 1933.
40 *Church of England Newspaper*, 26 January 1934.
41 From a widely printed press article, reprinted in *Moral Re-Armament*, edited by H. W. 'Bunny' Austin (Heinemann, 1938), pp. 58–9.
42 George Light, unpublished MS, 11 February 1946.
43 *The Times*, 6 October 1933.

Chapter 18

1   *Harper's*, August 1932.
2   William Gilliland to Buchman, 23 May 1932.
3   Buchman to Mrs Henry Ford, 16 June 1932.
4   Now Ruth Lamond.
5   *Ottawa Evening Citizen*, 15 November 1932.
6   *Church of England Newspaper*, 2 December 1932.
7   *Vancouver News*, 3 April 1933.
8   *Vancouver Daily Province*, 11 April 1933 and following days.
9   *Sunday Pictorial*, 25 June 1933.
10 *Calgary Herald*, 12 June 1934.
11 *Mail and Empire*, 20 March 1934 and 9 May 1934.
12 *Ottawa Evening Citizen*, 23 March 1934.
13 *The Colonist*, 3 June 1934.
14 *Ottawa Evening Journal*, 12 March 1934.
15 *Allentown Morning Call*, 24 April 1934.
16 *Toronto Evening Citizen*, 18 June 1934.
17 *Witness and Canadian Homestead*, 27 June 1934.
18 *Ottawa Evening Citizen*, 16 June 1934.
19 Report on 'The North American House Party, Banff, Canada', 6–11 June 1934.
20 See *Boston Evening Transcript*, 26 January 1935, article by Albert Diefenbaker headed 'The Conversion of Canada's Prime Minister'.

Chapter 19

1 Moni von Cramon recorded her experiences, related in this and following chapters, in two documents which she wrote in June 1954.
2 Buchman to Mrs William H. Woolverton, 23 September 1920.
3 Buchman to Miss Angélique Contostavlos, 22 September 1923. The doctor was probably Dr Schäfer of Bad Homburg.
4 Buchman to Mrs Tjader, 8 December 1927.
5 Professor D. Adolf Allwohn *Zum Gedenken an Justus Ferdinand Laun, 1899–1963*: (Prof. Adolf Allwohn, 1963).
6 Speech at Passau, 27 October 1928, quoted in *Une Eglise à croix gammée* by Bernard Reymond (L'age d'homme, Lausanne, 1980), p. 299.
7 Radio address 1 February 1933, in which Hitler said: 'The national government . . . will firmly protect Christianity which is the basis of our common morality . . . May God Almighty accept our work in His grace.'
8 Hjalmar Schacht: *Account Settled* (Weidenfeld and Nicolson, 1948), p. 66.
9 Karl Barth: *Eine Schweizer Stimme, 1938–1945*, under entry for 5 December 1938 (Evangelischer Verlag, 1945).
10 See Buchman to Gerhard Heine, 14 December 1921.
11 Ruth Bennett to Moni von Cramon, 18 June 1933.
12 Eberhard Bethge: *Dietrich Bonhoeffer* (Collins, 1970), p. 204.
13 *Church of England Newspaper*, 13 October 1933.
14 Diary of Moni von Cramon.
15 Quoted by Hans Stroh in an interview with Pierre Spoerri. Stroh was Fezer's assistant at that time.
16 cf. A. S. Duncan-Jones: *Struggle for Religious Freedom in Germany* (Gollancz, 1950), p. 60.
17 Klaus Scholder: *Die Kirchen und das Dritte Reich* (Propyläen Verlag, 1977), p. 39.
18 Bethge, pp. 282–4.
19 Emil Brunner to Buchman, 21 December 1933.
20 Buchman to Emil Brunner, 23 December 1933.
21 *Morning Post*, 16 January 1934.
22 H. von Krumhaar to Buchman, 7 January 1934.
23 Wurm: *Tagebuchaufzeichnungen aus der Zeit des Kirchenkampfes* (Quell Verlag, 1951). Bishop Wurm and his wife each made entries in the diary.
24 Bethge, p. 318.
25 Diary notes of Frau Elisabeth Münch, 1931–5.

Chapter 20

1 Buchman to Sir Lynden Macassey, 7 May 1935.
2 Trygve Bull: *Mot Dag av Erling Falk* (Cappelens Forlag, 1945).
3 *Stortingsforhandlingere*, 5 July 1957.
4 Buchman to Carl Hambro, 27 August 1934.
5 Unpublished account by Fredrik Ramm.

6   Victor Sparre: *The Flame in the Darkness* (Grosvenor, 1979), p. 116.
7   Loudon Hamilton to Beatrice Hamilton, 2 and 6 November 1934.
8   Basil Yates to author, 1981.
9   *Tidens Tegn*, 12 November 1934.
10 *Bergens Aftenblad*, 5 December 1934.
11 *Drammens Tidende*, 12 December 1934.
12 See Tore Stubberud: *Victor Sparre* (Aventura Forlag, 1984), p. 12.
13 *The Times*, 31 December 1934.
14 *Tidens Tegn*, 24 December 1934.
15 ibid., 1 May 1935.
16 At a meeting for 50th anniversary of Høsbjør house-party, 27 October 1984.
17 *The Spectator*, 1 February 1935.
18 ibid., 15 February 1935.
19 Quoted in Martin MSS.
20 *Drammens Tidende*, December 1933. Contemporary translation. Copies for 3 and 11 December missing from newspaper's own files. As Hambro spoke in London on 6 December, date of article is probably 11 December.
21 *Stortingsforhandlingere*, 23 January 1935.
22 ibid., 26 March 1935.
23 Bishop Arne Fjellbu: *En Biskop ser tilbake* (Gyldendal, 1960), p. 186.
24 *The Spectator*, 15 February 1935.
25 Buchman, pp. 6–9.
26 Einar Molland: *Church History from Hans Nielsen Hauge to Eivind Berggrav* (Gyldendal, 1968), pp. 78–81.
27 Eye-witness account related to author.
28 Molland, p. 86.
29 Eye-witness account of the story told by Mowinckel at the home of Advocate Erling Wikborg and related to the author by Svend Major.
30 *Kirke og Kultur*, No. XLIII (Oslo, 1936).
31 Personal account to author.
32 Karl F. Wisløff: *Norske Kirke Historie* (Lutherstiftelsen, Oslo, 1966–71), Vol. III, p. 423.
33 C. A. R. Christensen: *Vårt Folks Historie*, Vol. VIII (Aschehoug, 1961), p. 270.
34 Carl Hambro to Buchman, 7 February 1935.
35 Buchman to Carl Hambro, March 1935.
36 Ramm, unpublished MS.
37 Broadcast of 13 January 1935.
38 *Dagens Nyheder*, 14 January 1935.
39 Buchman to H. Kenaston Twitchell, 30 January 1935.
40 ibid.
41 *Berlingske Tidende*, 20 August 1935.
42 Undated contemporary typescript translation.
43 *Social-Demokraten*, 28 March 1935.
44 *Kristeligt Dagbladet*, 29 March 1935.
45 *Dagens Nyheder*, April 1935.

46　Buchman to Carl Henrik Clemmensen, 11 May 1935.

47　*Dagens Nyheder*, 10 June 1935.

48　For account of Danish campaign see Emil Blytgen-Petersen: *Oxford i Danmark* (Haase, 1935).

49　Conversation and letters from Alfred Nielsen to author, August 1981.

50　*Scandinavian Review*, February 1940.

51　*Berlingske Tidende*, 19 October 1935.

52　*Extrabladet*, April 1936.

53　See Henrik S. Nissen and Hening Poulsen: *På Dansk Friheds Grund*, for a description of his work in bringing understanding between Socialist politicians and the Danish army during the Occupation.

54　Irene Gates to Buchman, 23 October 1943, reporting conversation with Karen Petersen.

55　In September 1940 for his article on 'Loyalty' in *Kirke og Kultur*. See also: Bjarne Hoye and Trygve Ager: *The Fight of the Norwegian Church against Nazism* (Macmillan, 1943), pp. 15, 16, 51, 78.

56　*Everybody's Weekly*, 11 December 1944. For an account of Fredrik Ramm in prison and his journey to Odense, see Hiltgunt Zassenhaus: *Walls* (Coronet Books, 1977), pp. 71, 77–8, 123–31.

57　Bethge, pp. 656–8.

58　Confirmed in a two-page interview by Francis Goulding in *New World News*, June 1945. See also Christensen, p. 451: 'The Oxford Group . . . has played a part in reducing tensions in the religious life of Norway during the last decades, and it prepared the way for co-operation between the religious movements during the [German] occupation.'

59　Reported in *Everybody's Weekly* by Ronald Chamberlain, MP, 5 September 1946.

60　Buchman, p. 324.

Chapter 21

1　Secret instructions from the head of the Security Service (*Sicherheitsdienst*), NW Germany (Hamburg, Kiel, Bremen and Braunschweig), 20 May 1937. Further secret instructions warning against Oxford Group infiltration of the Party were issued on 3 December 1937 and 4 March 1938.

2　*Daily Telegraph*, 24 February 1936.

3　*Berlingske Aftenavis*, 25 February 1936.

4　Original in Bundesarchiv, Koblenz, dated 26 February 1936.

5　Original in Document Centre, Berlin.

6　Rosenberg: *Protestantische Rompilger* (Munich 1937), p. 69.

7　Ursula Bentinck to Buchman, April 1936 (Martin MSS).

8　*Flensborg Avis*, 2 January 1962.

9　Leitheft *Die Oxford- oder Gruppenbewegung*, herausgegeben vom Sicherheitshauptamt, November 1936. Geheim, Numeriertes Exemplar No. 1.

10　*New York World-Telegram*, 25 August 1936.

11　Hunter, pp. 29–33.

12 Martin diaries, 7 March 1940.
13 *Daily Express*, 17 September 1936.
14 *The Times*, 7 November 1938.
15 *Sicherheitsdienst RPSS*, Oberabschnitt Süd-West, Stuttgart, 18 July 1937.
16 Order of 26 February 1938.
17 Count John Bentinck to Buchman, 12 May 1938.
18 Buchman to Count John Bentinck, 14 May 1938.
19 *Die Oxford-Gruppenbewegung*, gedruckt im Reichssicherheitshauptamt, 1942, pp. 124–5.
20 *Heeresverordnungsblatt*, 21 October 1942.
21 Siegfried Ernst: *Dein ist das Reich* (Christiania Verlag, 1982), p. 138.
22 *Die Oxford-Gruppenbewegung*, pp. 90–91.
23 ibid., p. 59.
24 Press Association wire, 19 September 1945; see also *Manchester Guardian*, 18 September 1945; *Daily Telegraph*, 20 November 1945.
25 *Het Nieuwe Volk* (National Socialist), 10 May 1941.

Chapter 22

1 Templeton Award Speech, London, 10 May 1983.
2 *Journal de Genève*, 27 September 1935.
3 Spoerri: *La Dynamique du silence* (Editions de Caux, 1975), p. 117.
4 *Der Bund*, 20 September 1935.
5 *La Suisse*, 20 September 1935.
6 *Neue Zürcher Zeitung*, 31 December 1937.
7 Ebenezer Cunningham, *The Spectator*, 18 October 1935.
8 *Berlingske Aftenavis*, 25 April 1936.
9 *The Oxford Group in Geneva*, (1935), text of speeches made at luncheon given by Dr Eduard Benes. Also *Journal de Genève*, 27 September 1935.
10 *Time*, 23 September 1935.
11 Buchman to Carl Hambro, 2 October 1935.
12 Text of a speech made in many centres and variously reported in *Ottawa Citizen*, 15 November 1935; *The Lutheran*, 14 November 1935; *New York Herald Tribune*, 21 November 1935, etc.
13 *New York Times*, 30 May to 8 June 1936.
14 Privately reprinted by Dr Pfatteicher in pamphlet form, Christmas 1934.
15 Revd Edward Horn to Buchman, 19 May 1936.
16 *Dayton Daily News*, 13 June 1936.
17 19 June 1936, Buchman, p. 30.
18 *Leeds Mercury*, 23 July 1936.
19 Hansard, 20 March 1936.
20 Lady Hardinge in talks with the author and others.
21 Lady Hardinge in talks with the author and in a letter to *The Times*, 30 June 1975.
22 Note by Lord Salisbury on Hatfield weekend.
23 Lord Salisbury to Archbishop Lang, 14 October 1936.

24 Buchman to Lord Salisbury, 14 October 1936.
25 Lord Salisbury to Buchman, 15 October 1936.
26 H. Kenaston Twitchell to Buchman, 28 October 1936.
27 Kenneth Rose: *The Later Cecils* (Weidenfeld and Nicolson, 1975), p. 97.
28 Salisbury notes on Hatfield.
29 Rose, p. 96.
30 ibid., p. 102.
31 Verbal to Wilson and in letter from Wilson to author, 28 September 1981.
32 Lord Salisbury to H. Kenaston Twitchell, 27 July 1937.
33 H. Kenaston Twitchell to Lord Salisbury, 29 July 1937.
34 *The Times*, 7 August 1937.
35 July 1939.
36 Lord Salisbury to Roland Wilson, 2 December 1942.
37 Lord Grey to Archbishop Lang, 14 October 1936.
38 Buchman to H. Kenaston Twitchell, 16 November 1936.
39 Buchman to Theophil Spoerri, 11 and 15 December 1936.
40 *The Times*, 10 March 1935.
41 B. H. Streeter to Buchman, 6 April 1936.
42 ibid.
43 *Oxford Times*, 17 September 1937.
44 Thornton-Duesbery: *The Open Secret of MRA* (Blandford, 1964), pp. 74–5.
45 Buchman to William Gilliland, 25 July 1937.
46 *Het Volk*, 18 May 1937.
47 Buchman to Herman Salomonson, 24 May 1937.
48 *Sunday Times*, 18 April 1937.
49 *Daily Express*, 9 July 1937.
50 *World's Press News*, 18 September 1953.
51 *Daily Mirror*, 9 July 1937.
52 *Daily Sketch*, 14 July 1937.
53 On 13 July 1937.
54 H. W. Austin and Phyllis Konstam: *A Mixed Double* (Chatto and Windus, 1969), p. 89.
55 *Morning Post*, 17 August 1937.
56 Prebendary Wilson Carlile to Buchman, 28 June, 1 and 12 July 1937; 1 January 1938.
57 *The Times*, 7 August 1937.

Chapter 23

1 *Det tredje Standpunkt* (Denmark), November 1936, pp. 35–42. Article entitled 'The Christian Culture of Europe against Communism and Nazism'.
2 *Vi måste börja om* (Wahlström and Widstrand, 1937).
3 *New York Times Book Review*, 20 March 1938.
4 Geoffrey Gain: *A Basinful of Revolution – Tod Sloan's Story* (Grosvenor, 1957), p. 44.

5 Buchman, pp. 45–8.
6 Gain, pp. 28–38.
7 Tod Sloan to Buchman, 27 November 1938.
8 Buchman to Professor Runestam, 22 August 1935. Runestam later became Bishop of Karlstad.
9 Buchman to Cuthbert Bardsley, 21 February 1937.
10 Conversations between Graham Turner and Mr and Mrs Stolpe in November 1976. In various books, published between 1938 and these conversations, Stolpe made many comments, both appreciative and critical, on different aspects of Buchman and his work.
11 *Dagens Nyheter*, 13 August 1938.
12 Buchman, pp. 53–8.
13 Nils Gösta Ekman: *Experiment med Gud* (Gummersons, 1971), p. 8.
14 *Lund Dagblad*, 30 September 1941.
15 *Icke för skolan utam för livet* (Svenska Kyrkans Diakonistyrdses Bokförlag, 1943).
16 Speech in Melbourne, Australia, 25 December 1961.
17 At the Hotel Phoenix, Copenhagen. Unpublished record by Hans Wenck of the Danish Foreign Ministry, who was present.
18 *Politiken*, 14 August 1938.
19 *Scandinavian Review*, February 1940.
20 *New York World-Telegram*, 6 July 1938.
21 'A Spectator's Notebook', *The Spectator*, 15 December 1939.
22 Buchman, p. 3.
23 ibid., p. 33.
24 Paul Tournier: *Vivre à l'écoute* (Editions de Caux, 1984), p. 27.
25 Paul Tournier: *Médecine de la Personne* (Delachaux et Niestlé, 1940, 1983).
26 Malcolm Muggeridge to author, 17 February 1985.
27 *Landsforeningen til Arbejdsløshedens Bekämpelse (LAB), 1 August 1939–1 December 1965* (Copenhagen, August 1966), p. 12.
28 *Scandinavian Review*, February 1940.
29 ibid.
30 *LAB*, p. 21.
31 ibid., p. 28.
32 ibid., p. 11.
33 Martin MSS.

Chapter 24

1 Buchman, p. 60.
2 ibid., pp. 62–4.
3 Spoerri, *Dynamic out of Silence*, pp. 127–8.
4 Buchman, pp. 65–7.
5 ibid., p. 68.
6 ibid., pp. 77–8.
7 Jean Martin to other editors, 8 October 1938.

8   *The Times*, 1 September 1938.
9   ibid., 10 September 1938.
10 Said to Roland Wilson, who conveyed the letter, with Salisbury's covering letter, from Cranborne to *The Times*.
11 8 November 1938.
12 19 September 1938 in all Dutch papers.
13 J. A. Patijn to Buchman, 3 October 1938.
14 10 October 1938.
15 21 November 1938.
16 *Manchester Guardian*, 26 September 1938. The same group issued a second manifesto on 24 October, which appeared in *The Times* and other papers.
17 *The Scotsman*, 30 November 1938.
18 *Liverpool Post*, 11 November 1938.
19 *The Times*, 11 November 1938.
20 11 November 1938.
21 Buchman to King George of Greece, 10 October 1938.
22 Revd F. A. Iremonger to Buchman, 25 November 1938.
23 Archbishop Lang to Lord Salisbury, 28 July 1937.
24 Lord Salisbury to Buchman, 20 November 1938.
25 Message from Archbishop Lang to Buchman for 4 June 1938, signed at Lambeth 24 May 1938.
26 National broadcast by Archbishop Lang, 2 October 1938.
27 *Daily Telegraph*, 12 March 1941.
28 George Light: *Ben Tillett, Fighter and Pioneer*, speeches and tributes with a foreword by Lord Sankey (Blandford, 1943), pp. 12–13.
29 Buchman, pp. 85–6. 'MRA' now passed into general use.
30 Austin and Konstam, pp. 98–9.
31 ibid., p. 103.
32 William Jaeger to Buchman, 3 January 1939.
33 Buchman to Arthur Kirby, 20 January 1939.
34 *United States News*, 24 November 1938.
35 Quoted in letter from Buchman to Lord Salisbury, 3 March 1939.
36 *Saturday Evening Post*, August 1939.
37 Quoted in Reginald Pound: *A. P. Herbert* (Michael Joseph, 1976), pp. 155–6.
38 A. P. Herbert to 'Dear Sir', 17 February 1939.
39 *The Times*, 8 June 1939.
40 A. P. Herbert: *Independent Member* (Methuen, 1970), p. 133.
41 *Sunday Pictorial*, 2 July 1939.
42 *Hansard*, 1939, lot 1099–1100.
43 *Sunday Pictorial*, 2 July 1939.
44 Pound, p. 156.
45 Buchman to anon., 1939 (Martin MSS).

Chapter 25

1   Buchman, pp. 91–2.
2   *Washington Post*, 5 June 1939.
3   Austin and Konstam, p. 108.
4   *Los Angeles Times*, 20 July 1939.
5   Buchman, p. 25.
6   cf. Garry Cotton to General L. B. Hershey, Director, Selective Service System, 28 January 1943. Also Arthur Krock in *New York Times*, 28 February 1943.
7   Dale O. Reed, President of the Aeronautical District Lodge No. 727, International Association of Machinists, to General Hershey, 7 February 1943.
8   Morris Martin and Reginald Hale, who were at the interviews in San Francisco and Seattle respectively.
9   Public Records Office, A 1134/26/45 (FO.371.24227), A 4219 of 17/9/1940.
10 Hale, Vol. I, p. 74.
11 ibid.
12 Martin diaries, 17 January 1940.
13 ibid., 6 February 1940.
14 H. W. Austin: *Frank Buchman as I Knew Him* (Grosvenor, 1975), pp. 86–7.
15 ibid., p. 87.
16 Hale, Vol. I, p. 77.
17 See William Grogan: *John Riffe of the Steelworkers* (Coward, McCann, 1959), pp. 33, 74–82.
18 Martin MSS.

Chapter 26

1   Quoted by Buchman in world-wide broadcast from San Francisco, 4 June 1940. Quoted in part in Buchman, p. 97.
2   Colonel John Langston to Buchman, 19 January 1942.
3   cf. *Bristol under Blitz* by Alderman T. H. J. Underdown, Lord Mayor of Bristol, published in February 1941; also *Report on Work of Moral Re-Armament in Nottingham* by Councillor Wallis Binch, Lord Mayor 1939–40 (Hawthornes, Nottingham, July 1941); also *Nottingham Journal*, 1 March 1941.
4   Between 7 and 31 August 1940.
5   Peter Howard: *Innocent Men* (Heinemann, April 1941).
6   Daphne du Maurier: *Come Wind, Come Weather* (Heinemann, August 1940).
7   Alan Bullock: *The Life and Times of Ernest Bevin* (Heinemann, 1967), Vol. 2, pp. 98–101.
8   Hansard, 7 October 1941.
9   Peter Howard: *Fighters Ever* (Heinemann, 1941), p. 18.

10 Pound, pp. 178–179.
11 *The Times*, 9 October 1941.
12 Martin MSS.
13 Stephen Early to Fred D. Jordan, 19 November 1941.
14 Major-General Lewis B. Hershey to Admiral William D. Leahy, senior aide to President Roosevelt, 3 August 1942.
15 *Washington Star*, 15 May 1941, et al.
16 *Allentown Morning Call*, 15 May 1941.
17 *New York Times*, 21 April 1941.
18 *Daily Telegraph*, 10 November 1941.
19 Statement by Bishop Logan Roots to church leaders (Martin MSS).
20 Dr Irene Gates to Martin, (Martin MSS).
21 Buchman to Paul Musselman, 27 September 1941.
22 John Caulfeild, unpublished MS, 18 November 1941.
23 Buchman, p. 144.
24 20 May 1942.
25 Buchman to Henry Ford, drafted 21 June 1942.
26 Hale, Vol. I, p. 98.
27 Charles A. Lindbergh: *Wartime Diaries* (Harcourt, Brace & Jovanovitch, 1970), p. 674.
28 Contributed for, but not printed in, *Frank Buchman – Eighty* in 1958.
29 *Frank Buchman – Eighty*, p. 124.
30 Hale, Vol. I, p. 98; Martin MSS.
31 *Frank Buchman – Eighty*, p. 124.
32 Denis Foss, unpublished MS.
33 Harry S. Truman and others to President Roosevelt, 16 April 1942.
34 Letter dated 25 March 1942, printed in Frank David Ashburn: *Peabody of Groton, A Portrait* (Coward McCann, 1944), p. 350.

Chapter 27

1 Buchman to Ann Sumner, 28 November 1942.
2 Hale, Vol. II, p. 2.
3 *Frank Buchman – Eighty*, p. 176.
4 ibid.
5 *Daily Mirror*, 14 January 1943.
6 21 January 1943.
7 Congressman James Wadsworth to Buchman, 5 December 1942.
8 Hale, Vol. I, p. 102.
9 *Melbourne Age*, 25 February 1943.
10 *The Fight to Serve* (Moral Re-Armament, Washington, 1943), p. 80.
11 Buchman to Gudrun Hambro, 17 May 1943.
12 Carl Hambro to Buchman, 31 July 1943.

Chapter 28

1   Martin diaries, 29 June 1943.
2   Buchman, pp. 139–45.
3   Now Signe Strong.
4   Martin diaries.
5   *New York Herald Tribune*, 12 April 1943.
6   19 November 1943. For full speech, see Buchman, pp. 361–2.
7   Buchman to Cuthbert Bardsley, 13 June 1945.
8   A. R. K. Mackenzie to Buchman, 25 March 1945.
9   William D. Leahy: *I Was There* (Whittlesey House, 1950), p. 318.
10 Earl of Birkenhead: *Halifax* (Hamish Hamilton, 1965), p. 547.
11 ibid., pp. 547–8.
12 Martin diaries, 3 June 1945.
13 *Manchester Guardian*, 20 June 1945.
14 Martin diaries, 28 June 1945.
15 ibid., 29 June 1945.

Chapter 29

1   Martin diaries, 13 July 1945.
2   Public Records Office, AN 3313.
3   ibid., AN 2187 (FO 371 44582).
4   Martin diaries, 14 October 1945.
5   ibid., 25 and 26 November 1945.
6   Hale, Vol. III, p. 1.
7   *The Times*, 29 December 1945.
8   *Oregon Journal, Vancouver Daily Province*, etc., 10 December 1945.
9   Lt-Gen Sir Frederick Browning to author, 28 February 1947.

Chapter 30

1   Oxford University Sermon by Revd J. P. Thornton-Duesbery, 9 June 1946.
2   *Isis*, 6 March 1946.
3   *The Times*, 3 May 1946.
4   ibid., 6 July 1946.
5   Sir Alan Herbert: *Independent Member* (Methuen, 1950), p. 138.
6   Will Locke to Buchman, 2 January 1946.
7   Hansard, 29 January 1946.
8   S. Howard to Buchman, 3 July 1946.
9   Reg and Ivy Adams to Buchman, 3 July 1946.
10 *Doncaster Free Press*, 4 July 1946.
11 J. Deardon to Buchman, 2 July 1946.
12 Roland Wilson to Buchman, 9 April 1946.
13 Hale, Vol. III, p. 22.

14 *The Spectator*, 6 June 1947.
15 *Birmingham Post*, 2 December 1947.
16 Conversation with author, April 1949.
17 Confirmed by Alan Thornhill and Kenneth Belden.
18 John D. Wood to author, 11 May 1984.
19 *Manchester Guardian*, 22 February 1947.
20 *Daily Worker*, 22 February 1947.
21 *L'Osservatore Romano*, 21 May 1937.
22 ibid., 15 June 1939.
23 Broadcast on Swiss radio, 4 June 1947. (See Buchman, pp. 154–5.)

Chapter 31

1 Winston Churchill: *The Second World War* (Cassell, 1954), Vol. VI, p. 138 .
2 *Forrestal Diaries* (Cassell, 1952), p. 57.
3 At Harvard, 5 June 1947.
4 H. Kenaston Twitchell: *Regeneration in the Ruhr* (1981), pp. 8–12. I was present at the interview with Lord Pakenham (now Lord Longford) and personally confirmed this statement with him in 1981 in preparation for the publication of Twitchell's account.
5 Twitchell, p. 22.
6 Erich Peyer to Buchman, 15 April 1948.
7 Gabriel Marcel: *Fresh Hope for the World* (Longmans, 1960), p. 24.
8 *Tagespiegel*, 26 October 1947.
9 Leif Hovelsen: *The Struggle for Post-War Europe*, p. 3. (See 32 note 13.)
10 Hans von Herwarth: *Against Two Evils 1931–45* (Collins, 1981); *Zwischen Hitler und Stalin* (Propyläen Verlag, 1982).
11 *New World News*, June 1948.
12 Reinhold Maier: *Ein Grundstein wird gelegt 1945–47* (Tübingen, 1964), p. 383.
13 *Neue Zürcher Zeitung*, 5 October 1947.
14 Prittie in letter of 9 August 1979 to Price. (Price dissertation, *The Moral Re-Armament Movement and Post-War European Reconstruction*, p. 20.)
15 Schmid to Price, 8 October 1979. (ibid., p. 20.)
16 Hans Peters: *Problematik der deutschen Demokratie* (Origo Verlag, 1948).
17 Caux transcripts, 2 September 1947.
18 ibid., 13 September 1947.
19 For the complete story of Irène Laure and Peter Petersen, who later became a Member of Parliament, see Marcel, pp. 18–30.
20 Lord Pakenham to Jacob Kaiser, Chairman of the CDU in Berlin, 24 December 1947, quoted in Twitchell, pp. 32–3.
21 General Clay to Rear-Admiral Richard E. Byrd, 3 December 1947, quoted in Twitchell, p. 32. Twitchell includes a translation of *Es Muss Alles Anders Werden* (pp. 70–84).
22 Public Records Office, WD1111/1-2-4 of 6.1.50, FO371.70607, C81, C914, C10152, etc.

23   *New York Times*, 8 September 1947.
24   *Los Angeles Herald and Express*, 3 June 1948.
25   Twitchell, p. 40.
26   Buchman to Robert Schuman, 30 August 1948.
27   Caux transcripts, 12 September 1948. Adenauer's warm letter of thanks to Buchman, 22 September 1948, is reproduced in Hans Peter Mensing: *Adenauer Briefe 1947–1949* (Siedler Verlag, 1984).
28   Price, p. 31.

Chapter 32

1   H. Kenaston Twitchell to Senator Alexander Smith, 21 October 1948.
2   *News Chronicle*, 5 November 1948.
3   *Der Kominformplan für West-Deutschland* (Kurier, Berlin), 15 January 1948. Also published by the British Foreign Office, 26 January 1948.
4   *New World News*, September 1948.
5   Austin and Konstam, pp. 174–6.
6   Gudrun Egebjerg to Buchman, 4 December 1949.
7   Buchman, p. 172.
8   Duncan Corcoran to Buchman, 12 March 1949.
9   Buchman, p. 172.
10   'Communism in the British Zone', FO 371/64874. The report itself is still not available.
11   Hubert Stein, speaking in Oslo at a conference of European Socialists in the headquarters of the Building Workers' Union, 26 April 1953.
12   Artur Sträter, speaking on 25 November 1950.
13   Leif Hovelsen: *All Verden Venter* (Oslo, 1958). Hovelsen was confined in Grini, the notorious Nazi concentration camp in Norway, where he first met Moral Re-Armament. In his book and in an unpublished report, *The Struggle for Post-War Europe: Germany between East and West* (January 1962), Hovelsen gives an eye-witness account of these years. His book was published in English under the title *Out of the Evil Night* (Blandford, 1959).
14   Geoffrey Daukes to author, 19 February 1983.
15   *Frank Buchman – Eighty*, p. 119.
16   ibid., p. 117.
17   Hovelsen, *Out of the Evil Night*, p. 70.
18   Max Bladeck to Buchman, 31 October 1949.
19   *Manchester Guardian*, 8 February 1950.
20   Konrad Adenauer to Buchman, 28 April 1950.
21   Buchman, pp. 177–84.
22   *Essener Allgemeine Zeitung*, 29 May 1950.
23   *Frank Buchman – Eighty*, p. 118.
24   Hovelsen, *Out of the Evil Night*, p. 110.
25   Holvelson, *The Struggle for Post-war Europe*, p. 19.
26   For example, in a talk at Bonn to Ruhr miners who had taken their play

Hoffnung through the Ruhr and were about to take it on a world tour, 4 November 1959.

27 25 January 1949.
28 Müller-List, 'Eine neue Moral für Deutschland?', *Das Parlament*, 31 October 1981, p. 15.
29 ibid., p. 19.
30 ibid., pp. 20, 21.
31 Johnson, p. 584.
32 Müller-List, 'Kampf um die Mitbestimmung', *Das Parlament*, 25 April 1981.
33 Müller-List, 'Eine neue Moral für Deutschland?' p. 20.
34 ibid., p. 20.
35 Sydney Cook to Buchman, 28 March 1952.
36 Müller-List, 'Eine neue moral für Deutschland?', p. 15.
37 Martin's eye-witness account in MSS.
38 *New York Times*, 7 January 1951. A paper in the Bibliothèque Nationale in Paris, according to Price (research report for 1941), puts the proportion at two-thirds.
39 Caux transcripts, 8 June 1948.
40 ibid., 3 September 1948.
41 ibid., 27 September 1950.
42 ibid., 27 September 1948.
43 ibid., 23 September 1951.

Chapter 33

1 Files of the Chancery of the Legion of Honour, Paris, 15 June 1950.
2 *New York Times*, 18 December 1952; *The Times*, 19 December 1952.
3 *Evening Standard*, 10 June 1950.
4 *New Statesman*, 10 June 1950.
5 Robert Rochefort: *Robert Schuman* (Editions du Cerf, 1968), p. 234.
6 W. A. Visser 't Hooft: *Zeugnis eines Boten* 7, quoted by Eberhard Bethge: *Dietrich Bonhoeffer* (Collins, 1970), p. 648.
7 Rochefort, p. 51.
8 Georgette Elgey: *La République des Illusions* (Fayard, 1965), p. 304.
9 *France-Forum*, November 1963; Rochefort, p. 231.
10 Interview in Veronese *World Crisis and the Catholic*, p. 5; quoted by Price, p. 40.
11 Report by Juliet Boobbyer of visits to Jean Monnet Institute, 9 August 1982 and February 1983.
12 Henri Rieben: *Des Ententes de Maîtres de Forges au Plan Schuman* (Centre de recherches européennes, Lausanne, 1954), Part III, Section 1, Ch. 5, p. 327.
13 Reinhold Maier, Minister-President of Württemberg-Baden, speaking in Stuttgart, 11 October 1948, at an official reception for Buchman and *The Good Road*.

14 Caux transcripts, 13 September 1948.
15 *Neue Zürcher Zeitung*, 19 July 1959, 'Das Ruhrgebiet aus der Vogelschau'.
16 Philippe Mottu: *The Story of Caux* (Grosvenor, 1970), p. 118.
17 Martin MSS; cf. also Mottu, p. 118.
18 Spoerri, p. 166.
19 Caux transcripts, 13 September 1953.
20 Buchman: *Refaire le Monde* (La Compagnie du Livre, 1950), p. v.
21 Caux transcripts, 12 September 1953.
22 Buchman to Robert Schuman, 1 May 1949.
23 Buchman to Karl Arnold, 4 May 1949.
24 Konrad Adenauer to Buchman, 13 June 1949.
25 *L'Aube*, 20 September 1949; *New York Times*, 6 June 1949.
26 Johnson, p. 584.
27 Report of the Caux Conference, 1949 (German edition, p. 45).
28 Price, p. 56.
29 See Spoerri, *Dynamic out of Silence*, pp. 166–7.
30 Schuman: *Pour l'Europe* (Nagel, 1963), pp. 93–4.
31 Konrad Adenauer: *Memoirs* (Weidenfeld and Nicolson, 1966), p. 233.
32 Elgey, p. 441.
33 Memo of Robert Murphy, US political adviser to General Clay, FRUS 1948, II, pp. 444–5.
34 Conversations with the author at the time.
35 Elgey, p. 422.
36 R. C. Mowat: *Creating the European Community* (Blandford, 1973), pp. 91–3.
37 Unpublished memo from participants.
38 Jean Monnet: *Mémoires* (Fayard, 1976), p. 336.
39 Price, p. 50.
40 ibid., p. 51.
41 Rochefort, p. 264.
42 Richard Mayne: *Postwar* (Thames and Hudson, 1983), p. 302.
43 *New York Times*, 4 June 1951.
44 Price, p. 56.
45 Mowat, pp. 97–8.
46 *New York Herald-Tribune*, 4 June 1951.
47 *News Chronicle*, 10 May 1950. Also see Franz Rodens: *Konrad Adenauer* (Knaur, Munich/Zürich 1963), p. 119.
48 Caux transcripts: 12 September 1953.
49 *Frank Buchman – Eighty*, p. 203.
50 See Spoerri, *Dynamic out of Silence*, pp. 205–6.
51 Price, p. 3.
52 *The Times*, 4 June 1959.
53 Personal letter to Price, 3 September 1979, quoted Price, p. 6.
54 Event recorded in *Bonner Generalanzeiger*, 16 September 1982. Extract taken from verbatim copy of speech issued by President's office.
55 At German Embassy, Delhi, 17 December 1952.

Chapter 34

1   Martin MSS.
2   Basil Entwistle, unpublished memoirs, II, p. 6.
3   ibid., II, p. 9.
4   ibid., II, p. 11.
5   Buchman, p. 166.
6   ibid., p. 195.
7   Entwistle, II, p. 15.
8   Basil Entwistle: *Japan's Decisive Decade* (Grosvenor, 1985), p. 37.
9   ibid., p. 42.
10 ibid., p. 44.
11 Martin MSS.
12 *The Observer*, 25 July 1950.
13 24 July 1950.
14 *New York Times*, 19 July 1950.
15 *Saturday Evening Post*, 29 July 1950.
16 Entwistle: *Japan's Decisive Decade*, p. 67.
17 Martin diaries, 20 September 1951.

Chapter 35

1   Buchman to mother, 23 May 1918.
2   Mrs Adams to Mrs Buchman, 15 September 1922.
3   Hamilton, unpublished notes.
4   Martin diaries, 28 June 1951.
5   ibid., 10 May 1951.
6   Buchman to parents, 12 November 1899.
7   Austin and Konstam, pp. 198–200.
8   *Crossroad.*
9   *The Times*, 27 June 1960.
10 Charlotte van Beuningen: *A New World for my Grandchildren* (Himmat Publications, 1969), pp. 60–61, 64–6, 69–84.

Chapter 36

1   Roger Hicks, unpublished autobiographical MS, chapter 6, 'Living with Mahatma Gandhi'.
2   Martin, account of Asian trip.
3   Surya Sena: *Of Sri Lanka I Sing* (Ranco, Colombo, 1978), pp. 225–7.
4   Dudley Senanayake and S. W. R. D. Bandaranaike to Buchman, 21 November 1952.
5   R. G. Senanayake to Buchman, date unknown; Martin, Asian account.
6   Martin, Asian account.

7 *Bombay Chronicle*, 20 November 1952. This was in the first of thirteen special supplements devoted to the tour by leading Indian newspapers, published at their own initiative and expense.
8 25 November 1952.
9 Jawaharlal Nehru: *An Autobiography* (John Lane and Bodley Head, 1936), pp. 153–4.
10 Jawaharlal Nehru: *An Autobiography* (Jawaharlal Nehru Memorial Foundation, New Delhi, 1980), pp. 361–2.
11 Jawaharlal Nehru to Buchman, 1 May 1926.
12 Austin and Konstam, p. 191.
13 *Hindustan Times*, etc., 2 January 1953; Buchman, p. 205.
14 Duncan Corcoran to Buchman, 24 March 1953.
15 Peter Howard: *Frank Buchman's Secret* (Heinemann, 1961), p. 31.
16 Martin, Asian account.
17 ibid.
18 ibid.
19 A reference is made to this visit in Stanley Wolpert: *Jinnah of Pakistan* (OUP, 1984), p. 303.
20 Martin, Asian account.
21 Michael Brecher: *Nehru, A Political Biography* (OUP, 1959), pp. 607–8.
22 From speech by Sanjiva Reddi in Westminster Theatre, London, 1972.
23 Told to Hicks by Appadorai Aaron.
24 Mr and Mrs Albert H. Ely to Buchman, 4 June 1951.
25 ibid., 2 June 1949.
26 Gilbert Harris to Buchman, 23 October 1951.
27 Mrs John Henry Hammond to Buchman, 5 January 1957.
28 *New York Herald-Tribune*, 4 January 1951.
29 For further analysis see Thornton-Duesbery, pp. 94–95. The accounts of the Oxford Group in Britain are filed at the Companies Registry Department of the Board of Trade, where they can be inspected.

Chapter 37

1 Martin, Asian account.
2 Buchman, p. 161.
3 ibid., pp. 46–7.
4 ibid., p. 65.
5 ibid., p. 198.
6 Grogan, p. 140.
7 Foreword to *World Labour and Caux* (Caux, February 1950).
8 Mackinac transcripts, June 1952.
9 Marcel, p. 113.
10 Piguet and Sentis: *Ce Monde que Dieu nous confie* (Centurion, 1979), p. 64.
11 ibid., p. 46.
12 Dan Hurley to Buchman, (undated) 1950. Late September, as he spoke at Caux on 10 September.

13 *New York World-Telegram and Sun*, 14 July 1953; similar reports in *The Times*, 6 July 1953 *Daily Herald*, 8 July 1953.

14 ICFTU Information Bulletin, Vol. IV, No. 18 (84), 15 September 1953.

15 George Woodcock, General Secretary of the TUC, to James Haworth, 28 April 1954; statement by Len Williams, National Agent and later General Secretary of the Labour Party (*Eastern Standard*, 2 April 1954).

16 *Der Bund*, 27 September 1953.

17 *The New Leader*, 15 February 1954.

18 The full story is told in Grogan, pp. 147–51.

19 Thorton-Duesbery, pp. 120–22, Appendix VII, Haworth: 'Moral Re-Armament for Socialists'.

20 ICFTU Press and Radio Service, 18 August 1966.

21 11 May 1952.

22 *Coventry Evening Telegraph*, 7 June 1952.

23 Letter from Revd G. Johnson Jeffrey, 20 May 1952.

24 Minutes of Social and Industrial Council, 19 November 1952.

25 ibid., 26 February 1953.

26 Minutes of Standing Committee, 13 May 1953.

27 ibid. and 2 July 1953.

28 *Daily Telegraph*, 13 and 21 January 1954.

29 Observations by Sir Lynden Macassey, QC, in *Statement by the Council of Management of the Oxford Group* in regard to the method of making the Report on Moral Re-Armament adopted by the Social and Industrial Council (February 1955), pp. 24–30. It was Sir Lynden who had conducted an earlier investigation of the Oxford Group for the Bishop of London.

30 Archbishop Fisher to John Moncrieff, 22 and 26 January 1954.

31 Minutes of the Social and Industrial Council, 28 January 1954.

32 D. C. Grimshaw, Acting Secretary of the Oxford Group, to J. A. Guillam Scott, Secretary of the Social and Industrial Council, 17 February 1954.

33 J. A. Guillam Scott to Acting Secretary of Oxford Group, 22 February 1954.

34 ibid., 12 March and 12 April 1954.

35 Minutes of the Social and Industrial Council, 4 December 1954.

36 *The Times*, 16 February 1955.

37 Gerald Steel to Scott, 16 December 1954.

38 *The Times*, 17 February 1955.

39 ibid., 16 February 1955.

40 Buchman to Francis Woodlock, S.J., 23 October 1933.

41 Karl Adam writing in Tübingen *Theological Quarterly*, Spring edition 1952; reprinted *Vaterland*, Lucerne, 12 August 1952.

42 Werner Schöllgen: *Aktuelle Moralprobleme* (Patmos Verlag, September 1955).

43 *L'Osservatore Romano*, 9–10 December 1957.

44 Count Carlo Lovera di Castiglione to Philippe Mottu, 18 November 1951.

45 Gabriel Marcel: *En Chemin, vers quel éveil?* (Editions Gallimard, 1971), pp. 170–71.

46 Mgr Léon-Joseph Suenens (then Auxiliary Bishop of Malines): *Que penser du Réarmement moral* (Editions Universitaires, 1953), p. 90.

47 *Civiltà Cattolica*, issues of 14 June, 12 July, 13 September, 25 October and 13 December 1958, Vol. II, pp. 570–84; Vol. III, pp. 143–56, 584–90; Vol. IV, pp. 260–72 and 623–34 respectively.
48 *Monitor Ecclesiasticus* (Rome, 1957), Series III, pp. 451–503.

Chapter 38

1   Gabriel Marcel: *Plus décisif que la violence* (Plon, 1971), p. 65.
2   *Courrier du Maroc*, 3 October 1953.
3   Abdessadeq's doubts are confirmed in Gavin Maxwell's book *The Lords of the Atlas: The Rise and Fall of the House of Glaoua 1893–1956* (Longmans, 1966), p. 255. Maxwell gives credit to Abdessadeq, Chavanne and Guessous for their parts in El Glaoui's *volte-face*, while being unaware of many details related here and obtained from the participants.
4   Maxwell, p. 257.
5   ibid., p. 258.
6   *L'Express*, 26 October 1955: 'Le Glaoui Rappelle Ben Youssef!'.
7   *The Times*, 9 November 1955.
8   Si Bekkai to Buchman, August 1955.
9   Mottu, p. 30.
10 cf. *Courrier du Maroc*, 18 January and 2 June 1955.
11 Mottu, p. 132.
12 ibid.
13 *The Times*, 14 July 1954.
14 Leonard and Flora Kibuthu to Buchman, 13 December 1958.
15 Quoted in *Time and Tide*, London, 2 September 1965.
16 Gabriel Marcel speaking at Caux, 1956, quoted in *Frank Buchman – Eighty*, p. 50.
17 Marcel, *Fresh Hope for the World*, p. 174.
18 *Daily Worker*, 18 December 1949.
19 *Zik, Selected Speeches of Dr Nnamdi Azikiwe* (OUP, 1961), Ch. 14, 'Zik on Moral Re-Armament'.
20 *Frank Buchman – Eighty*, p. 100.
21 ibid.
22 MRA Information Service, 31 March 1972.
23 *Rand Daily Mail*, Johannesburg, 15 January 1972.
24 Bremer Hofmeyr to Buchman, 18 June 1960.
25 Buchman to Robert Schuman, 27 June 1960.
26 Grand Chief Kalumba to Buchman, 7 August 1961.

Chapter 39

1   Marcel, *Fresh Hope for the World*, pp. 89–90.
2   Howard, *Frank Buchman's Secret*, pp. 92–7.
3   Peter Howard to Roger Hicks, 1 April 1950.

4 Wolrige Gordon: *Peter Howard – Life and Letters* (Hodder and Stoughton, 1969), p. 156.
5 Signe Strong to author, 15 April 1984.
6 H. Kenaston Twitchell: *The Strength of a Nation* (Moral Re-Armament, Los Angeles, 1948), pp. 6–8.
7 Signe Strong to author, 25 April 1984.
8 Victor Sparre, *Stenene skal rope* (Tiden Norsk Forlag, 1974), p. 62.
9 Now Virginia Goulding.
10 Sparre, *The Flame in the Darkness*, pp. 121–2.

Chapter 40

1 *Afro-American*, 26 April 1955.
2 Peter Howard: *An Idea to Win the World* (Blandford, 1955), pp. 18–19. The detailed story of the preparations and journey of the 'World Mission' is told in this book.
3 Mottu, p. 132.
4 Martin MSS.
5 H. K. Twitchell to Buchman, 8 October 1955.
6 Howard, *An Idea to Win the World*, p. 52.
7 *Everybody's Weekly*, London, 16 June 1956.
8 Rossi tells the full story in Marcel, *Fresh Hope for the World*, pp. 74–9.
9 John Farquharson.
10 Oliver N. Warin to author, 4 January 1984.
11 *Sydney Morning Herald*, 16 January 1984.
12 James Baynard-Smith's notes on the tour.
13 *Reader's Digest*, Japan, May 1956.
14 *Frank Buchman – Eighty*, pp. 141–6.
15 Martin diaries, 7 May 1956.
16 Wilson to author, 21 January 1985.

Chapter 41

1 Buchman to Gilbert Harris, 15 December, 1955.
2 Entwistle, *Japan's Decisive Decade*, pp. 160–61.
3 ibid., p. 161.
4 ibid., pp. 161–2.
5 *Sydney Morning Herald*, 5 December 1957.
6 *Washington Evening Star*, 18 December 1957.
7 Entwistle, *Japan's Decisive Decade* p. 173.
8 ibid., p. 176.
9 ibid., p. 175.
10 Austin and Konstam, pp. 217–18.
11 ibid., p. 218.

12 *Detroit Free Press*, 21 September 1958. (Note: 'Drew Pearson is on a brief vacation. Today's column is written by an assistant, Tom McNamara.')
13 31 December 1959.
14 *Pittsburgh Courier*, 2 January 1960.
15 *Observer*, London, 23 January 1966.
16 Buchman to Ahmed el Mahdi, 29 December 1959.

Chapter 42

1 *Frankfurter Allgemeine Zeitung*, 4 June 1958.
2 Buchman to Prince Richard of Hesse, November/December 1959 (Martin MSS).
3 Caux transcripts, 9 September 1961.
4 *The Times*, 22 August 1958.
5 *Washington Post*, 25 August 1958.
6 *State Times*, Jackson, Miss. quoted in Charis Waddy: *The Muslim Mind*: (Longman, 1976, pp. 99–102), where the full story of this event is told.
7 Archbishop Gregorius to Buchman, quoted in Buchman, p. 262.
8 Klaus Bockmühl to author, 3 March 1984.

Chapter 43

1 Buchman, p. 251.
2 *Ideology and Co-Existence* (Moral Re-Armament, 1959), p. 30.
3 Buchman, p. 259.
4 Andrew Mackay to Buchman, 13 November 1958.
5 ibid., 28 February 1960.
6 Marcel, *En chemin, vers quel éveil?*, pp. 260–61.
7 Sven-Georg Adenauer to Buchman, 17 December 1959.
8 *New York Journal-American*, 31 January 1960.
9 *Arizona Daily Star*, 22 March 1960.
10 Spoerri, *Dynamic out of Silence*, p. 206.

Chapter 44

1 See Ravines: *The Yenan Way* (Scribners, 1951), pp. 145–63.
2 Martin MSS.
3 Buchman, pp. 386–8.
4 Buchman to Father Ling, 11 October 1960.
5 Buchman to Mary Reynolds, 26 December 1960.
6 Arturo Lanocita in *Corriere della Sera*, 23 June 1961.
7 Buchman, pp. 272–307.
8 Buchman to anon. (Martin MSS).
9 Nobusuke Kishi to Buchman, March 1961.

Chapter 45

1 *Daily Herald*, 9 August 1961.
2 *The Penguin Dictionary of Saints* (1966), pp. 10–11.
3 Dietmar Lamprecht: *Die Stadt auf dem Berge* (Vandenhoeck Ruprecht, 1976), Introduction.
4 Article in *Silva*, 25 March 1962.
5 Statement sent by Cardinal Franz König to author, 15 November 1984.
6 ibid., 18 November 1984.
7 Lord Blanch to Gordon Wise. Speaking at Tirley Garth, Cheshire, on 10 June 1984, Lord Blanch commented, 'MRA manages to mobilise its experience . . . expertly and quickly and is able to call upon a group of people who will go anywhere and do anything if they are called by God to do it.'
8 See Howard, *Frank Buchman's Secret*, p. 13.

ACKNOWLEDGEMENTS

I am grateful to three authors who have allowed me to quote from their books at length.

Irving Harris permitted me to quote his account of the first meeting between Buchman and Sam Shoemaker from his biography of Shoemaker, *The Breeze of the Spirit* (Seabury, 1978).

Katharine Makower in *Follow My Leader* (Kingsway, 1984) enlightened me further about the visit of two Cambridge men, Murrary Webb-Peploe and Godfrey Buxton, to America with Buchman in 1921.

In the chapters devoted to Japan and her people, I have relied greatly on unpublished memoirs and the recent book *Japan's Decisive Decade* by Basil Entwistle. Professor Ezra F. Vogel, Chairman of the Council on East Asian Studies at Harvard University, writes: 'Basil Entwistle was in an unusual position in the early post World War II period to come into contact with the people in Japan who were to emerge as the leaders in the economy and in the government directing the Japanese miracle . . . He has written an extremely careful, precise, informative and inspirational account of his experiences. For those of us who have read about these great leaders at a distance, it is a fascinating history.'

I would like also to thank the many other authors whom I have quoted more briefly, all of whom are acknowledged in the Source References.

I am also grateful to the staffs of the libraries mentioned in the Preface, to whom I would add the libraries of Oslo and Uppsala Universities

INDEX